THE EDINBURGH COMPANION TO THE EIGHTEENTH-CENTURY BRITISH NOVEL AND THE ARTS

Edinburgh Companions to Literature and the Humanities

These single-volume reference works present cutting-edge scholarship in areas of literary studies particularly those which reach out to other disciplines. They include volumes on key literary figures and their interaction with the arts, on major topics and on emerging forms of cross-disciplinary research.

For a complete list of titles in the series, please go to
https://edinburghuniversitypress.com/series/ecl

THE EDINBURGH COMPANION TO THE EIGHTEENTH-CENTURY BRITISH NOVEL AND THE ARTS

EDITED BY JAKUB LIPSKI AND M-C. NEWBOULD

EDINBURGH
University Press

Edinburgh University Press is one of the leading university presses in the UK. We publish academic books and journals in our selected subject areas across the humanities and social sciences, combining cutting-edge scholarship with high editorial and production values to produce academic works of lasting importance. For more information visit our website: edinburghuniversitypress.com

© editorial matter and organisation Jakub Lipski and M-C. Newbould 2024
© the chapters their several authors 2024

Published with the support of the University of Edinburgh Scholarly Publishing Initiatives Fund.

Edinburgh University Press Ltd
The Tun – Holyrood Road
12(2f) Jackson's Entry
Edinburgh EH8 8PJ

Typeset in 10/12 Adobe Sabon by
IDSUK (DataConnection) Ltd, and
printed and bound in Great Britain

A CIP record for this book is available from the British Library

ISBN 978 1 3995 0662 5 (hardback)
ISBN 978 1 3995 0663 2 (webready PDF)
ISBN 978 1 3995 0664 9 (epub)

The right of Jakub Lipski and M-C. Newbould to be identified as the editors of this work has been asserted in accordance with the Copyright, Designs and Patents Act 1988, and the Copyright and Related Rights Regulations 2003 (SI No. 2498).

CONTENTS

List of Illustrations	viii
Acknowledgements	xiii
The Eighteenth-Century British Novel and the Arts *Jakub Lipski and M-C. Newbould*	1

Part I: Styles and Discourses

1. Invisibility and Narration in Haywood (and Behn and Fielding) *Marcie Frank*	23
2. Orientalism and Sexuality in the Eighteenth-Century Novel *James Watt*	38
3. Crafting the Past: Antiquarianism, Decorative Handicrafts and the Novel at the Mid-Century *Katharina Boehm*	53
4. Anatomy, Invasion and Imagination: Reading Gender, Medicine and the Body in the Mid-Century Novel *Ashleigh Blackwood*	67

Part II: Visual Cultures

5. Before and After: Imagining Pleasure in Eighteenth-Century British Art and Literature, from Defoe and Hogarth to Sterne and Gainsborough *Frédéric Ogée*	89
6. The Art of Architecture and the Form of the Novel *Chris Ewers*	108
7. 'The statue cannot be formed, unless our inclination concur thereto': Statuary and Sculpture in the Eighteenth-Century Novel *M-C. Newbould*	123

vi CONTENTS

8. Depicting Beautiful Women in the Eighteenth-Century Novel 140
    Katherine Aske

9. Stories behind Pictures: Reconstructing a Pre-History of Horace
    Walpole's *The Castle of Otranto* 155
    Jakub Lipski

10. The Romances of Ann Radcliffe and the 'Total Work of Art' 176
    Hannah Moss

Part III: Modes and Spaces of Performance

11. Haywood's Whimsical Adventures: The Novel and the Rococo 195
    Joseph Drury

12. Song in the Novels of Samuel Richardson 211
    Elizabeth Kraft

13. Vexed Diversions: *Gulliver's Travels*, the Arts and Popular Entertainment 228
    Daniel Cook

14. Songs, Stories and Sentimentalism: The British Broadside Ballad as
    Sentimental Fiction 244
    Georgina Bartlett

15. 'Novel Romance makes me puke!': Burneys, Shakespeares and
    the Sentimental Plot 262
    Mascha Hansen

16. Polite Arts/The Arts of Politeness: Manners, Hypocrisy and
    the Performance of the Self 277
    Przemysław Uściński

17. Musical 'Epiphanies' in the Late Eighteenth-Century Novel 293
    Pierre Dubois

18. Jane Austen's Art of Elocution: Discerning Feeling in *Persuasion* 307
    Fraser Easton

Part IV: Networks and Interactions

19. Multimedia Coterie Romance 329
    Natasha Simonova

20. The Art of Reading and the Eighteenth-Century Novel: The Case of
    The History of Charlotte Summers, The Fortunate Parish Girl 348
    Joanna Maciulewicz

21. The Eighteenth-Century Novel and the Sociable Arts 362
    Emrys D. Jones

22. Novels, Paintings and the Half-Trained Eye in Mid-Eighteenth-Century
    Reading Culture 376
    Paul Goring

CONTENTS

Part V: Adaptations and Afterlives

23. From Visual to Material Culture: The Afterlives of Frontispieces to
    Robinson Crusoe — 397
    Nathalie Collé

24. Text Transformed into Silkwork: British Needlework Pictures and
    the Adaptation of *Charlotte at the Tomb of Werter* — 414
    Sandro Jung

25. Extra-Illustration and the Seduction of a 'Standard' Text:
    James Comerford's Erotic Books — 433
    Helen Williams

26. Eighteenth-Century Fiction and the Art of Graphic Satire, from Character
    to Constellation — 460
    Brigitte Friant-Kessler

27. Contemporary Art and the Eighteenth-Century Novel — 485
    Amelia Dale

28. Invoking the Implied Viewer in the Eighteenth-Century Novel on Film — 503
    Jennifer Preston Wilson

Notes on Contributors — 518

Index — 524

ILLUSTRATIONS

Plates

Plate 1   *Roxana in her Turkish Habit*. Probably an illustration to an abridgement of Daniel Defoe's *The Fortunate Mistress*, entitled *The Life and
Adventures of Roxana* (London, 1765?). Engraving. ART file R886
no. 1, Folger Shakespeare Library

Plate 2   Thomas Daniell, *Old Government House* (1788), in *Views of Calcutta*,
Plate 10. Aquatint. © The Trustees of the British Museum

Plate 3   Stourhead Garden (author's photograph)

Plate 4   Peter Lely, *Portrait of a young woman and child, as Venus and Cupid,
almost certainly Nell Gwyn (1650–87)* (mid-1660s). 48¾ x 61¾ in.
(123.8 x 156.8 cm). Public domain, via Wikimedia Commons

Plate 5   Jean-Antoine Watteau, *Pèlerinage à l'île de Cythère*, or *L'embarquement
pour Cythère (The Embarkation for Cythera)*, 1717, 50.7 x 76.3 in. (120
x 190 cm). Musée du Louvre. Public domain, via Wikimedia Commons

Plate 6   Thomas Gainsborough (British, 1727–88), *The Mall in St. James's
Park* (c.1783). Oil on canvas, 47 1/2 x 57 7/8 in. (120.7 x 147 cm).
The Frick Collection, New York. Photo: Joseph Coscia Jr. Copyright
The Frick Collection

Plate 7   Thomas Gainsborough, *Elizabeth and Mary Linley* (c.1772; retouched
1785). Oil on canvas, 199 x 153.5 cm. Dulwich Picture Gallery. Public
domain, via Wikimedia Commons

Plate 8   Thomas Gainsborough, *Mrs. Richard Brinsley Sheridan* (1785–87). Oil
on canvas, 219.7 x 153.7 cm. Andrew W. Mellon Collection. Courtesy
National Gallery of Art, Washington

Plate 9   Thomas Gainsborough, *Mrs. Mary Robinson (Perdita)* (1781). Oil on
canvas, 233.7 x 153 cm. The Wallace Collection. Public domain, via
Wikimedia Commons

Plate 10   James Gillray, *The Contrast, or Things as they Are* (1796). Courtesy of
the Lewis Walpole Library, Yale University

Plate 11   Marcus Geeraerts the Younger, *Henry Cary, 1st Viscount Falkland*
(c.1603). Oil on canvas. Sarah Campbell Blaffer Foundation, Houston

Plate 12   Watercolour copy of Jacopo Ligozzi's portrait of Bianca Capello. LWL
SH Contents Un58 no. 16 Box 120. Courtesy of the Lewis Walpole
Library, Yale University

ILLUSTRATIONS

Plate 13	William Hogarth, *William Wollaston and his Family in a Grand Interior* (1730). Oil on canvas. New Walk Museum and Art Gallery, Leicester. Public domain, via Wikimedia Commons
Plate 14	Silkwork of *Charlotte at the Tomb of Werter*, late eighteenth century. Reproduced from the copy in the author's collection
Plate 15	Silkwork of *Charlotte at the Tomb of Werter*, late eighteenth century. Reproduced courtesy of Needlework Antiques
Plate 16	Silkwork of *Charlotte at the Tomb of Werter*, late eighteenth century. Reproduced from the copy in the author's collection
Plate 17	Silkwork *Charlotte at the Tomb of Werter*, late eighteenth century. Reproduced, with permission, from the copy in the Collection of the Museum of Early Southern Decorative Arts (MESDA)
Plate 18	Silkwork of *Charlotte at the Tomb of Werter*, late eighteenth century. Reproduced from the copy in the author's collection
Plate 19	Silkwork of *Charlotte at the Tomb of Werter*, early nineteenth century. Reproduced from the copy in the author's collection
Plate 20	Silkwork of *Charlotte at the Tomb of Werter*, early nineteenth century. Reproduced from the copy in the author's collection
Plate 21	Silkwork of Poor Maria, late eighteenth century. Reproduced from the copy in the author's collection
Plate 22	Hand-coloured print, folded within the front endpapers of Comerford's *Voyage to Lethe* (1741): T. P. Hydrographer [Pseud.], *A Map or Chart of the Road of Love, and Harbour of Marriage* (1748, amended by hand to '1741'). British Library General Reference Collection Cup.1001.c.4. By permission of the British Library
Plate 23	Johann Michael Voltz, *Der neue Robinson auf der einsamen Ratten Insel im Süd-Meere St Helena genannt* (c.1815–16). G27593. © Paris Musées. Musée Carnavalet – Histoire de Paris
Plate 24	Udo J. Keppler Jr, *Robinson Crusoe Fairbanks*, cover for *Puck*, vol. 58, no. 1505, 3 January 1906. © Library of Congress Prints and Photographs Division
Plate 25	Peter Brookes, *Debased Currency*, *The Times*, 19 July 2017. Courtesy of Peter Brookes
Plate 26	John Baldessari, *The Life and Opinions of Tristram Shandy, Gentleman* (San Francisco: Arion Press, 1988). © John Baldessari 1988. Courtesy Estate of John Baldessari © 2023. Courtesy of Sprüth Magers
Plate 27	Meg Cranston, *The Complete Works of Jane Austen* (1991). Artspace. Courtesy of Meg Cranston
Plate 28	Paul Chan, *Font Drawings* (2008). Ink on paper, 84 x 54 inches each. Courtesy of the artist and Greene Naftali, New York

Figures

Figure 2.1	William Hogarth, *Credulity, Superstition, and Fanaticism. A Medley* (1762). Engraving. Courtesy of the Lewis Walpole Library, Yale University	42

X   ILLUSTRATIONS

Figure 2.2   Charles Grignion the Elder, after Thomas Rowlandson, *The Duke of N–'s Levee, an illustration from Tobias Smollett's 'The Expedition of Humphry Clinker' (London, 1793), Vol. 1*. Etching and engraving. The Metropolitan Museum of Art, New York. Accession Number 59.553.562(5), The Elisha Whittelsey Collection, The Elisha Whittelsey Fund, 1959. www.metmuseum.org   43
Figure 4.1   William Hogarth, *The dissection of the body of Tom Nero*, from *The Four Stages of Cruelty* (1751). Etching. Wellcome Collection   74
Figure 4.2   William Hogarth, *Mary Toft (Tofts) appearing to give birth to rabbits in the presence of several surgeons and man-midwives sent from London to examine her* (1726). Etching. Wellcome Collection   76
Figure 4.3   William Smellie, Table XXIV from *A sett of anatomical tables, with explanations, and an abridgment, of the practice of midwifery, with a view to illustrate a treatise on that subject, and collection of cases* (1754). Wellcome Collection   80
Figure 5.1   William Hogarth, *Before* and *After* (1736). Etching and engraving. Harris Brisbane Dick Fund, 1932. The Metropolitan Museum of Art, New York. www.metmuseum.org   96
Figure 5.2   William Hogarth, *A Harlot's Progress* (1732), plates 1 & 2. Etching and engraving. Harris Brisbane Dick Fund, 1932. The Metropolitan Museum of Art, New York. www.metmuseum.org   98
Figure 6.1   William Hogarth, *The Marriage Contract* (1743). Plate 1, *Marriage A-la-Mode*. Engraved from the original by Richard Earlom. Courtesy of the Lewis Walpole Library, Yale University   112
Figure 6.2   James Lambert, *Fonthill Abbey, Wiltshire* (1822). Courtesy of the Lewis Walpole Library, Yale University   115
Figure 6.3   *Strawberry Hill* (c.1822). Courtesy of the Lewis Walpole Library, Yale University   118
Figure 8.1   Illustration from *Pamela: or, Virtue rewarded. In a series of Familiar Letters from a Beautiful Young Damsel to her Parents* (1742) by Samuel Richardson, showing Mr B. intercepting Pamela's first letter home to her mother. Original engraving by Hubert Gravelot. Public domain, via Wikimedia Commons   144
Figure 8.2   *Tom Jones and Sophia Western are seated together on a sofa as Squire Western enters the room with a riding whip* [image has been cropped]. Stipple engraving by Peter Simon after J. Downman [1789?]. Reference: 28844i. ©Wellcome Collection. Public domain   149
Figure 9.1   Horace Walpole, *A Description of the Villa of Mr. Horace Walpole* (Strawberry Hill, 1784), page 101. LWL Folio 49 3582. Courtesy of the Lewis Walpole Library, Yale University   161
Figure 9.2   Horace Walpole's collection of George Vertue's *Original Drawings of Heads, Antiquities, Monuments, Views, &c.*, page 75. LWL Folio 49 3581. Courtesy of the Lewis Walpole Library, Yale University   163
Figure 9.3   Horace Walpole's collection of George Vertue's *Original Drawings of Heads, Antiquities, Monuments, Views, &c.*, page 36. LWL 49 2610. Courtesy of the Lewis Walpole Library, Yale University   164

ILLUSTRATIONS

Figure 9.4	Horace Walpole's sketch of Richard II in the 'Book of Materials', 1:64. LWL 49 2615 I. Courtesy of the Lewis Walpole Library, Yale University	170
Figure 12.1	Psalm-tunes for the Psalm CXXXVII, from John Chetham, *A Book of Psalmody, Containing a Variety of Tunes for all the Common Metres of the Psalms in the Old and New Versions* (1741)	213
Figure 12.2	'The Charms of Silvia', *The Monthly Melody: or Polite Amusement for Gentlemen and Ladies. Being a Collection of Vocal and Instrumental Music Composed by Dr. Arne* (London: G. Kearsley, 1760)	215
Figure 12.3	'Ode to Wisdom', inset lithograph, Samuel Richardson, *Clarissa* (1748), vol. 2, between pages 50 and 51	220
Figure 12.4	George Frederick Handel, 'Happy Pair', from *Alexander's Feast*, as reproduced in *The Muses Delight* (1754)	223
Figure 14.1	A slip ballad of 'The Sailor's Farewell' and 'The Rover of the Seas' (c.1800). Private collection	248
Figure 19.1	Honoré D'Urfé, *L'Astrée* (Paris, 1633). Source gallica.bnf.fr / Bibliothèque nationale de France	330
Figure 19.2	Honoré D'Urfé, *L'Astrée* (Paris, 1733). Source gallica.bnf.fr / Bibliothèque nationale de France	331
Figure 19.3	Honoré D'Urfé, *L'Astrée* (Paris, 1633). Source gallica.bnf.fr / Bibliothèque nationale de France	331
Figure 19.4	Mary Wroth, *The Countesse of Montgomeries Urania* (London, 1621). Folger Shakespeare Library, STC 26051 Copy 1	332
Figure 19.5	Amabel Hume-Campbell, Countess de Grey, *View of the Bowling-green Canal, Wrest*. Etching. © The Trustees of the British Museum	342
Figure 23.1	Unknown artist, frontispiece to *The Life and Strange Surprizing Adventures of Robinson Crusoe of York, Mariner* (London: W. Taylor, 1719). Etching by John Clark and John Pine. Courtesy of Beinecke Rare Book and Manuscript Library, Yale University	399
Figure 23.2	Bernard Picart, frontispiece to *La Vie et les avantures surprenantes de Robinson Crusoe* (Amsterdam: L'Honoré & Chatelain, 1720). Engraving. Courtesy of Beinecke Rare Book and Manuscript Library, Yale University	402
Figure 23.3	Thomas Stothard, *Robinson Crusoe in his island dress* (1782), engraved by C. Heath, in *Robinson Crusoe* (London: T. Cadell & W. Davis, 1820), facing p. 92. Engraving. Private collection	403
Figure 23.4	Statue of Alexander Selkirk at the site of his original house on Main Street, Lower Largo, Fife, Scotland (1885). Photograph by Sylvia Stanley (23 September 2009). SylviaStanley, CC BY-SA 3.0, https://creativecommons.org/licenses/by-sa/3.0, via Wikimedia Commons	405
Figure 23.5	Robinson Crusoe monument, in what is now Queen's Gardens, Hull but what would then have been Queens Dock (1973). Photograph by Steve F-E-Cameron (2007). Steve F-E-Cameron (Merlin-UK), CC BY-SA 3.0, http://creativecommons.org/licenses/by-sa/3.0/, via Wikimedia Commons	406

xii   ILLUSTRATIONS

Figure 24.1 Stipple print of *Charlotte at the Tomb of Werter*, engraved by J. R.
             Smith (1783). Reproduced from a copy in the author's collection   420
Figure 24.2 Intaglio print of *Charlotte at the Tomb of Werter*, engraved by
             R. S. Marcuard (1785). Reproduced from a copy in the author's
             collection   421
Figure 25.1 A print serving as a 'frontispiece' to Comerford's *Voyage to Lethe*
             (1741): H. Dodd, engraved by Andrew Birrell, *Captain James Cook,*
             F.R.S. (amended by hand to 'Saml. Cock') (1785). British Library
             General Reference Collection Cup.1001.c.4. By permission of the
             British Library   437
Figure 25.2 Thomas Rowlandson? after Velázquez, a Venus embracing Cupid
             (n.d.), facing p. 29 of Comerford's *Voyage to Lethe* (1741). British
             Library General Reference Collection Cup.1001.c.4. By permission
             of the British Library   439
Figure 25.3 Unidentified erotic print of a woman masturbating with carrots,
             extra-illustrating Comerford's *Voyage to Lethe* (1741), facing
             p. 35. British Library General Reference Collection Cup.1001.c.4.
             By permission of the British Library   439
Figure 25.4 Unidentified print of a group of people by a riverside facing the
             first page of Comerford's *Romance of a Day* (1760). British Library
             General Reference Collection 1459.a.60. By permission of the
             British Library   442
Figure 25.5 Unidentified print of two women looking from a balcony onto
             three men in a city street, extra-illustrating Comerford's *Romance*
             of a Day (1760), facing p. 45. British Library General Reference
             Collection 1459.a.60. By permission of the British Library   446
Figure 26.1 Honoré Daumier, *Une panique de Lilliputiens qui ont essayé de*
             garotter le Suffrage universel, Actualités no. 158. G 2857.
             Published in *Le Charivari* no. 179, 28 June 1851. © Paris Musées.
             Musée Carnavalet – Histoire de Paris   468
Figure 26.2 George Townshend, *The evacuation, or, An emetic for Old*
             England, by a Scot (1762). Courtesy of the Lewis Walpole Library,
             Yale University   471
Figure 26.3 Martin Rowson, *Gulliver's Travels Adapted and Updated* (2012),
             page 18. Courtesy of Martin Rowson   476
Figure 27.1 The phrase 'In Chan's work, character becomes font' rendered
             according to the Alternumeric 'Oh Blangis'. Courtesy of the artist
             and Greene Naftali, New York   495

Tables

Table 25.1 Prints in Comerford's *Voyage to Lethe* (1741)   450
Table 25.2 Prints in Comerford's *Romance of a Day* (1760)   455

Acknowledgements

Research for this book was funded by the National Science Centre, Poland, as part of the Opus project number 2020/37/B/HS2/02093: Inter-artistic contexts for the development of the early English novel.

The Eighteenth-Century British Novel and the Arts

Jakub Lipski and M-C. Newbould

NO ARTFORM IS an island. The cliché may urge a weary sigh for seeming gratuitous, but it neatly summarises some of the principal ideas explored in this volume: the arts do not germinate, evolve and exist in isolation but are inherently interconnected. The eighteenth century witnessed a complex set of circumstances in which this core principle found expression, for reasons we will outline here. But, of course, the notion that one artform somehow 'speaks' to another has deeper, older roots. Philip Sidney created perhaps the most memorable formula summarising a defining feature of early modern approaches to interartistic discourse in England:

> Poesy, therefore, is an art of imitation, for so Aristotle termeth it in the word *mimēsis*, that is to say, a representing, counterfeiting or figuring forth – to speak metaphorically, a speaking picture – with this end: to teach and delight.[1]

The sixteenth and seventeenth centuries offer multiple manifestations of theories about and expressions of this approach, in poetry, drama, painting, architecture and more.[2] Sidney, too, drew on it, but in order to reformulate long-standing ideas about these conversations across artforms, going back to Simonides, rerouted through Plutarch and Horace.[3] Simonides's concepts of painting as 'silent poetry' and poetry as 'speaking painting' (as related by Plutarch), as well as Horace's even more famous dictum, *ut pictura poesis* (as is painting so is poetry), have served as a running thread throughout discussions of what have been called the 'Sister Arts', encapsulating the shared, if distinctive, languages of communication between artforms.[4]

The classical roots of the flourishing interartistic discourse of the sixteenth and seventeenth centuries are significant to the period covered in this volume, the so-called 'long' eighteenth century, stretching from the latter end of the Restoration to the early nineteenth century. No precise date boundaries are observed in this volume precisely because the notion of strict divisions is antithetical to the approach we collectively take, where demarcations between periods (along traditional lines), concepts, practices and genres are considered to be fundamentally porous rather than clearly defined. It will nevertheless be shown in what follows that the long eighteenth century saw the fruition of interartistic ideas and practices that took different, innovative routes to those found in the early modern period which preceded it.

That said, a central axis of continuity was the significance of the classical world, which re-emerged in the various iterations of neoclassicism that stretch from the late seventeenth century to the Roman and especially Hellenistic revivals of the turn of the nineteenth century. This was driven in part by the acquisition and subsequent display of artworks purloined from greatly admired cradles of Western civilisation – which had, of course, featured prominently on the itineraries of travellers to continental

Europe – in private homes and in public spaces designed to facilitate access to art. The appearance of the earliest literary works discussed in this volume – the plays and prose narratives written by Aphra Behn – coincided with the establishment of the Ashmolean Museum in Oxford (1683), the founding of which documents a transformation of the cabinet of curiosities (with items ranging from smaller antiquities to the seventeenth-century mantle of King Powhatan, Pocahontas's father) – a testimony to the Western arrangement and ordering of knowledge as a practice of empowered objectification – into a more accessible museum space. The last dated prose fictions discussed in this volume, Jane Austen's *Northanger Abbey* and *Persuasion*, were published posthumously in 1817, not long after what were then known as the Elgin Marbles were purchased by the British government in 1816, amid a controversy that survives to this day; now re-termed the Parthenon Sculptures or Marbles in recognition of their original locus of creation and display, they were first exhibited at Montagu House, the original home of the British Museum (founded in 1753). The contention surrounding these sculptures now, as well as debates about former imperial powers' 'museumification' of the colonised heritage, reminds us of the politicised contexts in which 'art' was produced and consumed. These discourses and practices were rarely neutral. That the thread of classicism and the related activities of collection and display should run throughout the eighteenth century is itself a reminder of the often charged nature of aesthetic theory and praxis in the period. The neo- forms of classicism and the nature of exhibition culture, after all, were frequently weaponised to project old arguments in new forms about wealth, power and – that most loaded of early eighteenth-century concepts – Taste.

At the same time, as this volume explores, the eighteenth century saw an explosion of modes of artistic expression that seemingly transgressed, or even broke down barriers of educational or class privilege, social status and economic advantage (sometimes designated by 'connoisseurship'). While the expansion of public museums, galleries and 'popular' forms of entertainment – the theatre, street performances and so on[5] – allowed alternative iterations of what 'the arts' encompassed, new literary forms evolved in parallel with these developments, which catered for diverse types of reader in a rapidly expanding market for literacy across a wider social spectrum than had previously been known. The explosion in demotic print culture was aided by the exponential growth of a printing industry and a network of booksellers, circulating libraries and loci for sharing reading materials.

The centrality of the novel in this network continues to generate critical discussion. But the very term 'novel' is complicated and, in fact, historically inaccurate when used with reference to much eighteenth-century prose fiction. Few of the period's writers whom we often now identify as novelists (and who are identified as such in the essays that follow) would necessarily have laid claim to the term. 'Life and Adventures', 'History' and 'Romance' were often used instead, at times with confusing interchangeability. Nevertheless, when from the 1740s onwards fiction writers manifested a greater self-reflexive awareness in their writing, it was not untypical of the discourse of the genre, whatever it was called, to be informed by interartistic analogies and parallels. Henry Fielding's preface to *Joseph Andrews* (1742) as well as his metafictional commentaries in *Tom Jones* (1749) are perhaps among the best-known examples of how the other arts were integrated into the language of the novel – in the case of *Joseph Andrews*, theatre (tragedy, comedy and burlesque) and the pictorial arts (history painting, portraiture,

THE EIGHTEENTH-CENTURY BRITISH NOVEL AND THE ARTS   3

caricature and the natural character-drawing of Fielding's friend, William Hogarth).[6] But the history of this entanglement goes well beyond Fielding's metafiction. In the dedication opening *Oroonoko* (1688), dubbed 'a true history', Aphra Behn compares writing to painting, arguing in favour of the former: 'the pictures of the pen shall out-last those of the pencil, and even worlds themselves'.[7] The conceptual metaphor of the novel as a picture was a recurrent theme in subsequent fiction. It was similarly foregrounded in two more extensive definitions of the genre later in the period, by Tobias Smollett in *Ferdinand Count Fathom* (1753) and Clara Reeve in *The Progress of Romance* (1785), which also exemplify some of the earliest uses of the term 'novel' in a manner comparable to how it is typically adopted today. To Smollett, the novel was a 'diffused picture', to Reeve, 'a picture of real life and manners' – the former highlighting the openness of the form, the latter its realist poetics.[8]

While authors such as Fielding, Smollett and Reeve used interartistic discourse to differentiate their narratives from other types of writing, especially romance, taxonomically speaking these attempts remained inconsistent: to Fielding, 'a comic Romance is a comic Epic-Poem in Prose';[9] Smollett rearticulates his definition elsewhere, this time going with the label 'Romance';[10] while Reeve calls 'Romance' 'an Epic in prose', but lists among 'Novels and Stories Original and uncommon' an eclectic collection of titles, some of which we might now call novels (*Gulliver's Travels, Robinson Crusoe*) and some we might not (Swift's *Tale of a Tub*).[11] By 1810 Anna Letitia Barbauld was able to survey the history of the novel to the early nineteenth century, but while observing that 'the range of this kind of writing is so extensive', encompassing many different examples, she still favoured a terminologically conflicted descriptive formula: 'A good novel is an epic in prose.'[12] The fluidity of generic labelling in eighteenth-century critical writing about the novel stems, in part, from the diversity of a genre still in its early evolution, but also from the pejorative view many contemporary critics took of the novel as a lowly literary form. As Nicole Horejsi suggests of Reeve's argument, the 'prejudice in favour of ancient texts works hand in hand with ignorance of romance fiction to enshrine classical authors as literary authorities'; the attempt by Reeve and others to assert the novel's generic status alongside and against classical forms such as epic challenges 'canon formation' along the elitist lines privileged by contemporary (and male-dominated) cultural, connoisseurly discourse, to establish a more valued role for alternative types of fiction.[13]

The uncertainty regarding terminology and classification even among the writers of this period translated into a comparable turmoil in later criticism. Numerous critics have pointed out that the sheer diversity and evolutive growth of different types of prose fiction throughout the long eighteenth century make the term 'novel' restrictive and effectively redundant. When it is used as a normative generic marker, referring to realist prose fiction, it fails to capture the hybridity of 'the' genre throughout the long eighteenth century, its numerous and varied iterations and the historical contingencies which shaped them.[14] So why choose 'novel' in relation to 'the arts' for this volume? Terms such as 'fiction' or even 'literature' seem to encompass the breadth and diversity of these prose forms, but they are also capacious, suggesting not only a literary form but a theoretical concept, and they do not help to establish a set of readerly expectations for the type of text under discussion. Sometimes, a term – problematic though it is – comes to designate something with both critical valency and readerly comprehensibility, and it gains a currency that acquires value for being broadly understood, no matter its recognised flaws. 'Novel' carries specific assumptions and preconceptions, as often broken as they are met, and a broad-brush sense of what the term encompasses as a generic marker, and of the literary history to which it belongs.

The history of the emergence of 'the novel' in the long eighteenth century is nevertheless as fraught and contested as the terminology associated with it. Ian Watt's account of 'formal realism' in his classic *The Rise of the Novel* has encountered considerable subsequent critical contestation and reformulation since it first appeared in 1957 – not least for locating the starting point of novelistic fiction in Daniel Defoe and for consolidating a canon of white, male authors, to the neglect of significant precursors and contemporaries (including Behn, Eliza Haywood, Delarivier Manley and others).[15] But even such revisionist approaches to the 'rise' of the novel in the eighteenth century as Margaret Anne Doody's *The True Story of the Novel*, arguing against the romance-novel dialectic, agree that from the late seventeenth century onwards prose fiction took a new turn.[16] Stemming out of but also transforming earlier long prose narratives (Cervantes exerted an untold impact on the eighteenth century, after all[17]) and the romances popular in continental Europe, especially France, it told the lives of more ordinary citizens in more easily identifiable ways. Watt, in fact, pinpoints how this transformation took place in a way that brings us back to explaining why the long eighteenth century invested in and transformed interartistic discourse beyond its early modern iterations, and why the novel provides a rich locus for exploring it.

Watt argues that eighteenth-century philosophy – particularly in drawing on the legacy of John Locke, whose *Essay concerning Human Understanding* (1690) remained profoundly influential throughout the period – introduced new ways of thinking about human cognition, experience, consciousness and personal identity. Locke's arguments are complex, and Watt's exposition is of course far more detailed than can be summarised here, but the basic principle is that, in offering a schema for understanding how individual human experience can be understood – and how it can be expressed and communicated – Locke's ideas coagulated with a subsequent investment in individualised human experience and, in turn, its expression in new verbal forms. The novel offered an opportunity to capture that experience through narrative strategies demonstrating psychological complexity, interiority and a reaction to quotidian experiences within this empirical framework. What happens and how we think about it, external event and cognitive process, could be wrapped within an engaging fictive construct that drew readers to invest in a protagonist who, they found, reacted to and thought about those quotidian experiences in ways that seemed broadly familiar to their own. To illustrate his point, Watt made use of an interartistc parallel, arguing that the new type of fiction was registering a cultural change, a transition from universalism to particularism, also visible in, for example, the art of Dutch Golden Age painter Rembrandt.

Rembrandt's interests in particular experience and Locke's cognitive and verbal theories emerged at a time when empirical inquiry was itself challenged and invigorated, not only in the more abstract sense of theorising about thinking, but in a more mechanical way. How do we experience the world around us, in the most basic sense? What are the bodily mechanisms? And how does this relate to how we think? Locke famously formulated '*Ideas*' as '*Pictures drawn in our Minds*', drawn in the mind, which lie 'dormant' in the memory: 'secondary Perception' operates as a re-viewing of that internalised visual catalogue.[18] These pictures are first formed through visual experience, locating the primary sense organ in the eye. In parallel with an interest in ocularity similarly explored by René Descartes, Margaret Cavendish, and indeed in Isaac Newton's *Opticks* (1704), this organ was seen to be the primary mechanism for acquiring and subsequently processing sensory, primarily visual, experience.[19] The notion that ideas (as in thought) are inherently visual – contest it though we legitimately may, for aphantasia cannot be assumed to be universal – took hold with vigour. It informed, for example, Joseph Addison's discussion of visual memorial recall in his well-known 'Pleasures of the Imagination' essays, published in *The Spectator* in 1712.[20] It provided a core feature of the renewed investment in *ut pictura poesis*, too, and the various ways in which pictures, words and other forms of expressing 'what passes in a man's own mind' worked against, within and in relation to each other – to borrow from Laurence Sterne's redaction of Locke in *The Life and Opinions of Tristram Shandy, Gentleman* (1759–67), a text which challenges the applicability of 'novel' perhaps above all others of its period. In other words, the relationship between perception, cognitive processing and expression – meaning artistic representation, in whatever artform – was propelled into new territories by a discourse in which philosophic and aesthetic theory, literary and artistic practice combined, in the context of an expanding and increasingly diverse environment of readers, viewers, audience members, producers and consumers.

Among important milestones in the aesthetic theories that shaped these discourses, Charles Alphonse du Fresnoy's *De Arte Graphica*, first published in French in 1667 with notes by art theorist Roger de Piles, and translated into English in 1695, puts Horace's phrase at the forefront of Fresnoy's treatise. The preface to the English edition – 'A Parallel betwixt Painting and Poetry' – was penned by John Dryden (the work's translator), the most influential voice in English literary criticism of the day, who transformed the Horatian dictum to create a key term and concept that was to dominate much aesthetic theory and artistic practice in the ensuing century. As the opening lines of the translation have it, 'Painting and Poesy are two Sisters, which are so like in all things, that they mutually lend to each other both their Name and Office. One is call'd a dumb Poesy, and the other a speaking Picture.'[21] As subsequent entries into the debate came from representatives of various branches of the arts, it was not unusual for these treatises to undertake the task of ordering the arts.[22] In *An Essay on the Theory of Painting* (1715), for example, Jonathan Richardson argues for the primacy of the visual over the verbal:

> Words paint to the Imagination, but every Man forms the thing to himself in his own way: Language is very imperfect: There are innumerable Colours and Figures for which we have no name, and an Infinity of other Ideas which have no certain Words universally agreed upon as denoting them; whereas the Painter can convey his Ideas of these things clearly, and without Ambiguity; and what he says every one understands in the Sense he intends it.[23]

Richardson suggests a universality of visual language that – again to recall Locke – is more effective in the task of communicating ideas than words.

The hierarchisation of artforms permeated practice as well as theory, with writers (poets, novelists, dramatists and non-fiction writers) expanding long-standing methods of deploying figures of speech and techniques borrowed from non-verbal artistic practices, such as Sidney had earlier suggested. The inexpressibility topos, which again possessed an ancient pedigree, came to acquire new valency in the context of the verbal–visual debates that gathered in intensity throughout the eighteenth century. Phrases such as 'words cannot describe' or, tellingly, 'words cannot paint' became particularly commonplace in the prose fiction of the period to convey the apparent expressionistic limitations of the writer's chosen medium. Words are ambiguous, and can lead to miscommunication, and cannot convey with simple and comprehensible clarity the ideas, emotions and experiences more effectively presented by visual means. Novelists therefore often cast about for alternative, non-verbal methods of communicating experience, often borrowed from other artforms: typographical symbols and graphic elements abounded, notably in works such as Sterne's *Tristram Shandy* (and numerous, perhaps lesser-known texts which similarly deployed verbal–visual elements), while the frequent use of techniques such as literary pictorialism (verbal picture-painting) and the pseudo-theatrical 'scripting' of dialogue and the arrangement of characters as though in the scene of a play appeared to suggest that the novel-writer needed to use features more particular to other media when words alone seemed insufficient.

On the other hand, several theorists asserted the limitations of purely visual forms of expression, and instead promoted a logocentric approach. In Hildebrand Jacob's *Of the Sister Arts* (1734), for instance, we read that

> *Poetry* not only can express the external Signs of the Operation of the Mind, which are so livelily represented by *Painting*; but also its finest *abstracted* Thoughts, and most *pathetic* Reflections. *Painting* cannot convey its *Images* in such *great Numbers*, and with so *quick* and *unwearied* a *Succession* as *Poetry* does; and there are almost innumerable *Images* in *Poetry*, which *Painting* is not capable of forming, and which are often the greatest Ornaments in *Poetry*.[24]

We find a comparable idea in Lord Kames's later *Elements of Criticism* (1762), but with an important caveat. Kames revitalises Locke's theory of the connection or 'train' of ideas, and explores how it is formed and best communicated.[25] He affirms the superiority of the senses (the eye and the ear), but also the significance of the intellectual (conveyed verbally through connected ideas) to the process of understanding:

> Words are so far short of the eye in liveliness of impression, that in a description the connection of objects ought to be carefully studied, in order to make the deeper impression. For it is a known fact . . . that it is easier by words to introduce into the mind a related object, than one which is not connected with the preceding train. . . . different things are brought together without the slightest connection, if it be not what may be called verbal, *i. e.* taking the same word in different meanings.[26]

Kames suggests interdependence and symbiosis rather than exclusive superiority, the combination of the sensual and the intellectual. Indeed, the seeming competition for primacy between artforms was not a strict science, and throughout the century theorists and practitioners alike stressed the combination of artforms not as a solution to limitation, but as a more fecund opportunity for communication, and indeed for creativity. In Joseph Trapp's earlier *Praelectiones poeticae* (1711–19), translated into English as *Lectures on Poetry* by William Bowyer in 1742, we read that 'So near is their Affinity, that by a very natural and common Metaphor, Poetry is said to paint

THE EIGHTEENTH-CENTURY BRITISH NOVEL AND THE ARTS 7

Things, Painting to describe them. Both give us *Draughts* of the Body, as well as the Soul.'[27] As Ralph Cohen observes, in Trapp's aesthetic thought the two sister arts 'formed a complete example of human experience . . ., but singly they lacked this completeness'.[28] Indeed, as Jacob had pointed out, none of the sister arts can 'well be explain'd, without giving some Insight into the other at the same Time', and he adds that '[t]he nearer the *Poet* approaches to the *Painter*, the more perfect he is; and the more perfect the *Painter*, the more he imitates the *Poet*'.[29] Manifestations of novelistic – and indeed wider literary – self-deprecation over words' insufficiency was never a sincere confessional admission that purely verbal means of expression were somehow inadequate. The recurrence of the terminology, practices and concepts of non-verbal artforms frequently found in novelist texts is, instead, a conscious engagement with the possibilities of incorporating and remoulding other forms of artistic expression within a seemingly alien medium, showing the elasticity of artistic interaction rather than the limits of any one form. The rationale for this volume, therefore, is not so much an attempt at positioning novelistic discourse within a hierarchy of the arts in the period, but instead a wide-ranging investigation into how the genre developed in the context of other arts, and how interartistic dialogue imprinted itself on the novelistic text, based on the belief that various artistic practices feed upon one another rather than compete for a kind of mimetic supremacy.

The *ut pictura poesis* principle nevertheless encountered a marked backlash as the eighteenth century wore on. For one, the idea that there could be an easy correlation between word and image, that one speaks to the other, albeit in the unique language belonging to its own medium, troubled aesthetic theorists. Jacob's *Of the Sister Arts*, generally arguing in favour of the concept, already expresses some tentativeness: 'however they [the sister arts] may be reciprocally oblig'd to each other, and agree so well in the main, they have their *separate* Beauties too'.[30] David Hume, in his *Enquiry Concerning Human Understanding* (1748), expressed a reservation that 'All the colours of poetry, however splendid, can never paint natural objects in such a manner as to make the description be taken for a real landskip'; while Edmund Burke, in his *Philosophical Enquiry into the Origin of our Ideas of the Sublime and Beautiful* (1757), argued that words do not create mental images: their effect 'does not arise from their forming pictures of the several things they would represent in the imagination'.[31]

As Niklaus Schweizer demonstrates, recognition of the inherent differences between painting and poetry continued to motivate criticisms against sister arts discourse, which found their most elaborate expression in Gotthold Ephraim Lessing's *Laocoon* (1766), an aesthetic treatise which takes the celebrated Roman group statue depicting a key moment in the epic myth of the fall of Troy as a primary example.[32] Lessing argues that painting and poetry each have their own specific properties, drawing a distinction between them on spatial and temporal grounds: painting attains its narrative function through space, while poetry tells its story stretched over time. This differentiation was to exert lasting impact on eighteenth-century and subsequent approaches to the relationship between word and image, although recent criticism has asserted that the interaction between them is more nuanced (and 'confused') in Lessing's treatise than some subsequent redactions have suggested.[33] This counter approach was most powerfully promoted in Sir Joshua Reynolds's authoritative *Discourses*, published versions of the lectures he delivered as President of the Royal Academy he had co-founded in 1768. In the thirteenth discourse of 1786, Reynolds argues that no art can be grafted with success on another art. For though they all profess the same origin, and to proceed from the same stock, yet each has its own peculiar modes both of imitating nature, and of deviating from it, each for the accomplishment of its own particular purpose. These deviations, more especially, will not bear transplantation to another soil.[34]

Reynolds's language of territorial appropriation and expansion recalls *Laocoon*'s depiction of painting and poetry as 'two equitable friendly neighbouring states', each with their own 'empire'; but whereas for Reynolds sovereignty over the land is inviolable, for Lessing, once again, borders are to some degree permeable, infringements are inevitable, and each neighbour must exercise a 'mutual indulgence' towards the 'little infractions' that one might make on the 'extreme frontiers' of the other's territory.[35]

Such arguments (and their inherent conflicts) have resurfaced in more recent critical interventions recommending caution in researching the 'correspondences' of the arts. As René Wellek and Austin Warren's classic *Theory of Literature*, first published in 1942, suggests, difference lies in the reception as much as in the creation of art, but must be recognised as difference all the same:

> The parallels between the fine arts and literature usually amount to the assertion that this picture and that poem induce the same mood in me. . . . But this is the kind of parallelism which is of little worth for purposes of precise analysis. . . . Parallels between the arts which remain inside the individual reactions of a reader or spectator and are content with describing some emotional similarity of our reactions to two arts will, therefore, never lend themselves to verification and thus to a co-operative advance in our knowledge.[36]

Wellek and Warren were arguing against a tendency in comparative studies, which has never been abandoned and still finds its proponents, to elucidate readings of literary works with interartistic references that are not based on the textual reality, but are made on the grounds of indirect 'correspondences', by way of such vague concepts as comparable 'mood'. In fact, their corrective is not so far away from Lessing's motivation in attempting to define the medial specifics of painting and poetry more clearly, to rectify the tendency of 'witty' critics who fail to 'hold the scales equal between the two Arts'.[37] These reservations, however, do not necessarily hold for interdisciplinary dialogues established by specific instances of crossovers that have a formal or contextual rationale. Contemporary studies of these crossovers, accordingly, have departed from the concept of 'correspondences', and have opted for more specific notions capturing the diverse relationships established between artforms and artistic practices, visible especially in forms that by definition exist at the intersection of artistic modes of expression. Such terms as 'iconotext' or 'imagetext' have been coined (by Kristin Hallberg and W. J. T. Mitchell, respectively) to address the formal shape of artworks where the visual and verbal modes of expression are entangled by definition.[38] And while they have typically been used with reference to more contemporary genres, such as picturebooks, graphic novels and comic books, the long eighteenth century produced a variety of examples showing an analogical coexistence of word and image.[39] While the novel, unlike William Hogarth's graphic narrative cycles, illustrated broadsheet ballads or Willam Blake's poems, does not depend for its generic identity on this coexistence, recent perspectives from the fields of book history and print culture studies have firmly established that the material packaging of the novel text – from format and book binding to typeface and pictorial embellishments – is an integral formal component.[40] Mitchell's claim that 'all arts are "composite" arts (both text and image); all media are mixed media' is central to understanding the novel as an artistic entity that is not limited to the verbal.[41]

Studying the interartistic dialogues in which the eighteenth-century novel participated nevertheless goes beyond these cases of the integral coexistence of word and image. The 'correspondences' approach criticised by Wellek and Warren is now typically substituted by insights grounded in intermediality studies, where the novel is seen as an element of a wider network of media.[42] 'Intermedia' as a concept was first problematised by Fluxus artist Dick Higgins in 1966, who adopted Samuel Taylor Coleridge's term 'intermedium' (originally used with reference to Edmund Spenser's use of allegory in *The Faerie Queene*) to address artforms combining different media, in a manner later repeated by those critics who put forward the more specific concepts of 'iconotext' and 'imagetext'.[43] The notion of intermediality as it is used today, however, is much more comprehensive, and apart from elucidating relationships between media within specific genres and examples of artwork, it draws attention to the relationships established within a wider system of art practices. This broader perspective is aptly captured by Higgins's later 'Intermedia Chart' (1995), which includes genres that are inherently intermedial, such as concrete poetry or visual novels, but also those that are seemingly separate from others and formally autonomous. Yet even the latter, the chart shows us, are brought together by the all-encompassing circle of intermedia, indicating that there is no way for one artform to be effectively disconnected from others.[44]

As indicated in Higgins's chart, intermediality has now grown into a vast umbrella term that contains multimodal artforms and diverse interartistic relationships, but also the implied presence of other media, various aspects of which will be addressed in this volume. The conflicts and confluences noted by present-day theorists of intermediality are not, in fact, so very far removed from the seemingly inherent contradictions of eighteenth-century aesthetic discourse and artistic (including literary) practice. The essays gathered here reflect elements of the convergence between theorisations of these processes found in current discussions of the intermedial, flourishing in a period that witnessed a significant expansion and complication of connections between the arts. These processes did not develop unproblematically, or without contestation – just as 'the novel' was far from universally embraced as a wonderfully democratising and absorbing literary form by critics, readers or indeed some novelists.

So far, the discussion has principally revolved around the relations between word and image, poetry and painting. But as intermedial studies suggest – and as eighteenth-century theory and practice attest – the idea of related artforms expanded well beyond. The so-called family of sister arts encompassed music, architecture, sculpture, landscape gardening and more, to create a dynamic context for shared traits and distinctive differences to meet, exchange and sometimes clash when one artform encountered another. The aesthetic realms of discourse were tested out and contested on the terrain of practical application in numerous, sometimes surprising contexts. Peter de Bolla has explored these connections and their subsequent developments in *The Education of the Eye*, which puts forward the argument that the focus on the ocular as a key instrument for empirical inquiry and subsequent artistic creation in the eighteenth century was in turn shaped by the producers of art, whether in the decorative and architectural designs of James and Robert Adam, the landscape designs of Lancelot 'Capability' Brown and Humphry Repton, or the paintings of J. M. W. Turner. Producers and consumers alike operated within 'a *culture* based on the visual'.[45] De Bolla argues that what we might recognise as 'modern subjectivity' took shape through these processes – involving a consciousness of the self as a perceiving being – and peaked in the mid-eighteenth century. This coincides with some of the features of the new forms of prose fiction identified here as investing in interiority and shifting ideas about consciousness.[46] As he also stresses, it is important to recall that the cultural products of the period were the result of collaborative effort, and indeed of labour, with a largely unidentified group of individuals collectively embodied in the name of the single creator we might now metonymically use to represent that product. As de Bolla writes,

> the name *Adam* name stands for a complex mesh of interlocking signifiers, constituting a family architectural practice; a studio of draftsmen; an aggressive developers' and builders' empire; a group of subsidiary companies; and a vast and pretty stable cohort of subcontracted artisans, laborers, artists, and craftsmen. It was the product of all this that came to be known as the culturally disseminated style called 'the Adam style'.[47]

The makers of fiction, too, extend beyond named (or even anonymous) novelists to include typesetters, papermakers, ink mixers, bookbinders and other printshop workers besides. The technologies of print and bookmaking, and of artistic faction, provide a salient thread in some of the essays that follow, which trace the sometimes hard to identify labour behind craftwork, decorative skill and the manufacture of visual and textual artefacts.

De Bolla's work is situated within a vast and yielding field of critical interventions addressing how the arts 'interacted' in the varied ways suggested so far, and some of the reasons why. Many of these studies have similarly located an investment in 'the eye' and in the ways that verbal and visual expression (broadly defined) are intertwined in the eighteenth century.[48] Classic works, such as by Jean Hagstrum, Richard Wendorf and John Brewer, among others, variously address aspects of the sister arts, including what *ut pictura poesis* meant to eighteenth-century creators and how it found its expression; of what literary pictorialism was, and how practitioners from James Thomson to (differently) William Wordsworth pushed the boundaries of 'painting with words'; and of the audiences for different manifestations of the arts.[49] The expanding globalism of the century, through trade and economic as well as social commerce, and significantly through tourism, facilitated an exchange, and even an appropriation, of cultural styles, discourses and of course artefacts. These, in turn, shaped the visual aesthetic of Britain in manifestly visible ways, but also in more intangible senses, too, as the essays in this volume tease out through exploring variant discourses and expressions of the arts in the period's novelistic fiction. There is by now an extensive body of work that has established how the novel, in particular, provided an apt testing ground for the development of interartistic discourses, whether in specific case studies focusing on major figures (Samuel Richardson, Smollett, Sterne, Frances Burney, Austen), genres (the Gothic) or specific artforms (painting, for instance).[50] In many respects, these valuable studies consolidate and contribute further examples that endorse existing patterns of thinking about 'the novel' and 'the arts', and how they relate to each other. The collection of essays gathered here, in turn, performs an act of consolidation and subsequent expansion, focusing on British examples of novels, with salient reference to continental European works.

We have already set up some of the general ideas explored in this collection, where they come from and why they might matter, but some further precisions are needed in order for this volume's contribution to the field to be all the more discernible. The term 'the arts' itself is as loaded and as complicated as 'the novel'. Although this is, in many ways, a collection that reiterates and develops the principles of 'sister arts' discourse, at the same time it offers a wider perspective on what the arts meant in the language of the period beyond the conventional referents of the 'fine arts'. This expansiveness is, in fact, characteristic of eighteenth-century thought and practice. A typically insightful entry compiled by Samuel Johnson in his *Dictionary* confirms that 'art' was understood very broadly, as 'The power of doing something not taught by nature and instinct', 'A science', 'A trade', 'Artfulness; skill; dexterity', 'Cunning' and 'Speculation'.[51] This breadth of vision was inherited from earlier medieval and subsequent early modern concepts of art as allied to artistry, artifice, craft, imagination, manufacture and skilfulness, with manual and intellectual powers combining to create artistic products that were both aesthetically pleasing and/or served a practical purpose. Johnson's revitalisation of these concepts, however, is situated in the eighteenth-century – dare we say Enlightenment – crucible of new opportunities for developing cultural experience (through expanded travel, museums or reading, for instance) and emerging technologies for shaping and expressing knowledge in practical ways, as de Bolla's book, for one, attests. 'Arts', therefore, had a particular socio-performative dimension, and a cursory search alone into the uses of the word in the eighteenth-century corpus yields a plethora of results even when limited to titles. These range from such well-known instances as 'the art of walking' (as in John Gay's 1716 poem), 'the art of speaking' and 'the art of cookery' to more idiosyncratic examples: 'the art of angling' or the 'art of making soap'. In Jane Collier's satirical work, *An Essay on the Art of Ingeniously Tormenting* (1753), the parodic use of 'art' in the title implies a long-standing tradition of social behaviours perceived as 'arts'. Accordingly, several artistic practices understood in this broader way – such as the art of reading, the art of politeness, the art of elocution or the art of sociability – find their place in this volume as demonstrating how these modes meaningfully interacted with the period's novels.

The collection also recognises some problematic challenges inherent in the discourse of the arts as understood and practised in this period, and as its novelistic fiction testifies. In the eighteenth century, as now, the notion that 'fine arts' were feminised – whether in their depiction as draped Muses, or Graces, or in the notion that women were objects to be looked as, as though themselves artworks – reinforces gendered discourses of disempowerment, objectification and exploitation. Many of the examples of the intersections between gender and the arts explored in this collection precisely counter the notion of a weakly feminised concept of art, or indeed of the feminine being weak – even while a female character is depicted in just such terms. James Noggle, for one, identifies a mid-century shift in how women were situated in relation to the discourse of taste, which 'put women as objects into a particularly tense relation to their role as subjects'[52] – and which coincides with the mid-century period during which novelistic fiction flourished in quantity and diversity. Whether as the objects of artistic discourse, or its creators, women's engagements with the arts challenge (often by satirical means) the very premises on which they seem, in many respects, to be founded and promoted – especially by male connoisseurs.

The discourse of the arts, as woven into the novel, was frequently used to serve other types of power play, too – those of racial and class-based subjugation, for instance. On the one hand, depictions of the so-called lower classes in word and in image sometimes tended either towards caricatured stereotyping or decorative prettification, such as of a pastoral scene with aestheticised rustic poverty.[53] On the other, ownership over and aesthetic manipulation of marginalised social groups operated in the pernicious racial discourse of the period. Behn's depiction of Oroonoko in her eponymous novel, often discussed in critical studies as an example of reified aestheticisation, deploys literary pictorialism to admire its hero, but by bringing him to conform to European ideals of beauty while underscoring the racialised otherness that allows him to be traded as a commodity:[54]

> He was pretty tall, but of a shape the most exact that can be fancied. The most famous statuary could not form the figure of a man more admirably turned from head to foot. His face was not of that brown, rusty black which most of that nation are, but a perfect ebony, or polished jet. . . . His nose was rising and Roman, instead of African and flat. His mouth, the finest shaped that could be seen, far from those great turned lips, which are so natural to the rest of the Negroes. The whole proportion and air of his face was so noble and exactly formed that, bating his colour, there could be nothing in nature more beautiful, agreeable, and handsome.[55]

The closing scenes of *Oroonoko* create a spectacle of the execution of this 'ebony' artefact with a gory relish that, in many respects, parallels the (equally racially stereotyped) heroic dramas of Behn's day, as Catherine Gallagher suggests.[56] Behn's narrative layering, as some critics argue, no doubt lends greater complexity to such depictions, but from at least one perspective she seems to be reinforcing an aestheticisation of racialised otherness through literary pictorialism that was to endure.

Another memorable example is the familiar character sketch of Friday in *Robinson Crusoe* (1719). Shortly after their encounter, narrator Crusoe gives a detailed literary portrait of his new companion:

> He was a comely handsome Fellow, perfectly well made, with straight strong Limbs, not too large; tall and well shap'd . . . He had a very good Countenance, not a fierce and surly Aspect; but seem'd to have something very manly in his Face, and yet he had all the Sweetness and Softness of an *European* in his Countenance too, especially when he smil'd. His Hair was long and black, not curl'd like Wool; his Forehead very high, and large, and a great Vivacity and sparkling Sharpness in his Eyes. The Colour of his Skin was not quite black, but very tawny, and yet not of an ugly yellow nauseous tawny, as the *Brasilians*, and *Virginans*, and other Natives of *America* are; but of a bright kind of a dun olive Colour, that had in it something very agreeable; tho' not very easy to describe. His Face was round, and plump, his Nose small, not flat like the Negroes, a very good Mouth, thin Lips, and his fine Teeth well set, and white as Ivory.[57]

The description, echoing Behn's to some extent, is an object lesson in how diverse registers for depicting otherness were integrated in the language of the novel: we see a mix of Western expectations, deriving from the 'noble savage' imaginary; elements of a negative poetics deployed to differentiate Friday from other types of racialised others; traces of stock expressions coming from the romance tradition; and confusingly tentative constructions of masculinity. Defoe's famous passage is a very apt illustration of how the various conventions of literary pictorialism were implemented to aestheticise and at the same time objectify racial difference.

A much later work, the anonymous *The Woman of Colour* (1808), suggests the longevity of this type of literary pictorial representation – of the protagonist as artistically admirable but nonetheless othered – where 'blackness' is again a demarcation of visible difference set against Westernised perceptions of physical appearance and racial alterity.[58] As Olivia Carpenter suggests, the visual arts offer an important parallel narrative to how the novel's biracial heroine, Olivia, wishes to 'rub away her blackness' to attain the whiteness prized in European concepts of beauty.[59] At the same time, Olivia asserts that she is as 'clean' as her white counterparts, and so 'unsettles the racist notion that negative qualities remain inextricably wedded to permanent external characteristics'. As Carpenter argues, referring to David Dabydeen's work on depictions of blackness in eighteenth-century painting, these scenes attain their complex aesthetic force by their 'visual nature'.[60] Indeed, *The Woman of Colour* uses visualised language – 'picture', 'scene', 'draw', 'paint' – throughout to describe landscape and protagonists alike, both external appearance and internal character. Beyond simply reiterating commonplace descriptive clichés, these terms reinforce the extent to which this text is heavily invested in ways of seeing and of perceiving, and of the cultural and politicised dynamics in which interartistic discourse and its manifestation in novelistic practices operate.

While the format of a 'companion' enables a relatively broad and far-ranging coverage of the ideas and materials discussed so far, and for some aspects of these wider issues and debates to be addressed, no attempt is made in what follows at comprehensiveness, which would at best be illusory. We have opted against a typical companion-like structure with conventional sections and a mostly canonical scope, both in terms of the novelistic texts covered and the artforms read alongside these texts. As one would expect, this decision resulted in some unavoidable gaps in authorial and textual representation; deciding what 'should' be included or excluded can risk conforming to the constraints of canonicity in playing against a checklist of must-haves on the one hand, or attempting to subvert it by deliberately excluding them on the other. Meanwhile, there are several crossovers: sometimes the same authors or texts are discussed in multiple places, invariably to reveal the very diverse readings they can produce when perceived through alternative theoretical and aesthetic perspectives. In general, our idea was to reconcile the imperatives of consolidation and innovation. This rationale is visible in a combination of survey essays that systematise current approaches to the eighteenth-century novel and the arts with, by contrast, specialised studies that expand the field either by challenging the critical status quo or by breaking new ground. The expected overlaps in coverage, then, result from the volume's heterogeneity in terms of the types of scholarly material it collects and of the diversity of research perspectives and methodologies adopted. Our hope is that this arrangement results in the *Companion*'s suitability for a variety of readers: from students new to the field, to eighteenth-century scholars, to researchers in literature and visual cultures more broadly, among many other disciplines.

To make this volume's rich offering accessible and cogent we have divided the material into five sections that help readers to navigate the volume's conceptual scope by clustering together essays that share salient themes, ideas and perspectives, adapted to distinctive material examples. The first – 'Styles and Discourses' – gathers four studies mapping the novel's entanglement with contemporaneous discourses of art and aesthetics as well as art-related cultural practices and fashions. Marcie Frank addresses the issues of narrative and anonymity in Haywood's *Invisible Spy* (1755), acknowledging the author's indebtedness to the work of Behn and Fielding. James Watt discusses the problematic representations of empire as expressed in the relationship between Orientalism and sexuality in Defoe's *The Fortunate Mistress* (1724), Robert Bage's *The Fair Syrian* (1787) and Phebe Gibbes's *Hartly House, Calcutta* (1789). Katharina Boehm sheds new light on the discourse of antiquarianism by asserting the role of handicraft within it, and its significance to mid-century novels, focusing on Sarah Scott's *Millenium Hall* (1762). The convergence between novelistic and medical discourse, meanwhile, is addressed in the parallels Ashleigh Blackwood draws between the textual-visual didacticism of medical publications and contemporary novels, from Jane Barker's *A Patch-Work Screen for the Ladies* (1723), to Smollett's fiction, to Sterne's *Tristram Shandy*.

The subsequent cluster of essays on eighteenth-century 'Visual Cultures' shows how the novel occupied a crucial position in the broader terrain of the period's cultures of visuality, in its intersections between plastic, architectural and verbal arts, such as suggested by de Bolla's study of interartistic theory and practice. The essays in this section range from survey approaches to focused case studies. Frédéric Ogée shows how painting and the novel across the eighteenth century shared a common rationale in documenting modern subjectivity; his focus throughout are the affinities in these two artforms' representations of pleasure. Chris Ewers evaluates the importance of the architectural imagination for the formal aspects of the novel, using examples ranging from Fielding's *Tom Jones*, to Gothic fiction, to Austen's *Mansfield Park* (1814). M-C. Newbould traces the enduring presence of sculpture and the sculptural metaphor in the gendered discourses of prose fiction, tracing a thread between the lifelike inanimacy of heroines, such as Richardson's Clarissa or those found in Gothic fiction, and the temporary suspension of the (often male) protagonists of comic fiction, such as Smollett's, pictured as the 'statue of surprise'. Katherine Aske sketches the aesthetic background behind the novelistic conventions of describing beautiful women, in examples including *Pamela* (1740), *Tom Jones*, Charlotte Lennox's *The Female Quixote* (1752) and Burney's *Evelina* (1778). Jakub Lipski shows how Horace Walpole's fascination with word and image crossovers, as documented by materials ranging from handwritten annotations to private correspondence, resulted in *The Castle of Otranto* (1764); while Hannah Moss revisits the complex artistry of Ann Radcliffe's Gothic fiction, especially in *The Mysteries of Udolpho* (1794), and considers her romances as 'total works of art'.

Opening the section titled 'Modes and Spaces of Performance', Joseph Drury redefines the rococo, or the whimsical, as a performative practice, as visible in the fiction of Haywood. Elizabeth Kraft, in turn, recognises the unique functions of song in Richardson's fiction, with psalmody in *Clarissa* (1747–8) playing a key role. Daniel Cook explores the variety of popular forms of entertainment, as represented in Jonathan Swift's *Gulliver's Travels* (1726). These two perspectives are combined

THE EIGHTEENTH-CENTURY BRITISH NOVEL AND THE ARTS   15

in Georgina Bartlett's essay, which is concerned with broadside ballads in the context of sentimental fiction. The interartistic iterations of the culture of sensibility are also addressed by Mascha Hansen, who reads the work of the Burneys with reference to Shakespearean performances and sentimental plots. The subsequent three essays are all engaged with diverse performative acts of novelistic characters: Przemysław Uściński explains the prevalence of the 'polite arts' across eighteenth-century novels, including Oliver Goldsmith's *Vicar of Wakefield* (1766); Pierre Dubois argues for the central role of 'musical epiphanies' in the later fiction of the period, including the work of Sterne, Henry Mackenzie, Radcliffe and Burney; and Fraser Easton studies Austen's investment in the art of elocution, as represented by *Persuasion*.

While the whole volume is underpinned by a conviction that eighteenth-century novel writing was an interactive venture within a wider network of artistic practices, in Part IV – 'Networks and Interactions' – this conviction comes to the fore. This section includes two case studies: Natasha Simonova's investigation of the intermedial practices of the Wrest circle, partly in relation to *The Female Quixote* and the structures of romance; and the metafictional insights on the art of reading included in *The History of Charlotte Summers* (1749–50) brought out by Joanna Maciulewicz. Also in this section, Emrys Jones teases out the notion of 'sociable arts' with a look towards eighteenth-century conversation pieces, and of the confluences and divergences found in their novelistic equivalents, including *Robinson Crusoe*, *The Female Quixote* and *Evelina*. Paul Goring, meanwhile, challenges the critical assumptions sometimes prevalent in discussions of the visual arts in relation to seemingly demotic novelistic fiction, by reminding us that the widespread availability of examples of visual art cannot be taken for granted. His discussion lights upon Smollett, Defoe, Frances Sheridan and Haywood, among others.

The final section – 'Adaptations and Afterlives' – is concerned with the eighteenth-century novel's transmedial futures, offering studies of novelistic content reimagined in a diversity of artforms, from the eighteenth century to the present. Nathalie Collé surveys the endurance of some of the most popular frontispieces to eighteenth-century editions of *Robinson Crusoe*. Sandro Jung traces adaptations of the 'Charlotte at the Tomb of Werter' scene in British needlework pictures, drawing comparisons between Johann Wolfgang von Goethe's phenomenally successful novel of 1774 and Sterne's *A Sentimental Journey through France and Italy* (1768). Helen Williams studies nineteenth-century collector James Comerford's practice of extra-illustrating eighteenth-century erotic books in his collection, with particular emphasis on the anonymous *Voyage to Lethe* (1741) and John Cleland's novella *The Romance of a Day* (1760), and the digital afterlives of these books today. Brigitte Friant-Kessler revisits the continuing popularity of representations of eighteenth-century authors and novelistic characters in visual satire, tracing reiterations of eighteenth-century book illustrations to *Robinson Crusoe*, of the enduring appeal of disproportionate sizes in *Gulliver's Travels*, and of the iconic image of Austen in later political satire. The two essays closing the volume are concerned with artforms alien to the eighteenth century itself, but which nonetheless embrace the period's novelistic fiction and repurpose it in the new forms and contexts of radically alternative media, thus offering unique insights into afterlives and adaptations. Amelia Dale analyses how the work of Sterne, the Marquis de Sade and Austen has been reconfigured in contemporary conceptual art, including examples from John Baldessari, Meg Cranston and Paul Chan. Jennifer Wilson offers an essay that exemplifies novel-to-film studies, reminding us of the significant role that film media play in reimagining the characters, scenes, themes and dynamics of eighteenth-century fiction. Her focused analysis of Tony Richardson's *Tom Jones* (1963) and its construction of the implied viewer in comparison with Fielding's implied readers shows how adaptation can seek to recreate not just narrative, plot and character, but the atmosphere, energy and comic vitality of the novelistic text which inspires it.

The essays offered here, therefore, serve individually and collectively as reflections, meditations, interventions and at times provocations. They contribute towards rather than seek to define or delimit the critical thought surrounding and generated by the bountiful ways in which eighteenth-century novels embrace the ferment of artistic and cultural activity in which they were produced, and which undoubtedly helped to shape them. That process of discovery throughout the period was jagged and uneven, rather than having pursued a smooth and methodical course. There are undoubtedly many avenues of exploration not tested here, and many more of which we are all as yet unaware. Walter Scott may have stated in his 1815 review of Austen's *Emma* that 'A novel . . . is frequently "bread eaten in secret"' – voicing in order to critique long-standing and contemporary attacks on this literary form – but its very status as a seemingly unstable genre in the artistic hierarchies of its day in fact serves to assure its position within current evaluations of eighteenth-century cultural practice.[61] To return to the anti-hierarchising impulse in approaching the arts in general adopted here, when we broaden our perspective on what they encompassed throughout this period, so we can reassert the significance of the novel as crucial to their evolution, and vice versa.

Acknowledgement

This research was funded by the National Science Centre, Poland, as part of the Opus project number 2020/37/B/HS2/02093.

Notes

1. Philip Sidney, *Sidney's 'The Defence of Poesy' and Selected Renaissance Literary Criticism*, ed. Gavin Alexander (Harmondsworth: Penguin, 2004), 46.
2. See a classic overview by Rensselaer W. Lee, '*Ut Pictura Poesis*: The Humanistic Theory of Painting', *The Art Bulletin* 22, no. 4 (1940): 197–269.
3. Gavin Alexander, 'Introduction' to *Sidney's 'The Defence of Poesy'*, 29–30.
4. Henryk Markiewicz, 'Ut Pictura Poesis . . . A History of the Topos and the Problem', *New Literary History* 18, no. 3 (1987): 535–58.
5. See Richard Altick's classic study, *The Shows of London* (Cambridge, MA: Belknap Press of Harvard University Press, 1978).
6. See Henry Fielding, 'Preface' to *Joseph Andrews*, ed. Martin C. Battestin and Fredson Bowers, The Wesleyan Edition of the Works of Henry Fielding (1742; Middletown: Wesleyan University Press, 1966), 3–11, and the opening chapters to the six books of *Tom Jones* in Henry Fielding, *The History of Tom Jones, a Foundling*, ed. Fredson Bowers, The Wesleyan Edition of the Works of Henry Fielding (1749; Middletown: Wesleyan University Press, 1975).
7. Aphra Behn, *Oroonoko and Other Writings*, ed. Paul Salzman (1688; Oxford: Oxford University Press, 1994), 3.
8. Tobias Smollett, *The Adventures of Ferdinand Count Fathom*, ed. Jerry C. Beasley, The Works of Tobias Smollett (1753; Athens and London: University of Georgia Press, 1988), 4;

Clara Reeve, *The Progress of Romance, through Times, Countries, and Manners*, 2 vols (Colchester: Printed for the Author, 1785), 1:111.

9. Fielding, 'Preface' to *Joseph Andrews*, 4.

10. Reviewing *The Peregrinations of Jeremiah Grant* (1763), Smollett paraphrases his definition, this time using such terms as 'this kind of romance' and 'diffused comedy'. *Critical Review* 15 (1763): 13–14.

11. Reeve, *The Progress of Romance*, 1:13, 2:53.

12. Anna Letitia Barbauld, 'On the Origin and Progress of Novel-Writing', in *The British Novelists; with an Essay; and Prefaces, Critical and Biographical, by Mrs. Barbauld* (London: J. Rivington et al., 1810), 2–3.

13. Nicole Horejsi, *Novel Cleopatras: Romance Historiography and the Dido Tradition in English Fiction, 1688–1785* (Toronto: University of Toronto Press, 2019), 168–9.

14. See, for example, John J. Richetti, *Popular Fiction before Richardson: Narrative Patterns: 1700–1739* (Oxford: Clarendon Press, 1969), and Michael McKeon, *The Origins of the English Novel, 1600–1740* (Baltimore: Johns Hopkins University Press, 1987).

15. Ian Watt, *The Rise of the Novel: Studies in Defoe, Richardson, and Fielding* (Berkeley and Los Angeles: University of California Press, 1957).

16. Margaret Anne Doody, *The True Story of the Novel*, 2nd edn (New Brunswick: Rutgers University Press, 1997). Watt's theory has been revisited and revised by a number of critics. See, for example, McKeon, *The Origins of the English Novel*; J. Paul Hunter, *Before Novels: The Cultural Contexts of Eighteenth-Century English Fiction* (New York: W. W. Norton, 1990); and a very useful overview of Wattian, post-Wattian and anti-Wattian approaches, Nicholas Seager, *The Rise of the Novel: A Reader's Guide to Essential Criticism* (Basingstoke: Palgrave Macmillan, 2012).

17. See, for instance, Ronald Paulson, *Don Quixote in England: The Aesthetics of Laughter* (Baltimore, MD and London: Johns Hopkins University Press, 1998), and J. A. G. Ardila, ed., *The Cervantean Heritage: Reception and Influence of Cervantes in Britain* (London: Legenda, 2009).

18. John Locke, *An Essay concerning Human Understanding*, ed. Peter H. Nidditch (1690; Oxford: Clarendon Press, 1975), 152.

19. Isaac Newton, *Opticks: or, A Treatise of the Reflexions, Refractions, Inflexions and Colours of Light* (London: S. Smith and B. Walford, 1704).

20. Joseph Addison, *The Spectator*, 411–21, 21 June–3 July 1712.

21. Charles-Alphonse du Fresnoy, *De Arte Graphica. The Art of Painting. Translated into English, together with an Original Preface containing A Parallel betwixt Painting and Poetry by Mr. Dryden* (London: W. Rogers, 1695), 3.

22. See Lawrence Lipking, *The Ordering of the Arts in Eighteenth-Century England* (Princeton: Princeton University Press, 1970).

23. Jonathan Richardson, *An Essay on the Theory of Painting* (London: John Churchill, 1715), 5–6.

24. Hildebrand Jacob, *Of the Sister Arts: An Essay* (London: W. Lewis, 1734), 5.

25. Henry Home, Lord Kames, *Elements of Criticism*, 3 vols (London: A. Millar; Edinburgh: A. Kincaid & J. Bell, 1762). Chapter 1 is entitled 'Perception and ideas in a train'.

26. Kames, *Elements of Criticism*, 1:39.

27. Joseph Trapp, *Lectures on Poetry*, trans. William Bowyer (London: C. Hitch and C. Davis, 1742), 17.

28. Ralph Cohen, *The Art of Discrimination: Thomson's 'The Seasons' and the Language of Criticism* (Berkeley and Los Angeles: University of California Press, 1964), 192.

29. Jacob, *Of the Sister Arts*, 3–4.

30. Jacob, *Of the Sister Arts*, 5.

31. David Hume, *An Enquiry Concerning Human Understanding*, in *Enquiries Concerning Human Understanding and Concerning the Principles of Morals*, 3rd edn rev., ed. P. H. Nidditch (1748; Oxford: Clarendon Press, 1975), 17. Edmund Burke, *A Philosophical Enquiry into the Origin of Our Ideas of the Sublime and Beautiful*, ed. Adam Phillips (1757; Oxford: Oxford University Press, 1990), 152.
32. See Niklaus Schweizer, *The Ut pictura poesis Controversy in Eighteenth-Century England and Germany* (Bern: Peter Lang, 1972).
33. W. J. T. Mitchell, 'Foreword: Why Lessing's *Laocoon* Still Matters', in *Rethinking Lessing's 'Laocoon': Antiquity, Enlightenment, and the 'Limits' of Painting and Poetry*, ed. Avi Lifschitz and Michael Squire (Oxford: Oxford University Press, 2017), xxiii–xxxiv (xxvi).
34. Joshua Reynolds, *The Discourses of Sir Joshua Reynolds* (London: James Carpenter, 1842), 235.
35. Gotthold Ephraim Lessing, *Laocoon*, trans. Robert Phillimore (London: Routledge, 1910), 145. See also Mitchell, 'Foreword', xxvi.
36. René Wellek and Austin Warren, *Theory of Literature* (New York: Harcourt, Brace and Company, 1949), 127.
37. Lessing, *Laocoon*, 56.
38. See Kristin Hallberg, 'Litteraturvetenskapen och bilderboksforskningen', *Tidskrift för litteraturvetenskap* 3, no. 4 (1982): 163–8, and W. J. T. Mitchell, *Picture Theory: Essays on Verbal and Visual Representation* (Chicago and London: University of Chicago Press, 1995), 89. See also Peter Wagner, ed., *Icons – Texts – Iconotexts: Essays on Ekphrasis and Intermediality* (Berlin and Boston: De Gruyter, 1996), and Liliane Louvel, *Poetics of the Iconotext*, ed. Karen Jacobs, trans. Laurence Petit (Farnham: Ashgate, 2011).
39. Peter de Voogd, for example, writes about a 'coexistential' relationship between word and image with reference to eighteenth-century material (here in the work of Sterne), which is 'when the text's verbal and visual elements are so intimately interwoven that they form an aesthetic whole'. Peter de Voogd, '*Tristram Shandy* as Aesthetic Object', *Word & Image* 4, no. 1 (1988): 383–4.
40. The art of William Hogarth has been discussed comparatively with reference to eighteenth-century fiction by a number of critics. See, for example, Peter Jan de Voogd, *Henry Fielding and William Hogarth: The Correspondences of the Arts* (Amsterdam: Rodopi, 1981), and Ronald Paulson, *The Beautiful, Novel, and Strange: Aesthetics and Heterodoxy* (Baltimore and London: Johns Hopkins University Press, 1996). For a study of the narrative quality of Hogarth's art, see, for instance, Robert L. S. Cowley, *Marriage A-la-Mode: A Re-View of Hogarth's Narrative Art* (Manchester: Manchester University Press, 1983). To read more on the aesthetics of print, see, among others, Janine Barchas, *Graphic Design, Print Culture, and the Eighteenth-Century Novel* (Cambridge: Cambridge University Press, 2003), and Christopher Flint, *The Appearance of Print in Eighteenth-Century Fiction* (Cambridge: Cambridge University Press, 2011).
41. Mitchell, *Picture Theory*, 94–5.
42. See, for example, Leena Eilittä and Liliane Louvel, eds, *Intermedial Arts: Disrupting, Remembering and Transforming Media* (Newcastle upon Tyne: Cambridge Scholars Publishing, 2012), and Gabriele Rippl, ed., *Handbook of Intermediality: Literature – Image – Sound – Music* (Berlin: De Gruyter, 2015).
43. Dick Higgins, 'Intermedia', *Something Else Newsletter* (1965), reprinted in Dick Higgins, *Horizons: The Poetics and Theory of the Intermedia* (Carbondale and Edwardsville: Southern Illinois University Press, 1983); Samuel Taylor Coleridge, 'Spenser', *Coleridge's Miscellaneous Criticism*, ed. Thomas Middleton Raysor (London: Constable & Co., 1936), 33.
44. Dick Higgins, 'Intermedia Chart', 1995, https://dickhiggins.org/intermedia (accessed 7 November 2023).
45. Peter de Bolla, *The Education of the Eye: Painting, Landscape, and Architecture in Eighteenth-Century Britain* (Stanford: Stanford University Press, 2003), 4–5.

THE EIGHTEENTH-CENTURY BRITISH NOVEL AND THE ARTS   19

46. De Bolla, *The Education of the Eye*, 4.
47. De Bolla, *The Education of the Eye*, 159.
48. For a detailed overview of the field, see David Marshall and Dean Mace, 'Literature and the Other Arts', in *The Cambridge History of Literary Criticism*, vol. 4, ed. H. B. Nisbet and Claude Rawson (Cambridge: Cambridge University Press, 1997), 681–741.
49. See, for instance, Jean H. Hagstrum, *The Sister Arts: The Tradition of Literary Pictorialism and English Poetry from Dryden to Gray* (Chicago: University of Chicago Press, 1958); Richard Wendorf, ed., *Articulate Images: The Sister Arts from Hogarth to Tennyson* (Minneapolis: University of Minnesota Press, 1983); John Brewer, *The Pleasures of the Imagination: The Emergence of English Culture in the Eighteenth Century* (London: HarperCollins, 1997).
50. See, for instance, W. B. Gerard, *Laurence Sterne and the Visual Imagination* (Aldershot: Ashgate, 2006); William Gibson, *Art and Money in the Writings of Tobias Smollett* (Lewisburg: Bucknell University Press, 2007); Lynn Shepherd, *Clarissa's Painter: Portraiture, Illustration, and Representation in the Novels of Samuel Richardson* (Oxford: Oxford University Press, 2009); Natasha Duquette and Elisabeth Lenckos, eds, *Jane Austen and the Arts: Elegance, Propriety, and Harmony* (Bethlehem: Lehigh University Press, 2014); Francesca Saggini, ed., *Frances Burney and the Arts* (Cham: Palgrave Macmillan, 2022); Kamilla Elliott, *Portraiture and British Gothic Fiction: The Rise of Picture Identification, 1764–1835* (Baltimore: Johns Hopkins University Press, 2012); Joe Bray, *The Portrait in Fiction of the Romantic Period* (London and New York: Routledge, 2016); Jakub Lipski, *Painting the Novel: Pictorial Discourse in Eighteenth-Century English Fiction* (London and New York: Routledge, 2018).
51. Samuel Johnson, 'Art', *Samuel Johnson's Dictionary*, https://johnsonsdictionaryonline.com/views/search.php?term=art (accessed 7 November 2023).
52. James Noggle, *The Temporality of Taste in Eighteenth-Century Britain* (Cambridge: Cambridge University Press, 2012), 126.
53. In terms of painting, see John Barrell, *The Dark Side of the Landscape: The Rural Poor in English Painting 1730–1840* (Cambridge: Cambridge University Press, 1980), 1–2.
54. Catherine Gallagher, *Nobody's Story: The Vanishing Acts of Women Writers in the Marketplace, 1670–1820* (Oxford: Oxford University Press, 1995), 55–6, 67–72; Andrew Hiscock, '"'Tis there eternal spring": Mapping the Exotic in Aphra Behn's *Oroonoko*', *Journal of the Short Story in English* 29 (1997): §6, http://journals.openedition.org/jsse/70 (accessed 7 November 2023).
55. Behn, *Oroonoko and Other Writings*, 11–12.
56. Gallagher, *Nobody's Story*, 69.
57. Daniel Defoe, *The Life and Strange Surprizing Adventures of Robinson Crusoe*, ed. Maximillian E. Novak, Irving N. Rothman and Manuel Schonhorn (Lewisburg: Bucknell University Press, 2020), 171–2.
58. Anonymous, *The Woman of Colour*, ed. Lyndon Dominique (Ontario: Broadview Press, 2008).
59. Olivia Carpenter, '"Rendered Remarkable": Reading Race and Desire in *The Woman of Colour*', *Studies in Eighteenth-Century Culture* 50 (2021): 249. See also Jennifer DeVere Brody, *Impossible Purities: Blackness, Femininity, and Victorian Culture* (Durham, NC and London: Duke University Press, 1997), 15–17.
60. Carpenter, '"Rendered Remarkable"', 249. See also David Dabydeen, *Hogarth's Blacks: Images of Blacks in Eighteenth Century English Art* (Manchester: Manchester University Press, 1987).
61. Anonymous [Walter Scott], 'Art. IX. *Emma. a Novel*', *Quarterly Review*, vol. 14, issue 27 (October 1815), 188.

Part I:
Styles and Discourses

1

Invisibility and Narration in Haywood (and Behn and Fielding)

Marcie Frank

THE INVISIBLE SPY (1755), one of Eliza Haywood's last publications, has impressed readers from Clara Reeve, in *The Progress of Romance* (1785), to Kathryn R. King, in *A Political Biography of Eliza Haywood* (2012), as belonging among her most significant works.[1] In the introduction to her edition, Carol Stewart, like King, calls for more readings, yet the text has proved challenging to assess.[2] A four-volume compilation of stories narrated by an authorial persona, Explorabilis, who has the power to become invisible, *The Invisible Spy* includes letters from readers. It thus resembles a periodical, the kind of writing Haywood had produced and published earlier in *The Female Spectator* (1745–6) and *The Parrot* (1746); yet *The Invisible Spy* was not published periodically but all at once. As a result, Manushag Powell has proposed to treat *The Invisible Spy* as a mashup of novelistic and periodical conventions.[3] King, however, observes that 'To some extent Haywood is working out of the secret history tradition';[4] Eve Tavor Bannet and Rachel Carnell follow her lead by exploring *The Invisible Spy* as a secret history with connections to the novel.[5] Carnell notices that the terms 'secret history' and 'novel' appear interchangeably on the title pages of Haywood's prose fiction, and we should take into account that 'novel' did not regularly designate what we have come to expect before the end of the eighteenth century.[6]

Other critics avoid the vexed question of the genre of *The Invisible Spy* altogether. Daniel Froid, for instance, treats the text as Haywood's extended and self-conscious address to and exploitation of her reading public.[7] Karin Kukkonen, meanwhile, locates *The Invisible Spy* among Haywood's other fiction regardless of genre by using an amalgamation of semantics, narratology, rhetorical analysis and cognitive approaches to literature; she characterises the text as an 'uncooperative narration' because it flouts the conventions of Gricean pragmatics that derive meaning from language use.[8] In certain respects these approaches are mutually reinforcing, and in others they are mutually exclusive; but none captures the full extent of generic mixing in *The Invisible Spy*, which is more complicated than I have suggested so far.

The Invisible Spy is peppered with quotations from plays, and some of the stories rehash plots familiar from the stage. Haywood had been involved with the theatre before the Stage Licensing Act of 1737, both as a writer and an actor, and she published a work of dramatic criticism, *The Dramatick Historiographer*, in 1735. *The Invisible Spy* also bears marks of libertine erotica. In one episode, a jealous husband uses peepholes made in the wall of a brothel, like those to be found in John Cleland's *Memoirs of a Woman of Pleasure* (1748/9), to confirm his wife's adultery. In Denis

Diderot's *Les Bijoux indiscrets* (1748) the magical powers of the sultan Mangogul to make women's vaginas talk are given by a ring that, when worn on a different finger, confers the power of invisibility (that he does not use). Although it was translated anonymously into English almost immediately as *The Indiscreet Toys* (1749), Haywood could have read Diderot's novel in French: her eight translations included another work of erotic fiction, Crébillon *fils*'s *The Sopha* (1742), in collaboration with William Hatchett. Haywood tapped both drama and erotica for the links they exploited between invisibility and embodiment, but drama plays a bigger role in my analysis. The media differences between print and performance disclose that Haywood's navigation of the passage from actual to virtual embodiment in print was indebted to invisibility onstage, which is also the case for her most significant literary precursor, Aphra Behn, and her most important contemporary, Henry Fielding. Putting Haywood in dialogue with Behn and Fielding brings Haywood's experiment with invisibility into the history of the novel through its narration as well as through its generic markers.

Approaching invisibility as a narrative problem accommodates the generic range of *The Invisible Spy*, but I resist subsuming its diverse elements too quickly under the rubric of 'novelization' in order to bring the text into a genre- and medium-specific history of the novel that remains conscious of its ties to print.[9] In *Nobody's Story: The Vanishing Acts of Women Writers in the Marketplace*, Catherine Gallagher argued that eighteenth-century women authors forged a model of disembodied authorship that was crucial to the development of the literary marketplace.[10] Invisibility may readily be associated with anonymity as well as with disembodiment. Mark Vareschi has recently proposed to replace the category of the author, usually an organising principle of literary scholarship, by an account of anonymous publication that pervaded all genres and relied on a network of activities by producers and consumers that went beyond the achievement of any single individual, yet he leaves embodiment in the domain of performance.[11] Suggesting that the eighteenth-century novel has an apparitional history, Daniel J. Johnson has located the interest in invisible spirits taken by Daniel Defoe, among others, at the intersections of theology and print.[12] However, the recent infusion of invisibility and its flip side, visibility, by the struggle to achieve social, political and economic equity for racialised and other minorities makes the question of embodiment in literature a pressing matter, especially as it engages questions of both genre and media.

Charles W. Mills acknowledges in *Blackness Visible* that feminist thought helped to pave the way for a philosophy of race.[13] Like feminism, anti-racism has fastened on the importance of visibility and invisibility as markers of political empowerment and disempowerment in life as well as literature, for authors as well as for characters. Visibility and invisibility are here understood as more than mere metaphors; 'being seen' is believed to be capable of assuaging or inflicting hurts or wrongs insofar as they embed material experiences of embodiment. But this association has a history, one that reflects, in part, the forms that invisibility has taken in literature, forms that depend on material historical conditions, to be sure, but which are also shaped by narrative and other arts. This inquiry into Haywood's invisibility looks at the ways her narration drew on various genres and reflected the media of print and performance in which they occurred. Like Vareschi, I am interested in the intermediality of literature, and, like Johnson, I wonder to what extent invisibility expresses the effects of print. Therefore, I relocate Gallagher's focus on the disembodying processes women authors

INVISIBILITY AND NARRATION

used in a comparative analysis of the ways invisibility worked onstage and in print in light of the new weight the terms 'invisibility' and 'visibility' have acquired. By using Haywood's invisibility to work with, rather than trying to overcome, generic mixing, I aim to grasp her contributions to the long history of the novel so as to frame her achievement in relation to our current moment.

The Invisible Spy

The invisibility of Haywood's Invisible Spy is the product of an exotic magic the acquisition of which she playfully narrates in the introduction. Granted the choice of two gifts by a descendant of the Magi of Chaldea, Explorabilis opts for a belt of invisibility and a tablet that records a limited number of spoken transactions verbatim:

> The first thing that raised in me any covetous emotions was the apparatus of a belt, but seemed no more than a collection of attoms gathered together in that form and playing in the sun-beams. ---I could not persuade myself it was a real substance, till I took it down and then found it so light, that if I shut my eyes I knew not that I had any thing in my hand. ---The label annexed to it had these words:

> The BELT of INVISIBILITY,

> Which, fasten'd round the body, next to the skin, no sooner becomes warm than it renders the party invisible to all human eyes.
> A little farther, on the same side of the wall, was placed a Tablet, or Pocket book; which, on examining, I found was composed of a clear glassy substance, firm, yet thin as the bubbles which we sometimes see rise on the surface of the waters; – it was malleable, and doubled in many foldings, so that, when shut, it seemed very small; but when extended was more long and broad than any sheet I ever saw of imperial paper; – its uses were decipher'd in the following inscription:

> The WONDERFUL TABLET,

> Which, in whatever place it is spread open, receives the impression of every word that is spoken, in as distinct a manner as if engrav'd; and can no way be expunged except by the breath of a virgin. (10–11)

From the outset, the truth claims of the text are established as paradoxical: its stories are based on the evidence of the senses, described in meticulous detail, yet they are enhanced by magic. Furthermore, a curious gender dynamic supports the magical tablet, specifically. Its capacity to be useful depends upon the enforcement of female chastity. As Explorabilis explains, the tablet can be cleaned and therefore used again only when it is first breathed upon by a virgin who must be older than twelve and whose thoughts are pure, and then wiped by her hand with the first down of the left wing of an unfledged swan (11).

Strikingly, Haywood uses Explorabilis's invisibility to suspend the gender identity of her narrative persona. *The Invisible Spy* begins:

> When a new book begins to make any noise in the world, every one will desire to become acquainted with the author . . . Some doubtless will take me for a philosopher, others for a fool;---with some I will pass for a man of pleasure,----others for

26 MARCIE FRANK

a stoic ... But whether I am any one of these, or whether I am even a man or a woman, they will find it difficult to discover. (7)

Bannet calls Explorabilis 'Mr. Invisibility' throughout her discussion of *The Invisible Spy*, thereby following King, who treats Explorabilis as a male persona, a treatment partly justified by the late gender reveal.[14] Kukkonen, however, observing that the Latin ending 'ilis' is gender-ambiguous, uses the feminine gender pronoun to capture the ways Haywood uses Explorabilis to reflect on 'the varied roles that were ascribed to her in the course of her career'.[15] Haywood had associated herself across her prose fiction, dramatic writing and appearances on the stage with the adulterous female body, an association reinforced, as Ros Ballaster observes, by Alexander Pope and Richard Savage's satirical treatments of her in *The Dunciad* (1728/43) and *The Authors of the Town* (1725), respectively.[16] Ballaster characterises Haywood's 'signature style [as] a play of authorial presence and absence in the depiction of the strong effects of feeling, especially amatory passion, upon the reasoning self'.[17] The insistent gendering of Haywood's authorship makes Explorabilis's claim that invisibility can suspend gender identification all the more curious.

Bannet insightfully proposes that invisibility is a narrative strategy that can be found in Haywood's novels,[18] but to draw persuasive connections between Explorabilis's invisibility and Haywood's narrative third person will involve a more detailed consideration of the diverse generic roots of *The Invisible Spy* and their relations to the problem of embodiment. For instance, Bannet insists upon a definitive difference between spying and spectating that bars *The Invisible Spy* from being considered alongside *The Spectator*, or other periodical writing for that matter, but the striking similarity of their openings demands attention. In the first *Spectator* paper of 1711, Joseph Addison tells us that Mr Spectator is seen everywhere in London but known only to a few. He cultivates the privacy of obscurity so that he can more effectively observe everyone with a studied neutrality that underwrites the general applicability of his impartial judgements. Readers will want to know

> Whether the Writer of it be a black or a fair Man, of a mild or cholerick Disposition, Married or a Batchelor, with other Particulars of the like nature, that conduce very much to the right Understanding of an Author.[19]

Mr Spectator seeks both to satisfy and to limit what can be known about him, and print is the enabling condition that preserves this limited anonymity.

In a penetrating account of the gender politics of *The Spectator*, Powell points out that Mr Spectator both seeks occasionally to divest himself entirely of his body and imagines that he is instructing the men who read the paper in the coffeehouses how to behave as though there were ladies present.[20] Addison here exploits print's virtuality to accomplish a disembodiment that both expropriates for itself and judges the fashionable privileges associated with privileged women. He thereby inscribes a heterosexual male point of view that is presented as transcendental and gender neutral.[21] In adopting full rather than occasional invisibility and playing with Explorabilis's gender indeterminacy, Haywood takes the dynamics of Addison's periodical writing to one logical conclusion and exposes the stakes of this fantasy of print-authorship for women (and for other people with marked bodies).

But invisibility is not only a print-based fantasy; its long stage history indexes the powers and limits of that which embodiment can signify onstage, as the wide uptake of the term 'ghosting' within performance studies reflects.[22] Andrew Sofer has recently theorised the workings of invisibility onstage as the 'dark matter' of drama, theatre and performance itself.[23] Among the most famous instances would be the ghost of Hamlet's father, who appears to everyone in the play's opening scene, and Banquo's ghost, who appears only to Macbeth in the banquet scene. As in Haywood, invisibility was an important element of Behn's sex comedies and Fielding's metatheatrical plays, though it worked differently in each; it also informed the characteristic narrative strategies they each adopted in their own prose fiction. For neither Behn, Haywood nor Fielding did the virtuality of print determine the complete disembodiment of narrators, or author-surrogates, in prose fiction, which suggests that the association may flow not from the history of the novel 'itself' (whether it is told independent of or in relation to drama or the other arts), but instead from a preference for modern novels that speak for themselves over those with voluble or present narrators.[24] We can grasp this more fully if we turn first to Behn and then to Fielding to set the context for understanding Haywood's treatment of invisibility and embodiment in *The Invisible Spy*.

Invisibility in Behn

The Invisible Spy contains many allusions to Behn. An early episode (33) begins with Marcella reading *Love Letters between a Nobleman and his Sister* (1684–7), which, as Bannet observes, signals the resemblance between her story and that of Behn's Silvia.[25] Haywood had based her play *A Wife to be Lett* (1723) – in which she herself took the role of the virtuous wife, Mrs Graspall – on Behn's *The Luckey Chance* (1682).[26] Indeed, Behn's plays can also be found in *The Invisible Spy*.

Explorabilis compares the comic ending of the episode featuring two now married lovers, Melanthe and Dorimon, to the last act of a play upon which the curtain will drop, only to defer this ending to 'farther explanation' involving 'my great favorite, Florimel' (107). Having donned her brother Dorimon's clothes in order to disguise herself as Melanthe's lover, Florimel thereby prevents her from being married off to a rich old man at the same time as she sets the younger couple up. Although Florimel may be named after the archetypal damsel in distress of Spenser's *Fairie Queene*, she more closely resembles Behn's Hellena as if she had wandered off the set of *The Rover* (1677) and onto that of *The Luckey Chance*. The 'farther explanation' Explorabilis promises uses the extended temporality of prose fiction to grant Florimel the marriage she deserves, but the story thereby arrives at the familiar conclusion of stage comedy after all.

Sofer discusses the connections between invisibility and embodiment in terms of the functions of the mask and the signifying powers of female sexuality in *The Rover*, but Behn's last play to be performed, *The Emperor of the Moon* (1687), exploits the different ways this could work for characters and spectators. Perhaps because she had already begun to publish prose fiction, Behn connected the intersection of invisibility and embodiment in *The Emperor of the Moon* to reading.[27] Invisibility makes Dr Baliardo's madness concrete in two complementary scenes involving music, dance, courtship and, ultimately, marriage. He over-privileges his own visual powers, which are enhanced by his gigantic telescope, yet he twice fails to see what is occurring before his eyes in the courtship of his daughter, Elaria, and his niece, Bellamante, by lovers of whom he disapproves. In the first scene, the two couples become invisible to him when, having interrupted their courtship by returning home unexpectedly, they hide in plain sight behind a hanging. Their bodies remain visible and touchable, but he cannot determine their identities. This comic dynamic recurs in the final pageant in which the male lovers appear in disguise as lunar visitors, the Emperor of the Moon and his brother, Prince Thunderland. The play explicitly aligns invisibility and the power of theatrical illusion in the last scene in which the lovers are married off and Baliardo's sanity is restored.

Katherine Mannheimer argues that this play discloses Behn's rejection of the mind/body dualism and her exploration of the possibility that the imagination can feel and the body can convey abstract truths that signals her commitment to a materialism in which imagination, sensory perception and affect are not opposed or in conflict with each other but instead work together to produce knowledge and truth.[28] Reading is the source of the imagination's capacity to enhance or blunt the senses for Baliardo as well as for other characters, who read, write and are carried away by love letters. Behn draws upon the differences between embodied performance and disembodied reading to aid the consolidation of the idea of literature itself, according to Mannheimer, for whom drama is exemplary at bringing these differences to the fore. However, they also inspired the narrative strategies of Behn's prose fiction.

Scholars have connected Behn's plays to her prose fiction, though they have not yet discussed the relations between the embodiment of her narrators and her dramatic writing. According to Monika Fludernik, she adapted the unit of the dramatic scene for prose in *The History of the Nun*, thereby creating the 'scene of consciousness'; Anne F. Widemayer discusses her invention of narrative equivalents for dramaturgical practices and scenography.[29] In a fascinating essay, Harold Love connects the embodiment of her prose characters to the stage when he observes that the vocal performance style that John Harold Wilson called 'tone' can be found in the *Love Letters from a Nobleman to his Sister*, especially in moments of heightened emotion.[30]

In an early letter to Philander, for example, Silvia reflects on having repeatedly read his missive aloud to herself in an attempt to capture his amorous voice.[31] Relineating thirty-two lines of the letter in blank verse, Love shows that they contain the same mix of regular lines and broken off hemistiches that signified heightened emotion in many plays of the period. Silvia's virtual embodiment emanates, in part, from the actual, though invisible, sounds of the stage. She is a palimpsest (even if not all readers are aware of every element): Lady Henrietta Berkeley, the historical woman upon whom Silvia was loosely based, is overlaid with recollected or imagined stage performances of women musing on their absent lovers, and given voice, silently or aloud, by readers in sociable groups or those, like Silvia, who read aloud to themselves.[32]

The intersecting themes of sexual desire and the powers of the imagination occupied Behn as much in her prose fiction as in her plays. She brought them into relation on stage through scenes of non-recognition that question the meaning of that which can be seen and felt and that which remains invisible, most famously in the bed-trick scenes in *The Luckey Chance*.[33] In print, the intersection not only shapes the stories she tells; it also informs the embodiment of her narrators, the element of narrative the most alien to drama. Behn's narrators are consistently embodied even when they are not characters or participant-observers, as is the narrator of *Oroonoko* (1688). In *The Fair Jilt*, for example, Behn's narrator explains the story's significance with reference to her own experiences, even making occasional addresses directly to the reader; in *The History of the Nun*, she interrupts to tell readers her own opinion. Behn's eyewitnessing or tale-hearing narrators make interventions that indicate embodiment by emphasising their own locations and access to the stories they relay. Haywood's narrators, by contrast, are usually more distanced and aloof. Haywood's shaping hands orchestrate from no specifically locatable place; they point (more and less ironically) to social and biological forces beyond the control of any individual. This contrast cannot simply be understood in terms of the differences between the first- and third-person point of view, as becomes clear when we consider the ways Haywood's narrators moralise. Both Behn and Haywood use their narrators actively to guide readers' understanding: in crucial respects, their narratives do not speak for themselves. They do not always show rather than tell. Explorabilis, however, is an exception. Like the narrator of *Oroonoko*, the Invisible Spy is a participant-observer who draws attention to location and access to story, but, unlike her, Explorabilis's body remains, for the most part, unspecified. It is helpful to consider Explorabilis's invisibility in relation to Fielding as well as to Behn, for in many respects Haywood occupies a middle ground between them.

Invisibility in Fielding

The Invisible Spy contains fewer allusions to Fielding than to Behn, and those it makes are personal and political rather than textual. Haywood and Fielding had worked together at the Haymarket theatre in the 1730s. King documents their parting of ways in the 1740s due to conflicting political allegiances. She reads the references to Fielding in Explorabilis's treatment of the Elizabeth Canning affair in volume 4 of *The Invisible Spy*, like Haywood's earlier jab at 'F----'s scandal shop' at the 'little theatre in the Haymarket' in *Betsy Thoughtless* (1751), as evidence of their public antagonism, and not as a repudiation of their 'shared love of a bawdy stage play'.[34] Yet the ways in which his plays treat invisibility and embodiment not only affect his prose narratives but also inform *The Invisible Spy*.

Ghosts, which were not exclusive to tragedy, abound in Fielding's writing. Observing their prevalence in his plays and elsewhere, Ballaster describes his writing as 'ghost writing'.[35] In *Tom Thumb* (1730), Tom Thumb's death is caused by his having been swallowed by a cow, and his ghost appears, only itself to be killed off. In *Pasquin* (1736), the Ghost of Common-Sense appears and even speaks the epilogue. In both of these instances, ghosts make possible the repetition and intensification of an already absurd situation. To the flouting of social and political norms that Fielding exposes as ridiculous, ghosts add an interrogation of how embodiment can work on stage (or not) to solicit belief.

In these plays, ghosts are only one of the ways that Fielding probed the limits of embodiment. He frequently played the characteristics of the actor's body against the demands of the performance. Cross-gendered casting reinforced the comedy of scale in *Tom Thumb*, in which the great hero's miniature status was signalled by the actor's sex, youth and family ties. The role was taken by Miss Jones, the teenage daughter of Mrs Jones, who played Tom's beloved, Huncamunca.[36] Fielding challenged assumptions about aliveness as a condition of embodiment in *The Author's Farce* (1734) by having actors play the roles of puppets in Luckless's puppet show, 'The Pleasures of the Town'.[37] Fielding exploited the limits of embodiment in performance by reinforcing and calling into question the meanings it could convey: status, stature, age, sex, gender and kinship.

Haywood both participated in and contributed to Fielding's theatrical experiments with embodiment. When Fielding reworked the materials of *Tom Thumb* for *The Tragedy of Tragedies* (1731) he added the character of Glumdalca, the captive Queen of the Giants who is in love with Tom Thumb, to augment the Swiftian effects generated by scale. Haywood retained her in the successful adaptation, *The Opera of Operas* (1733), that she wrote in collaboration with Hatchett. During April 1730 Haywood had appeared on stage at the Haymarket both actually and virtually in two plays performed on alternating nights: in the role of Briseus in Hatchett's *The Rival Father* (1730) and as Mrs Novel in the puppet show of *The Author's Farce*, a role acted by Mrs Martin.[38] Haywood's other roles in Fielding's plays, including Mrs Screen in *The Historical Register* (1737) and the author's Muse in *Euridice Hiss'd* (1737), highlighted her capacity for a rambunctious kind of bawdry, as King appreciates.[39]

Ghosts are the only supernatural agents to be allowed to 'us Moderns' by Fielding's narrator in *Tom Jones* (1749), as Jayne E. Lewis has observed in her exposition of the ways they work alongside other invisible elements, like the air, to convey an atmosphere in which readers can be immersed.[40] Fastening on the capacity of the word 'machine' to mean both scientific engine and supernatural agency in poems or plays, Joseph Drury compares the performative narrator of *Tom Jones* to scientific demonstration in order to explore Fielding's delivery of the secular magic of fiction itself that, Drury claims, is continuous with and not opposed to scientific truth.[41] Both Lewis and Drury seek to redeem Fieldling's intrusive narrators from those critics who find them problematic, including Ian Watt and D. A. Miller. Watt had downgraded Fielding's contributions to formal realism, and for Miller Fielding's voice was that of a clubby gentleman and the antithesis of style itself, as epitomised by Jane Austen.[42] Yet as Walter J. Ong recognised in a classic essay, 'The Writer's Audience is Always a Fiction', writers must construct their audiences and cast them into some sort of role, and readers must correspondingly fictionalise themselves by following the cues the writers provide.[43] As he observed, novels did not fully accommodate themselves to print until Austen, and even then, the problem of the reader's role in prose narrative was not entirely resolved.[44] Like Behn, both Haywood and Fielding embodied their narrators to script roles for their readers; like her, they exploited their understanding of the powers and limits of that which embodiment could convey on the stage. For all three, narrators' embodiment was a source for establishing literature's imaginative powers, but unlike Behn, Haywood and Fielding found in third-person narration what they took to be a more effective way to deliver its moral truths.

Both Haywood and Fielding brought their attitudes towards and experiences with the powers and limits of embodiment onstage to their critiques of *Pamela* (1740), one of the most significant works of prose fiction with a didactic purpose. Fielding's *Shamela* (1741) and *Joseph Andrews* (1742), like Haywood's *Anti-Pamela* (1741), attacked Richardson's presentation of Pamela's virtual embodiment of virtue by means of the epistolary form. In *Shamela*, Fielding parodied these letters by using the form against itself: Pamela, as his title attests, is a sham, and her letters to her mama, instead of attesting to her innocence, describe the progress of her scheme to seduce Master

INVISIBILITY AND NARRATION   31

Booby into marriage.[45] For both, Richardson's first person needed to be exploded if the kind of belief that fictional representation elicited (on stage or in prose fiction) could have any claim to morality. For both, the hypocrisy of a self-representation that spoke of its own virtue and chastity betrayed its lack of modesty, which each used the third person to expose. *Joseph Andrews* begins with letters, but Fielding turned from them to a third-person narrator, influenced, perhaps, by the effects Haywood had achieved in her presentation of Syrena Tricksy's letters alongside explanations from the narrator of *Anti-Pamela*. In Explorabilis, Haywood provided a narrator whose invisibility made possible participation and observation, and who, in this respect, resembles the narrator of Behn's *Oroonoko*. But by linking Explorabilis's moralising judgements, frequently presented and frequently undercut, to invisibility, Haywood also borrowed (or shared) a page from Fielding's playbook.

The Invisibility of *The Invisible Spy*

Explorabilis's invisibility comes from magical, fantastical, or even vaguely Orientalised sources, but Haywood also exposes its morally compromising limitations in the actions taken to collect stories. The Invisible Spy enters private spaces, seeing and hearing that which people seek to hide. The Clelandesque episode involving peepholes takes this to a pornographic level (164–75). Roxana suspects that Sabina, who is married, has stolen her lover, so she gets her footman to make holes in the wainscotting of an adjoining room at the brothel to which she has tracked them. Not only do Roxana and the undetected Invisible Spy peep, so does the footman. If there is something ridiculous about the line-up of three peeping bodies, the whole scenario is repeated and amplified when Roxana exacts her revenge. She sends Germanicus, Sabina's husband, a letter telling him where he can find his wife. He and two friends

> agree they should all go together, not only to prevent any indiscreet effects of his rage on the persons who wronged him, in case the affair should prove as the letter had represented; but also to be his witnesses, if he thought proper to bring it before a court of judicature. They went, according to the directions given by Roxana [and] found every thing answered the description; – they were shewed up into the yellow chamber; I still accompanied them, and made a fourth person, unfelt, as well as unseen by any of them. (173)

Explorabilis's moral judgement is more explicitly undermined in the episode which immediately follows, in which invisibility makes it possible to pocket Belinda's correspondence with Selima, which is then reproduced to narrate Selima's love affairs. Headnote summaries to these chapters first characterise the theft as an 'act of petty larceny' performed to 'oblige the public' (175), and then warn readers with moral scruples to skip the episode entirely:

> If there be any reader, in this very pious and religious age, that may happen to have too tender and scrupulous a conscience to benefit himself by the receipt of stolen goods, the author thinks it highly necessary to give him this timely notice, that it will be best for his peace of mind to avoid looking either into this or some of the succeeding chapters. (179)

Readers who persist are thus as implicated, as they were in the pervy pleasures of the peepholes, alongside the transgressive actors of the stories and their invisible author. Haywood thus lays bare the trade-off between the fantastical and the moralising as it borders on the perverse, for which the gender indeterminacy of the Invisible Spy can serve as an emblem.

Ultimately, however, the Invisible Spy is revealed to be male in an episode near the end of the third volume fittingly dedicated to exposing the dangers of masquerade. The central characters are known to him, and he interacts with them without the aid of the magical belt. But if this revelation aims to stabilise his moral authority, its structural dependence on female chastity is emphasised at the end, when Explorabilis is suddenly forced to give up the writing project altogether because it has become impossible to erase the magical tablet: 'Nature has baffled all my vain precautions to preserve my little virgin's native purity' (466–7). The magical tablet becomes useless because she has caught sight of a portrait of a man and fallen in love. Relentless female desire works here much as it does in *Fantomina* (1725), when pregnancy puts an end to the heroine's adventures and to her story. The 'vain precautions' come retrospectively to vibrate with unwholesomeness, given Explorabilis's gender-reveal. Aware that the girl will have to be educated in social seclusion, as we are told in the Introduction, he has bought a three-year-old from a very poor widow with many children for a small sum, who he has brought up in a garret under the careful supervision of a discreet old woman:

> I frequently visited them in my Invisibility, and was highly pleased and diverted with the diligence of my good old woman; – she not only obey'd my orders with the utmost punctuality, but did many things of her own accord, which, though very requisite, I had not thought of. (12)

For example, to keep the girl's body limber, she has taught her to play badminton. This treatment, Explorabilis assures us, 'maintain'd my virgin's purity inviolate, as I did not fail to make an essay in a few days after she enter'd into her thirteenth year' (12). Authorship, for Haywood, may be embodied in the relays between presence and absence, following Ballaster, but only when the consequences of female embodiment can be suspended. Such suspension may produce its own perversities.

Working between the legacy of Behn's prose and Fielding's plays, Haywood literalises invisibility as a print-based fantasy. *The Invisible Spy* thereby takes up the possibilities for imagining disembodiment in the various genres it uses, including periodical writing, drama and libertine erotica, in order to explore their different constraints. It can thus represent a step in the adaptation of the novel as a genre to print. Together, Haywood, Behn and Fielding expose some critical features of the current discourse of visibility and invisibility for the purposes of empowering those with minoritised bodies insofar as it concerns the literary history of the novel.

The Politics of Invisibility

In a recent essay that gives a genealogy to the political importance now granted to invisibility and visibility, Leela Gandhi lays out the double bind produced by the widespread association of knowledge with the power to make things visible: invisibility in this system is an indicator of both epistemic violence, the exercise of keeping unwanted things unseen, and epistemic non-violence, the refuge of the hidden and a place of potential resistance.[46] For Gandhi, the contradictory logic of invisibility culminated during the Cold War with Salvador Dalí's claim that the nuclear world order that had everyone in its crosshairs called for total camouflage, and with Ralph Ellison's novel, *Invisible Man* (1952).

Invisibility is a problem of both race and narration for Ellison, but it is also a joint solution. From down the sewer to which he returns at the end of the book, having had the painful contradictions of hypervisibility and invisibility forced upon him, Ellison's unnamed narrator resolves them in the scene of writing. The novel ends:

> Being invisible and without substance, a disembodied voice, as it were, what else could I do? What else but try to tell you what was really happening when your eyes were looking through? And it is this which frightens me: Who knows but that, on the lower frequencies, I speak for you?[47]

In this powerful ending, Ellison lays bare the frightening logic binding narrative point of view to invisibility: it is impossible to separate the ability to speak for oneself, and for others, from either the history of racism or the experience of disembodiment. If our eyes can see through his, if the invisible man can speak for us, this is because of the disembodying power of novelistic narration. Marked by mid-century modernism and the Cold War logic Gandhi dissects, Ellison's questions open up the possibility of believing, or not believing, in the power of the novel as a genre.[48]

Virginia Woolf's treatment of invisibility in *Orlando* (1928) offers a bridge back to the eighteenth century even as it highlights a different experience of embodiment: that of gender. Having become female in the eighteenth century, Orlando cultivates the company of Pope, Addison and Swift not as the aspiring poet he had been the century before but as a *salonnière*. The writers, however, prove disappointing in person, where they supply no better wit than they do on the page. Reflecting upon this, Orlando is stirred by 'the very thought of a great writer to the pitch of belief that she almost believed him to be invisible. Her instinct was a sound one. One can only believe entirely, perhaps, in what one cannot see'.[49] Invisibility here is a fantasy that grows out of Orlando's author worship, which Woolf thereby gently deflates along with her literary ambitions. But in the context of the novel's mapping of gender transitivity onto English literary history, invisibility also reflects the ways that gender can enable or block access to a literary career. Ellison and Woolf, like Haywood, exploit invisibility's capacity to access literary authorship even as they expose its internal contradictions.

Haywood uses invisibility to examine the experience of female embodiment, much as Ellison, three centuries later, did so to examine the experience of Blackness. In both, invisibility represents the real social limits imposed by patriarchy or structural racism because it offers an escape from such limits, and, at the same time, gives access to a requisite condition of print-authorship that Woolf, significantly, represented as a matter of belief. Haywood and Woolf each played the transitivity of gendered and sexed embodiment off the fixed binaries of male and female, and Ellison probed the intransitivity of the Black/white binary from every possible angle. Fiction made it possible for all three to imagine disembodiment and alternative embodiments.

This interplay between disembodiment and embodiment is critical to the production of the novel, which, Gallagher argues, co-evolved with and helped to produce the literary marketplace for print. Haywood and Ellison each reached for invisibility, a fantastical possibility; in *Orlando*, Woolf developed a character who lived for a few centuries as a man and then a few more as a woman. Yet it can still feel like a stretch to call *The Invisible Spy* a novel, and a strain on sensitivity to think of Ellison's *Invisible Man* as related to H. G. Wells's *The Invisible Man* (1897). That Woolf identified invisibility as a component of authorship and a matter of belief, perhaps, makes it possible to perceive the lineaments of a more genre- and medium-specific history of the novel, the Trojan horse of Gallagher's literary history of fictionality.[50] I am suggesting that the suspension of embodiment required by fiction – that is to say, imaginative writing across the genres – can be connected more specifically to the genres and media in which it occurs. The genre- and medium-specific strategies and conventions for representing and/or delivering embodiment may elude observation if we do not read in search of fiction's traffic across genres and media.

Print-authorship has structured the modern literary field until now, including the boundaries between essay, novel and drama, but new media conditions have helped to blur the differences between memoir and novel, and the dominance of first-person narration in both can index the new weight recently acquired by invisibility and visibility. The consequences make themselves felt in the study of the long-eighteenth-century novel: Behn's first-person narratives seem to be more easily recuperated, once her attitudes towards race, class and gender are registered as historical phenomena, than Haywood and Fielding's third-person novels, which can seem retrograde. Yet paradoxically, although Behn can appear more recognisable, it is to Haywood and Fielding that the new infusion of visibility and invisibility with moral force owes a bigger debt. Certain elements of these eighteenth-century authors' navigation of their own media shift – that is, their adjustment to the then-new literary genres associated with print – reinforce the current expectation that the first-person voice will line up with the body of the author, especially when that author is a racialised or otherwise minoritised person, while other elements may have come to seem unrecognisable. But perhaps our own media shift is producing generic mixtures and new conventions for representing embodiment that will come presently to seem as strange to future readers as those of Haywood's literalisation of invisibility in *The Invisible Spy* can appear to us.

Notes

1. Clara Reeve cited in Rachel K. Carnell, 'Eliza Haywood and the Narratological Tropes of Secret History', *Journal for Early Modern Cultural Studies* 14, no. 4 (2014): 101; Kathryn R. King, *A Political Biography of Eliza Haywood* (London: Pickering & Chatto, 2012), 193–201.
2. Eliza Haywood, *The Invisible Spy*, ed. Carol Stewart (London: Pickering & Chatto, 2014), 107. Further references parenthetical.
3. Manushag N. Powell, 'Eliza Haywood, Periodicalist(?)', *Journal for Early Modern Cultural Studies* 14, no. 4 (2014): 163–86.
4. King, *A Political Biography of Eliza Haywood*, 197.
5. Rachel Carnell, 'Eliza Haywood and the Narratological Tropes of Secret History', *Journal for Early Modern Cultural Studies* 14, no. 4 (2014): 101–21; Eve Tavor Bannet, 'The Narrator as Invisible Spy: Eliza Haywood, Secret History and the Novel', *Journal for Early*

Modern Cultural Studies 14, no. 4 (2014): 143–62. The relations between the genre of secret history and the novel are established by Michael McKeon in *The Secret History of Domesticity: Public Private and the Division of Knowledge* (Baltimore: Johns Hopkins University Press, 2006).

6. See Cheryl Nixon, ed., *Novel Definitions: An Anthology of Commentary on the Novel 1688–1815* (Peterborough: Broadview Press, 2009), and Peter Garside, James Raven and Rainer Schöwerling, eds, *The English Novel, 1770–1829: A Bibliographical Survey of Prose Fiction Published in the British Isles* (Oxford: Oxford University Press, 2000).

7. Daniel Froid, 'The Virgin and the Spy: Authority, Legacy, and the Reading Public', *Eighteenth-Century Fiction* 30, no. 4 (2018): 485.

8. Karin Kukkonen, 'Flouting Figures: Uncooperative Narration in the Fiction of Eliza Haywood', *Language and Literature* 22, no. 3 (2013): 205–18.

9. On 'novelization', see Mikhail Bahktin, 'Epic and Novel', in *The Dialogic Imagination: Four Essays*, ed. Michael Holquist, trans. Caryl Emerson and Michael Holquist (Austin: University of Texas Press, 1982), 3–40; on using the recognition that all genres are always already mixed to resist the association of novelisation with modernisation, see Wolfram Schmidgen, 'Undividing the Subject of Literary History: From James Thomson's Poetry to Daniel Defoe's Novels', in *Eighteenth-Century Poetry and the Rise of the Novel Reconsidered*, ed. Kate Parker and Courtney Weiss Smith (Lewisburg: Bucknell University Press, 2014), 92.

10. Catherine Gallagher, *Nobody's Story: The Vanishing Acts of Women Writers in the Marketplace 1670–1920* (Berkeley: University of California Press, 1994).

11. Mark Vareschi, *Everywhere and Nowhere: Anonymity and Mediation in Eighteenth-Century Britain* (Minneapolis: University of Minnesota Press, 2018).

12. Daniel J. Johnson, '*Robinson Crusoe* and the Apparitional Eighteenth-Century Novel', *Eighteenth-Century Fiction* 28, no. 2 (2015–16): 240–2.

13. Charles W. Mills, *Blackness Visible: Essays on Philosophy and Race* (Ithaca: Cornell University Press, 1998).

14. Bannet, 'The Narrator as Invisible Spy', 143–62.

15. Kukkonen, 'Flouting Figures', 206.

16. Ros Ballaster, *Fictions of Presence: Theatre and Novel in Eighteenth-Century Britain* (Woodbridge: Boydell Press, 2020), 43–4.

17. Ballaster, *Fictions of Presence*, 43.

18. Bannet, 'The Narrator as Invisible Spy', 158–9.

19. Joseph Addison, 'No. 1', *The Spectator*, 1 March 1710–11.

20. Manushag Powell, 'See No Evil, Hear No Evil, Speak No Evil: Spectation and the Eighteenth-Century Public Sphere', *Eighteenth-Century Studies* 45, no. 2 (2012): 263.

21. For a complementary account of gender in *The Spectator*, see Erin Mackie, *Market à la Mode: Fashion, Commodity and Gender in the Tatler and the Spectator* (Baltimore: Johns Hopkins University Press, 2003).

22. Elin Diamond encapsulates the history of the term 'ghosting' in the work of performance theorists and theatre historians Herbert Blau, Joseph Roach and Marvin Carlson in a review of Marvin Carlson's *The Haunted Stage: The Theater as Memory Machine* (Ann Arbor: University of Michigan Press, 2003) in *Theater Journal* 55, no. 1 (2003): 192–4.

23. For a recent discussion of the significance of the invisible in theatre, see Andrew Sofer, *Dark Matter: Invisibility in Drama, Theater, and Performance* (Ann Arbor: University of Michigan Press, 2013).

24. Brian Boyd, 'Does Austen Need Narrators? Does Anyone?', *New Literary History* 48, no. 2 (2017): 285–308.

25. Bannet, 'The Narrator as Invisible Spy', 146.

26. Ballaster, *Fictions of Presence*, 38–9.

27. Aphra Behn, 'The Emperor of the Moon', in *The Works of Aphra Behn*, vol. 5, *The Plays, 1682–1696*, ed. Janet Todd (Columbus: Ohio State University Press, 1996), 153–208.
28. Katherine Mannheimer, *Restoration Drama and the Idea of Literature* (Charlottesville: University of Virginia Press, forthcoming), 155.
29. Monika Fludernik, *Towards a 'Natural' Narratology* (London and New York: Routledge, 2002), 106–20; Anne F. Widemayer, *Theatre and the Novel from Behn to Fielding* (Oxford: Oxford University Press, 2015), 43–7. I have suggested that Behn found narrative equivalents to the structure of generic relation used in tragicomedy: Marcie Frank, 'Tragedy, Comedy, Tragicomedy and the Incubation of New Genres', in *Emergent Nation: Early Modern Literature in Transition*, ed. Elizabeth Sauer (Cambridge: Cambridge University Press, 2019), 66–79.
30. John Harold Wilson, 'Rant, Cant, and Tone on the Restoration Stage', *Studies in Philology* 52, no. 4 (1955): 592–8. Cited in Harold Love, 'Vocal Register in Behn's *Love-letters Between a Nobleman and his Sister*', *English Language Notes* 41, no. 1 (2003): 44–53.
31. This letter can be found in Behn's *Love-letters*, ed. Janet Todd (London: Pickering & Chatto, 1993) 2:188.
32. See Abigail Williams, *The Social Life of Books: Reading Together in the Eighteenth-Century Home* (New Haven: Yale University Press, 2017). For Vareschi, the mediations of the elocutionary movement affect the attributions of authorship across the genres. Vareschi, *Everywhere and Nowhere*, 57–8.
33. See Catherine Gallagher's reading of the bed-tricks of *The Luckey Chance* in *Nobody's Story*, 45–7, which Mannheimer contests: *Restoration Drama and the Idea of Literature*, 122–32.
34. King, *A Political Biography of Eliza Haywood*, 65–72.
35. See Ballaster, *Fictions of Presence*, 55–74.
36. Henry Fielding, *Tom Thumb*, in *Plays*, vol. 1, *1728–1731*, ed. Thomas Lockwood, The Wesleyan Edition of the Works of Henry Fielding (Oxford: Clarendon Press, 2004), 367.
37. On the relations between puppets and ghosts in *The Author's Farce*, see Ballaster, *Fictions of Presence*, 58–9. See also David Brewer, 'Rethinking Fictionality in the Eighteenth-Century Puppet Theatre', in *The Afterlives of Eighteenth-Century Fiction*, ed. Daniel Cook and Nicholas Seager (Cambridge: Cambridge University Press, 2015), 174–92.
38. King, *A Political Biography of Eliza Haywood*, 65.
39. King, *A Political Biography of Eliza Haywood*, 70.
40. Henry Fielding, *The History of Tom Jones, a Foundling*, ed. Fredson Bowers (Middletown: Wesleyan University Press, 1975), 395–407 (398). Cited in Jayne E. Lewis, 'The Air of *Tom Jones*: Or What Rose from the Novel', *The Eighteenth Century* 52 nos. 3–4 (2011): 313.
41. Joseph Drury, 'Realism's Ghosts: Science and Spectacle in *Tom Jones*', *Novel: A Forum on Fiction* 46 no. 1 (2013): 50–72. Fielding, Drury proposes, harnessed spectacle to philosophy using the same legerdemain as those scientific lecturers who directed audiences to 'the wonder of God's providence and philosophical principles through the sensuous thrill of spectacular experiment' (66). 'The paradox of the realist novel that Fielding addresses', Drury concludes, 'is the same one that Bruno Latour has found at the core of the scientific fact: "It is because it is constructed that it is so very real, so autonomous, so independent of our own hands"' (68).
42. Ian Watt, *The Rise of the Novel: Studies in Defoe, Richardson, and Fielding* (Harmondsworth: Penguin, 1974); D. A. Miller, *Jane Austen, or The Secret of Style* (Princeton: Princeton University Press, 2003), 31–2.
43. Walter J. Ong, 'The Writer's Audience is Always a Fiction', *PMLA* 90, no. 1 (1975): 9–21.
44. Ong, 'The Writer's Audience is Always a Fiction', 17.
45. See Thomas Lockwood, 'Theatrical Fielding', *Studies in the Literary Imagination* 32, no. 2 (1999): 105–14; see also my discussion of Fielding's use of letters as props in Marcie Frank,

The Novel Stage: Narrative Form from the Restoration to Jane Austen (Lewisburg: Bucknell University Press, 2020), 77–81.

46. Leela Gandhi, 'Invisibility, Inc.', *ELH* 88, no. 2 (2021): 421–42.

47. Ralph Ellison, *Invisible Man* (1952; New York: Vintage, 1995), 575.

48. At the MLA 2021 conference, on the panel 'Ralph Ellison and Public Television', Paul Devlin and André Davenport each suggested that by 'the lower frequencies' Ellison meant television.

49. Virginia Woolf, *Orlando: A Biography* (London: Hogarth Press, 1928), 97.

50. For a similar critique, see Julie Orlemanski, 'Who Has Fiction? Modernity, Fictionality, and the Middle Ages', *New Literary History* 50, no. 2 (2019): 145–70.

2

ORIENTALISM AND SEXUALITY IN THE EIGHTEENTH-CENTURY NOVEL

James Watt

PLATE I COMES from a 1765 abridgement of Daniel Defoe's novel *The Fortunate Mistress* (1724), commonly known as *Roxana*, and it depicts the high point of the narrator's story when, having laundered the proceeds of her various affairs, Roxana appears in a 'Turkish habit' before an audience including Charles II at her newly acquired residence in Pall Mall: 'Now things began to work as I wou'd have them', she recollects.[1] Roxana aims at the king and gains his notice, and the affair that she goes on to have with him further establishes the symbolic freighting of her name by calling up the story of the slave-turned-empress wife of the sixteenth-century Ottoman sultan, Suleiman the Magnificent. As she 'makes a figure' through dance as well as dress, Roxana performs a relatively familiar 'Turkish' exoticism that is mediated via French aristocratic culture and defined against the less easily assimilable otherness of the Georgian and Armenian women, with their 'wild and *Bizarre*' air, who are also in attendance (179). Her masquerade costume constitutes an overtly sexualised form of self-fashioning, and she records the success of her performance when she describes how the assembly celebrated their hostess: 'they all call'd out Roxana' (180). She subsequently recognises, however, that the name by which she is hailed here is also a kind of branding, from which she spends most of the remainder of the novel trying to escape, and when she moves eastwards to the Minories she passes for a Quaker and wears her Turkish costume – 'not a decent Dress in this Country', she states – only once more, in a private exhibition for her husband, before hiding it away in a closet (247).

Shortly after marrying the Dutch merchant, Roxana declares that she would not want 'to be known by the Name of *Roxana*, no, not for ten Thousand Pounds' (271). In addition to presenting Roxana's Turkish performance as 'a domestication of the foreign as a delightful and exotic artifice', Srinivas Aravamudan argues, Defoe's novel thus goes on to demonstrate that 'the foreign can survive . . . only as an unacknowledged and hidden scandal within bourgeois conventionality'.[2] Later in the century, as John Mullan shows, the numerous endings of different editions of the novel encapsulate contemporary perceptions of its scandalous content by rewriting Defoe's abrupt conclusion and making Roxana a redemption-seeking figure who resigns herself to death.[3] Defoe's novel is a useful point of departure for this essay, then, both because it memorably stages an episode of sexualised Orientalist performance and because its production and reception help us to think about the changing terms on which features of the literary and visual register of 'Orientalism' – most notably the related ideas of its sexual allure and threat – could be admitted into, and deployed by, the British novel across our period.

The theatrical spectacle of Roxana's entrance at Pall Mall, depicted in 'painterly' terms by Defoe, is exemplary of the interplay between the novel and the arts across the eighteenth century, and the resonance of this widely revisited episode additionally exemplifies the self-referential character of contemporary Orientalist discourse, where the citation of recurrent tropes and received ideas helped to provide 'knowledge' of a largely undifferentiated East.[4] For much of the eighteenth century, in the sphere of material culture and the metropolitan realm of public exhibition and display as well as in prose fiction, this composite domain tended to be loosely aligned with Ottoman Turkey and the Near East rather than the more distant regions of India and China; China and things Chinese were not so easily integrated into a monolithic sense of the Orient. The parameters of the British imaginary of the East were significantly extended, however, by the new and increasingly specific understandings of cultural difference that were directly or indirectly produced by the Seven Years' War (1756–63), which established the East India Company's sovereignty in Bengal and made Britain the pre-eminent global power. As I will show, novels of the 1770s and 1780s continued to draw upon (and in turn perpetuate) the association of 'the East' with forms of deviant or transgressive sexuality, while also sometimes revising familiar representations of sultans and seraglios and acknowledging the changing circumstances of British imperial authority.

In what follows I will attempt to bring together two related strands of argument concerning the function of what might be termed 'sexual Orientalism' in the eighteenth-century novel and the shift in modes of representing the East in prose fiction. After a brief overview of some recent big-picture accounts of the relationship between Orientalism and eighteenth-century fiction, I will consider a diverse range of works produced in the aftermath of the Seven Years' War. Tobias Smollett's *The Expedition of Humphry Clinker* (1771) and Robert Bage's *The Fair Syrian* (1787), for example, respectively associate the Near East with 'unnatural' vice and sexual despotism for an immediate critical or satirical purpose, whereas William Beckford's *Vathek* (1786), by contrast, more fully and enthusiastically explores the social and sexual dynamics of despotic power from the vantage point of an Eastern sovereign. Beckford's work was inspired by the 'virtual seraglio' orchestrated by the painter and scenographer Philip James de Loutherbourg at Fonthill in 1781, and while it harnesses new media technologies, it additionally both incorporates specific ethnographic reference into its main text and (in its first published edition) provides extensive accompanying endnotes to explain this.[5] The final text I will discuss, Phebe Gibbes's *Hartly House, Calcutta* (1789), which remains decorous in its treatment of the sexual allure of the East, depicts a precisely realised colonial milieu rather than working with older and for the most part 'non-referential' traditions of literary Orientalism. It represents the closest engagement with India in eighteenth-century fiction, although in the work's troubling conclusion (which portrays colonialism as a theatre of sexual violence), I suggest, the narrator's story of her disengagement from India and subsequent return to England may also anticipate the marginalisation of Eastern empire and the East more generally in novels produced over the following century.

'Orientalism' and Eighteenth-Century Fiction

Aravamudan argues that the new form of the novel which came to be established by the 1740s defined itself against what he terms 'Enlightenment Orientalism' – a miscellany of playfully reflexive texts ('Oriental tales, pseudoethnographies, sexual fantasies, and political utopias') that were premised upon relativising comparison between cultures; this was an emphatically 'imaginative Orientalism', he states, 'circulating images . . . that were nine parts invented and one part referential', and it preceded the 'imperial turn' in British and French relations with the East.[6] The 'domestic' or 'national' realism of Henry Fielding and Samuel Richardson was, for Aravamudan and others, a self-consciously 'English' mode of narrative fiction that rejected such outlandish content, and in turn narrowed readers' horizons, and some contemporaries certainly recognised its novelty in such terms.[7] Francis Coventry, for example, approvingly noted the difference of Fielding's *Joseph Andrews* (1742) from some of the fictions that came before it, alluding to the earlier popularity of the *Arabian Nights' Entertainments* (translated from Antoine Galland's *Les Mille et Une Nuits* between c.1706 and 1721): 'For crystal Palaces and winged Horses, we find homely Cots and ambling nags, and instead of impossibility, what we experience every day.'[8] Samuel Johnson also appeared to acknowledge a shift in assumptions relating to the production and reception of prose fiction when he claimed in *Rambler* 4 (1750) that the works which were currently most popular were 'such as exhibit life in its true state, diversified only by accidents that daily happen in the world, and influenced by passions and qualities which really are to be found in conversing with mankind'.[9] Johnson here repudiated the 'help of wonder' in prose fiction, and in his philosophical tale *The History of Rasselas, Prince of Abissinia* (1759) he would eschew Orientalist exoticism and fantasy, notably by presenting the harem in which Pekuah (the attendant of the prince's sister) is briefly imprisoned as a locus of boredom rather than sexual energy.

One story to tell about the place of Orientalism in eighteenth-century fiction therefore concerns the increasing separation of what has been dubbed the 'novel proper' from the heterogeneous kinds of 'experimental', non-realist text that Aravamudan recovers, which 'resisted' the rise of the novel but became increasingly marginal as a result of its ascent.[10] An alternative reading of the apparently pivotal mid-century moment of separation referred to above is that older modes of literary Orientalism remained a structuring feature of the British novel, only in an embedded or mediated rather than overt manner. Ros Ballaster, for example, questions Aravamudan's reification of 'the novel' as a discrete cultural form and argues that a work such as Richardson's *Pamela* (1740) pays silent tribute to the frame tale of the *Arabian Nights* since it accords its heroine a narratorial eloquence comparable to that of Princess Scheherazade, who tells story after story because her life depends on it.[11]

Although they cannot be seen to present 'what we experience every day' (as Coventry put it) in the same way as *Pamela*, the diverse works that I will discuss exemplify the different kinds of traffic that took place between 'realistic' prose fiction and other flourishing forms of literary production, such as the informant narratives of fictional Oriental travellers and popular dramas featuring Eastern settings and/or based on *Arabian Nights*-derived stories. There were no counterparts of Defoe's 'wicked' heroine Roxana in the mid- to late eighteenth-century novel (at least some contemporary readers were likely to think that she merited

ORIENTALISM AND SEXUALITY

punishment, as noted), but there were figures on the stage, such as Roxolana in Isaac Bickerstaff's farce *The Sultan, or, A Peep into the Seraglio* (first performed in 1775), whose exploits likewise allude to the story of Sultan Suleiman's wife, as it was circulated by the French writers Jean-François Marmontel and Charles-Simon Favart.[12] Versions of this sultan/slave scenario would in turn feature in Bage's *The Fair Syrian* and then, perhaps most famously, in much later works such as Charlotte Brontë's *Jane Eyre* (1847) that are sometimes regarded as paradigmatically 'English'. That the charged dialogue between Jane Eyre and Mr Rochester – in which she likens him to a sultan who treats her as his slave – takes place at Thornfield Hall in deepest northern England, however, also invites us to consider the rhetorical mobility (not to say ubiquity) of 'Oriental' allusions and tropes in fiction of the eighteenth century and beyond. In the remainder of this chapter I will focus on the terms on which Orientalist content – especially the representation of sexual deviance and/or threat – is made a constituent component of four different works of the 1770s and 1780s, and in conclusion I will briefly consider what the use of such subject matter might indicate not only about the development of eighteenth-century fiction but also about Britons' imaginative relation to the wider world.

Smollett's Ambassador

In Smollett's epistolary novel *Humphry Clinker* Lydia Melford displays something of the enduring popular familiarity with literary Orientalism when she offers her much-cited first impression of the metropolis: 'All that you read of wealth and grandeur, in the Arabian Night's Entertainment, and the Persian Tales, concerning Bagdad, Diarbekir, Damascus, Ispahan, and Samarkand, is here realized.'[13] Although Lydia does not directly refer to it, the novel may thus allude to the popular Orientalism that was a constituent feature of what Richard D. Altick terms the 'shows of London' – those diverse 'public nontheatrical entertainments' which included the pleasure gardens of Ranelagh and Vauxhall that she mentions in this letter.[14] While they are in London her less impressionable brother Jery relays opinion of 'the Algerine ambassador' (whom he sees at a levee held by former prime minister the Duke of Newcastle) as a 'green-horn' in the city (119). The ambassador may initially appear to be a figure reminiscent of spectators and spies in the long-established mode of informant narrative (stretching back to Giovanni Marana's *Letters Writ by a Turkish Spy*, first translated from French in 1687) whose function is to offer an estranged perspective on the scenes that they witness. There is a near-contemporary visual representation of a – notably uncaricatured – 'Turkish' spectator in William Hogarth's 1762 engraving 'Credulity, Superstition and Fanaticism' (Figure 2.1), in which a turbaned man smoking a pipe looks quizzically through a window at a church congregation being harangued from a pulpit by a Methodist preacher; Ronald Paulson suggests that Hogarth may have responded to Oliver Goldsmith's use of a 'foreign commentator' in the 'Chinese Letters' which began to appear in the *Public Ledger* in 1760.[15] Thomas Rowlandson's depiction of the levee episode (from the 1793 edition of the novel), titled 'Turkish Ambassador introduced to the Duke of N—' (Figure 2.2), at first seems to bear out such an understanding of it, because it shows in the foreground the ambassador reacting with incredulity to the clownish appearance of the duke, while his 'dragoman, or interpreter', to the ambassador's right, is apparently too confounded to look.

Figure 2.1 William Hogarth, *Credulity, Superstition, and Fanaticism. A Medley* (1762). Engraving. Courtesy of the Lewis Walpole Library, Yale University.

Jery describes the duke as breaking off his ablutions to receive the ambassador:

> A door opening, he suddenly bolted out, with a shaving-cloth under his chin, his face frothed up to the eye with soap lather; and, running up to the ambassador, grinned hideous in his face—'My dear Mahomet! (said he) God love your long beard, I hope the dey will make you a horse-tail at the next promotion, ha, ha, ha!—Have but a moment's patience, and I'll send to you in a twinkling—' So saying, he retreated into his den, leaving the Turk in some confusion. (121)

After the duke thus demonstrates the superficiality of his knowledge, through his naming of the ambassador as 'Mahomet' and his fixation on stereotypical signifiers of cultural difference (the ambassador's beard) and status (the 'horse-tail'), the ambassador himself is described as misrecognising their encounter in a manner that is in keeping with the informant narrative tradition, where the observer is often a secondary object of satire. The 'conductor' of Jery and his party, 'captain C—', 'who conversed with the dragoman, as an old acquaintance', explains:

> Ibrahim, the ambassador . . . had mistaken the grace for the minister's fool, [and] was no sooner undeceived by the interpreter, than he exclaimed to this effect—'Holy prophet! I don't wonder that this nation prospers, seeing it is governed by the counsel of ideots; a series of men, whom all good mussulmen revere as the organs of immediate inspiration!' (121)

ORIENTALISM AND SEXUALITY 43

Figure 2.2 Charles Grignion the Elder, after Thomas Rowlandson, *The Duke of N–'s Levee*, an illustration from Tobias Smollett's *'The Expedition of Humphry Clinker'* (London, 1793), Vol. 1. Etching and engraving. The Metropolitan Museum of Art, New York. Accession Number 59.553.562(5), The Elisha Whittelsey Collection, The Elisha Whittelsey Fund, 1959. www.metmuseum.org

The understanding of the ambassador is still skewed even after it is explained to him that the duke is not a court jester, and from his nominally 'Muslim' perspective, which is presented as conjoining 'idiocy' and 'inspiration', he at once alludes to Hogarth's caricature of religious enthusiasm and attempts to account for British pre-eminence in the aftermath of the Seven Years' War: only a uniquely 'inspired' people could have achieved such apparent success, he suggests.

On a surface level, then, the apparent seriousness of the 'venerable Turk, with a long white beard' throws into relief the eccentricity of the superannuated duke, even as the 'green-horn' ambassador continues to misread his host. As Peter Miles argues, however, a closer contextualisation of this episode reveals a usually overlooked topicality that also shows Smollett's carefully inserted 'Oriental' reference to have a particular – strongly homophobic – satirical function. Although Miles's reading is too richly detailed to summarise (especially in what it has to say about the likely identity of 'captain C—'), some of its salient points concern the established innuendo (which Smollett had perpetuated in *The Adventures of an Atom* [1768]) surrounding the duke's sexuality, and the association made by at least some contemporaries of 'Algerines' from the state of Barbary with 'unnatural vices'.[16] Miles suggests that the tall figure to the duke's right in Rowlandson's image is 'Captain C—', 'posed as intermediary or pander between Newcastle and the ambassador', and he identifies the figure to the ambassador's right as Jery's irascible uncle Matt Bramble, who, he writes, 'glowers disapprovingly at the inward-facing circle of four'.[17] Considering text and image together, Miles suggests, it is possible to see Smollett's work as offering 'an invitation to read the duke's levée disparagingly as a sodomitical clique and indeed . . . as an outcrop of London's increasingly recognizable homosexual subculture'. What therefore 'comes into focus' in the illustration, he claims, 'is the all-male environment and the boyish Newcastle lathered with sexual excitement as much as with soap as he half-crouches in deference and eagerness before an Algerine ambassador posed as object of sexual desire'.[18]

'Eastern' Gallantry

This reading of Smollett's homophobic satire chimes with Matt Bramble's wider representation of London as a sink of corruption and vice, consequent upon its openness to and contamination by the wider world. It is also broadly consonant with Daniel O'Quinn's Foucauldian analysis of a significant shift in social relations from around 1770 whereby the 'consolidation of . . . middle-class hegemony' was achieved in part through a normalising regulation of sexuality which worked via the 'deployment' of Orientalist stereotypes.[19] Bickerstaff's play *The Sultan*, briefly mentioned above, can also be seen to exemplify such a shift because it represents the process by which the 'Turkish gallantry' of the title character is subject to reform by an English heroine who identifies as a 'free-born woman, prouder of that than all the pomp and splendour eastern monarchs can bestow'.[20] The role of Roxolana was written for the celebrity actress Frances Abington, who apparently pressured David Garrick into staging the drama, and Abington's individual fame and the baggage which came with it may have been somewhat at odds with the 'representative' function of the character that she played; some complained that 'Roxolana' was an inappropriate name for one credited with improving agency.[21] If Bickerstaff's Roxolana exerts her influence over the sultan in a coquettish manner, she is nonetheless more modest than her 'French' predecessors in works by Marmontel and Favart, lacking their sexual experience. Whereas the self-presentation of Defoe's Roxana at her Pall Mall gathering is overtly sexualised (and gains her a position as the king's mistress), Roxolana's influence over the sultan leads him to reject his harem wives and to embrace the idea of companionate marriage with her. The Drury Lane set for the first performances of the drama was lavishly Oriental (incorporating such items as a 'low, deep Turkish sopha covered with long carpets and cushions, a gold table, [a] rich gold sa[l]ver set with jewels, [and] a spoon made of the beak of an Indian bird'), but rather than show Roxolana as indulging in identity play and masquerade (like Defoe's Roxana), *The Sultan* culminates in her triumph over and 'conquest' of her captor through the force of her 'English' free speech.[22]

The Sultan was frequently performed despite its author's disgraced reputation, and – exemplifying the processes of citation and re-enactment referred to above – versions of its sultan/slave scenario are common across late eighteenth-century popular drama as well as being present in a dialogic text such as Bage's comic epistolary novel *The Fair Syrian*. The titular character of Bage's work, Honoria Warren, describes how she was born in Syria (hence her sobriquet) after her merchant father had settled there but later came to be separated from him when they were both seized by Saif Ebn Abu, the son of her father's business associate. As when Honoria describes the threat that Saif posed to her during her captivity, Bage's novel is more uncompromising than Bickerstaff's play in accentuating the rhetoric of Oriental sexual despotism. Honoria recounts that she carried a knife with which to ensure 'his death or my own', and that 'never, whilst I stayed in Asia, did I part with it from my person'; the attentions of a subsequent master, she states, likewise displayed 'the idea of property . . . that is visible in the regards of [all] the Orientals'.[23] Even as it invokes such unexamined notions of men's tyranny over women in a monolithic 'East' ('Asia'), however, *The Fair Syrian* also frequently plays this received idea for laughs. While she recalls the sexual danger that she faced, Honoria makes wryly detached reference to the 'lock-up houses' established in the era of 'that horrid bear, Mahomet', and then incongruously includes 'luxurious slippers' alongside 'wine, and women' in her list of the things that 'a Turk thinks of value upon earth' (2:36, 2:86). Bage meanwhile qualifies the actual sense of threat faced by his heroine by having her explain that she retained her chastity during her captivity because the man who bought her from Saif was impotent.

One further index of Bage's comic engagement with this subject matter is that his novel incorporates the figure of the free-speaking Georgian harem slave Amina, who combines Roxolana's instinct for free speech with a far greater degree of sexual candour. Without self-pity or sensation, Amina relates to Honoria how she spent nine years adorning the 'splendid harams' of eleven different owners, most of whom beat her because, as she puts it, she 'disturbed their . . . gravity with laughing' (2:78, 2:79). Honoria describes how 'this wild, untutored, sensible mad-cap' also laughed at her and her 'most serious arguments', ridiculing her principled assertion that she would 'prefer death a thousand times' to the kind of accommodation to harem life that her companion so blithely narrates (2:81). Amina is in some ways therefore a 're-Orientalised' Roxolana and her role in *The Fair Syrian* exemplifies the unconventional exploration of sexual politics across Bage's fiction more widely. It is significant, however, that (in contrast to Defoe's and Bickerstaff's heroines) Amina has only a cameo role in the text, and that her story is contained as a brief episode within Honoria's narrative: 'What became of her, I never heard', Honoria states after their separation (2:90). Rather than assume any reformist 'Scheherazadean' role over Eastern men, Amina exerts an influence over Honoria instead, by preparing her to laugh at (and thereby put in his place) an English suitor who attempts to make her his mistress.

When, back in England, Sir John Amington drunkenly attempts to seduce Honoria, she mockingly asks him to translate his raptures into a more comprehensible language, at which point he ventriloquises what he takes to be an 'Eastern' style of address, declaring his desire to 'improve felicity, and create a paradise for man' (1:246). After responding that this paradise would be 'a purgatory for women', Honoria ridicules the 'cold and lifeless' style as well as the substance of Sir John's indecent proposal. She then offers her own version of how to praise female beauty in what she presents to him as a properly (though knowingly inflated) Eastern idiom:

> Her eyes were large and black, like the eyes of the heifer of Yerak – their lustre surpassed the gems of Golconda – Her cheeks were the full blown rose of Damascus – Her teeth, the cypresses of Diarbekir – Her hair was black as the raven's plumes . . .
> (1:248)

Honoria's response to Sir John's clumsy attempt to play the sultan therefore appears to display her enjoyment of a fantastical, non-referential Orientalism, predicated on a sophisticated awareness of the gulf between euphonious fantasy and mundane reality. Even as (in comic dialogue reminiscent of Bickerstaff's play) she offers an alternative to Sir John's hackneyed rhetoric, however, Honoria here draws an implicit analogy between 'Turkish' and – broadly upper-class – 'English' gallantry.

Sir John's proposal to Honoria is framed as a momentary aberration because the pair go on to marry, and the novel moreover complicates any sense of class critique by describing Amington's friendship with the libertine Frenchman the Marquis de St. Claur (who freely enjoys 'Mingrelian' women while on a pleasure trip to Constantinople); like *The Sultan*, *The Fair Syrian* uses its Eastern setting as a means of reflecting on the meaning of liberty at a time when Britain's war with its American colonies had radically called this into question.[24] Bage's satire of Sir John's conduct in this episode is nonetheless convergent with the more sustained and polemical treatment, in works such as Mary Wollstonecraft's *A Vindication of the Rights of Woman* (1792), of how 'Eastern' manners were established – and women thus subordinated – in Britain. By the 1790s, Saree Makdisi argues, the seraglio (and the idea of male pleasure that it represented) provided 'the ideal surrogate for radical critique', and writers with reformist sympathies, especially, commonly projected such a shorthand notion of 'Oriental' excess, associated above all with deviant sexuality, onto the upper classes to define their own contrasting honesty, rationality and sobriety.[25] Two decades later, numerous print and graphic satires of the 1810s would depict a corpulent and sometimes explicitly Orientalised Prince Regent, while offering a debunking treatment of elite manners more widely.

Celebrating Despotism

Along with O'Quinn's account of a shift in social relations achieved through the regulation of sexuality, the ossification of what Makdisi identifies as a 'new' Orient – understood with reference to imaginary characteristics rather than any actual evidence – helps us now to appreciate the dissident performances of William Beckford. Ros Ballaster contrasts the celebrated figure of Lady Mary Wortley Montagu with Defoe's Roxana, her contemporary, stating that the former's class privilege enabled her to adopt Turkish dress during her travels 'to express her freedom from the constraints of western marriage and government'.[26] Beckford enjoyed comparable privilege to Montagu (to whom he was indirectly connected through her son Edward Wortley Montagu, who provided him with Arabic manuscripts), but while he similarly sought to evade social responsibility, his self-fashioning was considerably more audacious. At Fonthill, which he would later attempt to extend into a gigantic Gothic abbey, in December 1781, Beckford held a three-day Oriental extravaganza, orchestrated by the 'spectacle maestro' de Loutherbourg, at which he sought to immerse his guests in what Iain McCalman describes as 'a novel experiment in "virtual reality"', 'a visual and sensory space that integrate[d] them in a perceptual and emotional relationship with the surrounding images'. If this spectacle was, in effect, as McCalman puts it, a 'virtual seraglio', then Beckford himself was the sovereign within it, and in his correspondence he sometimes indeed imagined himself 'as if [he] were the Grand Turk'.[27] Beckford would later present the 'voluptuous festival' at Fonthill as part of a lifelong project of

ORIENTALISM AND SEXUALITY 47

fantasy and self-dramatisation, although, as McCalman notes, he organised the festivities with an immediate aim in mind too, 'want[ing] an Oriental spectacle that would completely ravish the senses of his guests, not least so that he could enjoy a sexual tryst with a thirteen-year-old boy, William Courtenay'.[28]

Beckford was socially ostracised following the circulation of gossip about his alleged liaison with Courtenay at Powderham Castle in 1784, and he would spend much of the rest of his life overseas. Before this scandal broke, however, he used the Fonthill festivities – so he later claimed, at least – as the creative stimulus for his best-known work, *Vathek*, which he probably wrote in 1782 although it was only published, without Beckford's consent, in 1786. While *Vathek* is structured as if it were a fable warning against the 'insatiable curiosity' that the title character displays, its main narrative appears to demonstrate what Aravamudan refers to as an 'uninhibited celebration of despotism';[29] in contrast to *The Sultan* and *The Fair Syrian* it only minimally acknowledges any 'subaltern' challenge to absolute male power. At one point Vathek declares himself 'not over-fond of resisting temptation', and Beckford seems to have revelled in the hedonism of the Caliph as a means of both escaping from the constraints of social expectation and of exploring an alternative world of sexual possibility: for Beckford, 'Orientalism' functions as a metaphorical stage on which socially transgressive forms of elite self-fashioning can be pursued.[30] The homoeroticism of the text is plain to see in Vathek's relations with the mysterious Giaour, as when he agrees to meet the latter's demand for 'the blood of fifty children' and goes on to undress himself as he sacrifices naked boys to the salivating stranger, to gain access to his 'portal of ebony' (20, 19). Later, after the ailing Vathek has been healed by an unspecified 'potion' supplied by the Giaour, we are told that he 'leaped upon the neck of the frightful Indian and kissed his horrid mouth and cheeks, as though they had been the coral lips and the lilies and roses of his most beautiful wives' (13).

Presenting *Vathek* as a pioneering example of 'queer Gothic', George Haggerty argues that the 'queerness' of the text is manifest not only in such content, but also in the way in which it self-consciously challenges 'all normative . . . configurations of human interaction'.[31] Vathek's mother Carathis, for example, surpasses her son in both ambition and villainy, and when some of the Caliph's faithful subjects attempt to rescue him from the fire spreading through his Babel-like tower in Samarah, she orders that they be asphyxiated by 'mutes and negresses' just as they are about to reach him. While punishment by strangulation was a signifier of the barbaric nature of Oriental despotism, here the narrator archly notes that 'Never before had the ceremony of strangling been performed with so much facility' (29). Thomas Keymer states of this episode that it demonstrates how, in *Vathek*, 'style . . . trump[s] mere morality', and he suggestively presents this privileging of style as central to the tonal ambiguity and formal hybridity of the work.[32] One especially relevant aspect of such formal hybridity for the purposes of this essay concerns the strikingly visual dimension of the text, which Eliza Bourque Dandridge likens to an 'action-adventure comic book'.[33] Episodes such as the one where the Giaour, assuming the shape of a ball, is kicked around Samarah by the Caliph's subjects, offended by the stranger's insolence, display an essentially 'cartoonish' mode of narration that is exaggeratedly graphic, and which for that reason (Dandridge argues) 'mitigates the unbearable violence of the scenario'.[34] Donna Landry's description of *Vathek* as 'a re-enactment of the three-day event he had staged at Fonthill, which was itself a re-enactment of the *Arabian Nights*', also helps us

48   JAMES WATT

to recognise how the distinctive atmospherics of the work can be seen both to extend
the virtual reality experiment of Beckford's Christmas party and to employ the visual
language of popular drama.[35] The five wings that the Caliph adds to his palace, 'destined for the particular gratification of each of the senses' (3), are initially described
almost as if they were stage sets designed by a scenographer such as de Loutherbourg.

Landry's account of *Vathek* as (indirectly) 'a re-enactment of the *Arabian Nights*'
presents it as offering a kind of tribute to old forms of storytelling as well as to new
visual technologies. The fact that *Vathek* was originally written in French – Samuel
Henley had to translate it for his pirated version – invites us to see it as in some ways
a consciously belated text, harking back to the creative licence of an earlier and more
intellectually cosmopolitan moment in the history of literary Orientalism, before the
rise of 'domestic' or 'national' realism reordered the field of prose fiction. One other
feature of the heterogeneity of the work relevant to mention here is that it combines
the fantastical fictionality that Aravamudan sees as characteristic of 'Enlightenment
Orientalism' with accurate historically and culturally specific reference, such as to the
figure of Vathek himself, described in the opening sentence as 'ninth Caliph of the race
of the Abassides, . . . and the grandson of Haroun al Raschid' (3). When Henley issued
his edition in 1786, he did so with an extensive apparatus of what he referred to in
his title as 'Notes Critical and Explanatory', designed to gloss terms such as 'Caliph':
'This title amongst the Mahometans implies the three characters of Prophet, Priest,
and King', Henley's first note begins (97). *Vathek* can be seen as the work of a maver-
ick author, and as a highly idiosyncratic text which in its gleeful amorality throws into
relief the ideological coding and the regulatory function of 'Eastern manners' in other
contemporary works. At the same time, however, it can be seen as a generative text for
subsequent writers (notably for poets – for example, Lord Byron and Robert Southey –
more than novelists), because of both its depiction of its overreaching protagonist and
the cultural and ethnographic specificity that its notes seek to explicate.

Renouncing the East

Beckford presents the Giaour who tempts Vathek with the promise of extraordinary
wealth as 'an Indian', hailing from 'a region of India . . . which is wholly unknown'
(13), and some contemporaries recognised the topical application of the mysterious
stranger's ultimately destructive allure: by one (albeit slightly tendentious) reading
Vathek allegorises the decline and fall of an imperial Britain fatally attracted to the
East. In several other fictions of the 1770s and 1780s, India is not specifically realised
even where it is, in plot terms, much more central than in *Vathek*: Charles Johnston's
The Pilgrim: or, A Picture of Life (1775), for example, an informant narrative modelled on Goldsmith's *The Citizen of the World*, engages with the politics of Indian
empire (notably by accentuating the horrors of the Black Hole of Calcutta) but nonetheless refers to India as 'Mogulstan' and to Bengal as 'a town'.[36] As its title suggests,
Phebe Gibbes's *Hartly House, Calcutta* by contrast provides a thicker description of its
milieu than any previous fiction of India, and even if it does not eschew the lexicon of
literary Orientalism, it renders its setting with reference to 'on the spot' observation.
Although Gibbes never travelled to the subcontinent, she probably based her work
upon letters which her son sent her from Calcutta, and the novel was widely praised as
(in *The Critical Review*'s terms) a source of 'much information' about India.[37]

Gibbes's heroine, Sophia, acknowledges the exotic aura of India when she describes herself on her approach to Calcutta as *'orientalised* at all points'.[38] Although her narrative voice remains flighty, she goes on to evoke everyday life on the ground for 'Calcuttonians' (26) – probably a coinage of Gibbes, as Michael Franklin suggests – and in her depiction of the colonial community established in Calcutta she notably rejects the prevalent anti-nabob stereotype concerning young British adventurers on the make in India. As if in response to Edmund Burke's charge that 'England has erected no churches, no hospitals, no palaces, no schools', Sophia's portrayal of Calcutta suggests that the presence of the East India Company in the city has helped to create a flourishing civil society where none existed before.[39] She refers to the infrastructure that 'originates from commerce and owes its support . . . to commerce', and she identifies as symbolic of this a hospital 'erected for the reception of *all* indisposed persons': quoting from Pope's *Epistle to Burlington*, she states that 'These are imperial works, and worthy kings' (44). A 1908 edition of *Hartly House* gave it the subtitle 'A Novel of the Days of Warren Hastings', and Sophia sometimes directly vindicates the former governor-general, who was famously under impeachment at the time of the work's publication. Sophia indeed conceives of British India as a reproach to Britain itself (theatres in England, she states, are 'far more censurable and licentious than any the Eastern world contains' [51–2]), and by thus presenting an at once prosperous and polite Calcutta, *Hartly House* can in some ways be seen as a literary analogue of 'views' of the city produced by the artists William Hodges and Thomas and William Daniell. One of Thomas Daniell's *Views of Calcutta* of 1788 (Plate 2) captures the neoclassical elegance of Old Government House on what appears to be 'a special day of formal viceregal celebration', presided over by the reforming governor-general Lord Cornwallis, at which, in the words of Hermione de Almeida and George H. Gilpin, 'English and India residents of all classes are shown gathering . . ., with the wealthiest arriving on elephants and by palanquin'.[40] Exemplifying the interplay between literary and visual sources that is a feature of many of the novels discussed in this essay, Sophia's glowing account of the Calcutta cityscape invites readers to share her spectatorial pleasures.

It is useful to conclude with a brief discussion of *Hartly House* because as well as offering an unprecedentedly precise and specific description of its setting (for example, in referring to the transfer of power from Hastings to Cornwallis), Gibbes's novel also engages, albeit indirectly and decorously, with the idea of 'Oriental' sexual decadence that provides one of the organising threads of this chapter. *Hartly House* counters the anti-nabob discourse which imagined India as at once corrupt and corrupting of Britons who went there, as noted, and it does this not only through its representation of Calcutta but also through attaching its protagonist to the inoffensive Edmund Doyly. This kind of 'English' companionate relationship might appear to complement the establishment of a new colonial regime under Cornwallis that defined itself against the cross-cultural exchange characteristic of the Hastings era. What complicates any such reading of Sophia's connection with Doyly, however, is that the novel also gives space to her fascination with a young Brahman, the nephew of her father's chief servant. Sophia idealises the Brahman, sometimes invoking him as a spectator of her conduct, and any sense that a 'colonial romance' might be developing between them is contained by the death of the nameless, unindividuated Indian. When at one point she presents herself as 'a convert to the Gentoo faith' (because, via the Brahman, she has become fascinated with Hinduism), Sophia nonetheless – if in a somewhat arch

50 JAMES WATT

fashion – performatively broaches the loss of identity popularly associated with the idea of 'turning Turk' (111).

There is a clearer frisson of sexual transgression in the later episode where Sophia imagines herself being carried off by the Muslim Nawab of Bengal, a man whose gaze – to the unease of Doyly, who 'turned pale' – generates 'ambitious throbs' in her heart (154). Kathryn Freeman identifies an 'embedded sequence of references to Shakespeare's *Othello*' across the novel, where Sophia assumes the position of Desdemona, and it is notable here too that Sophia compares herself with another figure from an earlier era, Lady Mary Wortley Montagu:[41]

> I thought of [her] account of . . . being noticed by the Grand Seignor, when spectator of a Turkish procession, on the Nabob's observation of me;—but there was this difference between the circumstances—namely, that the attention the Sultan paid that Lady was merely *en passant*; whereas this Nabob of Nabobs proved in the face of all the people, how long he bore me in mind—that is, how deeply he was wounded—and I hold myself in expectance of hearing more of him. (155)

Sophia's references to Montagu suggest that her enjoyment of this encounter is to some extent mediated, deriving in part from her self-conscious sense of participating in a kind of literary re-enactment that her social privilege makes possible. (Montagu described her exchange of gazes with a Sultan, who, she writes, 'looked upon us very attentively, so that we had full leisure to consider him'.)[42] As if to deflate the potency of the prince she goes on to record his 'astonishment' at a display of artillery firepower by East India Company troops. She again notes the jealousy of 'Poor Doyly', nonetheless, and the strength of her illicit fantasy is such that she calls up the memory of 'my Bramin' to compose herself (155).

What makes *Hartly House* especially interesting, as well as rhetorically unstable, however, is that immediately after this episode, the novel changes tack and moves from describing the Nawab as an alluring figure to presenting colonial Bengal as an arena of threat. In her penultimate letter Sophia recounts the story of an army officer's rape of an Indian woman and his subsequent murder of her father: 'There are monsters . . . in human shapes', she writes, 'and the Eastern world is . . . the scene of tragedies that dishonour mankind' (157). Sophia goes on to 'rejoice, more than ever, that I am about to leave a country, where fiend-like acts are, I fear, much oftener perpetrated than detected' (158), presenting India as a corrupt and dangerous foreign environment in terms that are compatible with anti-nabob discourse. It is crucial here, though, that the aggressor appears to be British rather than Indian, and that the degradation of 'the Eastern world' is therefore figured not as immanent but as contingent upon external agency; here at least this pro-Hastings novel seems to invoke his antagonists' sense of the East India Company as a ruthless predator despoiling innocent victims. Having enthusiastically declared herself 'orientalised' on her approach to Calcutta, Sophia in her final letter, written from Portsmouth, briefly and soberly records how she 'landed safe at this place, after a tedious, though not hazardous voyage'; 'Meet us then at Guildford' (159), she tells her female correspondent, as if to announce her return to the world of domestic realism. I do not want to overstate the wider symbolism of this episode as a watershed moment in the history of the eighteenth-century novel: older modes of literary Orientalism endured while (from the 1820s) new kinds of Anglo-Indian fiction would emerge.

It is nonetheless striking that a work which was credited with setting a new standard for accuracy in its portrayal of India should enact a novelistic retreat from the subject of Indian empire instead of inspiring other writers to follow its example. Through its minimal yet decisive acknowledgement of the quotidian violence of East India Company rule and its final departure from the scene of such crimes, *Hartly House* arguably broaches the idea that empire poses a problem of representation, and it thus anticipates not simply the marginal role of the subcontinent in later fiction but also its imaginative distance for metropolitan Britons more generally.

Notes

1. Daniel Defoe, *Roxana*, ed. John Mullan (1724; Oxford: Oxford University Press, 1996), 176. Further references parenthetical.
2. Srinivas Aravamudan, *Enlightenment Orientalism: Resisting the Rise of the Novel* (Chicago: University of Chicago Press, 2012), 65, 67.
3. John Mullan, 'Introduction' to Defoe, *Roxana*, vii.
4. Jakub Lipski, *Painting the Novel: Pictorial Discourse in Eighteenth-Century English Fiction* (New York and London: Routledge, 2018), 30–4.
5. Iain McCalman, 'The Virtual Infernal: Philippe de Loutherbourg, William Beckford and the Spectacle of the Sublime', *Romanticism on the Net* 46 (2007), https://www.erudit.org/en/journals/ron/1900-v1-n1-ron1782/016129ar/ (accessed 8 November 2023).
6. Aravamudan, *Enlightenment Orientalism*, 4.
7. Aravamudan, *Enlightenment Orientalism*, 6, 18.
8. Francis Coventry, 'An Essay on the New Species of Writing Founded by Mr Fielding' (1751), cited in William B. Warner, *Licensing Entertainment: The Elevation of Novel Reading in Britain, 1684–1750* (Berkeley: University of California Press, 1998), 33.
9. Samuel Johnson, *The Rambler*, ed. W. J. Bate and Albrecht B. Strauss, The Yale Edition of the Works of Samuel Johnson (New Haven: Yale University Press, 1990), 19.
10. Suvir Kaul, *Eighteenth-Century British Literature and Postcolonial Studies* (Edinburgh: Edinburgh University Press, 2009), 34n53.
11. Ros Ballaster, 'Narrative Transmigrations: The Oriental Tale and the Novel in Eighteenth-Century Britain', in *A Companion to the Eighteenth-Century English Novel and Culture*, ed. Paula R. Backscheider and Catherine Ingrassia (Oxford: Wiley Blackwell, 2009), 83.
12. Ruth Bernard Yeazell, *Harems of the Mind: Passages of Western Art and Literature* (New Haven: Yale University Press, 2000), 150–8.
13. Tobias Smollett, *The Expedition of Humphry Clinker*, ed. Evan Gottlieb (1771; New York: W. W. Norton, 2015), 99. Further references parenthetical.
14. Richard D. Altick, *The Shows of London* (Cambridge, MA: Belknap Press of Harvard University Press, 1978), 1.
15. Ronald Paulson, *Hogarth's Graphic Works*, 3rd edn, rev. (London: The Print Room, 1989), 177.
16. Peter Miles, 'Smollett, Rowlandson, and a Problem of Identity: Decoding Names, Bodies, and Gender in *Humphry Clinker*', *Eighteenth-Century Life* 20, no. 1 (1996): 12.
17. Miles, 'Smollett, Rowlandson, and a Problem of Identity', 17.
18. Miles, 'Smollett, Rowlandson, and a Problem of Identity', 16.
19. Daniel O'Quinn, *Staging Governance: Theatrical Imperialism in London, 1770–1800* (Baltimore: Johns Hopkins University Press, 2005), 7.
20. Isaac Bickerstaff, *The Sultan, or A Peep into the Seraglio* (London: Charles Dilly, 1787), 13.
21. *Middlesex Journal*, 12–14 December 1775, 1.

22. Cited in Berta Joncus, '"Nectar If You Taste and Go, Poison If You Stay": Struggling with the Orient in Eighteenth-Century British Musical Theatre', in *Scheherazade's Children: Global Encounters with the Arabian Nights*, ed. Philip F. Kennedy and Marina Warner (New York: New York University Press, 2013), 308.
23. Robert Bage, *The Fair Syrian*, 2 vols (1787; New York: Garland, 1979), 2:70, 2:85. Further references parenthetical.
24. James Watt, *British Orientalisms, 1759–1835* (Cambridge: Cambridge University Press, 2019), 103–5, 107–10.
25. Saree Makdisi, *William Blake and the Impossible History of the 1790s* (Chicago: University of Chicago Press, 2003), 206.
26. Ros Ballaster, *Fabulous Orients: Fictions of the East in England, 1662–1785* (Oxford: Oxford University Press, 2005), 65.
27. McCalman, 'The Virtual Infernal'. William Beckford, *Life at Fonthill, 1807–1822: With Interludes in Paris and London, from the Correspondence of William Beckford*, ed. Boyd Alexander (London: R. Hart-Davis, 1957), 65.
28. Thomas Keymer, 'Introduction' to William Beckford, *Vathek*, ed. Thomas Keymer (Oxford: Oxford University Press, 2013), xv; McCalman, 'The Virtual Infernal'.
29. Srinivas Aravamudan, *Tropicopolitans: Colonialism and Agency, 1688–1804* (Durham: Duke University Press, 1999), 214.
30. William Beckford, *Vathek*, ed. Thomas Keymer (Oxford: Oxford University Press, 2013), 80. Further references parenthetical. Donna Landry, 'William Beckford's *Vathek* and the Use of Oriental Re-enactment', in *The Arabian Nights in Historical Context: Between East and West*, ed. Saree Makdisi and Felicity Nussbaum (Oxford: Oxford University Press, 2008), 167–94.
31. George E. Haggerty, *Queer Gothic* (Urbana: University of Illinois Press, 2006), 3.
32. Keymer, 'Introduction' to Beckford, *Vathek*, xxviii.
33. Eliza Bourque Dandridge, 'William Beckford's Comic Book, or Visualizing Orientalism with Vathek', *Eighteenth-Century Fiction* 29, no. 3 (2017): 27.
34. Dandridge, 'William Beckford's Comic Book', 442.
35. Landry, 'William Beckford's *Vathek*', 178.
36. Charles Johnston, *The Pilgrim: Or, A Picture of Life*, 2 vols (London: T. Cadell, 1775), 1:7.
37. Cited in Michael Franklin, 'Introduction' to Phebe Gibbes, *Hartly House, Calcutta*, ed. Michael Franklin (Delhi: Oxford University Press, 2007), xxi.
38. Phebe Gibbes, *Hartly House, Calcutta*, ed. Michael Franklin (Delhi: Oxford University Press, 2007), 8. Further references parenthetical.
39. Edmund Burke, 'Speech on Fox's India Bill', in *The Writings and Speeches of Edmund Burke*, vol. 5, ed. P. J. Marshall (Oxford: Clarendon Press, 1981), 404.
40. Hermione de Almeida and George H. Gilpin, *Indian Renaissance: British Romantic Art and the Prospect of India* (London and New York: Routledge, 2016), 186–7.
41. Kathryn S. Freeman, '"She had eyes and chose me": Ambivalence and Miscegenation in Phebe Gibbes's *Hartly House, Calcutta* (1789)', *European Romantic Review* 22, no.1 (2011): 38.
42. Lady Mary Wortley Montagu, *Letters Written During Her Travels in Europe, Asia, and Africa* (1763), cited in Gibbes, *Hartly House*, 217.

3

CRAFTING THE PAST: ANTIQUARIANISM, DECORATIVE HANDICRAFTS AND THE NOVEL AT THE MID-CENTURY

Katharina Boehm

EXPLORING MID-EIGHTEENTH-CENTURY novelists' engagement with antiquarian practices can usefully expand our view of antiquarianism's contribution to the novel's emergence as an important medium of historical thought. Scholars have begun to reconstruct the considerable cultural reach that antiquarian approaches enjoyed in the long eighteenth century. However, accounts of antiquarianism's entanglement with literary writing have so far concentrated on the Romantic-era novel and on other fictional and non-fictional genres. Tellingly, Horace Walpole's *The Castle of Otranto* (1764) is the only novelistic work that receives extended discussion in Barrett Kalter's and Crystal B. Lake's excellent monographs on intersections between eighteenth-century antiquarian and literary cultures.[1] Other scholars have shown that, around 1800, novelistic renditions of antiquarianism and of the (often comic, socially awkward) figure of the antiquary were forged by, and in their turn intervened in, cultural debates about patriotism, national identity, masculinity and the rise of disciplinarity in different fields of historical inquiry.[2] This body of criticism has also explored how antiquarian research propelled the emergence of verisimilar realism as a key mode of historical representation at the turn of the nineteenth century. According to this argument, the labours of antiquaries provided comprehensive information on the 'costume' of earlier periods in history, which then allowed Romantic-era novelists to furnish their fictional worlds with a wealth of period detail.[3] Walter Scott's Waverley novels still loom large in these accounts, which dovetails with the long tradition, inaugurated by Georg Lukács's much-cited *The Historical Novel* (1937), of viewing these novels as the origin of the nineteenth-century realist historical novel.[4] At the same time, critics have also begun to unearth the much wider field of historical fiction as it emerged in the latter part of the eighteenth century.[5]

The mid-eighteenth-century novel displays comparatively few of the thematic and paratextual features that signal the late eighteenth-century novel's sustained attention to antiquarianism, such as historically remote settings, the presence of vividly drawn antiquaries in the diegesis or frame narratives of these novels and the inclusion of antiquarian paratexts including prefaces, appendices, glossaries, endnotes and footnotes. However, as my discussion of Sarah Scott's *Millenium Hall* (1762) in this chapter shows, the discourse of the sister arts provided a framework in which novelists were able to enter into dialogue with antiquarianism at the mid-century.[6] My essay focuses on Scott's figurations of decorative handicrafts: as I show, she uses handicraft practices and objects to explore material, epistemological and representational concerns that are born of an engagement with antiquarian approaches to the past. Most importantly, Scott's portrayal of what the novel refers to as the female 'arts' mediates between antiquarianism and the aesthetic ambitions and practices of the novel form. Throughout the essay, I am also concerned with *Millenium Hall*'s interest in women's marginal position both in antiquarian research and in much classical and eighteenth-century historiography. As we shall see, Scott proposes that consideration of the history of arts and crafts performed by women might not only expand opportunities for female participation in antiquarian research but also aid in unearthing forgotten spheres of female industry. I begin with a short survey of some of the cultural contexts in which men and women, including members of Scott's circle, encountered antiquarian approaches to the past, before discussing *Millenium Hall*'s sophisticated reflections on the domestic 'trifles' that women produced and which male and female antiquaries studied.

Antiquarianism at the Mid-Century

Eighteenth-century antiquaries were interested in the material remains of many different pasts. They variously studied Romano-British, Anglo-Saxon and medieval artefacts, pursued genealogical and heraldic studies, produced detailed accounts of the natural history and antiquities of particular counties or regions, inquired into native literary and oral traditions, and sought to elucidate the manners and customs of past periods.[7] The cheap publication schemes, picturesque print series and popular entertainments that would introduce much larger and diverse audiences to antiquarianism in the late eighteenth century were not yet in place at the mid-century. Indeed, antiquarian pursuits were by no means a mass phenomenon in the first half of the century: the majority of active antiquaries were clergymen, lawyers, doctors, heralds, librarians and archivists, whose educational and professional backgrounds facilitated their participation in antiquarian research. Women's ability to partake in antiquarian inquiries was hamstrung by a number of factors. Even aristocratic women were much less likely than their male peers to possess thorough facility with Latin and Greek. They were also barred from pursuing a professional career in the law, as archivists, or as librarians, which limited their ability to develop expertise in the handling of historical documents such as charters and chronicles.[8] However, as we shall see in what follows, by the mid-century the study and appreciation of antiquities had evolved into an interest pursued in many different private and newly emerging public spheres. Women and girls with an interest in antiquarianism continued to experience many limitations, but some were carving out opportunities to participate in antiquarian fieldwork, excavations and collecting.

Metropolitan and provincial societies offered forums in which like-minded antiquaries could come together, discuss their research projects and collections, and develop collaborative initiatives that required a pooling of expertise and financial backing. The re-establishment of the Society of Antiquaries of London (informally revived in 1707 and more formally re-established in 1718; henceforth SAL) was followed by the foundation of smaller provincial organisations, such as the Gentlemen's Society at Spalding (founded 1709) and the Gentlemen's Society of Peterborough (founded 1720s).[9] Women were barred from membership in all but one antiquarian society, the short-lived

Society of Roman Knights (founded 1722), which numbered two female members.[10] A degree of familiarity with antiquarian pursuits could also be gained without membership of an antiquarian society. Coffeehouses and taverns – key spaces in the emergence of a public sphere, again limited to male patrons in the great majority of cases – were important meeting places for antiquaries. In fact, they sometimes doubled as informal antiquarian museums. In the early eighteenth century, the Swan's enterprising owner in Pillbridge bought 'a great parcel of the littl [sic] stones of a [Roman] tesselated pavement found but two days before' to attract customers who 'came immediately out of curiosity'.[11] A much bigger collection of antiquities and natural history specimens was on show in London's first 'public museum': Don Saltero's coffeehouse, set up in 1695 by James Salter, which went from strength to strength until the collection was auctioned off in 1799.[12] Don Saltero's was far from the only popular venue that lured customers with antiques and exotic objects: Adam's Museum at the Royal Swan in Kingsland Road, which was active in the mid-eighteenth century, claimed to exhibit the boots of Charles of Sweden and Henry VIII's spurs alongside a large number of spurious and bizarre curiosities.[13] Richard Greene's more serious collection at Lichfield contained, for instance, a cabinet of coins, ancient urns and other vessels, armour and weapons.[14]

A different kind of 'public' museum opened its doors at the refurbished Montagu House in 1759: the British Museum was established when Parliament acquired the Irish naturalist and antiquarian Sir Hans Sloane's substantial collection, bequeathed to the nation, after his death. Six rooms were dedicated to medals, coins and manuscripts. In theory, the British Museum was Europe's first state-sponsored 'public' museum, in the sense that the regulations stipulated that it would be open to men and women of all social ranks. In practice, admission procedures were complicated and slow, and 'in its first years no more than sixty visitors a day visited the British Museum'.[15] Educated men and women of social rank, who constituted the museum's primary audience in its early decades, could also apply to visit the collections of antiquities that were held by many proprietors of stately homes. As part of the rise of domestic tourism, 'a remarkable apparatus of country-house visiting grew' in the middle of the eighteenth century, as estates such as Stowe, Wilton and Blenheim opened their doors to select visitors.[16]

As Andrew McRae has noted, '[t]ravelling one's own land for pleasure, or in the interest of acquiring knowledge, was one of the most peculiar things that a man or woman could do in the sixteenth and seventeenth centuries';[17] but from the early eighteenth century onwards, increasing numbers of leisured men and women as well as so-called commoners toured the country to see ancient monuments, the ruins of medieval monasteries, burial sites and other places of interest. For instance, in 1709, while he was still a student at Cambridge, William Stukeley – who later became a major figure in the revived SAL and published highly influential studies of Stonehenge and Avebury – undertook some of his earliest antiquarian excursions in the company of Martha Lucas, the young, unmarried sister of one of Stukeley's friends. 'We traveld together like Errant Vertuosos', Stukeley narrates in his memoirs, 'when we came to an old ruind Castle, &c, we climbd together thro' every story & staircase . . . Nor could travailing curiosity or Antiquarian Researches be rendered so agreeable as with a fair & witty Companion & Fellow laborer.'[18] Stonehenge attracted so many visitors in the first half of the eighteenth century that, in the 1730s, an enterprising local carpenter named Gaffer Hunt 'built a hut against' one of the megaliths and 'attended there daily with liquors, to entertain the traveller, and shew him the stones'.[19] Stukeley's lavishly illustrated domestic tour, *Itinerarium Curiosum* (1724), contains copperplate engravings that show mixed groups of men and women exploring sites of antiquarian interest together.

Decades before William Gilpin's famous guidebooks stoked the vogue for picturesque tourism, male and female travellers documented their antiquarian explorations in letters and diaries. Sarah Scott's social circle included many women who were keenly interested in antiquarian endeavours. Her sister, the bluestocking writer and salonnière Elizabeth Montagu, hosted travelling antiquaries – including eminent members of the SAL such as George Vertue – on her country estates in Berkshire and York, where Scott likely met them during her visits.[20] Montagu also went on such excursions herself, providing 'an account of our tour' in her letters, and demonstrating her antiquarian appreciation of ancient architecture.[21] Montagu's close friendship with the Duchess of Portland, a keen collector of antiquities and specimens of natural history, began when both women were teenagers and Montagu kept Scott informed of the rapid growth and variety of the Duchess's collection.[22] Another female antiquary – not a member of Montagu's inner circle but a mutual acquaintance of Montagu and Scott – was the Anglo-Saxon scholar Elizabeth Elstob, who had joined the Duchess of Portland's household as governess in 1739 and was part of Scott's social circle when she visited Tunbridge Wells in 1747.[23] Scott was also closely acquainted with the poet and classicist Elizabeth Carter and the scholar Catherine Talbot. Carter and Talbot's friendship began when they met through their mutual friend, the antiquary Thomas Wright, with whom Carter undertook antiquarian expeditions.[24] Talbot and Carter kept each other abreast of their antiquarian adventures in their letters. 'One of my late exploits', Talbot wrote to Carter in 1748, 'has been venturing myself a whole night in a moated castle [Sherbon Castle], that does really look as if a giant, or at least a score of knights armed cap-a-pié [*sic*] were to sally out over the draw-bridge.'[25] Talbot's association of Sherbon Castle's rugged architecture with the early modern romance is of a piece with the endeavours of influential contemporary antiquaries such as Thomas Warton and Richard Hurd, who combined their interest in the recovery of a native literary history, including what they referred to as 'Gothic romances', with a strong appreciation for the history of Gothic architecture in Britain.[26]

As Lake also notes, the full title of *Millenium Hall* evokes antiquarian travelogues and the literature of domestic travel.[27] *A Description of Millenium Hall, and the Country Adjacent; Together with the Characters of the Inhabitants, and Such Historical Anecdotes and Reflections as May Excite in the Reader proper Sentiments of Humanity, and the Mind to the Love of Virtue* calls to mind the domestic tours written by contemporary antiquaries such as Stukeley and William Borlase, which typically included ample topographical descriptions. As in *Millenium Hall*, these tours were sometimes offered to the reader in epistolary form. Educated, leisured, keenly interested in history and sociable, *Millenium Hall*'s male narrator has much in common with the friends and fellow antiquarian enthusiasts who joined Stukeley on his excursions and who figure as addressees of the epistles that make up his *Itinerarium Curiosum*.[28] After the narrator's chaise breaks down on the road in *Millenium Hall*, he finds shelter at the ladies' estate. In the manner of a travelling antiquary, he comments on 'the magnificence of the ancient structure' of the hall, and recounts how the ladies buy and restore other old country halls, including 'a very old, and formerly very fine mansion, but now much fallen to decay' which used to be a 'seat of ancient hospitality'.[29] It is important to note that right from the outset the novel's various nods to ancient architecture and to antiquarian interests are interlaced with comments that foreground differences between the ladies' and more prototypical antiquarian approaches to antiquities. For example, the penchant of Scott's protagonists for restoration and renovation complicates the antiquaries' typical preference for unrestored ruins and artefacts that are in an authentic state of decay. The narrator comments that he 'was pleased to see with how much art they repaired the decays of time, in things which well deserved better care, having once been the richest part of the furniture belonging to the opulent possessor [of one of the ancient halls]' (222). Throughout the novel, the ladies' endeavours to 'repair the decays of time' are associated with their skill at a range of decorative handicrafts. As I suggest below, Scott puts these practices and resulting objects to complex thematic and conceptual use: at various points in the novel, they showcase some limitations of antiquarianism as Scott perceived them, but they also come to figure the potential that she saw in antiquarianism's interest in previously neglected domains of history, and in approaches to the past that questioned the historical teleologies proposed by universal and conjectural historians.

History's 'Triflers': Antiquarianism and Decorative Handicrafts in *Millenium Hall*

From the moment the ladies of Millenium Hall enter the novel, their collective and individual identities, as well as their approach to the material world that surrounds them, are associated with domestic craft practices and the various 'arts [the narrator's] arrival had interrupted' (59):

> The room where they sat was about forty-five feet long . . . At the lower end of the room was a lady painting, with exquisite art indeed, a beautiful Madonna; near her another, drawing a landscape out of her own imagination; a third, carving a picture-frame in wood, in the finest manner; a fourth, engraving; . . . At the next window were placed a group of girls, from the age of ten years old to fourteen. Of these, one was drawing figures, another a landscape, a third a perspective view, a fourth engraving, a fifth carving, a sixth turning in wood, a seventh writing, an eighth cutting out linen, another making a gown, and by them an empty chair and a tent, with embroidery, finely fancied, before it[.] (59)

Whereas in earlier centuries the female 'arts' had consisted chiefly of sewing and embroidery, the activities listed here reflect the expanding repertoire of female accomplishments over the course of the eighteenth century. Advice manuals geared primarily towards female readers began to include chapters on japanning, varnishing, shellwork, filigree, woodturning, lacquering, painting on glass and many other crafts. Among early examples are *The Accomplish'd Female Instructor* (1704) and the pseudonymous 'Mrs Artlove's' *The Art of Japanning, Varnishing, Pollishing, and Gilding* (1730).[30] Demand for such publications appears to have picked up around the middle of the century: Robert Sayer's *The Ladies Amusement; or, Whole Art of Japanning Made Easy* (c.1759) and Hannah Robertson's *The Young Ladies School of Arts, Containing a Great Variety of*

Practical Receipts in Gum Flowers, Filigree, Japanning, Shellwork, Gilding, Painting (1766) ran to multiple editions within less than a decade.[31] As the title of Robertson's manual indicates, decorative arts – 'drawing a landscape', for instance – and handicrafts, such as 'carving' or 'turning in wood', were placed in the same domain as amateur arts, and will be treated as such in this essay. All these female endeavours, Ann Bermingham notes, were sharply distinguished from the realm of the male professional:

> The professional artist expressed his individual genius and imagination; the lady amateur practiced art for amusement and to display her taste and skill, to strengthen the domestic bonds of love and duty, to serve her community, and to improve her taste and that of the nation.[32]

The arts that are trained and perfected at Millenium Hall allow the ladies to trans-form the manmade and the natural world that surrounds them: dilapidated antique furniture gets a new lease of life when the ladies restore these pieces using 'shells, elegantly put together', or paint and decorate them with 'sea-weeds' (195); decayed old mansions become inhabitable once more; the cultivated landscape that surrounds the hall is rendered even more attractive by 'a most beautiful grotto, made of fossils, spars, coral, and . . . shells' (70) and by 'a temple dedicated to solitude' that is 'an exquisite piece of architecture' (69). It is equally significant that the objects the ladies enshrine in their renovated mansions, grottos and temples are not antiquities but their own craft productions. These include, for instance, a drawing of 'saint Cecilia, painted in crayons by Mrs. Mancel', 'a fine piece of carved wood over the chimney, done by Mrs. Trentham' (62), and the 'moon-light pieces, . . . workmanship of the ladies' (69), which decorate the temple. These objects displace the old furniture, paintings, antique weapons and classical sculptures that antiquaries valued and which we would expect to find more commonly in a manor house. The novel's celebration of female creativity and skill is thus directly intertwined with a critique of the naive and backward-looking reverence for ancient relics of which antiquaries were often accused. Indeed, the prominence of the ladies' shell-decorated grotto in the text must have reminded some of Scott's immediate readers of the derisive treatment which antiquarianism received by Alexander Pope, creator of another famous shell-encrusted grotto.[33] However, whereas Pope's criticism in *The Dunciad* is directed at antiquaries who are either duped by fakes or complicit in their production, *Millenium Hall* consigns a different class of objects to the dustheap of history. These objects centrally include the heirlooms and antiques that are passed down from one generation of landholders to the next as material signifiers of the descent of property through primogeniture and, in many cases, as mementos of the family's participation in events of national importance (such as military conflicts) and of its ties to the monarchy and other aristocratic dynasties. These objects could be marshalled to give credence to historical accounts of pivotal political and military events, accounts which usually give women a marginal role at best.

By contrast, the handicraft objects that the ladies of Millenium Hall produce and display point to their interest in the possibility of recovering the experiences and living conditions of women of the past. Scott, Montagu and their bluestocking friends were avid practitioners of many and varied crafts, including embroidery, sewing, painting, carving, engraving, filigree and shellwork, upholstery, japanning, gilding, the fabrication

ANTIQUARIANISM AND THE NOVEL   59

of artificial flowers and woodturning.[34] The topic of domestic handicrafts also found its way into some of their debates about history, where it often serves as a shorthand for aspects of (female) experience that historians tend to neglect. Scott and her female friends and correspondents studied the works of ancient historians, such as Thucydides, Xenophon and Herodotus, and they were also up to date with the works of modern English and French historians and antiquaries.[35] However, they often expressed dissatisfaction with the neglect of women in works of classical and modern historiography. In a letter to Carter, Talbot railed against the Athenian historian Thucydides: 'I am very much offended with him on behalf of all the Grecian ladies, whom he does not think fit to mention once through his whole history; and indeed of all ladies in general.'[36] Talbot discussed the place of women in history in another letter to Carter:

> [W]e shall . . . try to make every minute turn to the best account we can – and whether that be in knitting stockings, painting violets, or ruling kingdoms, what does it signify when the minute is over? I am sick of all human greatness and activity, and so would you be if you had been turning over with me five great folios of Mont- faucon's *French Antiquities*, where warriors, tyrants, queens, and favourites, have past before my eyes in a quick succession, . . . Here and there shines out a character remarkably good or great, but in general I have been forced to take refuge from the absolute detestation of human nature . . ., in the hope that the unillustrious in every age, the knitters, the triflers, the domestic folks, had quietly kept all the goodness and happiness among themselves, of which history preserves so few traces.[37]

History is understood here as a male-focused narrative of military and political events. Talbot suggests that her preoccupation with domestic activities – 'knitting stockings' and 'painting violets' – places her outside of history. However, the note of quiet resignation in Talbot's letter is misleading. She and other members of the bluestocking circle were aware that male historians had denied historical recognition both to women and to the craft practices in which they typically engaged – and this awareness led Talbot and her circle to take a broader approach to historical inquiry. They began to consider, often in a playful tone, how greater insight into the experience of previous generations of women might be extracted through engagement with the objects and material practices that had shaped these women's lives. In fact, the letters they exchanged are littered with comments indicating that they often imagined their craft projects as a way of engaging with the past. For instance, Talbot wrote to Carter in February 1743 that she regarded the working of 'muslin and lawn' as a 'laudable imitation of the quiet domestic virtues of our great grandmothers'.[38] Domestic handicrafts are here associated with an older model of femininity as well as with a female lineage of ancestors whose patterns and embroidery techniques are passed on through the generations. In a letter to Talbot from the same year, Carter gives an account of working a particularly complicated piece of embroidery, based on a pattern that is 'a perfect imitation of the gothic taste'.[39] And Talbot, in her turn, teased Carter, who was always eager to improve her pie recipes, by noting that 'in a list of the curiosities found in all these years at Herculaneum, I find nothing extraordinary but a silver roll . . . [a]nd a pye that had been in the oven 1000 years'.[40] Montagu, writing in 1741 to the Duchess of Portland, gave a detailed report of the antique furniture she had discovered in a friend's house:

I am now sitting in an old crimson velvet elbow chair I should imagine to be elder brother to that which is shewn in Westminster Abbey as Edward the Confessor's. . . . My toilette, I fancy, was worked by one of Queen Maud's maids of honour. There is a goodly chest of drawers in the figure of a cathedral, and a looking glass, which Rosamond or Jane Shore may have dressed their heads in.[41]

These letters evince an interest in matters of private and domestic life that combines with a typically antiquarian fascination with the material traces of the past. Montagu's fantasy that she is gazing into a looking glass that may once have caught the reflection of Jane Shore, like Talbot's observation that her working of muslin put her in touch with her female ancestors, treat bodily practice as a key to knowledge about the domestic labour and experience of women whose lives rarely figure in the work of historians. Antiquarian endeavours provided Scott and her bluestocking friends with welcome evidence of the important role that female expertise in the production of textiles and craft practices ought to play in such an enterprise.

Many eighteenth-century antiquaries were not only interested in the kinds of antiques removed from Millenium Hall – objects connected to political or military history – but also in quotidian household objects that shed light on historical manners and customs as well as on the evolution of practices of everyday life: tools, articles of clothing, kitchen utensils, vessels, objects relating to religious practice, some decorative items, and so on. These objects' seeming lack of aesthetic value and historical significance often became the punchline in satirical representations of antiquaries. Francis Grose's print 'Antiquarians Peeping into Boadicia's Night Urn' (c.1770) shows seven antiquaries crowded around a table, eagerly investigating an old chamber pot. Meanwhile, the introduction to *The Antiquarian Repertory* (1775), a miscellany dedicated to familiarising the general public with antiquarian endeavours, takes issue with the familiar cliché of antiquaries showing undue excitement over 'broken pipkins'.[42] However, antiquaries argued that historical household objects, articles of clothing, tools and other items of use served as important repositories of social practices. Some branches of this research also provided entry points for women interested in antiquarian pursuits. For instance, Cassandra Willoughby, a pioneering female antiquary, drew on her knowledge about needlework as well as on paintings and manuscript sources to date and research the sartorial fashions exemplified in the historical textiles that came into her hands.[43]

Antiquarianism was a varied field of inquiry, and the rich symbolic valences of the handicraft objects produced by the ladies of Millenium Hall co-ordinate different aspects of the novel's sophisticated engagement with antiquarian research: first, its disregard for the kinds of antiques that were often used to knit landed estates and their owners into the public history of the nation; and, second, its valorisation of two semantically related types of 'trifles' – the allegedly trivial, mundane household items that some antiquaries studied as well as the objects of female handicrafts, produced in households past and present, which were often treated as derivative and merely decorative. As I suggest in the remainder of this chapter, scenes that figure these handicraft 'trifles', their making and exchange also become an occasion for Scott to think about novel writing in analogy to the domestic 'arts' featured in the text. Serena Dyer and Chloe Wigston Smith point out that eighteenth-century women 'often engaged in literary pursuits during making', which they suggest encompasses 'decorative handicrafts'

ANTIQUARIANISM AND THE NOVEL 61

in the widest sense: 'reading aloud and literary conversations were frequent partners to making'.[44] Indeed, this is the case at Millenium Hall: the narrator's first glimpse of the ladies at work on their various 'arts', mentioned earlier, also features 'two ladies reading, with pen, ink, and paper on the table before them' (59). The scene reminds us that, like handicraft objects, novels and other written works were carefully and laboriously crafted by hand in the domestic realm. While working on *Millenium Hall*, Scott and her companion, Lady Bab, made ornaments for Lady Bab's room: 'we gilded cone corn acorns poppy heads & evergreens with flowers & leaves in lead & some fruit in pipe makers [*sic*] clay, with these made a frame to the glass, & continued the work in a light pattern'.[45] Of the different literary genres in which women were active, the mid-century novel had a particular affinity to handicraft objects: the imitative aesthetic of many craft practices (flowers and leaves made from lead; fruit sculpted from pipe-maker's clay) resonated with the novel's reliance on verisimilar modes of representation, while the then widespread view of female handicrafts as frivolous, trivial and ephemeral found an analogue in mid-century debates about novels as 'poor insignificant productions' geared towards middle-class female readers.[46]

Millenium Hall uses the ladies' 'arts' as a platform to explore a range of questions pertinent to the novel form, including its relationship to commerce, taste and the literary marketplace. However, I am especially interested in Scott's exploration of the novel's capacity for historical thought through the handcrafted 'trifles' that crowd into *Millenium Hall*. Scott's choice to insert these objects in the place of more traditional heirlooms and antiques drives home her interest in what we might call, adapting a term introduced by the philosopher of history Eelco Runia, as 'denotative' rather than 'connotative' elements in narratives about the past. Runia's brief but suggestive remarks contrast the dominance of connotative approaches in historiography – that is to say, of approaches that assemble discrete items of information into synthesising, interpretive, closed narratives – with the long neglect of the 'denotative level of historiography', that is, those aspects of historical research and writing that render the material record of the past available through thick descriptions that are metonymically open, and not yet (or not fully) slotted into larger interpretive narratives of causation and historical progress.[47] As Scott's bluestocking friends noted, the trifles that women – past and present – produced hardly ever found a place in traditional historiographies, but they offered rich opportunities for individuals to contemplate how their existence related, or did not relate in any straightforward sense, to the historical trajectories traced in the works of philosophical and stadial historians.

The narrative structure of *Millenium Hall* foregrounds two different potentials of the novel form and plays them off against each other. These are, first, the novel's ability to capture social realities and their slow evolution over time; and, second, the novel's capacity to imagine communal and individual life otherwise, which entails exploring possibilities that have not yet been realised in history. Scott's novel is structurally divided: the portions of the novel that describe the estate, the ladies' charitable projects and their 'arts' are firmly embedded in the mid-eighteenth-century present; meanwhile, the interpolated biographies of Miss Mancel, Mrs Morgan, Lady Mary Jones, Miss Selvyn and Miss Trentham are introduced as oral narratives that transmit the past and connect experiences of female exploitation and oppression across time. The insertion of embedded narratives, of course, was standard practice among eighteenth-century novelists, and before embarking on *Millenium Hall* Scott had produced a long work of fiction, *A Journey through Every Stage of Life* (1754), that drew on the tradition of French seventeenth-century romances and was made up almost entirely of embedded narratives. Scott took a markedly different approach to the insertion of interpolated oral tales in *Millenium Hall*, harnessing this old narrative structure to her exploration of the novel's relationship to history. Scott's interpolated tales emphasise the importance of understanding social and female oppression as historical phenomena that are systemic and that have developed over large swathes of time. The interpolated tales' interest in how the present is born out of a specific past that remains sedimented in the present shares an affinity with the work of then-contemporary philosophical and stadial historians such as William Robertson and David Hume. These historians' belief in slow and incremental societal change led them to disregard the possibility of more rapid shifts in the existing order of things. However, if Scott's interpolated tales invite a perspective on history that points to the family likeness between the early novel and the work of influential eighteenth-century historians, it is also important to note that other portions of *Millenium Hall* are more in sympathy with the antiquaries' appreciation of the 'trifling' materials that rarely found admission into the systematising, sweeping accounts of narrative historians.[48]

Indeed, Scott's description of Millenium Hall and the ladies' arts – parts of the novel which are in close dialogue with antiquarian approaches to the past – show a marked lack of interest in positing historical trajectories as fixed and inevitable. The patriarchal and economic structures that govern society at large are suspended at Millenium Hall: the estate is managed by financially independent women who are not or are no longer married, and who have turned Millenium Hall into a refuge for some of the most disadvantaged members of society. A group of old pensioners, some of whom suffer from disabilities, live in cottages on the estate. An old mansion houses thirty 'indigent gentlewomen' (115), and another part of the estate accommodates 'an asylum for those poor creatures who are rendered miserable from some natural deficiency or redundancy' (73). At Millenium Hall, an economy of alienable commodities that are bought and sold in commercial contexts is displaced by a ritualised exchange of handicraft gifts. Just as the ladies offer each other craft objects and decorate the communal spaces of their mansion and estate with them, the separate community of gentlewomen, the charity-school girls and the poor pensioners all produce and exchange handicraft objects, while the physically disadvantaged people who live in the 'inclosure' are expert cultivators of flowers, some of which they give to the ladies of Millenium Hall (75).

The inhabitants of Millenium Hall rely on the exchange of these objects to establish affective ties, to promote shared values such as industriousness and charity, and to maintain and symbolically enact a social contract of mutual obligation. These 'trifles' are imbued with the novel's transformative vision, which radically rethinks social and gender relations. The novel's utopian charge is future-directed, but Scott's insistent nods towards antiquarian activities reveal that this charge is galvanised by antiquarianism's potential to give women and their domestic work a more prominent place in history. As I have shown, participatory antiquarian practices invited men and women to engage with material remains of the past that were often ignored by historians, allowing them to imagine their own place in history. In *Millenium Hall*, this emancipatory impulse is deployed in order to envision a bold departure from the male-dominated socio-economic status quo. The novel acknowledges antiquarianism's more conservative

ANTIQUARIANISM AND THE NOVEL

strain. However, Scott ultimately gives more weight to antiquarianism's ability to unearth disaggregated and long-neglected objects and practices that invite revisionary perspectives on the past and its cultural uses in the present. In this sense, antiquarian modes of inquiry are deeply integrated into *Millenium Hall*: they make it possible to interrogate the seeming givenness of the teleological historical trajectories in which neither the past nor the future hold surprises or provide spaces for radical transformation.

Notes

1. See Barrett Kalter, *Modern Antiques: The Material Past in England, 1660–1780* (Lewisburg: Bucknell University Press, 2012), 149–90; Crystal B. Lake, *Artifacts: How We Write and Think about Found Objects* (Baltimore: Johns Hopkins University Press, 2020), 109–35.
2. See Katie Trumpener, *Bardic Nationalism: The Romantic Novel and the British Empire* (Princeton: Princeton University Press, 1997); Ina Ferris, 'Pedantry and the Question of Enlightenment History: The Figure of the Antiquary in Scott', *European Romantic Review* 13, no. 3 (2002): 273–83; Mike Goode, 'Dryasdust Antiquarianism and Soppy Masculinity': The *Waverley* Novels and the Gender of History', *Representations* 82, no. 1 (2003): 52–86; Richard Maxwell, 'Inundations of Time: A Definition of Scott's Originality', *ELH* 68, no. 2 (2001): 419–68.
3. See Cynthia Wall, *The Prose of Things* (Chicago: University of Chicago Press, 2006), 201–30; Mark Salber Phillips, 'Scott, Macaulay, and the Literary Challenge to Historiography', *Journal of the History of Ideas* 50, no. 1 (1989): 117–33.
4. George Lukács was among the first to point out the affinities between early nineteenth-century schools of objective history and the 'broad, objective, epic form' of Walter Scott's historical novel. Georg Lukács, *The Historical Novel*, trans. Hannah and Stanley Mitchell (London: Penguin, 1962), 32.
5. See, for instance, Anne H. Stevens, *British Historical Fiction before Scott* (Basingstoke: Palgrave Macmillan, 2010), and Fiona Price's *Reinventing Liberty: Nation, Commerce and the Historical Novel from Walpole to Scott* (Edinburgh: Edinburgh University Press, 2016).
6. For a pioneering reading of *Millenium Hall* as a text that was deeply informed by Scott's interest in antiquarianism, see Crystal B. Lake, 'Redecorating the Ruin: Women and Antiquarianism in Sarah Scott's *Millenium Hall*', *ELH* 76, no. 3 (2009): 661–86.
7. See Rosemary Sweet, *Antiquaries: The Discovery of the Past in Eighteenth-Century Britain* (London: Hambledon, 2004); Noah Heringman, *Sciences of Antiquity: Romantic Antiquarianism, Natural History, and Knowledge Work* (Oxford: Oxford University Press, 2013); Susan Pearce, ed., *Visions of Antiquity: The Society of Antiquaries of London, 1707–2007* (London: Society of Antiquaries, 2007).
8. See Sweet, *Antiquaries*, 71–9.
9. The standard history of the SAL is still Joan Evans, *A History of the Society of Antiquaries* (Oxford: Oxford University Press, 1956). The early history of the antiquarian activities of the Gentlemen's Society at Spalding is given in John Nichols, 'An Account of the Gentlemen's Society at Spalding', in *Antiquities in Lincolnshire, Being the Third Volume of Bibliotheca Topographica Britannica* (London: Nichols, 1790), i–lv.
10. The Countess of Hertford was an elected member as well as Stukeley's future wife, Frances Williamson. See Stuart Piggott, *William Stukeley: An Eighteenth-Century Antiquary*, rev. edn (London: Thames & Hudson, 1985), 53–5.
11. William Stukeley, *Itinerarium Curiosum, or, An Account of the Antiquitys and Remarkable Curiositys in Nature or Art, Observ'd in Travels thro' Great Brittan* (London: Printed for the Author, 1724), 147.

12. Richard Altick, *The Shows of London* (Cambridge, MA: Belknap Press of Harvard University Press, 1978), 17.
13. David Murray, *Museums, Their History and Their Use, Volume 1* (1904; London: Forgotten Books, 2013), 172.
14. See *A Descriptive Catalogue of the Rarities, in Mr. Greene's Museum at Lichfield* (Lichfield, 1773).
15. Altick, *The Shows of London*, 26. On the foundation of the British Museum and its development in the eighteenth century, see also Edward Miller, *That Noble Cabinet: A History of the British Museum* (London: André Deutsch, 1973), 19–90.
16. Peter Mandler, *The Fall and Rise of the Stately Home* (New Haven: Yale University Press, 1997), 9. See also Carole Fabricant, 'The Literature of Domestic Tourism and the Public Consumption of Private Property', in *The New Eighteenth Century: Theory, Politics, English Literature*, ed. Felicity A. Nussbaum and Laura Brown (New York: Methuen, 1987), 254–75.
17. Andrew McRae, *Literature and Domestic Travel in Early Modern England* (Cambridge: Cambridge University Press, 2009), 16.
18. William Stukeley, *The Family Memoirs of the Rev. William Stukeley*, ed. W. C. Lukis (Durham and London: The Surtees Society, 1882), 45.
19. John Smith, *Choir Gaur; The Grand Orrery of the Ancient Druids, Commonly Called Stonehenge on Salisbury Plain* (Salisbury: Easton, 1771), 58. Smith notes that Hunt must have set up his hut prior to the visit to Stonehenge of a fellow antiquary, John Wood, in 1739.
20. In 1747, Montagu reports in a letter to her father: 'Lord —— and George Vertue arrived here last night after a ramble, which the best geographer could hardly describe; they have been hunting churchyards, and reading the history of mankind upon gravestones.' Elizabeth Montagu, 'Letter to Matthew Robinson', undated [1740s], in *The Letters of Mrs. Elizabeth Montagu: With Some Letters of Her Correspondents*, ed. Matthew Montagu, 3 vols (Boston: Wells and Lilly, 1825), 1:197.
21. Elizabeth Montagu, 'Letter to Mrs Donnellan', 12 September [1747], in *The Letters of Mrs. Elizabeth Montagu*, 2:140. Montagu writes, for instance, about Winchester Cathedral, noting that 'the building . . . is of the neatest Gothic kind, and rather grown reverend than old by time; there is to the choir an extremely fine screen of more modern architecture, but in a still more ancient order of architecture, namely the Corinthian' (141).
22. See Elizabeth Montagu, 'Letter to the Duchess of Portland', 27 January [1741–3], in *The Letters of Mrs. Elizabeth Montagu*, 1:269–70.
23. For an overview of Elstob's research, see Mechthild Gretsch, 'Elizabeth Elstob: A Scholar's Fight for Anglo-Saxon Studies', *Anglia* 117 (1999): 163–300, 481–524. Scott mentions Elstob's and her stay in Tunbridge Wells in a letter to her sister. See Sarah Scott, 'Letter to Elizabeth Montagu', 28 August 1747, in *The Letters of Sarah Scott*, ed. Nicole Pohl, 2 vols (London: Pickering & Chatto, 2014), 1:91.
24. See Thomas Wright, 'Letter to Mrs Carter', in *A Series of Letters between Mrs. Elizabeth Carter and Miss Catherine Talbot*, 4 vols (London: Rivington, 1809), 1:1–2; Elizabeth Carter, 'Letter to Miss Talbot', in *A Series of Letters between Mrs. Elizabeth Carter and Miss Catherine Talbot*, 1:5.
25. Catherine Talbot, 'Letter to Elizabeth Carter', 10 October 1748, *A Series of Letters between Mrs. Elizabeth Carter and Miss Catherine Talbot*, 1:293. See also Elizabeth Carter, 'Letter to Mrs Underdown', 14 May 1739, in *Elizabeth Carter, 1717–1806: An Edition of Some Unpublished Letters*, ed. Gwen Hampshire (Newark: University of Delaware Press, 2005), 69.
26. Richard Hurd and Thomas Warton approached 'Gothic romances' as a rich mine of clues to the manners, customs and values dominant during the medieval and early modern period. The second edition of Warton's *Observations on the Faerie Queene of Spenser*, published

in 1762, contains his famous typological study of the evolution of Gothic architecture in England.

27. Lake, 'Redecorating the Ruin', 666.

28. Stukeley's *Itinerarium Curiosum* celebrates antiquarian sociability and collaboration. Each of the letters that make up the travelogue is dedicated to another of Stukeley's friends, fellow antiquaries, or patrons with whom Stukeley travelled through a particular part of the country.

29. Sarah Scott, *Millenium Hall*, ed. Gary Kelly (Peterborough, ON: Broadview Press, 2004), 219, 221. Further references parenthetical.

30. See [R. G.], *The Accomplish'd Female Instructor or a Very Useful Companion for Ladies, Gentlemen and Others in Two Parts* (London: Knapton, 1704); [Mrs Artlove], *The Art of Japanning, Varnishing, Pollishing, and Gilding Being a Collection of very Plain Directions and Receipts* (London: Warner, 1730).

31. See Robert Sayer, *The Ladies Amusement; or, Whole Art of Japanning Made Easy* (London: Printed for the Author, c.1759); Robert Dossie, *The Handmaid to the Arts* (London: Printed for the Author, 1758); Hannah Robertson, *The Young Ladies School of Art* (Edinburgh: Printed for the Author, 1766).

32. Ann Bermingham, *Learning to Draw: Studies in the Cultural History of a Polite and Useful Art* (New Haven: Yale University Press, 2000), 180.

33. Pope's Mummius is a 'Fool-renown'd' whose obsessive collecting of mummies makes him turn a blind eye to fraudulent specimens. See Alexander Pope, *The Dunciad in Four Books*, ed. Valerie Rumbold (New York: Routledge, 2009), 322, 322n371. On Pope's scepticism towards antiquarianism and his own, arguably antiquarian, project of annotating the *Dunciad*, see Pat Rogers, 'Pope and the Antiquarians', in *Essays on Pope* (Cambridge: Cambridge University Press, 1993), 240–60.

34. On the bluestockings' interest in making and mending textiles, see Nicole Pohl, '"To embroider what is wanting": Making, Consuming and Mending Textiles in the Lives of the Bluestockings', in *Material Literacy in 18th-Century Britain*, ed. Serena Dyer and Chloe Wigston Smith (London: Bloomsbury, 2022), 67–81. On the role of female 'accomplishments' in the cultivation of friendships among bluestockings, see Elizabeth Eger, 'Paper Trails and Eloquent Objects: Bluestocking Friendship and Material Culture', *Parergon* 26, no. 2 (2009): 109–38. Nicole Pohl and Betty A. Schellenberg discuss the bluestockings' thought on the relationship between 'female virtues' and the intellectual life of the mind in 'Introduction: A Bluestocking Historiography', *Huntington Library Quarterly* 65, no. 1 (2002): 1–19.

35. See Karen O'Brien, *Women and Enlightenment in Eighteenth-Century Britain* (Cambridge: Cambridge University Press, 2009), 201–36; Daniel Woolf, 'A Feminine Past? Gender, Genre, and Historical Knowledge in England, 1500–1800', *American Historical Review* 102 (1997): 645–56, and Daniel Woolf, '"A most indefatigable love of history": Carter, Montagu, and Female Discussions of History, 1740–1790', *Women's History Review* 20, no. 5 (2011): 689–718.

36. Catherine Talbot, 'Letter to Mrs Carter', 6 January 1745, in *A Series of Letters between Mrs. Elizabeth Carter and Miss Catherine Talbot*, 1:85.

37. Catherine Talbot, 'Letter to Mrs Carter', 24 October 1751, in *A Series of Letters between Mrs. Elizabeth Carter and Miss Catherine Talbot*, 2:58.

38. Catherine Talbot, 'Letter to Mrs Carter', 28 February 1743, in *A Series of Letters between Mrs. Elizabeth Carter and Miss Catherine Talbot*, 1:27.

39. Elizabeth Carter, 'Letter to Miss Talbot', 16 April 1743, in *A Series of Letters between Mrs. Elizabeth Carter and Miss Catherine Talbot*, 1:28.

40. Catherine Talbot, 'Letter to Mrs Carter', 26 November 1750, in *A Series of Letters between Mrs. Elizabeth Carter and Miss Catherine Talbot*, 1:363.

41. See Elizabeth Montagu, 'Letter to the Duchess of Portland', 8 April 1741, in *The Letters of Mrs Elizabeth Montagu: With Some Letters of Her Correspondents*, 1:87.
42. Anonymous [Francis Grose?], 'Introduction' to *The Antiquarian Repertory: A Miscellany Intended to Preserve and Illustrate Several Valuable Remains of Old Times, Volume 1* (London: Blyth and Evans, 1775), iii.
43. 'Extracts from Collections of Cassandra Willoughby, 1702', in *Report on the Manuscripts of Lord Middleton* [Historical Manuscripts Commission] (London: Hereford Times, 1911), 572–3).
44. Serena Dyer and Chloe Wigston Smith, 'Introduction', in *Material Literacy in 18th-Century Britain*, 5, 4.
45. Sarah Scott, 'Letter to Elizabeth Montagu', [December 1752], in *The Letters of Sarah Scott*, 1:142.
46. Review of *The Adventures of Sophie Hughes*, *Monthly Review* 23 (1760): 532. Quoted in Laura L. Runge, 'Gendered Strategies in the Criticism of Early Fiction', *Eighteenth-Century Studies* 28, no. 4 (1995): 365. As Runge notes, '[d]espite historical evidence that suggests a primarily male reading audience . . . [b]y the middle of the century, critics blamed women for the omnipresence of bad fictions' (365).
47. Eelco Runia, 'Spots of Time', *History and Theory* 45, no. 3 (2006): 315.
48. On the relationship between the eighteenth-century novel and different genres of narrative historiography, see, for instance, Devoney Looser, *British Women Writers and the Writing of History, 1670–1820* (Baltimore: Johns Hopkins University Press, 2000); Mark Salber Phillips, *Society and Sentiment: Genres of Historical Writing in Britain, 1740–1820* (Princeton: Princeton University Press, 2000); Ruth Mack, *Literary Historicity: Literature and Historical Experience in Eighteenth-Century Britain* (Stanford: Stanford University Press, 2009).

4

ANATOMY, INVASION AND IMAGINATION: READING GENDER, MEDICINE AND THE BODY IN THE MID-CENTURY NOVEL

Ashleigh Blackwood

LAURENCE STERNE'S CHARACTER-NARRATOR Tristram Shandy directs his reader in volume 6 of his comic novel *The Life and Opinions of Tristram Shandy, Gentleman* (1759–67) to leave their position as a passive consumer of the text and adopt a more proactive role in creating parts of the novel:

> To conceive this right,—call for pen and ink—here's paper ready to your hand.——
> Sit down Sir, paint her to your own mind——as like your mistress as you can——as
> unlike your wife as your conscience will let you—'tis all one to me——please but
> your own fancy in it.[1]

Intent on focusing the reader's mind on the visual attributes of the book just as much as – if not more than – its textual features, Sterne follows up this instruction with a subsequent page left blank to allow readers to insert their own vision of his female character the Widow Wadman (567). *Tristram Shandy* is well noted for its experimentation with visual and typographical features. As Helen Williams explains, those purchasing the book for the first time would not have known about the design work inherent in its construction, making its content 'surprising to readers, even to those approaching later volumes accustomed to the visual experimentation of earlier instalments'.[2]

Although few copies of the book have ever evidenced readers' direct engagement with this distinctive instruction, the blank page in *Tristram Shandy* has been the subject of much curiosity and fascination for readers, even inspiring an exhibition at Shandy Hall, the author's Yorkshire home.[3] Reflecting on the exhibition and Sterne's language, which gives rise to the blank page, Paul Munden and Paul Hetherington draw attention to the fact that Sterne intrinsically connects the visualisation of women's bodies with themes of biological exploration and the medicalisation of reproduction that was taking place during the eighteenth century.[4] The ambiguity and ambition of Sterne's words to his readers leaves open the ways in which Widow Wadman might be 'conceived' of in the minds of readers, and thereby depicted on the blank page itself, as a purely facial or full-length portrait. A small number of examples of readers' entries for this page have been found by David Brewer and by Brigitte Friant-Kessler, while Anne Bandry-Scubbi has examined one 29-line textual pen-portrait.[5] Even before 'call[ing] for pen and ink', or metaphorically handing the reader the useable paper that is the blank page, however, Tristram's employment of the word 'conceive' serves as a reminder to the reader of the importance of corporeal themes within the novel, specifically those surrounding reproductive health, and of the alliance between creative or imaginative conception and bodily procreation. As Day points out, '*The Life and Opinions of Tristram Shandy, Gentleman* is, among many other things, a work about conception.'[6] From beginning to end, the theme of procreation is inescapable and the gendering of bodies is loaded with humorous references to anatomy, genitalia, generation and, at times, impotence.[7]

The publication of *Tristram Shandy* coincided with a period of intense interest in the medical exploration and visual mapping of the human body and, more specifically, gendered and reproductive anatomies. Although anatomical studies had been developing in Britain for well over a century, progress in medical and surgical subjects that specifically concerned women was much slower than those concerning men. As Londa Schiebinger outlines, 'the drawings of the first female skeletons [only] appeared in England, France, and Germany between 1730 and 1790'.[8] Similarly, reproductive health care had long relied on translations of European works, such as Eucharius Rösslin's *Der Rosengarten* (1513), Jacob Rueff's *De Conceptu et generatione hominis* (1554) and Jacques Guillemeau's *De l'heureux accouchement des femmes* (1609), making progress in British research in these areas slow.[9] While a small number of original texts appeared in vernacular English print during the late seventeenth and early eighteenth centuries, notably Nicholas Culpeper's *A Directory for Midwives* (1651), William Harvey's *Anatomical Exercitations Concerning the Generation of Living Creatures* (1651) and Sarah Stone's *A Complete Practice of Midwifery* (1737), it was only in the 1750s that medical work on gendered physiology and the science of generation truly began to flourish. Landmark texts such as William Smellie's *A Treatise on the Theory and Practice of Midwifery* (1752–64) and *A Sett of Anatomical Tables, with Explanations, and an Abridgment, of the Practice of Midwifery* (1754) offered new insights into how the interiority of the human body was connected to the external world of medical practice. While the *Treatise* is a textual account of midwifery cases, the addition of the *Anatomical Tables* means that Smellie's works participate in the wider trend for book illustration by complementing the text with illustrated plates that help to explain and clarify to fellow medical professionals both the problems he encountered during deliveries and the technical solutions that he offered. To the wider reading public, however, these images played a dual role. As Tita Chico explains, 'cultural consumers in London [and across Britain] ate up science in an assortment of fora' alongside literature and the visual arts.[10] In addition to being demonstrative, Smellie's illustrations also constituted an opportunity to generate imaginative speculation about the human body and its biological role and cultural significance. These contributions, from both the literary and medical arts, therefore shaped for generations ideas of what anatomy, gender and sex had to do with science, and what these might, in turn, have to do with everyday life.

This chapter brings together these innovations of print culture to examine, for the first time, interactions between literary, medical and visual cultures that influenced depictions of human bodies, gender and associated health care in the mid-century novel. It first explores how a diverse range of visual sources – including Bernhard Siegfried Albinus's *Tabulae Sceleti Musculorum Corporis Humani* (1747) and Hogarth's *The Four Stages of Cruelty* (1751) – and imaginative texts – such as Jane Barker's *A Patch-Work Screen for the Ladies; or Love and Virtue Recommended* (1723) and

Tobias Smollett's *The Adventures of Roderick Random* (1748) – were deeply engaged in revealing and interpreting anatomical information and the contexts in which it was used. Second, the chapter turns towards how literary and visual cultures, focused specifically on gendered and reproductive anatomy and health care, were integrated into the development of the plot, characters and literary style of Sterne's *Tristram Shandy* and Smollett's *The Adventures of Peregrine Pickle* (1751). Both authors were acutely aware of the culture of scientific inquiry that would later come to mark their age as one of medical enlightenment, as well as the nature of medical and scientific questions that remained unanswered concerning how reproductive bodies functioned. Each utilises their literary creativity within the form of the novel to engage directly with medical debates of the period surrounding gendered anatomy and reproductive health, demonstrating how elements of visuality permeate the medical theories and practices being depicted, such as beliefs surrounding the maternal imagination and its impact on foetal development and the management of obstructed deliveries.[11] Their works appreciate the relevance of both textual and visual elements of medical knowledge, and employ current debates about and public fascination with medical manuals, anatomical artworks and popular fiction which employed text as well as visual devices simultaneously to inform and entertain their readers. As Angela Woods points out, '[v]isual arts provide a powerful, yet often overlooked, medium for understanding a diversity of perspectives about medicine and healthcare'.[12] This essay follows Woods's observation, examining how both anatomical art and ideas about the visual imagination served as key influences on the mid-century novel, and how these works both offer and respond to new ways of thinking about human bodies.

Dissecting the Body

The exploration and care of human bodies in the Western world has always necessitated elements of visual learning and communication and, as George Rousseau observes, 'medicine, viewed as a social institution, discursive practice, and visual medium, is an integral, even central, tile in the mosaic of *all* culture'.[13] Medicine offered subject matter for many types of visual artwork throughout the seventeenth and eighteenth centuries, including anatomical illustrations, sculpture and caricature. Produced both within and beyond the medical professions themselves, images became a core means through which the public began to understand their own bodies and those of others. Visual artworks that utilised medical themes came in many forms and had a multitude of purposes, including the mapping of human anatomy, the demonstration of diagnostic and treatment processes, the exposure of poor-quality practice or quackery, the advancement of political ideas, and satire. From William Hogarth and Thomas Rowlandson to Jacques Fabien Gautier D'Agoty, artists of many types became embroiled in investigating the body for the esoteric knowledge it had to offer. Artistic engagement with anatomy, in particular, had been growing since the sixteenth century as artists and medics alike sought to understand and represent the body in ever more accurate ways. As Jonathan Sawday indicates, the Renaissance had brought with it a drive towards acquiring and developing new knowledge and practice, and this involved

> an incisive recomposition of the human body, which entailed an equivalent refashioning of how people made sense of the world around them, in terms of

their philosophy of understanding, their theology, their poetry, their plays, their rituals of justice, their art, and their buildings.[14]

In the transformation of cultures and identities through natural philosophy, human dissection was a primary means through which new inquiries took place, and for which the recording of visual information became essential. During his education, physician and anatomist Andreas Vesalius became gripped by the process by which scientific findings could be made from dissection. He began to produce drawings based on his practical work. These efforts culminated in the publication of his *Tabulae Anatomicae Sex* (1538), *De Humani Corporis Fabrica Librorum Epitome* (1543) and *De Humani Corporis Fabrica* (1543), which has since become known as the *Fabrica*. Part of the strength of Vesalius's contribution to anatomy and medical authorship lay in the way in which the *Fabrica* combined text and images to inform readers about the human body in new ways. In his preface to the text, addressed to Emperor Charles V, he explains the pedagogical necessity of images as a central part of medical education: 'illustrations greatly assist the understanding, for they place more clearly before the eyes what the text, no matter how explicitly, describes'.[15] Furthermore, he argues for images as a means of increasing access to medical knowledge for

> those people who do not always have the opportunity of dissecting a human body or who, if they do have the opportunity, are so squeamish (a very inappropriate quality in a physician) that, although they are fascinated and delighted by the study of man (which attests, if anything does, to the wisdom of the infinite Creator), yet they cannot bring themselves to the point of ever actually attending a dissection.[16]

The result of his efforts, Valeria Finucci finds, was 'a radical shift away from the rambling and imprecise written *corpus* that had then defined medical knowledge', at least until that point.[17] So successful were his publications that, as Monique Kornell explains, 'its illustrations were disseminated through countless iterations of copies, only displaced in popularity by the appearance of Bernhard Siegfried Albinus's *Tabulae Sceleti Musculorum Corporis Humani* in 1747'.[18] For the first time, the body had been invaded by anatomists, artists and readers, united in the search for knowledge, and, as Katherine Park posits, during the sixteenth century vernacular medical texts and illustrations, particularly those from the *Fabrica*, became progressively more important to how individuals and communities understood and reflected on what it meant to be human.[19]

Between the production of Vesalius's and Albinus's respective works, an increasing number of literary authors came to share these interests with medical practitioners and artists, and sought to join the conversation about how the interiority of the body might be laid out and visualised by the public. Jane Barker's novel, *A Patch-Work Screen for the Ladies* (1723), addresses this same need for information about the human anatomy. A largely autobiographical work, the *Patch-Work Screen* offers a thinly veiled telling of Barker's own life as it follows the experiences of Galesia, a spinster, religious exile and female medical practitioner. Unlike other novels of the period, Barker's work has frequently been labelled as experimental for its inclusion of a variety of different literary forms and genres, including romance, verse, religious reflections and recipes, all of which combine to offer a fulsome and dynamic account of Galesia's abilities and encounters. One of Barker's poems that appears in the text, 'Anatomy', is a revised version of an earlier verse, 'A Farewell to Anatomy', which was originally printed in her *Poetical Recreations* (1688) and provides an effective example of literary work that employed pictorial forms of expression about the body.[20] She begins:

> Now BARTHOLINE, the first of all this Row,
> Does to me *Nature's Architecture* show;
> How the *Foundation*, first of *Earth* is Laid;
> Then, how the *Pillars* of *Strong-Bones* are made.
> The Walls consist of *Carneous-Parts* within,
> The Out-Side *pinguid*, overlay'd with *Skin*;
> The *Fret-work*, *Muscles*, *Arteries* and *Veins*,
> With their Implexures; and how from the *Brains*
> The *Nerves* descend; and how 'tis they dispense
> To every *Member* Motive-Power and Sense.[21]

Barker's poem observes, yet also penetrates the skin to offer a tour around the inner workings of the body in much the same way as an early eighteenth-century reader might expect to walk through an exhibition, property or, later, the pleasure gardens that appeared in London and other locations. In keeping with her attempts to use creative arts as a means of understanding medicine, writing further engages with the artistry of architecture, referring to the 'foundation' and 'pillars' of the human skeleton, before pointing out organs, muscles and nerves at every turn, allowing readers to visualise each part in relation to others and providing an imagined map of human anatomy. Although written in verse, her words would not appear out of place set alongside drawings in the pages of a book of anatomical artwork, such as that produced by Vesalius. Heather Meek argues that Barker's fiction 'both reflects the most modern and supposedly advanced medical wisdom, and rewrites and challenges such wisdom, sometimes drawing on older, humoural understandings of the body in unusual and inventive ways'.[22] Her interest in anatomy was personal, since she had trained in medicine informally and had practised as a physician, but for readers it continued to parallel wider curiosities about corporeality. That she sought to be so visual with her descriptions is indicative of the kinds of scientific inquiry that pervaded medical cultures of the late seventeenth and eighteenth centuries.

Beginning in 1724, the year after Barker published her novel, Albinus commenced work with artist Jan Wandelaar to make records of his dissection practice. No detail went unnoticed as the pair sought to negotiate matters of layering, detail, scale and aesthetics as part of their undertaking. Although it took over twenty years to complete, their timing in having the completed project printed in 1747 could scarcely have been better. A version of the text was reproduced in English in 1749 and sold in London under the title of *Tables of the Skeleton and Muscles of the Human Body* when, as Andrew Cunningham describes, 'the discipline [of anatomy] was flourishing as never before or since'.[23] By the 1740s, surgical skills constituted a valuable form of professional currency, and throughout Europe any enterprising medic required an up-to-date knowledge of anatomy. In cities such as London, Edinburgh, Paris, Amsterdam and Leiden, as well as Rome, Padua and Bologna, anatomy was vibrantly present within medical research and teaching as there was a need for a large surgical workforce in both the commercial and military communities, and, as Barker's language shows, interest in medical matters was increasingly widespread and manifested in multiple outlets, include those of imaginative fiction.[24] One such surgeon was Smollett.

Reports of Smollett's early medical experiences are somewhat mixed in terms of detail, but it is well established that he attended anatomy and medicine lectures at the University of Glasgow and became apprenticed to an apothecary and then to a surgeon in the city, Dr John Gordon, in approximately 1735. He was released early from his five-year term of indenture on the grounds of poor health and moved to London. By 1740 he had been examined by the Board of Surgeons at Surgeons' Hall and obtained a commission as surgeon's mate with rank of a third rate. His medical career heavily influenced his later literary works, and his early experiences of naval medicine onboard the HMS *Chichester* can be seen his first novel, *The Adventures of Roderick Random* (1748). Roderick, the novel's eponymous protagonist, enters the professional medical environment through the education he acquires at university and his association with the apothecary Mr Roger Potion, and with Potion's professional adversary, the surgeon and apothecary Mr Launcelot Crab. On Crab's proposal to house him, Roderick responds that

> I would willingly serve in your shop, by which means I may save you the expence of a journey-man, or porter at least, for I understand a little pharmacy, having employed some of my leisure hours in the practice of that art, while I lived with Mr. Potion, neither am I altogether ignorant of surgery, which I have studied with great pleasure and application.[25]

Crab accepts, and although he grants his young apprentice no salary beyond providing for his needs within the household, he sets Roderick off on a new professional path that will influence his longer-term future. While the surgeon appears to possess no particular affection for Random and, it is further suggested, intends to blame the young man for his indiscretions with a serving girl who has made known her pregnancy, it is also Crab who first initiates the advancement of his servant's medical skills and ability to earn a living, and he even loans him money to set out for London to make his ambitions a reality. He begins by commenting to Roderick:

> I am surprised that a young fellow like you discovers no inclination to push his fortune in the world.—Before I was your age, I was broiling on the coast of Guinea.— Damme! what's to hinder you from profiting by the war, which will certainly be declared in a short time against Spain?—You may easily get on board of a king's ship in quality of surgeon's mate, where you will certainly see a good deal of practice, and stand a good chance of getting prize-money. (39–40)

Although Roderick is eventually successful in his bid to become a naval surgeon, initially his knowledge of anatomy and medicines is not enough to secure him a place: he is confronted at first by the popularity of the surgical profession and the competition he faces from others attempting to secure a naval warrant for a position, like that taken up by Smollett himself. As Mr Cringer, a London contact of Mr Crab's to whom Roderick appeals for help, is heard to say:

READING GENDER, MEDICINE AND THE BODY 73

I believe it will be a difficult matter (continued he) to procure a warrant, there being already such a swarm of Scotch surgeons at the navy-office in the expectation of the next vacancy, that the commissioners are afraid of being torn in pieces. (77)

Here Smollett reflects on an unfortunate reality of the ecology of medical service provision in London during the eighteenth century. As W. F. Bynum explains, the medical contingent of the British Army and Navy was well populated with Scottish and Irish practitioners.[26] One reason for this is that Scottish universities were well placed to offer medical education, and there was no equivalent provider in London that could offer the same academic background to training.

Unlike the plentiful availability of surgeons, however, the supply of cadavers available for dissection was much more limited.[27] These restricted allocations of the criminal justice system, which allowed the use of a small number of criminal corpses for dissection, in no way matched up to the increasing interest in anatomical studies, resulting in a disconnect between supply and demand that persisted for the long term. As a result, there emerged a tacit acceptance that immoral means of acquiring cadavers constituted necessary routes for managing the needs of anatomists.[28] Such an uncomfortable reality generated an attendant cultural anxiety that surfaced in tales of body snatching. Sterne himself was famously rumoured to have been the victim of grave robbing, with a series of conflicting accounts circulating, all of which claimed that his corpse had reached one anatomist's table or another after its interment in March 1768.[29] Stories of this kind, both real and fictional, would remain in the public consciousness, paving the way for what would later become an integral feature of many eighteenth- and nineteenth-century Gothic narratives, including what has since become the most famous of these texts, Mary Shelley's *Frankenstein; or The Modern Prometheus* (1818).[30] Apprehensions concerning the sourcing of bodies were only fully realised with the now notorious events of 1827 and 1828 that took place in Edinburgh, which saw William Burke and William Hare confess to the murders of sixteen people whose bodies they then sold to surgeon Robert Knox for purposes of dissection. Their actions, vouchsafing their legacy as two of the most infamous criminals in British history, instigated parliamentary work that led to the introduction of the Anatomy Act of 1832, and even formed the basis for what would become the most celebrated example of literary murder and grave robbing, Robert Louis Stevenson's short story 'The Body Snatcher' (1884).[31]

Long before these gruesome events and their literary offspring, however, popular visual cultures had already set to work interpreting medical research and dissection on its own terms. William Hogarth's *The Four Stages of Cruelty* (1751) depicts the life and misdeeds of its central character Tom Nero and positions anatomical dissection as the ultimate punishment for his sins, as captured in three of the four engravings – animal cruelty, robbery, seduction and murder among them. The fourth plate of the series, 'The Reward of Cruelty' (Figure 4.1), shows Nero's body being used as the subject of a public dissection, his conviction and hanging for murder having secured his fate on the anatomist's table. Incidentally, while William Hare would be granted immunity for his confession of his own involvement, life mimicked art as Burke's ultimate sentence reflected a similar end to Nero's. David Boyle, the Lord Justice Clerk who presided over the case, summarised the decision to the accused:

William Burke, You now stand convicted, by the verdict of a most respectable jury of your country, of the atrocious murder charged against you in this indictment ... your body should not be exhibited in chains, in order to deter others from the like crimes in time coming ... [but] should be publicly dissected and anatomized.[32]

The Murder Act of 1752 that made this form of dissection legal had been implemented shortly after Hogarth produced this series of prints. Yet, although its key purpose was to regulate and satisfy the interest in and need for obtaining cadavers for medical work by approving the use of criminal corpses from hangings at Tyburn (which would later expand to include Newgate), the significant time lapse between these events, and the continued demand for cadavers well into the nineteenth century, reveals its ultimate failure to do so.[33] Those within the medical profession and beyond applied and maintained ongoing and significant pressure, as those seeking opportunities to study anatomy empirically were few, particularly where subjects for practical examination were in short supply. Novels, anatomical artworks, drawings and etchings therefore continued to serve an important purpose as a central source of information and creative space through which to map and explore the body's interior workings during the mid-eighteenth century. Novelists, including Barker and Smollett, brought health discourses and their attendant challenges closer to the lay public, where they might otherwise have remained largely within the confines of the elite professional medical communities.

Figure 4.1 William Hogarth, *The dissection of the body of Tom Nero*, from *The Four Stages of Cruelty* (1751). Etching. Wellcome Collection.

Imagining Maternity

By the time *Roderick Random* appeared on the print market, a sense of progress permeated the scientific and medical management of gendered anatomy and reproductive bodies. Lying-in hospitals were then being established in England and the practice of man-midwifery was growing, both in its professional appeal for physicians and surgeons and its popularity with birthing families, thus accelerating the production of print materials on these themes.[34] The four decades before *Roderick Random*'s publication had seen approximately twenty new medical texts discussing women's health and childbearing appear per decade, approximately half of which were original English vernacular texts (four in the 1710s, nine in the 1720s, twelve in the 1730s and twelve in the 1740s). Among them were Daniel Turner's *De Morbis Cutaneis. A Treatise of Diseases Incident to the Skin* (1726) and James Augustus Blondel's *The Strength of Imagination in Pregnant Women Examin'd* (1727).[35] These texts vigorously debated the influence of a woman's visual imagination on her unborn child, discussions that were precipitated, at least in part, by the occurrence of what became known as 'the Toft affair', an elaborate hoax that took place in the autumn of 1726.

Even in an environment where theories abounded about quite how gestation took place, and where natural philosophers were increasingly drawn to approaches towards the creation of knowledge based on empiricism, matters of myth and story still appeared to become a reality when a young woman from Godalming in Surrey, Mary Toft, claimed to have given birth to rabbits. Her story captured the imagination of curious physicians, enterprising journalists and commercially minded artists as the public followed the investigations with keen interest, as if the tale were a novel emerging a volume at a time as new information, both realistic and sensational, became available. The mass of published material in the form of medical books, pamphlets and images, such as Figure 4.2, was substantial, as tales of Toft's purported capacity for monstrous reproduction drew readers of all types. Each of the key players in the scene is identified as a recognisable character in the tale by Hogarth's labelling and annotations, and by their behaviours and dialogue, much as in a novel. Nathanael St André, for example, is labelled as individual 'A' in the image, although his name is not used directly; 'The Dancing Master or Preternatural Anatomist' (as he is described) turns out his feet as if in a dancing lesson, and announces 'The Great Birth' as Toft progresses through the agonies of an alleged delivery.[36] Here, Hogarth mocks St André's fervent belief in the authenticity of Toft's story, as well as his personal history as a dancing and fencing master prior to his taking up a surgical apprenticeship. Furthermore, the etching parodies archetypal scenes depicting the Adoration of the Magi, satirising those who would promote religious beliefs without bringing an analytical view to their ideas. Hogarth's work contrasts superstition and rational thought, contributing to contemporary discussions that surrounded popular and professional medical beliefs of the period.

Within just a few short months Toft's claims were found to be fraudulent when suspicions were quickly aroused and a confession obtained that she had arranged the hoax with her mother-in-law, Ann Toft, and an unnamed friend. When public confidence in the key medical figures involved in these investigations was shaken by the exposure of the hoax, a space was opened for new voices to enter the debates surrounding childbirth. Dr Blondel struck whilst the iron remained hot, publishing his *The Strength of Imagination in Pregnant Women Examin'd* the following year. As

Figure 4.2 William Hogarth, *Mary Toft (Tofts) appearing to give birth to rabbits in the presence of several surgeons and man-midwives sent from London to examine her* (1726). Etching. Wellcome Collection.

Jenifer Buckley explains, this Anti-Imaginationist work contested both the work of physicians who had been involved in the affair and Daniel Turner's earlier work on the same topic, which had been reprinted in the wake of this controversy.[37] Unlike many of his peers, Blondel was not enticed by ideas which alleged that the maternal imagination could have a profound physical influence on an unborn child. His 1729 text, *The Power of the Mother's Imagination over the Foetus Examin'd. In Answer to Dr. Daniel Turner's Book, Intitled 'A Defence of the XIIth Chapter of the First Part of a treatise, De Morbis Cutaneis'*, is firm about his reason for publishing at all. 'My design', he explains in the book's preface,

> is to attack a vulgar Error, which has been prevailing for many Years, in Opposition to Experience, sound Reason, and Anatomy: I mean the common Opinion, that Marks and Deformities, which Children are born with, are the sad Effect of the Mother's irregular Fancy and Imagination.[38]

His words reflect the turning of the tide within professional medicine away from these popular yet unproven theories, and the simultaneous need to address the fact that these beliefs still persisted among the wider population, for which superstitions and stories, no matter how fantastic, still held much sway.

Smollett's medical interests were keenly attuned to these ideas and debates, as well as the broader public interest they aroused. Literary fiction offered ample opportunity, therefore, for imaginative play based on the ambiguities that continued to exist concerning how unborn infants took on the physical forms and characteristics they would later come to exhibit. Of his mother's experience, Roderick explains:

> During her pregnancy, a dream discomposed my mother so much that her husband, tired with her importunity, at last consulted a highland seer, whose favourable interpretation he would have secured before-hand by a bribe, but found him incorruptible. She dreamed, she was delivered of a tennis-ball, which the devil (who, to her great surprize, acted the part of a midwife) struck so forcibly with a racket, that it disappeared in an instant; and she was for some time inconsolable for the loss of her off-spring; when all of a sudden, she beheld it return with equal violence, and enter the earth, beneath her feet, whence immediately sprung up a goodly tree covered with blossoms, the scent of which operated so strongly on her nerves that she awoke. (17)

Some scholars have noted this passage for its links to other literary texts, including John Webster's *The Duchess of Malfi* (c.1613) and Samuel Richardson's *Pamela; or Virtue Rewarded* (1740), both of which utilise the image of the tennis ball to indicate the unpredictable direction of 'fortune' for their characters, and even John Locke's *An Essay concerning Human Understanding* (1690), in which a tennis ball is an object with the potential to be moved in all directions. However, the influence of theories of maternal imagination on this passage is often neglected.[39] Although Smollett avoids embroiling his novel directly in what was quickly becoming an unfashionable medical argument by offering a clear opinion, his narrative does take advantage of the comic potential inherent in this surrounding scientific dialogue. His use of a dream in which a child's corporeality is affected by his mother's experiences, even for humorous purposes, indicates the continued difficulties of so many ambiguities and gaps in existing knowledge about how a mother's body was connected to, and influenced, that of her child. Smollett's writing constructs a space in which both popular beliefs and professional medical dialogue could be exposed to satirical scrutiny by both the author and their readers, who could consider in new ways the different forms of knowledge that made up the medical culture of the age.

After the success of *Roderick Random*, Smollett's next novel, *The Adventures of Peregrine Pickle*, once again turned to the theme of maternal imagination and foetal development to inform his imaginative plot. Another picaresque text, *Peregrine Pickle* tells the tale of a young man's misfortunes and triumphs as he makes his way through life. Unlike *Roderick Random*, however, *Peregrine Pickle* does not allow its chief character-narrator the opportunity to recount the story of his own birth at the novel's opening. In fact, the event of his birth does not take place until chapter 6. Smollett's detailed inclusion of Mrs Sally Pickle's gestation with her son Peregrine and his subsequent birth allowed him to integrate these public curiosities regarding the visualisation of reproductive bodies into his text. As Aileen Douglas highlights, 'the plot of *Peregrine Pickle* has more pregnancies, comic and tragic, than any eighteenth-century novel and none of them is straightforward', suggesting that Smollett cannot help but offer a more detailed position on maternal imagination in the process of his storytelling.[40] In this novel, his literary humour moves from general ideas of interpreting dreams in anticipation of the birth of his protagonist, whose birth is framed as being all-important to the survival of the Pickle family through the customs of primogeniture and patrilineal inheritance. In the interests of safeguarding the existence of the family, Mrs Pickle's sister-in-law, Mrs Grizzle, 'purchased Culpepper's [sic] Midwifery, which, with that sagacious performance dignified with Aristotle's name, she studied with indefatigable care'.[41] This choice of Culpeper's *Directory for Midwives* and the pseudo-medical work *Aristotle's Masterpiece*, which remained in print between 1684 and 1800, is deliberate, as Smollett opts for those most likely to be viewed as outdated and incongruous with the spirit of innovation and change that continued to grow rapidly in the field of human generation studies. In her attempts to adhere to conflicting and outmoded guidance, Mrs Grizzle turns not just to older, and potentially less scientific, books as in the case of the *Masterpiece*, but also to increasingly irrelevant theories of maternal imagination to ensure the preservation and continuation of the family. She panics when Mrs Pickle attempts to eat a piece of fruit for fear that it will cause her sister-in-law and unborn infant harm. As Smollett describes the exchange between the two:

> one day when Mrs. Pickle had plucked a peach with her own hand, and was in the very act of putting it between her teeth, Mrs. Grizzle perceived the rash attempt, and running up to her, fell upon her knees in the garden, intreating [sic] her, with tears in her eyes, to resist such a pernicious appetite. (38)

She quickly reverses her position, however, upon 'recollecting that if her sister's longing was baulked, the child might be affected with some disagreeable mark, or deplorable disease', with potential adverse effects including, but not limited to, the malformation or absence of limbs, spots or markings on the skin and other deformities.[42]

As an invasive and somewhat controlling influence within the household, it is not long before Mrs Grizzle's seemingly unending directives come to frustrate Sally Pickle. Smollett uses her character to highlight even further the absurdities of maternal imagination theory by having her deliberately seek to exaggerate her needs during pregnancy as a means of keeping her sister-in-law occupied. Sally's discussions about her longings include her thoughts of consuming a pineapple, pinching her husband's ear, wanting an 'opportunity of plucking three black hairs from [the commodore's] beard' (41), and requesting the use of a chamber pot belonging to a neighbour. These requests serve only to re-establish her power over her household, rather than being the product of any genuine desire for the items she lists. Her lies and her willingness to play along and engage with all kinds of foodstuffs and other items expose to the reader the truth that she has no fears for her own child, highlighting the ludicrous nature of the beliefs held by her sister-in-law. In both *Roderick Random* and *Peregrine Pickle*, Smollett persists in deploying concepts of maternal imagination for comic purposes and takes for granted that readers will likely be only too well aware of these debates about how the role of visual stimulation might affect women and children as gestation progressed, including the Toft affair. His characters and the respective plots of these novels also reveal how creative narratives involved themselves in medical commentary, with a unique ability to highlight the professional and popular influences that were brought to bear on understandings of anatomy and wider health care during the mid-eighteenth century.

Much like Smollett, Sterne was able to exploit the coexistence of popular and professional beliefs surrounding human reproduction for satirical purposes in *Tristram Shandy*. Yet the scientific developments that occurred in the intervening years between

Peregrine Pickle and Sterne's first volume appearing, and Sterne's particular interest in the technical innovations of obstetric medicine, meant that his novel made a distinctive contribution to the dialogue between arts and science to that of his predecessor. Elements of the division between popular and professional conceptualisations of medicine still infiltrate the novel's plot, most poignantly in the dispute between Mr and Mrs Shandy regarding their choice of a birthing attendant, between Dr Slop and the local female midwife; and Elizabeth Shandy's conception of her infant son and her subsequent pregnancy is no less chaotic than Sally Pickle's. But Sterne is far less concerned with the events of gestation, and rather more preoccupied with the development of the unborn Tristram himself. Sterne tells readers, as early as the third page of the first volume, that his character's pre-birth homunculus 'consists, as we do, of skin, hair, fat, flesh, veins, arteries, ligaments, nerves, cartileges [*sic*], bones, marrow, brains, glands, genitals, humours, and articulations' (3). In contrast with the myths and mystery that surround conceptions, pregnancies and births in Smollett's texts, Sterne's description of his as-yet-unborn character enables readers to build an altogether more tangible image of foetal development than other novels of the period. His description not only recalls the Rabelaisian influences for which *Tristram Shandy* is already so well known, but also Barker's poem and its excursion of '[t]he *Fret-work, Muscles, Arteries* and *Veins*' that make up human anatomy.[43] His depiction of the unborn foetus is closely related to the ways in which Barker and many experienced anatomists articulated how the fully grown adult human was formed. Sterne satirically invokes the (by then dated) theory of preformation, or the idea that an unborn foetus existed within the womb as a fully preformed miniature being that would simply grow in size during gestation. William Harvey's text had generated much controversial discussion in the late seventeenth century with the author's alternative suggestion that 'all animals whatsoever, even viviparous creatures, nay man himself, are all engendered from an egg, the first conceptions of all living creatures from which the foetus arises are some kind of egg', and that the foetus concerned would develop through 'the addition of parts budding out of one another', otherwise known as epigenesis.[44] While Harvey's ideas were not instantly accepted by the elite medical communities in which he was ensconced – as Matthew Cobb explains, his work both 'excited and perplexed its readers' – especially because he had been unable to offer full justifications for his findings, by the mid-eighteenth century his influence was sufficiently acknowledged to have been integrated into medical theories surrounding conception.[45] Sterne's use of older theories not only communicates key information about Tristram's personality, it also offers a distinctly pictorial form of writing, from which readers can more easily relate to Tristram as a fully developed character, even before he is born, than would otherwise have been the case had he attempted to employ embryogenesis as a means of describing his young character's progress.

Even though a preformed infant is much easier to depict as a protagonist than a foetus that is gradually being formed, this is not to say that Tristram Shandy is not also informed by Sterne's learned perspective on the latest medical research and publications that surrounded him as he progressed with his serialised novel.[46] Among the newest sources of which he was aware were the works of Dr William Smellie. The most influential obstetrician of the period, Smellie challenged the limits of midwifery both as an academic discipline and as an increasingly medicalised set of practices. Already towards the end of his career in the late 1750s, he had published two of the three volumes that would make up his best-known work, *A Treatise on the Theory and Practice of Midwifery* (1752–64), and had also recently collaborated with artist Jan van Rymsdyk and engraver Charles Grignion to produce his *A Sett of Anatomical Tables* (1754). As Lyle Massey outlines, prior to Smellie's ground-breaking work, reproductive anatomy and childbirth had not been principal subjects for the anatomist or the artists who illustrated their works.[47] While a scarcity of gravid cadavers was almost certainly still a factor in the relatively little attention these subjects were paid, it was only the growing position of famed man-midwives such as Smellie that could legitimise anatomical studies of this type, offering medical students and other readers an in-depth view of pregnant women's bodies. In terms of medical education, as Massey further suggests, while Smellie advocated hands-on teaching, he also clearly considered the *Anatomical Tables* a critical conduit of knowledge. That is, the atlas makes the case that only when one can 'see' the body correctly, from inside out, 'can one have a clear picture of birth'.[48] Figure 4.3 shows just one example of the images produced by Smellie, van Rymsdyk and Grignion, revealing the new levels of empirical and artistic detail that were offered to readers by the publication of the *Tables* and the irreversible change that took place once this visual information was placed on show for anyone who could access a copy.

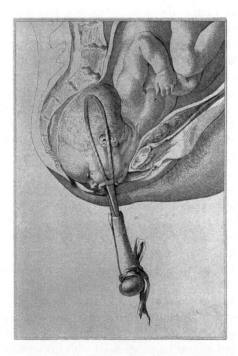

Figure 4.3 William Smellie, Table XXIV from *A sett of anatomical tables, with explanations, and an abridgment, of the practice of midwifery, with a view to illustrate a treatise on that subject, and collection of cases* (1754).
Wellcome Collection.

READING GENDER, MEDICINE AND THE BODY   81

Although Smollett was known to have been a friend of Smellie's and is even thought to have played an active role in the writing of his works, his use of gender and generation in his novels is not based on what medical professionals knew or may have been working on, or even whatever information to which he might have had privileged access himself, but rather the ways in which the public continued to harbour long-held cultural beliefs about gendered bodies and their reproductive capacity.[49] Sterne, on the other hand, revelled in developing satire that combined popular ideas with new scientific discourses, even if he did not necessarily communicate positive opinions regarding the illustrious Dr Smellie himself. Literary scholars have identified a parody of Smellie and his *Treatise* in volume 2 of *Tristram Shandy*, where Tristram details Walter's reading habits. He tells readers that

> My father who dipp'd into all kinds of books, upon looking into *Lithopœdus Senonesis de Partu difficili, published by Adrianus Smelvgot,* had found out, That the lax and pliable state of a child's head in parturition the bones of the cranium having no sutures at that time, was such,—that by the force of the woman's efforts, which, in strong labour-pains, was equal, upon an average, to a weight of 470 pounds averdupoise acting perpendicularly upon it. (175–6)

Arthur Cash, Donna Landry and Gerald MacLean agree that the fictional Smelvgot is based on Smellie himself.[50] His further detailing of the 'lax and pliable' nature of an infant's head is represented in many of Smellie's images, including Figure 4.3. These images are further paired with Smellie's descriptions of his experiences of delivering infants. In his chapter 'Of the Pelvis and the Child's Head', Smellie explains of such pliability that, 'in laborious cases, when the head is squeezed along with great force, we find it pressed into a very oblong form, the longest axis of which extends from the face to the *Vertex*'.[51] Sterne makes much of these circumstances in his discussion of Walter Shandy's selection of Dr Slop as a birthing attendant, even if his wife continued to insist on having only the support of the local female midwife. While this difference of opinion would be enough to parody current discussions of the appropriateness of engaging the services of the emerging man-midwife to enter the intimate and protected space of the birthing chamber which for centuries had been run by women, this is not enough for Sterne, who delves further into the world of what man-midwifery could offer in terms of knowledge, practice and technology. As Tristram explains to readers, Walter's chief apprehensions about his second child's arrival relate to the physical processes of birth itself. As he explains, Bobby, Walter and Elizabeth's first child, was delivered, 'with his head *foremost*,—and turning out afterwards a lad of wonderful slow parts,—my father spelt all these together into his opinion; and as he had failed at one end,—he was determined to try the other' (179).

Walter's parental role in Tristram's birth, as he perceives it, is to educate himself and guard against the possibility of a repeated, or even worse incident occurring. With this in mind, Tristram continues:

> Of all the men in the world, Dr. *Slop* was the fittest for my father's purpose;—for tho' his new-invented forceps was the armour he had proved, and what he maintained, to be the safest instrument of deliverance,—yet, it seems, he had scattered a word or two in his book, in favour of the very thing which ran in my father's

fancy;—tho' not with a view to the soul's good in extracting by the feet, as was my father's system,—but for reasons merely obstetrical. (180)

Slop is not intended to represent Smellie in his practice, and was in fact a parody of one of his peers, Dr John Burton of York, who also designed his own forceps and published a medical manual, *A Complete New System of Midwifery* (1751), which was illustrated by a young George Stubbs, who would become best known for his equine paintings. While both practitioners were successful in the years following the launch of their own forceps, with each undertaking the navigation of obstructed and complex births for years to come, it was Smellie who would gain the most fame for his work. Even in the early days after both books were published, Smellie's written works received the more favourable reviews, which permitted him to become the most illustrious name in obstetrics for some time.[52] Even without drawing further on Smellie's research and reputation, and as its reference to Smellie in the form of Smelvgot attests, *Tristram Shandy* cannot help but owe a debt to the Scottish physician who had, for the first time, opened reproductive bodies to public view in new ways by creating novel artistic tools for medical learning.

Literature, Medicine and the Arts

The literary and medical arts were equally, and collaboratively, involved in the search for new knowledge and practices during the mid-eighteenth century. Novels, medical texts and images were deeply engaged in the common goal to create, disseminate and critique as many new ideas about anatomy, gender and the science of generation as possible. Literary authors such as Barker, Smollett and Sterne were acutely aware of the difficulties experienced by medical practitioners and the reading public alike in attempting to visualise the inner workings of their bodies and respective abilities to procreate. Barker's work established a new precedent for the detailed exploration of anatomy in creative literature through pictorial writing and played a key role in educating readers in how the human body worked. Following in her footsteps, even if not consciously, both Smollett and Sterne used their novels to enter this same spirit of inquiry, although they utilised very different approaches to do so. Smollett's writing capitalises on the popular myth and misinformation that circulated as a dominating force within popular beliefs surrounding human gestation during the mid-eighteenth century. His use of lay and professional debates concerning theories of maternal imagination, including the by-then notorious Toft affair, allows readers a close-up view, through scrutinising satire, of the mixture of influences that were acting upon cultures of supporting pregnancy and birth. Sterne, on the other hand, brings human bodies and their functions into full view and draws readers into the rapidly changing world of professional anatomy and midwifery within his own satirical narrative. *Tristram Shandy* delights in being as specific as possible for readers in painting detailed pen portraits of human bodies where possible and the emerging health care practices that sought to attend to the complex needs of reproduction. Moreover, while Sterne might mock a range of medical figures such as Smellie and Burton, among others, he persists in uniting *Tristram Shandy* with medical texts and illustrations of his own time to further insert discussions about anatomy, gender and gestation into literary fiction. These authors' engagement with the visual, as well as textual, exploration of ideas about gender and the body helps readers to understand the transformation of medical

READING GENDER, MEDICINE AND THE BODY

knowledge and practice both as it happened and in the years after they were first published. The examination of literature and medicine together is productive to the study of places where scientific practitioners, artists and authors of the eighteenth century made key contributions to the evolution and advancements of both the creative and the scientific cultures that surrounded them.

Acknowledgement

This essay has received support from the Wellcome Trust project 'Thinking Through Things: Object Encounters in the Medical Humanities' and the Leverhulme Trust project 'Writing Doctors: Medical Representation and Personality, ca.1660–1832'. This research would not have been possible without the support of Professor Richard Terry (1962–2020).

Notes

1. Laurence Sterne, *The Life and Opinions of Tristram Shandy, Gentleman*, ed. Melvyn New and Joan New, The Florida Edition of the Works of Laurence Sterne (1759–68; Gainesville: The University Presses of Florida, 1978), 566. Further references parenthetical.
2. Helen Williams, *Laurence Sterne and the Eighteenth-Century Book* (Cambridge: Cambridge University Press, 2021), 3.
3. W. G. Day, 'Paint Her to Your Own Mind – The Blank Page Exhibition' was held at Shandy Hall and galleries across the north of England in 2016. See https://blankpage147.wordpress.com (accessed 9 November 2023).
4. Paul Munden and Paul Hetherington, 'Paint Her to Your Own Mind', *Axon: Creative Explorations* 8, no. 1 (2018): para. 5 of 28, https://www.axonjournal.com.au/issues/8-1/paint-her-your-own-mind (accessed 9 November 2023).
5. David Brewer, 'A Drawing on the Blank Page', *The Shandean* 17 (2006): 158–61; Brigitte Friant-Kessler, 'A Doodle, and More "Curious Cuts"', *The Shandean* 17 (2006): 162–8; Anne Bandry-Scubbi, 'Point blank – or Fulfilling Tristram's Command of "Painting" on the Blank Page', *The Shandean* 20 (2009): 126–30.
6. Day, 'The Blank Page' (2016), para. 5 of 10, https://blankpage147.wordpress.com/the-blank-page/ (accessed 9 November 2023).
7. For more on Sterne and male impotence, see Kirsten Juhas, 'Of Fribblers and Fumblers: Fashioning Male Impotence in the Long Eighteenth Century', in *Disease and Death in Eighteenth-Century Literature and Culture: Fashioning the Unfashionable*, ed. Allan Ingram and Leigh Wetherall Dickson (London: Palgrave Macmillan, 2016), 101–24.
8. Londa Schiebinger, 'Skeletons in the Closet: The First Illustrations of the Female Skeleton in Eighteenth-Century Anatomy', *Representations* 14 (1986): 42–82 (53).
9. Rösslin's text was first translated by Richard Jonas and retitled *The Byrth of Mankynde* in 1540 and was reprinted for over 150 years, the last edition appearing in 1654. Both Guillemeau's and Rueff's texts retained their original titles and authors' names in translation. See Richard Jonas, *The Byrth of Mankynde* (London: Thomas Raynalde, 1540); Jacques Guillemeau, *Child-Birth, or The Happy Delivery of Women* (London: Anne Griffin, 1635); Jacob Rueff, *The Expert-Midwife* (London: E. Griffin, 1637).
10. Tita Chico, *The Experimental Imagination: Literary Knowledge and Science in the British Enlightenment* (Stanford: Stanford University Press, 2018), 1.
11. Numerous studies have analysed the role of the novel in the wider ecosystem of medical communication of the period, but they have tended to focus on cognitive science and the

cultures of sensibility. See Katherine Kickel, *Novel Notions: Medical Discourse and the Mapping of the Imagination in Eighteenth-Century English Fiction* (London and New York: Routledge, 2007); Juliet McMaster, *Reading the Body in the Eighteenth-Century Novel* (Basingstoke: Palgrave Macmillan, 2004); Anne C. Vila, *Enlightenment and Pathology: Sensibility in the Literature and Medicine of Eighteenth-Century France* (Baltimore: Johns Hopkins University Press, 1998).

12. Angela Woods, 'The Limits of Narrative: Provocations for the Medical Humanities', *Medical Humanities* 37 (2011): 76.

13. George Rousseau, 'Sinews of Science, Medicine and Art During the Enlightenment: A Review Essay', *Eighteenth-Century Studies* 26, no.1 (1992): 85.

14. Jonathan Sawday, *The Body Emblazoned: Dissection and the Human Body in Renaissance Culture* (Abingdon and New York: Routledge, 2006), ix.

15. Andreas Vesalius, *On the Fabric of the Human Body, Book 1: The Bones and Cartilages*, trans. William Frank Richardson and John Burd Carman (San Francisco: Norman Publishing, 1998), lvi.

16. Vesalius, *On the Fabric of the Human Body*, lvi.

17. Valeria Finucci, 'Vesalius and the Languages of Anatomy', *Journal of Medieval and Early Modern Studies* 48, no. 1 (2018): 2.

18. Monique Kornell, *Flesh and Bones: The Art of Anatomy* (Los Angeles: Getty Research Institute, 2022), 3.

19. Katherine Park, *Secrets of Women: Gender, Generation, and the Origins of Human Dissection* (New York: Zone Books, 2006), 262.

20. Jane Barker, 'Anatomy', in *A Patch-Work Screen for the Ladies* (London: E. Curll, 1723), 16.

21. A more tentative, less confident, version of this poem had been published under the title of 'A Farewell to Poetry, with A Long Digression on Anatomy', in her earlier *Poetical Recreations* (1688). For more information on these two versions, see Karen Bloom Gevirtz, 'Philosophy and/in Verse Jane Barker's "Farewell to Poetry" and the Anatomy of Emotion', in *The Future of Feminist Eighteenth-Century Scholarship*, ed. Robin Rubina (New York and Abingdon: Routledge, 2018), 54–70.

22. Heather Meek, 'Jane Barker, Medical Discourse, and the Origins of the Novel', in *Literature and Medicine*, vol. 1, *The Eighteenth Century*, ed. Clark Lawlor and Andrew Mangham (Cambridge: Cambridge University Press, 2021), 51.

23. Andrew Cunningham, *The Anatomist Anatomis'd: An Experimental Discipline in Enlightenment Europe* (London and New York: Routledge, 2016), 8.

24. Cunningham, *The Anatomist Anatomis'd*, 83–4.

25. Tobias Smollett, *The Adventures of Roderick Random*, ed. James G. Basker, Paul-Gabriel Boucé, Nicole A. Seary and O. M. Brack, The Works of Tobias Smollett (Athens and London: University of Georgia Press, 2012), 37. Further references parenthetical.

26. W. F. Bynum, 'Physicians, Hospitals and Career Structures in Eighteenth-Century London', in *William Hunter and the Eighteenth-Century Medical World*, ed. W. F. Bynum and Roy Porter (Cambridge: Cambridge University Press, 2002), 119.

27. Laurence Talairach explains that the first legislation to cover anatomy in England was implemented in 1540 by Henry VIII to allow the bodies of four hanged criminals per year for dissection, while R. Allen Shotwell indicates that in Europe cadavers were supplied at a rate of two specimens per dissection – one male and one female – although this quota often went unfulfilled by the supply of only one body, or at times none. See Laurence Talairach, 'Anatomical Culture, Body-Snatching, and Nineteenth-Century Gothic', in *Literature and Medicine*, vol. 2, *The Nineteenth Century*, ed. Clark Lawlor and Andrew Mangham (Cambridge: Cambridge University Press, 2021), 75; R. Allen Shotwell, 'Animals, Pictures, and Skeletons: Andreas Vesalius's Reinvention of the Public Anatomy Lesson', *Journal of the History of Medicine and Allied Sciences* 71, no. 1 (2015): 4.

READING GENDER, MEDICINE AND THE BODY

28. Fiona Hutton, *The Study of Anatomy in Britain, 1700–1900* (Abingdon and New York: Routledge, 2016), 3.
29. See Warren L. Oakley, *A Culture of Mimicry: Laurence Sterne, His Readers, and the Art of Bodysnatching* (London: Maney Publishing, 2010), 2. Smollett allegedly promised his corpse to anatomist John Hunter in a letter written during the summer of 1771, but this wish was never realised. Smollett was buried in the Old English Cemetery in Livorno, Italy, where he had kept a home and died aged fifty. See Wendy Moore, *The Knife Man: Blood, Body-Snatching and the Birth of Modern Surgery* (London: Bantam Books, 2006), 321.
30. For further information on Mary Shelley's text and its contexts concerning grave robbing, see Tim Marshall, *Murder to Dissect: Grave-Robbing, Frankenstein and the Anatomy Literature* (Manchester and New York: Manchester University Press, 1995).
31. See Sandra M. Leonard, 'Grave Allegations: Victorian Bodysnatching and Plagiarism', in *The Graveyard in Literature: Liminality and Social Critique*, ed. Aoileann Ní Éigeartaigh (Newcastle upon Tyne: Cambridge Scholars Publishing, 2022), 342–57.
32. *Trial of William Burke and Helen M'Dougal Before the Court of Justiciary at Edinburgh, On Wednesday 24, 1828, for the Murder of Margery Campbell, or Docherty taken in shorthand by Mr. John Macnee* (Edinburgh and London: Robert Buchanan, William Hunter, John Stevenson, and Baldwin & Craddock, 1829), 198–9.
33. Talairach, 'Anatomical Culture, Body-Snatching, and Nineteenth-Century Gothic', 76.
34. The first of these had been Sir Richard Manningham's Jermyn Street establishment, which opened in 1739, offering approximately thirty beds for pregnant women to give birth with medical support.
35. Other texts that engaged with this debate include John Maubray's *The Female Physician* (London: J. Holland, 1724) and John Henry Mauclerc's *The Power of Imagination in Pregnant Women Discussed* (London: J. Robinson, 1740).
36. For more on the key medical figures involved in the Toft affair, and the events concerning these extraordinary claims and their exploration, see Karen Harvey, *The Imposteress Rabbit Breeder: Mary Toft and Eighteenth-Century England* (Oxford: Oxford University Press, 2020).
37. Anti-Imaginationist pamphlets are those that argued specifically against the concept of maternal imagination and its powerful influence on the formation of the unborn infant. Jenifer Buckley explains that this type of medical writing emerged in the months following the exposing of Toft's hoax. See, Jenifer Buckley, *Gender, Pregnancy and Power in Eighteenth-Century Literature: The Maternal Imagination* (Cham: Palgrave Macmillan, 2017), 62.
38. James Augustus Blondel, *The Power of the Mother's Imagination Over the Foetus Examin'd. In Answer to Dr. Daniel Turner's Book, Intitled 'A Defence of the XIIth Chapter of the First Part of a Treatise, De Morbis Cutaneis'* (London: John Brotherton, 1729), vi.
39. See Smollett, *Roderick Random*, 391n3.
40. Aileen Douglas, *Uneasy Sensations: Smollett and the Body* (Chicago and London: University of Chicago Press, 1995), xxv.
41. Tobias Smollett, *The Adventures of Peregrine Pickle*, ed. John P. Zomchick and George S. Rousseau, The Works of Tobias Smollett (Athens and London: University of Georgia Press, 2014), 38. Further references parenthetical.
42. Buckley, *Gender, Pregnancy and Power in Eighteenth-Century Literature*, 3.
43. Barker, *A Patch-Work Screen for the Ladies*, 16.
44. William Harvey, *Anatomical Exercitations Concerning the Generation of Living Creatures* (London: James Young, 1653), 2, 272.
45. Matthew Cobb, *The Egg & Sperm Race: The Seventeenth-Century Scientists Who Unravelled the Secrets of Sex, Life and Growth* (London: Pocket Books, 2007), 29.

46. See Judith Hawley, 'The Anatomy of *Tristram Shandy*', in *Literature and Medicine During the Eighteenth Century*, ed. Roy Porter and Marie Mulvey Roberts (London: Routledge, 1993), 84–100.
47. Lyle Massey, 'Pregnancy and Pathology: Picturing Childbirth in Eighteenth-Century Obstetric Atlases', *The Art Bulletin* 87, no.1 (2005): 74.
48. Massey, 'Pregnancy and Pathology', 77.
49. Robert Woods, 'Dr Smellie's Prescriptions for Pregnant Women', *Medical History* 52, no. 2 (2008): 257.
50. Donna Landry and Gerald MacLean, 'Of Forceps, Patents, and Paternity: *Tristram Shandy*', *Eighteenth-Century Studies* 23, no. 4 (1990): 526; Arthur Cash, 'The Birth of Tristram Shandy: Sterne and Dr. Burton', in *Studies in the Eighteenth Century*, ed. R. F. Brissenden (Canberra: ANU Press, 1968), 137n5.
51. William Smellie, *A Treatise on the Theory and Practice of Midwifery*, 5th edn, 3 vols (London: D. Wilson and T. Durham, 1786), 1:86.
52. For more on Smellie's legacy, see Adrian Wilson, *The Making of Man-Midwifery: Childbirth in England, 1660–1770* (Cambridge, MA: Harvard University Press), 124–5.

Part II:
Visual Cultures

5

BEFORE AND AFTER: IMAGINING PLEASURE IN EIGHTEENTH-CENTURY BRITISH ART AND LITERATURE, FROM DEFOE AND HOGARTH TO STERNE AND GAINSBOROUGH

Frédéric Ogée

ONE OF THE great English contributions to the Age of Enlightenment was the promotion of new conditions allowing not only the emergence of what has been called a public sphere, but also the opening of new spaces authorising individual expression. A century later, in Article 11 of the Declaration of the Rights of Man and of the Citizen of 1789, that expression was written into law (if not into reality): 'The free communication of ideas and opinions is one of the most precious of the rights of man. Every citizen may, accordingly, speak, write, and print with freedom, but shall be responsible for such abuses of this freedom as shall be defined by law.[1]

In Britain, such individual expression, tirelessly presented as 'modern', is urged and accounted for by the awareness of our experience of the world through a sensory apprehension of 'nature', considered as the source and foundation of all objective knowledge. Let us start from a blank page, writes John Locke, the blank page of our birth, and let our five senses apprehend the world and gradually fill this page with 'characters' (that is, sensory data). Ultimately, this apprehension of nature will lead us, quite naturally, to a rational comprehension of it, and in the process will shape our individual characters.[2]

As a result, the work of the senses and its complex relation to the 'pleasures of the imagination' became a central preoccupation of philosophers, scientists and artists, and in the second half of the eighteenth century 'the age of sensibility' increasingly conceived of sensory experience as a vital counterpoint to cold reason. 'The Pleasures of the Imagination' is the title of a well-known series of eleven consecutive essays published by Joseph Addison in June 1712 in the English periodical he edited with Richard Steele from 1711 to 1714, *The Spectator*. In the aftermath of the Glorious Revolution of 1688, which established parliamentary monarchy, habeas corpus and the freedom of the press, this paper proved a remarkable vector for the dissemination of new political, philosophical and scientific ideas (notably those of Isaac Newton and Locke) within a public sphere which it greatly contributed towards shaping.[3]

Addison's series is one of the founding texts of British Enlightenment aesthetics, echoes of which can be found throughout the century, from Francis Hutcheson to David Hume, Edmund Burke or Lord Kames. Within a neoclassical critical framework in which the emphasis was on the rules of creation of the work of art, Addison offers

90   FRÉDÉRIC OGÉE

one of the first discussions of the perception of this work, what Gérard Genette has aptly called the *work* of art:[4] 'Every thing that is new or uncommon raises a pleasure in the imagination, because it fills the soul with an agreeable surprise, gratifies its curiosity, and gives it an idea of which it was not before possessed.'[5]

The founding in the 1660s of The Royal Society of London for the Improving of Natural Knowledge encouraged the emergence of a new method of scientific investigation which, rather than seeking to verify preconceived hypotheses, recommended an objective and direct observation of the 'particulars' of nature and the writing of 'accounts' or narratives of the causes and effects of natural phenomena, from which the laws of nature could then be deduced. Writers and artists soon responded to and represented the consequences of all these changes, and began to conceive 'modern' forms of expression, clearly presented as English, idiomatic and free, allowing them to model and analyse this new approach to nature, including human nature. Quite remarkably, these new forms all appeared between the 1720s and 1740s.

In garden design, after trying to compete with French baroque grandeur (as at Castle Howard or Blenheim Palace), landscapists Charles Bridgeman, William Kent and Lancelot 'Capability' Brown gradually replaced the geometric and architectural framing of nature *à la Le Nôtre* as at Versailles by a more pictorial form of garden, increasingly irregular, serpentine and 'natural', which, while being in fact as artificial as its French anti-model, was presented as the emblem of English freedom, encouraging the visitor to develop a personal and sensory relation to the (national) land (see Plate 3). This Addisonian creation was primarily the sign of a new, self-conscious English relationship to nature, and it is indeed under that name – *jardin anglais*, *Englischer Garten*, *giardino inglese* and so on – that it was imitated and adapted throughout the European continent and North America in the second half of the century.

The de-geometrisation of space, on paper as much as in the field, makes the a priori perception and understanding of its design impossible. Sinuously drawn along an associative, meditative and increasingly free and personal course (*solitaire*, Jean-Jacques Rousseau will soon say), the visitor, guided by his five senses, acquires a knowledge of the garden through a progressive and cumulative experience of the space involved.

Such an aesthetic is primarily based on that pleasure of the pursuit which William Hogarth, in *The Analysis of Beauty* (1753), defined and theorised for a whole generation of designers:

> Pursuing is the business of our lives; and even abstracted from any other view, gives pleasure . . . Every arising difficulty, that for a while attends and interrupts the pursuit, gives a sort of spring to the mind, enhances the pleasure, and makes what would else be toil and labour, become sport and recreation. . . . The eye hath this sort of enjoyment in winding walks, and serpentine rivers, and all sorts of objects, whose forms, as we shall see hereafter, are composed principally of what, I call, the waving and serpentine lines. Intricacy in form, therefore, I shall define to be that peculiarity in the lines, which compose it, that *leads the eye a wanton kind of chace*, and from the pleasure that gives the mind, intitles it to the name of beautiful.[6]

In literature, Britain developed a passion for a new genre of long prose narrative – which gradually took on the name of 'novel' – and set out to represent the causes

IMAGINING PLEASURE 91

and effects of a 'modern' individual's integration in the new urban and market society of contemporary England. After Eliza Haywood's (*Love in Excess; Or, The Fatal Enquiry* [1719], *Fantomina; or Love in a Maze* [1724]) and Daniel Defoe's (*Robinson Crusoe* [1719], *Moll Flanders* [1722], *The Fortunate Mistress*, better known as *Roxana* [1724]) first experimental attempts, Samuel Richardson, with his bestsellers *Pamela* (1740) and *Clarissa* (1748), developed the epistolary genre to tap the epistemological friction released by the confrontation of several contiguous points of view, while his rival Henry Fielding, with *Joseph Andrews* (1742) and *Tom Jones* (1749), set out to explore what he called his 'new province of writing',[7] offering the epic, panoramic account of his heroes' progresses, painstakingly broken down into volumes and short chapters, in a format inspired by the daily instalments of the periodical press, which in a way had prepared its readership.

Defoe, Fiction and Pleasure

With his last two novels, Defoe approached the issue of pleasure in a remarkably innovative way by focusing on the new situation made for women by the rise of finance and the capitalist economy, the commodification of the female body and the leeway left to women to dispose of it at their discretion and to enjoy, as much as possible, the pleasure of freedom.

The plot of *The Fortunate Mistress* takes place in part at the time of the Restoration of Charles II (and the birth of Defoe), in the 1660s, when libertinism (above all a matter of commerce), amorality and political cynicism were set up as vengeful compensation for the rigours of the hard-line Calvinism imposed by Oliver Cromwell during his ten years of government. By shifting some of the temporal sequences of the novel from 1724 to the 1680s, or even earlier in the 1660s, Defoe re-summoned a libertine culture embodied by the character of Roxana, whose various permutations the reader follows as the novel progresses. Her protean character makes it possible to perceive the complexity of the radical changes which took place in England during these decades and the underlying tension, in Defoe's account, between the Restoration and the end of the Stuart years in the 1680s, and the beginning of Georgian England. Remarkably, the story plays on the antagonisms between the ideology and practices of the Court at the Restoration, and the new progressive values of the Dissenters and the new 'middling sort' which emerged after the Glorious Revolution.

The figure of the libertine during the Restoration period, driven by a sparkling and cynical *carpe diem*, challenged all forms of authority contained in social, political, religious and cultural norms. Encouraged by Charles II, courtiers proudly opposed any moral restraint, decimating their victims with flashes of sword or wit. The reopening of the theatres encouraged an exceptionally rich production of new plays in which performance, role playing, double meaning and masquerade were predominant, as can be seen throughout *Roxana*. Inspired by Thomas Hobbes's *Leviathan* (1651) and the flamboyant pornographic poetry of the king's favourite, John Wilmot, second Earl of Rochester (1647–80), the comedies of the Restoration – for example, William Wycherley's *The Country Wife* (1675), George Etherege's *The Man of Mode* (1676), Aphra Behn's *The Rover* (1677), even William Congreve's later *The Way of the World* (1700) – evince a linguistic virtuosity and moral cynicism in which sex is omnipresent. Sir Peter Lely, official painter to Charles II, painted hundreds of portraits of this court society, and his occasionally disturbing art provides remarkable visual evidence of the arrogance, cross-dressing and omnipresence of sex which predominated. Roxana's character is believed to have been in part inspired by one of Charles II's mistresses, Nell Gwyn, from whom she borrows the nickname 'the Protestant Whore' (see Plate 4). But Roxana's French origins also evoke another of Charles II's mistresses, Hortense Mancini, Duchess of Mazarin, whose disastrous life and marriage before coming to England in the 1670s was the subject of much gossip, speculation and fiction.

The complicated episodes of Roxana's sex and marital lives raise the controversial issue of what Mary Astell in her *Reflections on Marriage* (1700) called 'marital prostitution',[8] and open important questions about gender relations and women's loss of power with the new marriage laws. In the middle section of the novel, at the height of her prosperity, she refuses to marry a wealthy merchant and declares that 'the very nature of the marriage contract [is], in short, nothing but giving up liberty, estate, authority, and every-thing to the man, and the woman [is] indeed a mere woman ever after, that is to say, a slave'.[9] Turning libertine cynicism to her advantage to underline and embody the link – terrifying for men – between prostitution and female power, Roxana stigmatises what society calls 'whoredom', which in reality means sexual freedom. Written by a man with a female protagonist, *Roxana* remarkably explores some of the issues related to the social and sexual empowerment of women, including, with the return of her daughter Susan in the latter part of the novel, the alleged moral and practical incompatibilities between sexual freedom and motherhood, questions which remained at the heart of British culture until the end of the Victorian era.

The autobiography of Mademoiselle de Beleau (one of Roxana's many aliases) certainly offers the portrait of one of the most flamboyant libertines in English literature, whose final contrition is only the ambiguous puritanical reframing of a remarkably bold text. The case of Moll Flanders, two years her senior, is much less clear. The orphan of a criminal and deported mother and an unknown father, she recounts the successive stages of her career as a prostitute, a 'Harlot's Progress', as William Hogarth will describe it in pictures a few years later, a career which, from lovers to husbands, from solitude to setbacks, gradually leads her to pickpocketing, prison and deportation. Again, one of the most original features of the novel is the way Defoe engages with issues of sexual politics. Beyond the uneasiness that Moll's predominantly mercenary attitude to love and marriage may pose to today's readers, or, worse yet, her apparent absence of any maternal feeling towards a large number of offspring discreetly abandoned along the way, her zigzagging life and narrative reflect the complex changes that affected sexuality, gender relations and marriage in early eighteenth-century England, and the intricate, 'modern' connection between pleasure and commerce.

The new situation that the rise of capitalism created for women, the eminently problematic position they were suddenly led to occupy in a new economic and social environment – that of the great modern city, as fascinating as it was ruthless – redistributed gender roles and responsibilities. Urban life contributed to destroy previous communal ties and divide people into financially independent nuclear families. From the end of the seventeenth century, the family became the new principle of social organisation, a sort of survival cell in an increasingly complex and re-prioritised society. One of Moll's most poignant difficulties comes precisely from the fact that she never manages to fit into a stable family unit, and on the few occasions she does, she experiences the anxiety of seeing the husband either die or disappear. In addition, the separation of home and workplace completed the confinement of women in the domestic sphere, outside which it was very difficult for them to have any activity. The eviction of women from the new economic structures thus made them more and more dependent on the marriage they managed to achieve. As Moll's distress shows on numerous occasions, it was almost impossible, because highly suspect, for a woman to claim economic and therefore social autonomy. No place was made for them in urban society outside the home of the father and then of the husband, so Moll's only, obsessive and harrowing activity becomes the acquisition of a good husband, an issue that will dominate most eighteenth-century novels all the way to Jane Austen. Moll is perhaps the first of those new heroines whose identity is defined almost exclusively in the relationship they maintain with men and in their struggle to achieve what is presented to them as 'happiness' and some form of personal autonomy in a world where they are completely under guardianship. As Ruth Perry puts it, 'the very repetitive and sometimes silly fiction of this era is certainly an expression of an eminently unhealthy situation'.[10]

The difficulties women encountered were all the more acute as the status they acquired through marriage was very unfair. What the new patriarchal structures strove to present as the natural state and aspiration of women was in effect the legal form of a placement under tutelage and of a complete dependence, and this, clearly, invites us to reconsider the moral choice between 'whoredom' and marriage as being certainly more complex than it appears. This confinement by marriage of women to the domestic sphere actually had a dramatic effect on their social 'worth'. Gradually reduced to mere considerations of reproduction, they were increasingly considered exclusively in sexual terms. It was no longer their activity that gave them value and a place in the community, but only their gender. Their 'capital', as Moll Flanders often points out, was directly proportional to their charm and they began to make strategic use of these charms as bait to catch rich husbands. The way she manages her sexuality and her relationship with men, the way she trades in her body, the moving way in which she takes note of the tragic consequences of ageing, must therefore be read in this context, at a time when living without a family and in the city was, for a woman, a tightrope walk between virginity and pollution or defilement, between prostitution and marriage, or else between old-maid celibacy, sleazy cohabitation or penniless widowhood. As the true story of actress, poet and celebrity figure Mary Robinson (see below) or the fictionalised lives of Austen's Dashwood sisters sadly reveal, by the end of the century nothing much had changed.

Living in London in the first decades of the eighteenth century, at the heart or on the fringes of an urban expansion which sometimes looks like a proliferating malignant growth, with its dizzying spectacle of wealth and crime, staggering luxury and sordid misery – remarkably exposed in John Gay's 1728 ballad opera, *The Beggar's Opera* – meant being aware of the reality of the body at every moment. Whether covered in silk or exhibited in brothels, the body, which, as we said above, the empiricists considered as the key instrument of the acquisition of knowledge, became in a few years the central place of all exchanges.

Unlike many of his contemporaries, Defoe (like his contemporary, Jonathan Swift) never looked away from the darker realities of this new fact, and did not hesitate to impose on his readers the spectacle of the hidden demands of the body, from defecation to fornication, all those things that the most precious lace and silks sometimes had

94 FRÉDÉRIC OGÉE

a hard time covering. Flanders, above all else, designates a highly sought-after con-traband fabric, and Moll, like Roxana, is constantly engaged in a disguising exercise.

Indeed Moll's empirical strategies and the way in which, in a society where com-merce and money are the indices of modernity, she negotiates questions of sexuality and desire, with her body as sole capital,[11] explain what drives her to use masks and decoys, either to attract potential husbands or to dodge the consequences of her sinuous sex life. As *Roxana* would soon confirm, the masked ball was in those years the most fashionable and most scandalous way to explore the limits of sexual 'com-merce', and this burning topicality of the culture of cross-dressing, developed in *Moll Flanders*, is perhaps not unrelated to the narrative strategy of Defoe, who, like Moll and Roxana, chooses to disguise himself as a woman to write one of the first great modern European novels, suggesting a primordial link between novel and pleasure, between reading, dis-covering and eroticism.

The masquerade ball, which was one of the most popular court entertainments for many years, became, during the first decades of the eighteenth century and Defoe's novel writing period, the matrix of the first commercial entertainments, a new urban phenomenon which crossed, even undermined, the traditional lines of demarca-tion conferred by social rank and privilege. Swiss impresario and businessman John Heidegger saw the commercial potential of masked entertainments, which, from 1717, came to thrive most remarkably in the 'pleasure gardens' of Ranelagh and Vauxhall. Contemporary of the famous *scènes galantes* painted by Jean-Antoine Watteau (Plate 5), present in London during the same years, these gardens of pleasure inspired a new form of sociability, in fictitious and multi-sensory universes where music, gastronomy and painting (Hogarth exhibited his first genre scenes there) form the setting for a fantasised 'Embarkation for Cythera' (the title given to one of Watteau's most famous paintings. Incidentally, several visitors arrived by boat on the Thames, as if they were in Venice). The attraction and fascination exerted by these places can be explained by the fact that it was both a public and clandestine phenomenon allowing the manipula-tion of appearances in order to simulate, and often put in action, fictional scenarios. It may therefore not be a coincidence that this success occurred in the same years as the emergence of the modern novel, since both are based on a strategic use of fiction allowing the reader to experience situations which, in reality, are not quite possible in real life, often because they disturb the limitations imposed by social etiquette and morality.

Interestingly, we find descriptions of a masquerade in a number of major British novels of the period, in Defoe, Haywood, Fielding, Richardson, Tobias Smollett and Frances Burney, all of whom use it as the almost conventional backdrop for scenes of seduction and adultery.[12] Described at the time as the new work of the Devil, who donned a mask to tempt Eve, vilified as 'a libidinous Assembly contrived for the Advancement of Cuckoldom',[13] these masquerades removed the usual restraints of modesty. As Fielding noted in his 1728 poem *The Masquerade*, 'To masque the Face [is] t'unmasque the mind'.[14]

Defoe's *Moll Flanders* and *The Fortunate Mistress* are linked to this culture of disguise and cross-dressing. Both Moll and Roxana use masks to explore scenarios, to seduce and to taste the forbidden fruit. Whatever their situation, they are always playing a role, pretending to be what actually they are not, pretending not to be what they actually are. From one adventure to the next, aware of the intimate link between body and money, they are constantly consuming new bodies. At no point in their narratives, which nevertheless present themselves as autobiographies, do they move without a mask. Their real name is never revealed, and such a strategy allows them to experience a whole series of transgressive relationships (including incest) the subversive force of which never seems to affect them since the disguise ensures their anonymity. Defoe thus explores fictions of sexual emancipation and otherwise inconceivable independence which masks allow women. Disguising both identity and language, Moll and Roxana are able to make contact with strangers (including readers), initiate conversation, touch and kiss unknown men, and ultimately express sexual desire and impulses in a way that radically transgresses what 'modesty' usually prescribed for women.

By publishing his book without an author's name, by passing it off as the authentic memoirs of anonymous and clandestine characters, Defoe invites his readers to a similar masquerade, to identify themselves risklessly with an 'other', and perhaps experience the other in themselves.[15] Constantly sheltering behind the mask of edifying narrative, fiction is used here as a keyhole to peek into a world of sexual freedom and easy commerce, far more effectively and subversively than the pornographic novels of the period, such as John Cleland's *Memoirs of a Woman of Pleasure* (otherwise known as *Fanny Hill*, 1748–9), in which the keyhole peep show primarily reveals how sad the flesh is. Far more exciting than exposed sex, Defoe's narratives invite the reader to acknowledge and experience the complexities of 'a harlot's progress', a phrase William Hogarth (1697–1764), the first major English artist, chose for the title and pictorial programme of a famous series of pictures painted and then engraved in 1731–2.

William Hogarth's Narrative Art

Hogarth's paintings and engravings bear witness to the new practices of observation advocated by empiricist epistemology. Throughout his oeuvre, he seeks to account for very physical phenomena of evolution, progress, accumulation, and the new forms of the representation of reality he proposes describe very tangible experiments in proliferation and decomposition, analysed in a Newtonian dynamic of causes and effects. The emphasis placed on the activity of perception and the pleasure of an active and empirical 'wanton kind of chace' within the images is found most remarkably in the choice Hogarth made of a serial form of representation. Many of his works are conceived as sequences of images, in which the progress of his characters is in a way leveraged and deployed onto several images which follow one another in a visual sequence, a structural feature shared with the contemporary novel.

The functional principle of the series is illustrated in a very didactic way in the aptly named set of two images, *Before & After* (1733), the somewhat raw subject of which cleverly plays on the theme of seduction (Figure 5.1). The painted versions, devoid of any eroticism, clearly verge on pornography, and look like schoolboy pranks oozing with a familiarly sick masculinity.[16] In the engraved version, meanwhile, the visual and moral effect of the work results from the confrontation of the two images, and from the equally sick humour contained in the false suspense and playful withholding of information, in what is nothing less than a violent rape scene.

Figure 5.1 William Hogarth, *Before and After* (1736). Etching and engraving. Harris Brisbane Dick Fund, 1932. The Metropolitan Museum of Art, New York. www.metmuseum.org

The title of the first image is clearly programmatic, opening up a space of expectation, impatience even, and invites a temporal, left-to-right reading. The second image, on the other hand, acts like a candle snuffer, abruptly ending the broken 'sentence' on a note of frustration ('After what?'). At the same time, the suspended fall of the dressing table (a vanity) in the first image, metaphorically foreshadowing that of the young lady, underlines the artist's artificial interruption of the passing of time, just as its actual fall in the second image allows the spectator-voyeur to discover, in the displaced ray of the sun, a second image of Cupid, henceforth hilarious at having succeeded in 'firing his shot'. Finally, the 'progress' of the dog, erect in the first image, curled back at rest in the second, reads like the rather gritty transposition of the successive movements of the male character's 'animal parts'. Yet, of course, we also quickly realise that the central image is missing, a space left empty which the imagination of the spectator (who never lacks any) is invited to invest. In his definition of the line of beauty, Hogarth wrote that

> by its twisting so many different ways, [it] may be said to in close (tho' but a single line) varied contents; and therefore all its variety cannot be express'd on paper by one continued line, without the assistance of the imagination.[17]

Examined side by side, the couple's two positions form a suggestive V which seems to point temptingly towards the gap between the two images, the present tense of the narration, between past and future, the space that the spectator's voyeuristic 'pleasures of the imagination' will fill with explicit details. The two stages of the narration (before/after) create a tension which, a bit like dissonance in music, calls for a resolution.

The same dynamic principle informs the structure and perception of Hogarth's more elaborate series. The open space between plates 1 and 2 of *A Harlot's Progress* (Figure 5.2) is that of the young country girl's tragic corruption, the graphic details of which Hogarth leaves the spectator to imagine. Hogarth's novelty consists in introducing more variety and complexity into the simple two-image pattern by representing the successive rebounds of fate. *A Harlot's Progress*, *A Rake's Progress* (1733–5) or *Industry & Idleness* (1747) are genuine 'natural histories', unfolding as sequences of 'before, and after, and after, and after . . .'. Similarly, in *Marriage A-la-Mode* (1743–5), the first image serves as the trigger for a whole series of 'after-effects'. Their progressive discovery by the spectator, invited to make the connections and provide the missing links, produces a remarkably pathetic effect, of the kind Diderot so greatly admired in the work of Jean-Baptiste Greuze, the 'French Hogarth'.[18]

Hogarth's great series aim to fragment the temporal continuum into meaningful moments in order to make these stories of tragic fates even more dramatic by reducing them to a few crucial episodes (between two and twelve, depending on the series). Each of these wordless stories represents their characters' few and momentous 'Choices of Hercules', reducing the pantomime of their existence to a terrifyingly laconic sequence. The beholders, meanwhile, are invited not only to piece together the missing scenes, but also, in the end, to step back and question the very nature of these failures. The sequential acquisition of experience and knowledge is much more their business than that of the characters, to whom no chance seems given to make the slightest progress.

With the pressure of the new economic model, where the race for more and the headlong rush already predominated, could such a narrative drive, such an alleged

Figure 5.2 William Hogarth, *A Harlot's Progress* (1732), plates 1 & 2. Etching and engraving. Harris Brisbane Dick Fund, 1932. The Metropolitan Museum of Art, New York. www.metmuseum.org

'love of pursuit' at the heart of all these new forms of expression, also be seen as the first symptom of the new consumer society's obsessive desire for ever more 'progress', the tragic nature of which, remarkably perceived by Hogarth, feels like an early awareness of our civilisation's entry into the Anthropocene?

Such suspicious enthusiasm for the pursuit, for the narratives of journeys allowing upstarts to become parvenus, and almost always ending in consummation and marriages supposed to bring eternal happiness, is perhaps at the origin of the phenomenal success of all ensuing novels. The scope of the present essay does not allow for their close examination, but it can quickly be pointed out how Richardson in his two most famous epistolary stories, *Pamela* and *Clarissa*, places rape at the heart of his stories, fought and defeated in the first, perpetrated and dissected in the second. The reader-voyeur is invited to look over the characters' shoulders into their secret correspondences where intimate thoughts and details are revealed with a darkly rigorous realism which, while not denying the importance of desire, leaves no room for sauciness. This is what we perceive in Joseph Highmore's ambitious series of paintings, clearly inspired by Hogarth, which he produced to illustrate *Pamela*, hoping to capitalise on the book's phenomenal success. With *Joseph Andrews* and *Tom Jones*, Fielding, on the contrary, presents a much more benevolent, tolerant and decidedly comical vision of amorous commerce, a vision also clearly masculine and conservative of the patriarchal order. His female characters are either pot-bellied matrons, very 'natural' farm wenches, or fairly abstract icons of physical and moral perfection (Fanny, Sophia).

Sterne, Fiction and Sentiment

In 1768, just a few weeks before his death, the Anglican preacher and novelist Laurence Sterne published the first two books of *A Sentimental Journey through France and Italy*, which remained unfinished. After the thunderous nine volumes of his bestseller *The Life and Opinions of Tristram Shandy, Gentleman* (1759–67), this enigmatic travelogue, narrated by Parson Yorick (the name of the king's jester in *Hamlet* and a character in *Tristram Shandy*, which Sterne had also used to publish his *Sermons*) is a remarkably subtle attempt to achieve a form of balance between the demands of the body and those of the soul, between impulse and reason, between the sensory and the sensible, a balance that the word 'sentimental' was meant to encapsulate, thus foregrounding Sterne's final exploration of the link between sensibility and pleasure.

In fact, throughout the eighteenth century, under the combined influence of empiricist philosophers (Locke, and David Hume and Adam Smith later in the century) and those of the so-called 'moral sense' school (Anthony Ashley Cooper, Earl of Shaftesbury, Hutcheson and Henry Home Lord Kames) it became increasingly clear that there was perhaps little or no difference between feeling and thinking. In the 1760s, which offer us many representations of men openly crying, it was commonly believed that the private feelings of the heart were the main inspirers of moral behaviour, that through the pleasurable sensations we derive from our benevolent actions, from the fact that we feel 'loved', we come to understand the private benefits of an actively virtuous public life. In his *Elements of Criticism* (1762), Lord Kames defined sentiment as 'every thought prompted by passion'.[19] Our thoughts come from what we experience, from what we feel, and 'sentimental' therefore acquired the meaning of what makes us feel and therefore understand.

The development of sentimentalism was also linked to the new scientific approach to the study of our physical being, and the terms 'sensibility', 'sentiment' and 'sympathy', for instance, were commonly used in physiology and neurology, medical disciplines which developed greatly in the same decades.[20] A better understanding of the sensory system, of the vibrations and stimulation of the nerves, gave even more relief to the status of *l'homme sensible* and helped to flesh out the philosophical interconnections between feeling and thought.

A Sentimental Journey is nothing but a careful observation of the vibrations and reactions of men and women to impulses, in themselves as much as around them, with Yorick as priest-mediator, whose role is not only to experience sentimental receptivity by himself but also to try and make his readers-parishioners feel it too. The first lesson to be drawn is the extent to which a careful deciphering of the heart's emotions, as the body allows us to feel them, is conducive to better social understanding and 'commerce', better, that is, than through the imperfect mediation of language. As Yorick explains while holding the lady's hand in front of the remise door: 'The pulsations of the arteries along my fingers pressing across hers, told her what was passing within me: she looked down—a silence of some moments followed.'[21] Time and time again, in the 'unobserved corners', in the 'dark alleys', Yorick demonstrates this active connection between body and soul, each time emphasising the physical and physiological details. The primordial importance of touch, of the contact of 'hands' (one of the most frequently used words in the book) as a much more explicit vector of communication than language, encourages Yorick to search for ways of translating such feeling into its conceptualisation by language:

> There is not a secret so aiding to the progress of sociality, as to get master of this *short hand*, and be quick in rendering the several turns of looks and limbs, with all their inflections and delineations, into plain words. (47–8)

The double project of the book is first to show that the world in its most ordinary recesses, nature in her simplest attire, are full of vibrations which only those who have 'taste' – that is, who are ready to travel sentimentally – can perceive, and, secondly, to describe how the feeling of these vibrations can be written down and transformed into a kind of moral fluid essential to life. The book not only describes Yorick's journey (his 'transports'), it also allows us to see Yorick reasoning and writing about it (hence the importance of writing the Preface several chapters into the narrative). With such an internal vision of the operations of the external senses, Sterne's remarkable interest in the reciprocity of effects marks an important evolution in the Enlightenment understanding of the body's mediating function and of its reality as the physical container of individual existence (habeas corpus).

In 1769, with *Le Rêve de d'Alembert*, Diderot, following up on Sterne's intuitions (which he knew very well), also underlined the need to take into account the body's internal operations and their role in the construction of self-awareness. In his study of the history of what he calls 'the feeling of self' from the sixteenth to the twentieth century, Georges Vigarello has shown the extent to which, from the eighteenth century onwards, sensory impressions were increasingly felt to be not only mere transmitters of information about the outside world but also revealers of information on the self's inner realities.[22] The new English novel, from Defoe and Richardson to the Gothic

IMAGINING PLEASURE

novel or Jane Austen, focusing as it does on the representation of individual journeys (as announced by all its titles), attempts to describe exactly that.

The maid Yorick meets in the streets of Paris is especially interested in Crébillon's 1736 novel *Les Egarements du cœur et de l'esprit* (54). They spend a long time moving from one street corner to the next, and their discussion of itineraries ('—But is this the way, my dear' [55]) provides the metaphorical transposition of the heart's essential need to wander as well as of the high connectedness of all its avenues, its 'fine-spun threads': 'Tut! said I, are we not all relations?' Like the arteries and vessels which allow the heart to send blood around the whole body, the streets of Paris map out a network of possible 'relations' in which Yorick can experience 'the conviction of consanguinity' (56). In the landscape of the narrative they figure the avenues of imagination and are represented as yet untravelled, undiscovered potentialities. Structurally, the fragmented texture of the narrative tries to follow the sudden emotions of the heart and the resulting vibrations in the mind. As the few straight (that is, avowed) digressions help to point out, the narration embraces the ebb and flow of Yorick's (senti-)mental pulsation, with a high freedom of association and rhythm. Through the coloured glass of Yorick's observation, the world is indeed seen successively 'in yellow, blue, and green, running at the ring of pleasure' (41).

Unlike his predecessors in the genre, Sterne – who, like Diderot, constantly seeks a natural, spontaneous and conversational tone – refuses to order his material into artfully conceived plots, with symphonic beginnings and endings, and the final resolution of initial tensions. Life is just not like that; emotional tension and its consequences on behaviour are essentially erratic in nature and follow the internal logic of our private sensoriums. Both in its individual stories and in the whole setting, the book avoids questions of beginning and end, inviting us to understand their irrelevance. Once the body begins to feel, only death will interrupt its vibrations. Ann Jessie Van Sant noted how Sterne substituted an *in*vestigation of the interior world of private feeling, as mediated by the body and the senses, to an *ex*ploration of the outside world, which is traditionally the purpose of travel narratives: 'For Yorick, in quest of melancholy adventures means in search of exquisite sensations. . . . In *A Sentimental Journey*, not only is sensation the basic unit of experience; it replaces adventure as the basic unit of narrative.'[23]

Communication and conversation are reduced to essentials, like precipitates of experience: with the ladies, a few vibrant words, woven into minimalist dialogues; with the men, delicate conversations, with their punctuation of tears, sighs and bows, in which most of the meaning is conveyed between the lines. Such an internalisation of discourse, such a privatisation of experience, are perceptible in the recurring pattern of some of the main scenes of the book. With Madame de L***, the interview is gradually 'translated' from outside the remise door to the inside of the chaise; with the Grisset, the conversation imperceptibly glides from outward directions (the outside world) to inward explorations (the feeling of the pulse); the conversation with the fair *fille de chambre* moves from the rue de Nevers to the privacy of Yorick's hotel room; and the reader is warmly encouraged to consider the possibility of a similar movement from outside to inside in the last scene of the novel with the Piedmontese lady, the climax of the book: 'So that when I stretch'd out my hand, I caught hold of the *Fille de Chambre's* . . .' (104).

The sentimental, erotic teasing is also a means of exploring the limits of artistic representation and of going beyond simple feats of deliberate artificiality, as can occasionally be found in *Tristram Shandy*. In that first novel, Sterne had playfully shown the numerous communication barriers that make any verbal exchange so problematic. Such awareness is ultimately tragic because it signals the fundamental impossibility of any conversation other than with oneself (if that). The *Journey* is an attempt not to ignore but to bypass this difficulty, and sentimental travelling is 'a quiet journey of the heart in pursuit of NATURE, and those affections which rise out of her, which make us love each other—and the world, better than we do' (71). As Yorick had previously remarked, 'there are worse occupations in this world *than feeling a woman's pulse*' (44).

The enigmatic first sentence of the narrative – '——THEY order, said I, this matter better in France—' (3) – might wish to signal the advantages of travelling 'abroad', since such a journey excludes more or less radically and immediately the fluidity of verbal communication, reducing it to simple non-syntactic keywords (as any embarrassed tourist has experienced), while conversely, to compensate for it, it encourages the exploration of new forms of contact – the exchange of snuffboxes or the feeling of the pulse, for example. To invite the reader to accept what he calls 'the mere *Novelty of my Vehicle*' (10), Yorick makes use of a non-verbal form of language, that of the body, with its complex syntax of caresses, looks and sighs, which escapes the possibilities of verbal language:

> There are certain combined looks of simple subtlety—where whim, and sense, and seriousness, and nonsense, are so blended, that all the languages of Babel set loose together could not express them—they are communicated and caught so instantaneously, that you can scarce say which party is the infecter. (46)

The scene with the fair *fille de chambre*, aptly entitled 'The Temptation' (76–8), has a remarkably visual quality, not only in that it is mainly descriptive and centred around a few carefully selected and delineated objects (the pen, the desk, the bed, the purse, the strap) but also because it accurately records the bodily traces of emotions (the blush, the trembling of the hands, the fidgeting with the pen, the holding of hands, the brushing of the neck, the lifting of the foot). What we primarily have here is the duet of two bodies reacting like musical instruments to each other's vibrations. The sexual charge of their encounter is teasingly displaced by Sterne onto the metaphorical objects that symbolise them, both in their professional and sexual capacities: Yorick and his pen, the *fille de chambre* and her purse. She comes to his room to attend to his 'writing', and when he is too nervous to use his 'pen', she offers him the ink to dip it into. The minimalist dialogue is a masterpiece of double entendre: 'I have nothing, my dear, said I, to write upon.—Write it, said she, simply, upon any thing.— . . . If I do, said I, I shall perish—' (77). Using his 'pen' would lead Yorick to a form of *petite mort*.

The way Yorick plays with the maid's purse is animated with the same tension, a tension made tangible, textually by the abundant use of dashes, and syntactically by the ambiguous referentiality of the pronoun 'it':

> I'll just shew you, said the fair *fille de chambre*, the little purse I have been making to-day to hold your crown. So she put her hand into her right pocket, which was next me, and felt for it for some time—then into the left.—'She had lost it.'— I never bore expectation more quietly;—it was in her right pocket at last;—she

IMAGINING PLEASURE 103

pulled it out; it was of green taffeta, lined with a little bit of white quilted sattin, and just big enough to hold the crown—she put it into my hand—it was pretty; and I held it ten minutes with the back of my hand resting upon her lap—looking sometimes at the purse, sometimes on one side of it. (77–8)

Yorick's gaze, linking the purse and the young girl's lap, clearly contributes to the erotic charge. The images which follow, evoking the seam and the tying of the strap, are also strongly connoted and bring in the final climax:

A strap had given way in her walk, and the buckle of her shoe was just falling off—See, said the *fille de chambre*, holding up her foot—I could not for my soul but fasten the buckle in return, and putting in the strap—and lifting up the other foot with it, when I had done, to see both were right—in doing it too suddenly—it unavoidably threw the fair *fille de chambre* off her center—and then— (78)

As the next chapter, 'The Conquest', tries to make us believe, however, the climax is exclusively that of the episode, and Yorick concludes the scene not only chastely walking the girl to the door and giving her an innocent kiss, but also berating the reader for his (it is clearly a male reader we are talking about here) inability to resist the urge of imagining any consummation (78–9). As Tristram Shandy had elegantly put it: 'It is for this reason, an' please your Reverences, That key-holes are the occasions of more sin and wickedness, than all other holes in this world put together.'[24]

Eroticism becomes pornography when it succumbs to the temptation of being more explicit. The absence of a conclusion in the last chapter ('The Case of Delicacy') is most revealing in this regard. Sterne, after devoting the nine volumes of *Tristram Shandy* to the demonstration that it was impossible to finish a story, here continues to distract the reader from any narrative impulse and encourages them not to want to consume, to reach and demand consummation. Unlike that which Hogarth's images staged, imagining the 'after' of a scene like that involving the fair *fille de chambre* is to remain a victim of the weight of the temporality of experience, of a syntactic rhythm of apprehension, that goes against the form of sentimental vibration which the work tries to exalt. Far from encouraging the continuation of the story, the scene wants to figure a suspension in the story, because all narrativity is syntactic, therefore limited in time and potentially dead. Sterne refuses to give the story, or the narrated event, the central and prominent position from which meaning would radiate. By downsizing both plot and realism, it offers a form of sense that differs from its two common synonyms, 'meaning' and 'direction'. Sense in Sterne is found in his extension of the territory of fiction the 'pleasures' of which the book's assumed incompleteness leaves each reader to imagine.

In a way, *A Sentimental Journey* is like a new *Embarkation for Cythera*, a nostalgic journey of suspended sentimental exchanges, at a time when the whirlwind of modern history was gathering momentum, when, as we saw with Defoe, economic exchange became the core of all social conversation, at a time of ruthless commodification. With a touch of desperate humour, Sterne, living in a small village in Yorkshire, attempts to defy that constitutive feature of the modern capitalist and commercial world: the closing of transactions. Poetically, by means of the sketch or the vibration,[25] he tries to make non-conclusion the atemporal centre of his sentimental experiments, in a

104   FRÉDÉRIC OGÉE

manner remarkably similar to that of fellow amateur musician (they both played the viol) and contemporary artist, Thomas Gainsborough.

Gainsborough's 'kind of magic'

Born in 1727 in the pretty little market town of Sudbury in Suffolk, Gainsborough received his first training in London with the French draughtsman and illustrator Hubert-François Gravelot and then patiently developed his work as a portrait painter, first in Suffolk, then from 1759 in Bath, where all the fashionable came to spend the summer, before finally becoming one of London's adulated stars in the late 1770s.

Like Sterne, Gainsborough takes pleasure in shaking up expectations, in practising his art with the same insolent freedom; similarly, the very texture of his painting is playful, even paradoxical, in that it surreptitiously invites us to be wary of what we see (for instance, *Mr and Mrs Andrews* [1750], his ironic portrait of the pleasures of consummation). His pictures let out traces of the artist, pictorial marks that put the emphasis on their pictoriality. On his death, his colleague and rival Joshua Reynolds – President of the Royal Academy they had both contributed to create – had to admit, with minced words, that Gainsborough's manner, contrary as it was to academic precepts, nevertheless evinced something magical:

> those odd scratches and marks, which, on a close examination, are so observable in Gainsborough's pictures, and which even to experienced painters, appear rather the effect of accident than design . . . this chaos, this uncouth and shapeless appearance, by a kind of magic, at a certain distance, assumes form, and all the parts seem to drop into their proper places . . .[26]

The aesthetics of Gainsborough's paintings, made on the eve of the Romantic period, have their origin in the early decades of the eighteenth century, the Addisonian era with which we began this essay. The artist who most inspired the visual universe of Gainsborough is undoubtedly Watteau, who made a brief stay in London in 1719 where he had gone to consult Doctor Richard Mead, an avid collector of his work.[27] It was thanks to Gravelot that Gainsborough learnt about Watteau's mysterious and allusive scenes of couples in parks, enigmatic choreographies and sketchy eroticism, the irony of which he could perceive beneath the ghostly surface (see Plate 6). The imaginary park of the rococo is socially ambiguous, and as Moll and Roxana found out, a far cry from the decorative universe with which it is traditionally associated: the figures parading in beautiful dresses can be ladies or prostitutes, the harlequins who court them gentlemen or swindlers. Vauxhall, Ranelagh or St James's Park, urban transpositions of Watteau's gallant scenes, were new spaces of sociability where real and imaginary overlapped in a complex and volatile role-playing game.

In the early 1770s, when he was in Bath, Gainsborough came into contact with the Linleys, a famous musical family, who commissioned several portraits from him, including that of the two daughters in 1772 (Plate 7). The Linley sisters were singers, very close to the world of the theatre. In his painting, Gainsborough transforms them into gorgeous nymphs in a brilliant, satiny and fantastical pastoral, and while Elizabeth looks away, Mary makes direct eye contact with the artist, and beyond with us, with a frank, intense, somewhat ominous gaze.

Yet it was the elder Elizabeth who scandalised Bath when she fled with the rising star of the English stage, Richard Brinsley Sheridan. As in Sterne's very visual and tangible vignettes, the intimacy in Gainsborough's portraits is often unsettling, yet imbued with the same deep tolerance, a generosity free from any moralistic prudery. When, a dozen years later, Gainsborough painted a large, solitary portrait of Elizabeth Linley-Sheridan (Plate 8), he enshrined his model's resigned sadness within the sweetness of a splendid bower of nature. Now an MP, as famous in politics as he had been in the theatre, Sheridan, like many men of his day, racked up mistresses and debts, while removing his wife from the public eye by putting an end to her singing career. In Gainsborough's painting, Elizabeth, her hands nervously playing with her diaphanous shawl, gazes wistfully at us, seated in a remarkable wind-blown landscape. Gainsborough was one of the first European artists to use landscape not as a mere backdrop or neoclassical Arcadian construction intended to abstract his models from their everyday lives, but as the echo chamber of their torments and interior thoughts, like the chromatic joint powdering of their physical and psychological beings.

We find the same tension in the famous portrait of Perdita (Plate 9), also sitting in the midst of nature. Mary Robinson – nicknamed Perdita after the character in Shakespeare's *The Winter's Tale* she had often impersonated at the Theatre Royal, Drury Lane – was one of those many flamboyant and tragic victims of eighteenth-century Britain and of its stunning but deceptive social mobility. Born into a poor family, she married at the age of fifteen a certain Thomas Robinson, who soon found himself imprisoned for debt, forcing Mary to fend for herself, a new Roxana at the end of the eighteenth century, gifted with a certain talent for poetry and the stage. Her first collection of poems was published in 1775 and her abilities as a performer were noticed by actor and theatre manager David Garrick. Success and beauty drew to her a myriad of lovers, including politician Charles James Fox, and playwright and manager of Drury Lane theatre, the (in)famous Richard Brinsley Sheridan, whose marital status we have just mentioned. Like Nell Gwyn (as embodied by Defoe's Roxana) with Charles II a century earlier, Mary Robinson subsequently became one of the many mistresses of the Prince of Wales, the future George IV. When their story started to be rumoured (and caricatured) in the press in 1780, she quit the stage for her new royal role. Gainsborough's portrait of her was commissioned by the prince, but by the time the artist had completed it George had a new mistress, and Mary had lost everything, ending her life as the plaything of a sad series of passing lovers. In Gainsborough's portrait she seems stunned, absent, abandoned against her will in a dreamworld turned nightmare. The tiny carmine touch of the miniature portrait of the Prince of Wales she holds in her right hand seems infinitely distant from that on her lips, the portrait itself looking as if it were about to fall like a dead leaf. The famous stripes for which Reynolds criticised him here allow Gainsborough to infuse his painting with a nervous energy reinforced by the coldness of the blues and greens. Nature harmonises with the feelings of the young woman, not like some conventional rococo decor, but as the chromatic extension of this empathic exchange between artist and model.

The art of Sterne and Gainsborough marks the first culmination and epitome of the English approach to 'the pleasures of the imagination', as Addison had described them. A few years later, Jane Austen's novels, Thomas Lawrence's portraiture and J. M. W. Turner's landscapes were to propose the summation of a century of empiricist experimentation, bringing English literature and art to the top of European creation.

106   FRÉDÉRIC OGÉE

Notes

1. 'Declaration of the Rights of Man – 1789', *The Avalon Project: Documents in Law, History and Diplomacy*, Yale Law Scool, https://avalon.law.yale.edu/18th_century/rightsof. asp (accessed 9 November 2023).
2. John Locke, *An Essay concerning Human Understanding*, 4th edn, ed. Peter H. Nidditch (1700; Oxford: Clarendon Press, 1975), 105.
3. 'I have brought philosophy out of closets and libraries, schools and colleges, to dwell in clubs and assemblies, at tea tables and in coffeehouses.' Joseph Addison, 'No. 10', *The Spectator*, 12 March 1711. *The Spectator* was the product of a deliberate enterprise nourished by the discussions within the Kit-Cat Club in London.
4. Gérard Genette, *The Work of Art: Immanence and Transcendence*, trans. G. M. Goshgarian (Ithaca: Cornell University Press, 1997).
5. Joseph Addison, 'No. 412', *The Spectator*, 23 June 1712.
6. William Hogarth, *The Analysis of Beauty*, ed. Ronald Paulson (1753; New Haven: Yale University Press, 1997), 32–3.
7. Henry Fielding, *Tom Jones*, ed. John Bender and Simon Stern (1749; Oxford: Oxford University Press, 1996), 68.
8. See also Lady Mary Wortley Montagu's 1724 *Epistle from Mrs Yonge to Her Husband*, based on a real case: 'For wives ill used no remedy remains, / To daily racks condemned, and to eternal chains. / From whence is this unjust distinction grown?' (lines 23–5). Lady Mary Wortley Montagu, *Epistle from Mrs Yonge to Her Husband*, in *British Women Poets of the Long Eighteenth Century: An Anthology*, ed. Paula R. Backscheider and Catherine E. Ingrassia (Baltimore: Johns Hopkins University Press, 2009), 278.
9. Daniel Defoe, *Roxana: The Fortunate Mistress*, ed. David Blewett (1724; London: Penguin, 1982), 187.
10. Ruth Perry, *Women, Letters, and the Novel* (New York: AMS Press, 1980), 62.
11. Defoe was also the author of numerous important books on economics.
12. On the culture of cross-dressing in eighteenth-century England, see Terry Castle's definitive *Masquerade and Civilization: The Carnivalesque in Eighteenth-Century English Culture and Fiction* (Stanford: Stanford University Press, 1986); as well as her 'The Culture of Travesty: Sexuality and Masquerade in Eighteenth-Century England', in *Sexual Underworlds of the Enlightenment*, ed. G. S. Rousseau and Roy Porter (Manchester: Manchester University Press, 1987), 156–80.
13. Joseph Addison, 'No. 8', *The Spectator*, 9 March 1711.
14. Lemmuel Gulliver [Henry Fielding], *The Masquerade, a Poem* (London: J. Roberts and A. Dodd, 1728), line 10.
15. On the issue of anonymity, see Mark Vareschi, *Everywhere and Nowhere: Anonymity and Mediation in Eighteenth-Century England* (Minneapolis: University of Minnesota Press, 2018).
16. One version is in the Fitzwilliam Museum, Cambridge (UK), the other in the Getty Museum, Los Angeles (USA).
17. Hogarth, *The Analysis of Beauty*, 42.
18. See, for instance, his *Le fils ingrat* (1777) and *Le fils puni* (1778), both in the Louvre.
19. Henry Home, Lord Kames, *Elements of Criticism*, 6th edn, ed. Peter Jones, 2 vols (1762; Indianapolis: Liberty Fund, 2005), 1:311.
20. See G. J. Barker-Benfield, *The Culture of Sensibility: Sex and Society in Eighteenth-Century Britain* (Chicago and London: University of Chicago Press, 1992). In the same years, several books were published on this and related questions, with a particular emphasis on Sterne and the 'sentimental novel': for example, John Mullan, *Sentiment and Sociability: The Language of Feeling in the Eighteenth Century* (Oxford: Clarendon Press, 1988); Ann

IMAGINING PLEASURE

Jessie Van Sant, *Eighteenth-Century Sensibility and the Novel: The Senses in Social Context* (Cambridge: Cambridge University Press, 1993); Markman Ellis, *The Politics of Sensibility: Race, Gender and Commerce in the Sentimental Novel* (Cambridge: Cambridge University Press, 1996). See also Paul Goring, *The Rhetoric of Sensibility in Eighteenth-Century Culture* (Cambridge: Cambridge University Press, 2004), and Ildiko Csengei, *Sympathy, Sensibility and the Literature of Feeling in the Eighteenth Century* (London: Palgrave Macmillan, 2013).

21. Laurence Sterne, *A Sentimental Journey through France and Italy*, ed. Ian Jack and Tim Parnell (1768; Oxford: Oxford University Press, 2003), 16. Further references parenthetical.

22. Georges Vigarello, *Le sentiment de soi. Histoire de la perception du corps XVIe–XXe siècle* (Paris: Éditions du Seuil, 2014).

23. Van Sant, *Eighteenth-Century Sensibility and the Novel*, 100.

24. Laurence Sterne, *The Life and Opinions of Tristram Shandy, Gentleman: The Text*, 2 vols, ed. Melvyn New and Joan New, The Florida Edition of the Works of Laurence Sterne (1759–67; Gainesville: University Presses of Florida, 1978), 2:737.

25. On the fragmentary quality of Sterne's writing, see Elizabeth Wanning Harries, *The Unfinished Manner: Essays on the Fragment in the Later Eighteenth Century* (Charlottesville and London: University of Virginia Press, 1994), and W. B. Gerard, *Laurence Sterne and the Visual Imagination* (Aldershot: Ashgate, 2006).

26. Joshua Reynolds, 'Discourse 14', in *Sir Joshua Reynold's Discourses* (1788; Chiswick: C. Whittingham, 1830), 132.

27. He died two years later, probably of tuberculosis, but his stay in London left an important mark, notably through Philip Mercier, who arrived in London from Germany in 1716 following the Hanoverian German court, and who undoubtedly served as assistant to Watteau during his stay in the English capital.

6

THE ART OF ARCHITECTURE AND THE FORM OF THE NOVEL

Chris Ewers

The Art of Building

Architecture has rarely been regarded as a key lens through which to understand the early novel, partly because it is so often conceived of as an overarching structure that stands above – and almost separate from – the human. When we think of architecture, we tend to look upwards: to a frieze, a pediment, a vaulted ceiling, a dome. The early novel, by contrast, keeps its eyes fixed to the ground: Daniel Defoe's Moll Flanders or Colonel Jack ducking and diving at street level, Crusoe searching for footprints in the sand. The emergent prose form is partly a response to a new interest in human subjectivity and the lives of ordinary people, who typically inhabit a shapeless, confusing, contingent realm. And yet, of course, one of the other key innovations of the novel is that it places people in a specific built environment for the first time, rather than the 'general and vague' settings of earlier narrative forms.[1] Novels of the period do consider the way humans interact with buildings and interiors, yet this is initially checked by a sense that architecture as an artform is exterior to ordinary lives, projecting instead distance and power.

The fact that the early novel rarely connects to architecture is exacerbated by the emergent form's tendency to describe built environments in ways that are rarely fully realised. One of the challenges of studying novels in this period is to read the significance of these barely described spaces. Cynthia Wall suggests that the seeming blindness to space and detail in the early novel is partly because, for contemporaries, it was so obvious. Wall argues that 'early eighteenth-century readers were able to see – fill out, expand on, rehydrate – the local, immediate signs of a shared culture, a shared visual landscape of meaningful, referential detail'.[2] The spatial turn in literary studies has led to considerable excavation work, bringing these hidden layers to the surface, helped by key texts such as Alistair M. Duckworth's *The Improvement of the Estate: A Study of Jane Austen's Novels* (1971). Karen Lipsedge, for instance, has shown how, for a contemporary reader, the heroine's close connection to her dairy house in Samuel Richardson's *Clarissa* (1747–8) marks her as separate from the rest of her family's economic ambitions.[3]

This need for digging work is partly a consequence of how architecture was conceptualised in the early 1700s. Mark Girouard divides the period into the formal house (1630–1720), the social house (1720–70) and the arrival of informality (1770–1830).[4] The formal house, which dominated the early period of Daniel Defoe, Aphra Behn and Eliza Haywood, rigidly controlled human interaction in palaces and country estates, organised around a hierarchy of rooms, which led progressively to the inner sanctums

THE ART OF ARCHITECTURE AND THE FORM OF THE NOVEL   109

of power. The novel, so interested in connections between people, finds more material within the social and the informal room once people 'spent more time in the common rooms and less in their own apartments'.[5] At the start of *Vathek* (1786), William Beckford's Arabian tale about a fabulously opulent ruler, we are told that Vathek had improved on the magnificent buildings of his predecessors by adding 'five wings, or rather other palaces, which he destined for the particular gratification of each of the senses'.[6] Beckford points to the hedonism of his protagonist, but this is also a reminder that architecture is deeply enmeshed with the body, where buildings and people interact in specific ways. Novels increasingly start to furnish their rooms and houses with more detail. When, in Jane Austen's *Mansfield Park* (1814), the younger elements of the party to Sotherton escape through a door and step immediately into the grounds, this is part of an increasing connection between interior and exterior, joining 'nature' and house design (previously, the main rooms for sociability were on the first floor). If architecture starts as a distant presence, by the end of the century the human and the house are deeply connected.

A key issue, of course, is what we regard as 'architecture'. Does Crusoe's cave count? In reading *Moll Flanders* (1722) and *Colonel Jack* (1722), is there an architecture of the street? Does Eliza Haywood's *Fantomina* (1725) speak to sites of sociability, and, as its alternative title suggests, place 'Love in a Maze'? What Wall detects as a blindness, where the physical framework of houses and their interiors are not seen, could in fact be a reaction against a form of architecture that keeps the human at a remove, re-envisaging what constitutes the shaping of the built environment. Crusoe, Moll Flanders and Fantomina inhabit spaces in ways that the 'formal house' defined by Girouard actively tried to discourage. The modern mode is to define the discipline in the widest possible sense, where all forms of structure qualify as architecture – from a brick outhouse to a football stadium. This catholic approach is summed up by Léon Krier's simple dictum: 'Architecture and Building are only concerned with creating a built environment which is beautiful and solid, agreeable, habitable and elegant.'[7] The novel emerges as a major prose form in England partly as a response to a period of profound spatial reorganisation: the Great Fire of 1666 and the new geography of London, urbanisation and widening circuits of trade and roads. Yet few in the 1700s would have recognised this as having anything to do with architecture, reserving the term instead for signature buildings. The *Oxford English Dictionary* recognises this shift in meaning, describing architecture as 'the art or science of building or constructing edifices of any kind for human use', but adds that 'architecture is sometimes regarded solely as a fine art' with a 'narrower meaning'. For much of the eighteenth century, this narrower meaning was the dominant one. Johnson's *Dictionary* entry in 1755 simply calls architecture 'the art or science of building', observing that some 'contend that the rules of this art were delivered by God himself to Solomon'. Ephraim Chambers's *Cyclopaedia* (1728) charts a clear progress narrative in terms of the aesthetic hierarchies of building, stating that humans started by making huts and tents, but 'gradually advanced to more regular and stately Habitations'.[8] That the crowning achievement of architecture is to be 'regular' and 'stately' mirrors a period of massive investment in new buildings and country estates (fuelled by colonial trade, Enclosure Acts and improvement to rent rolls, and fortunes made from slavery). The 'high Art' of grand houses and great buildings dominated the conception of what counted as architecture.[9]

In a century where 'art' was a key word, taking in many areas of life we would not think of as artistic today (the art of conversation, the art of politeness, the art of walking), this conception of architecture as 'high art' cannot be underestimated. It was the most elite of all disciplines, often felt to encompass and even subsume the other arts, since a grand house might incorporate a music room, a library, a drawing room, as well as galleries and porticoes for statues, hangings and paintings. It was also a discipline that was increasingly formalised through the work of major figures such as William Kent and Inigo Jones, while others, such as Colen Campbell in *Vitruvius Brittanicus* (1725) or Robert and James Adam in *Works in Architecture* (1778), were remarkably successful in disseminating their designs and manifestos in print as well as practice. Lee Morrissey, who develops Peter Eisenman's argument that 'the distinction between building and architecture depends on "a sign of architecture"', considers the idea that to qualify as architecture, a building must provide an extra, aesthetic component, a 'sign' that it is special, or different.[10] In this reading, architecture involves an extra signification that moves beyond the functional. This helps Morrissey to link architecture and literature, observing: 'architecture is made of building materials, in the same way that literature is made of words. Anytime that one sees more than building materials arranged to provide shelter or to shape a space, one is falling for the metaphor'.[11] Thinking in these terms, it is possible to see architecture as a symbol of power, a fixed communication projecting outwards at the start of the century, only for it gradually to emphasise the interaction and connection between the human and the building. As the relationship moves closer to a dialogue than an emblem, novels start to change the architectural landscape. The Gothic novel is partly responsible for the 'ancient' follies that appeared like mushrooms in English parklands, while Sir Walter Scott's *Waverley* novels created their own Highland style, exemplified by Abbotsford.

Morrissey's focus on the 'rhetorics' of architecture is certainly in accord with a period when formal choices (of a building style, or a type of literary composition) had clear political and cultural connotations. Morrissey argues that when Alexander Pope decided to build a villa at Twickenham in the 1720s, it was a pointed rejection of the great houses of London.[12] Changes in taste were politically complex, and these cultural shifts took many forms in the period, involving ideas of the sublime and the picturesque, the neoclassical revival promoted by the architects Robert and James Adam from the 1760s onwards, fashions for faux rustic cottages towards the end of the century, or constant debates about landscape gardening. The major tectonic plates, however, are arranged around two architectural styles: the Classical and the Gothic. Johnson's *Dictionary* speaks to this fault line that runs throughout the period:

> Under Augustus, architecture arrived to its greatest glory; but it afterwards dwindled by degrees, and at last fell with the western empire, in the fifth century, when the Visigoths destroyed all the most beautiful monuments of antiquity; and a new manner of building took its rise, called the Gothick, coarse, artless, and massive.[13]

For Johnson, the Classical mode is unsurpassed, though by mid-century the Gothic was increasingly re-evaluated and championed. In some periods, literary and architectural movements are in accord: there are modernist novels and modernist buildings, as well as postmodern texts and postmodern architecture. In the eighteenth-century novel, this convergence between the art of building and the art of writing is centred on the Gothic, where the spaces of ruined abbeys, old castles and dungeons effectively shape Gothic narratives. Perhaps one of the questions to ask is: why is there a connection here, but not elsewhere? Should we be wary of expecting two such disparate artforms to speak to each other in any simple, shared language? Why does the Gothic novel cohere as a term, while the Classical novel is much more elusive, barely registering as a trace?

Locating the Classical Novel

When the new extended prose form, which we now call the novel, started to emerge in England in the early 1700s, the dominant architectural style was Classical, with its marble columns, pediments, architraves and appropriation of temple fascias, arranged in mathematically exact proportions. The most influential surviving classical text, Vitruvius's *De architectura* (c.27 BC), was endlessly modified and translated by later writers such as Alberti, Palladio and, in England, Sir Henry Wotton. Vitruvius emphasised the principles of timelessness, symmetry and simple grandeur. Robert Adam, the great proponent of the neoclassical, which modified this tradition from the 1760s onwards, observed that the epitome of Classical architecture, the Pantheon in Rome, had a sublime effect, impressing itself upon the viewer: 'the greatness and simplicity of parts fills the mind with extensive thoughts, stamps upon you the solemn, the grave and the majestic'.[14] Classical forms linked the great houses of the aristocracy to ancient Rome and Greece, regarded by the elite as the peak of Western civilisation, which they believed helped cement their right to privilege and authority as the inheritors of this patrician heritage. This is exactly what William Hogarth's Earl Squanderfield points to when he shows off his family tree in the first print of *Marriage A-la-Mode* (1743–5), 'The Marriage Settlement'. The centrepiece is not the loving couple, but a transfer of money from the city Alderman, through his lawyer, to Earl Squanderfield, and then to his architect (Figure 6.1). One of the ironies of this exchange is that neither the Alderman nor the lawyer sees the view of the courtyard and the grand new Palladian building under construction. In a very real sense, though, they have bought for their daughter what the Earl offers them: access to this columned symbol of tradition and lineage.

It is no accident that the city men are focused on the money and the contracts. To understand the art of architecture was to be part of an elite club that excluded the lower ranks. The main qualification for joining was to have experienced the ultimate luxury item, the Grand Tour. Reserved mostly for the sons of the aristocracy and the extremely wealthy, the Grand Tour in the late seventeenth and early eighteenth century provided a grounding in understanding Classical buildings and ruins. Many owners of great houses could return home boasting high levels of knowledge about architecture, such as the Earl of Burlington, the 'Architect Earl', credited with introducing the Palladian style to Britain in the 1720s. Until the Royal Institute of British Architects was founded in 1834, familiarity with the antique was the key qualification for becoming an architect. Architects were self-appointed: Sir John Vanbrugh moved swiftly – and with equal success – from writing plays to designing Castle Howard and Blenheim Palace. Vanbrugh was not alone; Pope took a great interest in the design of his villa at Twickenham, while Horace Walpole and Beckford were also fascinated by architecture. It may seem strange to a modern reader, who would not expect Margaret Atwood to design a Canadian eco lodge, but there was

Figure 6.1 William Hogarth, *The Marriage Contract* (1743). Plate 1, *Marriage A-la-Mode*. Engraved from the original by Richard Earlom. Courtesy of the Lewis Walpole Library, Yale University.

a clear correlation between the author of a text and the author of a building. Wotton, in his influential *The Elements of Architecture* (1624), stated that for the architect 'glory doth more consist, in the Designement and *Idea* of the whole *Worke*, and his truest ambition should be to make the *Forme*, which is the nobler Part (as it were) triumph over the *Matter*'.[15] Vanbrugh, dividing his plays into acts and conforming to a degree with the dramatic unities, and Pope with his metrical 'numbers' and the ordered simplicity of his couplets, translated their skill in the form of their compositions into the spatial form of buildings. Form, as Adrian Forty argues, was for most of the eighteenth century interchangeable with a signifying 'shape', connected to 'the belief that "form" exists to transmit meaning'.[16]

The emergent prose form, however, posed different questions. This was partly due to the fact early novelists, unlike poets or playwrights, were rarely from the highest ranks. If the Grand Tour, the finishing touch on the education of the elite, was chiefly responsible for promoting the taste for the Classical, the early novel reads more like Defoe's *A Tour Thro' the Whole Island of Great Britain* (1724–7), which is as interested in goods, industry, markets and roads as the great houses that dominated previous observations. Architecture is easy to find in poetry, with its long tradition of estate poems such as Pope's 'Epistle to Burlington', and in art, where the Wedgwood 1,000-piece dinner set the 'Green Frog Service' consisted of views of castles, great estates, cottages and villas; yet the emergent novel rarely fawns on the 'power houses' of the elite.[17] Defoe, whose Dissenting and business backgrounds set him at variance

THE ART OF ARCHITECTURE AND THE FORM OF THE NOVEL 113

with inherited power, prefers the 'middling sort' interests identified by Ian Watt's *The Rise of the Novel* (1957). The shipwrecked Crusoe's 'Country Seat' is a glorified lean-to shelter, and his great house is a cave, suggesting a different perspective on the 'art' of building.[18] The great houses project outwards, just as a pediment in Rome signified the rank of its owner; Crusoe's survival depends on his habitations being hidden from sight. Other waifs and strays such as Moll Flanders and Captain Singleton are more likely to be on the outside of the big houses and civic structures, allowed inside only on sufferance.

It is, however, possible that the novel becomes increasingly Classical as writers start to draw attention to the symmetry and order of their texts. Buildings also increasingly come to the fore. It has often been noted that titles of early novels focus on names (*Robinson Crusoe*, *Betsy Thoughtless*, *Pamela*), only to shift towards structures (physical or ethical), such as *The Old Manor House*, *Nature and Art* or *Mansfield Park*. There is a fascination with the de-structured self in the emergent novel, before a greater mid-century focus on how environment determines identity. In this reading, not only does the novel start to gentrify, like a London postcode, but it also increasingly moves from a focus on pathways to incorporate a fascination with structures. It is notable that the beginning of the crystallisation of the novel as a respectable form coincides with Samuel Richardson's grand house settings in *Pamela* (1740) and *Clarissa* (1747–8) and Henry Fielding's Paradise Hall in *Tom Jones* (1749). The Palladian style dealt in order and perfection, placing its owner as a form of moral epitome, just as Pamela, Clarissa and even Tom Jones have something heroic about them, making them closer to conceptions of the ideal.

Richardson and Fielding anchor their novels to buildings in a way that Defoe's adventurers, inhabiting the margins of society, can never manage. In looking for a Classical novel, *Tom Jones* is perhaps the most likely candidate. It has been described by Dorothy van Ghent as a 'Palladian palace', arranged simply and clearly, spacious and intelligible.[19] The novel divides its eighteen books into three equal parts: six in the country estate, six on the road, and six in the city (an edifice divided in three, the magic number for Classical architecture). The patrician Fielding, as Henry Power has argued, was involved in translating the past Roman and Greek forms into his narrative, moving towards a 'comic Epic-Poem in Prose'.[20] Central to this is the architectonics of *Tom Jones*, its building blocks foregrounded by the metafictional introductory chapters to each book, which point out how the narrative is being shaped and built on certain principles. Fielding, in looking to move the novel closer to the epic (to give it a Classical heritage), uses chapter divisions and books like columns, and engineers symmetrical relations between characters and events, to leave Samuel Taylor Coleridge famously exclaiming: 'What a master of composition Fielding was.'[21] Fielding's Dedication is addressed to George Lyttleton, the Cofferer to the Household, who was to turn Hagley into an impressive Palladian house, and also thanks the Duke of Bedford and Ralph Allen for their patronage. Like a visitor shown into a grand hall, this portico is intended to convince the reader of the quality to come, positioned at the 'very entrance on this work'.[22]

Tom Jones also places the description of a great house near the beginning, in a chapter which highlights some of the reasons why the Classical is more likely to connect to the novel in a form of productive friction rather than simple translation. If the Classical tradition proposes a sense of cosmic harmony born out of patrilinear order, where a single head rules (God, king, estate owner, husband), the prospect from the house, with Mr Allworthy shining his beneficence on the valleys and villages below, suggests Paradise Hall is aptly named. Great houses were built to dominate the view, to extend their influence to the wider community. Yet the perfections of Paradise Hall are suspect and are only described in chapter 4, one chapter after we have been told that a bastard child has been laid in Mr Allworthy's bed, and one chapter before his housekeeper, Mrs Wilkins, descends like a bird of prey to terrorise the local populace and discover the (female) culprit. Paradise Hall is also a mixed structure, seemingly Gothic, and yet also imbued with Classical virtues:

> The Gothic style of building could produce nothing nobler than Mr Allworthy's house. There was an air of grandeur in it that struck you with awe, and rivalled the beauties of the best Grecian architecture; and it was as commodious within as venerable without. (36)

Fielding's own technique similarly joins Classical beauties with the particularities of Gothic turnings and complexities; the imposing clarity of the edifice of the novel does not match the reading experience, with its misdirections.

The novel, of course, always resists static conceptions, even in a text as committed to stable values and providential ordering as *Tom Jones*. The sublime simplicity of the Classical does not sit easily with the emergent novel form, which constantly alters positions and perspectives. Fielding's text is a perfect example of how readers need to have a mobile conception of judgement in order to understand the contingent nature of characters such as Tom, Mr Square and Black George. Compared to the stricter rules of poetry and drama, the prose sentence has no exact rules; it can go anywhere and do anything. In *Tom Jones*, the reading experience is also explicitly imagined as a journey. The narrator's final trope to explain the writer–reader compact is that they are like two strangers travelling together in a stagecoach, who become better acquainted as they move from stage to stage. This is far from the awe inspired by the vertical axis of Classical architecture, offering instead a horizontal comradeship. The novel is the child of mobility, which puts it at variance with Classical stability. Paradise Hall takes up just a third of *Tom Jones*; the second section goes on the road; the final third lands in London. Fielding's novel bears out Rosalind Williams's observation that 'the outstanding feature of the modern cultural landscape is the dominance of pathways over settlements', adding that streets and highways increasingly gain more attention than 'the square, market, forum, or particular buildings'.[23] Architecture, so fixed and formal at the start of the century, increasingly speaks to the type of movement that so fascinates the novel form.

Many critics, such as Simon Varey, Rosa Mucignat, Nancy Armstrong and Peter de Bolla, have detected a shift in the representation of space and architecture after mid-century, where buildings started to gain greater agency and, in de Bolla's formulation, 'something recognizable as precisely a *culture* based on the visual, on modalities of visualization', came together in such a way that it became possible to 'identify something called visual *culture*'.[24] Perhaps the most ambitious attempt to connect architecture and the novel is Wall's *Grammars of Approach*, which suggests mobility is introduced into the way houses are viewed, centring on the increasing importance of the 'approach'. Wall's imaginative reading, which ties together changes in architecture, typography and sentence structure, argues that thinking in the period becomes increasingly 'prepositional'. Wall does this by analysing the changing nature of the approach to the house, outlining a gradual shift from the stately home being placed front and centre, which ensured that the object (signifying the power of the landowner) dominated the view, to a winding approach, through bends and trees, which put the subject – the observer's experience – to the fore. Compare the two views of Beckford's remarkable creation Fonthill Abbey (Figure 6.2). The first is full-frontal, dwarfing the human, and placing the emphasis on the power of the building, its spire connecting it to the heavens. The second is side-on, still impressive, but now seen from a vantage point that suggests a lower viewpoint, a different scale. The imposing full-frontal view (which retains something of a two-dimensional plan) is here given a third, 'human' dimension. According to James Ackerman, at the start of the century 'the plan dominated architecture as never before or since', functioning cognitively as a top-down, bird's-eye view.[25] From mid-century onwards, stately homes, as Girouard has observed, were drawn differently, no longer 'full-frontal, from a central axis', but obliquely, from an angle.[26] In the process, Wall argues, the focus is moved from the foursquare, monumental aspect of architecture 'to the *in-between*'.[27] In very broad terms, Wall argues that architecture shifts from the sublime – dominating the viewer – to a more human aesthetic, where the spectator's eye composes the scene. Wall gives an example of how these architectural conceptions collide at the level of prose in *Pride and Prejudice* (1813). Elizabeth Bennet takes a serpentine coach drive as she visits Pemberley for the first time, intermittently glimpsing the house as the path bends and curves, only for her to be shocked when she arrives and sees Darcy walk towards her. Wall argues: 'The description of the approach winds round and bursts upon. Darcy is the House, per eighteenth-century architectural theory; Darcy *is* the Noun of the narrative pattern. Elizabeth is the concept of approach.'[28]

Figure 6.2 James Lambert, *Fonthill Abbey, Wiltshire* (1822). Courtesy of the Lewis Walpole Library, Yale University.

116   CHRIS EWERS

The fact that 'Darcy is the House' indicates the importance of gender in considering these shifts in how buildings were represented. Architecture as high art was a masculine preserve, either as a nascent profession or as a popular gentlemanly pursuit, giving the elite male the chance to put his mark on the landscape for generations to come. The French painter André Rouquet observed that 'in England more than in any other country, every man would fain be his own architect', with the operative word being 'man'.[29] In the aptly named *Mansfield Park* (1814), Henry Crawford interests himself in the improvement of various estates and grounds as both a privileged hobby and on the assumption that he is the right person to master and arrange the land as he sees fit. The novel, perhaps, is hot-wired to question these architectural assumptions. As a form that focuses on the interior of the individual and their relationship to the environment, novels tend to be at variance with the monumental, the predetermined, and external, fixed roles. Even when houses are depicted, we often see the ground-level negotiations around these structures. It is notable that female protagonists, from Pamela Andrews to Elizabeth Bennet, typically experience the house and its environs from a low-level view, to some extent renegotiating these male spaces and introducing a sense of becoming, rather than a plan. In *Mansfield Park*, Fanny Price inhabits the rooms of the house that no one else wants, taking over the old schoolroom as she moves down from the white attic. Unlike the public rooms dominated by Sir Thomas Bertram and the rest of the family, she connects to the hidden spaces. The schoolroom is full of bric-a-brac: her cousins' transparencies of romantic scenery, her brother William's drawing of his ship, HMS *Antwerp*, a footstool and some 'profiles' that are deemed unworthy of being displayed downstairs. They are all rhetorical additions to the house, ways of seeing that emphasise imperialism and the accomplishments of the marriage market, or which focus on long-distance networks. Fanny Price, by contrast, makes the room 'most dear' to her by attaching the space to her memories and emotions.[30] In a century that seems defined by an imperative to master space, Fanny is one of the few characters to sidestep this desire for acquisition and control, redefining 'improvement' and suggesting the possibility of an extension of self that is not based on domination. It is a long way from a Classical idea of structure, which tries to stand above contingency, transmitting universal ideals. Here, the human is actively engaged in creating the significance of the building.

Gothic Architecture and the Gothic Novel

This discontent with the Classical had already been registered by the re-emergence of the Gothic from the mid-century onwards. The Gothic novel reverses the outward journey of a Tom Jones by sending its protagonists inwards to explore the rooms of old manor houses, ruined abbeys and castles, with the occasional 'subterranean passage' thrown in for good measure.[31] The Gothic reframes the epic male odyssey with an interior voyage, often allowing women to adventure in a more respectable domestic setting. The great Gothic novel factory, the Minerva Press, features a series of female heroines encountering forbidding spaces, such as *The Castle of Wolfenbach* (1793). The Gothic novel also sends the protagonist back to interrogate origins of authority, often to discover the unequal power structures that allowed the great house to become a symbol of patriarchy. In Walpole's foundational Gothic novel, *The Castle of Otranto* (1764), we are surely meant to laugh at masculine hegemony when the villain Manfred

THE ART OF ARCHITECTURE AND THE FORM OF THE NOVEL 117

starts to lose control, unbolting the castle doors when confronted by 'the knight of the gigantic sabre' (57). The Gothic has long been credited with bringing an interest in the past into the orbit of the novel, just as architecture always foregrounds a connection with what has gone before; buildings claim a posterity beyond the usual expectations of a human lifespan. Castles, abbeys, halls, great houses, even cottages, are all involved in a haunting of the present. It is no accident that *The Castle of Otranto* begins with Manfred's son Conrad 'buried under an enormous helmet' (18), since almost all houses subject their inhabitants to lines of force that are hard to escape. The helmet, like a giant statue, crushes the heir with the weight of expectation (of chivalry, of martial power, of lineage), just as so many characters have to accommodate themselves to the traditions and spaces of a structure built long ago.

The Gothic novel also traces a shift in British ideas about its own architectural legacy, where what was once described by Johnson as 'coarse, artless, and massive' is viewed as natural, native and impressive. The Goths, so long reviled as barbaric, were increasingly re-evaluated. The Ancient Britons and Anglo-Saxons formed a British Gothic tradition, in step with an increasing celebration of a less polished yet more natural native culture, which no longer needed to see itself as an imitation or pale heir to Rome and Greece. In 1749, the same year Fielding published his Palladian *Tom Jones*, the youngest son of his bête noire Sir Robert Walpole started to Gothicise his house at Strawberry Hill by adding turrets, crenelations and cloisters. It is tempting to range these two great modes of architecture in a series of polar opposites: rational/emotional, Tory/Whig, elite/democratic, imperial/feudal, simple grandeur/terror. Such binaries need to be treated warily, as Nick Groom points out: 'The Gothic myth was rooted in antiquity and antiquarian politics; it celebrated English history as progressive, Protestant, and parliamentarian; but it was also guiltily aware of its violent and bloody past.'[32] The Gothic could speak to a mythical, feudal connection between master and servant, emphasising mutual, shared obligations between high and low. It could also be seen as anarchy, especially after the shock of the French Revolution in 1789. The Classical, as James Gillray suggests in his 1796 print *The Contrast, or Things as They Are*, is seen as a bulwark of order, holding up the pillars of the English constitution, compared to the Gothicised ruins of revolutionary change (Plate 10). Gillray works in binaries, but again architectural forms are complex signifiers. With growing fears that riot and revolt might cross the Channel, the fashion for Gothic castles, turrets, towers and battlements could just as easily have a defensive, counter-revolutionary edge.

The re-evaluation of the Gothic created new options, both for architecture and the novel. Strawberry Hill (Figure 6.3) was the inspiration for *The Castle of Otranto*, tracing an umbilical cord between Gothic architecture and the nascent Gothic novel, with Horace Walpole teasing in the preface to the first edition that 'the author had some certain building in his eye' (7). In Walpole's tale, the castle is a main character, an overarching force that dominates even the most powerful of human figures, the tyrannical Manfred, who vainly tries to subject all around him to his will. The castle materialises giant objects, makes doors and escape routes mysteriously available, interacts with its inhabitants and communicates mood and atmosphere, with 'wind . . . whistling through the battlements in the tower above' (38) being mistaken for a human voice. As Mikhail Bakhtin has argued, the chronotopes (the time-space characteristics) of the Gothic tend to shape narrative in certain directions:

The castle is the place where the lords of the feudal era lived ... the traces of centuries and generations are arranged in it in visible form as various parts of its architecture, in furnishings, weapons, the ancestral portrait gallery, the family archives and in the particular human relationships involving dynastic primacy and the transfer of hereditary rights.[33]

The spaces of the castle help knot together the genre of the Gothic. The dungeons and secret passages point to subconscious levels and proto-Freudian encounters, the castle walls emphasise tropes of incarceration and liberty, figuring an often oppressive, limiting patriarchal structure, and the feudal associations of castles and abbeys encourage an engagement with the past.

The Gothic also tends to elicit a different type of response from its audience. Walpole argued: 'One must have taste to be sensible of the beauties of Grecian architecture; one only wants passions to feel Gothic. . . . Gothic churches infuse superstition – Grecian, admiration.'[34] Increasingly the novel became an affective machine; while the sentimental mode prompts the reader to put the book down and contemplate moments of sadness, the Gothic produces horror and hooked, anxious page-turners. Mark Blackwell brilliantly describes the narrative 'rollercoaster' of the Gothic narrative, the way it slows and speeds up, leaving the reader on the edge of a drop for as long as possible.[35] The architecture of a castle helps to shape this; the thresholds that open to side rooms, and dark rooms that defy immediate legibility, are very different to bright drawing rooms.

Figure 6.3 *Strawberry Hill* (c.1822). Courtesy of the Lewis Walpole Library, Yale University.

THE ART OF ARCHITECTURE AND THE FORM OF THE NOVEL   119

The turn of a corner in the castle characteristically shapes a turn in the narrative. This rollercoaster analogy suggests the degree to which the Gothic undoes the fixity of the domestic; we are presented with a house in motion – an arras that moves in the wind, candlelit animations, a dimly perceived shape. In *The Castle of Otranto*, the emphasis on cause and effect often manifested in the emergent novel is changed to a mode of surprise. This is matched by Manfred's own shifts in tone. At one point he starts to feel shame for his actions, but it takes just one paragraph until 'the next transition of his soul' changes to 'exquisite villainy' (36).

The legibility of the Classical is replaced by a wilful Gothic obscurity, a false trail of passageways and objects that promise to reveal secrets, but rarely do – like the figure behind the veil in Ann Radcliffe's *The Mysteries of Udolpho* (1794). The structure of the Gothic novel again borrows from Gothic architecture and its overload of fretwork, cornices and hangings. For the Adam brothers, 'when the eye is distracted, worn out, the subject loses patience with itself, becomes fractured, fragmentary'.[36] What they regarded as a failing was taken by Gothic novels as a structuring principle. Beckford's Oriental-Gothic hybrid *Vathek* is a restless text, lacking a centre, its panoply of palaces and pavilions reflecting the protagonist's unsustainably extended desires. It is tempting to make a connection between Beckford's writing and his architectural ambitions. Beckford, who inherited great wealth from the proceeds of slavery, translated this into a fantasy of his own, the 'immense, soaring, and, it turned out, structurally unsustainable mansion, Fonthill Abbey'.[37] Vitruvius emphasised proportion, famously fitting the human body inside a circle and insisting on the importance of scale. *Vathek*, like the giant swords and helmets of *The Castle of Otranto*, is not to be limited or restricted, allowing narrative to splinter. This is a deliberate formal choice, speaking to a different conception of identity and knowledge that modifies the possibilities of the novel. A writer such as Radcliffe may provide rational explanations for the supernatural events in the endings of her novels, but the reading experience of doubleness, suspense, the liminal, of an eye unable to rest, cannot be so easily explained away. Morrissey argues that when Walpole's castle self-implodes at the end of his remarkable Gothic novel, it leaves in ruins not only 'an individual building' but 'the idea of proportionate, orderly architecture which had governed British architectural theory for at least the preceding one hundred years'.[38] That may be overstated, considering that the popularity of the neoclassical mode was coterminous with the Gothic, but there is certainly a growing interest in a range of building types and their narrative possibilities. Thomas Love Peacock, who built and fitted out more fictional houses than any other writer (and probably more than most architects), ends the long eighteenth century with *Headlong Hall* (1815), *Melincourt* (1817), *Nightmare Abbey* (1818), *Crotchet Castle* (1831) and *Gryll Grange* (1861). The forms of architecture became hugely varied, and Peacock was fascinated by how these connected to narrative and the novel.

Architecture and the Temporalities of the Novel

Space is, of course, also linked to time, and I would like to finish with a speculative conclusion: the novel connects to architecture by using form as a way of encasing temporality. Both the novel and a great house, for all their histories, construction periods and traces of different pasts and genres, are still, in the moment of being made public, stuck in this temporality forever.[39] Each novel, and each architectural creation, speaks to its moment of production, while a play, or a poem, has a greater freedom to traverse time. They are 'novel', new; and yet, while representing a present moment, they instantly become the past. De Bolla, in a fine chapter on the significance of Kedleston Hall, argues that 'buildings have an exemplary relation to the etching of time. They register temporality, the passing of time, in very legible ways'.[40] He adds that this history of buildings does not make them museum pieces but instead forces those who inhabit them to confront these 'conceptual spaces' and their temporal associations.[41] De Bolla asks: 'What are we to understand by this forceful act or origination, the marking of time, of history in the monumentality of this building that writes, etched onto its stone fabric, the frozen moment of the present?'[42] Each novel has its precursors and its afterlives, but the original moment of production is always a privileged 'frozen moment', too.

The novel tends to pit the fluidity of its prose and the malleability of its characters against the fixity of a building and what it stands for, but it is perhaps also true that architecture lends some of its solidity to characters and narratives. An archetype – a character founded on a blueprint – is not that dissimilar to the architectural plan. In texts based around structures, such as the Gothic, or a great house novel such as *Mansfield Park*, with its 'state-of-the-nation' significance as an edifice of 'stable values', it is possible that characters have less individuality, their shaping more a form of the subtle ideological patterning identified by Georg Lukács in *The Historical Novel*.[43] Elizabeth Bennet changes her view of Darcy when she sees Pemberley, partly because it helps her reformulate his 'pride' as responsibility, but also because it gives him more substance; like a noun, it enables her to identify what he stands for.

Certainly, there is a persistent structure in the eighteenth-century novel that returns a character, however nomadic, to a building at the end of the final chapter. Tom Jones and Sophia will make everyone in the environs of Paradise Hall happy after their wanderings; few could doubt Pemberley will be a different place under Elizabeth Bennet; Mansfield Park will become less austere under the stewardship of Fanny Price; while Clarissa is brought back to Harlowe Place in sad (and motionless) triumph. When the novel, in its final pages, stretches out to the future, it often returns the protagonist to a building, as if they are being placed beyond change, gaining something of the fixity of the architecture they are being connected to, protected and shored up by these walls and fittings. When, after hundreds of pages journeying through *Tom Jones*, or *Clarissa*, or *Pride and Prejudice* the reader puts the book away, they are left distanced, increasingly able to make out only the skeletal outline – the form, the shape – seeing the text as a structure. Is this different to how we might try to take in or remember Blenheim Palace, or Strawberry Hill? Adrian Forty argues that in trying to represent architecture, language is more useful than drawing, stating:

> It is in the nature of language that words have to be spoken or written in a linear sequence. A drawing, on the other hand, presents its image all at once. In this respect, buildings are more like language than they are like drawings, for they cannot be experienced all at once – they have to be explored by moving through and around them in a sequence.[44]

But when we finish a novel, or when we leave a building, we do have to try to remember it all at once, and it is the shape that tends to leave the biggest imprint. Books

THE ART OF ARCHITECTURE AND THE FORM OF THE NOVEL

increasingly start to live on as an edifice, resembling a mode of architecture where 'the *Forme*' triumphs 'over the *Matter*', and the classics on our shelves are looked up to like the pediments of Classical buildings.

Notes

1. Ian Watt, *The Rise of the Novel: Studies in Defoe, Richardson and Fielding* (1957; London: Pimlico, 2000), 26.
2. Cynthia Wall, *The Prose of Things* (Chicago and London: University of Chicago Press, 2006), 9.
3. Alistair M. Duckworth, *The Improvement of the Estate: A Study of Jane Austen's Novels* (Baltimore: Johns Hopkins University Press, 1971); Karen Lipsedge, '"I was also absent at my dairy-house": The Representation and Symbolic Function of the Dairy House in Samuel Richardson's *Clarissa*', *Eighteenth-Century Fiction* 22, no. 1 (2009): 29–48.
4. Mark Girouard, *Life in the English Country House: A Social and Architectural History* (Harmondsworth: Penguin, 1980).
5. Girouard, *Life in the English Country House*, 205.
6. William Beckford, *Vathek*, ed. Thomas Keymer (1786; Oxford: Oxford University Press, 2013), 3.
7. Cited in David Watkin, *A History of Western Architecture*, 3rd edn (London: Laurence King, 2000), 7.
8. Ephraim Chambers, *Cyclopaedia: or, an Universal Dictionary of Arts and Sciences*, 2 vols (London: James and John Knapton, 1728), 1:129.
9. This definition does start to become broader and more democratic by the close of the century, with Wall observing that 'between 1790 and 1835 over sixty illustrated design books for cottages and small villas were published'. See Cynthia Wall, *Grammars of Approach: Landscape, Narrative, and the Linguistic Picturesque* (Chicago and London: University of Chicago Press, 2019), 55.
10. Cited in Lee Morrissey, *From the Temple to the Castle: An Architectural History of British Literature, 1660–1760* (Charlottesville and London: University Press of Virginia, 1999), 10.
11. Morrissey, *From the Temple to the Castle*, 10. These metaphors have power: Amitav Ghosh wonders how Austen's legacy may have contributed to the clipped green lawns maintained by unsustainable sprinkler systems in places far from Britain. See Amitav Ghosh, *The Great Derangement: Climate Change and the Unthinkable Account* (Chicago and London: University of Chicago Press, 2016), 10.
12. Morrissey, *From the Temple to the Castle*, 64.
13. Samuel Johnson, 'Architecture', in *A Dictionary of the English Language*, 2 vols (London: J. and P. Knapton, 1755), 1:n.p.
14. Cited in Peter de Bolla, *The Education of the Eye: Painting, Landscape, and Architecture in Eighteenth-Century Britain* (Stanford: Stanford University Press, 2003), 167. De Bolla argues that Robert Adam, the great populariser of the neoclassical, effectively repackaged how the Classical appeared to a Grand Tourist, making 'antique Roman culture come alive in the fantasy life of the mid-eighteenth-century British gentleman – enabling the identification of the present through the phantasmic construction of the past' (170–1). For Adam, de Bolla writes, 'in order to stimulate demand for this new look, the eye would need to be educated so that patrons might buy into the public collective fantasy that is the "antique style"' (159).
15. Sir Henry Wotton, *The Elements of Architecture, Collected by Henry Wotton Knight, from the Best Authors and Examples*, 2nd edn (London: I. Bill, 1624), 11–12.

16. Adrian Forty, *Words and Buildings: A Vocabulary of Modern Architecture* (London: Thames & Hudson, 2019), 149. My thanks to Jo Gill at Exeter for alerting me to this text.
17. Girouard, *Life in the English Country House*, 1.
18. Daniel Defoe, *Robinson Crusoe*, 2nd edn, ed. Michael Shinagel (New York and London: W. W. Norton, 1994), 110–11.
19. Dorothy Van Ghent, *The English Novel: Form and Function* (New York: Harper, 1961), 80.
20. Henry Power, *Epic into Novel* (Oxford: Oxford University Press, 2015); Henry Fielding, 'Preface', in *Joseph Andrews* and *Shamela*, ed. Judith Hawley (1742; London: Penguin, 1999), 49.
21. Samuel Taylor Coleridge, 'Table Talk', 5 July 1834, in *Complete Works*, ed. W. G. T. Shedd, 7 vols (New York: Harper and Brothers, 1856), 6:521.
22. Henry Fielding, *Tom Jones*, ed. John Bender and Simon Stern (1749; Oxford: Oxford University Press, 1998), 5. Further references parenthetical.
23. Rosalind Williams, 'Cultural Origins and Environmental Implications of Large Technological Systems', *Science in Context* 6, no. 2 (1993): 380–1.
24. See Simon Varey, *Space and the Eighteenth-Century English Novel* (Cambridge: Cambridge University Press, 1990); Nancy Armstrong, *Desire and Domestic Fiction: A Political History of the Novel* (Oxford: Oxford University Press, 1987); Rosa Mucignat, *Realism and Space in the Novel, 1795–1869* (Farnham: Ashgate, 2013); De Bolla, *The Education of the Eye*, 4.
25. Cited in Morrissey, *From the Temple to the Castle*, 36.
26. Girouard, *Life in the English Country House*, 212.
27. Wall, *Grammars of Approach*, 2.
28. Wall, *Grammars of Approach*, 48.
29. Cited in Morrissey, *From the Temple to the Castle*, 4.
30. Jane Austen, *Mansfield Park*, ed. Kathryn Sutherland, intr. Tony Tanner (1814; London: Penguin, 2003), 141.
31. Horace Walpole, *The Castle of Otranto: A Gothic Story*, ed. Nick Groom (1764; Oxford: Oxford University Press, 2014), 26. Further references parenthetical.
32. Nick Groom, 'Introduction' to Walpole, *The Castle of Otranto*, xv.
33. Mikhail Bakhtin, 'Forms of Time and Chronotope in the Novel', in *The Dialogic Imagination*, ed. Michael Holquist, trans. Caryl Emerson and Michael Holquist (1937; Austin: University of Texas Press, 2006), 246.
34. Horace Walpole, *Anecdotes of Painting in England; with Some Account of the Principal Artists*, 4 vols (Twickenham: Strawberry Hill Press, 1762–3), 1:107–8.
35. Mark R. Blackwell, 'The Gothic: Moving in the World of Novels', in *A Concise Companion to the Restoration and Eighteenth Century*, ed. Cynthia Wall (Oxford: Blackwell, 2005), 149.
36. Cited in De Bolla, *The Education of the Eye*, 181.
37. Thomas Keymer, 'Introduction' to Beckford, *Vathek*, ix.
38. Morrissey, *From the Temple to the Castle*, 130.
39. By contrast, plays may be restaged, or performed afresh, while poetry, despite its essential historical grounding, can often move through the centuries more freely than a novel (possibly because of its greater focus on connections of language).
40. De Bolla, *The Education of the Eye*, 153.
41. De Bolla, *The Education of the Eye*, 153.
42. De Bolla, *The Education of the Eye*, 151.
43. Tony Tanner, 'Introduction' to Austen, *Mansfield Park*, 463. See Georg Lukács, 'The Classical Form of the Historical Novel', *The Historical Novel*, trans. Hannah Mitchell and Stanley Mitchell (1937; London: Merlin Press, 1989), 19–63.
44. Forty, *Words and Buildings*, 39.

7

'THE STATUE CANNOT BE FORMED, UNLESS OUR INCLINATION CONCUR THERETO': STATUARY AND SCULPTURE IN THE EIGHTEENTH-CENTURY NOVEL

M-C. Newbould

SCULPTURE HELD A high position in the estimation of eighteenth-century British connoisseurs. Alongside architecture, it was one of the admired remnants of Greek and Roman antiquity, the ephemeral or degradable elements of which had long since disappeared.[1] Statuary, often aligned with painting in aesthetic discourses,[2] embodied concepts of the ideal form of beauty, and of art's ability not only to capture, but to surpass nature, especially in the sculpted human shape. Classical sculptures – Roman and Greek, originals and replicas – were among the most highly prized souvenirs collected by wealthier British Grand Tourists to adorn their homes and gardens; the trade in such artefacts was big business.[3] Statues of significant national figures (monarchs, prelates and writers) filled Britain's public spaces, too, from churches to parks and squares.[4]

Statues exerted an imaginative force in the eighteenth century as compelling as their impressive physical presence, and which saw them play a poignant role in the discourse of the sister arts in the novel. Of the diverse and complex ways in which this emerges, here I explore two contrasting contexts in which statuary is variously present in prose fiction from the 1740s to the 1790s. First, the metaphor of statuary was regularly applied in descriptions of the female body. Questions of agency and powerlessness arise concerning the oft-discussed male gaze, which reifies the object of its regard and immobilises her as powerless to move of her own accord, as (for instance) Samuel Richardson, Matthew Gregory Lewis and Frances Burney variously explore.[5] In this, sculpture again shares several similarities with painting in that many novels, and particularly the Gothic examples discussed here, employ animated sculptures and paintings to reinforce the uncanny lifelikeness of certain mimetic forms, but also the stereotyped gendered representation of certain protagonists. The statue-woman, possessable yet unattainable, is often both idealised and mocked as a desirable but frigid figure of resistance – a paradox captured in the ongoing association between 'fille de marbre' and 'prostitute'.[6]

By contrast, in contemporary comic fiction – by Henry Fielding, Eliza Haywood and Tobias Smollett, among others – the discourse of statuary recirculates to generate comic effects partly independent of gendered dynamics, but also in ways which fundamentally rely on them. To be 'frozen' like the 'Statue of Surprise' engages with dramatic artforms, especially pantomime and farce, partly to debunk serious stage drama and its pretensions. But the frozen figures of comic fiction are also a humorous version of the (often male) hero of romance for whom beholding a love object temporarily suspends animation, offering a stark counterpart to how the statue motif is adopted in the contemporaneous non-comic fiction discussed here, where villainous pseudo-heroes obsessively admire women they both idolise and violate.

'Sculpture' and 'statue' are, of course, distinct, just as to sculpt a three-dimensional figure is very different from moulding it: one works from the outside in, the other, the reverse. It may be formed of marble, stone, bronze, wood, wax, clay, porcelain, alabaster and more; it may be mocked by one hand, or many; it may represent any thing, from humans to other animals (sometimes together) to mythic creatures or inanimate objects. 'Statue' is the term typically used in the novels I discuss to refer to a human figure depicted either in stone, marble or wax, but also to the idea as much as to the fact of a sculpted form, as the conceptual and tangible dimensions held by the term 'inclination' in the titular quotation suggest.[7] Reality jostles alongside fantasy, as figures are caught in a suspended animation they rarely assume willingly, but which they are more, or less, able to abandon of their own volition.

Cold as Marble or 'Like pliant Wax'?: The Fantasy of the Female Statue

The sculpted human figure is as often male as it is female. Nonetheless, the issues just touched upon – about powerlessness and potency, aesthetic beauty and the real – assert themselves in representations of women's bodies in eighteenth-century novels more than they do those of men. The gendering of statuary in those arenas that brought direct contact with the artform, from continental Grand Tour travel to domestic tourism (among others), is enmeshed within the discourse of connoisseurship, the association of which with crass slang terms[8] suggests how the claim to be appreciating high art also permitted the intense perusal of female bodies, and especially of nudes, depicted on paper or canvas, and in marble, bronze or other lustrous materials that allowed the curvatures of represented flesh to attract the eye with alluring titillation – reinforcing the extent to which Grand Tour travel was as much to do with cultural as with sexual encounters.[9]

As Jana Funke and Jen Grove rightly argue, however, not all representations of the 'sculpted female body' are about 'gendered appropriations' or eroticisation, and, following Katharina Boehm,

> the female body was not merely reduced to an erotic object through its association with antique statuary . . . Far from being a passive object that lacks agency, the female body was seen by male antiquarians as a particularly valuable artefact that acts out, and thereby brings to life, ancient cultural sensibilities.[10]

These are important reminders that discussing the presence of statuary in eighteenth-century culture risks being viewed through the monolens of gender. Nor, indeed, is the statue-woman necessarily immured in stony passivity: some female protagonists take their cue from Hermione, who in *The Winter's Tale* purposely adopts a statue-like form to stimulate her husband's guilt and to assert her own superior moral solidity,

STATUARY AND SCULPTURE 125

attaining an empowerment denied in other contexts. For instance, Unca Eliza Winkfield, the first-person narrator of *The Female American* (1767), is an island castaway
of half-Indian, half-English birth who seeks to impose her own colonising 'civilisation'
on the island's natives through converting them to Christianity by entering into the
statue of a solar deity and speaking as though she herself were the idol, an authoritative voice against their 'bigotry'.[11]

The representation of women's bodies as gazed-upon objects nevertheless provides
a recurrent thread in how certain female protagonists are represented as statues in the
novels I discuss here. They are often immured by the eye of their beholder(s) with a
compromised ability for self-reanimation. The eponymous heroine of Frances Burney's
Evelina (1778), for one, is conscious of being an artefact to be looked at: '"Eye!"
cried the Lord (I don't know his name), "and is there any eye here, that can find
pleasure in looking at dead walls or statues, when such heavenly living objects as I
now see demand all their admiration?"'[12] Burney uses the first-person narrative voice
to ironise these spectatorial transactions by describing the vocal but homogenously
unidentifiable gaggle of apparently knowing male connoisseurs. The overworn but
pithy concept of the male gaze tallies with a mode of perceiving another human being
that, here as elsewhere, fixes the female form in place such that she becomes a static
object viewed at leisure, in the beholder's own time, and from any angle he chooses.
William Gibson's suggestion that the female nude seems to be 'frozen at the moment of
the tease' perhaps unwittingly coheres with the idea Burney satirises, that she is unwill-
ingly fixed in just such a way as to facilitate legitimated voyeurism.[13]

The consciousness of being perceived and the pseudo-tactile act of perception ripple
throughout the woman-as-statue metaphor, where – as Funke and Grove's 'brings to
life' suggests – ideal and real frequently clash and yet teasingly combine in 'dreams and
fantasies of animation'.[14] The best-known precedent is Pygmalion, who (in Dryden's
translation from Ovid), half in love with the figure he sculpts, half with his own art,
fantasises his desire into reality: his 'Idol' seems so lifelike 'One wou'd have thought
she cou'd have stirr'd'.[15] The widespread impact of this myth in the eighteenth century
and beyond has been widely documented.[16] Its significance to statuary in the novel,
as discussed here, revolves around how the lifelike but lifeless sculpture is animated
into being by the eroticised imagination of the creator who gazes upon it. Pygmalion's
desire hovers between disbelief, 'the Cheat' and the 'Deceit' of art, and the credulity
fired by desire: he touches the statue's marble 'Flesh' but, inflamed, 'believes it soft'
(166). As one critical formulation has it of the compelling appeal of the 'state of suspension', it 'has to do with a state of uncertainty between immobility and movement,
the possibility of bodies that are at once immobile and in becoming'.[17] Tactility is
crucial to Pygmalion's desperate attempt to realise his fantasy: he 'embrac'd her naked
Body o'er' so violently, 'straining hard the Statue', that he fears he 'hurt his Maid'
(166). Divine intervention nevertheless catalyses the 'becoming' of metamorphosis:

> Soft, and more soft at ev'ry Touch it grew;
> Like pliant Wax, when chafing Hands reduce
> The former Mass to Form, and frame for Use. (168)

The familiar representation of women and their bodies as pliant, waxlike or mouldable
provides a recurrent theme in the likening of female characters to statues. The frozen

statute that supposedly embodies this fantasy, while enabling the mute female object to be subjected to the moulding of desire, also renders that desire unachievable, impotent, frustrated – unless fulfilled either within the social convention of marriage, or through extra-marital sex that is either complicitly transgressive or attained by force. Not all gazers are male or objects female, and not all uses of the statue metaphor to describe either are violent, criminal or tragic. Nevertheless, it does allow some predatory or malicious characters to possess a gazed-upon object of desire whose reification teeters between that of untouchable idol, frigid marble and pliantly impressionable form.

Richardson's *Pamela: Or, Virtue Rewarded* (1740) anticipates the spectatorial motif which was to concern Burney in *Evelina* by incorporating the language of statuary into the conflicting terms of the heroine's commodification. As she continues to repudiate Mr B., he peevishly elaborates the ekphrastic comparison as another bead on the string of insults he repeatedly hurls at her with one breath – 'hussy', 'boldface', 'wench' – while with the other he tries false promises. He regularly teases Pamela with illusory assurances of her safety, only to rebuke her for her seeming lack of gratitude: 'Do you hear what I say to you, Statue! can you neither speak, nor be thankful?—'.[18] He attempts flattery, saying 'abundance of fond Things to me', but Pamela is all the warier as she overhears him tell his creature, Mrs Jewkes, that 'I will try once more; but I have begun wrong. For I see Terror does but add to her Frost; but, she is a charming Girl, and may be thaw'd by Kindness; and I should have melted her by Love, instead of freezing her by Fear.'[19] Mr B.'s fire/ice dichotomy, plucked from a thousand love sonnets lamenting the cruel mistress's frigidity, also blends lightly with the waxen metaphor Dryden employs in capturing the promising warmth of the 'melted', reanimating statue's body.[20] It also prefigures the impressionability of Pamela as a future wife, on whom her 'master' shall imprint his strictures, rules and ideals of her person and personhood.[21]

The notion of the shapeable woman destined to be an ideal wife jars against the cold, hard substances with which the intractable unmarried girl is frequently associated. Richardson's *Clarissa: Or, the History of a Young Lady* (1747–8) has attracted substantial attention for frequently aligning its heroine with the language of aesthetic representation, including statuary, and the material substances associated with it.[22] This is central to Lovelace's fantasised – and eventual – possession of her body. His initial description of her beauty to Belford, where he praises 'Her wax-like flesh', marries with his assurance of her eventual compliance: 'a woman's heart may be at one time *adamant*, at another *wax*—as I have often experienced', he claims.[23] Yet it is her mother, Mrs Harlowe, who first accuses Clarissa of stony frigidity in resisting marriage with Mr Soames, while she also anticipates the malleable pliability of the resolve she hopes her maternal influence will melt. Clarissa is 'speechless, absolutely speechless', overwhelmed with emotion but unable to 'weep nor speak'. Her mother 'folded the *warm statue*, as she was pleased to call me, in her arms; and entreated me, for God's sake, and for her sake, to comply', an action which animates the narrator back to sentience: 'Speech and tears were lent me at the same time. You have given me life, madam, said I, clasping my uplifted hands together, and falling on one knee . . .' (108).

Clarissa's adoption of the classical posture of supplication – where a figure, often female, pleads for mercy or pity from an authority figure, or seeks sanctuary in a sacred place – confirms the evolution of her story in parallel with the conventions of Greek tragedy.[24] Ancient supplication is inherently allied to statuary, too, in that suppliants

could as frequently clasp the knees of a statue as those of a living person;[25] they temporarily become part of the material substance they clasp and address as if it were a living
person or god, as the formulaic posture of the stone figures found on funerary stele
indicates.[26] These classical associations parallel Clarissa's own metamorphosis into a
statue-like figure, first figuratively and then in actuality. The proximity of her drugged
state to death again plays into the Ovidian ambiguity of the illusory lifelikeness of the
inanimate statue, and testifies to what Patricia Pulham identifies as the intersections
between death and 'burial', animation and eroticism that meet in the 'sculpted body'.[27]
As she anticipates her impending actual death, Clarissa recalls how this inanimacy had
enabled her violation when she fears that Lovelace might 'insist upon viewing *her dead*
whom he ONCE before saw in a manner dead' (1413).[28] Eventually, her corpse becomes
the venerated shrine of a saint, a monument marking metamorphosis from physical
vulnerability to spiritual untouchability.

Clarissa's deathlikeness and her literal demise reinforce eighteenth-century conceptions of death within the novel's Christian context, but they also revolve around the
proximity of life-and-death-likeness in the statue figure. This positions Richardson's
novel as crucial in the development of the lifelike corpse motif that played a significant
role in the Gothic novels that emerged in subsequent decades, as Yael Shapira shows.[29]
The genre's relationship with the plastic arts in particular has garnered widespread
critical attention.[30] Artforms that manipulate the liminality between lifelike and deathlike states and the illusion of animacy – primarily painting and sculpture – appealed
to the teasing sensationalism sought by the Gothic aesthetic and its reliance on various
iterations of suspension (of fear, of belief, of animation). Artworks decorate the austere architectural edifices that often feature in this type of fiction, including ancestral
homes riddled with Daedalian interior spaces, and decayed religious structures sheltering the relics and remnants of defunct (or at least neglected) devotional practices:
churches and crypts housing corpses, overseen by the once-living or the mythologically
saintly, figuratively represented in statues and monuments.[31] The stony piety of such
sculptural figures provides an analogue for the imperilled virtue or lives (or symbolic
death through lost virtue) of the protagonists that feature in Gothic fiction, where the
slippage between animacy and its suspension plays out repeatedly in metaphors of the
human artwork, especially when the narrative of virtue in distress exploits the idol-
woman motif with macabre fascination.

Gothic fiction firmly established its investment in animated artworks as part of the
deceptive probability of the genre in its founding text, *The Castle of Otranto* (1764),
which teases boundaries between the seeming and the real to heighten suspense and
to intensify troubling uncertainty over what to believe. Famously, Walpole brings to
life the portrait of Ricardo, the ancestral patriarch, to forbode the future doom of his
villainous heir Manfred, with *Ruddigore*-like melodramatic excess. Upon Manfred
proclaiming his intention to marry his dead son's betrothed, Isabella, 'the portrait
of his grandfather . . . began to move'; 'he saw it quit its pannel, and descend on the
floor with a grave and melancholy air'.[32] Lifelike art comes to life in a fantastically
oppressive moment that relies on simultaneous spectatorial enthralment and horror;
indeed, 'portraiture . . . tends to purposely vacillate between the two realms' of art and
life in the Gothic's manipulation of the uncanny, Jakub Lipski writes.[33] The portrait's
figure 'marched sedately' (26) about the chamber, giving three-dimensionality to the
image depicted on canvas, and closely allying the portrait to the statue representing a

revered ancestor, Alfonso the Good, which is animated in the novel's opening scene.[34] Manfred's son Conrad is dashed to pieces by a mysterious giant helmet, like that of the 'figure in black marble' (20) representing Alfonso in the nearby church; the statue's fragmented body parts provide a recurrent thread foreboding damnation throughout the ensuing scenes, a novelistic equivalent of *Don Giovanni*'s Commendatore. The impact on the 'spectators' of Walpole's vivified statue is telling: Conrad's mother faints and is taken to her chamber 'more dead than alive', while Manfred 'fixed his eyes' on the helmet (as he later does on Ricardo's portrait), temporarily suspended from moving or speaking at the 'horror of the spectacle' (19).[35] Through its inexplicable enlargement and motility the marble fragment briefly imposes a deathlike state upon the still living.

This supernatural phenomenon holds a powerful sway over the assembled peasant 'mob', too, who generate gossipy 'conjectures' as to its meaning (20–1). Superstition – especially among the so-called lower orders – is integral to the anti-Catholic sentiment frequently promoted by British Gothic novels, and in which painted icons and statuary, central to the maligned 'Romish rituals' of venerating holy figures, such as the Virgin Mary and the saints, play a key part. Although not immune to such crude stereotyping, Ann Radcliffe nevertheless sought to elevate the Gothic by providing non-supernatural explanations for seemingly inexplicable phenomena: famously, a wax sculpture is so lifelike that Emily St Aubert, the heroine of *The Mysteries of Udolpho* (1794), initially believes it to be a corpse. Whereas Radcliffe uses Emily's *éclaircissement* as an opportunity for consolidating the passage from superstition to enlightened reason, Matthew Gregory Lewis's *The Monk* (1796) – a novel heavily encumbered with statues and anti-Catholic sentiment alike – exploits the potential for distressed virtue to inhabit life-and-death-likeness to create a highly sensationalised version of *Clarissa*'s story.

Lewis's eponymous protagonist, Ambrosio, provides a Gothic equivalent to Lovelace, now as the come-to-life saintly figure who conceals diabolical desires, an eighteenth-century version of *Measure for Measure*'s ironically named Angelo. Ambrosio idolises to the point of obsessive fantasy a woman who turns out to be his own sister, his lustful thoughts significantly having taken shape early on, ironically, when contemplating the painting of a beautiful Madonna to discipline his resistance to 'Objects of temptation'.[36] On the first occasion of his attempted rape, Ambrosio is interrupted by Antonia's mother, Elvira, who wakes from a nightmare 'just in time to rescue her from the grasp of the Ravisher: His shame and her amazement seemed to have petrified into Statues both Elvira and the Monk: They remained gazing upon each other in silence. The Lady was the first to recover herself' (301). Petrification, where individuals are momentarily so frozen by horror that they seem to have turned to stone, creates a simultaneous vulnerability and impermeability. The paralysis of these two inanimate individuals, each acting synchronously as mirror-Gorgons, with melodramatic posturing that betrays Gothic's theatrical dimensions, suggests either suspended potency or tense magnetic equilibrium.[37] There is not just one gazer and one object but one of each, rendered impotent by their petrification, and yet with the capacity for potency only temporarily suspended. Elvira is the first to 'recover', but victory is short lived: it is partly by murdering Elvira that Ambrosio can finally realise his perverse desires in a scene of prurient horror which, as Laura Miller suggests, attains its force through using imagery of the 'marble statue' to reinforce underlying associations with necrophilia.[38] After drugging and imprisoning Antonia in a crypt,

STATUARY AND SCULPTURE 129

Ambrosio (unlike Lovelace) 'impatiently' waits for her to regain consciousness, as he does not feel his triumph will be as enjoyable if she is insensible:

> By the side of three putrid half-corrupted Bodies lay the sleeping Beauty. A lively red, the fore-runner of returning animation, had already spread itself over her cheek; and as wrapped in her shroud She reclined upon her funeral Bier, She seemed to smile at the Images of Death around her. (379)

When Antonia does revive, her revulsion paradoxically renders her statue-like, hence less 'useful' for Ambrosio's purpose: '"Unhand me, Father! . . . Why have you brought me to this place? Its appearance freezes me with horror!"' (382). In a reversal of Clarissa's fate, where deathlike inanimacy facilitates her rape, as a now-animated 'image of death' Antonia is wrenched away from the protection of being solely statue-like, in stony untouchability, to emerge as a very tangible victim.[39] But the idol becomes tainted such that Ambrosio is revolted immediately he has attained his ends; he 'dart[s] upon her looks of hate' (384) and is 'at once repulsed from and attracted towards her' (387).

Ambrosio, like Lovelace, breaches the fantasy of the idealised woman-statue: the seemingly impermeable substance of her body, once penetrated, destroys the fabric of the tempting illusion of her untouchability, and the effect is to repel in equal measure to the former attraction. Yet for all that Antonia is the victim of a vicious sexual crime, a partial exculpation underlying this moment is also troublingly offered to the reader – as, to some degree, might be perceived in Clarissa's black transaction. On the one hand, Antonia's inviting and vulnerable beauty is held partly responsible for inspiring what is presented as a human if grotesquely distorted lust, yanking the admittedly flawed man of God from his calling and incurring immediate repentance. It may seem a stretch to suggest that Lewis condones Ambrosio's act, or reverses the crime upon Antonia in a twisted gesture of victim-blaming, but when placed alongside the pseudo-romance strains of the passage an unsettling interpretation emerges, whereby the hero tasked with bringing the untutored woman into a sexual awakening – 'saving' her from an unnatural frigidity – becomes guilty of a crime instead, a reading supported by Lewis's fairy-tale allusion.

Charles Perrault's 1697 version of the 'sleeping beauty' legend had first been published in English in 1729, in a translation by Robert Samber that was to enter multiple new editions throughout the ensuing decades. A parallel French–English text, with a modified version of Samber's translation, was published in 1796, the same year as The Monk. 'The Sleeping Beauty in the Wood', invoked by Lewis, presents the questing knight who wakes the teenage princess from her hundred-year slumber, and is immediately recompensed with loving gratitude.[40] He adopts the posture of the pseudo-suppliant worshipper, like Ambrosio before his icon, as 'with trembling and admiration' he 'fell down before her upon his knees' – her 'bright, and in a manner resplendent beauty, had somewhat in it divine', her bed as bier-like as Antonia's (52). But this prince is also unequivocally portrayed as a 'valiant' saviour who courageously overcomes challenging obstacles to obtain his prize: 'every thing he saw might have frozen up the most fearless person with horror' (50). He confronts the terrible ambiguity of human life held in suspended animation as the whole court lies in a hundred-year sleep: 'the image of death every where showed itself, and there was nothing to be seen but stretched out bodies of men and animals, all seeming to be dead' (50). As such, Ambrosio acts as the valiant prince who awakens Antonia – a 'sleeping beauty' similarly surrounded by 'images of death' – from her sepulchral slumber to animated pleasure, the Romeo joining his Juliet in a happy ending. The immediate revulsion of Ambrosio's shattered illusion, in fact, partly anticipates the gruesome unravelling of Perrault's sleeping beauty story, as her ogress mother-in-law threatens to eat both her and her children.

If it might seem too far removed from the disgust Ambrosio's crime inspires to compare him to the valiant prince of a fairy tale, we need only juxtapose him with Lovelace, who similarly views himself as the salvific hero of romance, a self-perception which, tellingly, appropriates and repurposes the language of statuary elsewhere allied to Clarissa's body. Lovelace styles himself as the powerless 'hero in romance' who confronts challenging 'trials' (146) which perversely mirror Clarissa's, helplessly swayed by the cruel mistress who exacts virtue of her self-appointed knight. He hopes for his own Pygmalion-style resuscitation, 'when she is convinced of the sincerity of [my remorse and penitence], and when my mind is made such wax as to be fit to take what impression she pleases to give it' (1335). This faux humility is a performance of heroic virtue that toys with the materials with which Lovelace constructs his fantasy version of Clarissa. He calls her an 'unaccountable' figure, 'immovable as a statue' (830), who at once captivates and infuriates him; it is, of course, only by drugging her into the inanimacy of which he accuses her that he can realise his fantasy. Both Ambrosio and Lovelace simultaneously inhabit and detach themselves from the paradox of the statuesque idol-woman who is at once compellingly attractive and yet untouchably cold; both subsequently frame themselves within the language of victimhood when, by their own actions, they effect a metamorphosis in their Galateas that so horribly reflects their own image back upon them that they become repulsed, and blame their victims rather than themselves. They vie for '"animation of the inanimate"', the 'objective use' of which, according to the editors of *Bodies of Stone*, 'presupposes a conception of the inanimate as an empty and inert recipient ready to welcome the vitality that the living subject infuses in it'.[41]

The dishonest self-reflexivity of both Ambrosio and Lovelace, however, is undoubtedly rendered more integral to Richardson's character by the self-narration whereby he attains it – just as Clarissa's (self-)reification puts her statuification in a different light to Antonia's 'objective' petrification. And, as such, whereas Lewis's moral purpose in *The Monk* might arguably be at least secondary to the novel's sensational appeal, Richardson's didactic intent in *Clarissa* makes clear that the metamorphosis from moral corruption to redemption is impossible in a character such as Lovelace. The only other contender for the chivalric model, and who can be salvaged, is Belford, whose repentance and subsequent transformation is accomplished by gazing upon both the body and the symbol of the deceased Clarissa as monumentalised saint. Whereas Lovelace hubristically attempts to appropriate the statue metaphor to portray himself as the forlorn romantic hero, Belford becomes statue-like not as a competitor to Clarissa but as venerator of the relic, suppliant at her shrine, immobilised by ineffable emotion: 'And downstairs [Colonel Morden] went, and out of the house, leaving me a statue' (1363).

Belford's passage from libertine to reformed man of feeling anticipates the recurrence of statue motifs representing emotional overload in later sentimental fiction, the protagonists of which are frequently 'frozen' with temporary paralysis and aphasia. In

Jane Collier and Sarah Fielding's satirical, pseudo-sentimental novel *The Cry* (1754), for instance, Cylinda recalls moments of 'sorrow' so intense that 'the most eloquent philosophy might as well have been bestowed on an inanimate statue'.[42] The narrator of the anonymous *Adeline de Courcy* (1797) is 'fixed like a statue' on seeing her faithless lover from a distance: 'it was impossible for me to move.—My eyes were fixed upon that dear object of love'.[43] Mary Hays's narrator in *The Memoirs of Emma Courtney* (1794) presents the overpowering effects of romantic disappointment in similar terms of catatonic suspension: 'the colour forsook my lips and cheeks;—yet I neither wept, nor fainted. Mrs Denbeigh took my hands—they were frozen—the blood seemed congealed in my veins—and I sat motionless—my faculties suspended, stunned, locked up!'[44]

Like Clarissa, these narrator-protagonists partly wrest back some form of narrative agency in the retrospective description of a moment where they had found themselves powerless to act: in self-statuifying in this way, they vocalise the claim to self-represent on their own aesthetic terms in a manner similarly prompted by Burney's Evelina, conscious of themselves as looked-at objects, but asserting the authority to describe what they see for themselves. In such scenarios, the female narrators of sentimental fiction are in company with Belford. And yet his statue moment is an important step on the route towards his own salvation through a spiritual possession of Clarissa's symbolic value as embodied by her embalmed corpse, allowing his own metamorphosis into a better – and more potent – man, one who might quite feasibly have staked his claim to wake and win this princess from her eternal slumber. Do Emma Courtney, or Adeline de Courcy, enjoy a similar transition to greater power through their temporary suspended animation, 'like a statue'? These examples, in fact, are typical of the romantic abandonment often found in sentimental novels, where the hero aborts his quest as apparently not worth the effort after all, or when from fickle distractedness he tries his valiancy elsewhere, leaving a passively longing jilt behind him, forlornly gazing from a window upon a scene in which she exerts conditional agency, if any.

There is an undeniable, if brutal, comic underlining to this perpetuation of the gendered arc of potency versus powerlessness, agency against the ineffectual, with the Penelope-like woman always awaiting her saviour knight, even when she seems defiantly to tell her own story. Indeed, while it would be unthinkable for us to see humour in the fates of Clarissa or Antonia, the novelistic fiction of the period offers plenty of opportunity for eliding the comic and tragic in parallel scenarios, with imbalanced gender dynamics and sexual violence a common thread, and in which the language, idea and actuality of statuary are pivotal reference-points.

The 'Statue of Surprise': The Frozen Bodies of Comic Fiction

For all its estimation among the noblest of artforms and its admired association with classical antiquity, both the idea and the figure of the statue were clearly available to appropriation in comic contexts. Whereas Mary Wollstonecraft's heroine in her sentimental novel *Mary: A Fiction* (1788) displays the typical signs of excess emotion by temporarily becoming frozen, like the 'statue of despair',[45] the immobilised figures of comic fiction instead mimic the 'Statue of Surprise', the recognised method for performing astonishment and wonder in dramatic tragedy.[46] In Benjamin Martyn's play *Timoleon* (1730), for instance, the eponymous protagonist tells his astonished brother that 'Thou look'st a very Statue of Surprize, / As if a Light'ning Blast had dry'd thee up'.[47] The hammy tragedy of such scenes, typical of the eighteenth-century stage, is ripe for comic exploitation given its leaning towards an exaggerated expression that could be pushed to ridiculous extremes. There is only a short step from the melodramatically frozen posture of the tragic statue of surprise to the freeze-frame slapstick of the pantomime buffoon.

This motif recurs repeatedly in comic novels from the mid-century onwards, where to be 'frozen like a statue' becomes a stock way of depicting a protagonist suspended in such complete surprise or astonishment that he or she is unable to move – as we saw, a theatrical posturing transmuted into Gothic fiction, too. An antonym, perhaps, to the figure of sensibility immobilised by affect, the comic freeze helps to congeal a moment of humorous suspense that relies on a physicality which is often rendered in some way grotesque. Far from simply operating as a comic motif, however – a clichéd phrase appropriated from the stage and inverted – the comic potential of the statue of surprise operates within a gendered context seemingly removed from, and yet related to, those moments of compromised agency (performatively aped by the villains) seen in novels such as *Clarissa* and *The Monk*. Where Lovelace imagines himself as the powerless slave of his frigid mistress, in contemporary comic novels male protagonists are described as motionless statues by third-person narrators at moments of erotic tension to highlight the farcical dimensions and gendered eroticism of romantic comedy.

The anonymous *Adventures of Dick Hazard* (1755), for instance, offers a stock comic scene in which an interview between the hero and a lady is interrupted by the intrusion of his wife. The comic potential of the statue metaphor lies ready at hand:

> . . . *I hear a Knock at the Door*; so saying, she ran to the Stair-case, and ushered in— our Hero's Wife, and a charming Boy. Here all Description fails—for the Appearance of Things I must refer the Reader to his or her Imagination; and only say, that while his Wife fainted, *Dick* remained immovable, a Statue of Surprize.[48]

'*Hazard* rousing from the Lethargy of Astonishment' is swiftly reconciled with his wife, and meets his hitherto unknown child. This sequence operates as a series of short scenes with rapid transitions between them, of physical posture and of emotional register alike, to suggest the affinity between the 'Statue of Surprize' metaphor and the dramatic pantomime sequence. Making the reader emotionally immersed in this scene is not the chief ambition; instead, the author exploits rapid shifts in this pantomimic way to heighten a comic effect that relies on externalised emotional gesture and comic cliché.

Henry Fielding – former playwright turned novelist, of course – similarly repurposes the dramatic potential of the statue of surprise for comic effect in *The History of the Adventures of Joseph Andrews* (1742). The otherworldly Parson Adams is naively sleeping alongside the desirable Fanny when Joseph enters the room and naturally wonders what to make of it. Fanny awakes and is equally confounded, and the whole scene results in confusion:

> . . . *Fanny* skreamed, *Adams* leapt out of bed, and *Joseph* stood, as the Tragedians call it, like the *Statue of Surprize*. '*How came she into my Room?*' cry'd Adams. '*How came you into hers?*' cry'd *Joseph*, in an Astonishment. 'I know nothing of the matter,' answered *Adams*, 'but that she is a Vestal for me. As I am a Christian, I know not whether she is a Man or Woman . . .'[49]

STATUARY AND SCULPTURE   133

Uncertain chastity – for all three protagonists – is the source of 'astonishment' and momentary petrification. The easy comedy of this scene may seem far removed from some of the non-comic examples previously discussed, but it nevertheless engages with comparable issues relating to the reification of objects of desire, the disempowerment of the petrified object of the gaze, and even sexual threat, especially when this scene is juxtaposed with the first appearance of the statue of surprise in *Joseph Andrews*. When Lady Booby interviews Joseph, whom she desires, on a false pretence of reprimanding him, 'She viewed him some time in Silence' before accusing him of assaulting the maids: 'As a Person who is struck through the Heart with a Thunderbolt, looks extremely surprised, nay, and perhaps is so too.—Thus the poor *Joseph* received the false Accusation of his Mistress' (33–4). She cajoles him with words, then touches him '(*laying her Hand carelessly upon his*)' and the conversation turns to the topic of 'Kissing' (34). She asks,

> 'Would you be contented with [just] a Kiss? Would not your Inclinations be all on fire rather by such a Favour?' 'Madam,' said *Joseph*, 'if they were, I hope I should be able to controll them, without suffering them to get the better of my Virtue.'— You have heard, Reader, Poets talk of the *Statue of Surprize*; . . . You have seen the Faces, in the Eighteen-penny Gallery, when through the Trap-Door, to soft or no Musick, . . . [a] ghostly Appearance [rises] . . . but from none of these, nor from *Phidias*, or *Praxiteles*, if they should return to Life—no, not from the inimitable Pencil of my Friend *Hogarth*, could you receive such an Idea of Surprize, as would have entered in at your Eyes, had they beheld the Lady *Booby*, when those last Words issued out from the Lips of *Joseph*. (34–5)

Where Joseph is merely 'extremely surprised', Lady Booby performs 'astonishment' on a hyperbolic scale: the dramatic and the sculptural possibilities of the metaphor are pushed to extremes that surpass either sculpting tool, pen or 'pencil' to depict. The astonishing notion of Joseph's virtue becomes the contested topic now, revolving around a favoured term that reinforces Fielding's protracted satire on Richardson – Joseph reminds Lady Booby that he is 'the Brother of *Pamela*' – but also the comedic potential of a scene strengthened by these theatrical allusions. The sensational appearance of ghosts enjoyed by the 'Eighteen-penny gallery' makes a mockery of Lady Booby's mock-tragic reaction, but also, potentially, of male chastity: '"Did ever Mortal hear of a Man's Virtue!"' (35). The scene, furthermore, reinforces how the societal inequalities that, alongside her gender, make Pamela a prey to Mr B. are shared by her brother.

These moments in *Joseph Andrews* serve as a prelude to the recurrence of statuary in *The History of Tom Jones* (1749). Although the most familiar example is Fielding's comparison between Sophia's beauty and that of one of the most admired statues of classical antiquity – 'the highest beauties of the famous *Venus de Medicis* were outdone',[50] itself an elaboration of Joseph's admiration of Fanny's beauty, which surpasses that of 'all the Statues he ever beheld . . . capable of converting a Man into a Statue' (267) – *Tom Jones* is more interested in the dramatic than the sculptural connotations of statuary. Fielding leaves a 'surprized' and 'astonished' Jones suspended over a stretch of narrative while he discusses other matters: 'In this astonishment then we shall leave him a-while, in order to cure the surprize of the reader, who will likewise, probably, not a little wonder at the arrival of [Mrs Waters]' (760). The male protagonists in particular (Partridge, Allworthy, Jones, Square, Mr Western) are suspended in 'astonishment' at several points throughout the novel, rendering them temporarily speechless and 'motionless'. Indeed, 'motionless' was a popular alternative to 'surprise' in denoting frozen astonishment. Fielding prefers it in *Amelia* (1751).[51] It also surfaces in Eliza Haywood's *History of Miss Betsy Thoughtless* (1751), where Mrs Prinks 'stood . . . pale and motionless as a statue' in a mock-'mournful scene' staging Lady Mellasin's 'immoderate sorrow' when her husband, Mr Goodman, discovers her deception.[52] Haywood's scene plays on the disposition of figures as in a dramatic tableau: Lady Mellasin lying in bed, 'with all the tokens of despair and grief, in every feature of her face', Flora prostrate on the floor beside her, and Mrs Prinks as immobilised observer. *The Adventures of Mr. Loveill* (1750), meanwhile, mocks its hero's encounter with a new mistress in similar terms: 'The amazement that Loveill was in at seeing an object so vastly superior to every thing he had met with since the affair of Lady Juliet, had fix'd him motionless in his place.'[53] His admired Cynthia acts as the commanding mistress of chivalric romance, 'frequently drawing up herself into the attitude of a statue, and haughtily nodding her head in a slow and magisterial manner, that something was pronounced like *insolent!—and know your distance*'.[54]

In repurposing the statuary trope within the context of pseudo-chivalric romance, these texts are closer to non-comic novels than might at first appear. Tom Jones's replayed posture of astonishment later characterises his appearance as the romance hero, rendered statue-like in beholding the object of his veneration at the eventual moment of reconciliation, in a chapter '*In which the reader will be surprised*' (600).[55] As Sophia enters the room and checks herself in the mirror, 'the statue of Jones now stood motionless':

> In this glass it was, after contemplating her own lovely face, that she first discovered the said statue; when instantly turning about, she perceived the reality of the vision: upon which she gave a violent scream, and scarce preserved herself from fainting, till Jones was able to move to her, and support her in his arms. (600–1)

The mirrored state of suspension – both petrified as one regards the other – is reflected in the mirror itself in an inversion of the Perseus myth that anticipates Lewis's moment of interrupted villainy, here turned towards romantic resolution. When they both recover the power of speech, Jones states, 'with faultering accents . . . "I see, madam, you are surprized." – "Surprized!" answered she; "Oh heavens! Indeed, I am surprized. I almost doubt whether you are the person you seem"' (601). Astonishment in the statue-like beholder is mutual here, as both Jones and Sophia assist in reanimating the object of their desire, each a Pygmalion that chafes the other back to life. The mistress–admirer dynamic of chivalric romance is confused, the distance between the adoring observer and the desired object conflated. Sophia assumes an 'air of . . . coldness' in rebuking him for his misdemeanours, but her 'trembling' and 'throbbing' heart betray her animated desire, and she 'allowed him' to kiss and hold her 'without any resistance' before 'recollecting herself' (601–3). On the other hand, arguably this simply reconfigures a pattern where the male romance hero temporarily becomes a Perseus frozen by an actually desirable Gorgon, but once reanimated pursues his quest to 'save' her, reinforcing how the 'cruel' mistress (601) is less an active agent than a catalyst for the hero to realise his own agency.

STATUARY AND SCULPTURE   135

Smollett's *The Adventures of Peregrine Pickle* (1751) perhaps provides the most telling example of this twisted dynamic. An inveterate adventurer and debauchee, Pickle shamelessly pursues his love-object, Emilia, who reciprocates his affection but insists on marriage before consummation. Impatient, he attempts but fails to rape her. A little later, now penitent and seeking forgiveness, Pickle presents as the anti-hero of a pseudo-chivalric romance; he is frequently enraptured at glimpses of his mistress's physical attributes, climaxing in a scene of unsettling resolution. Temporarily concealed from her view, Mr B.-like, Pickle observes her unobserved until,

> unable to resist the impetuosity of his passion, he sprung from his lurking place, exclaiming, 'Here I surrender;' and rushing into her presence, was so dazzled with her beauty, that his speech failed: he was fixed, like a statue, to the floor; and all his faculties were absorpt in admiration.[56]

Animated astonishment now belongs to the female characters – 'The ladies screamed with surprize at his appearance' – while

> Emilia underwent such agitation as flushed every charm with irresistible energy: her cheeks glowed with a most delicate suffusion, and her bosom heaved with such bewitching undulation, that the cambrick could not conceal or contain the snowy hemispheres, that rose like a vision of paradise to his view. (774)

Emilia's reanimation resembles that of Pygmalion's vivified sculpture, of Antonia in the crypt, as she transitions from abstract idol to attainable object in a supposedly comic inversion of the myth, but one which exposes her body's desirability more potently. She captivates Pickle, 'bewitching' him, but the suspension is only momentary, quickly yielding to the satisfaction of initial physical contact, and the promise of a speedy marriage and even greater intimacy. Like Jones, he has the capacity to mobilise himself out of his temporary suspension in order to leap to Emilia's aid, knight-like, but here with questionable motivations:

> While he was almost fainting with unutterable delight, she seemed ready to sink under the tumults of tenderness and confusion; when our hero, perceiving her condition, obeyed the impulse of his love, and circled the charmer in his arms, without suffering the least frown or symptom of displeasure. (774)

Just as Sophia wears the temporary mask of reproof, so Emilia performs only to discard the role of lofty lady of the romance quest, in responding to a lover who (like Ambrosio?) merely 'obeys' his natural 'impulse':

> His mistress, having by this time recollected herself, replied with a most exhilarating smile, 'I ought to punish you, for your obstinacy, with the mortification of a twelve-months' trial; but 'tis dangerous to tamper with an admirer of your disposition, and therefore, I think, I must make sure of you while it is in my power.' (774–5)

'Mortification', of course, is a resonant term here, hinting at the deathlike suspension of animated desire, counterbalanced by Emilia's telling suggestion that her 'power' is only temporary and conditional. Smollett pushes into uncomfortable terrain the blander deployments of the 'statue of surprise' when placed in the contexts of mock-romance. The modulations between comedy, farce and mock-tragedy pit Peregrine Pickle as a supposedly comic version of Lovelace and Ambrosio.

As Simon Dickie argues in his discussion of eighteenth-century rape jokes, and as such moments in *Peregrine Pickle* suggest, simply recognising historical sensibilities in a sense of humour does not remove the unease it instils. As Dickie writes, 'Rape humor effaces consequences, persistently nudging situations across the divide between tragic and comic. But it does so only because there are ambiguities and contested meanings to exploit.'[57] Although not all appearances of the statue metaphor in comic (as in non-comic) fiction are by any means concerned with rape or sexual violence, they nonetheless participate in a wider pool of comic vitalities in which humour about such offences takes a prominent role, creating 'ambiguities' that align them with contemporary tragic novels. Such moments in both types of fiction render dangerously ridiculous the romantic excess of the questing hero infatuated with his idol-mistress, exposing his 'trials' and her imperious demands as belonging to the games of a courtship ritual which offers only a pseudo-power to a woman who, by the fact of her marriage, will cede all power, actual and metaphorical, over body and mind, to the husband who had played at hopelessly panting after her as her adoring suitor.

In the revised edition of *Clarissa* that Richardson produced in response to his readers' comments, and moreover to their apparent misreading of the narrative's moral purpose, he significantly expanded a proposal scene that pits the heroine and Lovelace in a tense encounter characterised by passivity and agency, power and impotence, once again through deploying motifs associated with statuary. Clarissa reports on Lovelace's vehemence, over-awed by his unobtainable idol:

> O Charmer of my heart! snatching my hand, and pressing it between both his, to his lips, in a strange wild way, Take me, take me to yourself: Mould me as you please: I am wax in your hands: Give me your own impression; and seal me for ever yours—[58]

William Beatty Warner has suggested that 'This experience [of Clarissa's overpowering beauty] induces Lovelace's awe, stillness, and passivity.' And yet the seemingly suspended potency of the waxen, mouldable lover is double-edged: 'He suddenly wants to assimilate himself to Clarissa. . . . Clarissa's gestures and statements trigger his physical desire to possess . . . the heroine.'[59] Lovelace, again, self-models as the hero of romance; frustrated by Clarissa's adamantine resistance, his posture of adulation is simultaneously violent, 'strangely wild and fervent'; driven by the conflicting energies of perverse adoration, lust and desire, he projects onto Clarissa vicarious responsibility for his intemperate anguish.[60] The passionate yet languishing lover displays a tyranny at such points that would become a marital right.

In Smollett's work, seemingly worlds apart from Richardson's, a similar dynamic emerges following Pickle and Emilia's reconciliation, when he urges an immediate marriage but she desires a brief postponement:

> Peregrine, maddening with desire, assaulted her with the most earnest entreaties, representing, that, as her mother's consent was already obtained, there was surely

STATUARY AND SCULPTURE   137

no necessity for a delay, that must infallibly make a dangerous impression upon his
brain and constitution. He fell at her feet, in all the agony of impatience; swore that
his life and intellects would actually be in jeopardy by her refusal; and when she
attempted to argue him out of his demand, began to rave with such extravagance,
that . . . the amiable Emilia was teized into compliance. (775)

That Pickle's extremes of madness, 'agony' and extravagant rage 'teize' – or com-
pel – the ductile Emilia into an alarm and 'compliance' not dissimilar to Clarissa's
suggests that the fault line between the tragic and comic configurations of such a
scenario is fragile indeed. Whether formed of wax or stone, of fire or of ice, the
seemingly irreconcilable ambiguities of those female protagonists immured within
statue-like metaphors position them as the impossible objects of fantasy, while the
male connoisseurs who gaze upon them with apparent awe only thereby expose their
own complexity of contradictions.

Acknowledgement

This research was funded by the National Science Centre, Poland, as part of the Opus
project number 2020/37/B/HS2/02093.

Notes

1. On the role of statuary in eighteenth-century culture, see Katharina Boehm, 'Antiquarian
    Pygmalions: The Female Body, Ancient Statuary, and the Idea of Imaginary Transport in
    the Eighteenth Century', in *Sculpture, Sexuality and History: Encounters in Literature,
    Culture and the Arts from the Eighteenth Century to the Present*, ed. Jana Funke and Jen
    Grove (Basingstoke: Palgrave Macmillan, 2019), 35–7.
2. See Jonathan Richardson Senior, 'Of Painting and Sculpture', in Jonathan Richardson Sen.
    and Jun., *An Account of Some of the Statues, Bas-reliefs, Drawings and Pictures in Italy,
    & c., with Remarks* (London: J. Knapton, 1722), 89.
3. Jeremy Black, *The British Abroad: The Grand Tour in the Eighteenth Century* (London:
    Sandpiper, 1992 repr. 1999), 280–3.
4. Simon Varey, *Space and the Eighteenth-Century English Novel* (Cambridge: Cambridge
    University Press, 1990), 19.
5. See Boehm, 'Antiquarian Pygmalions', 37.
6. On the conflicting dichotomies of the female statue, see Michael R. Finn, 'Doctors, Malady,
    and Creativity in Rachilde', *Nineteenth-Century French Studies* 34, nos. 1–2 (2005): 121–33;
    Laura Miller, 'Between Life and Death: Representing Necrophilia, Medicine, and the Figure
    of the Intercessor in M. G. Lewis's *The Monk*', in *Sex and Death in Eighteenth-Century Lit-
    erature*, ed. Jolene Zigarovich (London and New York: Routledge, 2013), 221n26.
7. The quotation is taken from Ephraim Chambers, 'Preface' to *Cyclopaedia: Or, an Univer-
    sal Dictionary of Arts and Sciences*, 5th edn, 2 vols (London: Midwinter et al., 1741), 1:xi.
8. William Gibson, *Art and Money in the Writings of Tobias Smollett* (Lewisburg: Bucknell
    University Press, 2007), 110–11.
9. On the wider cultural eroticisation of the female sculpted nude, see Jana Funke and
    Jen Grove, 'Introduction', in *Sculpture, Sexuality and History*, 2. On sexual encounters
    on the Grand Tour, see, for instance, Chloe Chard, *Pleasure and Guilt on the Grand
    Tour: Travel Writing and Imaginative Geography 1600–1830* (Manchester: Manchester
    University Press, 1999), 91–2. See also Patricia Pulham's discussion of the connections

between travel, collecting and the sexualisation of statuary in nineteenth-century British fiction, in *The Sculptural Body in Victorian Literature: Encrypted Sexualities* (Edinburgh: Edinburgh University Press, 2020), 1–9.

10. Funke and Grove, 'Introduction', 15; see also Boehm, 'Antiquarian Pygmalions', 37.

11. *The Female American; or, the Adventures of Unca Eliza Winkfield. Compiled by herself*, 2 vols (London: Francis Noble, 1767), 2:28.

12. Frances Burney, *Evelina; or, the History of a Young Lady's Entrance into the World* (1778; Harmondsworth: Penguin, 1994), 119.

13. Gibson, *Art and Money in the Writings of Tobias Smollett*, 114.

14. Funke and Grove, 'Introduction', 7.

15. John Dryden, 'Pygmalion and the Statue', in *Fables Ancient and Modern* (London: J. Tonson, 1700), 166. Further references parenthetical.

16. See George L. Hersey, *Falling in Love with Statues: Artificial Humans from Pygmalion to the Present* (Chicago and London: University of Chicago, 2008), 95ff. See also Pulham, *The Sculptural Body*, 29–33.

17. Alessandra Violi, Barbara Grespi, Andrea Pinotti and Pietro Conte, eds, 'Introduction: Learning from Stone', in *Bodies of Stone in the Media, Visual Culture and the Arts* (Amsterdam: Amsterdam University Press, 2020), 10. Cf. W. J. T. Mitchell, 'What Do Pictures "Really" Want?', *October* 77 (1996): 73n4.

18. Samuel Richardson, *Pamela: Or, Virtue Rewarded*, ed. Thomas Keymer and Alice Wakely (1740; Oxford: Oxford University Press, 2001), 58.

19. Richardson, *Pamela*, 208, 209.

20. On the dominance of discussion of two-dimensional artworks in relation to Richardson, see for instance Murray L. Brown, 'Learning to Read Richardson: *Pamela*, "Speaking Pictures", and the Visual Hermeneutic', *Studies in the Novel* 25, no. 2 (1993): 129–51; Lynn Shepherd, *Clarissa's Painter: Portraiture, Illustration, and Representation in the Novels of Samuel Richardson* (Oxford: Oxford University Press, 2009).

21. On 'impressions' and gender, see Amelia Dale, *The Printed Reader: Gender, Quixotism, and Textual Bodies in Eighteenth-Century Britain* (Lewisburg: Bucknell University Press, 2019), 8–13.

22. See, for instance, Hélène Dachez, 'Mise en scène de la métamorphose du corps dans *Clarissa; Or, the History of a Young Lady* (1747–48) de Samuel Richardson', *Miranda: Revue pluridisciplinaire du monde anglophone / Multidisciplinary Peer-Reviewed Journal on the English-Speaking World* 1 (2010): 29, https://doi.org/10.4000/miranda.406 (accessed 14 November 2023).

23. Samuel Richardson, *Clarissa: Or, the History of a Young Lady* (1747–8; Harmondsworth: Penguin, 1985), 399, 430. Further references parenthetical.

24. F. S. Naiden, *Ancient Supplication* (Oxford: Oxford University Press, 2006), 4, 14.

25. Naiden, *Ancient Supplication*, 8, 38, 49.

26. Naiden, *Ancient Supplication*, 32, 176.

27. Pulham, *The Sculptural Body*, 194. See also Jolene Zigarovich, 'Courting Death: Necrophilia in Samuel Richardson's *Clarissa*', in *Sex and Death*, 76, 82–3, 89.

28. On Clarissa's corpse, see Yael Shapira, *Inventing the Gothic Corpse: The Thrill of Human Remains in the Eighteenth-Century Novel* (Basingstoke: Palgrave Macmillan, 2018), 85–131, 191. See also Pulham, *The Sculptural Body*, 92–7.

29. Shapira, *Inventing the Gothic Corpse*, 117.

30. See, for example, *The Edinburgh Companion to the Gothic and the Arts*, ed. David Punter (Edinburgh: Edinburgh University Press, 2019).

31. On the complex connections between Gothic fiction and sculpture, see Peter N. Lindfield and Dale Townshend, 'Gothic and Sculpture: From Medieval Piety to Modern Horrors and Terrors', in *The Edinburgh Companion to the Gothic and the Arts*, 69–88.

STATUARY AND SCULPTURE 139

32. Horace Walpole, *The Castle of Otranto*, ed. W. S. Lewis, intr. E. J. Clery (1764; Oxford: Oxford University Press, 1998), 26. Further references parenthetical.
33. Jakub Lipski, *Painting the Novel: Pictorial Discourse in Eighteenth-Century English Fiction* (London and New York: Routledge, 2018), 83.
34. Lipski, *Painting the Novel*, 84–5.
35. Lindfield and Townshend, 'Gothic and Sculpture', 77–8.
36. Matthew Lewis, *The Monk*, ed. Howard Anderson (1796; Oxford: Oxford University Press, 1980), 40. Further references parenthetical.
37. On 'the mirror motif' and the Gothic uncanny, see Lipski, *Painting the Novel*, 86.
38. Miller, 'Between Life and Death', 208. See also Zigarovich, 'Courting Death', 78.
39. On Lewis's remodelling of *Clarissa*, see Shapira, *Inventing the Gothic Corpse*, 177–217.
40. Charles Perrault, 'The Sleeping Beauty in the Wood', in *Tales of Passed Times by Mother Goose. With Morals*, trans. Richard Samber, 7th edn (London: T. Boosey, 1796), 52. Further references parenthetical.
41. Violi, Grespi, Pinotti and Conte, 'Introduction', 13–14.
42. Sarah Fielding and Jane Collier, *The Cry: A New Dramatic Fable*, 3 vols (London: R. and J. Dodsley, 1754), 2:327.
43. Anonymous, *Adeline de Courcy*, 2 vols (London: T. Cadell and W. Davies, 1797), 2:107.
44. Mary Hays, *The Memoirs of Emma Courtney*, ed. Eleanor Ty (1794; Oxford: Oxford University Press, 2000), 135.
45. Mary Wollstonecraft, *Mary: A Fiction*, ed. Gary Kelly (1788; Oxford: Oxford University Press, 1998), 15.
46. See notes to Henry Fielding, *Joseph Andrews*, ed. Thomas Keymer (1742; Oxford: Oxford University Press), 34n381.
47. [Benjamin Martyn], *Timoleon: A Tragedy* (London: J. Watts, 1730), 47.
48. Anonymous, *The Adventures of Dick Hazard* (London: W. Reeve, 1755), 240.
49. Fielding, *Joseph Andrews*, 294. Further references parenthetical.
50. Henry Fielding, *The History of Tom Jones*, ed. R. P. C. Mutter (1749; Harmondsworth: Penguin, 1985), 123. Further references parenthetical.
51. For instance, in *Tom Jones*, 27, 70, 244, 435.
52. Eliza Haywood, *The History of Miss Betsy Thoughtless*, ed. Beth Fowkes Tobin (1751; Oxford: Oxford University Press, 1997), 229–30.
53. *The Adventures of Mr. Loveill, Interspers'd with Many Real Amours of the Modern Polite World*, 2 vols (London: M. Cooper, 1750), 1:235.
54. *Adventures of Mr. Loveill*, 1:241.
55. Simon Dickie, *Cruelty & Laughter: Forgotten Comic Literature and the Unsentimental Eighteenth Century* (Chicago and London: University of Chicago Press, 2004), 220.
56. Tobias Smollett, *The Adventures of Peregrine Pickle*, ed. James L. Clifford and Paul-Gabriel Boucé (Oxford: Oxford University Press, 1983), 774. Further references parenthetical.
57. Dickie, *Cruelty & Laughter*, 193.
58. Samuel Richardson, *Clarissa: Or, the History of a Young Lady*, 7 vols (London: S. Richardson et al., 1751), 2:407.
59. William Beatty Warner, 'Proposal and Habitation: The Temporality and Authority of Interpretation in and about a Scene of Richardson's Clarissa', *Boundary 2* 7, no. 2 (1979): 189.
60. Richardson, *Clarissa*, 2:407.

8

DEPICTING BEAUTIFUL WOMEN IN THE
EIGHTEENTH-CENTURY NOVEL

Katherine Aske

SAMUEL RICHARDSON WARNED in his didactic novel *Pamela* (1740), 'Be sure don't let people's telling you, you are pretty, puff you up; for you did not make yourself, and so can have no praise due to you for it. It is virtue and goodness only, that make the true beauty.'[1] This chapter argues that representations of women's beauty in a selection of eighteenth-century British novels drew on, engaged with, and at times challenged prevailing thoughts on beauty evident in aesthetic treatise and social commentaries. To a greater extent than visual representations in the period, written descriptions could create a truly beautiful figure by associating favourable characteristics, such as 'goodness and virtue', with the period's idealised physical features, including pale skin, rosy cheeks and slim, proportionate features, to create a hybrid that was commonly known as 'true' or 'complete' beauty. Through a close analysis, this discussion considers the ways the figure of 'complete' beauty is manifested in the epistolary and narrative depictions of the beautiful heroines in *Pamela*, Henry Fielding's *Tom Jones* (1749), Charlotte Lennox's *The Female Quixote* (1752) and Frances Burney's *Evelina* (1778). While correlations between appearance and character were also evident in male characters, such as in *Tom Jones* and Fielding's *Joseph Andrews* (1742), the explicit connections between beauty and the expectations of moral behaviour for women are the specific focus of this analysis.

The interpretation of the 'complete' beauty explored here can be found in one of the period's most influential treatises on the subject, Edmund Burke's *Philosophical Enquiry into the Origin of our Ideas of the Sublime and Beautiful* (1757). Burke defined women's physical beauty as 'a thing much too affecting not to depend on some positive qualities', including '*Gracefulness*': 'In this ease, this roundness, and delicacy of attitude and motion, it is that all the magic of grace consists, and what is called its *je ne scai quoi*.'[2] It was commonly argued that without a certain *je ne sais quoi*, a woman's physical beauty could not be 'complete'. To offer a comparison, the qualities of what did not make a 'complete beauty' were outlined in *Harris's List of Covent-Garden Ladies* (1772), a guide to ladies of pleasure in London. Miss Grafton, the author reports,

> has been considered by many as one of the finest women on town: by some as the *finest*: we allow she is pretty, a good figure, sparkling eyes, her features small and pleasing, and her shape genteel; yet we cannot think her the complete beauty, much, very much is wanted to form it—'tis not a lip, an eye, a cheek—'tis a just

DEPICTING BEAUTIFUL WOMEN   141

and pleasing assemblage of the whole; yet most authors allow there never was such a being—perfection is not in nature.[3]

Miss Grafton is not a 'complete' beauty, but she is physically beautiful. The 'complete beauty', as this unironic text suggests, cannot exist, because 'perfection is not in nature'. A beautiful, virtuous woman was, perhaps, too good to be true, but here I argue that the elusive 'complete' beauty was not a form of perfection but was instead found in expressions of 'aimable' imperfections. For Burke, 'Perfection' was 'not the cause of BEAUTY', and he claims that modesty, 'which is a tacit allowance of imperfection, is itself considered as an amiable quality'.[4] In this way, the figure of 'complete' beauty needed to be something of a paradox, at once perfect and imperfect – a form that could only be captured in fictional terms.[5]

Although these particular novels have received their fair share of critical analysis, a focus on the creation of beautiful, virtuous characters can offer new light on them. Where the works of Robert Jones, Morag Martin, Hannah Grieg and Kathryn Woods have paved the way for the study of beauty in light of women's social visibility and identity, most studies of beauty in the period have been narrowed to specific areas, such as aesthetics, or material and cultural histories.[6] However, with the exception of Jakub Lipski's *Painting the Novel*, research focused on women's beauty in the eighteenth-century novel remains sparse. We can fill this gap by considering to what extent contemporary cultural beliefs influenced depictions of beautiful characters, meaning that novel readers could envisage 'complete' beauties even in the absence of details about their physical appearance.[7] In this way, verbal descriptions of beautiful women in novelistic literature, more than visual portrayals, can offer opportunities to unpick the ways female beauty was understood (or misunderstood) in terms of both physical and moral qualities. It is only through these literary depictions that we can grasp how ideas about 'complete' beauty moved beyond the physical to explore the widespread interpretations of a certain amicably imperfect *je ne sais quoi*.

The characters of Pamela, Sophia in *Tom Jones*, Arabella in *The Female Quixote* and the eponymous Evelina can be seen to represent the epitome of beauty: seemingly perfect women with heavenly looks and untainted (but not always untested) virtue. They are all praised for their beauty and grace, which is often positioned in terms of their obscure birth, social rank or modest behaviour. In illustrations based on these novels, these women are depicted with slim, proportioned features and figures, pale skin and graceful postures. However, unlike their illustrated counterparts, their literary characters are active, 'heavenly living objects', as *Evelina*'s Sir Clement notes, whose 'charming airs serve only to heighten the bloom' of their complexions.[8] These 'charming airs' encapsulated the 'complete' beauty in the eighteenth century. As argued by Robert Jones, the exemplary and rare figure of a beautiful, 'virtuous woman' became a social 'spectacle', a body on which to assign a moral code of conduct and an ideal for women to aim towards.[9] According to Morag Martin, a 'mix of interior and exterior beauty would allow [women] to function at the height of taste in the new social hierarchy',[10] and the commentaries regarding female beauty, and its significant social power, infiltrated multiple genres, from artistic treatises to moral philosophies, attempting to answer just what made a woman beautiful, or more beautiful, than another.

During the period, appearances became tied to concerns regarding identity, social position and the expression of moral sensibilities, which began to rise to the forefront of public thinking. Commentaries began to question what physical appearances really meant, and how a person's character could, or should, be judged. As Roy Porter has argued, 'New Science' and the questioning of whether the body could be divorced from the soul 'pierced physiognomy to the quick'. Moreover, the 'civilization of facades' that saw fashion and sociability dominate socio-cultural life in eighteenth-century Britain added further room for concern.[11] But despite challenges to physiognomy, the principles of the pseudoscience – basing character assessments on static features, such as large noses or high foreheads – continued to underpin newly emerging ideas about expression, which were similarly grounded in first-sight impressions and stereotypes.

In 1711, for example, Joseph Addison considered the subject of physiognomy in issue number 86 of *The Spectator*. He argued that 'We are no sooner presented to any one we never saw before, but we are immediately struck with the Idea of a proud, a reserved, an affable, or a good-natured Man', and that 'we may be better known by our Looks than by our Words'. Although Addison also expresses hesitation about the pseudoscience, in using the pronoun 'we' he assumes there is a sense of mutual agreement in the judgement of 'Looks'. His attempt to offer a simple yet poignant explanation of physiognomic theory through expressions led him to suggest that each passion 'gives a particular Cast to the Countenance, and is apt to discover itself in some Feature or other'.[12] As a person's facial and bodily expressions are a more transient visual indicator of character than early physiognomy accounted for, the idea that they could leave a lasting impression on a person's countenance (such as dimples from smiling, or frown lines from frowning too much) enabled a connection between reading expression and physiognomy – a connection that would continue to reinforce the aesthetic thinking of the period.[13] This also meant that the terminology associated with reading expression and practising physiognomy was often used interchangeably. However, most significant in this early thinking was that ideas about expression allowed the somewhat restrictive nature of physiognomy to acknowledge that the body and character could be two separate (but not wholly unrelated) entities. In terms of beautiful appearances, this divide became intrinsic to the way beauty was conceptualised, often paradoxically, as beautiful bodies could be associated with virtue and grace, as well as more socially fuelled prejudices, such as folly, sexual attraction, manipulation, pride, artifice and temptation. The value placed upon faces, expressions and impressions is, in this way, crucial to understanding broader ideas about beauty, character and identity in the period's novels.

In *Characteristicks of Men, Manners, Opinions, Times* (1711), Anthony Ashley Cooper, Earl of Shaftesbury addressed the subject of expression in relation to beauty:

> We may imagine what we please of a substantial solid Part of Beauty: but were the Subject to be well criticiz'd, we shou'd find, perhaps, that what we most admir'd, even in the Turn of *outward* Features, was but a mysterious Expression, and a kind of shadow of something *inward* in the Temper: and that when we were struck with a *Majestic* Air, a *sprightly Look*, an *Amazon bold* Grace, or a contrary *soft* and *gentle* one; 'twas chiefly the Fancy of these Characters or Qualities that wrought on us.[14]

What Shaftesbury describes as a 'mysterious Expression' is an observation of the relationship between the '*inward*' character and '*outward*' appearance that physiognomy had so long purported. In remarking that one can be 'struck' by an expression of inner beauty, he suggests, like Addison, that there is an immediate and intuitive element to our perception of another's appearance, based on the feeling or 'Fancy' that an expression 'wrought on us'. However, the impression of character as perceived through an expression also left room for the viewer's self-delusion and potential misinterpretation, a factor that ultimately challenged the existing approaches towards traditional physiognomy. For example, in the use of 'Fancy' Shaftesbury implies that impressions of physical beauty are individualised, and that there are intuitive expectations that beauty will be accompanied by certain 'Qualities' – even contradictory qualities – which in turn influence the ways in which 'we' judge beautiful appearances.

The period's novels frequently played with this sense of intuition. Through their beautiful and virtuous characters, the authors considered here were able to engage with complex investigations into the judgement of beauty, particularly through issues of perspective, moral judgement, taste, expression and prejudice, and to create – with varying levels of success – the 'spectacle' of this exemplary woman. It should also be noted that the narrative voices in these novels play a pivotal role in this process of creation. In *Pamela* and *Evelina*, the epistolary form confuses the narrative, as various voices complicate issues of perspective and the judgement of beauty and virtue. The third-person narrative voice of *Tom Jones* and *The Female Quixote* leaves far less room for misinterpretation; the correlations formed between appearance and character are somewhat more stable, but nonetheless provocative, in their depiction of the 'complete' beauty.

Every Lady is not a Pamela

Richardson's first novel, the epistolary account of the beautiful, fifteen-year-old servant entrapped by her infatuated master, paved the way for future novelistic heroines in Pamela's complex and, at times, inconsistent portrayal of the 'complete' beauty. For all Pamela's descriptions as being 'pretty', Richardson, much like Burney in *Evelina*, provides no tangible physical attributes for his heroine beyond a description of her 'fair soft Hands, and that lovely Skin' (69). Nevertheless, in Joseph Highmore's series of paintings for the novel, Pamela is pictured as a brunette, with pale skin, rosy cheeks and red lips, delicate features and a slim figure – the quintessential eighteenth-century beauty. However, the visual portrayal of Pamela's ideal beauty does not fully engage with the complex nature of the interpretations of her appearance in the novel, and the subsequent doubts that her character faces as a result. 'Pretty' Pamela has 'the Love of every body' (15), and yet the fear that her beauty might endanger her virtue, or be proof against it, is never far behind such comments: Mrs Jervis tells her she is 'too pretty to live in a Batchelor's House' (16). While the term 'pretty' was often interchangeable with the word 'beauty', there is multiplicity here. The idea of being 'too pretty' supposes an understanding of the inherent risks that physical beauty can bring to a young woman; but Richardson also frequently uses this term in its etymological meaning as crafty or artful. The interplay between Pamela's appearance, her 'virtue rewarded', and the inconsistencies in the way her character is reported means that, even within the first few letters of the novel, Pamela's virtue – the supposed safeguard of her beauty – is cast into doubt. Mr B. suggests that 'the Girl has Vanity and Conceit, and Pride too, or I am mistaken . . . she is a subtle artful Gypsey, and time will

Figure 8.1 Illustration from *Pamela: or, Virtue rewarded. In a series of Familiar Letters from a Beautiful Young Damsel to her Parents* (1742) by Samuel Richardson, showing Mr B. intercepting Pamela's first letter home to her mother. Original engraving by Hubert Gravelot. Public domain, via Wikimedia Commons.

shew it you' (29). Pamela's account of Mr B.'s perception of her is followed by her report of his unwanted attentions – forcefully kissing her neck and lips and groping her bosom – all supposedly provoked by her attractive appearance (Figure 8.1).

However, Pamela admits that 'I begin to think he likes me, and can't help it; and yet strives to conquer it, and so finds no way but to be cross to me' (54). Pamela's awareness of Mr B.'s attraction to her, and her rationale for his behaviour, begins to complicate the innocence her 'complete' beauty relies on. Her pride, too, adds further complexity to the judgement of her virtue. In the same letter she details her 'new Garb', in which, she claims, 'I never lik'd myself so well in my Life' (55). Equally, she is keen to reiterate any praise given to her appearance in her letters to her parents, who have already warned her not to 'puff' herself up. For example, before their marriage, Pamela recounts Mr B.'s conversations with their visitors:

> Lady Jones said, She is a charming Creature, I see that, at this Distance. And Sir Simon . . . swore he never saw so easy an Air, so fine a Shape, and so graceful a Presence. – The Lady Darnford said, I was a sweet Girl. And Mrs. Peters said very handsome Things. Even the Parson said, I should be the Pride of the County. (284)

With a whole section of the narrative taking the form of a self-reflective journal, alongside these self-appreciating reports and the fact that Pamela's letters are only addressed to her parents, the reader apparently has further reason to doubt her innocence of the situation, and the truthfulness of her behaviour around Mr B. In this sense, the epistolary nature of Richardson's novel works to reiterate that beauty, and indeed virtue, are a matter of perception – and a woman's virtue can be easily cast into doubt.[15]

Indeed, in Mr B.'s initial undermining of Pamela's beauty – 'The Wench is well enough' – and in his assumptions about her pride and vanity, he juxtaposes other characters' opinions of Pamela as a beautiful and virtuous figure (51). As Stuart Wilson has claimed, Pamela 'is seen as either a meretricious young hussy or a paragon of virtue, and the paradox in her character is yet to be resolved'.[16] Richardson's too-good-to-be-true virtuous servant was mocked in both Henry Fielding's *Shamela* (1741) and Eliza Haywood's *Anti-Pamela* (1741), among other works in the so-called *Pamela* controversy, suggesting that the idea of beauty and virtue being united in the same person was not appropriate for such a low-ranking character. However, these critiques also highlight failures in the narrative construction of Pamela's character and the room for interpretation. The epistolary style leaves space for Pamela's beauty and character to be interpreted in various ways, especially as, unlike Burney's *Evelina*, Richardson's novel is predominantly written from Pamela's perspective – and the reader cannot be certain how reliable her perspective is, or whether she would be likely to convey every detail about her relationship with Mr B. to her parents. In this sense, Richardson's creation of Pamela as a beautiful, virtuous figure engages with ongoing debates regarding the uncertainty of beauty's nature – its perception and expression – which were filling the pages of aesthetic treatises, moral philosophies and periodical essays. The provocative and uncertain nature of Pamela's virtue is therefore underpinned by the similarly paradoxical perception of female beauty in the period. The novel insinuates that appearances can be deceptive, and that beauty was expected (although rarely believed) to be accompanied by good, moral behaviour.

A Character Too Celestial

Roy Porter has argued that 'Georgian novels exemplify' a growing crisis between appearances and characters; from 'Fielding to the Gothic vogue, they abound with good-natured heroes and heroines who put their trust in faces'.[17] For example, in *Tom Jones*, the idea that 'a good Countenance is a Letter of Recommendation' is ultimately challenged by several misperceptions of certain characters. Jones is enamoured of Molly, whose beauty, ironically, according to the narrator, 'was not of the most amiable kind', and for whom he had more 'regard for her virtue than she herself'; but she 'soon triumphed over all [his] virtuous resolutions'.[18] While this apprehension speaks to much larger concerns brewing throughout the century, a person's ability to judge someone else's character accurately also became a form of moral judgement – where, for example, Molly's unattractiveness is aligned with her vicious nature. According to Roxann Wheeler, 'Characters who mistake appearance for reality are not treated uniformly in novels', as some are cast as ignorant or foolish, while others 'are often so good themselves that their mistake is a testament to their virtue'.[19] This innocent naivety – a naivety that cannot see the bad in others – and the inability to judge appearances accurately (especially deceptive ones) is often assigned to beautiful heroines, but also male examples, like Jones. On the other hand, the framing of such a misjudgement as ignorance, or as an internalised corruption (that is, jealousy) affecting the ability to perceive goodness, is more commonly pinned on older, or less beautiful women, or on rakish men, such as Mr B. or *Clarissa*'s Lovelace. A clear example is in *Evelina*, when Sir Clement, responding to Evelina's refusal of his advances, suggests duplicity: 'is it possible you can be so cruel? Can your nature and your countenance be so totally opposite?' (99). Although Sir Clement has supposedly misjudged Evelina's beauty as virtue, in perceiving her to be 'cruel', he now reveals his own moral character. In this way, to be thought both beautiful and virtuous requires a level of inexperience of the world and an ability always to see the best in others, however naively.

In the complexity of beauty's judgement, as well as the navigations of its paradoxical associations with both moral and immoral behaviours, discussions of women's beauty often had a didactic edge, underscoring the moral qualities that would make a woman, such as Pamela or Evelina, worthy of their beauty. Such observations became more prominent from the turn of the eighteenth century, and early periodical literature, such as *The Tatler* and *The Spectator*, often featured essays about women's beauty and character. Such discussions frequently concluded that a person could be physically beautiful but not necessarily virtuous, and that physical beauty should therefore be complemented by moral qualities. In *The Spectator* in February 1712, Richard Steele discussed the pleasing combination of beauty and virtue:

> the happy Concurrence of both these Excellencies in the same Person, is a Character too celestial to be frequently met with. Beauty is an over-weaning self-sufficient Thing, careless of providing itself any more substantial Ornaments; nay, so little does it consult its own Interests, that it too often defeats itself, by betraying that Innocence which renders it lovely and desirable. As therefore Virtue makes a beautiful Woman appear more beautiful, so Beauty makes a virtuous Woman really more virtuous.[20]

The idea that beauty 'too often defeats itself' and that the 'happy Concurrence' of all those qualities are too rare 'to be frequently met with', meant that beautiful and virtuous heroines in the period's novels had to walk a fine line; a line that entirely depended on others' perceptions of whether they were morally worthy of their beauty, or not.

The issue of perception was addressed in John Hawkesworth's essay for *The Adventurer* on 'the art of Being PRETTY' (1753). He writes, somewhat facetiously, that it should be 'wished at least, that beauty was in some degree dependent upon SENTIMENT and MANNERS, that so high a privilege might not be possessed by the unworthy'. Setting out to consider 'that species of beauty which is expressed in the countenance', the essayist argued that the 'finest features, ranged in the most exact symmetry, and heightened by the most blooming complexion, must be animated before they can strike; and when they are animated, will generally excite the same passions which they express'. Suggesting that faces will 'excite the same passions' they express, Hawkesworth draws on issues of perception, proposing that if a beautiful face does 'not express kindness' then the person 'will be beheld without love', and that all expressions 'will be reflected, as from a mirror, by every countenance on which they are turned'.[21] As Shaftesbury similarly argued, the idea that one could be struck by an expression on a beautiful face, and have an immediate impression of a person's good or bad character, was given weight in the judgement of appearances – but Hawkesworth gives further reason to trust that this reaction is a true reflection of another's character.

The idea that a beautiful and virtuous woman was something of a rarity meant that novelists could play with this idea of misjudgement. For example, in *Evelina*, Burney demonstrates how a 'first sight' reaction – mistaking appearance for reality – could be influenced by prejudice, or ignorance. In a letter from Lady Howard to the Reverend Mr Villars, Evelina is described as 'a little angel', and her

> face and person answer my most refined ideas of complete beauty: and this, though a subject of praise less important to you, or to me, than any other, is yet so striking, it is not possible to pass it unnoticed. Had I not known from whom she received her education, I should at first sight of so perfect a face, have been in pain for her understanding; since it has been long and justly remarked, that folly has ever sought alliance with beauty. (22)

Commenting on Evelina's 'charming face' and 'striking' beauty, Lady Howard's assurance that such beauty is often aligned with 'folly' serves as commendation of Evelina's virtue, as well as suggesting its rarity. But it also positions Lady Howard in the role of the ignorant interpreter. By acknowledging an assumption that beautiful girls often rely on their looks, whether from a place of jealousy or a genuine belief, Burney's satire on the erroneous correlations between beauty, virtue and folly plays with the distinction between ignorance and naivety. In this passage, Burney not only highlights common social prejudices, and the misjudgement such a 'striking' beauty could face, but also plays with this duplicity to justify Evelina's position as a 'complete beauty'.

Despite the attention Burney pays to other characters' interpretations of Evelina's appearance, there is surprisingly little actual description of it. According to Lipski, the novel contains

> a sketch of Evelina's personality and manners, but tellingly enough, there is hardly any mention of the looks, except for a cursory remark on her 'perfect face'. There is nothing for the reader on which to base his or her projection of Evelina but for the vague 'ideas of complete beauty'.[22]

However, Evelina's 'complete beauty' is, in Burney's witty style, depicted through her comparison with the other women in the novel – specifically her opposite in age and character, Madame Duval, and to some extent Maria, whom Captain Mirvin rudely describes (according to Evelina) in terms of 'the bad shape of her nose' and of her being 'a tall, ill-formed thing' (40). Through these descriptions, we can infer that Evelina, in contrast, is well formed, of a medium height, with a blooming complexion and proportioned features; such an interpretation, at least, is evident in the novel's illustrations, particularly the frontispiece to volume 2 of the novel's fourth edition, which depicts Evelina helping the dishevelled Madame Duval.[23]

Burney did not need to include any physical specifics for Evelina, because they are secondary to the qualities of Evelina's 'person'. Evelina is praised for the 'gentleness in her manners' and the 'natural grace in her motions'. Her character is described as 'ingenuous and simple', yet she has an 'excellent understanding, and great quickness of parts', with an 'air of inexperience and innocency that is extremely interesting' (22). In her mix of 'striking' physical beauty with the carefully balanced qualities of both 'understanding' and 'inexperience', Evelina, like Pamela, demonstrates the paradoxical imperfections of the 'complete' beauty. Evelina is conscious that her uncertain social status, repeated faux pas and ignorance of society make her unworthy of Lord Orville's interest – meaning that she simultaneously displays folly together with modest behaviour. In highlighting this inconsistency, Burney insinuates the idea that 'virtue' is not 'understanding' in an intellectual sense, but a type of natural naivety, where being ignorant of the world is both a practical disadvantage and a facilitator of moral character. The real complexity in crafting a 'complete' beauty therefore comes in creating the perfectly imperfect character worthy of their physical beauty.

A Thousand Amiable Qualities

Where the narrative biases in the epistolary novels explored here create space for both imperfection and misjudgement, the narrative voices in *Tom Jones* and *The Female Quixote* present their own set of challenges. In *Tom Jones*, Fielding, with an avid interest in physiognomy, describes every beautiful feature of Sophia:

> *Sophia* then, the only Daughter of Mr. *Western*, was a middle-sized Woman; but rather inclining to tall. Her Shape was not only exact, but extremely delicate; and the nice Proportion of her Arms promised the truest Symmetry in her Limbs. Her Hair, which was black, was so luxuriant, that it reached her Middle, before she cut it, to comply with the modern Fashion; and it was now curled so gracefully in her Neck, that few would believe it to be her own. If Envy could find any Part of her Face which demanded less Commendation than the rest, it might possibly think her Forehead might have been higher without Prejudice to her. . . . Her Complexion had rather more of the Lily than of the Rose; but when Exercise, or Modesty, increased her natural Colour, no Vermilion could equal it. . . . Her Neck was long and finely turned; and here, if I was not afraid of offending her Delicacy, I might justly say, the highest Beauties of the famous *Venus de Medicis* were outdone. Here was Whiteness which no Lilies, Ivory, nor Alabaster could match. (157)

With her dark hair, pale skin, 'Vermilion' cheeks and proportioned features, Sophia's physical beauty is, again, typical of the period – and evident in the novel's illustrations (Figure 8.2). However, in the suggestion that her 'Forehead might have been higher', and in the assurance that such a comparison with 'the highest Beauties' may offend 'her Delicacy', and therefore her modesty, Fielding adds the all-important 'imperfect' charm to Sophia's description. Her expression of modesty is furthered in the description of her behaviour around her love-interest, Tom Jones:

> Notwithstanding the nicest guard which Sophia endeavoured to set on her behaviour, she could not avoid letting some appearances now and then slip forth: for love may again be likened to a disease in this, that when it is denied a vent in one part, it will certainly break out in another. What her lips, therefore, concealed, her eyes, her blushes, and many little involuntary actions, betrayed. (115)

In these expressions – her 'blushes' and 'little involuntary actions', answering Burke's ideas of gracefulness, and the 'tacit allowance of imperfection' – Sophia becomes the

Figure 8.2 *Tom Jones and Sophia Western are seated together on a sofa as Squire Western enters the room with a riding whip* [image has been cropped]. Stipple engraving by Peter Simon after J. Downman [1789?]. Reference: 28844i. ©Wellcome Collection. Public domain.

very picture of female sensibility, beautiful and delicately expressive. The 'guard' she places on her behaviour is framed as a polite modesty, where her 'little involuntary' expressions reveal her true self.

As Roy Porter argues, 'Expression' could show the 'involuntary pulses of the nerves: tremblings, palpitations, blushing, weeping, quivering, swooning, all those indices of true feeling over which the contriving brain thankfully had no control'.[24] If a woman feigned modesty and virtue, it was believed that something would eventually slip, as with Lovelace's trial of Clarissa, where 'every step' is monitored 'to find one sliding one', or to 'catch her once tripping'.[25] While there were reasons to doubt displays of moral behaviour, particularly in a period of increasing social visibility, ideas surrounding involuntary expression, underpinned by new understandings of the nervous system, meant that there could be a truth to reading expression. Regarding beauty and expression, in the way it could be framed to justify a 'complete' beauty, Joseph Spence highlighted the importance of moderation:

> the chief Rule of the beauty of the Passions is Moderation; and that the Part in which they appear most strongly, is the Eyes. It is there that Love holds all his tenderest Language: It is there that Virtue commands, Modesty charms, Joy enlivens, Sorrow engages, and Inclination fires the Hearts of the Beholders[.] But all these, to be charming, must be kept within their due Bounds and Limits; for too sullen

an Appearance of Virtue, a violent and prostitute Swell of Passion, a rustic and overwhelming Modesty, a deep Sadness, or too wild and impetuous a Joy, become all either oppressive or disagreeable.[26]

Extreme passions could easily overshadow physical beauty, creating sites for ridicule or disgust, whereas moderate passions could complement a beautiful face and reflect inner virtues. In these limitations, the interpretation of the beautiful character is placed back on the viewer. Safely within 'due Bounds and Limits', the expressions assigned to beauty – that is, 'Virtue', 'Modesty', 'Joy' and even 'Sorrow' – align with notions of physical completeness.

The power of the involuntary action, and the focus on non-visible qualities to ensure beauty was not just skin deep, allowed, to an extent, a greater freedom in women's self-creation and their expression of virtuous qualities. The eighteenth century saw a surge in fashions, cosmetics and hairstyles – trends that blurred the lines between the upper and lower ranks, virtuous and not-so-virtuous ladies. The potential for a woman to cover her skin, and incidentally disguise her blushes (or lack thereof), was a cause for concern, but in trying to identify a true lady from a beautiful deceiver, the judgement of her character necessarily shifted to interpreting actions more than faces. This shift meant there was greater room for women who used cosmetics or followed the latest trends – like Sophia, who has cut her hair to 'comply with the modern Fashion' – to be considered as 'complete' beauties, rather than being accused of pride or deception. This is evident in Arabella's physical description in *The Female Quixote*, where dressing to her 'greatest Advantage' in no way lessens her presentation as a 'complete' beauty:

> Nature had indeed given her a most charming Face, a Shape easy and delicate, a sweet and insinuating Voice, and an Air so full of Dignity and Grace, as drew the Admiration of all that saw her. . . . Her Dress, tho' singular, was far from being unbecoming. All the Beauties of her Neck and Shape were set off to the greatest Advantage by the Fashion of her Gown, which, in the Manner of Robes, was made to fit tight to her Body; and fastened on the Breast with a Knot of Diamonds. Her fine black hair, hung upon her Neck in Curls, which had so much the Appearance of being artless, that all but her Maid, whose Employment it was to give them their Form, imagined they were so.[27]

Much like Sophia, Arabella is described as a stereotypical eighteenth-century beauty: her skin is fair, her dark hair is curled, and she has a 'delicate' shape. There are, again, small details that imply her 'aimable' imperfections, such as her dress being 'singular', but not 'unbecoming'. With all the makings of a 'complete' beauty, Arabella's seemingly 'artless' curls and her tight-fitting dress could easily be interpreted as her taking advantage of her beauty, but such possible intentions are quieted by the assurance that she is 'full of Dignity and Grace'.

Lennox similarly plays with the interpretation of Arabella's beauty through her, at times, immodest beliefs about her own beauty: ''Tis very certain, my Beauty has produced very deplorable Effects' (175). While her reaction is ironic, and hyperbolises the devasting effect of her beauty on her admirers, the reader is also assured that she is remorseful. Arabella is equipped with a naivety that lessens any possible intention for her to use her physical beauty for her own benefit. This is further demonstrated by her comparison with her cousin Charlotte Glanville, who not only purposely tries to appear more beautiful than Arabella, 'in order, if possible, to eclipse her lovely Cousin', but is also 'resolved to be present while her Cousin was dressing, that she might have an Opportunity to make some Remarks to her Disadvantage' (83–4). According to G. J. Barker-Benfield, 'Novelists taught the moral value of taste by contrasting tasteful heroines of sensibility with tasteless women of the world';[28] through these assurances of character, these two women, despite sitting at the same dressing table, wearing the same cosmetics and fashions, and both being physically attractive, are cast in opposition through their moral characters. Arabella's beauty, framed through her quixotic behaviour, is (unbeknownst to her) harmless, and her inability to judge appearance from reality accurately further proves her virtuous naivety. In this way, Lennox manages to preserve Arabella's character as a 'complete' beauty, even at the height of her quixotism, and with her use of cosmetics and fashion.

For Robert Jones, writers like Lennox provided 'a means of representing chaste and virtuous women while also enabling their young heroines to be attractive'.[29] He argues that Arabella's quixotism accepts and yet distorts the period's aesthetic theories that beautiful 'women were assumed to be both "lovely" and capable of virtue on the basis of their physical appearance', suggesting that 'Arabella believes that her status as a Beauty fits her automatically for the public sphere and, consequently, secures her virtue'.[30] But Arabella, because of her high-blown notions of romance, is well aware of her physical beauty and genuinely apprehensive of the attention it can invite – she, like Sophia and yet unlike Charlotte, is unwilling to use her beauty to her advantage. Her folly, in this way, acts in place of her modesty. Lennox presents her quixotic character as a means for Arabella to avoid engaging with the potential threats to her virtue invited by her beautiful appearance, by having her exaggerate the influence of her beauty. Where Evelina was misjudged for her potential lack of understanding, Arabella circumvents the frequently opposed judgements of beauty's association with both virtue and folly. Lennox instead uses her naivety and extreme behaviour to justify her virtuous character, although the moral closure of the novel suggests that her behaviour needs some moderation. In later demonstrating Arabella's ability to learn from her mistakes, Lennox arguably creates the most perfectly imperfect beauty.

The epitome of Arabella's 'complete' beauty can be found in Glanville's description of her character. Despite her 'unaccountable' behaviour, he accepts her romantic notions and 'Follies', because

> her Beauty had made a deep Impression on his Heart: He admired the Strength of her Understanding; her lively Wit; the Sweetness of her Temper; and a Thousand amiable Qualities which distinguished her from the rest of her Sex: Her Follies, when opposed to all those Charms of Mind and Person, seemed inconsiderable and weak; and, though they were capable of giving him great Uneasiness, yet they could not lessen a Passion which every Sight of her so much the more confirmed. (117)

A feeling or impression, especially one that accompanies the viewing of a beautiful woman, is often taken to be, as William Hogarth argued, a 'true and legible representation of the mind'.[31] The 'Passion' that 'every Sight' of Arabella stirs in Glanville reverberates with the ideas proposed by Hawkesworth in *The Adventurer*, and in Shaftesbury's earlier acknowledgement that the appeal of beauty is what our feelings 'wrought on us'.[32] As Glanville's description of Arabella's 'Beauty' is almost entirely based on her non-physical attributes, Lennox underscores that it is Arabella's character, and the assurance that her beauty is not skin deep, that makes her beauty 'complete'.

Conclusion

The depictions of beautiful women in these eighteenth-century novels engaged with ongoing discussions about appearances and character, and the often paradoxical expectations placed on female beauty. When forming a picture of beauty, or of any physical signifier, character is an essential part in how appearance is understood or misunderstood. When considering the commentaries that argued a woman's physical beauty was a useless adornment, if not a danger – without an accompanying grace, or the delicacy associated with feminine sensibility – to create their virtuous heroines novelists needed far more than a description of a pretty face. The predominant idea explored through each of these characters is that to be physically beautiful is also to entertain a correlation with moral beauty in a way that stereotypes of female beauty as deceptive, manipulative and artful undermine. Where issues of perception, identity and the interpretation of expressions abounded in the period's philosophies and social commentaries, for the eighteenth-century novelist these discussions became chances to explore appearances and realities. As readers, we are meant to believe that Sophia is more beautiful than Molly, and that Arabella is more beautiful than Charlotte, because they are more virtuous and worthy characters. As Steele concluded in *The Spectator*, 'Virtue makes a beautiful Woman appear more beautiful, so Beauty makes a virtuous Woman really more virtuous.'[33] Equally, we are meant to understand that Evelina is a 'complete beauty', even in the absence of her physical description, from her aimable qualities: she is equipped 'with a virtuous mind, a cultivated understanding, and a feeling heart' (9). Pamela, too, withstands her trials, accusations of pride and the inconsistent judgements of her beauty, and ultimately proves her virtue to Mr B.

Even where detailed descriptions of their appearances are lacking, these young women's characters are evidence enough that their beauty is indeed 'complete'. Yet the cautionary experiences detailed in Pamela's accusations and lack of social status; Sophia's comparison with Molly and her debilitating modesty; Arabella's ridiculous behaviour; and Lady Howard's initial misjudgement of Evelina, as well as Evelina's own naivety, all engage with, but also challenge, the idea that beautiful women can, and often will, depend on their looks. The 'true' or 'complete' figure of beauty will therefore always be tainted by the potential for deception, manipulation and temptation, alongside notions of superiority or pride, and provoking jealousy. However, to avoid the accusation that a perfect beauty is indeed too good to be true, these authors have created, in their small but present flaws – Pamela's inexperience, Evelina's obscurity, Sophia's modesty and Arabella's folly – 'complete' beauties; beauties that are evidenced by their imperfections, which leave room for them to grow from their experiences. To be truly beautiful, women in eighteenth-century novels had to be both art and artless, perfect and imperfect, complete and incomplete.

DEPICTING BEAUTIFUL WOMEN

Notes

1. Samuel Richardson, *Pamela; or, Virtue Rewarded*, ed. Thomas Keymer and Alice Wakely (1740; Oxford: Oxford University Press, 2001), 20. Further references parenthetical.
2. Edmund Burke, *Philosophical Enquiry into the Origin of our Ideas of the Sublime and Beautiful* (London: R. and J. Dodsley, 1757), 95, 107.
3. Harris [pseudonym], *Harris's List of Covent-Garden Ladies: Or Man of Pleasure's Kalendar, for the Year 1773. Containing an Exact Description of the Most Celebrated Ladies of Pleasure who Frequent Covent-Garden, and Other Parts of this Metropolis* (London: H. Ranger, 1773), 4.
4. Burke, *Philosophical Enquiry*, 91.
5. Burke, *Philosophical Enquiry*, 91.
6. See Robert W. Jones, *Gender and the Formation of Taste in Eighteenth-Century Britain: The Analysis of Beauty* (Cambridge: Cambridge University Press, 1998, repr. 2009); Morag Martin, *Selling Beauty: Cosmetics, Commerce and French Society 1750–1830* (Baltimore: Johns Hopkins University Press, 2009); Hannah Grieg, *The Beau Monde* (Oxford: Oxford University Press, 2013); Kathryn Woods, '"Facing" Identity in a "Faceless" Society: Physiognomy, Facial Appearance and Identity Perception in Eighteenth-Century London', *Cultural and Social History* 14, no. 2 (2017): 137–53; Martin Porter, *Windows of the Soul: The Art of Physiognomy in European Culture, 1470–1760* (Oxford: Oxford University Press, 2005); Roy Porter, 'Making Faces: Physiognomy and Fashion in Eighteenth-Century England', *Études Anglaises* 38, no. 4 (1985): 385–96; Paul Guyer, 'Eighteenth-Century Aesthetics', in *A Companion to Aesthetics*, ed. Stephen Davies, Kathleen Marie Higgins, Robert Hopkins and others (Oxford: Blackwell, 2009), 32–50; Paul Guyer, *Values of Beauty: Historical Essays in Aesthetics* (Cambridge: Cambridge University Press, 2005); Juliet McMaster, *Reading the Body in the Eighteenth-Century Novel* (London: Palgrave Macmillan, 2004), xi–xiii, 1; Sean Shesgreen, *Literary Portraits in the Novels of Henry Fielding* (DeKalb: Northern Illinois University Press, 1972); Peter McNeil, *Pretty Gentlemen: Macaroni Men and the Eighteenth-Century Fashion World* (New Haven: Yale University Press, 2018); Jakub Lipski, *Painting the Novel: Pictorial Discourse in Eighteenth-Century English Fiction* (London and New York: Routledge, 2018), especially 102–17.
7. The labels of 'true' or 'complete' beauty not only assigned a value or hierarchy to beauty, but also implied proportion, sincerity and 'real' or 'natural' beauty, as well as inner beauty and character. See D. Christopher Gabbard, 'The Complete, Common Form: Disability and the Literature of the British Enlightenment', in *Disability and the Literature of the British Enlightenment, Part III: Professional Identity and Culture*, ed. Clark Lawlor and Andrew Mangham (Cambridge: Cambridge University Press, 2021), 219–41. See also Katherine Aske, '"Such Gaudy Tulips Raised from Dung": Cosmetics, Disease and Morality in Jonathan Swift's Dressing-Room Poetry', *Journal for Eighteenth-Century Studies* 40, no. 4 (2017): 503–17.
8. Frances Burney, *Evelina*, ed. Margaret Anne Doody (1778; London: Penguin, 1994), 108, 46. Further references parenthetical.
9. Jones, *Gender and the Formation of Taste*, 115.
10. Martin, *Selling Beauty*, 74.
11. Porter, 'Making Faces', 386–7.
12. Joseph Addison, 'No. 86', *The Spectator*, 8 June 1711.
13. Porter, *Windows of the Soul*, 172, 186.
14. Anthony Ashley Cooper, Earl of Shaftesbury, *Characteristicks of Men, Manners, Opinions and Times*, 3 vols (London: John Darby, 1711), 2:138.
15. Julia Epstein, 'Marginality in Frances Burney's Novels', in *The Cambridge Companion to the Eighteenth Century Novel*, ed. John Richetti (Cambridge: Cambridge University Press, 1996, repr. 2002), 203.

16. Stuart Wilson, 'Richardson's *Pamela*: An Interpretation', *PMLA* 88, no.1 (1973): 79.
17. Porter, 'Making Faces', 386.
18. Henry Fielding, *Tom Jones*, ed. Fredson Bowers, The Wesleyan Edition of the Works of Henry Fielding (1749; Middletown: Wesleyan University Press, 1975), 92–3. Further references parenthetical.
19. Roxann Wheeler, 'Racial Legacies: The Speaking Countenance and the Character Sketch in the Novel', in *A Companion to Eighteenth-Century English Novel and Culture*, ed. Paula R. Backsheider and Catherine Ingrassia (Oxford: Blackwell, 2009), 436.
20. [Richard Steele], 'No. 302', *The Spectator*, 15 February 1712.
21. John Hawkesworth, 'Number LXXXII [82]. Saturday, August 18, 1753', in *The Adventurer*, 2 vols (London: J. Payne, 1752–4), 2:67–9. Throughout the article, Hawkesworth uses the terms 'pretty' and 'beautiful' interchangeably.
22. Lipski, *Painting the Novel*, 106.
23. See the frontispiece to volume 2 of Fanny Burney's *Evelina*; Evelina and Miss Mirvan surprised by Sir Clement Willoughby. Engraving by Anthony Walker after John Hamilton Mortimer (London: T. Lowndes, 1779). The British Museum: 1867,1214.300.
24. Porter, 'Making Faces', 393.
25. Samuel Richardson, *Clarissa; Or, The History of a Young Lady*, 3rd edn, 8 vols (London: S. Richardson, 1751), reprinted as *The Clarissa Project*, ed. Florian Stuber (New York: AMS Press, 1990), 88.
26. Joseph Spence [under Harry Beaumont], *Crito, or, a Dialogue on Beauty* (London: R. Dodsley, 1752), 28.
27. Charlotte Lennox, *The Female Quixote*, ed. Margaret Dalziel (1752; Oxford: Oxford University Press, 2008), 6–9. Further references parenthetical.
28. G. J. Barker-Benfield, *The Culture of Sensibility: Sex and Society in Eighteenth-Century Britain* (Chicago and London: University of Chicago Press, 1992), 206.
29. Jones, *Gender and the Formation of Taste*, 156.
30. Jones, *Gender and the Formation of Taste*, 162.
31. William Hogarth, *The Analysis of Beauty, with the Rejected Passages from the Manuscript Drafts and Autobiographical Notes*, ed. Joseph Burke (1753; Oxford: Clarendon Press, 1955), 136.
32. Shaftesbury, *Characteristicks of Men, Manners, Opinions and Times*, 2:138.
33. [Richard Steele], 'No. 302', *The Spectator*, 15 February 1712.

9

STORIES BEHIND PICTURES: RECONSTRUCTING A PRE-HISTORY OF HORACE WALPOLE'S *THE CASTLE OF OTRANTO*

Jakub Lipski

Not a picture here, but recalls a history.
– Horace Walpole, on Houghton Hall, 1761[1]

AN ARTIST HIMSELF,[2] Horace Walpole continuously revealed in his versatile writings something more than a conventional, connoisseurly interest and expertise in the arts. His profound knowledge and deepened understanding – both practical and theoretical – of painting, drawing, sculpture, architecture and garden design is reflected in a number of publications, of varying genres and objectives, written at different moments of his life and career as author, collector, salonnier and the period's arbiter of taste. His monumental corpus of correspondence is rich in art commentaries, ranging from critical evaluation to practical aspects of purchase, transport and display. His published work is also invariably concerned with the arts, from catalogue-like presentations, such as *Aedes Walpolianae: Or, A Description of the Collection of Pictures at Houghton-Hall in Norfolk* (1747) and *A Description of Mr. Walpole's Villa at Strawberry Hill* (1774), to biographical pieces, most notably his seminal *Anecdotes of Painting in England* (1762–80) and *A Catalogue of Engravers* (1782), both based on the notes of engraver and antiquary George Vertue, purchased by Walpole after his death in 1756. The common denominator for these works is not only what might be termed an ekphrastic agenda, rendering the visual with words, but also a desire to narrate, to construct a story that endows spatial artistic forms with temporal meaning (in the case of biographies and anecdotes), and to rely on narrative sequencing in explaining the spatial dimension of displayed artwork as well as garden and architectural design. For example, Walpole's own extra-illustrated edition of *A Description of Strawberry Hill* (1784) makes it clear that, to him, the villa depended for its aesthetic effect on the interplay of narrative and the visual arts, as can be seen in the imposed pattern for visiting the subsequent rooms, collectively making up a series of scenes to be admired on the house tour, and a series of images with captions and commentaries on the pages of the volume.[3]

In what follows, by focusing on the pictorial arts, I would like to concretise this narrative dimension of Walpole's verbal take on the arts and concentrate on his tendency to uncover stories behind images, to treat visual representations as an incentive for storytelling. Walpole's proneness to yield to what might be termed the narrative appeal of the image had profound consequences for the history of the eighteenth-century novel. His pioneering 'Gothic story', *The Castle of Otranto* (1764), features images as narrative catalysts: the mysterious portraits of Ricardo and Alfonso, which become literally or metaphorically animated, breaking the frames of non-temporality, precipitating major plot developments and constituting tangible representations of the novel's ideological concerns with ancestry, inheritance, family identification and – more broadly – history's haunting presence that is central to Gothic fiction.[4] The well-known story behind the writing of *Otranto*, included in a letter to his friend William Cole and repeated in *A Description*, provides an insight into the way Walpole approached the image: in both the letter and the catalogue Walpole points to the portrait of Lord Falkland in his Strawberry Hill collection (Plate 11) and comments on its inspirational role for the scene featuring a portrait walking out of its frame: 'When you read of the picture quitting its panel, did not you recollect the portrait of Lord Falkland all in white in my gallery?'[5]

In *The Castle of Otranto*, the referenced scene is narrated as follows:

> the portrait of [Manfred's] grandfather, which hung over the bench where [Manfred and Isabella] had been sitting, uttered a deep sigh and heaved its breast . . . still looking backwards on the portrait . . . [Manfred] saw it quit its pannel, and descend on the floor with a grave and melancholy air.[6]

The real portrait's narrative appeal, its potential to inspire stories in the recipient, as realised in the scene quoted, resulted from the crossover of form and reception. The painting is characterised by uncanny formal qualities that undermine the non-temporality of pictorial art: the *trompe l'oeil* effect created by the foot transcending the picture frame and the – not necessarily well-painted – rendition of the falling glove. While the form might have been the immediate inspiration, Walpole's narrative use of the portrait would also have been prompted by the genre's ideological contexts, most notably, its function to exude a spectral atmosphere of the past in the present. As such, the animated portrait of Ricardo and the portrait of Alfonso the Great, the object of heroine Matilda's 'uncommon adoration',[7] become emblematic of the Gothic tradition in general in as much as they animate the past and represent the ways in which it continues to haunt the here and now.

This essay aims to uncover the early traces of these dynamics, especially from the two decades preceding the publication of *Otranto*, the novel in which Walpole's recognition of the narrative potential of the image found its fullest articulation. The material that comes under scrutiny includes Walpole's early catalogue *Aedes Walpolianae*, the first two volumes of his *Anecdotes*, and his immediate responses to artwork, as recorded in his correspondence, manuscript annotations to the collected catalogues – including his own copies of *Aedes* and *Anecdotes* – descriptions of collections, drawings and engravings, as well as in the so-called 'Book of Materials'.[8] My aim is to show that the larger-scale achievements, such as Strawberry Hill and *Otranto*, which both testify to Walpole's attraction to the storytelling potential of the visual, originated in the collector's narrative perspective on the image. I am interested in identifying Walpole's tendency to yield to the desire to narrate, as manifested in a shift from description to narrative, from *ekphrasis* to *mythos* – a shift that is illustrative of the wider concerns of the contemporary sister arts debate, such as the spatiality–temporality divide and questions relating to the translatability of the visual into the verbal and literary.

In Walpole's time, the spatiality–temporality divide was a central aspect of the criticism against the traditional *ut pictura poesis* standpoint, that is, a way of undermining the argumentative and creative practice of establishing affinities between painting and literature. In 1766 it was memorably conceptualised by Gotthold Ephraim Lessing in his *Laocoon*:

> If it be true that painting employs wholly different signs or means of imitation from poetry, – the one using forms and colors in space, the other articulate sounds in time, – and if signs must unquestionably stand in convenient relation with the thing signified, then signs arranged side by side can represent only objects existing side by side, or whose parts so exist, while consecutive signs can express only objects which succeed each other, or whose parts succeed each other, in time.[9]

As Niklaus Schweizer demonstrates, Lessing's argument was not revolutionary and stemmed from a vibrant critical discussion in the eighteenth century, in England as much as in continental Europe, about the limits of the word–image parallel – the '*ut pictura poesis* controversy', in Schweizer's words – a significant element of which was the space–time distinction.[10] Meanwhile, however, mid-eighteenth-century creative practice in the field of visual arts explored ways to go beyond it. While the traditional painterly techniques discussed above offered only a metaphorical or implied reconciliation of space and time, the art of William Hogarth is perhaps the strongest voice against the unbridgeability of the divide. The temporal quality of Hogarth's images is produced, on the one hand, by serialisation (in the narrative cycles that were his claim to fame), and, on the other, by an inherently narrative dimension created by the iconographic arrangements within single pictures, '*lead[ing] the eye*', as Hogarth himself puts it in his *Analysis of Beauty*, on '*a wanton kind of chace*'.[11] The suspension of the divide then takes place at the moment of reception, which is always situated in time. And this is also how the narrative appeal of the visual is recognised by Walpole: it lies in the eye of the beholder. By drawing a broader panorama of Walpole's engagement with the image, this essay attempts to contextualise the origin of *Otranto*, to show that elaborating on the narrative potential of the portrait of Lord Falkland stemmed from Walpole's years-long fascination with the image, and with the stories behind and prompted by it.

Aedes Walpolianae and *Anecdotes of Painting*

Aedes Walpolianae, which describes the collection of his father, Sir Robert Walpole, at Houghton Hall in Norfolk, is early testimony to Walpole's habit of treating the catalogued pictures as gateways to stories of the figures represented and the painters who created them. The volume opens with an introduction in which Walpole, shortly after his return from Italy in 1743, fashions himself as a talented and knowledgeable art historian. His aim in this introduction is to describe the main schools of painting, for the most part Italian, but before his does so, he offers a paraphrase of Matthew Prior's poem about the rivalry between Apelles and Protogenes – an allegorical tale about the conflict between line and colour in painting.

158   JAKUB LIPSKI

When the actual description of the collection begins, Walpole assumes the role of a guide leading the reader through a series of rooms, in a previously determined sequence (Walpole will do the same in his description of Strawberry Hill). The guide already establishes his procedure in the description of the first room: some pictures are only titled and attributed to painters; others merit a longer description of the represented scene, sometimes with judgemental comments; at other occasions attributions are complemented with further information about the affiliations of the painter or the represented figure; and finally, some pictures constitute an incentive for narrative. The first of these is a portrait of Walpole's distant ancestor, Sir Edward Walpole:

> He was made a Knight of the Bath at the Coronation of King *Charles* the Second, and made a great Figure in Parliament. Once on a very warm Dispute in the House, he propos'd an Expedient, to which both Parties immediately concurred: *Waller* the Poet moved that he might be sent to the Tower, for not having composed the Heats sooner, when he had it in his Power. He married *Susan*, Daughter to Sir *Robert Crane*, on whose Death he wrote these Verses in his Bible, which is now in the Church here:

> > She Lives, reigns, triumphs in a State of Bliss:
> > My Life no Life, a daily Dying is.
> > . . .[12]

The brief account that follows the entry combines the narrative strategies Walpole will repeatedly adopt: mentions of credentials and family affiliations, anecdotes (often humorous) and literary embellishments – here excerpts of poetry, elsewhere, long passages taken from classical authors such as Zosimus, Livy or Scipio. The references to the ancients make for the most 'literary' dimension of the catalogue, and they were made according to the conventions established by a classical education and the sister arts tradition. Walpole's library featured a number of works adopting a classical *ut pictura poesis* standpoint. For example, John Spence's *Polymetis: Or, an Enquiry Concerning the Agreement Between the Works of the Roman Poets, and the Remains of the Antient Artists. Being an Attempt to Illustrate Them Mutually from One Another* (1747) elaborates on such parallels *in extenso*, and it is also worthwhile to notice that one of the major objects of interest to Spence are visual progresses, such as cycles of reliefs illustrating the life of Hercules, which explore the temporal and narrative possibility behind the sequencing of the pictorial.

With other entries in *Aedes*, one can only speculate about Walpole's reasons for turning certain pictures into narratives: there is no identifiable systematic approach and there is no way of justifying why certain exhibits are given more attention other than the guide's immediate associations. The catalogue is coherently organised in terms of movement through space – the description of each room begins with a capitalised heading helping the reader navigate through the pages and the house – but there is a clear lack of a preconceived organisation in terms of the presented content. The impression one has is of a loose guide-like talk, with an occasional pause determined by Walpole's associations. A similar impression can be gained from the numerous descriptions of the seats of nobility included in the 'Book of Materials'. These were not published in the author's lifetime and take the form of loose sketches, peppered with longer – narrative or descriptive – digressions here and there.

RECONSTRUCTING A PRE-HISTORY OF *THE CASTLE OF OTRANTO*   159

Aedes also reveals a feature that determines Walpole's writing on art in general: anecdotes. Walpole is for the most part interested in curiosities, background information about how the picture was created, who bought the portrait and how much it cost, who offered to buy it but was declined, to whose collection(s) the picture belonged and how it changed its owners,[13] and – last but not least – social affairs (matrimonial and otherwise). The monumental corpus of Walpole's letters is full of such connoisseurly or collector-oriented entries, with correspondents exchanging practical information embellished with witty anecdotal remarks. In *Aedes*, one good example is the portrait of Charles I by Anthony van Dyck, in which 'both the Gauntlets' seem to have been 'drawn for the Right Hand'. It is annotated (in print) as follows:

> When this Picture was in the *Wharton* Collection, old *Jacob Tonson*, who had remarkably ugly Legs, was finding fault with the two Gauntlets; Lady *Wharton* said, Mr. *Tonson*, why might not one Man have two Right Hands, as well as another two Left Legs?[14]

Another case in point is the portrait of Pope Innocent X by Diego Velàzquez:[15]

> he [the painter] was sent by the King of *Spain* to draw this Pope's Picture; when the Pope sent his Chamberlain to pay him, he would not receive the Money, saying the King his Master always paid him with his own Hand: The Pope humoured him. This Pope was of the *Pamphilii* Family, was reckoned the ugliest Man of his Time, and was raised to the Papacy by the Intrigues of his Sister-in-law *Donna Olimpia*, a most beautiful Woman and his Mistress.[16]

This chaotic sketch, which is further developed in a footnote, represents in a nutshell things that interested Walpole in his gossipy storytelling: money, sex, bodily deformities and the life of the court. Walpole's manner, deriving from a longer tradition of anecdotal biographical writing, as exemplified by John Aubrey's *Brief Lives* (1669–96), found its fullest articulation in *Anecdotes of Painting in England*.[17]

Anecdotes of Painting solidifies Walpole's narrative persona as the charismatic guide. The anecdotes included vary in content, but collectively they highlight aspects of court life, painters' affiliations, aristocratic collections and the ways in which they were gathered, as well as attributions and identifications. This is how, as Karen Junod demonstrates, Walpole enlivened George Vertue's fact-laden and meticulous notes; a tedious collection of antiquarian details turned into an entertaining narrative, with the eponymous concept understood as 'an entertaining textual instance, a good story, an unusual incident, a captivating tale told to enthral and amuse his readers'.[18] The crux of *Anecdotes* is a name-based history of English painting, but before it begins, the book includes period-based chapters, at certain points interspersed with engravings that are commented upon. Walpole's treatment of the incorporated engravings shows attempts at oscillating between ekphrastic and narrative modes. Writing about the picture of 'Henry 5th his Queen and Family', he begins with background information, then proceeds to a meticulous description in which the identification of characters plays an important role; the sketchy narrative bits included are limited to matrimonial issues. Walpole's main focus here is to identify the characters involved correctly:

It has been supposed that the two elder [ladies] were the wives of the Dukes of Clarence and Bedford, and the two younger their sisters; but this clashes with all history and chronology. Blanche and Philippa were both married early in their father's reign: and to suppose the two younger ladies the brides of Clarence and Bedford would be groundless, for Margaret Holland the wife of the former was a widow when he married her.[19]

Walpole's pedantry in correcting misidentifications,[20] a tendency manifested throughout the annotated catalogues of exhibitions, might also be seen in the context of the so-called secret histories that were popular in the period, which conceptualised reading as an identification process. Walpole's description of the following engraving, representing the 'Marriage of Henry 6th', depends on the same convention: most of the passage is devoted to identification and family associations. In Walpole's own copy of the first edition of *Anecdotes*, the passage devoted to this engraving is given a handwritten annotation establishing links between the described picture and the related items in the author's possession.[21] This exemplifies a quality we would today label hypertextuality. In a way, then, the space of the image is expanded both vertically (by in-depth storytelling) and horizontally (by establishing associational links), which shows affinities with a word–image practice in which Walpole excelled: extra-illustration, as testified to by his impressive copy of *A Description of Mr. Walpole's Villa at Strawberry Hill*, which through the author's, as it were, compulsive practice of annotation, correction and illustration, became a monumental artist's book (Figure 9.1).

But in *Anecdotes of Painting* it is the print layout that already foregrounds the entanglement of image and narrative. A number of entries begin with the painter's engraved portrait, which Junod considers to be '[o]ne of the major appeals of the *Anecdotes*', and the follow-up is a biographical sketch.[22] It is somehow surprising that in this painter-based section no direct links are established between the biographical narrative and the opening picture – surprising given the fact that the other illustrations included in the volumes are duly commented upon. Arguably, Walpole's agenda was to imply that the link was to be taken for granted, and the reader was invited to see the narrative as a direct follow-up on the portrait, perhaps recognising the specific realities of life as imprinted on the portrait and, conversely, the character traits depicted as translating into the life.[23] Junod points to similar strategies in eighteenth-century 'lives' in general, as exemplified by Joseph Ames's *Catalogue of English Heads* (1748) and Thomas Birch's *Heads of Illustrious Persons of Great Britain* (1743–51), and aptly remarks that 'British writers increasingly interpreted history through the lives and the faces of the country's most eminent individuals'.[24]

Dispersed Annotations and Manuscripts

Similar tendencies are also reflected in Walpole's handwritten annotations to the collected artwork, the many catalogues and collection descriptions he owned and perused, and in the manuscript reports of visits to the houses of nobility preserved in the 'Book of Materials'. One typical form of annotation that he practised was literary quotation, as evidenced by what has remained of Walpole's extensive collection of portraiture. For example, J. Faber's engraving of Godfrey Kneller's portrait of Richard Temple (c.1732) is annotated with excerpts from William Congreve's

RECONSTRUCTING A PRE-HISTORY OF *THE CASTLE OF OTRANTO* 161

Figure 9.1 Horace Walpole, *A Description of the Villa of Mr. Horace Walpole* (Strawberry Hill, 1784), page 101. LWL Folio 49 3582. Courtesy of the Lewis Walpole Library, Yale University.

'Of Pleasing, An Epistle to Sir Richard Temple' and Alexander Pope's 'Epistle to Sir Richard Temple, Lord Cobham',[25] while to the back of a framed pastel of Hugh Douglas Hamilton's *Margaret Smith, Wife of Sr. Charles Bingham, an Excellent Paintress* (1774), Walpole glued his own poem about the woman's genius:

> Without a rival long on painting's throne,
> Urbino's modest artist sat alone.
> At last a British fair's unerring eyes,
> In five short moons contests the glorious prize,
> Raphael by genuis [*sic*] nurs'd by labour gain'd it,
> Bingham but saw perfection, and attain'd it.[26]

The verses come from the post-*Otranto* period but merit attention here in as much as they capture the typically Walpolean blend of art criticism and family history. Some of the collected drawings by George Vertue in *Original drawings of heads, antiquities, monuments, views, &c. by George Vertue and others* (c.1757) are similarly annotated. For example, the picture of a Restoration gentleman is commented on with a motto: 'Time swift doth Run / to Judgement thou must come. / prepare for Death lest hee / send thee to woe & Miserie',[27] while the subsequent drawing, of another character type, is complemented with a passage from Henry Carey's ballad farce *The Honest Yorkshireman* (1736) (Figure 9.2).

Such literary annotations, however, are arguably outshone by Walpole's more individualised remarks, revealing his storyteller disposition, as he is drawing attention to things that are attractive, but not necessarily by virtue of artistic merit. In a bound collection of Vertue's drawings, he ridicules one Hatchard 'a Gent of Berkshire. dead.', who 'was so very fatt; that he could not get into a hackney Coach' (Figure 9.3); he also appends a newly sketched pearl to the volume, noting: 'This pearle was taken out of the Ear of my Grandfather after his head was cutt off and given to the princess Royal.'[28]

Walpole's copy of Abraham van der Doort's *A Catalogue and Description of King Charles the First's Capital Collection* features a more extensive handwritten annotation; Walpole comments on van Dyck's 'The Lady Shirley in fantastic habit' thus:

> Sr Antony Shirley had the extraordinary fate of being sent Embassador <u>from</u> Persia <u>to</u> his own country. Whom he married, I cannot discover; but it is certain, that there was something extraordinary either in his Wife or his Match. Here she is drawn in a fantastic or Persian habit; in p. 50(?40) she appears naked. Some very particular words in a letter in the Sidney papers lead one to think that her being a native of Persia either led him thither or that her whimsical humour drove him thither. Rowland White says to Sr Robt Sidney, Sr Ant. Shirley goes forward on his voyage very well furnisht, led by the strange fortune of his marriage, to undertake any course that may occupy his mind, from thinking on her vainest words. . . .[29]

An even longer version of this annotation appears in 'Book of Materials',[30] and some of the observations are repeated and extended in a manuscript note now appended to the engraving owned by Walpole.[31] But already this shorter passage perfectly illustrates what I term the 'narrative appeal' of the image. The vocabulary Walpole avails himself of illustrates a shift from curiosities confined within the representation

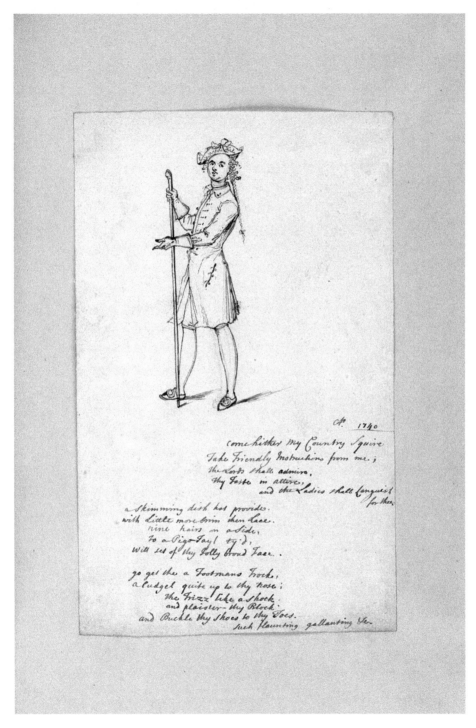

Figure 9.2 Horace Walpole's collection of George Vertue's *Original Drawings of Heads, Antiquities, Monuments, Views, &c.*, page 75. LWL Folio 49 3581. Courtesy of the Lewis Walpole Library, Yale University.

Figure 9.3 Horace Walpole's collection of George Vertue's *Original Drawings of Heads, Antiquities, Monuments, Views, &c.*, page 36. LWL 49 2610. Courtesy of the Lewis Walpole Library, Yale University.

(exemplified by the previously mentioned gauntlets or bodily deformities) to curiosities transcending the picture frame and opening up a narrative space: Walpole's starting point is the lady's 'fantastic' dress, but this leads him to the alluring story behind it, sketched with the use of such phrases as 'extraordinary fate', 'whimsical humour' or 'strange fortune', reminiscent of the typical language of romance fictions. A similar strategy of elaborating on a curiosity can be found in his 1759 manuscript account of a visit to Woburn Abbey, which he toured in October 1751. When describing the gallery, Walpole comments on 'Two heads of the Two Elder Sons of Francis Earl of Bedford':

> the tradition of the family says, that the story of these young Men gave rise to the play of the Orphan; & their pictures have something very remarkable. Edward the Eldest (aet. 22, 1573) holds snakes in his hand, with these words, 'fides hominis serpentibus fraus'; and above, 'fata viam invent', & on one side a Man in a Maze. This I take to be Castalio. He died before his father, having married Jane Sibylla, Daughter of Sir Richard Morrison. The Earl his father had married Sir Richard's widow, by which means it is probable her Daughter lived in the House. His Brother who outlived him long, married the widow Lady Hobby, by whom he had two Daughters, & who certainly was not the Monimia. His Brother's picture has a ship on one side, & a woman on the other.[32]

Walpole's anecdotal approach to art history is also reflected in the 'Book of Materials', in which there are several sections titled 'Anecdotes relating to Painters & other artists'.[33] The entries are scanty and chaotic, but some reveal Walpole's interest in attracting attention in a rather unscholarly manner. For example, one concerns 'Mr Miller – the architect', who 'went mad the end of 1759'.[34] Similar pieces of sketchy and anecdotal narrative can also be found in the manuscript annotations to the catalogues of artwork Walpole perused, such as those of exhibitions held by the Society of the Encouragement of Arts, Manufactures, and Commerce. These were organised from 1760 onwards, and, as reflected in the numerous catalogues of subsequent events in his possession, Walpole was an avid follower of these events. In his copy of *A Catalogue of the Pictures, Sculptures, Models, Drawings, Prints, &c. of the Present Artists, Exhibited in the Great Room of the Society of the Encouragement of Arts, Manufactures, and Commerce, on the 21st of April, 1760*, we read about Mr Ramsay, who never sent his pictures for these exhibitions:

> Mr Ramsay never sent any picture to any of the Exhibitions; nor Mr Adam the Architect any Designs. After Ramsay became King's Painter, He seldom painted but for the Royal family & their pictures for Embassadors.
>   When Ramsay had left off, & painted only the Royal Portraits, & of Lord Bute his Patron, at that time very unpopular, Sterne visiting him, said 'I see, Mr Ramsay, you deal only in court-cards, Kings, Queens & Knaves'.[35]

In the *Catalogue* for 9 May 1761, in turn, the commentary on the entry for 'Picquet, or virtue in danger' says: 'It is a young officer who has won a Lady's money at cards, and offers it to her again as the price of her favours. his head very fine.'[36]

Uncanny Animation and Proto-Gothic Storytelling

The examples given so far point to some of the major strategies of responding to artwork that Walpole repeatedly adopted in the two decades preceding *Otranto*. They may reveal some aspects of the author's storyteller charisma and his gossipy disposition, but, by and large, they do not significantly distinguish Walpole from his contemporaries, who shared his classical education, took the sister arts approach for granted, and had similar connoisseurly pursuits. They may shed more light on Walpole's treatment of the portrait of Lord Falkland, in as much as it prompted the author to tell a story of family affairs and the nobility's 'dark secrets' in *Otranto*, but is not enough in order to contextualise its inspirational role for Walpole's idea of a 'Gothic story' meaningfully. The portrait turned out to be an incentive for Gothic narrative by virtue of the history behind it and its uncanny painterly qualities (as discussed), but its catalysing function should be seen as grounded in the wider context of Walpole's understanding of the potential uncanniness of the visual arts, also in the decades preceding *Otranto*, which resulted in the narrative of animation.

In *Otranto*, the narrative voice stages the animation as a phenomenon first observed by villain Manfred. The preceding 'sigh' uttered by the figure in the picture, which is heard by victimised Isabella, leaves no doubt as to the actuality of the ensuing animation, but Manfred's first reaction – 'Do I dream?' – hints at the possibility of a counterfactual vision.[37] The villain is aware that the portrait may only seem as if alive to him. And while in this particular novelistic context, the antagonist is considering the hallucinatory effects of the doing of the evil powers, the hint has significant metacritical implications; namely, it points to the uncanniness of the portrait as a genre as such, created by painterly tricks, including, apart from the mentioned *trompe l'oeil*, the illusion of eye contact irrespective of the observer's position. This idea – of the portrait as if alive – as part of the critical discourse of portraiture recurs in Walpole's art commentary before *Otranto*. Indeed, as Thomas Gray put it in a 1739 letter to Walpole, who was then spending his time at Houghton Hall, '[Y]ou'll rather choose to converse with the living dead that adorn the walls of your apartments, than with the dead living that deck the middles of them.'[38]

In his responses to portraiture, Walpole obfuscates the binary of life and death, the animate and the inanimate, in several ways. He pays special attention to the countenance, which cannot surprise when responding to portraits is concerned. He tends to highlight 'curious', 'particular' or 'extraordinary' facial expressions. For example, when visiting Lord Hyde's seat, The Grove (in September 1761), he comments on the portrait of Lord Clarendon by Gerard Soest as characterised by 'a very particular countenance'.[39] At times, he explicitly invokes the 'as if alive' category. In this, he praises Raphael, who, as we read in volume 1 of *Anecdotes*, 'struck out that majestic freedom, which has since animated painting, and delivered it from the servility of coldly copying motionless nature'.[40] Taking the idea of portrait animation even further, he thus reports to his friend Horace Mann on a masquerade ball that he attended: 'quantities of pretty Vandykes, and all kinds of old pictures, walked out of their frames'.[41]

Arguably, the most complex proto-Gothic conceptualisation of portraiture's uncanniness can be discerned from the narratives surrounding Walpole's attraction to portraits of Bianca Cappello, as reflected in his correspondence. Jacqueline Musacchio has rightly considered Walpole's interest in Grand Duchess Bianca Cappello, the wife of

RECONSTRUCTING A PRE-HISTORY OF *THE CASTLE OF OTRANTO* 167

Francesco I de' Medici, as an expression of his 'gothic sensibility' given the duchess's own 'strikingly gothic biography', including an extramarital pregnancy, elopement, life in hiding, political intrigue, murder and scandalous marriage, which Walpole would have learnt about from such sources as the Florentine manuscript he acquired: the *Secret History of the House of Medici*.[42] As his letters from Italy testify, Walpole brought back two portraits he believed represented Bianca from his sojourns in Florence in 1739–40 and 1740–1. There was a miniature he thought had been created by Agnolo Bronzino, which, as Musacchio demonstrates, could not have been painted by this artist, nor would it have represented Bianca.[43] The second was a watercolour copy of Jacopo Ligozzi's portrait of Bianca (Plate 12), which Walpole would have seen in the Medici Villa del Poggio Imperiale outside Florence.

In line with the narrative strategies discussed above, the verso displays a short handwritten history of her life:

Bianca Capello [*sic*], a Venetian lady, mistress and afterwards second wife to Francis the First, Grand Duke. She married first a noble Florentine, for wch. his Father disinherited him, and being reduced, she maintained herself & Husband by washing Linen; the Gr. D. saw & fell in love with her. He made her Husband his minister, who used her very ill, and the people tyrannically; at last upon a murder he committed, the Gr. D. to whom she had often interceded for him, told her he wd. no longer protect him, upon wch. the relations of the murdered Person killed him. The Gr. Duke then married her, & they were both poisoned together by Ferdinand the Great, his Brother, then Cardinal, & on his Brother's Death Duke. Francis had Mary of Medicis Q. of France by a former wife. I have a small Head of this Bianca by Bronzino, when she was much younger & in her full Beauty.

There is no need to discuss the historical inaccuracies of this sketch; its literary qualities – the smoothing of the narrative line for the sake of partly factual and partly fictional emplotment – successfully demonstrate the transition from the image to Gothic storytelling.

Walpole's continuing interest in further representations of the noblewoman is evidenced in an exchange of letters with Horace Mann, who seems to share Walpole's sentiment. In a letter dated 9 November 1753, Mann writes:

[The picture I sent] is an old acquaintance of yours, and once much admired by you, though not quite in the bloom of her wrinkles. In short, it is the portrait you so often went to see in Casa Vitelli of the Bianca Cappello by Vassari, to which, as your proxy, I have made love to a long while, and will now own to you that I have been in possession of it some little time. It has hung in my bedchamber and reproached me indeed of infidelity, in depriving you of what I originally designed for you, but as I had determined to be honest at last I could not part with it too hastily.[44]

Walpole's response follows on in the same vein:

HER Serene Highness the Great Duchess Bianca Capello [*sic*] is arrived safe at a palace lately taken for her in Arlington Street: she has been much visited by the quality and gentry, and pleases universally by the graces of her person and comeliness of her deportment. . . . I have bespoken a frame for her, with the grand ducal coronet at top, her story on a label at bottom, which Gray is to compose in Latin as short and expressive as Tacitus (one is lucky when one can bespeak and have executed such an inscription!)[45]

There is of course a great deal of light-hearted irony in both letters, but this kind of fascination with a portrait finds its echoes in *Otranto*, where, as mentioned before, apart from the animated portrait of Riccardo (a fictional version of Falkland), there is another portrait, of Alfonso the Great, to which Matilda repeatedly addresses her sighs. The motif of desire for an inanimate canvas would find its transformations in the later Gothic tradition, most notably in Clara Reeve's *The Old English Baron* (1778) and in Matthew Gregory Lewis's *The Monk* (1796).[46] In the latter novel, the villainous monk Ambrosio's gradual transformation into a sexual predator is foreshadowed by his troubling idolatry:

> He fixed his eyes upon a picture of the Virgin, which was suspended opposite to him: This for two years had been the Object of his increasing wonder and adoration. He paused, and gazed upon it with delight.
> 'What Beauty in that countenance!' He continued after a silence of some minutes; 'How graceful is the turn of that head! What sweetness, yet what majesty in her divine eyes! How softly her cheek reclines upon her hand! Can the Rose vie with the blush of that cheek? Can the Lily rival the whiteness of that hand? Oh! if such a Creature existed, and existed but for me!'[47]

While Walpole's exchange of letters with Mann about Bianca is mostly concerned with biographical details, such ideas as 'making love' to a portrait or endowing it with agency, even if used ironically and intended to be taken with a pinch of salt, constitute a major step towards Gothic narrative as exemplified by *The Monk*.

The portrait they discuss has not yet been identified, but it could not have been painted by Giorgio Vassari: Mann speculates that 'The portrait was certainly the last that was made of her, and a very little time before she died, as appears by the age.'[48] Vassari, in turn, died thirteen years before Bianca (in 1574). It is likely that the portrait did not even represent her, but such factual details are secondary to the Gothic concept that emerges from this exchange of letters and the connoisseurly fascination that reconciles the collector's objectification and romance-like fantasy. In 1761 Mann sent Walpole another portrait of Cappello – an engraving by Francesco Allegrini, who published a catalogue of the Medici portraits, *Chronologica series simulacrorum regiae familiae mediceae* (1761). Walpole considered the representation 'curious',[49] but the gift did not provoke an exchange comparable to that relating to the supposed Vassari piece.

By extension, portraits endowed with quasi-agency, shrouded in an aura of curiosity and metaphorically animated, gave way to the idea of an enchanted or haunted gallery, which was fundamental to the making of *Otranto*. As Luisa Calè has demonstrated, Walpole was preoccupied with King Charles I's dispersed collection: he speculated about what English painting would have been like if the collection had not been broken up during the Civil War and toyed with the idea of recreating it, as suggested by some of his arrangements at Strawberry Hill and his commentaries on artwork (such as those on provenance, attribution and previous owners).[50] In a typically Gothic manner of reconciling diverse temporal layers, indicating the persistent presence of the past, Walpole approaches paintings as transhistorical objects or agents of change and mobility, uncannily merging recollections of the figures represented, creators and owners, and eluding the stability of spatial display for which they were supposedly destined. In the later decades of the century, Walpole was similarly anxious about what was happening to the gallery at Houghton, when the resident, George Walpole, third Earl of Orford, decided to sell the collection to Empress Catherine the Great of Russia. The deal was finalised in 1779, and Walpole expressed his dissatisfaction in his correspondence, calling his nephew, the Houghton descendant, 'the mad master' and lamenting: 'thus end all my visions about Houghton, which I never will *see*'.[51] It is ironic that an author who had devoted so much creative energy to mapping one famous dispersed collection should be directly exposed to the gradual disintegration of another.

But the haunting dimension of Houghton and its enchanting qualities were recognised by Walpole long before the sale. The distinction of 'visions' and 'seeing' in the excerpt quoted above is an apt illustration of how, to Walpole, the actual contact with the image produces a visionary after-effect – a more creative cognitive experience. The suspension of pictorial stasis, not only in the picture but also of its spatial and temporal context, is for Walpole a persistently vibrant idea, with painting exercising its powers of enchantment. In one of his letters to George Montagu, Walpole thus reports his return to Houghton Hall after sixteen years:

> HERE I am, at Houghton! and alone! in this spot, where (except two hours last month) I have not been in sixteen years! Think, what a crowd of reflections!—No, Gray and forty churchyards could not furnish so many. . . .
>
> The surprise the pictures gave me is again renewed—accustomed for many years to see nothing but wretched daubs and varnished copies at auctions, I look at these as enchantment. . . . Does great youth feel with poetic limbs, as well as see with poetic eyes? In one respect I am very young; I cannot satiate myself with looking . . .[52]

Walpole repeatedly remarked on the enchanting powers exercised by displayed artwork and appropriate architectural surroundings, especially such as those at Houghton Hall and Strawberry Hill, which depended on a powerful interplay of exhibits, architectural forms and interior design.[53] Two years later, in another letter to Montagu, he writes about the 'the air of enchantment and fairyism' exuded by his cabinet at Strawberry Hill, an idea to which he returns elsewhere, calling his house 'enchanted castle' or 'enchanted palace'.[54] As Dale Townshend demonstrates, Walpole derived the idea of an 'enchanted castle' from romance fiction, and as such it lends credence to the conceptual link between Strawberry Hill and the Castle of Otranto, given that the architectural forms of the latter seem to have little in common with the design of Walpole's villa.[55] One might find similar sentiments expressed after the publication of *Otranto*, and with reference to other spaces. In a letter to John Chute, Walpole writes about his experience at the Chartreuse near Paris:

> I am more enchanted with those paintings than ever. If it is not the first work in the world, and must yield to the Vatican, yet in simplicity and harmony it

beats Raphael himself. There is a vapour over all the pictures that makes them more natural than any representation of objects—I cannot conceive how it is effected![56]

These enchanting qualities, as recognised by Walpole, constitute what might be termed the supernaturalised portrait: endowed with quasi-agency, existing in between spatial and temporal contexts, casting a spell of enchantment, metaphorically animated and as if alive.

The gap between these ideas and Gothic narrative was bridged by Walpole at least twice in the years preceding *Otranto*, as documented by two manuscript notes conveying sketchy stories of the uncanny animation of artwork. These show how Walpole's narrative perspective on the image followed a trajectory from conventional responses to exhibited visuals, to enchanted galleries, and finally to proto-Gothic storytelling. The first is the story of a dream that Walpole wrote down in the first volume of his 'Book of Materials': a fantasy about King Charles I's dispersed collection. The dream followed Walpole's visit to Westminster Hall, and might also have been prompted by his work on George Vertue's notes on Abraham van der Doort's inventory cataloguing the then non-existent collection, which Walpole published in 1757. As Calè explains, the dream merges the spaces of Charles I's gallery at Westminster Hall with those of Whitehall, where some of the pictures were burned, and the planned gallery for Strawberry Hill.[57] The passage including a scene of animation features an 'odd' portrait of Richard II:

> I then went into another like gallery. At the end was a very odd picture; it seem'd a young King in his robes to the Knees, sleeping & leaning on one hand thus. [Sketch – see Figure 9.4[58]]

Figure 9.4 Horace Walpole's sketch of Richard II in the 'Book of Materials', 1:64. LWL 49 2615 I. Courtesy of the Lewis Walpole Library, Yale University.

> I immediately knew it to be Richard the 2d. He waked, and came out of the frame, & was extremely kind to me, & pressed me to stay with him – no, thought I, I know the Assassins are coming to murder you; it is not in my power to save you, & I cannot bear to see it.[59]

The passage uncannily conflates the spatial realities, as discussed by Calè, but also plays with the temporal level, endowing the time-travelling 'I' with an anachronistic historical consciousness. Walpole explores the word and image dynamic by inserting a visual sketch within the narrative; the sketch depicts the posture mentioned, 'sleeping & leaning on one hand', which evidences Walpole's awareness of iconographic conventions suspending the binary of stasis–motion. Just as he narrativises the *trompe l'oeil* of Lord Falkland's portrait in *Otranto*, so he explores here the emblematic meanings of the side-on half-lying posture, which in Renaissance tomb sculpture – which seems to be alluded to here – conveyed the idea of the dead's readiness to rise and leave the sepulchre at the moment of Christ's second coming and universal resurrection. Like in the case of *Otranto*, the animation is, in a sense, provoked by the specific formal arrangement that Walpole foregrounds.

The second proto-Gothic story is a handwritten annotation on the final page of a catalogue from an April 1763 exhibition of the Society for the Encouragement of Arts, Manufacturers, and Commerce, only a year before the publication of *The Castle of Otranto*:

> In this exhibition was a whole figure of an elderly man sitting, cast in (--) plaister of Paris and coloured, so very near to life that everybody mistook it for real. It was removed, on having frightened an apothecary. It was the performance of Rackstrow, Statuary.[60]

This brief note features a sculpture rather than a portrait, but in the realm of Walpole's connoisseurly storytelling the difference is not substantial, similar to his practice as a collector. And admittedly, the most memorable narrative of animation in *Otranto* features a gigantic statue of Alfonso, while the motif of mistaking a sculpted figure for real would reach its Gothic momentum in Ann Radcliffe's *The Mysteries of Udolpho* (1794), when heroine Emily faints, terrified on seeing a wax figure she takes for a corpse – a mystery that is resolved when the narrative draws to a close, long after the actual scene takes place:

> Emily passed on with faltering steps, and having paused a moment at the door, before she attempted to open it, she then hastily entered the chamber, and went towards the picture, which appeared to be enclosed in a frame of uncommon size, that hung in a dark part of the room. She paused again, and then, with a timid hand, lifted the veil; but instantly let it fall—perceiving that what it had concealed was no picture, and, before she could leave the chamber, she dropped senseless on the floor.[61]

Unlike the story of actual animation in the 'Book of Materials', Walpole's narrative annotation, just as Radcliffe's famous scene, capitalises on a quality central to Gothic aesthetics: confusion regarding the animate or inanimate state of things, with a cultural history ranging from 'haunted' objects to the zombie, from automata to humanoid robots.[62]

Neither of these very short narratives is told in a manner that is 'Gothic' enough in a generic sense, but the relative proximity to Walpole's work on *Otranto* (between 1 June and 6 August 1764)[63] and to the mentions of the enchanting powers of art

172 JAKUB LIPSKI

galleries in the correspondence suggests that the origins of Walpole's 'Gothic story' can be seen in a broader context, one that transcends the Strawberry Hill-based narrative presented to William Cole. As corroborated by the variety of textual material discussed here, Walpole frequently yielded to what might be considered a desire to narrate when responding to the visual. In doing so, he often suspended the binaries of stasis and motion, past and present, life and death, the real and the unreal, and the animate and the inanimate. This suspension of binaries – which is central to the Gothic tradition, as exemplified by *The Castle of Otranto* – is the effect produced at the word and image crossover, when the visual is translated into the narrative, when pictures provoke stories. The story of Walpole's fascination with the narrative potential of the image is thus not only the historical context for the making of *Otranto*. It provides a broader conceptual framework for the Gothic novel in general, given the continuous appeal of such stock motifs as the animated portrait, the haunted gallery and ontological ambiguity – a framework that goes beyond the eighteenth century, from Mary Shelley's *Frankenstein*, to Oscar Wilde's *The Picture of Dorian Gray* and to Stanley Kubrick's adaptation of Stephen King's *The Shining*.

Acknowledgement

This research was funded by the National Science Centre, Poland, as part of the Opus project number 2020/37/B/HS2/02093.

Notes

1. Horace Walpole to George Montagu, 25–30 March 1761, in *The Yale Edition of Horace Walpole's Correspondence*, ed. W. S. Lewis et al., 48 vols (New Haven: Yale University Press, 1937–83), 9:348.
2. Walpole's own attempts at painting and drawing are included and discussed in W. S. Lewis, *Horace Walpole* (New York: Pantheon, 1961).
3. Horace Walpole, *A Description of the Villa of Mr. Horace Walpole* (Strawberry Hill: Thomas Kirgate, 1784), Walpole's own extra-illustrated and annotated copy (The Lewis Walpole Library call number: LWL Folio 49 3582).
4. I discuss the uncanniness of the motif and its uses and meanings after Walpole in *Painting the Novel* (London and New York: Routledge, 2018), 79–101.
5. Horace Walpole to William Cole, 9 March 1765, in *The Yale Edition of Horace Walpole's Correspondence*, 1:88.
6. Horace Walpole, *The Castle of Otranto*, ed. Nick Groom (1764; Oxford: Oxford University Press, 2014), 25.
7. Walpole, *The Castle of Otranto*, 38.
8. Horace Walpole, *Aedes Walpolianae*, 3rd edn (London: J. Hughes, 1767), Walpole's own extra-illustrated and annotated copy (LWL 49 3932). Horace Walpole, *Anecdotes of Painting in England*, 4 vols (Twickenham: Strawberry Hill, 1762–71), Walpole's own extra-illustrated and annotated copy (LWL 49 2519). Horace Walpole, 'Book of Materials', 3 vols (1759–86, LWL 49 2615). I am grateful to the Lewis Walpole Library for awarding me a travel grant to access and study these and other Walpole materials.
9. Gotthold Ephraim Lessing, *Laocoon: An Essay upon the Limits of Painting and Poetry*, trans. Ellen Frothingham (Boston: Roberts Brothers, 1890), 91.
10. Niklaus Schweizer, *The Ut Pictura Poesis Controversy in Eighteenth-Century England and Germany* (Bern: Peter Lang, 1972).

RECONSTRUCTING A PRE-HISTORY OF *THE CASTLE OF OTRANTO*   173

11. William Hogarth, *The Analysis of Beauty*, ed. Ronald Paulson (New Haven and London: Yale University Press, 1997), 33. For the narrative quality of single pictures, see Robert L. S. Cowley, *Marriage A-la-Mode: A Re-View of Hogarth's Narrative Art* (Manchester: Manchester University Press, 1983), 51.
12. Walpole, *Aedes Walpolianae*, 38–9.
13. Luisa Calè argues that Walpole was persistently concerned with historical collections and what happened to them. See 'Horace Walpole's Dream: Remembering the Dispersed Collection', *Critical Quarterly* 55, no. 4 (2013): 42–53.
14. Walpole, *Aedes Walpolianae*, 51.
15. The referenced painting is not the famous portrait exhibited in the Doria Pamphilj Gallery in Rome, but the one now held in the National Gallery of Art in Washington, attributed to the circle of Velazquez.
16. Walpole, *Aedes Walpolianae*, 67.
17. Volume 3 of 'Book of Materials' begins with a reference to volume 4 of Aubrey's *Natural History and Antiquities of Surrey* (London: E. Curll, 1718). 'Book of Materials', 3:1.
18. Karen Junod, *'Writing the Lives of Painters': Biography and Artistic Identity in Britain, 1760–1810* (Oxford: Oxford University Press, 2011), 57–8.
19. Walpole, *Anecdotes of Painting in England*, 1:32.
20. Walpole is in general very pedantic about correcting all sorts of errors. A vivid testimony to this are his handwritten annotations to *The History and Antiquities of Windsor Castle* by Joseph Pote (1749, LWL 49 637). Walpole, unsurprisingly, for the most part focused on chapter XXVI, containing 'A Description of the Royal Apartments in WINDSOR CASTLE'. He meticulously corrects misattributions, wrong titles, as well as spelling errors. At one point, he gives vent to his irritation: 'This is one of the grossest blunders in this blundering book. The picture here mentioned is one of the finest in England, and painted by Giorgione' (annotation on page 421). It is ironic that in attributing *A Bohemian Family* to Giorgione, Walpole was also in the wrong. Nineteenth-century guidebooks unanimously attribute the piece to Pordenone.
21. Walpole, *Anecdotes of Painting in England*, 1:34.
22. Junod, *'Writing the Lives of Painters'*, 54.
23. For the prevalence of the biography-portrait analogy in the period, see Richard Wendorf, *The Elements of Life: Biography and Portrait-Painting in Stuart and Georgian England* (Oxford: Clarendon Press, 1991).
24. Junod points out that this was also a nod towards art-historiographic tradition and discusses similar structures of Renaissance and seventeenth-century lives of painters published on the Continent. Her other suggestion is that Walpole might have first written the text and then extra-illustrated it with what he possessed in his collections. Junod, *'Writing the Lives of Painters'*, 54–5, 68.
25. John Faber, after Sir Godfrey Kneller, *Richard Temple, Viscount Cobham*, c.1732, LWL SH Contents K68 no. 3+ Box 200, https://findit.library.yale.edu/catalog/digcoll:553768 (accessed 14 November 2023).
26. Hugh Douglas Hamilton, *Margaret Smith, Wife of Sr. Charles Bingham, an Excellent Paintress*, 1774, LWL SH Contents H217 no. 1 Framed, shelved in LFS Bin 33, https://findit. library.yale.edu/catalog/digcoll:4695259 (accessed 14 November 2023).
27. Horace Walpole, *Original Drawings of Heads, Antiquities, Monuments, Views, &c. by George Vertue and Others*, c.1757, LWL Folio 49 3581, 73, https://findit.library.yale.edu/bookreader/BookReaderDemo/index.html?oid=15950971&page=10#page/58/mode/1up (accessed 14 November 2023).
28. George Vertue, [*Drawings, Mostly Done by Vertue, of Various People and of Antiquities*], 1723–35, LWL Folio 49 3581, 75, 42, https://findit.library.yale.edu/catalog/digcoll:2794988 (accessed 14 November 2023).

29. Abraham van der Doort, *A Catalogue and Description of King Charles the First's Capital Collection* (London: W. Bathoe, 1757), LWL 49 2478, 163.
30. Walpole, 'Book of Materials', 1:13–14.
31. 'Horace Walpole Collection, 1725–1797', LWL MSS 1, Box 40, Folder 19.
32. Horace Walpole, *Horace Walpole's Journals of Visits to Country Seats*. The Sixteenth Volume of the Walpole Society, 1927–1928 (Oxford: Printed for the Walpole Society by John Johnson at the University Press, 1928), 20.
33. See, for example, Walpole, 'Book of Materials', 1:5–8.
34. Walpole, 'Book of Materials', 1:7.
35. *A Catalogue of the Pictures, Sculptures, Models, Drawings, Prints, &c. of the Present Artists, Exhibited in the Great Room of the Society of the Encouragement of Arts, Manufactures, and Commerce, on the 21st of April, 1760* (London: Society of Artists of Great Britain, 1760), LWL 49 3885.2, 16.
36. *A Catalogue of the Pictures, Sculptures, Models, Drawings, Prints, &c. of the Present Artists, Exhibited in the Great Room of the Society of the Encouragement of Arts, Manufactures, and Commerce, on the 9th of May, 1761* (London: Society of Artists of Great Britain, 1761), LWL 49 3885.2, 6.
37. Walpole, *The Castle of Otranto*, 25.
38. Thomas Gray to Horace Walpole, 15 July 1739, *The Yale Edition of Horace Walpole's Correspondence*, 13:104.
39. Walpole, *Horace Walpole's Journals of Visits to Country Seats*, 38.
40. Walpole, *Anecdotes of Painting in England*, 1:51.
41. Horace Walpole to Horace Mann, 18 February 1742, in *The Yale Edition of Horace Walpole's Correspondence*, 17:339.
42. Jacqueline Marie Musacchio, 'Florence, the Medici, and Bianca Cappello in the collections of Horace Walpole (1717–1797)', *The British Art Journal* 20, no. 1 (2019): 50–1, 53–4.
43. Musacchio, 'Florence, the Medici, and Bianca Cappello', 55.
44. Horace Mann to Horace Walpole, 9 November 1753, in *The Yale Edition of Horace Walpole's Correspondence*, 20:398.
45. Horace Walpole to Horace Mann, 28 January 1754, in *The Yale Edition of Horace Walpole's Correspondence*, 20:407.
46. I discuss the motif of desire for animation in *Painting the Novel*, 92–6.
47. Matthew Gregory Lewis, *The Monk*, ed. Nick Groom (1796; Oxford: Oxford University Press, 2008), 32.
48. Horace Mann to Horace Walpole, 9 November 1753, in *The Yale Edition of Horace Walpole's Correspondence*, 20:399.
49. Horace Walpole to Horace Mann, 4 January 1762, in *The Yale Edition of Horace Walpole's Correspondence*, 21:561.
50. Calè, 'Horace Walpole's Dream', 42–53.
51. Horace Walpole to Horace Mann, 18 December 1778, in *The Yale Edition of Horace Walpole's Correspondence*, 24:427–8.
52. Horace Walpole to George Montagu, 25–30 March 1761, in *The Yale Edition of Horace Walpole's Correspondence*, 9:347–8.
53. The gallery at Houghton was 'enchanting' even though Walpole was not keen on the house's Palladian form and thought of his own Strawberry Hill villa as a kind of corrective. See Marion Harney, *Place-Making for the Imagination: Horace Walpole and Strawberry Hill* (Farnham: Ashgate, 2013), 21–2.
54. Horace Walpole to George Montagu, 17 May 1763, in *The Yale Edition of Horace Walpole's Correspondence*, 10:72.
55. Dale Townshend, *Gothic Antiquity: History, Romance, and the Architectural Imagination, 1760–1840* (Oxford: Oxford University Press, 2019), 89, 91. Townshend also traces the critical

afterlife of the Strawberry Hill–Otranto parallels, confronting the 'critical orthodoxy' of under-lining the correspondences with approaches pointing out the incompatibilities (97–100).

56. Horace Walpole to John Chute, 5 August 1771, in *The Yale Edition of Horace Walpole Correspondence*, 35:126.
57. Calè, 'Horace Walpole's Dream', 48.
58. Horace Walpole's sketch of Richard II in the 'Book of Materials', 1:64. LWL 49 2615 I. Courtesy of the Lewis Walpole Library, Yale University.
59. Walpole, 'Book of Materials', 1:64.
60. *A Catalogue of the Paintings, Sculptures, Architecture, Models, Drawings, Engravings, Etc. Now Exhibiting under the Patronage of the Society for the Encouragement of Arts, Manufacturers, and Commerce, at their Great Room in the Strand* (London: James Harrison, 1763), LWL 49 3885.2 v. 4: No. 5, 16.
61. Ann Radcliffe, *The Mysteries of Udolpho*, ed. Donamy Dobrée, intr. and notes Terry Castle (1794; Oxford: Oxford University Press, 2008), 248–9.
62. This quality has been explored in the foundational critical work on the aesthetic of the uncanny. See Ernst Jentsch, 'On the Psychology of the Uncanny', trans. Roy Sellars, in *Uncanny Modernity*, ed. Jo Collins and John Jervis (1906; London: Palgrave Macmillan, 2008), 216–28; Sigmund Freud, 'The 'Uncanny'', trans. Alix Strachey (1919), http://web.mit.edu/allanmc/www/freud1.pdf (accessed 14 November 2023).
63. Horace Walpole, 'Short Notes of the Life of Horatio Walpole', LWL Mss Vol. 149, 15.

10

THE ROMANCES OF ANN RADCLIFFE AND THE 'TOTAL WORK OF ART'

Hannah Moss

ANN RADCLIFFE WAS one of the most respected, and highly paid, authors of the eighteenth century, publishing five Gothic romances between 1789 and 1797, as well as a travelogue, *A Journey Made in the Summer of 1794* (1795).[1] Read eagerly and breathlessly by readers and would-be authors alike, she was hailed by many as the first in her field. Sir Walter Scott, for one, viewed her as 'the first poetess of Romantic fiction',[2] whilst Thomas J. Mathias saw Radcliffe as 'a poetess whom Ariosto would with rapture have acknowledged', calling her 'the mighty magician of THE MYSTERIES OF UDOLPHO'.[3] To the accolades of poetess and magician, commentators also drew her into the discourse of the fine arts as her craft developed. For Scott, Radcliffe's rich and detailed descriptions of scenery combined 'the eye of the painter, with the spirit of the poet', whereas others used art as a means of distinguishing her travel writing from her fiction.[4] *The English Review*, for example, drew a distinction between painting and drawing with the comparative observation that 'in her romances she paints fancy-pieces; here [in her travelogue] she draws from nature'.[5] The contrast drawn between the precise realism of a draughtsman and the imaginative flair of the fancy piece suggests a firm stylistic divide between genres. However, it is worth considering how Radcliffe's travel writing, and the works of art she saw, informed the technique of her fiction. Radcliffe's use of poems, songs and tales, as well as lengthy passages of painterly landscape description, are all elements that contribute to her being recognised as the originator of a new style of romance, yet readers and reviewers, including Samuel Taylor Coleridge, have remarked upon the tendency for these aspects to slow down the pace of her narratives.[6] My aim is to reappraise Radcliffe's writing technique by analysing the frequent 'artistic interruptions' in the narrative as part of a wider aesthetic project that sees her experimenting with the boundaries of artistic form.

Jakub Lipski has proposed that Radcliffe employs a three-part 'sister arts' model, whereby music, painting and poetry are combined in her fiction in a way that pre-empts the idea of the 'total work of art'.[7] Typically translated as 'total work of art', 'synthesis of the arts', 'comprehensive artwork' or 'all-embracing artform', the term *Gesamtkunstwerk* was developed by the German writer and philosopher K. F. E. Trahndorff in an 1827 essay to refer to a work of art that makes use of many artforms, or at least strives to do so.[8] Building upon Lipski's assertion, I will extend my analysis to incorporate Radcliffe's travel journals as I demonstrate how her prose attempts to recreate her aesthetic experience of viewing an Arcadian landscape by Claude Lorrain, whereby the interdependency of the arts is highlighted as particular strains of music and poetry are brought to mind by the scene depicted. I will begin by reviewing the status of Radcliffe's inserted poetry, before moving on to analyse how the aesthetic encounters recounted in her travel journals shaped her romances. The essay will then conclude by considering how her imperilled, and often imprisoned, heroines draw on the arts, with a particular focus on Emily St Aubert's development as a poet in *The Mysteries of Udolpho* (1794).

The Problem of Form

Adding to the list of Radcliffe's innovations, George G. Dekker emphasises the point that her adaptation of the chivalric romance through the 'imaginative re-presentation of the tourist experience', then very much in vogue, made her 'the first to put tourism at the service and centre of the Romantic novel'.[9] Radcliffe was adept at drawing on other literary genres, as well as other artforms, and yet her particular blend of poetry and prose continues to divide critical opinion, even though Dahlia Porter notes that it was far from unusual to find verse and prose appearing 'next to each other on the page throughout the eighteenth century in drama, essays, and in various miscellaneous collections'.[10]

The choice to publish *The Mysteries of Udolpho* as 'A Romance; interspersed with some pieces of poetry' did not go unnoticed by the reviewer for *The British Critic*, who in August 1794 commented that 'The verses which are interspersed are announced on the title-page, and are consequently intended to be pointed out to particular notice.' However, the critic was ultimately unimpressed by the juxtaposition of poetry and prose:

> We have had occasion to observe that the introduction of verses in publications like the present is becoming a fashion, but we confess that they appear to us to be misplaced. However fond the reader may be of poetry, and however excellent the verses themselves, we will venture to assert that few will choose to peruse them whilst eagerly and anxiously pursuing the thread of a tale, a plain proof that, in such a situation, at least they are impertinent. Having said this, we are ready to confess that Mrs Radcliffe's poetical abilities are of the superior kind, and we shall be glad to see her compositions separately published.[11]

Barbara Benedict suggests that authors such as Radcliffe may actually have 'woven mottos and poetry into their novels with an eye to their afterlife in anthologies',[12] whilst Dahlia Porter notes the degree of commercial awareness behind the insertion of poetry: 'both authors and publishers recognized the value of compact, ready-made snippets for promoting novels through conventional reprinting practices and for directing how the novel would be represented in reviews'.[13] Radcliffe was clearly invested in both the aesthetic and commercial aspects of her artistic practice.

Radcliffe's poetry was instantly extracted and quoted by reviewers. The poem 'The Sea-Nymph' is the example Coleridge inserts in his review of *Udolpho*, printed in *The Critical Review* in August 1794, to demonstrate Radcliffe's 'beautiful', 'pleasing' but 'rather monotonous' poetry. Echoing *The British Critic*, Coleridge also argues that 'poetical beauties have not a fair chance of being attended to, amidst the stronger interest inspired by such a series of adventures'. There is a sense that here, quoted in isolation, it can be more greatly appreciated than when it is embedded in a narrative where readers are too eager for resolution to pause and enjoy the poetry. For Coleridge, 'The love of poetry is a taste; curiosity is a kind of appetite, and hurries headlong on, impatient for its complete gratification.'[14] This sentiment was also echoed by Anna Letitia Barbauld, who lamented that 'true lovers of poetry are almost apt to regret its being brought in as an accompaniment to narrative, where it is generally neglected'.[15]

Leah Price has noted the effect of such reviews on the readership: when 'reviewers project the divided structure of her texts onto her audience . . . The pace of reading becomes a test of taste'.[16] Distinguishing the discerning lover of poetry from the 'common reader', 'Appreciation of style proves the self-control needed to resist "impatient" greed for plot.'[17] This is still seen to this day in *Goodreads* reviews, as some readers confess to skipping the poetry, and others position themselves as more discerning by reading cover to cover.[18] Although eighteenth-century reading habits are difficult to recover, James Boswell observed that Samuel Johnson would not always finish a book he was reading, and recorded that his ability to skip sections to get 'at the substance of a book directly' was admired by a Mrs Knowles.[19] At a time when anthologies of fiction were increasingly popular, the style of composition favoured by Radcliffe similarly encourages readers to select what they want to read. Price argues that Radcliffe effectively 'turned narrative into a hook to hang anthology pieces on', prioritising the poetry over the prose.[20] Price, thus, provides a counter-argument to Mary Favret's assertion that the poetry is to be considered the dispensable aspect. Identifying no logic or pattern behind the insertion of quotations, she states that excerpts of poetry are merely used to make the novel 'look good'; that is, to enhance the realism of prose.[21] Ingrid Horrocks's analysis nonetheless highlights the 'self-consciousness with which Radcliffe uses quotations and poems within her novels', proving that 'there were thematic as well as generic issues at stake in the use of this form'.[22] For Horrocks, poetry is a form of sympathetic communication with the capacity to widen the perspective of the isolated heroine as she draws upon other voices. That said, the companionship provided by these other voices tellingly disappears once Emily is imprisoned at Udolpho, where she feels unable to read or write. Associating creativity with liberty, Horrocks proposes that 'the presence and absence of poetry becomes a tool for explaining the implications of the gothic itself'.[23] Horrocks's close reading of *Udolpho* demonstrates that there are gains to be made from a careful reading of the text as a whole. As one of the poems purportedly composed by Emily St Aubert, 'The Sea-Nymph' needs to be considered in relation to Radcliffe's wider aesthetic project, rather than extracted and read in isolation. The reader is told how this poem is inspired by the pageant Emily sees upon her arrival in Venice. Described as a spectacle that 'appeared like the vision of a poet suddenly embodied',[24] the account of the pageant illustrates the tendency for one artform to overlap with, and inspire, another. Where Horrocks focuses on the connection between imaginative and political freedom, my own approach will develop this idea to consider the interartistic discourse surrounding female creativity.

Radcliffe's Artistic Education

The lack of firm biographical knowledge about Ann Radcliffe can be attested to by the fact that Christina Rossetti abandoned her attempt to write a biography of the author in 1883 due to the scarcity of information available.[25] More recently, the research

ANN RADCLIFFE AND THE 'TOTAL WORK OF ART' 179

of Robert Miles and Rictor Norton has increased our understanding of Radcliffe's life and writing.[26] Nonetheless, Thomas Noon Talfourd's short and sanitised text, 'A Memoir of the Author, with Extracts from her Journals', prefixed to the posthumously published *Gaston De Blondeville, or the Court of Henry III Keeping Festival in Ardenne* (1826), remains a key source largely owing to the extracts of Radcliffe's travel diaries he embeds, to which I will turn later.

Despite going on to achieve a high degree of fame for her published works, Radcliffe did not court attention and avoided joining the literary coteries of the age. According to Talfourd's memoir, she had a 'natural repugnance to authorship'.[27] In this text, likely composed by Talfourd under the guidance of Radcliffe's husband, William, there is a careful attempt to secure her posthumous legacy as a woman quietly and contentedly confined to her 'domestic duties and pleasures', and who, with no children to take care of, wrote merely to entertain herself during her husband's absences from home when reporting on parliamentary debates.[28] The implication is that they were comfortably well-off, respectable people, and Mrs Radcliffe did not need to write in order to earn a living, despite her family background.

Ann Radcliffe was the only child of William Ward, a haberdasher, and Ann Oates. In Talfourd's memoir, her parents are described as 'persons of great respectability, who, though engaged in trade, were allied to families of independent fortune and high character'.[29] There is a clear reluctance to position Radcliffe as the daughter of a tradesman, although the family did enjoy a more illustrious connection to trade through their association with Josiah Wedgwood. Radcliffe's uncle, Thomas Bentley, was a partner in Wedgwood's pottery business from 1768 until his death in 1780. When the Wards' haberdashery business collapsed, Ann spent long periods with the Bentleys whilst her father re-established himself managing the Wedgwood showroom at Bath. Described as intelligent without being precocious, the 'docile' young Ann was a welcome guest in the Bentley household. In terms of her education, she is presented by Talfourd as suitably proficient, being 'instructed in all womanly accomplishments after the fashion of the time, but [she] was not exercised in the classics'.[30] Readers were, therefore, encouraged to see Radcliffe as curious, observant and talented, but not threateningly so, given that we are told that she entertained no ambition to raise herself beyond the usual confines of female education. However, it was through the Bentleys that she would have encountered luminaries including Hester Lynch Piozzi, Elizabeth Montagu and James 'Athenian' Stuart. Even if she was not schooled in the classics, she was surrounded by those actively engaged with literature, art and the proliferation of classical aesthetics.

The picture of Radcliffe Talfourd's short memoir provides is of a woman who enjoyed the arts in all its forms throughout her life. Aside from reading poetry and prose works, she liked to sing and regularly attended plays and operas. Furthermore, Radcliffe's novels are themselves populated by artistic heroines who regularly turn to their artistic skills by painting landscapes, playing musical instruments or composing poetry. Noting that the heroine of *The Italian* (1797) is a woman who engages in commercial activities by selling her artwork, Rictor Norton claims that the portrayal of Ellena Rosalba 'may reflect some of the feelings experienced by the daughter of a tradesman', as 'the author goes to some length to defend "the means of making this industry profitable without being dishonourable"'.[31] Furthermore, Norton suggests that Ellena's particular artistic talents are based upon those of Radcliffe's own aunt, Elizabeth, who drew copies from the antique for Wedgwood designs.[32]

Radcliffe's keen interest in art is evident in the extracts Talfourd quotes from her travel journals, as she dutifully yet enthusiastically follows the familiar itinerary of the domestic tourist. She describes seeing the great works of Anthony van Dyck, Peter Paul Rubens, Hans Holbein and Claude Lorrain on visits to Blenheim Palace, Warwick Castle and Knole, alongside contemporary works by Angelica Kauffman, Joshua Reynolds, Benjamin West and John Hoppner. Displaying a confident level of discernment in her critical assessment of these works, she notices the similarities and differences between the prestigious art collections she visits, noting that Warwick had the 'greatest number of Vandyke's pictures', and judging 'that fine picture of Lord Gowrie and Vandyke, by the latter; the finest portrait I ever saw, except one of Rubens, by himself, at Buckingham House'.[33] Radcliffe is not merely a tourist ticking off 'must see' items: her connoisseurship would lead her to discern at Blenheim that 'Vandyke's portrait of Charles the First's Queen is not so fine as his picture of her in the domestic drawing-room at Warwick Castle'.[34] Although she does not go into detail regarding what makes these particular portraits so 'fine', Radcliffe appears to have based her critiques of portraiture upon the ability of the artist to convey the character of their sitter. At Knole, she analyses the portraits of Elizabeth I's court based on their physiognomy: 'Salisbury, civil, sagacious and fastidious; effeminate, very fair: Burleigh, with a steady penetrating, grey eye, high forehead, with black hair; a cast of humour: Leicester, sturdy and crafty'.[35] However, it is not certain whether she actually surveys these images to confirm what she already knows of such historical figures from her reading of travel guides or history texts. On the same visit, she views the portraits of a group of celebrated literary figures and bases her appraisal of these portraits on their respective facial features, noting that Goldsmith's brow had 'nothing of the goodness of Johnson'. She also compares how these portraits relate to other images of the sitters she was more familiar with, recording how Dryden looked 'younger than usual', whilst Pope's 'old, wrinkled, spectre-like' image means that Swift appeared 'gentle in comparison'.[36] Here, the immediate context of the paintings and prior knowledge of other portraits of the sitters combine to create a subjective evaluation.

The space between the appearance of these portraits and the pre-existing ideal Radcliffe has in mind from other artworks she has seen, either in person or circulated as prints, is particularly illustrative of the instability and unreliability of likeness in Radcliffe's novels. In *Udolpho*, for example, the aged Laurentini not only laments that her own appearance has drastically changed since the miniature portrait of her was painted, but mistakenly takes the 'resemblance between Emily and her unfortunate aunt' as evidence to make the 'bold assertion' that 'Emily was the daughter of the Marchioness de Villeroi' (661). As Joe Bray observes, 'the portrait, rather than a transparent signifier of identity, is in fact a complex site of debate'.[37] An image on its own can all too easily fail to convey the precise information required, and in *Udolpho* Emily rightly resists identifying the portrait of the Marchioness until she has textual evidence to confirm the precise nature of their familial relationship.

Radcliffe would not hold back from criticising paintings that she thought failed to convey emotion or meaning. On a visit to Hampshire in September 1798, Radcliffe recorded her opinion of Benjamin West's *The Raising of Lazarus* (1780), commissioned as an altarpiece for Winchester Cathedral.[38] Radcliffe was far from impressed: 'The attitude of Lazarus is indeed such, that he might be taken for a person dying rather than one returning to life.'[39] Furthermore, she noted that 'The faces of the

ANN RADCLIFFE AND THE 'TOTAL WORK OF ART' 181

spectators do not sufficiently speak astonishment, awe and adoration.'[40] A painting's success, or indeed failure, depended on the artist's ability to convey the human emotions required of the narrative. Furthermore, for Radcliffe, there is more to art than the realistic representation of a scene; a viewer should see and experience more than that which is directly represented on canvas – as can be seen in Radcliffe's appreciation of landscapes, particularly the work of Claude.

Travel Writing and Art

Talfourd embeds extracts from Radcliffe's travel journals in his memoir as a 'means of watching the development of her faculties and tastes in her daily pursuits'.[41] According to Radcliffe, writing her notebooks allowed her to relive events, 'prolonging those vivid pleasures of life' and 'preserv[ing] the impressions of the living picture of the memory in its own colours'.[42] Statements like this, which present writing as akin to painting a scene, reinforce the by now long-standing critical assessment of Radcliffe's novels as painterly in their description. In 1798, Nathan Drake described Radcliffe as a writer 'who to the wild landscapes of Salvator Rosa added the softer graces of a Claude'.[43] These particular associations remained attached to her. Angela Wright and Dale Townshend note that it was through such comparisons that 'Radcliffe's fictions were construed as "masterpieces"', with the author herself 'elevated to the sublime status of Artist'.[44] Talfourd similarly praises Radcliffe with the observation that 'Perhaps no writer in prose, or verse, has been so happy in describing the varied effects of light in winged words.'[45] Indeed, Radcliffe took delight in observing the ever-evolving effect of light on a landscape; for instance, she described the sunset over the Isle of Wight in such terms numerous times. On a visit there in 1801 she captured a 'Lovely sun-set; a roseate, melting into saffron and shades of blue; some light purple streaks';[46] returning to the same spot in 1811, she remarked that it was 'Delightful to catch the different saffron, crimson, or fiery tints among the purple streaks.'[47] Like an artist carefully mixing their colour palette, Radcliffe documents the changing effects of the sunlight and sea vapour upon the waves in a manner reminiscent of Claude, who, according to Joachim von Sandrart's *Teutsche Academie* (1675), 'tried by every means to penetrate nature, lying in the fields before the break of day and until night in order to learn to represent very exactly the red morning sky, sunrise and sunset and the evening hours'.[48] Radcliffe's observations of light can be seen in a passage from *A Sicilian Romance* (1790) in which she describes the visual effect of the setting sun on the sublime landscape, combined with the sound of the waves and the sensation of the light breeze, as being conducive to creativity:

> The purple flush of evening was diffused over the heavens. The sun, involved in clouds of splendid and innumerable hues, was setting o'er the distant waters, whose clear bosom glowed with rich reflection. The beauty of the scene, the soothing murmur of the high trees, waved by the light air which overshadowed her, and the soft shelling of the waves that flowed gently in upon the shores, insensibly sunk her mind into a state of repose.[49]

In such a state of repose, Julia is in the perfect mindset for artistic creativity to flow and proceeds to compose an ode 'To Evening'. Julia experiences the power of music and poetry to reunite her with those she loves when, on singing this ode, her beloved Hippolitus suddenly appears. Here, visual, musical and poetical imagination combine, and serve to drive the plot. What is more, Radcliffe puts a woman in the privileged position of a poet responding to nature.

Hailing Radcliffe as a writer who unites 'the eye of the painter, with the spirit of the poet', Scott identifies *A Sicilian Romance* as the first work to introduce 'a tone of fanciful description and impressive narrative, which had hitherto been exclusively applied to poetry'.[50] Scott goes on to state, however, that Radcliffe's 'poetry partakes of the rich and beautiful colouring which distinguishes her prose composition, and has, perhaps, the same fault, of not being in every case quite precise in expressing the meaning of the author'.[51] For Scott, Radcliffe's poetry and prose blur within the novel. A distinction between the sister arts was nonetheless important to Radcliffe, as she drew on the creative potential for one artform to inspire another.

In its depiction of poetic creativity inspired by the journey through a sublime land-scape, this episode from *A Sicilian Romance* mirrors the composition of Radcliffe's own work. In *A Journey Made in the Summer of 1794*, for instance, she describes how the scenery around Ullswater awakens the 'poet's eye':

> The effect of Ulls-water is, that, awful as its scenery appears, it awakens the mind to expectations still more awful, and, touching all the powers of imagination, inspires that 'fine phrensy' descriptive of the poet's eye, which not only bodies forth unreal forms, but imparts to substantial objects a character higher than their own.[52]

There is space for fiction in the travelogue as the landscape stimulates the poet's imagi-nation. Yet Walter Scott's critical assessment of Radcliffe contrasted the clarity of her travel writing with the indistinct style of her fiction. Echoing *The English Review*'s comment that 'in her romances she paints fancy-pieces; here she draws from nature', he similarly declared: '*Udolpho* is an exquisite effect-piece, *Hardwick* a striking and faithful portrait'.[53] By contrast, when Talfourd describes the composition of *The Mys-teries of Udolpho* as a process of 'bringing out into distinctness all the hints and dim pictures, which have long floated in the mind', he more fully captures the essence of Radcliffe's tactic of delayed revelation in visual terms: a metaphorical clearing of the mist over the rugged landscape.[54] As opposed to the dichotomy suggested by Scott, nature and fancy are held in tension. Furthermore, Radcliffe's travel journals show how the 'real' stimulated her more imaginative output, suggesting that her travel writ-ing and her novel writing were not totally separate projects. Close attention to her references to Claude reveal the interartistic effect she strove to emulate.

Claude and the Total Work of Art

Like Radcliffe, Claude was recognised for doing something different; Katharine Baetjer describes how his 'observation and transcription of light falling on landscape were unique in his time'.[55] Radcliffe never visited Italy, so she initially relied upon scenes like those painted by Claude to fuel her imagination. As noted, the similarity between Radcliffe's landscapes and those of Claude is frequently remarked upon even though Radcliffe only names three artists in her novels: Salvator Rosa and Domenichino in *The Mysteries of Udolpho*, and Guido Reni in *The Italian*; but her admiration of

ANN RADCLIFFE AND THE 'TOTAL WORK OF ART'

Claude is evident in her travel writings. In *A Journey Made in the Summer of 1794*, for instance, Radcliffe compares the sublime Rhineland scenery of Godesberg to a Claudian landscape:

> To the west, under the glow of sun-set, the landscape melted into the horizon in tints so soft, so clear, so delicately roseate as Claude only could have painted. Viewed, as we then saw it, beyond a deep and dark arch of the ruin, its effect was enchanting; it was to the eye, what the finest strains of Paisiello are to the heart, or the poetry of Collins is to the fancy – all tender, sweet, elegant and glowing . . .[56]

In this instance, artistic representation becomes the original by which to appraise a real-life situation. Knowledge of Claude sets a precedent for Radcliffe's appreciation of natural scenery, following the craze for tourists using a tinted, convex mirror, or 'Claude glass', to help them view their surroundings as a Claudian landscape and to facilitate their artistic attempts to recreate the composition and tones of his work. Whilst art is Radcliffe's reference point, there is more to the relationship between writer and painter than a useful stock of images to draw upon.

The interartistic comparison, whereby the viewing experience is described as akin to the effect of listening to the music of Paisiello or the poetry of Collins, allows for similarity and difference through the acknowledgement that music appeals to the heart whilst poetry fuels imaginative thought. Collins is particularly evoked as the light begins to fade and Radcliffe turns to view the prospect over the 'wild and awful mountains'. As the vision becomes obscure, she appeals to another artform, in this case, poetry. In line with her novelistic practice, the words of Collins brought to mind by the scene are embedded with the acknowledgement that 'we seemed to have found the spot, for which Collins wished':

> Now let me rove some wild and heathy scene,
> Or find some ruin 'midst its dreary dells,
> Whose walls more awful nod
> By thy religious gleams.[57]

Unlike the disappointed traveller in Radcliffe's *Gaston de Blondeville*, who fails to find the forest of Arden as described in *As You Like It*, she successfully matches appropriate works of art and literature to real-life experiences in terms of the mood evoked.

Whether Radcliffe is viewing a sublime landscape in person or viewing an artistic representation of it, the effect is similar, in that her description draws on visual art, music and poetry, as seen in her record of a visit to Lord Eardley's art collection at Belvedere House in June 1805. There is nonetheless a notable difference in terms of the pleasurable blend between artforms conjured by Claude's canvas:

> In a shaded corner, near the chimney, a most exquisite Claude, an evening view, perhaps over the Campagna of Rome. The sight of this picture imparted much of the luxurious repose and satisfaction, which we derive from contemplating the finest scenes of Nature. Here was the poet, as well as the painter, touching the imagination, and making you see more than the picture contained. You saw the real light of the sun, you breathed the air of the country, you felt all the circumstances of a luxurious

climate on the most serene and beautiful landscape; and, the mind being thus soft-ened, you almost fancied you heard Italian music on the air – the music of Paisiello; and such, doubtless, were the scenes that inspired him.[58]

Radcliffe describes Claude's work as that of the poet and the painter combined. By this she means that his work is not merely a direct representation of a scene on canvas: it fires the imaginative faculties. Radcliffe describes being transported by the image before her to the extent that all her senses are awakened, and she can almost hear Italian music and feel the warmth of the sun upon her skin. She speculates that the Claudian landscape must have inspired Paisiello, thus presenting a chain of influence whereby the combined visual and audio effect created inspires her own writing. The reference to the Italian composer Giovanni Paisiello is particularly significant given that he is most connected to opera, an artform often considered a 'total work of art' owing to the combination of music and theatre. Where Lipski proposes that Radcliffe's fiction makes a 'multi-faceted contribution to the development of European Romanti-cism' by 'uniting literature, music and painting' in her romances, such qualities are also present in her travel writing.[59]

With Claude's landscapes described as combining the work of the poet and the painter, distinctions between artistic modes become blurred, with the effect here verg-ing on the supernatural. Claude's image has the ability to conjure music in Radcliffe's mind, but her mention of Paisiello means that the music evoked does not fit with the time of the painting's production. The description, thus, collapses time and place as well as artistic mode. The fact that Radcliffe moves seamlessly between her descrip-tions of paintings and the scenery she observes out of the windows at Belvedere House further exemplifies the unity between artistic modes fostered by an immersive viewing experience.

The praise of Claude as a poet mirrors the celebration of Radcliffe's painterly abili-ties, positioning them as kindred spirits with complementary aesthetic aims. Where James V. Mirollo presents ekphrasis as a technique writers could use to assert their dominance, describing it as a kind of 'ventriloquism' by which the literary practitio-ner appropriates the visual for their own ends, the picture Radcliffe develops through interartistic references places the sister arts in a supportive, symbiotic relationship.[60] The aesthetic experience of viewing a Claude painting thus exemplifies what she tries to accomplish in writing, with other artforms embedded as they are brought to mind. When combined with poetry, such as the verse embedded in *Udolpho*, such interartis-tic experiences help to shape and comment upon the heroine's aesthetic development.

The Heroine as an Artist and a Poet

In Radcliffe's first work of fiction, *The Castles of Athlin and Dunbayne* (1789), she illustrates the damage done to society when artistic women like her heroine, Laura, are kept locked away:

> The progress which she made in music and drawing, and in the lighter subjects of literature, while it pleased the Baroness, who was her sole instructress, brought with it bitter apprehension, that these accomplishments would probably be buried in the obscurity of a prison; still, however, they were not useless, since they served

at present to cheat affliction of many a weary moment, and would in future delude the melancholy hours of solitude.[61]

For Laura, the primary aim of her artistic accomplishment may be to attract male attention, rather than to amuse herself, but it is made clear that the civilising effects of the arts are lost when women are imprisoned; female influence is needed to polish society.

To return to the argument put forward by Horrocks, introduced at the start of this chapter, liberty is fundamental to Radcliffe's conception of creativity, and this idea is written into the very structure of *Udolpho*: 'In the politically charged atmosphere of the mid-1790s, *Udolpho* amounts to a historically situated argument for the need for imaginative freedom and its associated sympathies.'[62] Horrocks points to the significance behind Radcliffe's particular choice of extracts. For example, James Thomson's *Britannia, A Poem* (1729) provides an anachronistic yet effective way of promoting political virtue after gaining new-found popularity in the wake of the French Revolution.[63] Horrocks's close reading demonstrates how 'Emily's desires and need for release from the pressures she is under are aligned with the needs of Britain itself';[64] my intention, however, is to chart Emily's artistic development. Following Emily St Aubert's journey from the rural idyll of La Vallée to the fairyland of Venice, and on to the threatening towers of Udolpho, travel serves a key function in charting the heroine's development. Emily's impressions of her surroundings are often influenced by external aesthetic forces. The possibility for music, art and poetry to alter her perceptions, and to encourage speculation on the supernatural, can be traced from the opening scenes at La Vallée.

The picture Radcliffe paints of Emily's upbringing is one of order and harmony. This rural idyll, with Gascony presented as a prelapsarian Garden of Eden, reveals a reciprocal relationship between character and setting. The family home and its surroundings have played a role in Emily's development, with the internal spaces of the house, including Emily's room, flowing seamlessly into this landscape: 'The windows of this room . . . descended to the floor, and, opening upon the little lawn that surrounded the house, the eye was led between groves of almond, palm-trees, flowering-ash, and myrtle, to the distant landscape' (3). The well-stocked library is characterised as a similarly accessible space. Peter Otto likens the movement from room to room to Enlightenment education, noting 'an axis that extends in smooth progression from the domestic to acquired knowledge, experiment, and then, beyond the limits of La Vallée, to the world of nature'.[65] With the library opening 'upon a grove', the architectural layout is symbolic of an unobstructed flow of ideas from ancient and modern scholars to that which can be observed in the natural world. Otto's emphasis on experiment and observation particularly marks La Vallée as a place of empirical thought. However, with no restraining boundaries, it is possible to take ideas too far, and the inhabitants are not exempt from excessive sentiment, an over-active imagination or supernatural fancy.

An overly sentimental attachment to home is something Emily learns from her father, but he is anxious to educate her on the dangers of excess sensibility: '"A well-informed mind" he would say, "is the best security against the contagion of folly and of vice"' (6). In spite of this aim, Emily's education arms her with only a 'general view of the sciences' as opposed to 'an exact acquaintance with every part of elegant literature' (6). Her fanciful disposition means that when she sees strange lights in the woods her first thoughts are of fairies, before her father recommends using observation to find a rational explanation for the light source: '"Are you such an admirer of nature," said St. Aubert, "and so little acquainted with her appearances as not to know that for the glow-worm? But come," added he gaily, "step a little further, and we shall see fairies, perhaps; they are often companions"' (15). The willingness to indulge in such fancy himself shows how the supernatural is simultaneously accepted and rejected in the text. Radcliffe herself took delight in the supernatural appearance of glow worms. Recalling the inspiration behind one of Emily's early poems, she recorded in her journal that 'Glow worms, in great numbers, shone silently and faintly on the dewy banks, like something supernatural.'[66]

The poem 'The Glow-Worm', composed by Emily, is readily acknowledged to be lacking in style: 'The lines go in a sort of tripping measure, which I thought might suit the subject well enough, but I fear they are too irregular' (16). Although her father would never discourage Emily's attempts at composition, his taste is not deluded by his devotion:

> Whatever St. Aubert might think of the stanzas, he would not deny his daughter the pleasure of believing that he approved them; and, having given his commendation, he sunk into a reverie, and they walked in silence.

> A faint erroneous ray
> Glanc'd from th' imperfect surfaces of things,
> Flung half an image on the straining eye;
> While waving woods, and villages, and streams,
> And rocks, and mountain-tops, that long retain
> The ascending gleam, are all one swimming scene,
> Uncertain if beheld. (17)

The lines of poetry inserted to accompany St Aubert's reverie are taken from Thomson's 'Summer' (1727, II, lines 1687–93), providing a point of comparison with Emily's as yet undeveloped talent. Stefani Lethbridge notes that Thomson's *Seasons* was read in the manner of an anthology in that readers could select whatever particular 'beauties' appealed to them.[67] With certain extracts inserted in *Udolpho*, the effect is akin to an anthology. According to Leah Price, in fact, Radcliffe is 'Like an anthologist' in that she 'juxtaposes without justifying'. What is more, 'The anachronism of her quotations and the slackness of her transitions call attention to the gulf separating decoration from motivation, style from plot: the rules of the anthology from the rules of the novel.'[68] However, a close reading of chapter 3, when Emily and her father leave La Vallée, shows the value of reading in detail, and the significance of the insertion of poetry.

Chapter 3 opens with the following epigraph, taken from James Beattie's *The Minstrel* (1771, I, lines 73–83):

> O how canst thou renounce the boundless store
> Of charms which to her vot'ry yields!
> The warbling woodland, the resounding shore,
> The pomp of groves, and garniture of fields;

All that the genial ray of morning gilds,
And all that echoes to the song of even;
All that the mountain's shelt'ring bosom shields,
And all the dread magnificence of heaven;
O how canst thou renounce, and hope to be forgiven!
. . . .
These Charms shall work thy soul's eternal health,
And love, and gentleness, and joy, impart. (27)

Within the context of *Udolpho*, this extract not only highlights the significance of landscape, but hints that Emily should perhaps be wary of leaving the pastoral delights of home. Published in two parts, the first appearing in 1771 followed by the second in 1774, *The Minstrel* constitutes an early example of Romantic poetry as it follows the development of a poet's mind under the influence of 'nature'. As Beattie explained in his preface to the work:

> The design was to trace the progress of a Poetical Genius, born in a rude age, from the first dawning of fancy and reason, till that period at which he may be supposed capable of appearing in the world as a MINSTREL, that is, as an itinerant Poet and Musician; – a character, which, according to the notions of our fore-fathers, was not only respectable, but sacred.[69]

For Ian C. Robertson, Edwin, the minstrel of the piece, 'is not a construct created to make a philosophical point; he is a poetical portrayal of Beattie's own ado-lescent spirit'.[70] In the autobiographical preoccupation with poetic genius, which would become a central concern of the Romantic movement, Beattie's influence can be seen through to Wordsworth's *The Prelude* (1799–1850). Radcliffe's use of extracts from *The Minstrel* in *Udolpho* can thus provide an opportunity to consider Emily St Aubert's creative development and, in turn, Radcliffe's own position as a poet.

Further lines from *The Minstrel* are woven into the text as Emily leaves La Vallée to embark on what will be a transformative journey through wild landscapes:

> Leaving the splendour of extensive prospects, they now entered this narrow valley, screened by
>
> > Rocks on rocks piled, as if by magic spell,
> > Here scorch'd by lightenings, there with ivy green.[71]
>
> . . . This was such a scene as *Salvator* would have chosen, had he then existed, for his canvas; St. Aubert, impressed with the romantic character of the place, almost expected to see banditti start from behind some projecting rock, and he kept his hand upon the arms with which he always travelled. (30)

Radcliffe is well aware that her reference to Rosa and her quotation of Beattie are anachronistic in a text set in 1584. On one level, this is merely a shorthand means of setting a scene and creating a mood through referring to popular works of which the reader may be aware, yet the insertion of more contemporaneous references also implicitly asks the reader to consider that the dangers Emily faces are not restricted to the past. Furthermore, given that Emily chooses to sketch this rugged landscape, she is positioned as an originator who precedes rather than follows Rosa: a woman of taste, an artist and poet, setting off on a journey of self-discovery that pre-empts Wordsworth.

The chapter ends with Emily and her father meeting the man she will eventually marry, Valancourt – a reader of Homer, Horace and Petrarch. In a text where literary references abound, his reading is to be seen as a positive character trait, in contrast with the villain, Montoni, who tellingly does not quote any literary works. Following her father's instructions, 'to resist first impressions, and to acquire the steady dignity of mind, that can alone counterbalance the passions' (5), Emily constantly re-evaluates her perceptions of Montoni and seeks to work out what the architectural surroundings of his Venetian villa reveal about him. Indeed, the description of Venice, akin to a theatre set, divides the public facade from private reality behind the scenes, whilst also stimulating Emily's creative impulses:

> If Emily had admired the magnificence of the saloon, she was not less surprised, on observing the half-furnished and forlorn appearance of the apartments she passed in the way to her chamber . . . It brought gloomy images to her mind, but the view of the Adriatic soon gave her others more airy, among which was that of the sea-nymph, whose delights she had before amused herself with picturing; and, anxious to escape from serious reflections, she now endeavoured to throw her fanciful ideas into a train. (178–9)

The pomp and pageantry of Venice is no more than a performance. And yet the procession of Neptune she witnesses, accompanied by music, singing and performances of the poetry of Ariosto and Petrarch, acts as a contagion to her imagination: 'the fanciful images, which it awakened in Emily's mind, lingered there long after the procession had passed away' (178). The poems and songs Emily hears the gondoliers perform, and those she composes herself, transport her to an imaginary world, but she remains alert to the situation in which she finds herself.

Earlier I proposed that the poem 'The Sea-Nymph', which Emily composes whilst in Venice, should be read within the context of the novel as a whole, where the theme of female suppression under patriarchal power reflects Montoni's hold over Emily and her aunt. The mermaid Emily writes of in the first person is no deadly siren; she uses her voice to save sailors, but finds herself punished by Neptune for her good deeds:

> And thus the lonely hours I cheat,
> Soothing the ship-wreck'd sailor's heart,
> Till from the waves the storms retreat,
> And o'er the east the day-beams dart.
>
> Neptune for this oft binds me fast
> To rocks below, with coral chain,
> Till all the tempest's over-past,
> And drowning seamen cry in vain. (181)

ANN RADCLIFFE AND THE 'TOTAL WORK OF ART'   189

A pre-chapter epigraph taken from *Julius Caesar* (1.2. lines 202–9) follows on directly from 'The Sea-Nymph':

He is a great observer, and he looks
Quite through the deeds of men: he loves no plays, he hears no music;
Seldom he smiles; and smiles in such a sort,
As if he mock'd himself, and scorn'd his spirit
That could be mov'd to smile at any thing.
Such men as he be never at heart's ease,
While they behold a greater than themselves. (182)

Montoni loves no plays, hears no music; and, as Horrocks reminds us, Emily stops composing at Udolpho, her creativity stifled under his control. Whilst some readers have readily admitted to skipping or skim reading the poetry, its significance is perhaps emphasised even more potently by its absence in the Udolpho sections. The poetry Emily does compose, therefore, deserves closer scrutiny for what it reveals about her state of mind, character and aesthetic development.

Answering the call for Radcliffe's poetry to be extracted to be more fully appreciated, a collection of verse taken from her novels was published in 1816. Entitled *The Poems of Mrs. Ann Radcliffe: Author of 'The Mysteries of Udolpho'* (1816), the volume nevertheless implies her legacy was as a novelist rather than as a poet. Dahlia Porter's research into the publication history of Radcliffe's poetry through the course of the nineteenth century has found that 'Radcliffe's novels actively defined her verse even as she was anthologized as a poet', citing the example that when *The Gentleman's Magazine* reprinted 'Song of a Spirit' from *The Romance of the Forest* (1791), it was attributed to the heroine, Adeline.[72] The hold the original novelistic context exerts over these poems illustrates their place within Radcliffe's wider aesthetic project. For Radcliffe, the arts are supportive sisters; poetry, music and visual art can work together to enhance a mood, appeal to different senses and stimulate creativity.

Notes

1. Radcliffe received £500 for *The Mysteries of Udolpho* and £800 for *The Italian*. See Rictor Norton, *Mistress of Udolpho: The Life of Ann Radcliffe* (London and New York: Leicester University Press, 1999), 94–5.
2. Walter Scott, *Biographical Memoirs of Eminent Novelists, and Other Distinguished Persons*, in *The Miscellaneous Prose Works of Sir Walter Scott*, 20 vols (Edinburgh: Robert Cadell; London: Whittaker & Co, 1834), 1:342.
3. T. J. Mathias, 'The Pursuits of Literature: A Satirical Poem in Four Dialogues', 8th edn (Dublin: J. Milliken, 1798), 58.
4. Walter Scott, 'Prefatory Memoir', in *The Works of Mrs. Ann Radcliffe*, Ballantyne's Novelist's Library, 10 vols (London: Hurst, Robinson, and Co., 1821–4), 10:vi.
5. 'Review of *A Journey Made in the Summer of 1794 . . .*', *English Review* (July 1795), 1.
6. My use of the term 'Romance' is in line with Radcliffe's description of her work. The categorisation 'A Romance' on the title page not only signals to readers that her work will combine the real with the extraordinary, but also highlights the importance of a transformative journey. For Samuel Taylor Coleridge's review of *The Mysteries of Udolpho*, see *The Critical Review* (August 1794), 361–72.

7. Jakub Lipski, 'Ann Radcliffe and the Sister Arts Ideal', in *The Enchantress of Words, Sounds and Images: Anniversary Essays on Ann Radcliffe (1764–1823)*, ed. Jakub Lipski and Jacek Mydla (Palo Alto: Academica Press, 2015), 18.

8. K. F. E Trahndorff, *Ästhetik oder Lehre von Weltanschauung und Kunst*, 2 vols (Berlin: Maurersche Buchhandlung, 1827).

9. George G. Dekker, *Fictions of Romantic Tourism: Radcliffe, Scott, and Mary Shelley* (Stanford: Stanford University Press, 2005), 93, 71.

10. Dahlia Porter, 'The Spectral Iamb: The Poetic Afterlives of the Late Eighteenth-Century Novel', in *The Afterlives of Eighteenth-Century Fiction*, ed. Daniel Cook and Nick Seager (Cambridge: Cambridge University Press, 2015), 153.

11. 'Review of *The Mysteries of Udolpho*', *The British Critic* 4 (August 1794), 120. Charlotte Smith and Mary Robinson were also known for inserting poetry into their prose works.

12. Barbara Benedict, 'The Paradox of the Anthology: Collecting and *Différence* in Eighteenth-Century Britain', *New Literary History* 34, no. 2 (2003): 234.

13. Porter, 'The Spectral Iamb', 155.

14. Samuel Taylor Coleridge, 'Review of *The Mysteries of Udolpho*', *The Critical Review* (August 1794), 369.

15. Anna Letitia Barbauld, 'Mrs. Radcliffe', *The British Novelists*, 50 vols (London: F. C. and J. Rivington, 1810), 43:viii.

16. Leah Price, *The Anthology and the Rise of the Novel: From Richardson to George Eliot* (Cambridge: Cambridge University Press, 2000, repr. 2014), 97.

17. Price, *The Anthology and the Rise of the Novel*.

18. 'The Mysteries of Udolpho by Ann Radcliffe', *Goodreads*, https://www.goodreads.com/book/show/93134.The_Mysteries_of_Udolpho (accessed 10 February 2023).

19. For Boswell's quotation of Mrs Knowles, see John Brewer, *The Pleasures of the Imagination: English Culture in the Eighteenth Century* (London: HarperCollins, 1997), 192.

20. Price, *The Anthology and the Rise of the Novel*, 91.

21. Mary Favret, 'Telling Tales About Genre: Poetry in the Romantic Novel', *Studies in the Novel* 26, no. 1/2 (1994): 166.

22. Ingrid Horrocks, '"Her Ideas Arranged Themselves": Re-Membering Poetry in Radcliffe', *Studies in Romanticism* 47, no. 4 (2008): 508.

23. Horrocks, 'Re-Membering Poetry in Radcliffe', 508.

24. Ann Radcliffe, *The Mysteries of Udolpho*, ed. Bonamy Dobrée (Oxford: Oxford University Press, 1998), 178. Further references parenthetical.

25. Aside from her published works, Radcliffe only left behind a commonplace book, now held in Boston Public Library, documenting her health during her final months (November 1822–February 1823), and a letter to her mother-in-law regarding the financial support they provide her, discovered at the British Library in 2014. See The Evelyn Papers, Vol. DXXII, Add MS 78689.

26. See Robert Miles, *Ann Radcliffe: The Great Enchantress* (Manchester: Manchester University Press, 1995); Norton, *Mistress of Udolpho*.

27. [Thomas Noon Talfourd], *A Memoir of the Author, with Extracts from her Journals*, prefixed to Ann Radcliffe, *Gaston De Blondeville; Or, The Court of Henry III. Keeping Festival in Ardenne, A Romance*, 4 vols (London: Henry Colburn, 1826), 1:7. Contains approximately 6,000 words covering Radcliffe's travels around England post-1797.

28. Talfourd, *A Memoir of the Author*, 1:3.

29. Talfourd, *A Memoir of the Author*, 1:5.

30. Talfourd, *A Memoir of the Author*, 1:6.

31. Norton, *Mistress of Udolpho*, 44, quoting Ann Radcliffe, *The Italian*, ed. Frederick Garber (Oxford: Oxford University Press, 2017), 364.

32. See also Hannah Moss, 'Sister Artists: The Artist Heroine in British Women's Writing, 1760–1830', PhD thesis, University of Sheffield (2020).

33. Talfourd, *A Memoir of the Author*, 1:69, 1:72.
34. Talfourd, *A Memoir of the Author*, 1:63.
35. Talfourd, *A Memoir of the Author*, 1:70.
36. Talfourd, *A Memoir of the Author*, 1:72.
37. Joe Bray, 'Ann Radcliffe, Precursors and Portraits', in *Ann Radcliffe, Romanticism and the Gothic*, ed. Dale Townshend and Angela Wright (Cambridge: Cambridge University Press, 2014), 35. For further discussion of the significance of picture identification to Gothic fiction, see Kamilla Elliott, *Portraiture and British Gothic Fiction: The Rise of Picture Identification, 1764–1835* (Baltimore: Johns Hopkins University Press, 2012).
38. The painting remained in situ from 1782 until 1900 when it was sold to J. Pierpont Morgan. It is now in the collection of the Wadsworth Atheneum, Connecticut. Object ID: 1900.3.
39. Talfourd, *A Memoir of the Author*, 1:32.
40. Talfourd, *A Memoir of the Author*, 1:33.
41. Talfourd, *A Memoir of the Author*, 1:5.
42. Talfourd, *A Memoir of the Author*, 1:30.
43. See Nathan Drake, *Literary Hours: Or, Sketches Critical and Narrative* (London: T. Cadell and W. Davies, 1798), 249.
44. Dale Townshend and Angela Wright, 'Gothic and Romantic Engagements: The Critical Reception of Ann Radcliffe, 1789–1850', in *Ann Radcliffe, Romanticism and the Gothic*, ed. Dale Townshend and Angela Wright (Cambridge: Cambridge University Press, 2014), 19–20.
45. Talfourd, *A Memoir of the Author*, 1:119.
46. Talfourd, *A Memoir of the Author*, 1:54.
47. Talfourd, *A Memoir of the Author*, 1:74.
48. Sandrart quoted in Katharine Baetjer, 'Claude Lorrain (1604/5?–1682)', in *Heilbrunn Timeline of Art History* (New York: The Metropolitan Museum of Art, 2014), http://www.metmuseum.org/toah/hd/clau/hd_clau.html (accessed 15 November 2023).
49. Ann Radcliffe, *A Sicilian Romance*, ed. Alison Milbank (Oxford: Oxford University Press, 1993), 42.
50. Scott, 'Prefatory Memoir', iv.
51. Scott, 'Prefatory Memoir', xxxv.
52. Ann Radcliffe, *A Journey Made in the Summer of 1794 Through Holland and the Western Frontier of Germany . . .* (Dublin: William Porter, 1795), 477.
53. Scott, *Biographical Memoirs of Eminent Novelists*, 381.
54. Talfourd, *A Memoir of the Author*, 1:9.
55. Baetjer, 'Claude Lorrain'.
56. Radcliffe, *A Journey Made in the Summer of 1794*, 138–9.
57. Radcliffe, *A Journey Made in the Summer of 1794*, 138–9, quoting William Collins, 'Ode To Evening' (1747), lines 29–32.
58. Talfourd, *A Memoir of the Author*, 1:65.
59. Lipski, 'Ann Radcliffe and the Sister Arts Ideal', 18.
60. James V. Mirollo, 'Sibling Rivalry in the Sister Arts Family: The Case of Poetry vs. Painting in the Italian Renaissance', in *So Rich a Tapestry: The Sister Arts and Cultural Studies*, ed. Ann Hurley and Kate Greenspan (Lewisburg: Bucknell University Press; London: Associated University Presses, 1995), 39–40.
61. Ann Radcliffe, *The Castles of Athlin and Dunbayne*, ed. Alison Milbank (Oxford and New York: Oxford University Press, 1995), 65.
62. Horrocks, 'Re-Membering Poetry in Radcliffe', 527.
63. Horrocks, 'Re-Membering Poetry in Radcliffe', 515; see also John Barrell and Harriet Guest, 'Thomson in the 1790s', in *James Thomson: Essays for the Tercentenary*, ed. Richard Terry (Liverpool: Liverpool University Press, 2000), 217–34.
64. Horrocks, 'Re-Membering Poetry in Radcliffe', 515.

65. Peter Otto, '"Where am I, and what?" – Architecture, Environment, and the Transformation of Experience in Radcliffe's *The Mysteries of Udolpho*', *European Romantic Review* 25, no. 3 (2014): 302.
66. Talfourd, *A Memoir of the Author*, 1:42.
67. Stefani Lethbridge, 'Anthological Reading Habits in the Eighteenth Century: The Case of Thomson's *Seasons*', in *Anthologies of British Poetry: Critical Perspectives from Literary and Cultural Studies*, ed. Barbara Korte, Stefanie Lethbridge and Ralf Schneider (Amsterdam: Rodopi, 2000), 89–103.
68. Price, *The Anthology and the Rise of the Novel*, 94.
69. James Beattie, 'Preface' to *The Minstrel; Or, the Progress of Genius* (London: John Sharpe, 1817), 4.
70. Ian C. Robertson, 'The Minstrel: A Missing Link in Scottish Poetry', *Studies in Scottish Poetry* 43, no. 2 (2017): 250.
71. Quoting James Beattie, *The Minstrel* (1774), II, lines 56–7.
72. Porter, 'The Spectral Iamb', 164.

Part III:

Modes and Spaces of Performance

11

HAYWOOD'S WHIMSICAL ADVENTURES: THE NOVEL AND THE ROCOCO

Joseph Drury

Whim. *n.s.* A freak; an odd fancy; a caprice; an irregular motion of desire.
     – Samuel Johnson, *A Dictionary of the English Language* (1755)[1]

SCHOLARLY EFFORTS TO draw parallels between eighteenth-century literature and the rococo in the arts have always struggled with the fundamental incommensurability of different artistic mediums. As René Wellek argued many years ago, 'the various arts – the plastic arts, literature, and music – have each their individual evolution, with a different tempo and a different internal structure of elements'. Taking aim at the German tradition of *Geistesgeschichte* popularised by Oswald Spengler, Wellek questioned the value of comparative studies of literature and other arts that invoked a vague, mystical 'time-spirit' to discover only 'the slightest and most tenuous thematic or emotional similarities'. Instead of unhelpful parallels between the theories of artists working in different mediums that revealed little about the work they actually produced, or subjective claims about the similar 'moods' their work inspired, Wellek wanted comparisons of the arts to begin with their 'common social and cultural background' before proceeding to 'an analysis of the works themselves'.[2]

Wellek's call went largely unheeded by Helmut Hatzfeld, who opened his 1972 comparative study of the rococo with the rather astonishing claim that 'all the literary works of the eighteenth century display the same spirit or cultural style'.[3] But the tendentious analogising in Wylie Sypher's *Rococo to Cubism in Art and Literature* (1960) did at least acquire a new specificity, thanks to his robust engagement with the intellectual context of the Enlightenment and careful reading of the meticulous, austerely descriptive work of art historian Fiske Kimball.[4] Milton's complex Latinate epic verse was now said to resemble 'the bulging high relief in Grinling Gibbons' carvings with their swags, consoles, garlands, and baroque cartouches', while Pope's simplified, 'minutely precise' poetic diction was compared to 'the simple, almost prosaic, language of grasses, fronds, and tendrils in rococo panels'.[5] Still frustrated by what he saw as the spuriousness of such comparisons, Patrick Brady sought to bring structuralist rigour to the field of 'comparative aesthetics', as he called it, by identifying a higher-order set of 'psycho-cultural drives' that might mediate the analysis of works of art in different mediums.[6] But as Brady himself acknowledged, the effort to identify these drives at their deepest, 'semantic' level relied on 'almost pure intuition and hypothesis', with the result that it quickly reverted to the formulation of abstractions – 'compensation' for the 'loss of transcendence', or the 'pleasure in plurality' that arises from humanity's 'loss of a fixed centre or single meaning' – little different from the idealist time-spirits he was trying to leave behind.

Literary scholarship on the rococo has been further complicated by the lack of consensus on the term's meaning within art history. A coinage of nineteenth-century painters that was taken up by art historians, the word 'rococo' has only the faintest of connections to the eighteenth century through its derivation from *rocaille*, the French term for the colourful rockwork used to adorn grottoes and fountains that was later adapted by early eighteenth-century French interior designers and architects. Some scholars still use 'the rococo' narrowly to refer to this decorative style, but for many others it has become a much broader, and thus vaguer term for a pan-European 'formal idiom', the influence of which extends to painting, sculpture, ceramics, jewellery, furniture and gardening, as well as music and literature. Most recently, the rococo even seems to have lost its moorings in the eighteenth century, with one art historian noting that 'it has become possible to speak of rococo as a cultural mode of being, thought, and representation', traces of which can be found as far afield as Art Nouveau, post-war Pop Art and contemporary cinema.[7] The relatively small repertoire of impressionistic adjectives that recur in accounts of rococo art hints tantalisingly at some stable underlying referent; favourites include 'frivolous', 'playful', 'exuberant' and 'feminine' (or 'effeminate'). But even those scholars who view it as a period style rather than a way of life do not agree on such basic questions as whether it is best understood as sensuous or abstract, naturalistic or fantastic, an extension of the baroque or a revolt against it. These inconsistencies have reduced the term's explanatory power so much that the best definition one recent literary study could come up with was that the rococo is 'the aesthetic expression of individual uniqueness'.[8]

My own attempt to grapple with these difficulties involves, in part, simply changing the subject. Narrowing the focus to the idea of the 'whimsical' in the eighteenth century allows me to sidestep some of the historiographical problems presented by the concept of the rococo. Rather than an abstraction imposed on the art of the period by later scholars, the word 'whimsical' and its variants are not only native to the eighteenth century but emerged in response to the concrete social and material changes of the period. As Jonathan Sheehan and Dror Wahrman have noted, the word 'whim' belongs to a cluster of terms (the others they mention are 'caprice' and 'spontaneous') signifying 'unpredictable and unpredetermined behaviour' that entered the language in the late seventeenth century, a development they attribute to the period's financial and consumer revolutions. The rise of financial speculation and the growth in spending on consumer goods led to an expansion in the experience of what they call 'indifferent agency', the arbitrary form of action involved when one chooses between 'symmetrical' options, such as different lottery numbers or differently styled but functionally identical commodities.[9] 'Whimsical' also happens to be a key English word in the period for the style of artwork that art historians now identify as rococo. As evidence of the vogue for rococo interiors in mid-eighteenth-century Britain, for example, scholars often cite the French enamel painter Jean-André Rouquet's observation that 'the taste called *contrast*, a taste so ridiculous and whimsical, when applied to objects susceptible of symmetry, has reached as far as England, where it every day produces, as it does elsewhere, some new monster'.[10] Brigid von Preussen identifies the 'famous artist' to whom Rouquet attributes the 'invention' of this taste as the French goldsmith and interior designer Juste-Aurèle Meissonnier, and 'contrast' as 'the style known in eighteenth-century France as the "style moderne" . . . and today described as "the Rococo"'.[11] In mid-eighteenth-century periodicals, meanwhile, the whimsical functioned as a catch-all term of critique for a range of modern aberrations of taste that included masquerades, elaborate hairstyles, chinoiserie and rococo design. In addition to being an eighteenth-century coinage that captured some of the broad phenomenological aspects of far-reaching socio-economic change, therefore, whimsy had a more specific function in a discourse on taste that emerged in the period in part to facilitate the comparison of works of art across different mediums.

The eighteenth century's whimsical aesthetic ought thus to provide a stronger, more historically grounded basis than speculative time-spirits and psycho-cultural drives for the analogy I wish to draw in this essay between 'rococo' material culture and the narrative episodes involving arbitrary, capricious or indifferent agency in Eliza Haywood's fiction from *Fantomina* (1725) to *The History of Miss Betsy Thoughtless* (1751). In making this connection, however, I am also responding to Jennifer Milam's call some years ago for interdisciplinary studies that question 'the received wisdom that the rococo style reflects the shallowness of an aristocracy engaging only in superficial forms of entertainment' by recovering the 'primacy of ludicity in eighteenth-century culture' and reframing 'rococo "frivolity" in relationship to serious creativity and imagination rather than insouciance and decadence'.[12] Patricia Crown and Anne Puetz have both shown that, at least in the British context, the 'modern style' of decoration was more likely to be linked to new money than to the aristocracy, while the dominance of an academic art history that privileged the 'fine' arts of painting and sculpture over the more commercially oriented arts of design and ornamentation has meant that the rococo has only recently begun to shake off its long-standing associations with triviality.[13] Haywood's whimsical episodes are alert to the associations of whimsical agency with frivolity and luxury, but they also suggest an alternative, more sympathetic attitude to the opportunities for imaginative play newly available – to women in particular – in Britain's emerging consumer culture.

Whimsy and the Eighteenth-Century Discourse on Taste

Whims and caprices in the eighteenth-century discourse on taste were the indiscriminate impulses whose proliferation within the new consumer culture made necessary the discriminations of aesthetic judgement. Haywood seems to make her commitment to these habits of discrimination clear at the beginning of the first volume of her periodical *The Female Spectator* (1744–6), when she declares 'it is very much, by the Choice we make of Subjects for our Entertainment, that the refin'd Taste distinguishes itself from the vulgar and more gross'.[14] Not only do those who throw away their time on 'Trifles' show they lack the taste for 'any thing more elegant', they also ensure that they will never acquire such a taste, because 'to be transported with every new Caprice, and incessantly hurrying from one Folly to another, soon confounds the best Understanding and makes a kind of Chaos in the Mind' (3:137–8). Conversely, to have good taste – a 'distinguishing Power' (3:129) that inclines us to 'what will render us *better* and *wiser*' – implies a person's possession of 'whatever is great and valuable' (3:128). One of the stated purposes of *The Female Spectator* is thus to help Haywood's young, mainly female, mainly middling-sort readers distinguish between the kind of behaviour that displays '*true Taste*' from the kind that betrays a habit of merely 'following the Dictates of some irregular Propensity and Caprice' (3:128). Rather than chasing the local, ephemeral pleasures of the fashionable world – balls, masquerades, pleasure gardens and gossip – Haywood wants her readers to become 'Connoisseurs' (3:139) of the more rational, permanent pleasures of natural philosophy, reading and polite conversation. The stakes in this project are high, for, as she warns later on, the giddy pleasures of the town, 'in this Age of Luxury, serve as Decoys to draw the Thoughtless and Unwary together, and, as it were, prepare the Way for other more vicious Excesses' (1:204). The most immediate danger for a woman devoted to such pleasures was that she would spend too much time in company and thereby acquire the reputation of a coquette, a figure whose delight in flirtation, Theresa Braunschneider has shown, was viewed in the period 'as an inadvertent by-product of her passion for *au courant* luxuries'.[15]

Haywood's warning in *The Female Spectator* about the moral consequences of aesthetic misjudgements reads like a programmatic statement of one of the key didactic concerns animating her later fiction. *Betsy Thoughtless* culminates with the heroine experiencing an epiphany in which she resolves to act in future with more caution and consistency: 'even in the greatest, and most serious affair of life – that of marriage', she reflects after a quarrel with her husband that reveals how mistaken she was to marry him, 'have I not been governed wholly by caprice!'[16] She is thinking of her suitor Trueworth, whom she spurned because she thought she did not love him enough, only to marry Munden, whom she knew she did not love at all. But she might just as well be thinking of many other episodes in her career as a coquette 'too volatile for reflection' (31). An early adventure in a pleasure garden in Oxford, for example, results in Betsy's public humiliation after a sexual assault that she is able to repel ends up embroiling her brother in a duel: 'I confess', she admits to her confidante Lady Trusty, 'I have been too often misled by the prevalence of example, and my own idle caprice' (213).

As Braunschneider argues, the novel charts 'a shift from indiscriminate desire to discriminating choice', following a reformed coquette plot in which the heroine eventually chooses to give up the pleasures of polyamorous flirtation and homoerotic intimacy for the greater security afforded by heterosexuality and marriage.[17] Braunschneider focuses on the scrapes into which Betsy is led by her friendship with her schoolfriend Miss Forward, but Haywood's heroine has far more obviously erotic feelings for the mysterious Mademoiselle de Roquelair. On meeting at a mercer's shop, Mademoiselle de Roquelair is said to have 'attracted her in a peculiar way', prompting Betsy to make 'several overtures' (534) of friendship. Betsy later learns that she is the French mistress whom her older brother Thomas has brought back from his travels in Europe, a revelation that, along with her intimacy with the fashionable mercer and her name – suggesting *rocaille* perhaps as well as *roquelaure*, a fashionable type of coat – establishes her as the novel's key figure representing continental luxury: 'she loved variety', Haywood observes, when explaining the affair she has with the mercer while living under Thomas's roof: 'she longed for change, without consulting whether the object was suitable or not' (578). By showing Betsy acquiring a taste for Trueworth instead of variety, the novel suggests her education is aesthetic as well as moral and sexual.

Haywood's cautions against indulging whimsical desires align her with the period's civic humanist discourse on taste. Writing in the *Guardian* in 1713, George Berkeley had divided the 'Pleasures which constitute Human Happiness' into two classes: the 'Natural' and the 'Fantastical':

> *Natural Pleasures* I call those, which not depending on the Fashion and Caprice of any particular Age or Nation, are suited to Humane Nature in general, and were intended by Providence as Rewards for the using our Faculties agreeably to the Ends for which they were given us.

Since these pleasures are the object of 'Natural Desires', they are generally 'cheap or easie to be obtained' and produce 'the greatest Satisfaction' when enjoyed. Examples include 'fresh Air and Rural Enjoyments', good weather, moonlight and paintings of beautiful landscapes. Fantastical pleasures, on the other hand, are 'those which having no natural Fitness to delight our Minds, presuppose some particular Whim or Taste accidentally prevailing in a Sett of People, to which it is owing that they please'.[18]

The contrast Berkeley draws here between natural and fantastical pleasures closely resembles the distinction that sociologist Colin Campbell makes between the 'traditional hedonism' of elites prior to the eighteenth-century consumer revolution and the 'imaginative, autonomous hedonism' of the modern consumer. Whereas traditional hedonists seek only to maximise their enjoyment of life's pleasurable sensations (eating, drinking, sex, dancing and so on), he argues, their modern counterparts seek pleasure in the emotional stimulation afforded by mental images that are 'either imaginatively created or modified by the individual for self-consumption, there being little reliance upon the presence of "real" stimuli'.[19] Unlike the natural pleasures of the traditional hedonist, which Berkeley views as divinely ordained and common to all human beings, fantastical pleasures arise only among affluent members of commercial societies. Their 'sensitive Appetites being easily satisfied', modern consumers acquire a taste for objects – money, 'outward Distinctions', or the possession of things 'meerly because they are New or Foreign' – that in themselves neither delight the senses nor satisfy any needs. Disdaining the cheap and easy happiness afforded them by the 'Bounty of Providence', they bring misery upon themselves by pursuing 'imaginary Goods, in which there is nothing can raise Desire but the Difficulty of obtaining them'. Of those of his fellow creatures who waste their lives in the 'toilsome and absurd Pursuit of Trifles', Berkeley observes wonderingly, one is driven by the desire 'to be called a particular Appellation; another, that he may wear a particular Ornament'. As in *The Female Spectator*, 'real', universal, properly aesthetic pleasure, ordained by God and confined to the pleasures of the senses, is defined in opposition to the 'imaginary', culturally contingent, merely ornamental kind associated with the whims of fashion and emulative consumption.

The civic humanist distinction between true taste and mere whim would form the basis of the contrast that Joshua Reynolds later sought to draw between the 'Liberal' art of painting and the merely mechanical arts of decoration and design. Artists who failed to study 'the genuine habits of nature, as distinguished from those of fashion', he argued, resemble those 'dancing-masters, hair-dressers, and tailors' who indulge the 'vanity and caprice' of their customers with monstrous distortions of the human form: 'However the mechanick and ornamental arts may sacrifice to fashion', he warned his students at the newly founded Royal Academy, 'she must be entirely excluded from the Art of Painting; the painter must never mistake this capricious changeling for the genuine offspring of nature.' Unlike the fashionable decorative artist, who seeks to 'amuse mankind with the minute neatness of his imitations', the painter must elevate his eye beyond 'singular forms, local customs, particularities and details of every kind' towards the representation of 'Ideal Beauty'.[20] As Elizabeth Bohls has shown, this theory drew on a set of very old political and moral assumptions that extended well beyond the arts. Reynolds's elevation of 'general nature' over local particulars and of transcendent and ideal beauty over ephemeral fashions was founded on a familiar Platonic analogy between the state, the mind and the work of art:

> Good form in painting entails subordinating objects and figures to the idea, or subject, of the work . . . If not subordinate to form, in these related meanings of the term, details metaphorically threaten proper order in both mind and state. They are associated with 'low', potentially unruly elements in each: the senses and their disorderly desires, in need of regulation by the intellect; and the groups of people – 'mechanics' and women – more subject to those desires and hence more likely to form political disorder if not well ruled by citizens, in whose own minds, in turn, the senses are firmly under control.[21]

If an inclination for fashionable whims was portrayed as a consequence of the 'effeminate' self-indulgence typical of women and the lower orders, good taste indicated the masculine self-discipline of the virtuous landowning gentry: 'the vocabulary of the civic discourse', observes John Barrell, 'which could describe acquisitive and especially commercial activity in the same terms as it described sexual indulgence . . . enabled emancipation from sexual desire to stand as a mark of emancipation from material desire and vice-versa'.[22] To exhibit good taste was to demonstrate one's freedom from the arbitrary and thus illegitimate power of both consumer culture and sexual desire.

Whimsy's association with sexual self-indulgence informs Francis Coventry's acerbic 1753 satire of rococo architecture and gardens in the *World*, the popular mid-century periodical. Writing in the persona of the *World*'s editor Adam Fitz-Adam, Coventry opens his essay with a brief history of the 'whimsical variations of GARDENING' that 'have contributed so effectually to new-dress our island' since medieval times. As 'fatal proofs of the degeneracy of our national taste', he points to the 'grotesque little villas' that have sprung up along the banks of the Thames in recent years. The owner of one of these 'whimsical nothings' is a certain ''squire Mushroom'. Born to an attorney in a 'little dirty village in Hertfordshire', Mushroom has acquired a fortune from trade and is now 'ambitious of introducing himself to the world as a man of taste and pleasure'. His first steps – adding an edging of silver lace to his servants' waistcoats and taking a 'brace of whores' into his keeping – establish a pattern of garish display and sensual self-indulgence that is repeated in the farmhouse he converts:

> The old mansion immediately shot up Gothic spires, and was plastered over with stucco; the walls were notched into battlements; uncouth animals were set grinning at one another over the gate-posts, and the hall was fortified with three rusty swords, five brace of pistols, and a *Medusa*'s head staring tremendous over the chimney.[23]

The target of Coventry's satire here is mid-century 'Rococo-Gothic' architecture, which art historian Peter Lindfield has argued was defined by 'the whimsical application of

Gothic motifs to architectural elevations'. Later examples of the eighteenth-century Gothic Revival took a more scholarly, antiquarian interest in medieval architecture. But Richard Bentley's mid-century designs for Horace Walpole's Thames-side villa at Strawberry Hill, or the 'improvements' Sanderson Miller added to various houses across the Midlands and the West Country in the same period, were quite different. What connected these projects was 'a shared application of Gothic motifs arranged for fanciful, exuberant and decorative effect' that displayed little concern for archaeological authenticity or stylistic and structural coherence.[24] The wealth of these Rococo-Gothic enthusiasts was often derived from trade. Although Walpole came from an old Norfolk family, his father had notoriously enriched himself by exploiting the fallout from the South Sea Bubble. Dickie Bateman, whose Rococo-Gothic home nearby at Old Windsor was one of the inspirations for Strawberry Hill, was the son of a banker who became Lord Mayor, while Miller's father was a successful wool merchant.

The houses of these men were surrounded by gardens that have also been called rococo because of their playful 'sense of experiment', 'fantasy and imagination' and relatively small scale in comparison to the larger, grander parks landscaped by Lancelot 'Capability' Brown for the gentry and nobility in the same period.[25] Squire Mushroom's garden is said to be the 'triumph' of his genius. Though it covers only two acres of ground, it features a 'yellow serpentine river' twenty yards in length, with a toy ship floating in it, and a bridge, *partly in the chinese manner*. Crossing the river, the visitor encounters a grove of 'crooked walks' and a labyrinth of hedges; then a 'hermitage'; a little fountain surrounded by flowerbeds that the squire, *by way of whim*, has named *little Marybon* (after the pleasure gardens at Marylebone); and, finally, a 'pompous, clumsy, and gilded building, said to be a temple, and consecrated to Venus', for no other reason than that the squire 'riots here sometimes in vulgar love with a couple of orange-wenches taken from the purlieus of the playhouse'. The civic humanist discourse on taste was thus an attempt to regulate the indifferent agency of consumers by infusing it with moral weight. Apparently trifling decisions about the goods and amusements people chose to enjoy in fact revealed a great deal about their moral character. The possession of good taste indicated the virtues of self-discipline and public-spiritedness, while susceptibility to fashionable whims and caprices betrayed an immodest appetite for sensual gratification and a sordidly competitive, mercantile hankering after public admiration.

In his strictures on architecture and gardening, Coventry applied the same canons of taste that he had used two years earlier to distinguish between the enlightened realism of Henry Fielding's 'new Species of Writing' and what he attacked as the outrageously improbable fictions produced by the novelists that preceded him. Before Fielding's works appeared, he claimed,

> the World had been pester'd with Volumes, commonly known by the Name of Romances, or Novels, Tales, *&c.* fill'd with any thing which the wildest Imagination could suggest . . . Diamond Palaces, flying Horses, brazen Towers, *&c.* were here look'd upon as proper, and in Taste. In short, the most finish'd Piece of this kind, was nothing but Chaos and Incoherency.

Like rococo design, improbable fiction was a fashionable 'Monster' that originated in France before being carried across to England 'among the rest of her Neighbour's Follies'. Just as Coventry sought to convince his readers that rococo houses and gardens were aberrations of taste that betrayed the vulgar origins of their creators, so, he argued, Fielding's achievement in *Joseph Andrews* (1742) and *Tom Jones* (1749) had been to persuade 'Ladies to leave this Extravagance to their *Abigails* [that is, their maids] with their cast Cloaths', among whom 'it has ever since been observ'd to be peculiarly predominant'.[26] Charlotte Lennox seems likely to have had Coventry's essay in mind when she conceived *The Female Quixote* (1752), which depicts the 'bad Effects' of a young woman's 'whimsical Study' of seventeenth-century French romances.[27] Not only does Arabella's whimsical taste for romances cause lapses of judgement in which she mistakes a cast-off mistress, a prostitute and an actress for princesses in disguise, but the worthy divine who effects the 'Cure' (368) of her mind at the end of the novel does so, in part, by suggesting that her whims are the expression of an unruly sexual desire. Romances 'soften the Heart to Love' (380) by teaching women to view it as the 'ruling Principle of the World' (7) and the 'Sole Business of Ladies' (381) in particular – a truth that Arabella appears to acknowledge with her blushes.

Fantomina and the Arts of Ornamentation

As many critics have shown, however, the effects of Arabella's whimsical study of romances are more equivocal than the the the divine's cure implies. Her belated romantic idealism is favourably contrasted with her fashionable cousin Charlotte's worldly egotism and is shown to give her an admirably critical distance from the idleness and vanity she encounters on her travels to Bath and London.[28] In Haywood's work, this equivocation extends to even the most fashionable amusements – perhaps because her earliest fictions predate the mid-century shift in taste that Coventry describes. Even in *The Female Spectator*, as Robert Jones points out, 'Haywood rarely suggests simple abstention, preferring instead to recommend to readers that they regulate their appetites and entertainments within proper bounds.'[29] The problem, she argues, is not the amusements themselves, which are perfectly appropriate forms of recreation for the great, but the harm they do to 'People of an inferior Condition, only by being indulged to an Excess' (1:369). When a correspondent, Sarah Oldfashion, writes in seeking support for the reproofs she has been giving her daughter for her 'giddy Rambles' (1:265) at Ranelagh, the Female Spectator warns against any rash exercise of parental authority. Imposing severe constraints on the young, if they have any spirit, only prompts them to run risks more dangerous than those from which one seeks to protect them, a point she illustrates with the story of Christabella and Alvario. Christabella is a vain, though 'perfectly innocent' (1:272) young coquette devoted to 'Dress, Equipage, and Admiration' (1:271); her father Alvario locks her up after she refuses to moderate her behaviour. Deprived of her usual opportunities for self-display, Christabella contrives a new, more desperate one. She scribbles notes complaining of her father's cruelty and throws them into the street outside her window. One of these notes is picked up by a penniless gambler, who finds something 'so whimsical in the Adventure' that he resolves to be 'Knight-Errant enough to attempt the Relief of this distress'd Damsel' (1:276). He soon discerns an opportunity to enrich himself and, having persuaded Christabella to elope and then marry him by pretending to be the scion of a great family, he seizes her fortune for himself and sets off abroad to spend it, 'leaving her at Home to lament alone her wretched State' (1:286). Rather than sending her daughter into the country, therefore, the Female Spectator suggests that Mrs Oldfashion wean her daughter from her passion for Ranelagh by carrying her abroad, ideally to France, the birthplace of all fashionable whims, 'where she would find so vast a Variety, as would give a quite different Turn to her Temper, and make her despise all that before seem'd so enchanting to her' (1:287). If the attempt to suppress one form of whimsical behaviour simply provokes a worse kind, then the best way to cure a young woman of her whims is to expose her to more of them until she acquires a taste for something better.

Haywood's suggestion in *The Female Spectator* that 'whimsical' adventures are natural expressions of the female appetite for pleasure recalls the opening of what has become her best-known narrative, *Fantomina*, a work that illustrates the extent of her differences with civic humanist discourse at an earlier moment in her career. Although much of the recent scholarship on *Fantomina* has focused on the nature and implications of the protagonist's desire – its performativity, its subversion of androcentric constructions of female sexuality, its resonance with poststructuralist theories of subjectivity and so on – little notice has been taken of the explanation the narrator herself gives of the decision made by the unknown 'young Lady of distinguished Birth, Beauty, Wit, and Spirit' at the beginning to go to the theatre dressed as a prostitute.[30] Curiosity, the great ruling passion of the Enlightenment, provides the initial impulse: having been raised mainly in the country, the young lady wants to know how it feels to be addressed the way men address such a woman, without the reserve that her rank and reputation demand from them. But the method she devises to gratify this impulse, perhaps suggested by the contemporary fashion for masquerades, is described first as a 'little Whim' and later as a 'Frolick' (another late seventeenth-century coinage) – words that construe it as something more playful and indeterminate than the disciplined, instrumental curiosity of the Enlightenment philosopher.[31] The young lady uses the playhouse the way Squire Mushroom uses his garden, as a recreational space for realising fantasies.

The consequences of the young lady's playhouse frolic initially seem to indicate that the story will be a cautionary tale, in the civic humanist mode, about the dangers to which young women expose themselves when they indulge their taste for fantastical rather than natural pleasures. Of the crowd of men the young lady attracts in her disguise she is most drawn to Beauplaisir, whom she rashly agrees to meet again the following night: 'Strange and unaccountable were the Whimsies she was possess'd of,—wild and incoherent her Desires,—unfix'd and undetermin'd her Resolutions, but in that of seeing *Beauplaisir* in the Manner she had lately done' (44). Beyond extending the thrill of flirting with him, her endgame at this point seems merely to be the pleasure of witnessing his surprise when 'he finds himself refused by a Woman, who he supposed granted her Favours without Exception' (44). However, by the time they meet, she has rented some rooms to which she takes him for supper after the play; having encouraged Beauplaisir this far, she now finds herself unable to retreat without exposing herself to public ridicule and disgrace. Though she withholds her name, she confesses herself a virgin who was only pretending to be a prostitute to attract his attention. But Beauplaisir either does not believe her or does not care; he rapes her, unable to imagine why a woman who had gone to such pains to engage him should balk at 'the last Test' (47). No longer an innocent frolic, the young lady's whimsy has become a reckless aberration for which she pays a terrible price.

Yet if the first part of the narrative proceeds like a cautionary tale, what happens next does not align quite so easily with the civic humanist discourse on taste. The appetite for novelty that Braunschneider argues is characteristic of the coquette turns out to be the defining trait not of the young lady but of Beauplaisir, who, Haywood notes, 'varied not so much from his Sex as to be able to prolong Desire, to any great Length after Possession' (50), and soon begins to look for fresh conquests.[32] The young lady, by contrast, feels that it is 'only he whose Solicitations could give her Pleasure' and seeks to reignite her lover's waning passion by adopting a succession of new disguises: a maid at a country inn; an amorous widow inspired by the Ephesian matron; and finally, in the last of her 'whimsical Adventures' (68), an amorous lady of quality, similar in wealth and status to the young lady herself, who summons Beauplaisir to an assignation in the dark using the name Incognita. Far from moving distractedly from one shiny object to the next, in other words, the young lady remains doggedly focused on her original object of desire: 'her Design was once more to engage him, to hear him sigh, to see him languish, to feel the strenuous Pressures of his eager Arms' (51). Instead of changing her lover, she changes her clothes, hair and accent, assuming a higher social position with each persona to gain greater control over the fulfilment of her fantasy. Rather than ending up deceived and abandoned like Christabella, the young lady turns the tables on Beauplaisir, congratulating herself for having 'outwitted even the most Subtle of the deceiving Kind', and for arranging matters so that he who 'thinks to fool me, is himself the only beguiled Person' (59). Although the young lady's adventures eventually come to an end when her mother returns to discover her daughter is pregnant, Haywood declines to moralise, closing instead only with an observation about the entertainment she hopes her narrative has afforded her readers: 'Thus ended an Intreague, which, considering the Time it lasted, was as full of Variety as any, perhaps, that many Ages has produced' (71).

If the young lady's adventures suggest the behaviour of the modern consumer, then, it is not because of her coquetry, but rather her stubborn, quixotic idealism: she refuses to accept the reality, as Haywood presents it, that 'Possession' naturally abates the vigour of male desire, and uses her imagination and ingenuity to contrive an ideal relationship in which her lover is 'always raving, wild, impatient, longing, dying' (65). Just as the 'dress of nature', as Fitz-Adam calls gardening, allows Squire Mushroom to explore various versions of the man of taste and pleasure, so the costumes the young lady acquires enable her to realise her own romantic fantasies. Indeed, *Fantomina*'s subtitle – *Love in a Maze* – points to the structural correspondences between Haywood's episodic narrative and Fitz-Adam's tour through the squire's garden, in which each horticultural feature functions as a new whimsical adventure. In both cases, the pursuit of an ideal through a potentially endless series of self-reinventions exemplifies the autonomous imaginative hedonism of modern consumers, who are driven, Campbell argues, not by their appetite for sensory pleasures or novel material objects as such, but by 'the desire to experience in reality the pleasurable dramas that they have already enjoyed in imagination', such that 'each "new" product is seen as offering a possibility of realizing this ambition'.[33] The 'handsome Supper, and Wine' (45) the young lady lays on as Fantomina, the dress she has made for her performance as the Widow Bloomer, and the 'magnificent' (65) ballgown and vizard mask she wears as Incognita are all simply the material means, used up or discarded almost as soon as they are acquired, to an essentially immaterial end, the realisation of a fantasy that does not change because it can never be fully or permanently satisfied. The dim-witted Beauplaisir, meanwhile, exemplifies the simpler psychology of the traditional hedonist doomed to 'repeat cycles of sensory pleasure-seeking' over which he has little control, since the stimulation he seeks depends on the presence of a limited supply of real, physical objects rather than the manipulation of a potentially infinite variety of mental images.[34]

In portraying the superior delights of cultivating a variety of novel emotional experiences over a narrow round of familiar sensations, *Fantomina* also argues for the aesthetic values of the rococo decorative arts scorned by the civic humanist discourse on taste. The pattern-drawer is 'paid according to the Variety and Value of his Designs', observes Robert Campbell in *The London Tradesman* (1747). Creating them 'requires no great Taste in Painting', but 'a wild kind of Imagination', 'a fruitful Fancy' and the ability 'to invent Whims to please the changeable Foible of the Ladies, for whose Use their Work is chiefly intended'.[35] To realise her own design, Haywood's young lady must distort and disfigure the human form using the ornamental, merely 'mechanick' arts that Reynolds had contrasted with the 'Liberal' art of painting: those of the tailor for the dresses she has made; the hairdresser for the look – tied back straight and covered with 'Pinners' (54) – that she devises for the Widow Bloomer; and those, if not of the dancing-master, then of the 'Comedians' at the playhouse for the work of forming 'her Behaviour to the Character she represented' (57). Unlike Reynolds, who wanted painters to forgo minute imitation and learn instead how 'to reduce the variety of nature to the abstract idea', Haywood's young lady delights in the careful contrivance of intricate ornamental surfaces. When dressed as Incognita, she compensates for the want of 'those Beauties' she conceals behind her mask by setting forth the others – 'her fine Shape, and Air, and Neck' – with 'the greatest Care and Exactness' (65).

In her celebration of the arts of ornamentation, Hayward aligns herself not with the civic humanism of Berkeley and Reynolds, therefore, but with the practitioner aesthetics of William Hogarth, who defended the ornamental arts from the condescension of gentlemen connoisseurs in his *Analysis of Beauty* (1753). Hogarth argued that the delight the mind takes in tracing intricate decorative patterns – such as the ribbon twisted round a stick used to decorate frames, chimneypieces and doorways – resembles that excited by the contemporary ladies' fashion of 'interlacing the hair in distinct varied quantities'. The pleasure afforded by decorative forms derives not from the intimations they provide of a divine order or ideal, as Berkeley and Reynolds had argued, but from the stimulus they gave to the 'active mind', which is 'ever bent to be employ'd' and turns every difficulty that arises from tracing an ornamental pattern or following the 'well-connected thread of a play, or a novel' into 'sport and recreation'.[36] As Annie Richardson observes, 'for Hogarth, the notion of the active mind underwrites the pleasure in action, the legitimacy of the pleasures of appetite, and the close relation between arts and industry, leisure and work'.[37] If the civic humanist discourse on taste viewed the taste for ideal beauty over ornamental variety as an expression of the virtuous disinterestedness of the landowning gentleman, the young lady's imaginative pursuit of Beauplaisir – of beautiful pleasure, that is – through a series of intricate stratagems and disguises suggests not just the luxurious appetite of the female consumer, but the industrious ingenuity of the tradesman.

Although Haywood's later marriage plots treat the indulgence of whims rather more critically than *Fantomina*, it is striking that in *Betsy Thoughtless* the transformation of the heroine's taste is mediated by a whimsical adventure involving an apparently trivial decorative object. Not long after he rescues her from the clutches of a penniless suitor who pretends to be a baronet, Betsy hears by chance that her old flame Trueworth has had his portrait painted in miniature as a gift for his fiancée. The knowledge of this object immediately excites a desire to possess it. Haywood compares the various schemes Betsy entertains to acquire the miniature to the efforts a plastic artist makes to realise a design: 'she had got a caprice in her brain, which raised ideas there, she was in pain till she had modelled, and brought to the perfection she wanted' (444–5). Early next morning, she dresses herself in a riding habit and hunting cap she knows Trueworth has never seen her wearing, hires a 'handsome' equipage with a coachman and two servants, and calls on the artist claiming she has been sent to pick up the picture for its owner, eventually carrying it home in triumph.

The exact motives behind this whimsical adventure are once again obscure. Betsy tells herself that the picture will help remind her of her obligations to Trueworth, which she might otherwise forget. In her reading of this episode, Alison Conway notes the miniature portrait's contemporary associations with 'the aesthetics of the decorative and the rococo' – miniatures were often set in watches or jewellery and worn on the body – but also its power as a form to render 'precious what in negative accounts of portraiture is denigrated as the genre's necessary attachment to merely local details of character'. Betsy's theft of the miniature could therefore be read more broadly as a sign that 'a desire for contemplation and introspection has replaced a love for the superficial pleasures of London society'.[38] But the narrator notes that her scheme to acquire the miniature has the additional effect of helping her get over the shock of her humiliation by the mock baronet: 'all her remorse, – all her vexation, for the base design' to which she had been subjected 'were dissipated the moment she took it into her head to get possession of the picture' (447). Conway argues that this suggests the theft of the miniature might also be interpreted as 'an attempt to restore control over the events unfolding around her', which by this point include her brothers' plans for her to marry Munden. To relieve this pressure, Betsy concocts a disguise that enables her to acquire an object onto which she projects 'all of her desires for a marriage that will somehow not end up in her degradation'. This is a fantasy far more in keeping with the 'pleasing labour of the mind' stimulated by the intricacy of the decorative object than the civic humanist virtues of contemplation and introspection.[39] The quixotic ideal sustained by this adventure is ultimately rewarded at the end of the novel. Betsy has retreated to a house belonging to her attorney's sister-in-law on the banks of the Thames, and Trueworth finds her gazing at the miniature in a 'beautiful garden, decorated with plots of flowers, statues, and trees cut in a most elegant manner' (605), which leads to an erotic scene worthy of Squire Mushroom's temple of Venus. In a process that recalls the solution Haywood had urged upon Mrs Oldfashion in *The Female Spectator*, Betsy stumbles on true taste by indulging rather than disciplining her whims. In Haywood's fiction, the whimsical adventures made possible by the rise of consumer culture involve fantasies of deliverance from the constraints and injustices of the patriarchy.

On Whimsy

The equivocal nature of Haywood's representation of fashionable whimsy in her fiction reflects a broader cultural ambivalence about the imaginative hedonism licensed by an emerging consumer culture. This intensified during the 1740s, when the Jacobite Rebellion prompted fears of a French invasion and gave a new urgency to the decades-old debates about luxury. On the one hand, whimsical objects and designs were viewed as vulgar, self-indulgent fantasies that, taken to an extreme, seemed to undermine the foundations of social and civic life. Thus Fitz-Adam complains of being led through yet another maze of walks in Squire Mushroom's garden, in which 'the last error is much worse than the first'; Beauplaisir revolts when the young lady, disguised as Incognita, refuses to let him see her face; and Trueworth, in despair at Betsy's wilfulness, gives up his suit and looks for a wife elsewhere. These exasperated rejections of the whimsical object mirror the contempt articulated in the contemporary discourse on taste for intricate rococo works of art and design that seemed to flout the aesthetic principles of mainstream classicism and the virtues of self-restraint and public-spiritedness with which they were associated.

On the other hand, Haywood's depiction of her heroines' whimsical adventures also suggests the delightful feelings of freedom and power these objects could excite – especially in those who felt excluded by classicism's rigid social and moral norms – in a way that validates recent scholarly speculations about the appeal of rococo decorative art. David Porter, for example, discerns in the eighteenth-century passion for chinoiserie – often featured in rococo design and gardens – 'an oppositional aesthetic widely embraced by contemporary women'. What critics attacked as chinoiserie's monstrous hybridity, he argues, would have evoked for consumers excluded from the male aristocratic elite 'a corresponding social process of experimental self-fashioning'. Its 'irreverent disregard for authenticity' suggested 'an aesthetic subject cut loose from naturalized hierarchies of taste and status', able to enjoy 'a degree of self-determination beyond the bounds of rigidly prescribed roles'.[40] Matthew Reeve attributes a similar impatience with authenticity in the Rococo-Gothic aesthetics of Walpole and his circle to an 'oppositional queer sensibility' that turned the heteronormativity of the civic humanist tradition on its head. Rather than a form of childish or effeminate egotism, Walpole saw the ability to 'assert one's alterity through object choice outside of established convention' as an elegant expression of modern refinement.[41] To the Squire Mushrooms of the world, in other words, whimsy was not a failed attempt to rise to the aesthetic standards of the elite, but a liberating form of imaginative hedonism that reflected modern sensibilities less beholden to traditional hierarchies.

The whimsical might therefore be understood as one of the eighteenth century's 'minor aesthetic categories', similar in its affective weakness and ideological ambiguity to the terms recently explored by Sianne Ngai in the context of postmodern American culture. Although the whimsical in this period denotes some 'differences from a norm', these differences typically elicit a 'low, hard-to-register flicker of affect' rather than the 'powerfully uplifting and shattering emotions' excited by a major category like the sublime. This is in part because, as with other minor aesthetic categories, the judgement that an object is whimsical is often 'strikingly equivocal', the 'mixture of contradictory feelings' evoked by the term leaving it ambiguous as to whether it is being judged positively or negatively. Just as the initially protective response to the vulnerability of the 'cute' object, for example, is undermined by a secondary feeling of aggression, so the delightful sense of liberation excited by whimsy is counteracted by a simultaneous feeling of exasperated revolt against a self-indulgent fantasy. If sublime works of art transcend aesthetic norms in pursuit of grandeur, whimsy's modest, playful deviations typically result in something trivial, the smallness of the whimsical object signifying its implicit recognition of the authority and legitimacy of the norms from which it departs but never quite leaves behind.[42]

208   JOSEPH DRURY

The equivocal nature of minor aesthetic judgements is ideological as well as affective, the ambiguity of each category, in Ngai's view, registering conflicted feelings
about a different aspect of Western capitalism. The combination of protective concern
and aggression elicited by the cute object, for example, reflects consumers' complex
relation to the commodity form; the sensuous appeal of cuteness inspires a 'pastoral
fantasy' of rescuing the commodity's use-value from the rule of exchange that requires
'so much counterfactual force on the part of the imagination' that its 'use' becomes a
form of 'abuse'.[43] If whimsy retains its affective ambiguity today – and I would argue
that it does – my account of its origins suggests that this is because it speaks to ongoing tensions in our attitude towards the imaginative hedonism that sustains modern
consumer culture. On the one hand, the feeling of exasperated subjection provoked
by whimsical adventures in art and literature responds to what the political scientist
Benjamin Barber has called the 'infantilist ethos' of mass consumerism – its indulgence
of our narcissistic desire to prolong childhood and escape adulthood – which threatens
the political autonomy of citizens by undermining the habits of mature deliberation on
which civic life depends.[44] On the other hand, the delightful feeling of freedom excited
by whimsy's circuitous paths exemplifies the new opportunities for experimental self-
fashioning and libidinal fulfilment promised by consumer capitalism's restless search
for appetites to satisfy. From this perspective, the expansion of the realm of imaginative play in modern consumer societies has looked less like a threat to civic life than a
potent form of liberation.

Notes

1. Samuel Johnson, 'Whim', in *A Dictionary of the English Language* (London: W. Strahan,
    1755), vol. 2.
2. René Wellek, 'The Parallelism between Literature and the Arts', *English Institute Annual
    for 1941* (New York: Columbia University Press, 1942), 61, 49, 53–4, 56.
3. Helmut Hatzfeld, *The Rococo: Eroticism, Wit, and Elegance in European Literature*
    (New York: Pegasus, 1972), vii.
4. See Fiske Kimball, *The Creation of the Rococo* (Philadelphia: Philadelphia Museum of Art,
    1943).
5. Wylie Sypher, *Rococo to Cubism in Art and Literature* (New York: Random House, 1960),
    43. The New Critical approach to the rococo also yielded one compelling analysis of a liter-
    ary text, Roger Robinson's reading of Fielding's *Tom Jones* through the lens of Hogarth's
    theory and practice. But even this occasionally lapses into fanciful analogies, as when he
    compares the 'rich verbal surface of Fielding's prose' to the 'lavish and open brushwork
    of Hogarth's technique'. See Roger Robinson, 'Henry Fielding and the English Rococo', in
    *Studies in the Eighteenth Century II: Papers Presented at the Second David Nichol Smith
    Memorial Seminar, Canberra 1970*, ed. R. F. Brissenden (Toronto: University of Toronto
    Press, 1973), 108.
6. Patrick Brady, 'Towards a Theory of the Rococo', *The Comparatist* 9 (1985): 10, 17.
7. Melissa Lee Hyde, 'Rococo Redux: From the Style Moderne of the Eighteenth Century to
    Art Nouveau', in *Rococo: The Continuing Curve, 1730–2008*, ed. Sarah D. Coffin, Gail S.
    Davidson, Ellen Lupton and Penelope Hunter-Stiebel (New York: Smithsonian, 2008), 14.
8. Allison Stedman, *Rococo Fiction in France, 1600–1715: Seditious Frivolity* (Lewisburg:
    Bucknell University Press, 2012), 5.
9. Jonathan Sheehan and Dror Wahrman, *Invisible Hands: Self-Organization and the
    Eighteenth Century* (Chicago: University of Chicago Press, 2015), 78, 80.

HAYWOOD'S WHIMSICAL ADVENTURES 209

10. Jean-André Rouquet, *The Present State of the Arts in England* (London: J. Nourse, 1755), 85.
11. Brigid von Preussen, '"A Wild Kind of Imagination": Eclecticism and Excess in the English Rococo Designs of Thomas Johnson', in *Rococo Echo: Art, History and Historiography*, ed. Melissa Lee Hyde and Katie Scott (Oxford: Voltaire Foundation, 2014), 191. See also Michael Snodin, 'English Rococo and Its Continental Origins', in *Rococo Art and Design in Hogarth's England*, ed. Michael Snodin and Elspeth Moncrieff (London: Victoria & Albert Museum, 1984), 33.
12. Jennifer Milam, 'Play Between Disciplines: The Problem of the Ludic in Rococo Art and Enlightenment Culture', in *The Interdisciplinary Century: Tensions and Convergences in Eighteenth-Century Art, History, and Literature*, ed. Julia V. Douthwaite and Mary Vidal (Oxford: Voltaire Foundation, 2003), 109, 104.
13. See Anne Puetz, 'Drawing from Fancy: The Intersection of Art and Design in Mid-Eighteenth-Century London', *RIHA Journal* (2014), para. 6, https://doi.org/10.11588/riha.2014.1.69968; Patricia Crown, 'British Rococo as Social and Political Style', *Eighteenth-Century Studies* 23, no. 3 (1990): 269–82.
14. Eliza Haywood, *The Female Spectator*, 4 vols (London: T. Gardner, 1744–6), 1:1. Further references parenthetical.
15. Theresa Braunschneider, *Our Coquettes: Capacious Desire in the Eighteenth Century* (Charlottesville: University of Virginia Press, 2009), 44.
16. Eliza Haywood, *The History of Miss Betsy Thoughtless*, ed. Christine Blouch (1751; Peterborough: Broadview Press, 1998), 558. Further references parenthetical.
17. Branunschneider, *Our Coquettes*, 126.
18. *The Guardian*, ed. John Calhoun Stephens (Lexington: University Press of Kentucky, 1982), 192–5. 'No. 49', 7 May 1713.
19. Colin Campbell, *The Romantic Ethic and the Spirit of Modern Consumerism*, 2nd edn (London: Palgrave Macmillan, 2018), 131.
20. Sir Joshua Reynolds, *Discourses on Art*, ed. Robert R. Wark (1769–90; New Haven: Yale University Press, 1997), 50, 48, 42, 44–5.
21. Elizabeth A. Bohls, 'Disinterestedness and Denial of the Particular: Locke, Adam Smith, and the Subject of Aesthetics', in *Eighteenth-Century Aesthetics and the Reconstruction of Art*, ed. Paul Mattick, Jr (Cambridge: Cambridge University Press, 1993), 25.
22. John Barrell, '"The Dangerous Goddess": Masculinity, Prestige, and the Aesthetic in Early Eighteenth-Century Britain', *Cultural Critique* 12 (1989): 103–4.
23. 'No. 15', *The World*, 12 April 1753.
24. Peter N. Lindfield, *Georgian Gothic: Medievalist Architecture, Furniture and Interiors, 1730–1840* (Woodbridge: Boydell Press, 2016), 81, 82.
25. Michael Symes, *The English Rococo Garden* (Oxford: Shire Publications, 2011), 6.
26. Francis Coventry, *An Essay on the New Species of Writing Founded by Mr. Fielding* (London: W. Owen, 1751), 13–14, 14–15.
27. Charlotte Lennox, *The Female Quixote*, ed. Margaret Dalziel and Margaret Ann Doody (1752; Oxford: Oxford University Press, 1989), 5. Further references parenthetical.
28. See Scott Paul Gordon, 'The Space of Romance in Lennox's *The Female Quixote*', *Studies in English Literature, 1600–1900* 38 (1998): 499–516; Sharon Smith Palo, 'The Good Effects of a Whimsical Study: Romance and Woman's Learning in Charlotte Lennox's *The Female Quixote*', *Eighteenth-Century Fiction* 18, no. 2 (2005–6): 203–28.
29. Robert W. Jones, 'Eliza Haywood and the Discourse of Taste', in *Authorship, Commerce and the Public: Scenes of Writing, 1750–1850*, ed. E. J. Clery, Caroline Franklin and Peter Garside (Basingstoke: Palgrave Macmillan, 2002), 111.
30. Critical treatments of desire in Haywood's fiction are now legion. Those alluded to here are, respectively, Emily Hodgson Anderson, 'Performing the Passions in Eliza Haywood's *Fantomina* and *Miss Betsy Thoughtless*', *The Eighteenth Century* 46, no. 1 (2005): 1–15; Tiffany

Potter, 'The Language of Feminised Sexuality: Gendered Voice in Eliza Haywood's *Love in Excess* and *Fantomina*', *Women's Writing* 10, no. 1 (2003): 169–86; Helen Thompson, 'Plotting Materialism: W. Charleton's *The Ephesian Matron*, E. Haywood's *Fantomina*, and Feminine Consistency', *Eighteenth-Century Studies* 35, no. 2 (2002): 195–214.

31. Eliza Haywood, *Fantomina and Other Works*, ed. Alexander Pettit, Margaret Case Croskery and Anna C. Patchias (1725; Peterborough: Broadview Press, 2004), 41, 42, 44. Further references parenthetical.

32. Braunschneider, *Our Coquettes*, 4.

33. Campbell, *The Romantic Ethic*, 145.

34. Campbell, *The Romantic Ethic*, 15.

35. Robert Campbell, *The London Tradesman* (London: T. Gardner, 1747), 118, 115.

36. William Hogarth, *The Analysis of Beauty*, ed. Robert Paulson (1753; New Haven: Yale University Press, 1197), 32–4.

37. Annie Richardson, 'From the Moral Mound to the Material Maze: Hogarth's *Analysis of Beauty*', in *Luxury in the Eighteenth Century: Debates, Desires, and Delectable Goods*, ed. Maxine Berg and Elizabeth Eger (Basingstoke: Palgrave Macmillan, 2003), 130.

38. Alison Conway, *Private Interests: Women, Portraits, and the Visual Culture of the English Novel, 1709–1791* (Toronto: University of Toronto Press, 2001), 117, 133.

39. Conway, *Private Interests*, 129; Hogarth, *The Analysis of Beauty*, 33.

40. David Porter, *The Chinese Taste in Eighteenth-Century England* (Cambridge: Cambridge University Press, 2010), 11, 32–3, 34–5.

41. Matthew Reeve, *Gothic Architecture and Sexuality in the Circle of Horace Walpole* (University Park: Pennsylvania State University Press, 2020), 29, 26.

42. On the aesthetics of the small in this period, see Chloe Wigston Smith and Beth Fowkes Tobin, eds, *Small Things in the Eighteenth Century: The Political and Personal Value of the Miniature* (Cambridge: Cambridge University Press, 2022).

43. Sianne Ngai, *Our Aesthetic Categories: Zany, Cute, Interesting* (Cambridge, MA: Harvard University Press, 2010), 18–19, 66.

44. See Benjamin R. Barber, *Consumed: How Markets Corrupt Children, Infantilize Adults, and Swallow Citizens Whole* (New York: W. W. Norton, 2007).

12

Song in the Novels of Samuel Richardson

Elizabeth Kraft

A T THE CONCLUSION of her expansive essay on the origins of novel writing, written in preface to her 1810 fifty-volume *British Novelists*, Anna Letitia Barbauld quotes the Scottish writer and politician Andrew Fletcher of Saltoun, and modifies his observation to suit her thought:

> It was said by Fletcher of Saltoun, 'Let me make the ballads of a nation, and I care not who makes the laws'. Might it not be said with as much propriety, Let me make the novels of a country, and let who will make the systems.[1]

The connection Barbauld makes between the ballad and the novel harks back to her earliest literary criticism – criticism advanced in response to *Essays on Song-Writing* (1774) written by her brother, John Aikin. In that work, Aikin describes song writing as 'the faithful copyist of external objects and real emotions', later elaborated by imagination and wit.[2] Barbauld's commentary came in the form of a poem, 'The Origin of Song-Writing', wherein she speaks of the central subject of song as female suffering. In her work on the history of the novel, she found that a similar emphasis shaped the novel as it emerged in the eighteenth century. Indeed, the story she tells of Cupid in 'The Origin of Song-Writing' is very similar to the narrative she later fashions of the career of Samuel Richardson, whose works occupy a central place in her conception of the British novel. Like Barbauld's Cupid, Richardson found, by acquaintance with the 'Daughters of Jove' (l. 39), that 'love inspires the poet's song' (l. 66), producing works focused on the suffering of women. The genealogy tracked in Barbauld's poem includes Thomas Otway's Monimia, Virgil's (and Henry Purcell's) Dido and Alexander Pope's Eloisa, a list in which Richardson's heroines would find equitable companionship.[3] The lamentations of women – Pamela, Clarissa and *Sir Charles Grandison*'s Clementina – are central to Richardson's novels, but celebration is possible, too. After all, epithalamium, as G. Gabrielle Starr notes, ultimately controls the narrative of *Pamela* and one strain of the story (Harriet's) of *Sir Charles Grandison*, too.[4] *Pamela* (1740), *Clarissa* (1748) and *Sir Charles Grandison* (1753) all highlight emotion through the evocation of song, an important, though underacknowledged, source of their power and appeal.

Harmony

> I thought I had the Harmony of the Spheres all around me; and every Word that dropt from his Lips was sweet as the Honey of Hybla to me.
>
> – Samuel Richardson, *Pamela* (1740)[5]

The passage quoted as epigraph above offers an entrée into Richardson's sense of the musicality of love. The remark is Pamela's, of course, and it occurs in a letter that recounts a conversation after Mr B.'s 'conversion', that is, his admission of love for Pamela and his determination to marry her. What he says to her is not particularly pleasant, for he points out that the change in Pamela's status will aggravate many, and it is likely that, as his wife, Pamela will be subjected to social stigmas and personal sanctions despite (or even because of) her elevation through marriage:

> Sister Davers . . . will never be reconciled to you. The other Ladies will not visit you; and you will, with a Merit transcending them all, be treated as if unworthy their Notice. . . . [H]ow will my Girl relish all this? Won't these be cutting things to my Fair-one? (242)

Pamela calls these sentiments 'condescending' and 'generous' (242), and, indeed that seems to be why she finds in them resonance with the 'Harmony of the Spheres', for 'condescending', which has a pejorative connotation in our time, signified in 1740 the voluntary and gracious choice to renounce the privileges of station and to address a social inferior on equal terms.[6] While the notion of innate class inequality is one we do not countenance today, for Pamela (and for Richardson's readers) the hierarchies of society were so entrenched as to make the concept of even temporary equality radical. Earlier, Mr B. himself had petulantly noted that Pamela's innocence and simplicity were enough to 'corrupt a Nation' (149); here, he embraces both the woman and the 'corruption', which he now sees as a rectification of a truly corrupt world, a world that has been, like himself, out of tune with the moral universe.

In *Pamela*, song signals a retuning, a recalibrating of the moral order: following her betrothal to Mr B., Pamela sings a five-stanza composition at the request of visiting ladies, proving herself to be accomplished in the graceful arts expected of a woman of the landed classes (thanks to her 'Lady' who taught her the song). The implication of this scene is that any prejudice Pamela is to suffer will be based on snobbery rather than refined response to her natural or acquired talents. Having established that point, Richardson moves his narrative towards the marriage ceremony itself, in a more reflective musical direction with a long section focused on psalms. In this section, the meditation on class continues as sacred song unites the lowly (even the vulgar) and the refined, elevating the one and tempering the other.

First are psalms sung at Sabbath services the Sunday prior to the wedding. There is discussion of skipping the psalms 'for want of a Clerk', but it turns out that Pamela's father is equipped to 'perform that Office' for he had 'learnt Psalmody formerly in his Youth, and had constantly practised it in private, at home, of Sunday Evenings', so Pamela felt 'in no Pain for his undertaking it in this little Congregation' (289). Pamela describes his rendering of the 23rd Psalm as 'so intirely affected with the Duty, that he went thro' it distinctly, calmly, and fervently at the same time'. The edifying effect on the well-born congregation is represented in the reaction of Lady Jones who whispers to Pamela '[t]hat good Men were fit for all Companies and present to every laudable Occasion' (290).

Sabbath supper is devoted to a comparison of Psalm 137 and Pamela's revision based on her own captivity. Mrs Jewkes, surprisingly, had been the inspiration for the revision in two ways. First, we are told that she had asked Pamela one Sunday 'to sing a Psalm', but Pamela, being in poor spirits, declined. After Mrs Jewkes had left, however, Pamela remembered 'that the cxxxvii[th] Psalm was applicable to her own Case' (292) and rewrote it as an expression of her own sorrow. We have already read her version in the journal entry that recounts the tale; here, we revisit the poem in a verse-by-verse comparison as the dinner guests, including Mr Andrews and the ladies who had been at the church service, comment on and praise it. Five stanzas of Psalm 104 are sung by Mr Andrews at the afternoon service, 'suitably magnifying the holy Name of God for all his Mercies' (297). This extended reference to psalms and psalmody would likely have read tunefully to an age in which even a sacrilegious, vulgar housekeeper can plausibly be presented as having a taste for such songs. Indeed, many readers would have enjoyed fitting Pamela's revision of Psalm 137 to the tune they knew from church (Figure 12.1).

Figure 12.1 Psalm-tunes for the Psalm CXXXVII, from John Chetham, *A Book of Psalmody, Containing a Variety of Tunes for all the Common Metres of the Psalms in the Old and New Versions* (1741).

214 ELIZABETH KRAFT

The marriage ceremony itself is recounted briefly with abbreviated reference to the vows, the witnesses and the order of service (318);[7] afterwards, of course, the plot develops with some dark undertones (Lady Davers's mean-spiritedness, the revelation that Mr B. has a 'natural' daughter), but these are also occasions for the couple to demonstrate their devotion to one another and their ability to restore harmony in the aftermath of discordant events. To signal the lastingness of the happiness the two have found, the novel concludes with a poem written and sung by Mr B. for his wife. There are four stanzas, beginning with the following:

All Nature blooms when you appear;
The Fields their richest Liv'ries wear;
Oaks, Elms and Pines, blest with your View,
Shoot out fresh Greens, and bud anew.
   The varying Seasons you supply;
   And when you're gone, they fade and die. (454)

While speculation has assigned authorship of this song both to Richardson and to Aaron Hill, there is no agreement.[8] One thing is certain, however: when the verses appeared as Mr B.'s in 1740 they were known to a tune, for they had been printed in 1729 in volume 3 of *The Hive: A Collection of the Most Celebrated Songs* under the title 'To His Mistress'.[9] The tunes are not reproduced in *The Hive*, but by 1760, as we find in the musical anthology entitled *The Monthly Melody*, these verses had been retitled 'The Charms of Silvia' and set to music by Thomas Arne – or, to be more accurate, the first two verses were now so named as they were the only ones reproduced for 'the Polite Amusement of Gentlemen and Ladies', which this songbook promised to provide (Figure 12.2).[10] The first two verses appeared again in 1775 under the title 'The Charms of Sylvia' in *Apollo: Or the Songster's Universal Library*, an anthology helpfully subtitled 'Being a collection of all the new and old songs on love, mirth, war, hunting, and drinking'.[11] It is the design of the work to provide accurate lyrics of the songs heard at 'the Gardens and the Theatres' that will please the youthful singer/reader, as well as 'old merry ballads' that will remind older singers/readers of 'the Delights they tasted of in the Days of Yore'.[12] In 1885, the song was reunited with Mr B. in a curious publication entitled *Songs from the Novelists*. The four verses of the poem beginning 'All Nature blooms when you appear' were printed under the title 'Mr. B's Song' along with the five verses of the song taught to Pamela by her Lady, titled here 'Pamela's Song'.[13]

Richardson's *Pamela II* (1742) begins with song as Pamela describes the apartment that Mr B., whom she still calls her 'Master', plans to construct in the farmhouse in which he has situated Pamela's parents. This apartment will be for his and Pamela's use, and he will make modifications for their comfort, which Pamela duly describes. Most importantly, he will preserve 'the old Bow-windows',[14] adding larger panes of glass to let in more of the night air and of the song of the nightingales, which inspires Mr B. to ask his wife to sing for him, dubbing her the 'Sweetest of all Nightingales' when she does so (6). Later, though, the nightingale is invoked negatively as Pamela relates her first visit to the opera in a letter to her sister-in-law. Bemoaning (like many eighteenth-century English critics)[15] the unfortunate divorce of pleasure and instruction when librettos are in Italian, Pamela admits that a nightingale, 'all Voice, . . . all

Figure 12.2 'The Charms of Silvia', *The Monthly Melody: or Polite Amusement for Gentlemen and Ladies. Being a Collection of Vocal and Instrumental Music Composed by Dr. Arne* (London: G. Kearsley, 1760).

216 ELIZABETH KRAFT

Ear and lost to every Sense but that, and Harmony', might find '*Italian* opera . . . a transporting Thing', but those who value 'good Sense, and Instruction, and Propriety' regret that Italian opera sacrifices all three 'to the Charms of Sound' (361). Pamela quotes her husband in support: 'when once Sound is preferr'd to Sense, we shall depart from all our own Worthiness' (362). She seems ready to reject song altogether as she continues to ponder the topic and the impossibility of 'describ[ing] Sound' until Mr B. offers further commentary, in which he explains that while in England Italian opera is 'incongruous nonsense' (364), in Italy the sound and sense are 'very compatible' (363). Moreover, such compositions allow the poet (the librettist) 'to express the Passions without Offence to the Ear' (364). To put it another way, Mr B. understands that music can serve to intensify the claim words make upon us by enlisting our senses in support of their 'good sense'.[16] This is an idea that Richardson would continue to develop in *Clarissa* and *Sir Charles Grandison*.

Lyricism

What an example she set! . . . How she sung! How she played! Her voice music! Her accent harmony!

– Samuel Richardson, *Clarissa* (1748)[17]

Richardson's second novel, *Clarissa*, is notable for including, early on, a lithograph of the tune to which Clarissa has set three verses of Elizabeth Carter's 'Ode to Wisdom', a fact that has received insightful literary commentary. Clarissa has composed the tune to settle her mind after a confrontation with her parents. Song, which in *Pamela* had derived from and contributed to social harmony, functions more subversively in this episode.[18] It provides occasion for Clarissa to steady her nerves, to achieve a kind of self-harmony. And it also serves to define a community outside of her family. As both Leslie Ritchie and Scott Sanders note, the lithograph itself seems to reach beyond the text. The reader, like Anna Howe, finds the page folded within the book so that, in Sanders's words, he or she 'could discover Clarissa's song almost as though it were a sheet of music inserted into a letter'.[19] Ritchie imagines the reader playing the tune as Anna would have done, while Sanders recreates in detail the sonic affect of Clarissa's performance in her closed room:

> For Clarissa's musical performance, I imagine how the sound of her voice moves and resonates within the wooden interior of her bedchamber – an acoustically rich space whose materiality would modify Clarissa's voice. Given that Clarissa is constantly eavesdropping on her family, her voice, though contained within her room, might seep out through the door of her sister's adjoining parlor. We can assume that her room includes a few traditional items (curtains, rugs, wainscoting). With closed shutters and doors, these sonically reflective wooden surfaces would enhance the resonant capacity of her acoustic space. With little ambient noise, her voice would fill her bedchamber and reverberate after each verse.[20]

Pierre Dubois comments on the way the ode 'left the world of fiction to become, as it were, "real" – a piece of poetry and music that existed in the world out there, outside

SONG IN THE NOVELS OF SAMUEL RICHARDSON 217

the confines of the written text'.[21] In this sense, the 'Ode' is the opposite of the psalms sung by Mr Andrews and others in *Pamela*, though akin to the songs of Mr B. and Pamela as included in *The Monthly Melody* and other texts. Indeed, the author of the melody of the 'Ode' has never been determined, and, as Dubois notes, it tended to be attributed to Clarissa herself.[22]

Dubois also treats the relationship of Clarissa's song to the emergent eighteenth-century distinction between (Italian) opera and (English) oratorio; like the oratorio and unlike Italian opera, Clarissa's ode, and indeed the entirety of *Clarissa* itself, is focused on 'a moral message, an exemplary lesson'.[23] But the affective nature of Clarissa's tale (and her ode) is also the point, rendering this narrative one of the most powerful in the English language. In other words, while *Clarissa*'s message is conveyed in words, the lyricism of those words and the emotional intensity they create move the passions in a way similar to a musical score.

In her commentary on *Clarissa*, Barbauld points to the ballad-like nature of the narrative:

Nothing can be more simple than the story,—A young lady, pressed by her parents to marry a man every way disagreeable to her, and placed under the most cruel restraint, leaves her father's house, and throws herself upon the protection of her lover, a man of sense and spirit, but a libertine. When he finds her in his power he artfully declines marriage, and conveys her to a house kept for the worst of purposes. There, after many fruitless attempts to ensnare her virtue, he at length violates her person. She escapes from further outrage: he finds her out in her retreat; offers her marriage, which she rejects. Her friends are obdurate. She retires to solitary lodgings; grief and shame overwhelm her, and she dies broken-hearted; her friends lament their severity when too late. Her violator is transiently stung with remorse, but not reformed; he leaves the kingdom in order to dissipate his chagrin, and is killed in a duel by a relation of the lady's.[24]

'On this slight foundation, and on a story not very agreeable or promising in its rude outline', she concludes, 'has our author founded a most pathetic tale, and raised a noble temple to female virtue.'[25] The effect on the reader is one of dissonance and distress, but eventually harmony is restored:

As the work advances, the character rises; the distress is deepened; our hearts are torn with pity and indignation; bursts of grief succeed one another, till at length the mind is composed and harmonized with emotions of milder sorrow; we are calmed into resignation, elevated with pious hope, and dismissed glowing with the conscious triumphs of virtue.[26]

Barbauld's use of 'harmonized' here is interesting in that the term and its cognates are more often found in Lovelace's letters than in Clarissa's. It is true that Lovelace associates harmony with Clarissa's voice, but, unlike Mr B., he does not attempt to fashion his own songs or to accompany hers. Instead, he seeks to exploit harmonic resonances to forward his own plots against Clarissa. Relating to Belford his plan to escort Clarissa to a production of Thomas Otway's tragedy *Venice Preserv'd*, Lovelace remarks,

The woes of others so well represented, as those of Belvidera particularly will be, must, I hope, unlock, and open, my charmer's heart. Whenever I have been able to prevail upon a girl to permit me to attend her to a play, I have thought myself sure of her. The female heart, all gentleness and harmony, when obliged, expands, and forgets its forms, when attention is carried out of itself, at an agreeable or affecting entertainment: Music, and perhaps a collation afterwards, co-operating. (4:101)

Belvidera is pure and moral, and very much in the lineage of ballad-heroines defined by Barbauld in 'The Origin of Song-Writing'. She is the victim of the struggle between versions of masculinity and the quest for power, as is Clarissa. Both Belvidera and Clarissa live in worlds of dissonance and confusion; the harmony they achieve is with the viewer or the reader as their sufferings provoke sympathetic tears.

Starr has argued that 'lyric expression in the long eighteenth century is cross-implicated by and in the languages of emotion in early novels', reorganising 'lyric conventions' as well as 'private experience and the inner world'.[27] *Clarissa*, in her view (and I concur) makes significant strides in opening up the affective power of fiction, in developing language that, similar to the dialogue in Otway's she-tragedies, creates community outside of a text in which alienation and fragmentation prevail. Starr describes Clarissa's longing for 'consensus – feeling-with, a concord of heart and mind' as denied her in her relationships with individuals but made available through literature – the book of Job and the verse of George Herbert and John Donne, especially, which Richardson drew on as 'models for emotional intensity'.[28] In *Clarissa*, Starr observes, 'Richardson turned toward a form concerned with melding public and private experience; these lyrics provide models of emotional consensus imagined, lost, and ultimately reconstructed.'[29] 'Ode to Wisdom' offers insight into the way Richardson conceives of and creates the affective tempo and harmonic ideal that underwrite the emotional consensus to which Starr refers.

The ode's title indicates the addressee, Wisdom, but as the poem begins there is description rather than apostrophe. 'The solitary Bird of Night' is portrayed as 'wing[ing] Flight' through 'the thick Shades' from the 'Time-shook Tow'r' where he spends his day 'shelter'd' in 'Philosophic Gloom' (2:48). The impression of darkness and melancholy is deep, the scene nocturnal, but the diurnal that is left behind is also sombre. The first verse suggests that the road to wisdom is through suffering, a thought central to Stoic philosophy (the work of Epictetus, which the true author of the poem, Elizabeth Carter, would go on to translate), to Job, whose sufferings prefigure those of *Clarissa*, and to *Night Thoughts* (1742–5), the poem authored by Edward Young, Richardson's friend and correspondent. The second verse shifts to the speaker's internal response to the owl's flight – a 'Joy' at the 'solemn Sound' echoing through the night of 'sighing Gales', causing the speaker to 'bend / At Wisdom's awful Seat' in a kind of worshipful awe (2:48). The reference to joy in this atmosphere gestures towards feelings of the sublime, the typical mood of the ode, but one generally achieved through exaltation and praise rather than through confrontation with the awful mystery of melancholy which this verse references.[30] A third verse returns to descriptive language to divorce Wisdom from 'false Shews of Life' and the 'vain Disguise' often adopted by 'Folly'. Wisdom is simple and open, though most comfortable in 'the cool, the silent Eve' rather than 'in the Beam of Day' (2:49).

SONG IN THE NOVELS OF SAMUEL RICHARDSON

Finally, with the fourth verse, the apostrophe begins as the odist addresses 'Pallas', the Goddess of Wisdom, directly and continues to refer to 'thy' and 'thee' through to the tenth verse. The ninth and tenth verses seem particularly pertinent to Clarissa's case:

By Thee protected, I defy
The Coxcomb's Sneer, the stupid Lye
    Of Ignorance and Spite:
Alike contemn the leaden Fool,
And all the pointed Ridicule
    Of undiscerning Wit.

From Envy, Hurry, Noise, and Strife,
The dull Impertinence of Life,
    In thy Retreat I rest:
Pursue thee to the peaceful Groves,
Where Plato's sacred Spirit roves,
    In all thy Beauties drest. (2:50)

The next three verses elaborate on Plato's significance to the culture of Athens, Greece and (of course, by extension) to Europe. His focus on the 'Perfect, Fair, and Good' redeems a 'wild, licentious Youth'. Wisdom tames the passions in the pursuit of virtue and underwrites national strength through the works of Poets, Patriots, Heroes and all who participate in 'still, domestic Life' (2:50). Similarly, Clarissa's story, through its affective power, its ability to engage readers in lyrical moments of sympathy, advances the cause of virtue and wisdom. The corrective of national manners and taste in terms of combating the fashion for licentiousness and libertinism is a stated aim of Richardson's, and infuses all his fiction.

That the love of wisdom and virtue should permeate national life from the private home to the Halls of Parliament to the battlefields of foreign lands is an ideal with which Richardson would have had great sympathy. But it is the last three verses of Carter's poem that he chose to have set to music and engraved for his inset lithograph (Figure 12.3).[31] These verses again direct the gaze inward to the speaker's psychology and the emotional, even spiritual, benefit of the pursuit of Wisdom. Here the gloomy, dark imagery of the poem's opening is reinvoked and set in opposition to the 'Intellectual Light', 'Happiness and Good' and 'solid Joys' conferred by Wisdom. From the celebration of Platonic philosophy, the poem shifts to language more evocative of Christianity as the speaker leads thought to 'the Supreme all-perfect Mind', and relies on Wisdom to help 'direct my Soul' on 'Life's perplexing Road' through 'Mists of Error' and 'Gloom', before concluding with these Ecclesiastical lines:

Beneath Her clear discerning Eye
The visionary Shadows fly
    Of folly's painted Show.
She sees thro' ev'ry fair Disguise,
That All but Virtue's solid Joys,
    Are Vanity and Woe. (musical inset 2:50)

220 ELIZABETH KRAFT

Figure 12.3 'Ode to Wisdom', inset lithograph, Samuel Richardson, *Clarissa* (1748), vol. 2, between pages 50 and 51.

And, of course, the music reinforces all. To be played andante, moderately slow, the tune is in E major, with repetitions of lines 3 and 6 of each stanza scored which slows the pace as well. An averagely accomplished harpsichord player would soon master this piece or 'lesson', as Clarissa hopes Anna Howe will do. As Janine Barchas has noted, one obvious intention of including the inset was to establish Clarissa's participation in a 'community' or 'fellowship' of musical friends.[32] This is a female society centred on a taste for music and the thoughts and emotions that music scores and underscores. While the song, played and sung, creates a performance that reading the novel (even reading the novel aloud) cannot simulate, the musical lines serve as a synecdoche of the affective nature of Clarissa's suffering, a uniquely gendered suffering, that conjoins feeling characters within the text as well as responsive readers of the text.

Chorus

[I]t is the noblest composition that ever was produced by man.
– Samuel Richardson, *The History of Sir Charles Grandison* (1753)[33]

The quotation above is Sir Charles Grandison's opinion of Handel's *Alexander's Feast*, which, as Margaret Anne Doody notes, 'runs as a kind of *leit-motif* throughout [Richardson's third and final] novel'.[34] Charlotte conveys her brother's assessment in order to persuade Harriet to 'give ... a lesson on the harpsichord' after tea at Grandison's home in St James's Square. Harriet, it turns out, is something of

SONG IN THE NOVELS OF SAMUEL RICHARDSON

a Handel expert, having been heard by others in the company, namely her cousins Mr and Mrs Reeves, 'sing[ing] several songs out of the Pastoral, and out of some of his finest Oratorio's' (254). It is Sir Charles who, hearing of this expertise, requests Handel. Harriet demurs, not from shyness as much as from the nature of the piece itself: 'As you know . . . that great part of the beauty of this performance arises from the proper transitions from one different strain to another, any one song must lose greatly, by being taken out of its place, and I fear--' (254). Sir Charles interrupts her and tells her not to fear. They will make 'allowances' for any deficiency. But there is no need, for Harriet astutely chooses an air from the work that will not suffer from the displacement:

> I then turned to that fine piece of accompanied recitative:
> *Softly sweet, in Lydian measures*
> *Soon he sooth'd his soul to pleasures.*
> Which not being set so full with accompanying symphonies, as most of Mr. Handel's are, I performed with the more ease to myself, tho' I had never but once before played it over. (254)

Her performance is a success; she is asked to 'play and sing it once more' (254).

The libretto of Handel's work is adapted from John Dryden's poem of the same title, an ode written for the celebration of St Cecilia's Day (22 November) in 1697. Dryden had composed an ode for the same occasion, titled 'Song for St. Cecilia's Day', earlier in 1683. Handel set both to music in the 1730s – 'Alexander's Feast' in 1736 and 'Ode for St. Cecilia's Day' in 1739. These works share with the English oratorio, as Handel would go on to develop it, an emphasis on choruses rather than operatic arias – the joining of voices in communal reflection or response rather than the celebration of the individual voice.[35] Further, like the oratorio, they are preoccupied with the sacred. In Dryden's time, the poems were associated with high church Anglicanism or Catholicism in their celebration of the power of music, and particularly in the concluding reference in each poem to organ music, which Puritan services eschewed (organs had been destroyed in many churches during the English Civil War). By the mid-1750s, church music was not such a controversial issue, but there is surely significance in the fact that the Protestant Harriet sings a song written in celebration of the Roman Catholic patron saint of musicians who embraced virginity and, eventually, death for the sake of her religion. The devoutly Roman Catholic, though unmusical, Clementina seems drawn to St Cecilia's fate, although she does not eventually die a martyr and seems poised to marry as the novel concludes. In a work which the author himself styled as a kind of reconciliation between Protestantism and Roman Catholicism, the choice of leitmotif could not be more appropriate.

The songs invoked from Handel's *Alexander's Feast* are, also appropriately (given *Grandison*'s plot and theme), about love and marriage; but these songs, as every reader of 1753 would have known, are bright moments in a complex musical score which treats of a range of emotions – the point being that music has the power to drive human feeling and, therefore, behaviour. Eventually, Harriet and the reader learn the full story of the events that occurred the afternoon of the recital, and, as the full situation becomes clear, we recognise that the undertones of anger and fear, frustration and pride could have been activated by music had design or desire so dictated. During dinner, before the impromptu concert, Sir Charles is called from the room to meet with Mr Bagenhall who has arrived with a demand from Sir Hargrave Pollexfen. Sir Hargrave is a villain in the vein of *Clarissa*'s Lovelace, having abducted Harriet from a masquerade. His shenanigans, though violent in themselves, had ended without the violation of Harriet; she was rescued from Sir Hargrave by Sir Charles and returned to the London home of her cousins. These are the circumstances under which the Reeveses came to know Sir Charles; the dinner at St James's Square is the first occasion for a post-traumatic gathering of the two families, an opening gesture of friendship. When Sir Charles is called from the room to meet an emissary of Sir Hargrave, he asks Mr Reeves to accompany him – and so both hear the demand that Sir Hargrave be allowed to meet with Harriet, and if refused, to be given 'the satisfaction of a gentleman' (257). While Sir Charles has no intention of fighting a duel, he does agree to attend Sir Hargrave the next day. There is clearly some danger in the situation, which is evident on Mr Reeves's face when he returns to the company, but which Sir Charles does not evince. The soothing melody Harriet plays is unnecessary for Sir Charles's composure, but it likely contributes to the restoration of her cousin's equanimity. Harriet performs as the situation demands. She complies with a request for a particular musical work and chooses from that work an air commensurate with her talents. As it happens, she also ensures a social harmony where harmony is (though unbeknownst to her) at risk – a role that will continue to define her presence throughout the novel.[36]

The Grandison circle's familiarity with *Alexander's Feast*, in particular, affords a kind of shorthand. The very tune played and sung so gracefully by Harriet in the episode described above serves as an entry point into the resolution of a quarrel between Lord and Lady G. shortly after their marriage. Charlotte, Sir Charles's sister, is lively and irreverent; her new husband, earnest and easily offended. Their early wedded life is fraught with misunderstandings and petulance. As Emily, Sir Charles's ward who is living with the newly married couple, puts it when Harriet arrives at the troubled home: 'Ah, madam! We are all to pieces. One *so* careless, the other *so* passionate!' (915). Instead of explaining the situation to Harriet when she appears, Charlotte runs to the harpsichord and begins to sing soft, sweet 'Lydian measures'. Before she completes the last line of the couplet, she is interrupted by her husband who (slow though he is on some occasions) recognises immediately that Charlotte is sending him a message. 'I know what this is for', he says (915). Charlotte picks up on the hint and bemoans her state: 'Harmony! harmony! is a charming thing! But I, poor I! know not any but what this poor instrument affords me' (915). Harriet, too, understands: 'you have both, like children, been at play, until you have fallen out' (915). Like the mediator she is, Harriet assigns blame on both sides, requiring Charlotte to apologise and Lord G. to forgive, introducing the chance of harmony, if not complete accord, at this point.

For the Grandison set, marriage is filtered through the choruses of *Alexander's Feast*. Another air from the work is featured at Charlotte's wedding. Sir Charles himself sings to Harriet's accompaniment the following chorus (Figure 12.4), modified from the original to reflect his and the company's values:

Happy, happy, happy pair!
None but the good deserves the fair. (857)

Figure 12.4 George Frederick Handel, 'Happy Pair', from *Alexander's Feast*, as reproduced in *The Muses Delight* (1754).

While I agree with Doody that the substitution of 'good' for 'brave' is somewhat priggish,[37] it is also an economical underscoring (pun intended) of the novel's theme, a theme Richardson had been pursuing since *Pamela*: heroes are changing, just as the world is changing. Art reflects and helps direct that change. Dianne Dugaw has usefully summarised the old style or classical ballad as featuring 'feudal objects and settings', medieval 'social roles and practices' and premodern 'beliefs and mores'.[38] In a way, Sir Charles seems like a hero of that tradition, one who, out of a sense of responsibility towards his fiefdom, mounts his steed and gallops off to rescue those in distress. The two plot strands in *Sir Charles Grandison* are initiated by such rescues (of Jeronymo and of Harriet) with the potential reward of marriage at the end of each. Charles's antagonists, on the other hand, seem to derive from the world of broadside ballads. Jeronymo falls under the influence of a woman 'less celebrated for virtue than beauty' (625) and is attacked by a group of 'Brescian bravoes' on behalf of another of her admirers. His story is not that of George Barnwell exactly, as Jeronymo hails from a family of means and significance.[39] Libertinism, not greed, is his downfall – but the result is seedy and scandalous nonetheless, with a whiff of broadside interest in the sordid and the sensational. The same can be said of Sir Hargrave and his team of thugs who appear periodically throughout the narrative with ever-increasing degradation. Such enemies are brave enough themselves, if bravery can be defined as the willingness to undertake physical risk in pursuit of one's aims and designs. But they do not 'deserve the fair'; in a world of venality and corruption, it is not prowess but commitment to morality and ethics that points a way forward.

The final reference to *Alexander's Feast* is spoken not sung – and as such it refers us back to the very first invocation of the work, which was also a spoken allusion that, in a sense, announced the novel's theme long before the eponymous subject of the novel appeared. The final reference is made just before the wedding which will unite Harriet Byron and Sir Charles Grandison. It is uttered by Greville, one of Harriet's long-suffering, insufferable suitors whom we first meet in volume 1. By the time he appears here in volume 5, he has discovered that his suit is irrevocably lost, and Harriet will marry the incomparable Sir Charles Grandison. He has also emulated another of Harriet's suitors and challenged Sir Charles to a duel, which Sir Charles refuses; although he does draw his sword when Greville offers a parry, it is only to disarm his rival and to warn him that 'if you are either wise, or would be thought a man of honour, tempt not again your fate' (1279). Following this altercation, Greville attends the church service at which Sir Charles and Harriet make their first official appearance as a betrothed couple. Afterwards, Greville gives what he calls his 'dying speech' resigning all pretensions to Harriet and handing her, histrionically, to Sir Charles with the words '*Happy, happy, happy pair!—None but the brave deserves the fair!*' restoring the word 'brave' to the description of the good man. He flounces off following this dramatic gesture, not fully redeemed in the eyes of most of the company nor in the opinion of most readers. Yet, we are told, 'hurrying away', he was 'sobbing as he flew', a detail that provokes a kind remark from Harriet's friend Lucy and a similar kindness from Sir Charles, who was 'generously uneasy for him' (1297).

In fact, Harriet's query to Sir Charles is '[d]on't you pity Mr. Greville, my dear?' (1297). And he certainly does. He pities all the violent, undisciplined, wayward individuals he encounters throughout the long novel, from the headstrong Olivia who

SONG IN THE NOVELS OF SAMUEL RICHARDSON

stabs him with a poniard to his late father's mistress, Mrs Oldham, to Sir Hargrave Pollexfen himself. Therefore, it is oddly fitting that the very first citation of a line from *Alexander's Feast* should occur in a discussion between the Reeveses and Harriet about the relationship between pity and love, and the ability to settle on one suitor or another. Mr Reeves asks her, in fact, if she does not pity Mr Greville and Sir Hargrave, both of whom have just left after overlapping visits that included Harriet's playing (at their request) two songs on the harpsichord and a discussion about the musical pleasures offered in London society. Handel is praised for his 'English' compositions, and Mr Reeves, still thinking of the relationship between pity and love, slightly misquotes Dryden's lines from 'Alexander's Feast': 'For Pity melts the Soul to Love', changing 'Mind' in the original to 'Soul'.[40] This line describes, he says, the course of his own love for Mrs Reeves who first pitied, then loved him and then entered into the state of holy matrimony with him. Harriet dismisses the application to her own situation with regard to her various suitors: 'to say I *pity* a man who professes to love me, because I cannot consent to be his, carries with it, I think, an air of arrogance, and looks as if I believed he must be unhappy without me' (117). As the novel ends, however, both 'pity' and 'love' have acquired broader meanings. In a traditional opera or ballad, Clementina would have been cast as Harriet's rival to be rejected when Harriet is selected by the 'hero'. In *Sir Charles Grandison*, however, compassion for Clementina and for her family (whom Sir Charles early designates a 'family of harmony and love' [708]) leads to bonds of lasting commitment. Harriet, Sir Charles and Clementina form, in Sir Charles's words, a 'triple friendship' which 'will make . . . a safe bridge over the narrow seas . . . [and] cut an easy passage thro' rocks and mountains, and make England and Italy one Country' (1685).

The hope for reconciliation of Catholic and Protestant Christianity is clearly one metaphorical lesson to extract from the *Grandison* narrative, but another, equally important moral has to do with song. When Handel began to compose for London audiences, his librettos were in Italian, though his friend Aaron Hill, also a friend of Richardson, urged him to 'deliver us from our Italian bondage. . . . by reconciling reason and dignity with musick and fine machinery [to] . . . charm the *ear* and hold fast the *heart*, together'.[41] When he did so with *Alexander's Feast*, the success was immediate and spawned many other works that married word and sound and turned 'Air, well-beaten and play'd upon' (*Pamela II*, 362) into meaning, a moral one could take away in words, and articulated thoughts to the accompaniment of the feelings, emotion and visceral response generated by music and other sounds (the very theme of *Alexander's Feast*). Song derived from such productions could then make its way into music rooms and private 'lessons'; performances of single songs could call to mind an entire narrative; the marriage of word and sound thus expanded a brief articulation of feeling into a story with characters, plot and theme.

Alexander's Feast's celebration of the power of music stands testament to the relationship between harmony, lyricism and the creation of human community, a sentiment Samuel Richardson's novels confirm. 'From Harmony, from heav'nly Harmony / This universal frame began', says Dryden, sings Handel;[42] and to harmony, heavenly harmony, Richardson adds, we can return. *Pamela*, *Clarissa* and *Sir Charles Grandison* teach compassion for the sufferings of others, and, through their invocation of song – hymn, ballad and ode – they also offer participation in the comforts and joys of sympathetic community.

Notes

1. Anna Letitia Barbauld, 'On the Origins and Progress of Novel-Writing', in *The British Novelists* (London: F. C. and J. Rivington, et al., 1810), 1:62.
2. John Aikin, *Essays on Song-Writing* (London: Joseph Johnson, 1774), 6.
3. Anna Letitia Barbauld, 'The Origin of Song-Writing', in *The Poems, Revised*, ed. William McCarthy, vol. 1 of The Collected Works of Anna Letitia Barbauld (Oxford: Oxford University Press, 2019), 82–5. John Aikin's poem on the same theme, 'Cupid and His Tutor', does not include the suffering of women. He focuses only on the pleasures of love. *Poems by J. Aikin, M.D.* (London: J. Johnson, 1791), 94–5.
4. G. Gabrielle Starr, *Lyric Generations: Poetry and the Novel in the Long Eighteenth Century* (Baltimore: Johns Hopkins University Press, 2004), 114.
5. Samuel Richardson, *Pamela: or, Virtue Rewarded*, ed. Albert J. Rivero, The Cambridge Edition of the Works of Samuel Richardson (1740; Cambridge: Cambridge University Press, 2011), 242. Further references parenthetical
6. See *OED*, 'condescend, *v*'. For the third definition, Samuel Johnson's *Dictionary* (1755) is quoted: 'To depart willingly from the privileges of superiority by a voluntary submission; to sink willingly to equal terms with inferiours.'
7. On the liturgical authenticity of Pamela's marriage ceremony, see Lisa O'Connell, *The Origins of the English Marriage Plot: Literature, Politics and Religion in the Eighteenth Century* (Cambridge: Cambridge University Press, 2019), 11.
8. See Richardson, *Pamela*, ed. Rivero, 575n.
9. 'To His Mistress', *The Hive. A Collection of the Most Celebrated Songs* (London: J. Walthoe, [1729]), 3:259.
10. 'The Charms of Silvia', in *The Monthly Melody, or Polite Amusement for Gentlemen and Ladies* (London: Kearsley, 1760), 25.
11. 'The Charms of Sylvia', in *Apollo. Or the Songster's Universal Library* (Dublin: James Hoey, Jun., 1775?), 1:127.
12. *Apollo. Or the Songster's Universal Library*, 1:[iv].
13. *Songs from the Novelists from Elizabeth to Victoria*, ed. William Davenport Adams (London: Ward and Downey, 1885), 13–14.
14. Samuel Richardson, *Pamela in Her Exalted Condition*, ed. Albert J. Rivero, The Cambridge Edition of the Works of Samuel Richardson (1742; Cambridge: Cambridge University Press, 2012), 6. Further references parenthetical.
15. See, for example, John Dennis, *An Essay on the Opera's* [*sic*] *After the Italian Manner* (London: John Nutt, 1706); Joseph Addison, 'No. 18', *The Spectator*, 21 March 1711; William Popple, *The Prompter* 13 (24 December 1734).
16. See Michael Burden's discussion of the operatic afterlife of *Pamela* in 'The Novel in the Musical Theatre: *Pamela, Caleb Williams, Frankenstein,* and *Ivanhoe*', in *The Afterlives of Eighteenth-Century Fiction*, ed. Daniel Cook and Nicholas Seager (Cambridge: Cambridge University Press, 2015), 194–5.
17. Samuel Richardson, *Clarissa; or the History of a Young Lady* (London: Richardson, 1748), 7:353. Further references parenthetical.
18. See Leslie Ritchie, *Women Writing Music in Late Eighteenth-Century England: Social Harmony in Literature and Performance* (Aldershot: Ashgate, 2008), 48.
19. Scott Sanders, *Voices from Beyond: Physiology, Sentience and the Uncanny in Eighteenth-Century French Literature* (Charlottesville: University of Virginia Press, 2022), 65.
20. Ritchie, *Women Writing Music in Late Eighteenth-Century England*, 49; Sanders, *Voices from Beyond*, 67.
21. Pierre Dubois, *Music in the Georgian Novel* (Cambridge: Cambridge University Press, 2015), 44.

SONG IN THE NOVELS OF SAMUEL RICHARDSON

22. Dubois, *Music in the Georgian Novel*, 44. Dubois quotes Thomas McGeary's comment that 'Richardson created in Clarissa Harlowe a composer who would have ranked among the more highly skilled composers of the day'. 'Clarissa Harlowe's "Ode to Wisdom": Composition, Publishing History, and the Semiotics of Printed Music', *Eighteenth-Century Fiction* 24, no. 3 (2012): 437. For a list of other eighteenth-century novels (primarily French) that included insets of musical scores, see Sanders, *Voices from Beyond*, 193n22.

23. Dubois, *Music in the Georgian Novel*, 46.

24. Anna Letitia Barbauld, 'Life of Samuel Richardson, with Remarks on His Writing', in *The Correspondence of Samuel Richardson* (London: Richard Phillips, 1804), 1:lxxxi–ii.

25. Barbauld, 'Life of Samuel Richardson', 1:lxxxii.

26. Barbauld, 'Life of Samuel Richardson', 1:lxxxii.

27. Starr, *Lyric Generations*, 7.

28. Starr, *Lyric Generations*, 15–16.

29. Starr, *Lyric Generations*, 18. Barbauld's analysis of *Clarissa* reinforces Starr in that she herself responds to the emotional power of the work with quotations from poetry. Barbauld, 'Life of Samuel Richardson', 1:xcvi.

30. See Margaret Koehler on the shift in the mid-eighteenth century from the histrionic or 'calling' ode to the 'ode of absorption'. 'Odes of Absorption in the Restoration and Early Eighteenth Century', *Studies in English Literature, 1500–1900* 47, no. 3 (2007): 659–78.

31. As Janine Barchas notes, Richardson's '"ornamentation" of the ode has built a visible as well as audible crescendo, emphasising those passages Clarissa says she deems the most important moral "Lesson" of the poem'. Janine Barchas, *Graphic Design, Print Culture, and the Eighteenth-Century Novel* (Cambridge: Cambridge University Press, 2003), 98.

32. Barchas, *Graphic Design, Print Culture, and the Eighteenth-Century Novel*, 105.

33. Samuel Richardson, *The History of Sir Charles Grandison*, ed. E. Derek Taylor, Melvyn New and Elizabeth Kraft, The Cambridge Edition of the Works of Samuel Richardson (1753; Cambridge: Cambridge University Press, 2022), 254. Further references parenthetical.

34. Margaret Anne Doody, *A Natural Passion: A Study of the Novels of Samuel Richardson* (Oxford: Oxford University Press, 1974), 357.

35. On Handel's use of the chorus, see Ruth Smith, *Handel's Oratorios and Eighteenth-Century Thought* (Cambridge: Cambridge University Press, 1996), 62–70.

36. For more on Harriet's 'generosity and compassion', see Doody, *A Natural Passion*, 328.

37. Doody, *A Natural Passion*, 357.

38. Dianne Dugaw, 'Ballad', *Princeton Encyclopedia of Poetry and Poetics* (Princeton: Princeton University Press, 2012), 116.

39. In George Lillo's 1731 tragedy *The London Merchant*, George Barnwell, an apprentice who is seduced by a woman, Millwood, commits robbery and murder at her behest. The play was based on a seventeenth-century ballad.

40. John Dryden, 'Alexander's Feast', in *Poems 1697–1700*, ed. Vinton A. Dearing, Alan Roper and William Frost, The Works of John Dryden (Berkeley: University of California Press, 2000), 3–9, l. 96.

41. Letter from Aaron Hill to George Frederick Handel, quoted by Chester L. Alwes, *A History of Western Choral Music* (Oxford: Oxford University Press, 2015), 1:271.

42. John Dryden, 'A Song for St. Cecilia's Day, 1687', in *Poems 1685–1692*, ed. Earl Miner and Vinton A. Dearing, The Works of John Dryden (Berkeley: University of California Press, 1969), 202.

13

VEXED DIVERSIONS: *GULLIVER'S TRAVELS*, THE ARTS AND POPULAR ENTERTAINMENT

Daniel Cook

LEMUEL GULLIVER EXPRESSES little interest in Lilliputian architecture or country shows, beyond practical considerations. Later, his Brobdingnagian owners force him to entertain hostile gatherings in pubs. Exhausted by the constant and repetitive performances, the accidental actor wastes away to the point of death. He finds respite in Glumdalclitch's hastily built baby-box, but it lacks the comforts provided by fashionable designers for the top-end doll's houses back home. Farcically trying to play a colossal spinet for the court, Gulliver quickly admits defeat. In turn, their violent music drives him to the back of the room. Exposed to apparently advanced civilisations in the later voyages, our self-professedly virtuosic traveller may finally appreciate and even emulate their grandiose arts. Even then, he prefers the austerity of Houyhnhnm odes, though he provides no evidence of poetry from any of the remote nations. And the operatic world of Laputa overwhelms him. While he describes at length the extraordinary feat of reading Brobdingnagian books and prints, despite his size, he barely discusses the contents of the materials.

What about his author? According to Irvin Ehrenpreis, 'Swift had no ear for music, no eye for painting or sculpture, little understanding of architecture, not the faintest interest in dancing.'[1] Joseph McMinn has challenged this assumption in a book-length study, *Jonathan Swift and the Arts*. Such interest was not always positive, McMinn concedes, but that does not mean the arts did not influence Swift's literary practice.[2] We should add entertainments too. 'Popular entertainments are present in *Gulliver's Travels*', argues Dennis Todd, 'as evidence of man's thoughtlessness.' 'Literal-minded and superficial', he adds, 'Gulliver travels through the world like the stereotypical tourist, staring at everything and seeing nothing.'[3] Michael J. Conlon, too, has meticulously traced Swift's ironic connections between performances in the sciences and performances on stages and in texts.[4] Building on Todd's and Conlon's accounts of popular culture and performativity, I want to expose other seemingly more tangential portrayals of the arts and popular entertainments in *Travels*. A military exercise conducted on Gulliver's hand, in my reading, becomes a pragmatic type of dramatic spectacle devoid of the decorative or protective accoutrements associated with a theatrical house. Corrupted or otherwise mingled artforms even seep into early extensions of the book by Alexander Pope, Henry Fielding and others. As we shall see in the final section of this chapter, some of these Gulliverian extenders even turn the philistine protagonist into a mock-poet laureate or jobbing balladist; more often, they endorse his philistinism with 'missing scenes' set more explicitly in a playhouse and other recognisable cultural fora.

Together, Swift and his extenders embolden the primary author's claim that the 'chief end' of his project was to 'vex the world rather than divert it'.[5] Put another way, as an inept connoisseur Gulliver persistently vexes diversions.

What about Gulliver's inadvertent showmanship? Richard D. Altick straightforwardly characterises Gulliver as 'the showman' who became a 'show'.[6] In my reading, Gulliver remains throughout a reluctant showman and a failed show. Facing severe logistical impediments and lacking any discernible talent, Gulliver is both gawped at and the gawper during his travels; rarely can he simply be an audience member, and never willingly. Unlike Gulliver, the people or animals he meets have not had their senses of wonder worn down by the ubiquitous wares of the London fairs. Responding to the Man Mountain in the way unsuspecting spectators reacted to monster shows in England, the Lilliputians collectively convey 'a thousand Marks of Wonder and Astonishment' at the mere sight of him.[7] When he finally rises to walk, 'the Noise and Astonishment of the People . . . [were] not to be expressed' (42). Brobdingnagians similarly marvel at Gulliver, who 'was shewn ten Times a Day to the Wonder and Satisfaction of all People' (141). The Laputans 'beheld [him] with all the Marks and Circumstances of Wonder' (226). Even the highly rational Houyhnhnms cannot hide their astonishment: 'The Horse started a little when he came near me, but soon recovering himself, looked full in my Face with manifest Tokens of Wonder' (336). Gulliver does not react in quite the same way: he has seen it all. 'Many of the sights that Gulliver observes in these far-away nations, sights which he regards as utterly singular and alien', as Todd observes, 'could have been seen in London.'[8] Through analogy, however fleetingly, Gulliver invokes the puppet shows, peep shows, scale models, painted scenes, mechanical toys and street performers that Swift could not have avoided at Bartholomew Fair, Leicester Square, Soho, Piccadilly and elsewhere on a regular basis.

Shrunk to finger-length proportions, the Lilliputians are essentially autonomous puppets – but smaller and less animated than the fairground marionettes found in England.[9] Laputan communication is as nonsensical as Italian opera to Gulliver. The sorcerers of Glubbdubdrib stage a type of improvisatory theatre with long dead heroes and thinkers akin to animated effigies, but to no real purpose beyond correcting history books. Waxwork exhibits back home might seem more realistic and certainly more in sync with common perceptions of the subjects. Indifferent to the ingenuity of artifice, Gulliver nevertheless imposes English standards of beauty on what he cares to report about. More often than not, he neglects to complete the analogies Swift sets up, whether it pertains to the political arts of Lilliput or the moving parts of Brobdingnag, or even the cacophonous mathematics of Laputa and beyond. Read in a broader purview, *Travels* travesties any boundary between fiction (in its written form) and an immersive culture of popular entertainment and 'the arts' (theatre, music, architecture, gardening and literature broadly defined). Toggling between wonder and incredulity, as Sarah Tindal Kareem puts it, *Travels* challenged early readers' engagement with 'the novel', according to Johnson and Scott.[10] Gulliver refuses to be a character in 'a meer Fiction' (his words; 13). If so, he also cannot be an actor, musician, architect, gardener or a poet, let alone a consumer or connoisseur. Above all, the objects associated with the period's everyday entertainment industries had become too common, and Gulliver's own contrived sense of wonder barely conceals a collective show weariness.

Political Arts

There is little art in Lilliput, as far as our narrator cares to mention. On rare occasions, Gulliver explicitly draws on the performing or material arts in his description of the place, as in: 'I viewed the Town on my left Hand, which looked like the painted Scene of a City in a Theatre' (43). Fittingly for a character lacking artistry, the simile is insipid. Judged as a vehicle of personal impression, the simile becomes marginally more effective: to a man of Gulliver's stature an entire town looks like a mere stage set. Mildendo, the metropolis, looks like a model village to him too. In private, to bring in a telling contrast, the author had conveyed a far grander sense of wonder for precisely this type of artifice. Having attended a series of shows involving a 'moving Picture' in 1713, Swift revealed 'I never saw any thing so pretty. Y[ou] see a Sea ten miles wide, a Town on tothr end, & Ships sailing in t[h]e Sea, & discharging their Canon'.[11] 'The presence of actual miniatures in the emerging eighteenth-century culture of things', writes Melinda Alliker Rabb, 'introduces a distinctive source of irony because it bridges (at times it effaces) the division between the imagined (or the merely represented) and the real.'[12] We might expect more wonder in such surprising new worlds, but we would be looking in the wrong place and with the wrong guide.

In that opening paragraph in chapter 2, the nondescript stage painting, like the seven-foot trees that would have seemed massive to the Lilliputians, seems bathetic to Gulliver and his reader. Rather than attend to comparative aesthetics, our narrator plots out dimensions for the sake of it: 'The Houses are from three to five Stories. The Shops and Markets well provided.' More interested in urban planning than interior design, Gulliver repeatedly describes his difficult navigation around the buildings: 'it was impossible for me to stride over them, without infinite Damage to the Pile' (67). The only extended allusion to English arts and entertainments in the first voyage functions more as sport than anything else. Gulliver calls the rope-dancing a diversion. For the Lilliputians, though, rope-dancing held a careerist imperative – applied art, in other words. Here, in chapter 3, Gulliver even frames this section as an interlude in which the 'Emperor had a mind one Day to entertain me with several of the Country Shows; wherein they exceed all Nations I have known, both for Dexterity and Magnificence' (56). The word 'shows', as Pat Rogers points out in his study of popular culture in the eighteenth century, 'is loaded with associations of low pantomimic entertainment', namely harlequinades, raree shows, peep shows, punch-drama, waxworks and the like.[13] Taking the association as read, perhaps, Gulliver does not expand further: what happens at the country shows? How long do they last? In what ways do they excel all others in dexterity and magnificence? Are they lavish spectacles, or is this a forum for cheap street entertainment? To what extent is individual merit, even genius, celebrated – or is mere technical achievement prioritised? Our narrator instead dwells on the single event that caught his attention: 'I was diverted with none so much as that of the Rope-Dancers, performed upon a slender white Thread, extended about two Foot, and twelve Inches from the Ground' (56). Is he interested in the excellence of the participants or in the novelty of the sight? Is he a casual spectator or a curious observer?

Elsewhere in his account of the first voyage, Gulliver had happily refocalised the narratorial perspective, as in the Frelocks' bemused itinerary of the Man Mountain's objects. At no point in the rope-dancing section does he switch to the Lilliputian perspective. Instead, the funambulism remains at the level of spectacle. Before that spectacle,

GULLIVER'S TRAVELS, THE ARTS AND POPULAR ENTERTAINMENT 231

Gulliver explains the context for us: 'This Diversion is only practised by those Persons, who are Candidates for great Employments, and high Favour, at Court. They are trained in this Art from their Youth, and are not always of noble Birth, or liberal Education'. He continues:

> When a great Office is vacant, either by Death or Disgrace, (which often happens) five or six of those Candidates petition the Emperor to entertain his Majesty and the Court with a Dance on the Rope; and whoever jumps the highest without falling, succeeds in the Office. (56–7)

A popular entertainment among the Romans, rope-dancing distracted audiences from real dramatic art, according to Terence: 'ita populus studio stupidus in funambulo / animum occuparat' (the audience took a foolish fancy to a tightrope walker who claimed their attention).[14] Juvenal similarly dismissed such acrobatics as unedifying.[15] Horace used rope-dancing as an ironic metaphor for poetic ability.[16] Legal commentators in seventeenth-century England identified rope-dancing as a public nuisance, while religious commentators viewed it as an image of corrupt churchmen. Gulliver either ignores or is ignorant of this long and contradictory history of cultural funambulism.[17] This ignorance becomes all the more glaring when we consider the famous case of the 'little Child' who performed with a troupe of rope dancers at the Old Tennis Court in St James's Street in the vicinity of Swift's usual lodgings in late 1713, to great acclaim, before mysteriously vanishing not long into the new year.[18] Even if Gulliver did not pick up the analogy, many of his early readers would have done so.

Gulliver then introduces 'another Diversion', which is 'only shewn before the Emperor and Empress, and first Minister, upon particular Occasions' (58). Comparably far less meritocratic than rope-dancing, the dance of the silken threads has a privileged audience. The spectacles nevertheless share a purpose; that is, 'the Candidates are to undergo a Tryal of Dexterity':

> The Emperor holds a Stick in his Hands, both Ends parallel to the Horizon, while the Candidates advancing one by one, sometimes leap over the Stick, sometimes creep under it backwards and forwards several times, according as the Stick is advanced or depressed. (58–9)

While Gulliver gestures towards individual interpretation, the activity still looks closer to sport than to the arts – both rely on individual skill but one favours brawn over brains: 'Whoever performs his Part with most Agility, and holds out the longest in *leaping* and *creeping*, is rewarded with the Blue-coloured Silk' (59). As a metaphor for political subserviency, stick-leaping appeared throughout seventeenth-century verse and prose, to such an extent that *Gulliver Decypher'd* (1726) attacked Swift for apparently copying the section 'Word for Word' from earlier works.[19] Within the framework of the sporting spectacle, against the backdrop of this literary cliché, Swift ingeniously conflates physical and mental endurance: '*creeping*', in particular, carries connotations from both areas. Swift further emphasises the spectacle's mingling of art and sport through colours: in addition to the winner receiving 'the Blue-coloured Silk', 'the Red is given to the next, and the Green to the third, which they all wear girt twice round about the Middle' (59). For early

232   DANIEL COOK

readers, Edmund Curll's *Key, Being Observations and Explanatory Notes, upon the Travels of Lemuel Gulliver* (1726) had deciphered the colour scheme as referring to the British orders of the Garter, the Bath and the Thistle, ignoring the fact that the colours had been purple, yellow and white in the first edition of *Gulliver's Travels*. Besides, George I had only revived the Order of the Bath in May 1725, after Swift had written the Lilliput chapters. Coincidentally, Robert Walpole received the Garter in the following May, while the text was in press.

Political imagery often equates to spectacle. As Rogers points out, even today we refer to 'moral acrobatics' or 'a political tightrope'.[20] In one of Swift's earliest poems, 'Ode to Sir William Temple', the aspiring satirist had made a like-minded connection between politics and showmanship:

> The wily Shafts of State, those Juggler's Tricks
> Which we call deep Design and Politicks
> (As in a Theatre the Ignorant Fry,
> Because the Cords escape their Eye
> Wonder to see the Motions fly).[21]

Seemingly without irony, in the expanded purview of Swift's prior works, Gulliver soon makes his own spectacles of a similar if less outwardly political kind: 'I had the good Fortune to divert the Emperor one Day, after a very extraordinary Manner.' He continues:

> I desired he would order several Sticks of two Foot high, and the Thickness of an ordinary Cane, to be brought me; whereupon his Majesty commanded the Master of his Woods to give Directions accordingly; and the next Morning six Wood-men arrived with as many Carriages, drawn by eight Horses to each. I took nine of these Sticks, and fixing them firmly in the Ground in a Quadrangular Figure, two Foot and a half square; I took four other Sticks, and tyed them parallel at each Corner, about two Foot from the Ground; then I fastened my Handkerchief to the nine Sticks that stood erect; and extended it on all Sides, till it was as tight as the Top of a Drum; and the four parallel Sticks rising about five Inches higher than the Handkerchief, served as Ledges on each Side. (59)

Literally a supporter of the dramatic arts here, Gulliver oversees the building of a stage. Anticipating a stunning scene after such an elaborate account, we face disappointment: 'When I had finished my Work, I desired the Emperor to let a Troop of his best Horse, Twenty-four in Number, come and exercise upon this Plain' (59). Despite the mundanity of Gulliver's description, however, the exercise becomes an impromptu play of sorts, performed by the military in full regalia but using props: 'As soon as they got into Order, they divided into two Parties, performed mock Skirmishes, discharged blunt Arrows, drew their Swords, fled and pursued, attacked and retired' (60). The performance has no plot, or so we can only assume. As ever, Gulliver prioritises the practical aspects over aesthetics ('the best military Discipline I ever beheld'). The Emperor, meanwhile, 'was so much delighted, that he ordered this Entertainment to be repeated several Days', and the Empress practically sat on the stage, 'from whence she was able to take a full View of the whole Performance' (60). Lacking a basic plot, unless the repetition of movement counts, the militaristic play still deserved rapt attention from the in-text audience. Gulliver reduces an artform to an activity; the Emperor shifts military exercise to the arts.

Moving Parts

Owing to his Gargantuan proportions, Gulliver is unavoidably a spectacle to the Lilliputians. Largely limiting his movements, they effectively turn him into a horrifying statue, 'like a *Colossus*, with my Legs as far asunder as I conveniently could' (61–2). For the Brobdingnagians, Gulliver instead works best as an entertaining object when put into motion. To them, he is a mechanical toy, an inaudible actor or a miniature musician. An overarching plot line in the second voyage concerns Gulliver's rapid rise to fame, from his first show in an inn to his repeat performances in the queen's court. Along the way he battles jealous rivals, gains increasingly lavish sleeping quarters and endures occupational hazards. Gulliver begins his acting tour in a box lacking interior design ('The Box was close on every Side, with a little Door for me to go in and out, and a few Gimlet-holes to let in Air' [138]). Nothing more than an exotic pet, Gulliver receives little comfort save for a doll's quilt from his young nurse. Doll's houses could be ornate, a costly hobby rather than a plaything. Some even included scaled-down libraries; and skilled cabinetmakers such as Adam, Chippendale and Sheraton were involved in their design or production for elite customers.[22] Our miniature entertainer is not yet ready for such rewards. Forced to please a select audience of no more than thirty gawpers at a time, Gulliver first performs on an undecorated table. The canny innkeeper hired the 'cryer' (the '*grultrud*') to notify the town about the presence of a 'strange Creature to be seen at the Sign of the Green *Eagle*, not so big as a *Splacnuck* [and which] . . . could speak several Words, and perform an Hundred diverting Tricks' (138), thereby signalling that Gulliver must be both a curious object and a theatrical actor of sorts.

Without a script or routine, aside from some 'Speeches I had been taught', Gulliver mainly answers questions from Glumdalclitch, who 'direct[s] what I should do' (138–9). He is both a personal plaything and a public object. An obsolete definition of 'puppet' refers to a child's doll, or surrogate baby (puppa, poppet), as in Joseph Addison's observation in *The Spectator* (1712) about the 'Motherly Airs of my little Daughters when they are playing with their Puppets'.[23] In sum, these sorts of contradictions can be explained away. But the performing creature cannot stay in such a setting. Demand for repeat performances soars, 'till I was half dead with Weariness and Vexation'. Gulliver's actions seem comically dull: 'I turned about several Times to the Company, paid my humble Respects, said they were welcome.' He routinely 'took up a Thimble filled with Liquor . . . and drank their Health' (138–9). However, these little feats resemble the real 'monster shows' performed in England.[24] Handbills, as Todd reveals, indicate that monkeys performed similar tricks for paying audiences. To take one example: a 'Noble Creature, which much resembles a Wild *Hairy Man* . . . pulls off his Hat, and pays his Respects to the Company' and then 'drinks a Glass of Ale'.[25] Gulliver may think of himself as an actor delivering speeches, but, as an early reader familiar with London shows would have noticed, he looks more like a trained monkey, or 'the Girl at *Bartholomew*-Fair, who gets a Penny by turning round a hundred Times, with Swords in her Hands', as Swift mentions in *The Examiner*.[26] Like many amateur actors or animals forced to work in a public arena, Gulliver faces audience violence. A mischievous schoolboy fires a hazelnut directly at his head. And his de facto management team enjoy high takings with little personal risk: 'my Master demanded the Rate of a full Room whenever he shewed me at Home, although it were only to a single Family' (139). Sensing high profits, the master-showman arranges for a long excursion to the metropolis, 3,000 miles away.

Fortunately for the accidental actor, the travelling conditions have slightly improved: 'The Girl had lined [the box] on all Sides with the softest Cloth she could get' (140). Within a matter of paragraphs, in the next chapter, Gulliver climbs the somewhat unusual ladder of success. The queen buys him for a thousand pieces of gold and retains the services of Glumdalclitch. Evidently thrilled with her purchase, the queen carries Gulliver around the court as a unique curiosity. The king, meanwhile, dismisses him as a mere Splacknuck, a native animal. Then he assumes Gulliver must be a piece of clockwork – possibly a renegade from a British puppet theatre, we might surmise. Not all puppets relied on human handlers, after all, if we take at face value John Arbuthnot's remarks in *Law is a Bottomless-Pit* (1712): 'You look like a Puppet mov'd by Clock-work.'[27] An apt analogy for Gulliver's diminished autonomy in Brobdingnag, the clockwork man poses an arresting conundrum about agency. Seemingly able to move of its own volition, an automaton challenges the boundary between mechanical, replicable artifice and individual artistry. It can mimic differing levels of complex movement but fundamentally lacks reactiveness, a hallmark of invention. Finally astonished when Gulliver speaks unaided, the king nevertheless still dismisses the tiny human's abilities: he 'thought it a Story concerted between *Glumdalclitch* and her Father, who had taught me a Sett of Words to make me sell at a higher Price' (145). This goes against his wife's more attentive observation: 'The Queen giving great Allowance for my Defectiveness in speaking, was however surprised at so much Wit and good Sense in so diminutive an Animal' (144). For the queen, Gulliver is human because of his flaws. For the king, Gulliver can only be a mechanical spectacle, however impressive.

Regardless, the queen provides for the creature an improved box which, though lacking interior design, has more artistic flourish, thanks to the contribution of a 'Nice Workman, who was famous for little Curiosities' (148). Despite this set-up, Gulliver shares barely any detail and instead fixates on practical elements (the hinged ceiling for access, quilted sides to soften jolting and a lock against intruders). Even the respected cabinetmaker is relegated to 'Workman'. Besides, Gulliver's main function in the court is to attend the queen during mealtimes: 'her Diversion was to see me eat in Miniature'. Reversing the spectacle, in fact, Gulliver describes in excruciating detail the monstrosity of the Brobdingnagian queen's mastication: 'She would craunch the Wing of a Lark, Bones and all, between her Teeth, although it were nine Times as large as that of a full grown Turkey' (149). Less formally than in his inn-based theatre, Gulliver regales audiences with his strange conversations about Europe and, we learn many pages later, his sailing skills aboard a pleasure boat in a 300-foot trough filled with water. Risking serious injury on the water bellowed into waves by servants, Gulliver at turns astonishes and amuses the audience in a politer if no safer counterpart to the street shows of London.

Aside from the novelty value, or his apparent aptitude for speeches, Gulliver's success at court owes little to his talents in the performing arts, however. Towards the end of this part of the book, in chapter 6 of Part II, Gulliver declares 'I had learned in my Youth to play a little upon the Spinet' (177), a small instrument resembling a harpsichord. Glumdalclitch happened to have a spinet in her chamber, upon which she received music lessons twice a week. Hoping to impress the king and queen 'with an *English* Tune upon this Instrument', Gulliver faces blatant physical challenges: 'For, the Spinet was near sixty Foot long, each Key being almost a Foot wide; so that, with my Arms extended, I could not reach to above five Keys; and to press them down required a good smart stroak with my Fist, which would be too great a Labour, and to no purpose' (178). Ever the pragmatist, he finds a solution:

> I prepared two round Sticks about the Bigness of common Cudgels; they were thicker at one End than the other; and I covered the thicker End with a Piece of a Mouse's Skin, and by rapping on them, I might neither Damage the Tops of the Keys, nor interrupt the Sound. (178)

By his claim, Gulliver adapts the instrument without sacrificing musicality. Forced to use his fists rather than his fingers, however, he cannot complete the task properly: 'it was the most violent Exercise I ever underwent' (178). Unable to strike more than sixteen keys, he cannot play bass and treble together. As a musical performance it fails; it is a one-man sporting spectacle more than an artistic one. At the same time, Gulliver has little interest in Brobdingnagian music, even though it clearly mattered to the hosts: 'The King, who delighted in Musick, had frequent Consorts at Court, to which I was some-times carried, and set in my Box on a Table to hear them' (177).

At best, Gulliver finds the Brobdingnagian sound 'not disagreeable' only after being seated far away, 'hardly' able to 'distinguish the Tunes' (177) owing to their high vol-ume. Ehrenpreis and McMinn have identified Swift's own physical discomfort with instrumental sounds as a key context for understanding such passages.[28] More than that, in his metapoetry, Swift spoofed his lack of knowledge of the art: 'Grave D. of St P— ho[w] comes it to pass / That y[ou] . . . know musick no more than an ass'.[29] As McMinn points out, however, Swift had more to say about music than any of literature's other sister arts. Such views were contradictory. Swift recognises talent; the absence of it irks him: 'Singers like their brothers the Poets must be very good, or they are good for Nothing.'[30] Swift also said, sweepingly, in a letter to Lady Carteret: 'I would not give a farthing for all the musick in the universe.'[31] These comments must be read in the more specific circumstances of public worship: he acknowledges that others find music a useful accompaniment, but that he would prefer to say his prayers without it. As a form of entertainment, music bored Swift. In correspondence with Esther Johnson and Rebecca Dingley he mentions a 'musick-meeting' at Windsor, though 'I . . . was weary in half an hour of their fine stuff, and stole out so privately that every body saw me'.[32] But Swift understood the social function of music, beyond his personal discomfort.

Gulliver's reaction to the king's concerts may stem from similar aesthetic disre-gard, or some other reasons entirely, but he gives little away. Fully focused on the cacophony, he says nothing about the assembled musicians, their instruments, or any other visual aspect. We receive few if any insights into the Brobdingnagian arts in general, seemingly because they do not conform to neoclassical ideals of reason and order. Despite being 'very desirous to see the chief Temple, and particularly the Tower belonging to it' (161), Gulliver refers to even the most important architectural sites as 'an Heap of Buildings' (158). Although keen to satisfy 'my curious Reader', our guide reduces the cityscape to crude measurements: Lorbrulgrud 'contains above eighty thousand Houses'; 'It is in Length three *Glonglungs* . . . and two and a half in Breadth, as I measured it myself in the Royal Map' (157). The temple disappoints him, not for aesthetic reasons, as we might assume, but in scale: 'I may truly say I came back disappointed; for, the Height is not above three thousand Foot' (161). By implication, the building would not conform to European standards of beauty based on symmetry for it was not 'equal in Proportion'. Gulliver neglects to mention it, but he may have seen on display at St Paul's Christopher Wren's famous scale model of the cathedral, which was completed by August 1674 at a cost of about £600 – as much as a good London house. Instead, Gulliver blandly praises the temple's 'Beauty and Strength', though he again dwells on materiality not appearances; that is, the thickness of the walls caught his attention. Even when the would-be antiquary steals a finger that had fallen off a statue of one of their gods or emperors – he does not provide details – he reduces it to one of Glumdalclitch's 'Trinkets, of which the Girl was very fond, as Children at her Age usually are' (161). Much later, Gulliver casually describes the education of the Brobdingnagians, which 'is very defective; consisting only in Morality, History, Poetry and Mathematicks; wherein they must be allowed to excel' (195). In what ways do they excel? What is missing from the 'defective' list? Gulliver cannot or will not say.

No poetry is sampled. Any such poetry would presumably appear unpoetic to us since, 'as to Ideas, Entities, Abstractions and Transcendentals', Gulliver 'could never drive the least Conception into their Heads' (195). As for general literariness, our guide notes that their 'Stile is clear, masculine, and smooth, but not Florid' (197). Pragmatism trumps flourish, 'for they avoid nothing more than multiplying unnecessary Words, or using various Expressions' (197). To Gulliver's mind they have a diminished kind of poetry, which he cannot improve to his standards, however forcefully. The Brobdingnagians have had the art of printing for a long time, but still 'their Libraries are not very Large' (196). Lacking interpretative skills, they cannot produce reams of battling books, and even the writing of a law commentary has become a capital crime. What they do have remains a mystery, aside from an unnamed philosophical treatise on human weakness read by 'Women and the Vulgar' (197–8). Our feckless guide instead treats the library as a physical space in which he comically fetishises his moveable ladder ('a Kind of wooden Machine five and twenty Foot high' [197]). Like playing the gargantuan spinet, reading has become an endurance sport for someone of Gulliver's size: 'The Book I had a Mind to read was put up leaning against the Wall'. Mounting the ladder, he walks 'to the Right and Left about eight or ten Paces according to the Length of the Lines' (197). What the lines contain, we do not know: Gulliver does not deem them important enough for us.

Music, Maths and Magic

A medley of diversions among different groups of people, Gulliver's third voyage obliquely alludes to relatively modern arts enjoyed back in England, from landscape gardening to Italian opera to urban architecture. The episodes in Glubbdubdrib also feature a kind of improvisatory auto-theatre, where sorcerers conjure up the illustrious dead for short periods of enforced conversation. I propose we read such scenes in the purview of the dramatic arts, analogously. Some of the cultures encountered in

GULLIVER'S TRAVELS, THE ARTS AND POPULAR ENTERTAINMENT 237

Part III are so permeated with a specific artform it ceases to be mere entertainment. Viewed in panorama by Gulliver, Lilliput had looked like a nondescript painted scene from a theatrical stage. When he sees Laputa looming into view, by contrast, the scene appears impossibly ambitious: 'I took out my Pocket-Perspective, and could plainly discover Numbers of People moving up and down the Sides of it, which appeared to be sloping, but what those People were doing, I was not able to distinguish' (223). Opera glasses were not common in London until after 1800. Before then, patrons would have used a monocular spyglass not unlike Gulliver's maritime pocket telescope, though not with any regularity until the middle of the eighteenth century. And the floating island's dimensions, running to two miles in height, seem far too large to invite a serious parallel with even the major stages in Europe. But the Laputans are essentially an operatic people on a comically exaggerated scale. Despite the sheer size of their island, men 'were able (as it should seem) to raise, or sink, or put it into a progressive Motion, as they pleased' (223) – just like the trained stagehands on a movable set.

Visually, the island resembles an auditorium: 'I could see the Sides of it, encompassed with several Gradations of Galleries and Stairs, at certain Intervals, to descend from one to the other' (224). Gulliver walks into the set, though the distinction between performance stage and audience seating in his retelling remains unclear. Not just visually, but aurally, Laputa is operatic: 'At length one of them called out in a clear, polite, smooth Dialect, not unlike in Sound to the *Italian*' (224). Swift might have remembered Addison's attack on the new fashion for opera in England. In *The Spectator*, Addison mocked the ineffective correspondence between words and musical notes when the Italian lyrics were translated into English.[33] More concerned with staging, in a 1706 treatise, John Dennis warned of irreparable damage about to be wrought by operettists on British audiences.[34] Unable to understand each other, the Laputan and the Englishman nevertheless somehow make contact. If we can read the melophilic Laputans as barely functioning embodiments of the operatic, or visual music at large, we must concede that they corrupt the artform. As McMinn observes: 'Music in Laputa, far from being a sensuous delight to the ear and the imagination, is the unlikely but certain product of abstract, even mystical, contemplation without any grounding in the natural rhythms of language.'[35]

David B. Kesterson surmises that Swift and Addison opposed opera as an irrational form of entertainment in which, for them, the melodies and lyrics lacked meaning.[36] The Laputans literally lack words until cued to speak. Emptying the Laputans of their operatic verbosity, temporarily at least, Swift diverts our attention to their bizarre physicality:

> Their outward Garments were adorned with the Figures of Suns, Moons, and Stars, interwoven with those of Fiddles, Flutes, Harps, Trumpets, Guittars, Harpsicords, and many more Instruments of Musick, unknown to us in *Europe*. (226–7)

Relying on visual context, Gulliver assumes all the figures are instruments based on appearances. He seems to have missed off perhaps the most important instrument in Laputa, one not designed for entertainment. On the contrary, the blown bladders containing little pebbles are entirely functional. Without having a servant flapping their mouths and ears, the absent-minded Laputans would barely survive as human beings. Puppet handlers of sorts, the servants materially haunt their props, to adopt

Stallybrass and Jones's phrase, until the 'lifeless' Laputan intellectuals have been adequately flapped from their abstractions.[37] The flying island also recalls what George Speaight identifies as the 'machines' of moving scenery set into Martin Powell's popular Piazza Puppet Theatre, and which featured prominently on promotional playbills.[38] Speaight even noticed odd angles in contemporary engravings of Powell's stages, which, he conjectures, allowed 'servants' (Powell's word) to operate the elaborate sky pieces. Such structural irregularities fit with Gulliver's strange description of Laputa's exterior, 'which appeared to be sloping' (223). Without acknowledging it, Gulliver has really walked into an oversized puppet theatre masquerading as a mock-operatic auditorium in disguise.

Music and mathematics are so central to high Laputan society the people consume food cut into triangles, rhomboids and cycloids. Ducks are 'trussed up into the Form of Fiddles', sausages and puddings resemble 'Flutes and Haut-boys', and veal is formed into 'the Shape of a Harp' (229). Put another way, Gulliver can only comprehend Laputan maths and music as mere objects. A language tutor had helped to translate the names of instruments, as well as 'the general Terms of Art in playing on each of them' (230), but our narrator cannot elaborate for us. Even if he understands the theory, by his claim, the practice means little to him: 'about Eleven o'Clock, the King himself in Person, attended by his Nobility, Courtiers, and Officer, having prepared all their Musical Instruments, played on them for three Hours without Intermission' (232). Rather than describe, let alone enjoy, any aspect of the spectacle, Gulliver flatly states: 'I was quite stunned with the Noise' (232). He is not a willing cultural tourist: the art seems too alien. In the company of the outcast Lord Munodi, a relative dunce in the Laputan arts, Gulliver surveys Lagado more successfully. The houses look 'ill contrived' and 'ruinous', except that of Munodi, whose house, a 'noble Structure', had evidently been built 'according to the best Rules of ancient Architecture', along with the surrounding gardens. Failing to conform to 'a Form as modern Usage required' (254), the building will have to come down. Instead, the arts and sciences alike must adhere to modern principles, however ridiculous, as established in the Academy of Projectors at Lagado.

Many of the experiments conducted in the Academy parody real-world projects in a range of disciplines, including the extraction of sunbeams out of cucumbers (based on Stephen Hales's experiments on the respiration of plants). Such disciplines suffer inversion: 'There was a most ingenious Architect who had contrived a new Method for building Houses, by beginning at the Roof, and working downwards to the Foundation' (261). Swift reduces the labour-intensive art of book production to a mechanised randomiser of sentence fragments: 'at every Turn the Engine was so contrived, that the Words shifted into new Places, as the square Bits of Wood moved upside down' (269). Knowledge becomes a body of 'rich Materials', and sense has been lost. The tools of literature itself come under threat. 'The first Project was to shorten Discourse by cutting Polysyllables into one', reports Gulliver, 'and leaving out Verbs and Participles' (270). A second, more extreme linguistic project would abolish words as we know them: 'since Words are only Names for *Things*, it would be more convenient for all Men to carry about them, such *Things* as were necessary to express the particular Business they are to discourse on' (271). Literary, or even figurative, language has been jettisoned. A notable model for Swift's satire in the Academy episode, the Royal Society, had posed an uncannily similar proposal, 'to reject all the amplifications, digressions,

GULLIVER'S TRAVELS, THE ARTS AND POPULAR ENTERTAINMENT   239

and swellings of style', in the curiously stylised words of their spokesman Thomas Sprat.[39] Objectifying words confers quantifiable value on language, but inventiveness evaporates. Peddlers still find work: words, not books, weigh down their sacks. And the women, along with 'the Vulgar and Illiterate' who oppose the new system, presumably keep literary nuance alive, even if Gulliver has no interest in exploring that.

Taking a detour to Glubbdubdrib, the island of sorcerers, Gulliver meets historical and literary figures in a live-action version of a genre still read in the period, even if the titular author ignores the connection, namely, Dialogues of the Dead. Classical precedents include the *Odyssey* (XI), the *Aeneid* (VI) and Lucian's *The True History*, as well as works by Fontenelle, Brown and other modern exponents. If the School of Languages had raised the possibility of abolishing excessive language, the interaction with Homer reveals a more comical variation on that theme of literary diminishment. Following behind Homer we witness a train of textual commentators in a line so long that 'some Hundreds were forced to attend in the Court and outward Rooms of the Palace' (294). The commentators have hidden in the shadows away from Homer 'through a Consciousness of Shame and Guilt, because they had so horribly misrepresented the Meaning of those Authors to Posterity' (294–5). Swift's Aristotle similarly has no patience for Scotus and Ramus. Having spent at least five days conversing with the dead, Gulliver ought to have many new insights to share with us. Aside from some biographical particulars, his necromantic salon has instead become a gallery of horror and despair. Throughout the third voyage our guide becomes overwhelmed by the alien arts he encounters, expressly in the vast, immersive auditorium of Laputa. As the Laputan way of being resembles an extreme version of modern modes, from Italian opera to urban architecture, Gulliver at once exposes his lack of virtuosity and rejects curious connoisseurship.

Beyond Houyhnhnm-Land

Considering his comparative lack of wonder in the prior voyages, Gulliver's reaction to the grey and brown horses in Houyhnhnm-Land indicates the English tourist still expects tricksy artfulness: 'the Behaviour of these Animals was so orderly and rational, so acute and judicious, that I at last concluded, they must needs be Magicians, who had thus metamorphosed themselves upon some Design' (337). Gulliver's depiction of the arts so far has relied on the ludicrously visual, including even the massive spinet and the operatic mathematics of Laputa. But the straightforwardly equine appearances of the Houyhnhnms somehow instils confusion in Gulliver. Although unstated here, other than in the casual reference to classical metamorphosis, our guide may be alluding to a long literary tradition of bestial transformation, and perhaps inverting Apuleius' *Metamorphoses*, in which the narrator Lucius is turned into an ass and back again. By the third chapter we realise that Gulliver's first reaction proved misjudged. Artifice apparently has no place among the Houyhnhnms, who have no concept of lying and therefore the imagination ('*the thing which was not*' [349]), and lack 'the least Idea of Books or Literature' (348). Gulliver even comes to think of salt as a luxury since the culinary arts here lack basic flavouring. Such blandness contrasts with what purports to be an extensive discourse on European 'Arts and Sciences' (361). Instead we receive disturbing accounts of the 'Art of War' (366), courtroom cunning, charlatan doctors 'in the Profession or Pretence of curing the Sick' (377–8), and political doublespeak. More broadly, Gulliver characterises England not as a place of high culture but of gaming, theft and forgery.

In passing, he praises the Houyhnhnms' arts, despite their lack of books. Unlike the impractical design of Laputan architecture, the ancient-leaning Lord Munodi excepted, to Gulliver their houses are pleasingly functional, 'well contrived to defend them from all Injuries of Cold and Heat' (412). Most strangely of all, their poetry 'must be allowed to excel all other Mortals; wherein the Justness of their Similes, and the Minuteness, as well as Exactness of their Descriptions, are indeed inimitable' (412). Gulliver had expressed little interest in poetry during his travels so far, but a preference for oral Houyhnhnm verse suits his philistine character. While Gulliver lacks the critical vocabulary, we might infer from his account that the poetry resembles the ode and epistle forms still popular in the period, containing 'some exalted Notions of Friendship and Benevolence, or the Praises of those who were Victors in Races, and other bodily Exercises' (412). Swift the poet produced odes and epistles, even as late as the 1720s, but usually in a bantering, familiar style. Indeed, there may be an elaborate in-joke here for Swift's literary circle, especially the memoirist Laetitia Pilkington, who Swift said 'knew no more of Poetry than a Horse'.[40] In any case, Gulliver does not provide any samples. And, as in Lilliput, he gestures to forthcoming books beyond *Travels* that might appease the more curious reader, particularly a philosophical treatise 'upon the Manners and Virtues of this excellent People' (415). Not writing the book is, paradoxically, a truly Houyhnhnm act as they prioritise using 'the fewest and most significant Words' in communication of any kind (418–19). Rendering himself obsolete, Gulliver commits to the unbookishness of his favoured nation.

Where Swift's Gulliver spurned the arts, in his post-*Travels* adventures the author-explorer often engaged with poetry and drama. Henry Fielding's pseudonymously published *The Masquerade, A Poem* (1728) has a suggestive tagline: 'By LEMUEL GULLIVER, Poet Laureat to the King of LILLIPUT'.[41] Despite the absurdly grandiose title, he downplays his artistry – 'I am no poet, I assure you' – but only to appease his grubby audience ('if it will allure you'). After all, in the culturally bankrupt London depicted by Fielding's Gulliver, 'No man of any fashion wou'd / Appear a poet in a crowd'. This Gulliver nevertheless revels in the dubious marketplace: 'I appear'd / In the strange habit of a bard', he declares; 'Thus when equipp'd, I call'd a chair, / Go, to th' Haymarket theatre' (2–3). Not expecting much literary success, all he begs from his dedicatee C—t H—d—g—r (Count Heidegger), crassly, is 'a ticket for your next ball' ('The Dedication'). Elsewhere, and under different masters, he writes ballads too, including 'An Excellent New Ballad on the Wedding of Pritty Miss S—lly to Jolly Old J—o' (1730), a fairly conventional piece of street verse: 'Ye *Gallants* of *Dublin*, come listen a while, / A Story I'll tell you, will make you to Smile'.[42] Conscripted to Edmund Curll's army of hacks, Captain Gulliver takes on 'The Totness Address Transversed' (1727). Lemuel was not the only poet in the family. As early as 1727, the abandoned wife had aired her grievances in Pope's 'Mary Gulliver to Capt. Lemuel Gulliver', one of five poems added to the second edition of *Travels*.[43]

Early prose Gulliveriana written under Gulliver's name often samples original Lilliputian poetry, contra Swift. One of the major such extensions, long attributed to Eliza Haywood, devotes most of a chapter to a diversion 'left out' of Swift's original account of the first voyage: stage theatre. In *Memoirs of the Court of Lilliput* (1727) we hear about the rope-dancing we have become accustomed to, along with tumbling

GULLIVER'S TRAVELS, THE ARTS AND POPULAR ENTERTAINMENT   241

and some sort of comedy in a recognisable type of performance space: an ornate play-house. 'Most of the People of Quality', reports Gulliver, 'had frequently express'd a great desire that I should be present at the publick Diversions of the Country.'[44] Gulliver – this Gulliver, at least – reports that the Lilliputians view their art as inherently valuable, and yet contingent upon the body of the viewer. Or, rather than identify the unique properties of Lilliputian aesthetics, they compare it negatively with the art of Gulliver and his people: 'what appears so very beautiful among us, must needs be monstrous, and appear rather terrifying than delightful to the Eye, when perform'd by a Creature of so vast a bulk as you are' (93). Wearied by their discourses, Gulliver finally volunteers to 'look in' at the window of their theatre during a scheduled play. The Lilliputian performance space is 'not much unlike our Play-Houses in *England*', we learn; if anything, they are 'more richly adorn'd' (94), even to Gulliver's giant eye. Perhaps he means the big playhouses at Covent Garden or Drury Lane, or perhaps the scaled down high-end puppet theatres built at the London fairs, which, at their most ambitious, had boxes, pits, galleries, curtains, moveable scenery and other standard features associated with the theatre districts.[45] Like Swift's Gulliver, this Gulliver shows more interest in the materiality of the spectacle than the act itself. After describing the box seating at great length, he immediately grows bored of the show: 'I was soon sick of the monkey Tricks and Postures in which the Actors seem'd to endeavour to vie with each other' (97). To even a casual frequenter of raree shows, there's nothing new to see here.

With informed irony, the author of *Memoirs* harks back, or rather looks ahead to, Gulliver's performances in the pubs and later the court of Brobdingnag, when he becomes the relatively small actor of some celebrity. Whereas Swift's Gulliver executes banal acts such as quaffing drink and curtsying, the Lilliputian players here perform in a manner he now claims not to understand. This Gulliver can only describe the act as what looks like gurning – 'who should most distort his Body, or appear to have least of the human Form'. We lack a discernible plot or stagecraft. That said, Gulliver 'turn'd my Eyes from the Stage on the Assembly' (97), rendering him an unreliable reporter. *Memoirs*, in short, expands the scope of Lilliputian life beyond *Travels* to include a more legitimate form of theatre, against the mock-military displays undertaken on Gulliver's hand. But, in keeping with the attitudes of Swift's philistine protagonist, the new narrator fails to detail the qualities of the spectacle beyond vague references to its public importance. Ironically, despite Swift's and the Memoirist's concerted depiction of an unenthused theatregoer, the one area in which Gulliveriana thrived most was the dramatic arts. Lilliputian dances enjoyed great vogue well into the next century, and numerous acting companies riffed on the bankable name 'Lilliputian'. Records of performances of theatrical Gulliveriana before 1800 number around six hundred, accounting for prologues and epilogues, dances and plays.[46] Not that Lemuel Gulliver would have had any interest in arts or entertainments produced in his honour.

Notes

1. Irvin Ehrenpreis, *Swift: The Man, His Works, and the Age*, 3 vols (Cambridge, MA: Harvard University Press, 1962–83), 2:301.
2. Joseph McMinn, *Jonathan Swift and the Arts* (Newark: University of Delaware Press, 2010), 9.

242 DANIEL COOK

3. Dennis Todd, *Imagining Monsters: Miscreations of the Self in Eighteenth-Century England* (Chicago and London: University of Chicago Press, 1995), 150. See Darryl P. Domingo, *The Rhetoric of Diversion in English Literature and Culture, 1690–1760* (Cambridge: Cambridge University Press, 2016), 142–7.
4. Michael J. Conlon, 'Performance as Response in Swift's *Gulliver's Travels*', in *Gulliver's Travels*, ed. Christopher Fox (Boston and New York: Bedford Books of St Martin's Press, 1995), 408–24.
5. Jonathan Swift to Alexander Pope, 29 September 1725, in *The Correspondence of Jonathan Swift*, ed. Harold Williams, 5 vols (Oxford: Clarendon Press, 1963–5), 3:102.
6. Richard D. Altick, *The Shows of London: A Panoramic History of Exhibitions, 1600–1862* (Cambridge, MA and London: Belknap Press of Harvard University Press, 1978), 43.
7. Jonathan Swift, *Gulliver's Travels*, ed. David Womersley (1726; Cambridge: Cambridge University Press, 2010), 36. Further references parenthetical and to this edition unless stated otherwise.
8. Todd, *Imagining Monsters*, 140.
9. See David A. Brewer, 'Rethinking Fictionality in the Eighteenth-Century Puppet Theatre', in *The Afterlives of Eighteenth-Century Fiction*, ed. Daniel Cook and Nicholas Seager (Cambridge: Cambridge University Press, 2015), 177–9. On Swift and puppetry, see Hugh Ormsby-Lennon, *Hey Presto! Swift and the Quacks* (Newark: University of Delaware Press, 2011), 180–95.
10. Sarah Tindal Kareem, *Eighteenth-Century Fiction and the Reinvention of Wonder* (Oxford: Oxford University Press, 2014), 104–8.
11. Letter 62, in *Journal to Stella: Letters to Esther Johnson and Rebecca Dingley, 1710–1713*, ed. Abigail Williams (1766; Cambridge: Cambridge University Press, 2013), 519. See also Aline Mackenzie Taylor, 'Sights and Monsters and Gulliver's *Voyage to Brobdingnag*', *Tulane Studies in English* 7 (1957): 62, and A. H. Scouten, 'Swift at the Moving Pictures', *Notes and Queries* 188, no. 2 (1945): 38–9.
12. Melinda Alliker Rabb, *Miniature and the English Imagination: Literature, Cognition, and Small-Scale Culture, 1650–1765* (Cambridge: Cambridge University Press, 2019), 53.
13. Pat Rogers, *Literature and Popular Culture in Eighteenth-Century England* (Hassocks, Sussex: Harvester Press; New Jersey: Barnes & Noble, 1985), 73.
14. Terence, *Phormio. The Mother-in-Law. The Brothers*, trans. John Barsby (Cambridge, MA: Harvard University Press, 2001), 149.
15. Satire XIV, in *Juvenal and Persius*, trans. G. G. Ramsay (Cambridge, MA: Harvard University Press, 1969), 284.
16. Epistle II.I, in *Horace: Satires, Epistles and Ars Poetica*, trans. H. Rushton Fairclough (Cambridge, MA and London: Harvard University Press, 1999), 414.
17. See *Gulliver's Travels*, ed. Womersley, 477–81.
18. Taylor, 'Sights and Monsters', 68.
19. *Gulliver's Travels*, ed. Womersley, 58n10.
20. Rogers, *Literature and Popular Culture*, 81.
21. *The Poems of Jonathan Swift*, ed. Harold Williams, 2nd edn, 3 vols (Oxford: Clarendon Press, 1966), 1:29.
22. Rabb, *Miniature and the English Imagination*, 44.
23. Addison is quoted in *OED*, 'puppet', 2.b. For *poupette* ('little doll') and other etymological resonances, see Scott Cutler Shershow, *Puppets & "Popular" Culture* (Ithaca and London: Cornell University Press, 1995), 68–72.
24. *Gulliver's Travels*, ed. Womersley, 137n10.
25. Todd, *Imagining Monsters*, 145.
26. Jonathan Swift, 'No. 39', 3 May 1711, in *The Examiner and Other Pieces Written in 1710–11*, ed. Herbert Davis (Oxford: Basil Blackwell, 1966), 147.

27. *OED*, 'puppet', 3.a.
28. Ehrenpreis, *Swift*, 3:352–4; Joseph McMinn, 'Was Swift a Philistine? The Evidence of Music', *Swift Studies* 17 (2002): 59–74. See also McMinn, *Jonathan Swift and the Arts*, 27–50; Clive Probyn, '"Players and Scrapers": Dean Swift Goes Shopping, for Music', *Script & Print* 33, nos. 1–4 (2009): 109–24; Arno Löffler, '"Suit Your Words to Your Musick Well": Swift and the Poetic Harmonists', in *Swift: The Enigmatic Dean: Festschrift for Hermann Josef Real*, ed. Rudolf Freiburg, Arno Löffler and Wolfgang Zach (Tübingen: Stauffenburg Verlag, 1998), 99–112; Frank Llewelyn Harrison, 'Music, Poetry and Polity in the Age of Swift', *Eighteenth-Century Ireland / Iris an dá chultúr* 1 (1986): 37–63; David B. Kesterson, 'Swift and Music', *Texas Studies in Literature and Language* 11, no. 1 (1969): 687–94.
29. 'The Dean to Himself on St Cecilia's Day', in *The Poems of Jonathan Swift*, ed. Harold Williams, 2:522.
30. Jonathan Swift to Edward Harley, 9 February 1720, in *The Correspondence of Jonathan Swift*, ed. Harold Williams, 2:339.
31. Quoted in McMinn, *Jonathan Swift and the Arts*, 30.
32. Letter 31, in *Journal to Stella*, ed. Abigail Williams, 292.
33. See Kesterson, 'Swift and Music', 690.
34. John Dennis, *An Essay on the Operas After the Italian Manner, Which are about to be Establish'd on the English Stage* (London: John Nutt, 1706).
35. McMinn, *Jonathan Swift and the Arts*, 41.
36. Kesterson, 'Swift and Music', 694.
37. Peter Stallybrass and Ann Rosalind Jones, 'Fetishizing the Glove in Renaissance Europe', *Critical Inquiry* 28, no. 3 (2001): 126.
38. George Speaight, *The History of English Puppet Theatre*, 2nd edn (London: Robert Hale, 1990), 98–9.
39. *Gulliver's Travels*, ed. Womersley, 271n47.
40. *Gulliver's Travels*, ed. Womersley, 412n17.
41. Lemuel Gulliver [Henry Fielding], *The Masquerade, a Poem* (London: J. Roberts and A. Dodd, 1728), title page.
42. 'An Excellent New Ballad' is reproduced in *Gulliveriana VI: Book Two*, ed. Jeanne K. Welcher and George E. Bush, Jr (New York: Scholars' Facsimiles & Reprints, 1976).
43. See Norman Ault, *New Light on Pope* (Hamden: Archon Books, 1967), 231–42, and Thomas Van der Goten, 'The Lilliputian Ode, 1726–1826', *ANQ* 28, no. 2 (2015): 94–104.
44. *Memoirs of the Court of Lilliput*, 2nd edn (London: J. Roberts, 1727), 93. Further references parenthetical. For de-attribution, see Leah Orr, 'The Basis for Attribution in the Canon of Eliza Haywood', *The Library* 12, no. 4 (2011): 374.
45. See Brewer, 'Rethinking Fictionality in the Eighteenth-Century Puppet Theatre', 176.
46. *Gulliveriana VIII: An Annotated List of Gulliveriana, 1721–1800*, ed. Jeanne K. Welcher (New York: Scholars' Facsimiles & Reprints, 1988), 19.

14

SONGS, STORIES AND SENTIMENTALISM: THE BRITISH BROADSIDE BALLAD AS SENTIMENTAL FICTION

Georgina Bartlett

LIKE THE PROSE novel, the broadside ballad was a form of literature that could only come into being because of the printing press: broadsides appeared shortly after the invention of Gutenberg's moveable-type technology around 1450 and quickly proliferated across Europe, finding particular popularity and longevity in Britain, where the broadside tradition thrived uninterrupted for nearly 400 years.[1] What set the broadside apart from other print traditions of the early modern and Enlightenment periods was its affordability: it was a form of cheap literature that was accessible to the 'working classes' – wage earners, in other words – costing between a halfpenny and a penny.

The Stationers' Company, which had regulated printing in England since receiving its royal charter in 1557, defined a 'broadside' as a sheet that was only printed on one side.[2] Typically, this single page would include a song in strophic form, also known as 'ballad form', with verse after verse set to the same repeated melody. Until the early eighteenth century ballad verses were typically formatted in landscape orientation, accompanied by a woodcut illustration and a tune reference that would suggest a common or popular melody to which the verses could be sung.[3] The textual mode of these ballads was predominantly narrative: they told both newly written and traditional stories that had beginnings, middles and ends, following usually only two or three characters through the vicissitudes of their lives, which often ended sadly. The verses usually consisted of six or eight lines, sometimes followed by a repeated chorus that lent the song to communal performance (though often the 'chorus' was simply the first verse repeated). The verses of these songs gave their stories a sense of structure: they were episodic, with one event or set of events described in one verse before moving on to the next, like brief chapters or scenes in a play. In the seventeenth and early eighteenth centuries, broadside ballads could consist of a dozen or more verses, using only a little melody to sing a very long story. Each verse formed a link in a chain of variable and limitless length. That was the brilliance of strophic musical forms.

As a form of cheap literature and song, the broadside was sold by ballad singers on the streets and bought primarily by wage earners. The broadside tradition provides a wealth of information about the British working classes because it reflects what they cared about, what intrigued them, what moved them, and what tempted them to part with their meagre expendable income (18d a day for the common labourer in London in the 1770s).[4] Professional and leisure classes also invested heavily and meaningfully in the broadside ballad throughout its long history, however – not least as collectors, who amassed the vast collections of broadside materials that still exist in libraries across the world, especially in Britain and the United States. For while the broadside was the cheapest form of literature in its day, it was also rich, complicated and multivalent: the broadside interacted in many cultural spheres, and thus its identity in British culture was complex. It was a tradition that was both contemporaneous and historical, material and aural, literary and musical, factual and fictional. And, by the latter half of the eighteenth century, the broadside had become increasingly focused on realism and moralism as it engaged with sentimental literature and with theatre.

The Complexities of the Broadside in British Culture

The first complexity to consider is that the broadside tradition can be approached both synchronically and diachronically: that is to say, for nearly 400 years the broadside was both a living and a historical tradition in British culture. As new broadside songs were being penned and sold on the streets, reacting to current trends and events, ballads from a hundred years earlier remained pasted on 'the walls of cottages and little alehouses'.[5] The broadside, not only as a tradition, but in and through its constituent members, had remarkable longevity in British culture, and it lived in the shadow of its own history. In fact, the broadside tradition was considered to be 'old-fashioned' by the eighteenth century – but this was one of its selling points: printers kept the broadside's format, content and music quite consistent up to about 1750, long after other forms of print culture had adopted innovations in typeface and layouts, partly because that is what people liked.[6] Even in the eighteenth century, Britons looked back nostalgically at their country's (imagined) past, longing for the simplicity and rootedness that the 'olden days' seemed to provide: the broadside offered a touchstone of continuity and tradition to an industrialising and urbanising British society.[7]

Nevertheless, the broadside was a fully synchronic tradition as well, and it was nothing to its audiences if not relevant. It was, after all, what the broadside collector John Johnson (1882–1956) termed 'ephemeral' literature: print literature that was not intended to last.[8] Like newspapers, broadsides were cheap, disposable and often occasional (relating to a specific event). Examples would include political broadsides like 'A Song for the Independent Burgesses of Newcastle' (1774) written by an anonymous lady on the 1774 parliamentary election in Newcastle, or the many 'murder ballads' that reported the news of crimes or the subsequent remorse of their perpetrators. And, even when they were not focused on specific events, eighteenth-century broadsides became increasingly contemporary and relatable in their settings and content – much like literary novels of the day. The broadside tradition was an old frame in a diorama of continuously updated images of modern life.

The second complexity of the broadside – and perhaps the most profound – is that the tradition simultaneously belonged to material and to oral culture. Its materiality was important: the broadside allowed for the working classes to engage with print (literary) culture and also, by default, with material culture. As Britain became increasingly industrialised, all classes became interested in the accumulation of things, and the broadside was a printed item that could be collected by wage earners – just as small, illustrated octavo novels were collected by the professional classes.[9] But the value of the broadside was only partially vested in its materiality: it also had value as an item that enabled performative acts, such as reading, speaking or singing.

As John Moulden has argued, printed broadside sheets were the access points through which new song materials entered the oral sphere; print was a vehicle which allowed songs to be coded and then decoded, and to re-enter the world of sound at different times and places.[10] The broadside thus maintained a symbiotic relationship between the written and the spoken word that dated back to the middle ages: according to Walter J. Ong, in the medieval era 'writing served largely to recycle knowledge back into the oral world . . . in the reading of literary and other texts to groups, and in reading aloud even when reading to oneself'.[11] As Abigail Williams has shown, the culture of reading books aloud continued to thrive during the eighteenth century in middle-class domestic spaces – but the connection between literature and performance remained important in working-class life as well.[12] The broadside was a child of the printing press, but it was also the descendant of British oral balladry. Nineteenth-century folk song collectors such as Gordon Hall Gerould and Francis James Child held that the broadside was the nemesis of Britain's oral folk music: they believed that the birth of the broadside as a print tradition had sullied the 'pure', oral national song of Britain and eventually stamped it out entirely.[13] However, subsequent scholarship has indicated that the interchange between oral and broadside balladry was sufficiently active throughout its long history to make maintaining the distinction between British 'folk' traditions and printed broadside song nearly impossible, and also unprofitable.[14] In the late eighteenth and nineteenth centuries, popular song was no longer purely oral, nor was it primarily rural: it was printed and urban – in short, it was the broadside ballad, the default heir of Britain's oral musical past.

This brings us to a third and related complexity: the broadside belonged to both literary and musical culture. Like contemporaneous graphic satire, the broadside tradition fused words with non-verbal media to create a hybrid genre. The most extensive work on the broadside to date has been conducted by literary scholars,[15] perhaps because the literary side of the tradition is now the easiest to access: the words are printed and still exist in special collections across the world. Ballad lyrics may be transcribed and analysed for content and meaning, rhyme schemes and verse structures, as we see in 'Answer to the Cabin Boy', transcribed from a broadside printed by John Pitts between 1802 and 1819 in London:

WHEN clouds obscured the distant sky,
  And fate had mark'd my portion,
Devoid of fear and danger high,
  I braved the foaming ocean.

Returning home from distant plains,
  My heart was light and glad,
But wreck'd upon the briny main,
  A hapless sailor lad.

To distant clime I bid adieu,
  Salt waves are now my pillow,
Dear Annabell I thought on you,
  While floating on the billow.[16]

THE BRITISH BROADSIDE BALLAD AS SENTIMENTAL FICTION   247

The printed broadside has preserved this ballad's poetic structure and content: it consists of three verses of four lines, alternating iambic tetrameter and occasionally hypermetric iambic trimeter, with a rhyme scheme of *abab*, etc.; we can also access the ballad's poetic imagery and syntax through the transcription. But the problem with approaching broadsides exclusively as verbal texts is that it becomes easy to ignore what is not printed: their music. Some nineteenth-century broadsides were not intended to be sung at all, and were printed in prose rather than poetic form (many news ballads would fall into this category), but broadsides were traditionally intended to be sung and performed. Throughout the seventeenth century, tune references for common songs were standard on broadside ballads; in the late eighteenth and nineteenth centuries, broadsides were still mostly sung, according to contemporaneous accounts, though tune references largely disappeared from the printed sheets (as will be discussed later).[17] The broadside tradition was a significant feature in the sound-world of eighteenth- and nineteenth-century Britain, and it was an important part of British musical as well as print history: eighteenth-century city dwellers who had never touched a broadside sheet themselves would have been familiar with the tradition nonetheless, unable to escape its sonic presence around markets and on street corners. The broadside belonged to literary and material culture, but also to oral and musical culture.

The fourth complexity of the broadside is that printed broadside sheets were both textual and visual; this means that the broadside might both tell a story and show it – much like the fictional novels printed for the professional classes that featured engraved illustrations. Broadside printers used woodcut illustrations to adorn broadsides because they were cheap and interchangeable: the same woodcut stamp could be used for many different broadsides – very often accompanying ballads that had nothing whatsoever to do with the subject of the illustration, although as Alexandra Franklin suggests, even illustrations that seemed disconnected from the ballad might have contributed to their interpretative meaning.[18] Woodcuts had been included on broadsides throughout the seventeenth century and continued to be used in the eighteenth and nineteenth centuries, albeit in evolving ways. In the seventeenth century, sizeable woodcuts would often be placed just beneath the title of the ballad, before the columns of text were printed in landscape orientation. Come the mid-eighteenth century, new formats and layouts became common in broadside printing: one popular format, called the 'slip ballad', had only a small illustration or even just an ornamental woodcut accompanying each of two ballads, printed in portrait orientation and cut down the middle to be sold separately. In Figure 14.1, two ballads have been printed on a single sheet, which may have been sold in this format, or cut and sold separately. The two ballads have a similar topic (sailors), but they are accompanied by different types of woodcuts: the first, 'The Sailor's Farewell', has an illustration of a lady and gentleman being chased by a tradesman, a scene which has no particular relation to the subject of the ballad; the second, 'The Rover of the Seas', sports only an ornamental woodcut of a lyre rather than an illustration, but again, the lyre motif bears no particular relationship to the theme or topic of the ballad itself. This modernised, simplified layout effectively reduced the role of woodcut illustrations on broadsides, but the slip ballad was not the only format used by broadside printers for street sale in the later eighteenth century. Some broadsides emphasised rather than diminished the role of illustrations on the page, such as some versions of Charles Dibdin Sr's song 'Lovely Nan' (printed between 1802 and 1819), which tells the tale of a sailor's departure from his love.[19]

THE SAILOR'S FAREWELL.

Farewell, Mary! I must leave thee,
  The anchor's weigh'd—I must aboard;
Do not let my absence grieve thee,
  Of sorrow do not breathe a word:
What though the foaming ocean sever
  Me from thee, yet still my heart
Loves you, Mary, and will ever,
  Though stern duty bids us part.

Farewell, Mary! dearest Mary!
  Do not grieve,—I shall return,
Crowned with laurels,—pray, do smother
  That sad sigh, oh, do not mourn!
You unman me with your kindness:
  Oh! chase these tears from off my brow;
Now round thy lips sweet smiles are creeping,
  Bless thee, Mary, farewell now!

Farewell, Mary! do not weep so,
  Though I leave thee for awhile,
I'll love thee still when on the deep, now
  Cheer my heart with thy sweet smile;
Soothe my parents with thy kindness,
  And I'll bless thee when far away
Oh! forgive my youthful blindness,
  For I can no longer stay.

Dearest parents! farewell kindly;
  Rest content whilst I'm away;
Mark yon gun, 'tis to remind me,
  On shore I can no longer stay:
The anchor's weighed, the sails are spreading,
  The boat is waiting in the bay:
Farewell, now, all kind relations,
  Pray for me when far away.

THE ROVER OF THE SEAS.

I'm the rover of the seas,
  And chief of a daring band,
Who obey all my decrees,
  And laugh at the laws of the land.
Wherever my swift bark steers,
  Desolation and rapine are spread,
And the names of the famed buccaneers
  Fill the bosoms of all with dread.
      For I'm the Rover of the Seas—
          Ha! ha
      For I'm the Rover of the Seas.

King of the waves am I,
  And rule with despotic sway,
As over the waves I fly,
  In search of my lawless prey.
No mercy I ever show
  To any I chance to meet;
But 'neath the billows they go,
  For dead men no tales repeat.

I'm the terror of the main,
  For none yet has conquered me,
And every victory I gain
  Makes me firmer lord of the sea,
In calm, or in storm, or in fight,
  I ever am the same,
And dearly have earned the right
  To claim my blood-stained name.

I envy no king on shore,
  For there's none has power like me.
They're bound by the oath they swore,
  While I am reckless and free!
And tho' danger I meet each day,
  Yet merry my life is passed,
For let there come what may,
  I can but die at last.

Song 225.

Figure 14.1 A slip ballad of 'The Sailor's Farewell' and 'The Rover of the Seas' (c.1800). Private collection.

THE BRITISH BROADSIDE BALLAD AS SENTIMENTAL FICTION 249

Elaborate prints like these formed an important minority of late eighteenth- and early nineteenth-century broadsides; they appear to have been cheap, street-literature versions of the luxurious, high-art mezzotints printed for the professional and leisure classes.[20] In the 'Lovely Nan' example, the central image is not only exceptionally large, it is also very beautiful and as intricately hewn as a woodblock could be. In the background, there is a ship in full sail, ready to go to sea, gulls soaring high above it. The lightness of the sky around the ship makes the sea a cheerful prospect, while the land-based cottage on the other side of the image looks dreary, in shadow. The contrasting halves of the illustration's background force the eye to the couple, the focus of the work. But the figures are drawn in such a way as to indicate movement, action and relationship rather than mere presence: the sailor, although looking at Nan, gestures to the ship with his hat, perhaps by way of explanation – he must leave ('I love my duty . . . love truth and merit to defend'). The poetry, and therefore the music, of the ballad take secondary roles on this broadside: as well as being pushed to the borders, the verses are in an aesthetically pleasing – but hard-to-read – cursive script. Attention is wholly focused on the illustrated vignette presented in the woodcut, which acts as an ekphrastic interpretation of Dibdin's song; as will be discussed later, the vignette became an important feature of broadside literature in the period. The broadside could be an item of aesthetic value, collected to adorn the domestic spaces of the working classes, as well as to pass any leisure time in reading or singing. In short, the broadside was not only literature and music; as Kevin D. Murphy and Sally O'Driscoll have highlighted, it was also the common Briton's visual art.[21]

The fifth complexity of the broadside tradition is that it functioned as both news and fiction, although – as the ambiguous etymology and meanings of 'novel' suggest, in their relation to 'nouvelles' but also to fiction – the distinction between the two is not as clear as one might assume. Since its earliest days, the broadside ballad had sold the thrilling and scandalous: ever-popular 'murder ballads' recounted the grisly details of slayings or circulated murderers' final words before going to the gallows, sometimes even before the day of execution. Nevertheless, the confessions and accounts of tragedies on broadsides claimed to be factual, and in many cases they held a kernel of truth. One ballad seller interviewed by the social reformer Henry Mayhew (1812–87) asserted that the information of the street sellers in London could be better than that of the newspapers, as their extensive network of 'correspondents' was the quickest to reach the scene of any tragedy or event in the city.[22] Through the eighteenth and into the nineteenth centuries, broadsides continued to be used as a medium for news as well as entertainment: some 'news' stories were cast into verse (murderers' confessions were often rendered in verse form), but other stories were printed in prose for reading, presenting news-like accounts of criminal, social or political events.[23] The Stamp Act of 1712 had made newspapers so expensive that the working classes could not reasonably afford them (in fact, that was one goal of this particular tax). As such, the working classes either had to band together to purchase newspapers, or find out their news through a more affordable source – namely, through broadsides, which were not subject to the tax.[24] Technically, broadside printers had to register their broadsides with the Stationers' Company, but in actuality, the organisation did not concern itself greatly with the broadside trade, which ran largely unlicensed and unchecked by the Company or the government.[25] It seems an odd oversight of the government not to have regulated a trade that had tremendous penetration across society: according to contemporaneous collector Charles Hindley, tens of thousands of sheets of a single ballad could have been sold by London printers in the first half of the nineteenth century, and this at a time when the city's population was between just one and three million people.[26] In any case, the broadside trade remained largely free to disseminate news and political pamphlets to anyone who could pay a penny or halfpenny for them.

The distinction between 'truth' and 'fiction' in broadside literature was blurred further because – in England at least – broadside songs that did not purport to be 'news' still favoured the realistic over the fantastic, less concerned with dragons and fairies (although some do crop up in the ballads) than in stories that could be true: stories about loss and departure, death and longing, about love stories that end happily and many that end sadly. British broadsides tended to focus on commonplace events and people that could be used to make moral points, much like fables. As with fables, the historical veracity of the stories (that is, whether they actually took place) did not itself determine their truth-value; rather, the value of the ballad was in the aptness of its moral. For by the late eighteenth and early nineteenth centuries, the ballad song was seen to be a tool for moral teaching in Britain.[27] The stories told in these ballads – whether truth, fable or both – were compelling to the working classes (and, in fact, all classes of British society to some extent) because they boasted verisimilitude. A similar vacillation between the 'realism' of the emergent novel form (in Ian Watt's classic, if since contested, formulation) and the fantastical extremes of romances blurred both the terminology associated with contemporary prose fiction and the narrative shapes it took. The novel's relation to veracity also held potent relevance to its ability to fulfil the didact function prose fiction increasingly strove to assert, as manifested in the literary prefaces of authors including Daniel Defoe and Samuel Richardson.[28] In fact, broadsides had been interested in realistic, everyday people long before literature or opera deigned seriously to care about them. While Metastasio still reigned on the opera stage, his aristocratic characters modelling superhuman morality and self-denial for his audiences, the everyday ins and outs of pedestrian love affairs were being worked out in the broadside ballad. It is no coincidence that one of England's major contributions to operatic history, the genre of ballad opera, of which John Gay's *The Beggar's Opera* (1727) is the best-known example, was a vehicle for social satire built around ballads: ballads spoke truths through stories, when truth was comedic and especially when it was uncomfortable.[29]

The Broadside as Sentimental Literature

The broadside was part of perhaps the oldest contiguous tradition of storytelling in Britain, with its roots in oral balladry, and which continued unbroken – yet constantly replenished – through to the industrial era. In the eighteenth century, however, the broadside ballad experienced material changes. While never entirely eschewing its connections with tradition, the broadside was slowly updated in format and content. Changes in the broadside's typeface and layout have already been noted, as has its shifting relationship with music during this century, when tune references began to disappear from broadside sheets. This latter phenomenon remains something of a mystery, but recent research shows that a significant minority of broadside songs from the late eighteenth and early nineteenth centuries came from the playhouse stage: popular songs from London's theatres were regularly pirated by broadside printers for street

THE BRITISH BROADSIDE BALLAD AS SENTIMENTAL FICTION   251

performance and sale.[30] These songs were printed without tune references because they did not need them: the songs had presumably already become sufficiently popular from theatrical performances that their tunes were integrated within Britain's contemporaneous sound-world.

Naturally, the broadside was affected by this crossover of songs from the playhouse to the street – and not least by the sentimentalism that pervaded English theatre music in the second half of the century.[31] By the 1770s and 1780s the playhouse had absorbed the sentimentalism that had become popular in printed literature by that time. Samuel Richardson's *Pamela: or, Virtue Rewarded* of 1740 was critical in the development of the English sentimental novel, which focused on moral instruction through the manipulation of the reader's feelings and sympathies. The literary genre reached its apex in the 1770s, although it was satirised even during the height of its popularity.[32] By around 1800, the sentimental novel was considered by many to be merely a literary embarrassment, but it was undergirded by influential philosophical approaches to moral formation and social relationships, as developed variously by Anthony Ashley Cooper, third Earl of Shaftesbury (1671–1713), Francis Hutcheson (1694–1746), David Hume (1711–76), Adam Smith (1723–90) and the Scottish clergyman Hugh Blair (1718–1800), whose popular sermons preached morality and works-based religion.[33] The philosophical movement, indeed, was closely associated with the Scottish Enlightenment, but also influenced later Romantic thought. Sentimental philosophers theorised that human morality was based on the autonomous judgement of the individual, guided and informed by a natural sympathy for one's fellow man rather than obedience to an external moral system. This morality is, by its nature, relative, and as such sentimental philosophers relied on the judgement of a hypothetical 'impartial observer' to adjudicate moral actions: in other words, one human's sympathy-driven morality is deemed 'sound' only if it can be judged to be so by another, disinterested party.[34] While sentimentalist philosophy may appear to have been antithetical to the prevailing rationalism of the Enlightenment, philosophers such as Hume viewed sentiment and reason as uniting to guide man's autonomous, self-guided morality.[35]

Sentimentalism resonated with the seventeenth-century concept of the 'noble savage', which commended the natural sympathy, dignity and humanity of the 'uncivilised' man, who supposedly remained unsullied by the sophistry and corruption of civilisation.[36] As such, sentimental literature often presented 'uncivilised' characters as inherently moral beings, guided by their natural sympathy for fellow men. The sentimental novels by Richardson (along with those by Oliver Goldsmith, Mary Wollstonecraft, Laurence Sterne, Mary Hays and Henry Mackenzie, among others) encouraged readers to respond sympathetically to descriptions of human suffering – particularly the suffering of the moral poor – thereby reinforcing their moral formation.[37] Mackenzie's Harley from *The Man of Feeling* would be an example of this, who was very moved by the degraded state of a woman he encounters at Bedlam.[38] Very often, an epistolary form was used by sentimental novelists to help focus the reader's attention on particular incidents or people, eschewing a cohesive or complex narrative structure to invest in emotional exploration through loosely connected vignettes: both Mary Hays and Samuel Richardson used this approach. Another common form for the sentimental novel was the *manuscrit trouvé*: a narrative that is fragmented because part of the story has supposedly been lost before reaching the reader. Again, Mackenzie's *Man of Feeling* would be an example of this structure. Like the epistolary form, this model allowed the

252   GEORGINA BARTLETT

author to break the story up into individual, disconnected vignettes which could form character studies.

The functions of both the narrator and the reader were critical to the framing of the sentimental novel. Stories were often told through narrators who had ostensibly witnessed the scenes personally, or otherwise had some glancing connection to the characters or events in the plot. As Barbara Benedict has explored, this framing added a layer of interest – and mystery – to the novel, as the reader is required to simultaneously engage with both the novel's characters and the narrator's perspective on them as they are described.[39] Novels in epistolary form allowed the reader to perceive the characters and unfolding drama through a range of different narrative voices, while novels that were framed as discovered manuscripts allowed for an introduction to be added by the manuscript's ostensible discoverer or compiler, adding a 'frame tale' which provided readers with direction for interpreting the material and even guided them to the underlying moral of the story. The reader also has an important role in the sentimental novel: it was understood by mid-century readers that the 'correct' response to sentimental literature was to be moved oneself by the sufferings of those less fortunate in the story, meaning that readers themselves participated in the construction of sentimentalist virtue.[40]

Sentimentalism came into vogue on the stage not long after its popularisation in literature: Richardson's *Pamela* was adapted for the stage, first by Voltaire as *Nanine, ou le Préjugé vaincu* (1749), and then by Carlo Goldoni as *La Pamela* (1750).[41] Continental opera was also influenced by sentimentalism: after creating his stage play based on *Pamela*, Goldoni turned the story into an opera, *La buona figliuola*, with music by Niccolò Piccinni, beginning a trend for sentimentalism in the genre during the late eighteenth century.[42] In Britain, the 'sentimental comedy' – a much-debated form of English stage play that was concerned with the presentation of virtue and the sentimental depiction of characters, particularly of the lower classes – increased in popularity, reaching its height in the 1770s (in step with literary sentimentalism), as epitomised by works such as Richard Cumberland's *West Indian* (1771).[43] Sentimentalism came to the fore in the English comic opera, too – a variable tradition of English-language, full-length spoken plays with songs and an overture – which also became popular in London in the 1770s and 1780s, and typically focused on patriotic themes, martial commoners and sentimental heroines, with plots that revolved around two or three love pairs. *Poor Soldier* (1783), written by John O'Keeffe with music by William Shield, would be a prime example.[44] These hybridised forms of entertainment were not always well received: in his *Essay on the Theatre* (1773), Oliver Goldsmith suggested that sentimental theatre, in trying to combine the weight of high drama with the lightness of comedy, became a 'bastard form of tragedy, which is only applauded because it is new'.[45]

English comic operas boasted sentimental plots but also sentimental music. The songs or 'airs' of English operas of the late eighteenth century were of a peculiar kind: they tended to be stylistically simplistic and in strophic or ballad form. In fact, John Gay's ballad operas adopted actual street melodies, as well as music from other sources, as interpolated songs for his musical stage plays. By this time, musical simplicity had already become associated with 'Englishness' in popular culture, in contrast to the florid vocal displays and ternary forms of 'continental' opera arias.[46] English opera songs tended to be discrete with little or no recitative (intoned speech) to connect them, and they were often unrelated to the characters in the opera's plot: like real-life street songs, these ballads might present a story to listeners within the drama, from which a moral could be derived for their edification.[47] These little moralistic 'dramas within dramas' reflected the sentimentalism that shaped the dramatic work as a whole. And because the songs often had ballad structures and their own plots, they were easy pickings for piratical printers who copied down their verses to be sold as broadside ballads on the street.[48]

Of course, there were already many elements of the traditional broadside that resonated with these new, sentimental theatre songs: broadsides had long been concerned with ordinary people and focused on events and circumstances that evoked an emotional response from the listener, usually based on longing or regret, such as in the seventeenth-century ballad 'Joy after Sorrow'.[49] Even the 'gallows literature' ostensibly written by convicted murderers usually centred around remorse. And, of course, like sentimental fiction, broadside songs were expected to convey a moral meaning implicitly, or explicitly stated in a final verse or in the ballad's title, as found in 'The True Lovers Admonition', or 'The Married Wives [sic] Complaint of Her Unkind Husband; A Caution for Maids to Beware How They Marry'.[50] The advent of sentimentalism in prose fiction and on the stage in the late eighteenth century affected the broadside in perceptible ways, specifically through the proliferation of songs that were structured as a series of vignettes rather than a cohesive narrative. These focused on the suffering of virtuous characters (particularly those of the lower classes), presented morality as a product of natural sympathy, and emphasised the crucial role of the narrator both as a participant in the story told and as an interpreter of its moral meaning.

The songs of Charles Dibdin Sr (1745–1814) were instrumental in establishing eighteenth-century sentimentalism in broadside songs.[51] Though little remembered now, Dibdin wrote dozens of extremely popular songs for the playhouse and pleasure garden stages, as well as one-man entertainments and concerts. He was a brilliant melodist (though not necessarily a brilliant arranger or musician), but his true gift was in his ability to create relatable and sympathetic characters in his songs: his sentimental and moralistic songs affected the stage, the street and the domestic parlour alike.[52] Dibdin was responsible for many of the theatrical songs that transitioned to the street, and his character-types were widely imitated by other broadside writers.[53] As shown by 'Lovely Nan', discussed earlier, he was particularly famed for his sentimental 'sea songs' concerning the British naval sailor – or 'Jack Tar' as he was known in popular culture. The ennobling of the commoner, and particularly the martial or naval commoner, had become an important cultural movement in Britain by the end of the eighteenth century, as the future of Britain increasingly depended on the faithfulness and courage of the Royal Navy sailor, who guarded the 'wooden walls' of England during the turbulent French Revolutionary and then Napoleonic Wars. As Betty T. Bennett explains, at this time 'the epithets once reserved only for officers of the army and navy were applied to ordinary fighting men. They were ennobled not only in their military role, but given credit for excellent, albeit rough, intelligence, and sensitivity as well'.[54]

Dibdin was a crucial figure in the development of this 'sensitive' Jack Tar – a character who inspired patriotism and unity during politically uncertain times. Dibdin achieved this through creating his own brand of sentimentalism, which drew on both philosophical and literary models. 'Tom Bowling' (written 1789) is perhaps the best known of his songs today.[55] The song's links to literature are palpable: it was framed as an elegy to a common seaman (written after the death of the author's brother, Captain Thomas Dibdin), but it took its name from the rough but goodhearted character Tom Bowling from Tobias Smollett's picaresque novel *The Adventures of Roderick Random* (1748).[56] The three verses of Dibdin's song are reproduced below from a broadside printed in 1791 by John Evans:

> Here, a sheer hulk, likes poor Tom Bowling, the darling of our crew.
> No more he'll hear the tempest howling, for death has called him to [*sic*].
> His form was of the manliest beauty, his heart was kind and soft.
> Faithful below he did his duty, but now he is gone aloft.

> Tom never from his word departed, his virtues were so rare:
> His [friends] were many and true hearted, his Poll was kind and fair;
> And then he'd sing so blithe and jolly, ah! Many's the time and oft;
> But mirth is turn'd to melancholy, for Tom is gone aloft.

> Yet shall poor Tom find pleasant weather when He, who all commands,
> Shall give to call life's crew together the word to pipe all hands:
> Thus Death, who kings and tars despatches, Tom's life hath vainly doft.
> For tho' his body's under hatches, his soul is gone aloft.[57]

Tom, as a typical example of a Dibdin-esque sailor, is not a refined character: he is no gentleman, but a British commoner who works before the mast and sings before the mast. However, the elegiac form of the song allows the narrator to dwell on the sailor's lofty virtues, namely his 'soft' heart, faithfulness, integrity and joyfulness while doing his duty, 'blithe and jolly'. Dibdin depicts Tom as a model of virtue through his innate, uncomplicated and unsophisticated goodness, similarly to how Smollett characterised the original Tom Bowling in *Roderick Random*: 'a good seaman he is, as ever stept [*sic*] upon forecastle—and a brave fellow as ever crackt biskit;—none of your guinea-pigs, nor your fresh-water, wishy-washy, fair-weather, fowls. Many a taught gale of wind has honest Tom Bowling and I weathered together'.[58] It is because of Tom's natural goodness that the narrator (and therefore the reader or listener) mourns his passing: Tom was a good man felled by the vicissitudes of life. His death provides those more fortunate than him with the opportunity to have their own 'soft' hearts moved to pity. Such sentimental scenes involving sailors making sacrifices for the sake of duty, engaging the reader's/listener's admiration and sympathy, proved popular choices for ballads, as 'The Sailor's Farewell' and 'Lovely Nan' show.

'Tom Bowling' eschews a strict narrative form to focus on individual vignettes. The reader or listener hears about individual scenes rather than a chronological narrative: the first verse opens with the image of the poor dead man, then contrasts it with a description of his form in life; the second verse focuses on Tom's character and community, then again contrasts these images with the emptiness left by his passing; the third and last verse brings the threads of death and life together as the narrator points us forward to the resurrection, when the virtuous (namely, Tom) will see their heavenly reward. This vignette-based structure creates a similar effect to the epistolary form or manuscript fragmentation common in sentimental literature: the reader or listener is forced to focus on character studies and/or particular scenes rather than narratives, as

THE BRITISH BROADSIDE BALLAD AS SENTIMENTAL FICTION   255

would be traditional for broadside songs.[59] Additionally, the voice of the narrator provides a commentary that is both removed from the subject itself (Tom) yet proximate to it: he was the 'darling of our crew', implying that the narrator was his crewmate. The result is that the reader or listener feels as though they overhear the eulogy themselves: the song does not tell a story, it becomes a part of a story. Put another way, the song makes the narrator into a sort of dramatis persona in an implied drama of which the song is a part; indeed, Dibdin's clever framing of this song demonstrates his theatrical experience and his adeptness at creating engaging drama. The implied relationship between the narrator and Tom gives the song credibility – the narrator appears to be talking about an old friend – while also giving him authority to draw moral lessons from the subject of the song. In this particular case, the narrator, as Tom's crewmate, is ideally placed both to describe the character of the late Tom Bowling and to commend him to the audience as a model of human virtue.

Other broadside songs focused even more explicitly on sentimentalism, not only depicting sentimental scenes and characters, but propounding (in broad brushstrokes) what can only be termed sentimentalist philosophy, as contemporaneous novels were exploring. An anonymous broadside song published between 1790 and 1840 by Jennings of London, entitled 'The Heart That Can Feel for Another' (but more typically published under the title 'Jack Stedfast' in broadside literature, a play on the name of Jack Tar), demonstrates this trend:

Jack steadfast and I were both messmates at sea,
And plough'd half the world o'er together,
And many hot battles enounter'd have we,
Strange climates and all sorts of weather;
But seamen, you know, are inur'd to hard gales
Determin'd to stand by each other,
And the heart of a tar, wheresoever he sail,
Is the heart that can feel for another.[60]

Like 'Tom Bowling', this song consists of a series of images that are described by a narrator who – though not the subject of the song himself – features in it. 'Jack Steadfast' is described as a common sailor who has endured considerable suffering in the course of his duty. Nevertheless, he has remained unwavering in his natural sympathy throughout – his ability to 'feel for another'. Through this pithy concluding 'moral', the narrator effectively describes sentimentalist philosophy, while also inviting the audience to participate in it: first, the narrator establishes Jack's natural sympathy through description; second, he demonstrates his own natural sympathy by commending his friend's; third, readers or listeners, by pitying the crewmates' trials in 'all sorts of weather', are invited to establish their own sympathies by indulging their soft hearts in pitying the sailors and approving of their admirable morality. In a great chain of fellow feeling, the song encapsulates both the essence and the intended process of sentimental fiction, from subject to narrator to reader.

Sentimentalist philosophy is even more explicitly advanced in another of Dibdin's popular theatre songs-turned-broadside-ballads: 'True Courage', written c.1798. Its first verse, as found in a broadside edition printed by Pitts of London (printed between 1819 and 1844), runs:[61]

Why what's that to you, if my eyes I'm a wiping,
A tear is a pleasure, d'ye see, in its way;
'Tis nonsense for trifles I own to be piping,
But they that han't pity, why I pities they:
Says the Captain, says he, (I shall never forget it)
If of courage you'd know lads the true from the sham,
'Tis a furious lion in battle, so let it,
But duty appeas'd, 'tis in mercy a lamb.[62]

There are many familiar sentimental elements in this song: as in 'Tom Bowling', there is a focus on a particular vignette in the verse (the Captain giving his sage advice to the crew) rather than on a developing narrative; there is also a narrator who is ostensibly recounting the tale as a witness to and participant in it. But in this song, the narrator opens with his own gloss, addressing the audience itself both to defend his sentimentalism and exhort others to partake of the 'pleasure' of an apt tear: 'Why what's that to you if my eyes I'm a wiping / A tear is a pleasure, d'ye see, in its way'. As a sentimental hero, the narrator avers that human virtue (including that of common fighting men) is the product of sympathy-driven action.

Sentimental Broadsides as Fiction and Performance

When sentimental songs like these were performed, the voice of the narrator inevitably merged with the voice of the singer who realised them, and thus a singer himself could become an actor in the story he was telling, ostensibly recounting scenes and describing people that he himself knew. The song created a character for the singer, and in many sentimental songs (including all those discussed above) this character was as pitiable and/or honourable as the subject described – for example, the grieving crewmate of Tom Bowling, the true-hearted messmate of Jack Steadfast, and the sympathetic sailor who is 'in mercy a lamb'.

The characterisation of narrators in sentimental songs inevitably played into the public image of ballad singers themselves, who belonged to what is called the 'grey economy' of eighteenth-century Britain, an impoverished social group that relied variously on selling wares, picking pockets and receiving charity to survive.[63] As such, singers' public personae were crucial to their success, as Oskar Cox Jensen has discussed: the most successful singers would 'dress the part' to engage the emotions of their audiences.[64] For women, that might mean looking tragic, innocent, dirty and pitiable, perhaps even carrying infants on their hips as they sang their touching songs. For men, that might mean advertising (or assuming) a connection with the navy or army, presenting themselves as real-life 'Tom Bowlings' or 'Jack Steadfasts' – sailors who had been faithful to their country but had fallen on hard times.[65] Some ballad singers even resorted to wearing overt costuming: Joseph Johnson, a black ballad singer in London who was a former merchant sailor, wore a model ship on his head and sung only naval songs, advertising his own connection to the sea and establishing a public image for himself on the London streets.[66] Ballad singers were effectively actors as well as musicians. Therefore – through their use of sentimental language popularised by contemporary novelistic fiction and by stage plays, their presentation of worthy 'commoners', their explicit sentimentalist morals, and their creation of endearing narrators – sentimental broadside songs gave ballad singers repertoire to sing and also roles to play, providing passers-by with the opportunity to shed a 'pleasing' tear for the very real sufferings of the worthy poor.

Notes

1. For an exploration of British broadsides since their invention, see Patricia Fumerton, Anita Guerrini and Kris McAbee, eds, *Ballads and Broadsides in Britain, 1500–1800* (Farnham: Ashgate, 2010).
2. Cyprian Blagden, *The Stationers' Company: A History, 1403–1959* (Stanford: Stanford University Press, 1977), 20.
3. David Atkinson points out that singers were not limited to printed tune suggestions, however, and may well have used other melodies. David Atkinson, *The Anglo-Scottish Ballad and Its Imaginary Contexts* (Cambridge: Cambridge University Press, 2014), xiv.
4. See Robert D. Hume, 'The Value of Money in Eighteenth-Century England: Incomes, Prices, Buying Power – and Some Problems in Cultural Economics', *Huntington Library Quarterly* 77, no. 4 (2014): 380. See also Adam Smith, *An Inquiry into the Nature and Causes of the Wealth of Nations*, ed. R. H. Campbell, A. S. Skinner and W. B. Todd, 2 vols (1776; Indianapolis: Liberty Fund, 1981), 1:92.
5. Thomas Holcroft and William Hazlitt, *Memoirs of Thomas Holcroft* (1816; London: Humphrey Milford: 1926), 55.
6. This is best summarised by Gerald Egan: 'black letter is an actual vehicle for cultural significance, a formal property of a text that means something . . . as early as the seventeenth century black letter had a specific cultural meaning . . . it both constructed and evoked a nostalgia for a traditional, communal English past'. See Gerald Egan, 'Black Letter and the Broadside Ballad', *English Broadside Ballad Archive* (University of California, 2007), https://ebba.english.ucsb.edu/page/black-letter (accessed 16 November 2023); Zachary Lesser, 'Typographic Nostalgia: Playreading, Popularity and the Meanings of Black Letter', in *The Book of the Play: Playwrights, Stationers, and Readers in Early Modern England*, ed. Marta Straznicky (Amherst: University of Massachusetts Press, 2006), 99–126.
7. For more, see Suzanne Aspden, 'Ballads and Britons: Imagined Community and the Continuity of "English" Opera', *Journal of the Royal Musical Association* 122, no. 1 (1997): 24–51.
8. See M.L. Turner, 'John Johnson and His Collection of Printed Ephemera', in *The John Johnson Collection: Catalogue of an Exhibition* (Oxford: Bodleian Library, 1971), 5–18. For a further discussion on ephemera of this period, see Kevin D. Murphy and Sally O'Driscoll, eds, *Studies in Ephemera: Text and Image in in Eighteenth-century Print* (Lewisburg: Bucknell University Press, 2013), particularly the editors' Introduction entitled '"Fugitive Pieces" and "Gaudy Books": Textual, Historical, and Visual Interpretations of Ephemera in the Long Eighteenth Century', 1–30. See also 'A Song for the Independent Burgesses of Newcastle', Edition – Bod18318 (n.l., n.p., [1774]), *Broadside Ballads Online*, http://ballads.bodleian.ox.ac.uk/view/edition/18318 (accessed 16 November 2023). All of the Bodleian Library's approximately 30,000 broadside ballads may be accessed through the digitised database *Broadside Ballads Online* (BBO). Note that broadside ballads rarely had an imprint date, so date ranges are usually approximated from historical information gathered about printers and their locations during their careers.
9. Regarding eighteenth-century consumer culture, see John Styles and Amanda Vickery, eds, *Gender, Taste, and Material Culture in Britain and North America, 1700–1830* (New Haven: Yale Center for British Art, 2007); Neil McKendrick, John Brewer and J. H. Plumb, eds, *The Birth of a Consumer Society: The Commercialization of Eighteenth-Century England* (Bloomington: Indiana University Press, 1982); Carole Shammas, *The Pre-Industrial Consumer in England and America* (Oxford: Clarendon Press, 1990).

10. John Moulden, 'The Printed Ballad in Ireland: A Guide to the Popular Printing of Songs in Ireland, 1760–1920', PhD thesis, National University of Ireland (2006), 124, 214 and 230.
11. Walter J. Ong, *Orality and Literacy: The Technologizing of the Word* (London and New York: Routledge, 2002), 117.
12. On the culture of reading aloud in the eighteenth century, see Abigail Williams, *The Social Life of Books: Reading Together in the Eighteenth-Century Home* (New Haven: Yale University Press, 2017).
13. See Francis James Child, *English and Scottish Ballads, Selected and Edited by F.J. Child* (Boston: Little, Brown, and Co., 1857), and Gordon Hall Gerould, *The Ballad of Tradition* (Oxford: Clarendon Press, 1932), particularly 244. See also Mary Ellen Brown, 'Child's Ballads and the Broadside Conundrum', in *Ballads and Broadsides in Britain, 1500–1800*, 57–72.
14. Although he considered the broadside to be a corrupting influence on English 'folk' music, Child used broadside ballads to compile his 'folk' song collections. See Roy Palmer, *A Ballad History of England from 1588 to the Present Day* (London: B. T. Batsford, 1979) and '"Veritable Dunghills": Professor Child and the Ballad', *Folk Music Journal* 7, no. 2 (1996): 155–66. See also Steve Roud, *Folk Song in England* (London: Faber & Faber, 2017), and David Atkinson, *The Anglo-Scottish Ballad and Its Imaginary Contexts* (Cambridge: Open Book Publishers, 2014).
15. See the works of Patricia Fumerton, Gerald Egan and other scholars at the *English Broadside Ballad Archive*, https://ebba.english.ucsb.edu/, which has spearheaded the digitisation of many libraries' broadside collections and contributed significantly to broadside research, focusing on English broadsides of the seventeenth century.
16. See 'Answer to the Cabin Boy', Edition – Bod5665 (London: John Pitts, 1802–19), *Broadside Ballads Online*, http://ballads.bodleian.ox.ac.uk/view/edition/5665 (accessed 16 November 2023).
17. See Henry Mayhew, *London and the London Poor* (1861; London: Chatto & Windus, 1966); Charles Hindley, *Curiosities of Street Literature* (1871; Cambridge: Cambridge University Press, 2012); *Life and Times of James Catnach, Late of Seven Dials, Ballad Monger* (1878; Cambridge: Cambridge University Press, 2011); *The History of the Catnach Press, at Berwick-Upon-Tweed, Alnwick and Newcastle-Upon-Tyne, in Northumberland, and Seven Dials, London* (1886; Cambridge: Cambridge University Press, 2009); John Thomas Smith, *Vagabondiana; Or, Anecdotes of Mendicant Wanderers through the Streets of London, with Portraits of the Most Remarkable Drawn from Life* (London: Author, 1817); *The Cries of London: Exhibiting Several of the Itinerant Traders of Antient [sic] and Modern Times* (London: Author, 1839); *Antiquarian Ramble in the Streets of London: with Anecdotes of Their More Celebrated Residents* (London: Bentley, 1846).
18. 'The Sailor's Farewell' and 'The Rover of the Seas' (n.l., n.p., c. 1800), author's own collection. See similar editions in the *Broadside Ballads Online* collections: Edition – Bod7472 (n.l., n.p., n.d.), http://ballads.bodleian.ox.ac.uk/view/edition/7472 (accessed 16 November 2023); Edition – Bod8209 (Durham: Walker, 1797–1834), http://ballads.bodleian.ox.ac.uk/view/edition/8209 (accessed 16 November 2023). See also Alexandra Franklin, 'Making Sense of Broadside Ballad Illustrations in the Seventeenth and Eighteenth Centuries', in *Studies in Ephemera*, 166–94, particularly 171.
19. Charles Dibdin Sr, 'Lovely Nan', Edition – Bod2614 (London: Pitts, 1802–19), *Broadside Ballads Online*, http://ballads.bodleian.ox.ac.uk/view/edition/2614 (accessed 16 November 2023).
20. Nicholas Grindle, 'Dibdin and John Raphael Smith: Print Culture and Fine Art', in *Charles Dibdin and Late Georgian Culture*, ed. Oskar Cox Jensen, David Kennerley and Ian Newman (Oxford: Oxford University Press, 2018), 158. And again, see Hume, 'The Value of Money'.

21. See Kevin D. Murphy and Sally O'Driscoll, '"Fugitive Pieces" and "Gaudy Books"', and Alexandra Franklin, 'Making Sense of Broadside Ballad Illustrations in the Seventeenth and Eighteenth Centuries', both in *Studies in Ephemera*.

22. Mayhew, *London and the London Poor*, vol. 1, 236.

23. See Thomas Pettitt, 'Journalism vs. Tradition in the English Ballads of the Murdered Sweetheart', in *Ballads and Broadsides in Britain, 1500–1800*, 75–89.

24. Percy H. Muir, *Victorian Illustrated Books* (London: Portman, 1989), 2.

25. Robert Stark Thomson, 'The Development of the Broadside Ballad Trade and Its Influence upon the Transmission of English Folksongs', PhD thesis, Cambridge University (1974), 31.

26. The first two decades of the nineteenth century saw an immense surge in London's population, which jumped from approximately 1.1 million in 1801 to more than 1.4 million by 1815 and continued to rise as the century wore on, with over 3 million inhabitants by 1860. See Clive Emsley, Tim Hitchcock and Robert Shoemaker, 'London History – A Population History of London', *Old Bailey Proceedings Online*, https://www.oldbaileyonline.org/static/Population-history-of-london.jsp (accessed 16 November 2023), and Hindley, *Curiosities of Street Literature*, 118.

27. Berta Joncus, 'Ballad Opera: Commercial Song in Enlightenment Garb', in *The Oxford Handbook of the British Musical*, ed. Robert Gordon and Olaf Jubin (Oxford: Oxford University Press, 2017), 31–64.

28. Ian Watt, *The Rise of the Novel: Studies in Defoe, Richardson and Fielding* (Berkeley: University of California Press, 1957).

29. See Georgina Bartlett, 'Transformation or Conformation? The English Broadside Ballad and the Playhouse, 1797–1844', *Music & Letters* 103, no. 4 (2022): 662–84.

30. See Georgina Bartlett, 'From the Stage to the Street: Theatre Music and the Broadside Ballad in London, 1797–1844', PhD thesis, Oxford University (2020).

31. See Frank Ellis, *Sentimental Comedy: Theory and Practice* (Cambridge: Cambridge University Press, 1991), and Stefano Castelvecchi, *Sentimental Opera: Questions of Genre in the Age of Bourgeois Drama* (Cambridge: Cambridge University Press, 2013).

32. For a fuller exposition on the definitions of the genre, see Albert J. Rivero, 'Introduction', in *The Sentimental Novel in the Eighteenth Century*, ed. Albert J. Rivero (Cambridge: Cambridge University Press, 2019), 1–14. See also William Burling, 'A "Sickly Sort of Refinement": The Problem of Sentimentalism in Mackenzie's *The Man of Feeling*', *Studies in Scottish Literature* 23 (1988): 137–8.

33. Anthony Ashley Cooper, third Earl of Shaftesbury, *An Inquiry Concerning Virtue or Merit*, ed. David Walford (1699; Manchester: Manchester University Press, 1977); David Hume, *A Treatise of Human Nature* (1739–40; London: Longmans, 1874) and *Of the Standard of Taste, and Other Essays* (Edinburgh: A. Millar, 1757); Francis Hutcheson, *A System of Moral Philosophy, in Three Books* (London: A. Millar, 1755); Adam Smith, *Theory of Moral Sentiments* (Edinburgh: A. Millar, 1759). For more on Blair, see Richard B. Sher, *Church and University in the Scottish Enlightenment: The Moderate Literati of Edinburgh* (Edinburgh: Edinburgh University Press, 1985). For more on the philosophy of sentimentalism, see Michael Slote, *Moral Sentimentalism* (Oxford: Oxford University Press, 2009), and Hina Nazar, *Enlightened Sentiments: Judgment and Autonomy in the Age of Sensibility* (New York: Fordham University Press, 2012), 20.

34. Nazar, *Enlightened Sentiments*, 23: 'The spectator garners importance in Hume's writings owing to his understanding that not all sentiments are "moral sentiments" or have normative significance. As already noted, for sentimentalists like Hume and Smith, only the sentiments of approval or disapproval that have been reflectively endorsed from a standpoint of relative impartiality, or a "general of point of view", have such significance.'

35. Nazar, *Enlightened Sentiments*, 25–6.

36. R. Peter Burnham, 'The Social Ethos of Mackenzie's *The Man of Feeling*', *Studies in Scottish Literature* 18 (1983): 133–4.
37. John Dwyer, 'Clio and Ethics: Practical Morality in Enlightened Scotland', *The Eighteenth Century: Theory and Interpretation* 30 (1989): 65.
38. Henry Mackenzie, *The Man of Feeling* (London: Cadell, 1771), 46–54.
39. See Barbara M. Benedict, *Framing Feeling: Sentiment and Style in English Prose Fiction, 1745–1800* (New York: AMS Press, 1994).
40. Burling, 'A "Sickly Sort of Refinement"', 137: 'By popular consensus, the "ideal" sentimental person possessed an elevated sympathy for the joys and sorrows of others and reacted to even insignificant occurrences of life to an extreme degree.'
41. See Thomas Keymer and Peter Sabor on Richardson's novel and its dramatic adaptations: *The Pamela Controversy: Criticisms and Adaptations of Samuel Richardson's 'Pamela', 1740–1750*, vol. 6 (London: Pickering & Chatto, 2001), and also *'Pamela' in the Marketplace: Literary Controversy and Print Culture in Eighteenth-Century Britain and Ireland* (Cambridge: Cambridge University Press, 2005).
42. See Castelvecchi, *Sentimental Opera*.
43. For more on the genre and representatives of English sentimental comedy, see Ellis, *Sentimental Comedy: Theory and Practice*.
44. *Poor Soldier* premiered in London on 7 April 1783 after being premiered in Dublin at Crow Street Theatre on 15 April 1777. See John O'Keeffe (wordbook) and William Shield (music), *Poor Soldier* (London: Harrison Cluse, 1783). For more on English comic opera, see Roger Fiske, *English Theatre Music in the Eighteenth Century* (Oxford: Oxford University Press, 1986).
45. See Oliver Goldsmith, *The Works of Oliver Goldsmith: Life of Goldsmith. Vicar of Wakefield. Essays, Letters* (London: Bell, 1884), 401.
46. Oskar Cox Jensen, 'True Courage', in *Charles Dibdin and Late Georgian Culture*, 117.
47. A good example of a moralistic theatre song would be 'A Traveller Stopped at a Widow's Gate' from *The Iron Chest* (premiered 12 March 1796 at Drury Lane) by George Colman (wordbook) and Stephen Storace (music).
48. The crossover of other forms of literature into the broadside tradition could be direct: for example, in the late eighteenth and early nineteenth centuries, broadside copies abounded in England of 'A Red, Red Rose', 'Bannockburn' and other poems by Robert Burns (1759–96), who was himself much affected by Adam Smith's moral philosophy and venerated Mackenzie's *The Man of Feeling* next to the Bible. Burns supposedly always carried a copy of Mackenzie's book with him. See Robert Burns, *The Letters of Robert Burns*, ed. James Logie Robertson (London: Scott, 1887), 11–12; see the nine broadside ballads collected under Roud Number: V2890 ('A Red, Red Rose'), Broadside Ballads Online, http://ballads.bodleian.ox.ac.uk/search/roud/V2890 (accessed 16 November 2023), and the seventeen broadside ballads collected under Roud Number: V1089 ('Bannockburn'), *Broadside Ballads Online*, http://ballads.bodleian.ox.ac.uk/search/roud/V1089 (accessed 16 November 2023).
49. 'Joy after Sorrow: Being the Seamans return from Jamaico [sic]', Edition – Bod4169 (London: Vere, 1644–80), *Broadside Ballads Online*, http://ballads.bodleian.ox.ac.uk/view/edition/4169 (accessed 16 November 2023).
50. See 'The True Lovers Admonition', Edition – Bod4960 (London: Brooksby, 1672–96), *Broadside Ballads Online*, http://ballads.bodleian.ox.ac.uk/view/edition/4960 (accessed 16 November 2023), and 'The Married Wives [sic] Complaint of Her Unkind Husband; A Caution for Maids to Beware How They Marry', Edition – Bod23752 (London: Brooksby, 1672–96), *Broadside Ballads Online*, http://ballads.bodleian.ox.ac.uk/view/edition/23752 (accessed 16 November 2023).
51. Other theatre composers whose songs became particularly popular on the street were William Reeve (1757–1815) and William Shield (bap.1748/9, d.1829).

THE BRITISH BROADSIDE BALLAD AS SENTIMENTAL FICTION   261

52. Derek B. Scott, 'Music, Morality and Rational Amusement at the Victorian Middle-Class Soirée', in *Music and Performance Culture in Britain: Essays in Honour of Nicholas Temperley*, ed. Bennet Zon (London: Routledge, 2016), 83.
53. Ian Newman, Oskar Cox Jensen and David Kennerley, 'Introduction', in *Charles Dibdin and Late Georgian Culture*, 15. The development and depiction of the Jack Tar figure in British popular culture is too broad a topic to cover here, but I refer the reader to Isaac Land, *War, Nationalism, and the British Sailor, 1750–1850* (New York: Palgrave Macmillan, 2009); Harold F. Watson, *The Sailor in English Fiction and Drama, 1550–1800* (New York: Columbia University Press, 1931); Terrence M. Freeman, *Dramatic Representations of British Soldiers and Sailors on the London Stage, 1660–1800: Britons Strike Home* (Lewiston: E. Mellen, 1995).
54. Betty T. Bennett, *British War Poetry in the Age of Romanticism: 1793–1815* (New York: Garland, 1976), 66.
55. The song is traditionally played on the last night of the BBC Proms.
56. See Tobias Smollett, *The Adventures of Roderick Random*, ed. Paul-Gabriel Boucé (1748; Oxford: Oxford University Press, 2020), particularly 221.
57. 'Tom Bowling or the Sailor's Epitaph', Edition – Bod23092 (London: John Evans, 1791), *Broadside Ballads Online*, http://ballads.bodleian.ox.ac.uk/view/edition/23092 (accessed 16 November 2023). This song was sung by Charles Bannister at Covent Garden Theatre on 23 November 1790 as a part *of A Divertisement,* but it was previously performed as a part of *The Oddities*, which was one of Dibdin's so-called 'table entertainments', first performed at the Lyceum, 7 December 1789.
58. Smollett, *The Adventures of Roderick Random*, 221.
59. See Benedict, *Framing Feeling*.
60. 'The Heart that Feels for Another', Edition – Bod16955 (London: Jennings, 1790–1840), *Broadside Ballads Online*, http://ballads.bodleian.ox.ac.uk/view/edition/16955 (accessed 16 November 2023).
61. 'True Courage' was performed in London on 1 November 1798 in Dibdin's solo entertainment, *A Tour to the Land's End*. See Robert Fahrner, *The Theatre Career of Charles Dibdin the Elder (1745–1814)* (New York: Lang, 1989), 225, 149, and Oskar Cox Jensen, 'True Courage', 124.
62. 'True Corurage [*sic*]', Edition – Bod13826 (London: Pitts, 1819–44), *Broadside Ballads Online*, http://ballads.bodleian.ox.ac.uk/view/edition/13826 (accessed 16 November 2023).
63. See Oskar Cox Jensen, 'The Travels of John Magee', *Cultural and Social History* 11 no. 2 (2014): 195–216 (196).
64. See Oskar Cox Jensen, *The Ballad-Singer in Georgian and Victorian London* (Cambridge: Cambridge University Press, 2021), 145.
65. See Oskar Cox Jensen, 'Joseph Johnson's Hat, Or, The Storm on Tower Hill', *Studies in Romanticism* 58, no. 4 (2019): 545–69, and also Tim Hitchcock, 'Begging on the Streets of Eighteenth-Century London', *Journal of British Studies* 44, no. 3 (2005): 478–98 (496–8).
66. Oskar Cox Jensen, 'Joseph Johnson's Hat'.

15

'NOVEL ROMANCE MAKES ME PUKE!': BURNEYS, SHAKESPEARES AND THE SENTIMENTAL PLOT

Mascha Hansen

THE BURNEYS' NOVELS tend to be classified as novels of manners, and for good reasons.[1] In this essay, however, I will look at them as sentimental works in order to highlight a dilemma both Frances and Sarah Harriet Burney faced: whether to adapt or reject the language of sensibility in the attempt to impress the reader with sympathy for their protagonists' plights. As writers, both were well aware of the prevailing taste for the language of sensibility and sentimental comedy, which they condemned but made use of nonetheless: while they employed the sentimental mode on purpose to enhance the market value of their novels, they struggled – and in some instances failed – to find a different language for the emotional distress their heroes and heroines faced. Both studied other writers, and particularly Shakespeare, to find inspiration for how to carry away their audience. They reverted to eighteenth-century editions as well as productions of Shakespeare's plays: critical of the adaptations of his works that circulated in the eighteenth century, the sisters nevertheless learnt from them how to spice up their own productions for greater entertainment value. Shakespeare's craft helped them refine their techniques: by mixing pathos with humour, dramatic scenes and intertextual references, they widened the scope of the novel of manners. Shakespeare adaptations, moreover, allowed them to make use of sentimental plot elements without fully endorsing the novel of sensibility.

By the time Sarah Harriet published her first novel, *Clarentine*, in 1796 – the same year in which her sister's *Camilla* appeared – the taste for the sentimental was waning, and by the early nineteenth century the cult of sensibility had passed, as Sarah Harriet's overt ridicule in her novel *Country Neighbours* (1820) suggests.[2] At around the same time, in 1819, William Hazlitt castigated the 'endless affectation of sentiment' of Frances Burney's novels in his lecture 'On the English Novelists', but curiously, he also compared her to William Shakespeare, albeit to the credit of neither: 'It has been said of Shakespeare, that you may always assign his speeches to the proper characters; – and you may infallibly do the same thing with Mme D'Arblay's, for they always say the same thing.'[3] Yet Shakespeare, Samuel Johnson had maintained, was 'the poet that holds up to his readers a faithful mirrour of manners and of life'.[4] When reading Frances Burney's works as sentimental novels of manners, we do well to keep Johnson's Shakespeare in mind, and a Shakespeare-inspired idea of what the notion of 'manners' might actually entail.[5] The definition given by the *OED*, '[c]ustomary mode of acting or behaviour; habitual practice; usage, custom, fashion', ties the notion of manners to that of performance: doing one's manners rather than having good manners.[6]

The theatricality of Frances Burney's novels has long been noted, proof of the as yet close connection between the theatre and the novel at the time: 'many eighteenth-century readers and writers were concurrently spectators, performers, and playwrights', as Emily Hodgson Anderson puts it.[7] The novel of manners emphasises that the protagonists, and especially the heroines, are acting a part, and that they are continuously watched and rated for their performances by the other characters: in Burney's *Camilla*, for instance, the hero, Edgar, determines to watch Camilla's every move and then rejoices to find that she 'has but acted a part'.[8] Critics so far have tended to focus on the restrictions placed on characters by custom in the novel of manners rather than teasing out the opportunities for dramatic writing that the emphasis on (doing one's) manners also provides. In its stress on performance, the novel of manners is still closely attuned to the fashionable novel of sensibility, highlighting the difficulties especially women writers had with the sentimental: while trying to avoid the excesses of sentimental pathos, even considering them dangerous in real life, writers who wished to sell their novels to a contemporary readership, such as the Burneys, were rarely squeamish when it came to lifting popular sentimental plot elements or characters, such as that of the dutiful daughter reconciled to her (previously absent, estranged or imprisoned) father. Both Sarah Harriet and Frances ridiculed the language of sensibility (for example, Melmond's high-flown prose in *Camilla* or Lady Earlsford's in *Country Neighbours*), but Frances in particular struggled to describe her protagonists' emotional states, and especially feelings of sympathy, without having recourse to the language of sensibility. Even rational Edgar's 'eyes copiously overflowed with delight' (325) to show his sympathy with the heroine in *Camilla*, a performance on his part that is meant to demonstrate appropriate sensibility to the reader in a hero who might otherwise appear rather cold and phlegmatic.[9]

The terms 'sensibility' and 'sentimental' are part of a complex web of shifting meanings and often obscure significance, or, to borrow the words of Markman Ellis, 'a philosophical nightmare of muddled ideas, weak logic, and bad writing'; mostly used interchangeably, these two terms 'offer no obvious distinction'.[10] The sentimental novel is a genre characterised by various overlapping discourses, containing a mix of elements taken from other genres, and even the kinds of plots that scholars associate with it differ considerably. Patricia Meyer Spacks sees a looser plot form emerge, less reliant on providential intervention to test the hero and distribute rewards and punishments.[11] In the works focusing on female protagonists, however, providence continues to play with the heroine, rewarding and punishing both her and the reader, whose emotions are closely intertwined with her fate. The currency of tears and blushes to indicate a character's moral worth and good breeding, a dimension of sentimental novels that invites readers to visualise themselves watching a stage performance, is a typical plot element, reminiscent of sentimental comedy. At the same time, Gary Kelly notes how the female protagonist, 'a conventional figure of disempowerment', emphasises the need for the sentimental public to find a way to effect political participation while providing an opportunity for women writers to raise their voices in the public sphere.[12] Moreover, Lisa Freeman has convincingly argued that

> entry into the social order of sentimental comedy requires an act of 'submission' to the economic system that gives the social order its shape. Social status in this realm is governed by economic status as money, property, and exchange relations shape the 'reality' of sentimental comedies, circumscribing characters and motivating plots.[13]

The emergence of the sentimental novel in the eighteenth century is thus linked to broader social changes furthering the expansion of the middle classes and their commercial interests.[14]

'Sentimentalism remains polyphonic', according to Ellis, and indeed, even Shakespeare can be said to have joined the chorus, however unwittingly. On the one hand, the new, 'natural', less declamatory style of acting introduced by Garrick also required that actors concern themselves with the real-life equivalents and the historical details of their role: Garrick visited Bedlam to study inmates for his rendition of King Lear, and his fellow actor Charles Macklin studied the customs, dress and manner of Italian Jews to play Shylock.[15] On the other hand, Garrick added sentimental scenes to his stage adaptations of Shakespeare because he knew, and could not afford to ignore, what his audience wanted.[16] Sentimental plot changes and speeches in eighteenth-century productions of Shakespeare in turn influenced the Burneys' novels in ways that have not yet been teased out, touching commercial as well as authorial decisions that prove these writers to have privileged business before personal taste in some of their plot choices. Shakespeare helped them create emotional responses in their readers that were less trite than those of the common run of sentimental novels.[17] As Kate Rumbold explains, 'Shakespeare's theatricality is a vital part of his function in prose fiction', one which budding authors had to learn to exploit in their novels.[18] Reading both Burneys allows us to discern progress in women writers' use of Shakespeare's theatricality in the respectable, sentimental novel of manners.

Twenty years younger than her more famous sister, Sarah Harriet Burney (1772–1844) used Shakespeare in innovative ways to overcome some of the restrictions placed on women writers' heroines, and on their choice of plots. The youngest daughter of Dr Charles Burney, she would hardly have remembered Garrick's playful family visits, and while there are many references to Shakespeare's plays in her surviving letters, there are fewer indications of her theatregoing.[19] Fiona Ritchie and Peter Sabor have recently proved that Shakespeare's plays were central to both Burneys' writings in various ways, but it is still far from clear which versions of the plays – staged or written, adapted or 'original' – dominated their imaginations. If there seems to be more evidence for the impact of dramatic actions in the case of Frances, and more evidence for the influence of Shakespeare on plot decisions in Sarah Harriet's works, as Ritchie and Sabor claim, that difference may reflect the changes in 'proper' Shakespeare appreciation that began to dominate at the turn of the century.[20] Changes to Shakespeare's 'original' text had become dubious by 1811, and 'a new way of reading Shakespeare had appeared', the focus now being on the printed text rather than the (text in) performance.[21] By the end of the century, exploiting Shakespeare to arouse readers' attention was no longer an easy feat: as Kate Rumbold has argued, the use of Shakespearean quotations in contemporary novels had descended into banality, especially through the ubiquitous availability of selections such as William Dodd's *The Beauties of Shakespear*, published in 1752 and reprinted through the rest of the century. These little helpers allowed all and sundry to quote Shakespeare without having 'properly' read his plays.[22] Novelists were aware of the danger of overusing Shakespeare: novel techniques as well as a certain finesse were now required when handling his work to vitalise characters and plot.

Eighteenth-century productions of Shakespeare served various purposes which we no longer recognise as Shakespearean now. To Michael Dobson, successful mid-eighteenth-century adaptations such as Garrick's *Florizel and Perdita* (1758) 'present a domestic

Shakespeare who is at the same time eminently patriotic, identified at once with virtuous family life, vigorous trade, and British glory'.[23] The Shakespeare performed at the time was made to suit an eighteenth-century ideal, and the text was accordingly adapted to contemporary taste: characters were added, new scenes introduced and musical parts invented.[24] Both seventeenth- and eighteenth-century adaptations of Shakespeare's plays emphasised women's roles, even adding female characters (especially servants) and extra speeches. Yet while the seventeenth century's female parts, to quote Jean Marsden, were made 'to suffer helplessly and to act as erotic objects', the eighteenth century redefined Shakespeare's women in a more sentimental mode as loving, loyal and long-suffering wives and daughters.[25] Frances and Sarah Burney were familiar with the heavily abridged and even largely rewritten stage versions as well as the Folio texts, as edited by various scholars and poets at the time, and thus with the full Shakespearean canon that was part of eighteenth-century culture.[26] Both frequently used the sentimental father–daughter–lover plots which were a hallmark of eighteenth-century adaptations of Shakespeare's plays. Moreover, they were well aware of the need to show that their protagonists could attend to his plays with the appropriate amount of sensibility in their responses, as witnessed especially by their heroines.[27] The use of staple plot elements, in the Burneys' case, is not to be confused with hackneyed storytelling: both found ways to enliven their father–daughter plots to highlight the plight of women in contemporary society, for instance by using Shakespearean techniques and plot devices, as evinced by the frequently dramatic nature of their scenes. Marsden has outlined how eighteenth-century Shakespeare adaptations conjoined 'daughterly duty and national identity' so that '[t]he bond between father and daughter becomes a necessary pillar of patriarchy'.[28] The insistence on a daughter's duty in these adaptations of Shakespeare's plays had reverberations for the novels of the period, too: filial duty remained paramount, especially in the case of daughters. And yet for all the emphasis on the father–daughter plot, Jenny Davidson points out that during the eighteenth century, heroines began to resemble their mothers rather than their fathers, and that Shakespeare's plays were rewritten accordingly, as in Garrick's adaptation of *The Winter's Tale*. In Shakespeare's version, it is necessary that Perdita should look like her father, but in Garrick's *Florizel and Perdita*, Perdita looks like her mother.[29] In *Evelina* (1778), the heroine's resemblance to her mother is of vital importance to convince her father of his error, and reinstate her as the rightful daughter in a lengthy scene that is mostly made up of dialogue, with Evelina showing rather than telling how their complex emotional states unfold during the first and second 'unspeakably painful' meetings.[30]

Appropriating Shakespeare: Frances Burney and the Heroine as Cordelia

Most, but by no means all, quotations in Frances's novels are from plays that were popular on the eighteenth-century stage: *Romeo and Juliet*, *Richard III*, *Hamlet*, *King Lear*, *Othello*, *The Merchant of Venice*. She also quotes from plays that were less well known, but she seems to do so in her diaries with more frequency than in her novels, indicating that she envisioned an audience familiar with the spoken rather than the written Shakespeare. Stumbling across a Shakespeare quotation in Frances Burney's novels, then, we can never be quite sure whether we are to think primarily of a textual reference to a play Burney assumed her audience would have read, or a reference to a public performance which she assumed her audience would have seen, and in which a particular actor or actress had spoken that line in a memorable way.[31]

Frances did not relish the sentimental adaptations of Shakespeare's plays, and this may be a reason why her novels seem to waver between endorsing the sentimental plot and rejecting it. She voiced her dislike of both seventeenth- and eighteenth-century adaptations in her diaries, dismissing both John Dryden's *The Tempest, or The Enchanted Isle* (1667) and the 1773 version of *King Lear*, despite her admiration of Garrick's performance in it:

> We had yesterday the – I know not whether to say *pain* or *pleasure*, – of seeing Mr Garrick in the part of Lear. He was exquisitely Great . . . [but] I am sorry that this play is acted with Cibber's Alterations, as every Line of his, is immediately to be distinguished from Shakespeare, – who, with all his imperfections, is too superiour to any other Dramatic Writer, for them to bear so near a comparison: & to my Ears, every Line of Cibber's, is feeble & paltry.[32]

Lars Troide points out that Burney is partly mistaken: Cibber adapted *Richard III* but not *Lear*, and the play acted was in fact Garrick's adaptation (1768) of Nahum Tate's adaptation (1681) of *King Lear*.[33] Garrick gradually replaced many of the lines Tate himself had added to the play with lines actually written by Shakespeare.[34] His new versions of *King Lear* (he adapted it several times) were hugely successful, not least because they tapped into the taste for sentimental pathos that his audience had developed through novel reading: spectators wept openly and copiously throughout.[35] Yet even though his audience began to get used to original Shakespeare again, Garrick kept most of the plot changes that Tate introduced, such as the love scenes in which especially Cordelia is given more prominence.[36] From the start, Cordelia makes it clear that she must displease her father since she is in love with Edgar while Lear wants her to marry Burgundy. Garrick's version does cut down on the love plot a little to keep the focus on Lear instead, but eventually, Cordelia is united with the hero in a happy ending. These love scenes, while they do not at all resemble Shakespeare's, are reminiscent of the meetings between Burney's own heroes and heroines: Tate's Edgar pleads his love with becoming modesty, and Cordelia graciously accepts his vows – as do Burney's Edgar and Camilla, Orville and Evelina.

Burney may have disliked the additional scenes, but she does not say so; instead, she objects to the speeches. It is interesting to note that most of the lines written by Tate that Garrick kept are extra speeches given to Cordelia. Cordelia fits into the current dramatic vogue particularly well: according to Marsden, 'pathos as a dramatic device' pervades eighteenth-century plays, and 'the object of this pathos is almost inevitably a woman' – a virtuous woman in distress. Love plots were usually added to enhance women's roles (and sex appeal), Marsden continues, requiring 'a wholesale revision' of Shakespeare's heroines.[37] Tate's additions to *King Lear* are a case in point: audiences relished the pathos of a suffering daughter torn between her lover and her father. This new Cordelia nonetheless evinces quite some strength in her apparent helplessness, calling 'For an arm / Like the fierce Thunderer's when the earth-born sons / Storm'd Heav'n, to fight this injur'd father's battle!' in a monologue Tate first inserted.[38] 'Cordelia's scene has great merit', the editor of Garrick's version, Francis

Plate 1 *Roxana in her Turkish Habit*. Probably an illustration to an abridgement of Daniel Defoe's *The Fortunate Mistress*, entitled *The Life and Adventures of Roxana* (London, 1765?). Engraving. ART file R886 no. 1, Folger Shakespeare Library.

Plate 2 Thomas Daniell, *Old Government House* (1788), in *Views of Calcutta*, Plate 10. Aquatint. © The Trustees of the British Museum.

Plate 3 Stourhead Garden (author's photograph).

Plate 4 Peter Lely, *Portrait of a young woman and child, as Venus and Cupid, almost certainly Nell Gwyn (1650–87)* (mid-1660s). 48¾ x 61¾ in. (123.8 x 156.8 cm). Public domain, via Wikimedia Commons.

Plate 5 Jean-Antoine Watteau, *Pèlerinage à l'île de Cythère*, or *L'embarquement pour Cythère* (*The Embarkation for Cythera*), 1717, 50.7 x 76.3 in (120 x 190 cm). Musée du Louvre. Public domain, via Wikimedia Commons.

Plate 6 Thomas Gainsborough (British, 1727–88), *The Mall in St. James's Park* (c.1783). Oil on canvas, 47 1/2 x 57 7/8 in. (120.7 x 147 cm). The Frick Collection, New York. Photo: Joseph Coscia Jr. Copyright The Frick Collection.

Plate 7 Thomas Gainsborough, *Elizabeth and Mary Linley* (c.1772; retouched 1785). Oil on canvas, 199 x 153.5 cm. Dulwich Picture Gallery. Public domain, via Wikimedia Commons.

Plate 8 Thomas Gainsborough, *Mrs. Richard Brinsley Sheridan* (1785–87). Oil on canvas, 219.7 x 153.7 cm. Andrew W. Mellon Collection. Courtesy National Gallery of Art, Washington.

Plate 9 Thomas Gainsborough, *Mrs. Mary Robinson (Perdita)* (1781). Oil on canvas, 233.7 x 153 cm. The Wallace Collection. Public domain, via Wikimedia Commons.

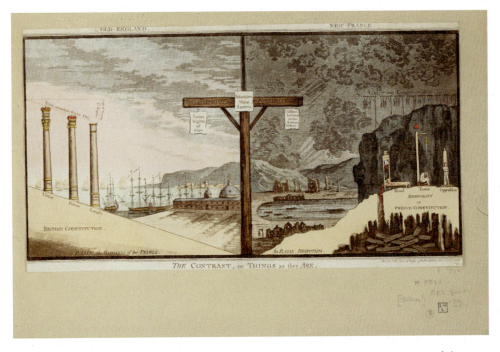

Plate 10 James Gillray, *The Contrast, or Things as they Are* (1796). Courtesy of the Lewis Walpole Library, Yale University.

Plate 11 Marcus Geeraerts the Younger, *Henry Cary, 1st Viscount Falkland* (c.1603). Oil on canvas. Sarah Campbell Blaffer Foundation, Houston.

Plate 12 Watercolour copy of Jacopo Ligozzi's portrait of Bianca Capello. LWL SH Contents Un58 no. 16 Box 120. Courtesy of the Lewis Walpole Library, Yale University.

Plate 13 William Hogarth, *William Wollaston and his Family in a Grand Interior* (1730). Oil on canvas. New Walk Museum and Art Gallery, Leicester. Public domain, via Wikimedia Commons.

Plate 14 Silkwork of *Charlotte at the Tomb of Werter*, late eighteenth century. Reproduced from the copy in the author's collection.

Plate 15 Silkwork of *Charlotte at the Tomb of Werter*, late eighteenth century. Reproduced courtesy of Needlework Antiques.

Plate 16 Silkwork of *Charlotte at the Tomb of Werter*, late eighteenth century. Reproduced from the copy in the author's collection.

Plate 17 Silkwork *Charlotte at the Tomb of Werter*, late eighteenth century. Reproduced, with permission, from the copy in the Collection of the Museum of Early Southern Decorative Arts (MESDA).

Plate 18 Silkwork of *Charlotte at the Tomb of Werter*, late eighteenth century. Reproduced from the copy in the author's collection.

Plate 19 Silkwork of *Charlotte at the Tomb of Werter*, early nineteenth century. Reproduced from the copy in the author's collection.

Plate 20 Silkwork of *Charlotte at the Tomb of Werter*, early nineteenth century. Reproduced from the copy in the author's collection.

Plate 21 Silkwork of Poor Maria, late eighteenth century. Reproduced from the copy in the author's collection.

Plate 22 Hand-coloured print, folded within the front endpapers of Comerford's *Voyage to Lethe* (1741): T. P. Hydrographer [Pseud.], *A Map or Chart of the Road of Love, and Harbour of Marriage* (1748, amended by hand to '1741'). British Library General Reference Collection Cup.1001.c.4. By permission of the British Library.

Plate 23 Johann Michael Voltz, *Der neue Robinson auf der einsamen Ratten Insel im Süd-Meere St Helena genannt* (c.1815–16). G27593. © Paris Musées. Musée Carnavalet – Histoire de Paris.

Plate 24 Udo J. Keppler Jr, *Robinson Crusoe Fairbanks*, cover for *Puck*, vol. 58, no. 1505, 3 January 1906. © Library of Congress Prints and Photographs Division.

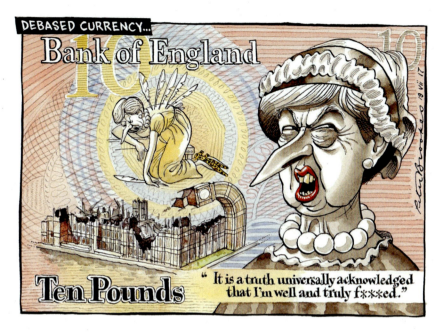

Plate 25 Peter Brookes, *Debased Currency*, *The Times*, 19 July 2017. Courtesy of Peter Brookes.

Plate 26 John Baldessari, *The Life and Opinions of Tristram Shandy, Gentleman* (San Francisco: Arion Press, 1988). © John Baldessari 1988. Courtesy Estate of John Baldessari © 2023. Courtesy of Sprüth Magers.

Plate 27 Meg Cranston, *The Complete Works of Jane Austen* (1991). Artspace. Courtesy of Meg Cranston.

Plate 28 Paul Chan, *Font Drawings* (2008). Ink on paper, 84 x 54 inches each. Courtesy of the artist and Greene Naftali, New York.

Gentleman, approvingly commented.[39] Garrick's Cordelia still speaks much more than Shakespeare's, but Cordelia's new lines weaken the impact of her short 'Nothing, my lord' in the very first scene: her stark refusal to say what her father wants her to say. Not surprisingly, the editor felt he had to add a note here, too, anxiously pointing out that Cordelia is not rebellious but merely showing her 'silent modesty' in her inability to speak.[40] Cordelia, far from being able to differentiate between a tyrannical request and the need to speak up for herself, is allowed to speak only to rouse the audience's emotional response. Evelina, in turn, watches Garrick play, but on coming home, the usually eloquent heroine can only laconically note that it has made her very sad – despite the fact that Garrick kept Cordelia alive, a change even Samuel Johnson endorsed.[41]

Marsden contends that 'the power of Lear's pathos was attributed not to his position as fallen king but almost universally to his position as wronged father'.[42] The father–daughter relationship is central to the plot of *Evelina*, and the public entertainment provided by Garrick's version of *Lear* may point to the fact that Burney consciously exploited this relation in her novel. Several critics, notably Margaret Anne Doody, have discussed Frances Burney's use of, and changes to, the sentimental father–daughter plot in her novels and plays, linking the choice to her close connection with, reverence for and occasional resentment of her own father.[43] Lorna Clark notes how both Frances and Sarah Harriet rely on similar plot elements, with the sentimental staple, the long-lost daughter, a favourite of both.[44] Both focus on the young heroine about to find her role in life at the side of a promising partner, a search that is hampered by the demands of a patriarchal father figure – a character type typical of the sentimental novel – but ultimately happily resolved in mutual understanding and acceptance.[45] Yet in their focus on the Burney daughters' relations with their own father, critics have somewhat neglected to look at the public interest *Evelina*'s sentimental attitude satisfies. The prolonged reconciliation scene engulfed her readers, and it is quite possible that Frances uses this sentimental insistence on the father–daughter plot – represented on various levels of the novel if Evelina's guardian, or second father, Mr Villars, is taken into account – to imitate the success of other sentimental productions, notably those on stage.

Cordelia's plight on finding her father incarcerated also seems to foreshadow Camilla's distress when she hears that her father is in prison.[46] *Camilla* uses comparatively few Shakespearean quotes, but continuously evokes the reader's knowledge of his plays. Thus, while Camilla herself is impervious to Major Cerwood's wooing her with 'the tenderest lines of Romeo' (never specified), the hero hears him only to blame Camilla for allowing the Major's passionate declarations of love, which 'passed off as quotations' (262–3). *Camilla*'s most notable Shakespeare adaptation, the 'disastrous Buskins' playing *Othello*, is about Shakespeare's language 'deformed' in the mouths of speakers using their regional dialects, and Shakespeare's tragedy is inadvertently turned into a comedy that Camilla, for one, finds wondrously entertaining. Burney includes a substantial thirty-three lines from the play, some of which she slightly misquotes, suggesting that – as usual – she quotes from memory, but her reading seems to have been based on Johnson's edition: for example, Othello's 'beseech you let her vill [will] / Have a free vay [way]', in Q1 but not in the Folio, is given in Johnson.[47] Desdemona's speech balancing the duty she owes to her father with that she owes to her husband is burlesqued next – a speech that, properly performed, would have been bound to please an eighteenth-century audience; Francis Gentleman commends it in a little note appended to Bell's edition: 'There is a beautiful degree of modest confidence in this delicate speech.'[48] It is surely no coincidence that the lines quoted end with Brabantio's aspersion on his daughter, 'A haz deceiv'd 'ur veather, and may thee.—' (320), but this mangled version takes the sting out of his prediction: Desdemona does not have to die in this particularly unsentimental adaptation.

Camilla's pathos was to be alternated with laughter, even horse laughter such as that provoked by the performance of *Othello*. Yet the very lines chosen from *Othello* in the 'original' appeal to the sentimental nature of audiences, and it is the sentimental that Burney chooses to make fun of here. This paradoxical stance runs through the novel, with the demands placed on the reader to sympathise with the youthful Camilla's errors in the language of sentimental pathos interspersed with injunctions not to credit the language of sensibility. There is space for proper sentimentality, Burney seems to suggest, and there is dangerous sensibility, but it is not quite clear where the one ends and the other begins. *Camilla* is a novel about distrust, jealousy and misunderstandings, but it is also a novel about performances: all the characters keep watching each other, and Camilla perpetually schemes in the best comic fashion how to win (back) her beloved – reminiscent of Hannah Cowley's *The Belle's Stratagem* (1780).[49] As Edward and Lillian Bloom surmise in their edition of the novel, Burney had meant to exploit her readers' propensity for sensibility by making them cry at tender scenes – a strategy that had previously paid off: readers had wept copiously over Evelina's tender reunion with her father and *Cecilia*'s conclusion.[50]

Burney's *Evelina* is frequently cited as an example of the novel's reinforcement of notions of filial duty so important to the age.[51] In her other works, however, Frances makes use of Shakespeare to rewrite the father–daughter bond and its patriarchal implications; for instance, she evokes *Romeo and Juliet* in *Cecilia* (1782), the plot of which hinges on a surname, to show that parental authority must have limits. Critics have noted Burney's sentimental rewriting of the play's ending here, but this, of course, is how eighteenth-century adaptations such as Garrick's had refashioned this play, and what audiences had begun to demand by force of habit. Cecilia is allowed to marry Delvile, a hero who quotes Romeo, admittedly using a rather well-known quotation ('He jests at scars') such as might be found in one of the popular anthologies of the day, making him a more 'banal' character than the heroine.[52] For Cecilia to be happy, however, another heroine has to die: Anderson points out the emotional importance of the story of Albany's lost fiancée, a fallen woman who starves herself to death, refusing to speak.[53]

Melissa Sodeman avers that by the beginning of the nineteenth century, novels such as Frances Burney's *The Wanderer* (1814), which adhered to the sentimental cast of the 'identity-mystery romance', were beginning to feel anachronistic, '[i]nvoking the novel's sentimental past at a moment when everybody else had moved on'.[54] Burney's last novel, which centres on a 'lost daughter' plot but does not present a sentimental reunion between father and daughter (albeit providing an uncle–daughter and a guardian–daughter reunion), does link the novel's sentimental past to the stage: the heroine, Ellis/Juliet, appears as Lady Townly in Cibber's *The Provok'd Husband* (1728, after Vanbrugh) in a privately staged play. While Burney tries to defend her heroine from the accusation of being a consummate actress – her powers are due to 'nature . . . not art that strove to be displayed' – the narrator goes on to evoke 'the attributes of good acting' in a self-reflective passage on the powers of both the author and the hero who fail to live up to the part they might have performed:

> That address, which gives life and meaning to every phrase; that ingenuity, which beguiles the audience into an illusion, which, for the current moment, inspires the sympathy due to reality; that skill which brings forth on the very instant, all the effect which, to the closet reader, an author can hope to produce from reflection . . . were now . . . beyond his reach, though within his powers.[55]

The Provok'd Husband was considered a sentimental comedy at the time, and the un-Shakesperean Juliet's 'serious, penitent, and pathetic' performance in the last act has the audience in sympathetic tears, due more to her 'penetrating countenance' than the 'words of the author'.[56] Perhaps Burney had still not forgiven Colley Cibber for mangling Shakespeare.

Plotting Shakespeare: Sarah Harriet Burney and the Heroine as Lear

'I cannot define [the only sort of sentimentality I like], but one of the appellations I would give it, would be that of genuine, and really virtuous & good sentimentality. Nervous hippishness is quite another thing – And Novel Romance makes me puke!', Sarah Harriet told her niece Charlotte Barrett in 1811.[57] She disclaimed any personal interest in the love stories she felt obliged to write: 'if I could give them humour and wit, however, I should make bold to skip the love'.[58] As she reminded her niece, she was writing for a literary market which craved love plots. Lorna Clark notes how diffident the younger Burney was with regard to her own writing, and that, to borrow Sarah Harriet's own words, 'scribbling by trade' to her seemed 'very ungenteel'; and yet she had to scribble to improve her scant income of about £100 per annum. She did have a nose for business, as Clark remarks: 'The only aspect of her work of which she speaks with unabashed enthusiasm is the money that she makes.'[59] Sarah Harriet's early work, *Clarentine* (1796), relies on the heroine's modest sentimental blushing to indicate her moral worth, but lacks a plot: not surprisingly, the book did not cut ice with a readership that was already hooked on the action-driven Gothic feasts of Ann Radcliffe. Her second publication, *Geraldine Fauconberg* (1808), accordingly contains a Gothic interlude to please the market or the circulating libraries, but as in *Camilla* there is too much reliance on the doubts in each other's feelings by the fastidious hero, Ferdinand (a name that links him to *The Tempest*), and the eponymous heroine, to keep tension alive over three volumes.[60] Both works make ample use of Shakespearean quotations in the manner described by Kate Rumbold, demonstrating Sarah Harriet's excellent knowledge of his works.

Whatever their flaws, Sarah Harriet's novels were not unsuccessful. For her third work, *Traits of Nature* (1812), she negotiated a substantial £50 per volume.[61] This novel, too, revolves around a sentimental father–daughter plot, and, as Lorna Clark writes, the novel 'conveys, powerfully, a sense of emotional rejection' on the part of the heroine during the scenes in which she suffers from her father's disapproval.[62] The plot of the novel does not stray far from the path of Sarah Harriet's earlier publications, but she makes a few striking moves: not only does the heroine's divorced mother fall for an impostor and into alcoholism, the hero also marries the wrong girl. In addition, Sarah Harriet wrote a 'prologue': the first few chapters deal entirely with Shakespeare, here evoked to characterise the heroine's guardian. Dr Hampden is an early example of the Victorian country physician, with one unusual trait: an 'ungovernable passion for reading'.[63] Burney uses an episode in which Dr Hampden borrows some volumes of a new edition of Shakespeare as an opportunity to insert a brief discussion of different editions of his works, and to demonstrate her own critical knowledge to the reader through Dr Hampden's instruction of his ignorant wife.[64] We do not learn which edition Hampden has obtained, but there may be a subtle nod to Johnson's version in the choice of play, *Henry IV, Part 1*; in his *Preface to Shakespeare* (1765), after all, Johnson claimed that 'None of Shakespeare's plays are more read than the First and Second Parts of Henry the Fourth'.[65] From now on, neither wife nor children have any power to disturb Hampden in what turns out to be a glowing picture of proper Shakespeare (re)reading:

> at every page, enraptured by the flashes of genius, the sublime morality, or the sterling wit of the sentiments and expressions; – bewitched by the interest of the tale, which, as he read with scrupulous and unbroken continuity, gradually unfolded itself, – he was being transported into another world – and descried, or fancied he every moment descried, new beauties, which had never struck him before.[66]

The unfolding tale is to be read rather than watched, and to be savoured, but that Sarah Harriet kept the stage in mind is made obvious in what follows: not only does the reader watch Hampden's performance of reading Shakespeare, the father's absorption also intrigues the children in the room. They place a cat on his lap and, as expected, it devours the doctor's tea and toast, much to the delight of the audience.[67] Reading Shakespeare, Dr Hampden has himself been cast as a comic part in an impromptu play.

The link between reading and performing Shakespeare clearly intrigued Sarah Harriet. Unlike Frances, she was a great fan of 'sweet Mrs Siddons': in 1810, she went to see Siddons in a performance of King John, where she was 'magnificent' as Constance, and 'for a week after, [Sarah] could do nothing but read Shakespeare'.[68] Indeed, the spectacle of the respectable Sarah Siddons playing Hamlet (repeatedly over three decades from 1775 to 1805) may have encouraged Sarah Harriet to take up the topic of cross-dressing in a novella, *The Shipwreck*, and it is here that we can see the influence of the Shakespearean heroine most clearly. In *The Shipwreck* – the first volume of her *Tales of Fancy* (1816) – Sarah Harriet merges at least two of Shakespeare's plays, *The Tempest* and *Twelfth Night*, with the usual sentimental plot involving a father–daughter conflict.[69] This time, the daughter – named Viola – and her mother are on their way to Bengal, where Viola is due to marry a man of her father's choice, when their ship is torn asunder in a violent storm. They manage to reach an island and find shelter in a simple cave. Unlike Prospero, however, Lady Earlingford cannot assure her daughter that no harm was done, and Viola continues to hear 'the dreadful cries of the drowning wretches in the vessel'.[70] There seem to be no other survivors, but a day later a chest washes up on shore containing, among other classics, Shakespeare's plays, 'bound in a single volume' (44). Viola, like Dr Hampden, is 'passionately fond of books', and reads as if she were watching a sentimental stage production: 'she hoped or desponded, wept or exulted in sympathy with the supposed feelings of which she read, and in happy oblivion of all that related to self' (44). The chest besides contains the clothes of Viola's male cousin, who had left the ship before the storm. Once they find that they are not alone on the island, Lady Earlingford persuades her daughter to don male attire, cut her hair and pretend that she is her own male cousin: a rare instance of cross-dressing in a tale intended for a respectable readership. What is more, Viola's mother openly hints at the threat of rape.[71] In this case, her fears prove to be unfounded, though the other survivor is a young gentleman.[72] Disguised as a young man herself, Viola is free to roam the island with this hero, Fitz Aymer, in an obvious parallel to *Twelfth Night*. Only on finally being able to leave the island does Viola change back into women's clothes (313), and six pages are then devoted to explaining the hero's surprise: apparently Fitz Aymer had felt attached to Viola without particularly noticing her appearance, but now he finds that even her voice has changed. He quotes Lear's words to Cordelia – still alive at this point in Garrick's version – 'ever soft / Gentle, and low – an excellent thing in a woman', realigning the heroine with the dutiful daughter that Viola, at present, is not (320). On the journey home, the hero tries to persuade her to get married without her father's blessing but she refuses, and although Fitz Aymer's friend advises him that 'the best pledge a woman can give of her intention to make a good wife, is that of performing the part of a good daughter' (330). Fitz Aymer, an unsentimental hero, is not convinced by 'all these axioms of duty and submission' (331). Viola's fears of her father's disapproval prove to be without foundation in the anti-climax to this stirring tale. However, she does become a truly sentimental heroine when she believes herself forsaken by the hero during a second storm. The narrator evokes Lear's ravings and, like him, the heroine no longer heeds the actual storm. Burney seems to be quoting the play from memory: 'The tempest in her mind / Did from her senses take all feelings else / Save what beat there' (247), applying Shakespeare's words to the heroine by changing the pronouns to highlight the performative drama of this scene. The emphasis on the sufferings of love experienced by the heroine aligns the novel with the pathetic tradition: Burney depicts a raging pain rather than the mind-numbing tears of sentimental lovelornness. Yet Viola is only mistaken, and, perhaps to warn her readers not to give in to sensibility, Burney refuses to build on a scene that might have had more interesting repercussions for the heroine.

To conclude, eighteenth-century notions of propriety and Shakespearean heroines do not necessarily make for a happy blend, as Sarah Harriet Burney's novels prove. Yet Burney not only studied Shakespeare's heroines, she also copied his dramatic art, quickening the pace and intensity of her later novels. To her, it is the ability to read Shakespeare properly – with absorption, like Dr Hampden in *Traits of Nature*, like Viola in *The Shipwreck*, or aloud like the hero Tremayne in *Country Neighbours* – that is the ultimate test of character. If the sentimental novel of manners relied on a reaffirmation of social order and the link between property and propriety, it also provided women writers, such as Frances and Sarah Harriet Burney, with an entry to the literary marketplace, and Shakespeare, in various ways, supported them in this effort. The novel of manners does not provide 'a faithful mirrour of manners and of life', but like the sentimental novel its aesthetics similarly revolve around the 'trope of inexpressibility' that is resolved by showing, rather than telling, what is felt: *doing* manners, even if these are restrained by an idealised notion of politeness – Othello's 'tyrant custom'.[73] Writing the sentimental novel without the language of sensibility requires the genius of

Shakespeare – or, as Sarah Harriet's next work, *Country Neighbours* (1820), suggests, that of Jane Austen. But hereby hangs another tale.

Notes

1. See, for instance, Patricia Meyer Spacks, *Novel Beginnings: Experiments in Eighteenth-Century English Fiction* (New Haven and London: Yale University Press, 2006), 168. The boundaries between the sentimental novel and the novel of manners are blurred: compare Frank Ellis's secondary characteristics of sentimental comedy, which can all be found in the novel of manners, too: 'B1: tender melancholy Conversation, B2: Reckless, self-sacrificing virtue, B3: Undeserved distress, B4: Overt moralizing'. Frank Ellis, *Sentimental Comedy: Theory and Practice* (Cambridge: Cambridge University Press, 1991), 20–1.
2. In *Country Neighbours*, Sarah Harriet pokes fun at the hero's mother, Lady Earlsford, 'the only decidedly romantic, soft, heroine-like fine lady' in the neighbourhood, and her sentimental attitudes. Sarah Harriet Burney, *Country Neighbours*, in *Tales of Fancy*, 3 vols (London: Henry Colburn, 1816–20), 2:209.
3. William Hazlitt, 'On the English Novelists', in *The Complete Works of William Hazlitt*, 21 vols, ed. P. P. Howe (London and Toronto: J. M. Dent, 1931), 6:124. Samuel Johnson denied Alexander Pope's claim that 'every speech may be assigned to its proper speaker' in his *Preface to Shakespeare* (1765). *The Johnson–Steevens Edition of the Plays of William Shakespeare*, intr. Nick Groom (London and Tokyo: Routledge/Thoemmes, 1995), 1:6.
4. Johnson, *Preface*, 4.
5. Johnson gave various definitions of 'manner' in the *Dictionary of the English Language* (1755); see '2. Custom; habit; fashion', for which he cites the New Testament, and 'Mien; cast of the look', for which his example is taken from Samuel Richardson's *Clarissa* (174). Samuel Johnson, *Dictionary of the English Language*, https://johnsonsdictionaryonline.com/views/search.php?term=manner (accessed 16 November 2023). Compare the entry in Hester Lynch Piozzi's *British Synonymy*, where 'good manners' are similarly equated with 'showing'. Hester Piozzi, *British Synonymy; or, An Attempt at Regulating the Choice of Words in Familiar Conversation* (London: G. G. and J. Robinson, 1794), 261.
6. *OED*, s.v. 'manner', https://www.oed.com/view/Entry/113569?redirectedFrom=manner& (accessed 16 November 2023).
7. Emily Hodgson Anderson, *Eighteenth-Century Authorship and the Play of Fiction: Novels and the Theatre* (New York: Routledge, 2009), 3. Anderson comments on Frances Burney's 'intense, vexed personal investment in the theatre . . . what Burney found attractive about the theater was exactly what she found problematic about it' (46–7). For the links between heroines and actresses in Burney's works, see also Nora Nachumi, *Acting Like a Lady: British Women Novelists and the Eighteenth-Century Theater* (New York: AMS Press, 2008). For a discussion of Burney's theatrical novels, see Francesca Saggini, *Backstage in the Novel: Frances Burney and the Theater Arts*, trans. Laura Kopp (Charlottesville: University of Virginia Press, 2012).
8. Frances Burney, *Camilla, or A Picture of Youth*, ed. Edward A. Bloom and Lillian D. Bloom (1796; Oxford: Oxford University Press (1999), 299. Further references parenthetical.
9. Leaving the age of sensibility behind, Burney struggled to excise sentimentalisms from *Camilla* as late as 1836; see Bloom and Bloom, 'Introduction' to Frances Burney, *Camilla*, xxv.
10. Markman Ellis, *The Politics of Sensibility: Race, Gender and Commerce in the Sentimental Novel* (Cambridge: Cambridge University Press, 1996), 7.
11. Patricia Meyer Spacks, *Desire and Truth: Functions of Plot in Eighteenth-Century English Novels* (Chicago: University of Chicago Press, 1990), 116, 131.

BURNEYS, SHAKESPEARES AND THE SENTIMENTAL PLOT

12. Gary Kelly, 'The Sentimental Novel and Politics', in *The Sentimental Novel in the Eighteenth Century*, ed. Albert J. Riveiro (Cambridge: Cambridge University Press, 2019), 26.
13. Lisa Freeman, *Character's Theater: Genre and Identity on the Eighteenth-Century English Stage* (Philadelphia: University of Pennsylvania Press, 2002), 202–3.
14. See also Ellis, *The Politics of Sensibility*, 17.
15. Saggini, *Backstage in the Novel*, 88. Frances Burney was familiarised with productions of Shakespeare plays first and foremost by David Garrick, a staunch Burney family friend. This may explain her later objection to Mrs Siddons's quite different style. See Fiona Ritchie and Peter Sabor, 'Part of an Englishwoman's Constitution: Frances Burney, Sarah Harriet Burney, and Shakespeare', *Women's Writing* 28, no. 3 (2021): 324; Linda Engel, 'Close Encounters: Frances Burney, Actresses, and Models for Female Celebrity', *The Burney Journal* 12 (2012): 12–14. For Garrick's innovative acting style, see, for example, Peter Thompson, 'Acting and Actors from Garrick to Kean', in *The Cambridge Companion to British Theatre, 1730–1830*, ed. Jane Moody and Daniel O'Quin (Cambridge: Cambridge University Press, 2007), 3–20.
16. For instance, in *The Winter's Tale*; see Vanessa Cunningham, *Shakespeare and Garrick* (Cambridge: Cambridge University Press, 2008), 85.
17. Ellis, *The Politics of Sensibility*, 3.
18. Kate Rumbold, *Shakespeare and the Eighteenth-Century Novel: Cultures of Quotation from Samuel Richardson to Jane Austen* (Cambridge: Cambridge University Press, 2016), 77.
19. That Sarah Harriet, too, at least occasionally went to see plays is evinced by a report she made to her niece, Charlotte Barrett, of having seen *King John* in 1810, in which Mrs Siddons 'was Magnificent'. *The Letters of Sarah Harriet Burney*, ed. Lorna J. Clark (Athens and London: University of Georgia Press, 1997), 116. Sarah Harriet's vision must have been very good, since she adds a drawing of Mrs Siddons's mouth when pronouncing the word 'Coward'.
20. Ritchie and Sabor, 'Part of an Englishwoman's Constitution', 234. For a detailed discussion of Shakespeare's influence on the eighteenth-century novel, see, for example, Michael Dobson, *The Making of the National Poet: Shakespeare, Adaptation, and Authorship, 1660–1769* (Oxford: Clarendon Press, 1992); Thomas Keymer, 'Shakespeare in the Novel', *Shakespeare in the Eighteenth Century*, ed. Fiona Ritchie and Peter Sabor (Cambridge: Cambridge University Press, 2012), 118–39; Michael Caines, *Shakespeare and the Eighteenth Century* (Oxford: Oxford University Press, 2013); Rumbold, *Shakespeare and the Eighteenth-Century Novel*.
21. Cunningham, *Shakespeare and Garrick*, 167.
22. Rumbold, *Shakespeare and the Eighteenth-Century Novel*, 24, 106ff; cf. Caines, *Shakespeare and the Eighteenth Century*, 124ff.
23. Dobson, *The Making of the National Poet*, 187.
24. Jean I. Marsden, 'Daddy's Girls: Shakespearean Daughters and Eighteenth-Century Ideology', *Shakespeare Survey* 51 (1998): 18.
25. Marsden, 'Daddy's Girls', 19.
26. Dr Charles Burney owned seven editions of Shakespeare's works by the time he died in 1840. See Ritchie and Sabor, 'Part of an Englishwoman's Constitution', 323.
27. Fiona Ritchie, *Women and Shakespeare in the Eighteenth Century* (Cambridge: Cambridge University Press, 2014), 168–9.
28. Marsden, 'Daddy's Girls', 19–20.
29. David Garrick, *Florizel and Perdita: A Dramatic Pastoral* (London: Tonson, 1758), 52. Jenny Davidson, 'Why Girls Look Like their Mothers: David Garrick Rewrites', in *Shakespeare and the Eighteenth Century*, ed. Peter Sabor and Paul Yachnin (New York: Routledge, 2016), 168.

30. Frances Burney, *Evelina, or The History of a Young Lady's Entrance into the World*, ed. Steward J. Cooke (1778; New York and London: W. W. Norton, 1998), 308, 318.
31. Thus, even in 1820, Sarah Harriet assumed her audience knew what she meant when she wrote 'in the words of Garrick' – presumably a reference to George Farquhar's *The Beaux' Stratagem* – in *Country Neighbours*, 2:225. Burney might have been influenced by Garrick's appearances as Romeo, as Janice Farrar Thaddeus surmises in *Frances Burney: A Literary Life* (Basingstoke and London: Macmillan, 2000), 79; but since Garrick had already given up playing Romeo in 1760, that seems unlikely. See Peter Holland, 'The Age of Garrick', in *Shakespeare: An Illustrated Stage History*, ed. Jonathan Bate and Russell Johnson (Oxford: Oxford University Press, 1996), 79.
32. *The Early Journals and Letters of Fanny Burney*, ed. Lars E. Troide and Stewart J. Cooke, 5 vols (Kingston and Montreal: McGill-Queen's University Press, 1988–2012), 1:242, 3:393.
33. *Early Journals and Letters*, ed. Troide and Cooke, 1:242 and note.
34. For a more detailed discussion of Tate's changes, see Naomi Klein Maguire, 'Nahum Tate's King Lear: "The King's Blest Restoration"', in *The Appropriation of Shakespeare: Post-Renaissance Reconstructions of the Works and the Myth*, ed. Jean Marsden (New York: Harvester Wheatsheaf, 1991), 29–42.
35. Jean Marsden, 'Shakespeare and Sympathy', in *Shakespeare and the Eighteenth Century*, ed. Sabor and Yachnin, 34–5. According to Cunningham, Garrick's emphasis on feelings in Shakespeare made him reconsider reinstating the Fool, since he thought the Fool would distract from the emotional impact of Lear on his audience. He preferred to keep Tate's emphasis on Cordelia in order to enhance the play's appeal to the audience's sensibility. Cunningham, *Shakespeare and Garrick*, 128, 134.
36. Holland, 'The Age of Garrick', 85. Garrick's version first appeared in print in 1773 in volume II of the Bell edition: *Bell's Edition of Shakespeare's Plays, as They are Now Performed at the Theatres Royal in London; Regulated from the Prompt Books*, 2 vols (London: John Bell, 1773).
37. Jean Marsden, 'Rewritten Women: Shakespearean Heroines in the Restoration', in *The Appropriation of Shakespeare*, ed. Marsden, 44, 48.
38. *King Lear, a tragedy by Shakespeare, as performed at the Theatre-Royal, Drury-Lane*, ed. Francis Gentleman (London: J. Bell, 1773), 2:69.
39. *King Lear*, ed. Gentleman, 2:53.
40. *King Lear*, ed. Gentleman, 2:8.
41. Frances Burney, *Evelina*, 31; Cunningham, *Shakespeare and Garrick*, 13.
42. Marsden, 'Shakespeare and Sympathy', 35.
43. Margaret Anne Doody, *Frances Burney: The Life in the Works* (New Brunswick: Rutgers University Press, 1988), 185; Barbara Darby, *Frances Burney, Dramatist: Gender, Performance, and the Late Eighteenth-Century Stage* (Lexington: University of Kentucky Press, 1997), 95.
44. Lorna Clark, 'Frances and Sarah Harriet Burney: The Novels in the Family and the Family in the Novels', in *A Celebration of Frances Burney*, ed. Lorna Clark (Newcastle upon Tyne: Cambridge Scholars Publishing, 2007), 45–7.
45. However, if, as Laura Freeman avers, the main purpose of the imperative conciliatory ending is to accentuate the patriarchal order of exchange, reducing the daughter's function to that of being her father's property, the Burneys' imperative of making money with their novels gives a bitter twist to their chosen endings. Freeman, *Character's Theater*, 220–1.
46. *King Lear*, ed. Gentleman, 2:64. For a discussion of the pervasive influence of *Othello* on Burney's third novel, see Farrar Thaddeus, *Frances Burney*, 123–4.
47. *The Johnson–Steevens Edition*, 10:467.

48. *Othello, a Tragedy, by Shakespeare, as performed at the Theatre Royal* (London: John Bell, 1777), 18.
49. See Farrar Thaddeus, *Frances Burney*, 123–5.
50. Bloom and Bloom, 'Introduction' to Frances Burney, *Camilla*, xvi; Joyce Hemlow, *The History of Fanny Burney* (Oxford: Clarendon Press, 1958), 97.
51. Marsden, 'Daddy's Girls', 21.
52. Farrar Thaddeus, *Frances Burney*, 79–80.
53. Anderson, *Eighteenth-Century Authorship*, 57; Frances Burney, *Cecilia; or, Memoirs of an Heiress*, ed. Peter Sabor and Margaret A. Doody (1782; Oxford: Oxford University Press, 1988), 707–8. Albany's name may be a reference to *King Lear*: the editors of the novel note that Burney toyed with the idea of calling the Delvile family Albany (962n65). *Cecilia* is set in 1779, and the novel reflects the highlights of the London season of that year (962n69). Already in January that year, several of Shakespeare's plays were on at Drury Lane Theatre. *King Lear* was on in March, April and May. See *London Stage Database*, https://londonstagedatabase.uoregon.edu/sphinx-results.php?sortBy=relevanc e&theatre=111Drury+Lane&date-type=1&start-year=1779&performance=&author=&actor%5B%5D=&role%5B%5D=&keyword= (accessed 16 November 2023).
54. Melissa Sodeman, 'Novel Anachronisms: Sophia Lee's *The Life of a Lover* and Frances Burney's *The Wanderer*', in *The Sentimental Novel*, ed. Riveiro, 191, 194.
55. Frances Burney, *The Wanderer; or, Female Difficulties*, ed. Margaret A. Doody, Robert L. Mack and Peter Sabor (1814; Oxford: Oxford University Press, 1991), 95.
56. Frances Burney, *The Wanderer*, 96. Frank H. Ellis claims that there is no sentimentality in *The Provok'd Husband* (*Sentimental Comedy*, 19), but it was considered a sentimental comedy already in 1812 by James Plumptre, *The English Drama Purified* (Cambridge: F. Hodson, 1812), 2:341.
57. *The Letters of Sarah Harriet Burney*, ed. Clark, 125.
58. *The Letters of Sarah Harriet Burney*, ed. Clark, 201; see also lx.
59. *The Letters of Sarah Harriet Burney*, ed. Clark, lxii, 197.
60. Ferdinand has an obvious resemblance to Edgar in *Camilla*, a novel Sarah Harriet admired. See Sarah Harriet Burney, 'To Frances d'Arblay', in *The Letters of Sarah Harriet Burney*, ed. Clark, 17–19, for her admiration of *Camilla*. Sarah Harriet Burney, *Geraldine Fauconberg*, 3 vols (London: G. Wilkie and J. Robinson, 1808).
61. *The Letters of Sarah Harriet Burney*, ed. Clark, 157; see also lvii. For the money, see Sarah Harriet Burney, 'To Charles Burney', in *The Letters of Sarah Harriet Burney*, ed. Clark, 66, 157.
62. Clark, 'Frances and Sarah Harriet Burney', 45.
63. Sarah Harriet Burney, *Traits of Nature*, 3 vols (London: Henry Colburn, 1812), 1:5, 1:8.
64. Sarah Harriet Burney, *Traits of Nature*, 1:20. This also substantiates Kate Rumbold's claim that novelists were aware of the various competing editions of Shakespeare; *Shakespeare and the Eighteenth-Century Novel*, 23.
65. Sarah Harriet Burney, *Traits of Nature*, 1:20; *The Plays of William Shakespeare*, ed. Johnson and Steevens, 5:611.
66. Sarah Harriet Burney, *Traits of Nature*, 1:23.
67. Sarah Harriet Burney, *Traits of Nature*, 1:25–9.
68. *The Letters of Sarah Harriet Burney*, ed. Clark, 116.
69. Thomas Keymer notes similarities between Shakespeare's *The Tempest* and Defoe's *Robinson Crusoe*, yet concludes that Defoe probably knew only an adaptation of the play by John Dryden and William Davenant. Keymer, 'Shakespeare in the Novel', 117–20.
70. Sarah Harriet Burney, *The Shipwreck*, in *Tales of Fancy*, 1:13. Further references parenthetical.
71. *The Monthly Review*, which calls the heroine 'a sort of female Robinson Crusoe', does not mention Shakespeare, but praises the cross-dressing scene as 'masterly': 'This part of

the tale is well delineated, and shews the difference between a masterly and a hacknied [sic] pen'. 'Tales of Fancy by S. H. Burney', *The Monthly Review* 79 (1816): 215.
72. Marsden contends that the threat of rape, too, was introduced to the sentimental plot via adaptations of Shakespeare's plays. In Tate's *King Lear*, Edmund goes so far as to plan Cordelia's rape. Marsden, 'Rewritten Women', 52.
73. Compare Meyer Spacks, *Novel Beginnings*, 134–5.

16

POLITE ARTS/THE ARTS OF POLITENESS: MANNERS, HYPOCRISY AND THE PERFORMANCE OF THE SELF

Przemysław Uściński

IN AN EARLY review of Jane Austen's novels, Sir Walter Scott underscored how the novelist replaces 'the splendid scenes of an imaginary word' with 'a correct and striking representation of that which is daily taking place'.[1] What Scott pinpoints in Austen's work may also be discussed as a larger tendency in the eighteenth-century novel of manners, namely, the propensity to refrain from employing fantastical or supernatural elements in fiction in order to rely on probability and to offer what Ian Watt calls 'the impression of fidelity to human experience'.[2] Speaking even more broadly, the interest in 'that which is daily taking place' characterises much eighteenth-century writing: certainly for most of the journal-keepers, letter-writers, novelists and biographers of the period, 'ordinary lives mattered. They were illuminating and instructive', as John Brewer argues, noticing, however, a certain departure from earlier, seventeenth-century Protestant journal-keeping: 'Traditional Christian works saw life as a journey, a passage from this world to the next, observed by God; politeness represented the world as a theatre in which one was obliged to perform before one's fellow men.'[3] Although the metaphor of life as a journey is still present in eighteenth-century writing, Brewer accurately emphasises the growing importance of sociability and its moral value in the period, as well as the common attendant trope that links manners and polite culture with theatricality and artifice. Daily life is perceived less as a journey that leads to an attainment of experience or wisdom and increasingly as a theatrical play, where it is the quality of the performance of one's social presence that acquires particular significance. Alongside the celebration of 'the sincere and sentimentalist forms of politeness' there is, therefore, a marked tendency in the period to acknowledge the possible divergence between virtue and politeness, extending to the body and bodily performance, which, 'instead of a truthful mirror of the inner self, [became] an opaque canvas on which polite appearance could be painted while hiding the true self carefully from sight'.[4] That shift from mirror to painting signals the acknowledgement of the discontinuity between the 'truth' of the inner self and the artful modes of self-presentation.

The cultural tendency in the eighteenth century to advocate for civility and politeness and to call for the reformation of manners was prompted by many factors. After the Restoration period – noted for its libertinism, bawdy songs, rakes, playhouses, alehouses and a prevailing atmosphere of irreverence and licentiousness – a puritan ethic of work, self-scrutiny, modesty and cleanliness advanced, slowly but steadily, into the cultural mainstream, supported by several evangelical and other reformatory movements. As G. J. Barker-Benfield puts it, 'To the [eighteenth-century] reformers of manners the Restoration theatre, as well as the alehouse, was a vortex of immorality.'[5] One crucial factor in this process was the increase in literacy, indeed there was a 'transition to mass literacy' in the period, which allowed for the distribution of a new and vast literature on manners, family, personal conduct and an array of topics connected with politeness.[6] Although 'the hegemony of the aristocracy was left largely uncontested for much of the eighteenth century', the patrician values of courtesy, honour and civility were being supplemented with the more ascetic virtues of bourgeois ethics: industriousness, modesty and self-improvement.[7] Novels such as Samuel Richardson's *Pamela* (1740) and Oliver Goldsmith's *The Vicar of Wakefield* (1766) would systematically challenge and ultimately reject 'the traditional aristocratic maxim that outward status means inward virtue'.[8] Furthermore, courtesy and politeness as seen in connection with disguise, fashion and masquerade were typically associated with the city. In Brewer's words, 'The critique of politeness drew on this association to condemn it as deeply implicated in the luxury, deception and vice of urban life, in contrast to the simplicities associated with rural and provincial life.'[9] As the century progressed, notions of sentiment, sensibility and benevolence were increasingly perceived as necessary supplements to the urban or aristocratic ideas of civility and politeness. Arguably, the cult of sensibility did not replace the culture of politeness but rather transformed some of its tenets, placing emphasis on sincerity, spontaneity and feeling.

The male heroes of sentimental fiction, for instance, needed to be 'benevolent, compassionate, and humane', while a degree of 'delicacy' was expected of both men and women.[10] If necessary, politeness could be compromised by a passionate outburst of sincerity, as for the advocates of sensibility the requirements of the heart were to take precedence over empty forms of politeness. Needless to say, sensibility and sentimentalism themselves were also depicted as conventional and self-indulgent manifestations of feeling and delicacy.[11] Romanticism explored the value of emotion and spontaneity, though it tended to see sentimentalism as a 'feigned' manifestation of feeling, or an expression of 'self-indulgent suffering'.[12] The Romantic belief in the power and value of sincerity was expressed, among others, by William Godwin: 'There is an energy in the sincerity of a virtuous mind that nothing human can resist.'[13] Like Godwin, many eighteenth-century novelists contrasted righteous sincerity with various forms of dissimulation, sometimes advocating for sincerity even at the cost of appearing rude or insolent: such a 'demand for openness . . . corresponds with the growing fascination with the fictional rendering of interiority', as April London remarks.[14] Nevertheless, because acting politely may also communicate sensitivity towards the feelings and needs of others, politeness and sensibility, far from being divergent, may actually strengthen and support one another.

While politeness continued to be valued as a proof of refinement and the condition of sociability, in eighteenth-century fiction it was often treated with a degree of ambivalence, as both indispensable and insufficient to secure ethical behaviour. From Richardson to Austen, politeness is an important concern in the British novel: it is seen as valuable, even necessary, but for most authors polite manners do not automatically translate into good deeds or ethical conduct. Likewise, polite society is not necessarily a moral or just one, notably also from the point of view of women: 'the spread of politeness in the [eighteenth] century' was a chief component of what Laura Runge refs to as 'the progressive or enlightened model of patriarchy', a socio-cultural paradigm that manifestly opposed brutality, but effectively cemented gender inequality. Within that paradigm, 'men protected and exerted authority over compliant, elegant, but clearly subordinate women'.[15] To reflect the period's ambivalent views on the art of politeness, I begin by discussing how it was seen as requisite for sociability and refinement, later turning to more critical assessments of politeness in terms of artifice and hypocrisy.

From Luxury to Taste: Politeness, Refinement and the Arts

Although the ideal of politeness often proved vague and ambiguous, the word 'polite' was conspicuous in the discourses of the time: phrases including 'polite learning', 'polite arts', 'polite conversation' or 'polite literature' were ubiquitous. The interconnections between taste, refinement and politeness are crucial to understanding the broader implications of the eighteenth-century 'culture of politeness'. As Brewer argues, the ideals of politeness required a 'polite identity' of sorts, an identity fashioned by 'regulating and refining [one's] passions, a goal that could best be achieved through the medium of literature and the arts'.[16] Lawrence E. Klein notes that

> expressions such as 'polite arts', 'polite letters', and 'polite learning' could be used to make the broad distinction between humanistic and artistic endeavours, on one side, and philosophical, mathematical and scientific inquiry, on the other. However, 'polite' could be used to make more subtle distinctions, for instance, to indicate a 'polite' approach to literature as opposed to mere philological criticism.[17]

The idea of politeness was thus conveying an approach different from a practical, professional or scientific one, underlining the need for general rather than 'technical' knowledge for the purposes of sociable, polite conversation. Moreover, politeness as an ideal was to be attained through instruction and acquired habit, with literature and art playing a pivotal role in its formation and display. Contentions often arose, however, as to the question of 'proper' or 'correct' taste and the specific moral qualities that art and literature should promulgate. Alexander Pope valued the art of the Italian Renaissance but mocked the enthusiasm for Italian opera among London's polite society; William Hogarth despised historical painting; Johnson denigrated popular novels. Lord Shaftesbury did much to promote the view that art and taste are inseparable from virtue – his Hellenism meant that he frequently evoked ancient Greece as 'that sole polite, most civilized and accomplished nation' which gave rise to 'arts and sciences'.[18] David Hume appreciated the role of sociability and polite conversation, for instance in his essay 'Of Refinement in the Arts' (1752), while Sir Joshua Reynolds supported the idea of establishing the Royal Academy because he, too, believed that the 'moral instruction of the nation' could be conducted 'through the exhibition of fine arts'.[19]

The discourse of politeness was intimately connected with the discourse of art – and with the vocabulary pertaining to visual arts, acting and artifice. Arguably, however, the focus on performance and artifice holds a dubious relation with the construction of class and gender identity in the period, since it functions alongside the continued discursive emphasis on notions of naturalness and spontaneity, with artifice and affectation often seen as unwelcome departures from the purported standards and regulations of 'nature'. Convictions about inborn qualities and social status often guarded access to the means of polite self-improvement. The ideal of politeness was thus both potentially inclusive ('polite' taste and refined manners could be acquired through study and instruction) and exclusive ('polite society' served as a code name for social distinction more than a universally available ideal). Understood not only in terms of good manners but also of varied 'accomplishments', politeness was to be combined with taste and refinement to offer a marker for social distinction: 'Taste was simultaneously a condition to which one was born and a state one achieved', Gary Day notes, for 'the aesthetic was the basis of sociability but, in being factored into the make-up of a gentleman, it also becomes a tool of discrimination'.[20]

In the preface to her debut novel *Evelina* (1778), Frances Burney presents her heroine as 'educated in most secluded retirement', so that 'her ignorance of the forms, and inexperience in the manners, of the world' provide the chief explanation for 'all the little incidents which these volumes record'.[21] Evelina's 'artlessness' is praised by Lady Howard:

> She has the same gentleness in her manners, the same natural graces in her motions, that I formerly so much admired in her mother. Her character seems truly ingenuous and simple; and at the same time that nature has blessed her with an excellent understanding and great quickness of parts, she has a certain air of inexperience and innocency that is extremely interesting.
>
> You have not reason to regret the retirement in which she has lived; since that politeness which is acquired by an acquaintance with high life, is in her so well supplied by a natural desire of obliging, joined to a deportment infinitely engaging.[22]

The positive evaluation of Evelina's 'natural graces' and her 'air of inexperience' positions personal or inborn traits as legitimate sources of politeness, which may be supplied without 'an acquaintance with high life'. A tension between the value of art or artfulness and the growing emphasis on naturalness and spontaneity is widely reflected in eighteenth-century art. The shift from the baroque formal garden to the English landscape garden is often given as a paradigmatic example: the formal garden with its 'clipped hedges and shaped trees, its expanse, its multishaped, geometric parterres, fountains, pools, and water mirrors' confidently exhibited the design, the intellect and the systematic work as well as exorbitant expense that were all employed to curb, correct and systematise nature; in the landscape garden, by contrast, 'beauty' was to be found in 'the given, empirical, experienced nature' – the charms of natural scenery were merely aided by the discreet labour of the designers and gardeners.[23] What is paradigmatic about this transition in garden design is not only the broad shift in the 'metaphysics of nature' but also the separation of art from mere luxury and ostentation – a process significant to the shaping of eighteenth-century aesthetic concepts and a precondition for the possibility that art could hold moral value.

David H. Solkin focuses on mid-century 'conversations' or 'conversation-piece portraiture' as illustrative of the shift from the virulent condemnation of luxury and idleness to a gradual appreciation of the moral benefits of polite conversation and company, now praised through the painterly representation of subjects including 'the communal rituals of tea-drinking and card-playing'.[24] Unlike some earlier or contemporary representations of similar scenes, paintings such as Joseph Van Aken's *An English Family at*

Tea (c.1720), William Hogarth's *William Wollaston and his Family in a Grand Interior* (1730 [Plate 13]) or Charles Phillips's *A Tea Party at Lord Harrington's House* (c.1730) introduce no satiric touches, reflecting instead the ideal of harmonious and instructive sociability, supportive of the acquisition of knowledge and polite taste, and hence suggesting that a public benefit may arise from enjoyable private interaction with good company. Such paintings tended to move away from concerns about luxury and symbolically to underscore 'mutual improvement' as well as 'an ostensible equality in status, replacing a vertical hierarchy of power with a horizontal pattern of relationships based on sympathy and civility'.[25] In terms of composition, the conversation pieces avoided formal poses and focused on the ease and 'naturalness' of sociable interaction 'to naturalise the outward forms of correct etiquette as the visible expression of an inherently refined sensibility', in Solkin's words.[26] Naturalness thus becomes an ideal to which art aspires – and politeness functions best when it is, artfully, made to appear as sincere and spontaneous. When discussing Hogarth's portrait of the Wollaston family (1730), Solkin emphasises 'the use of informal postures' in conversation-piece portraiture, as well as the creation of an illusion whereby the presented figures might seem 'oblivious to the fact that they are being observed', which 'serves to reinforce the impression that they are simply – and politely – being themselves'.[27]

Oliver Goldsmith, in *The Vicar of Wakefield* (1766), expresses a humorously sceptical attitude towards the idea that spending time in polite company means improvement. After a night of talking about 'nothing but high life, and high-lived society', Dr Primrose's impoverished family exhibits some significant alterations in its behaviour:

> The distinctions lately paid us by our betters awaked that pride which I had laid asleep, but not removed. Our windows again, as formerly, were filled with washes for the neck and face. The sun was dreaded as an enemy to the skin without doors, and the fire as a spoiler of the complexion within. My wife observed, that rising too early would hurt her daughters' eyes, that working after dinner would redden their noses, and she convinced me that the hands never looked so white as when they did nothing. Instead therefore of finishing George's shirts, we now had them new modelling their old gauzes, or flourishing upon catgut. The poor Miss Flamboroughs, their former gay companions, were cast off as mean acquaintance, and the whole conversation ran upon high life and high lived company, with pictures, taste, Shakespeare, and the musical glasses.[28]

Here, Goldsmith mocks the idea that polite conversation extends horizontal relations of equality, noticing instead how the strong focus on fashion, taste and refinement serves to underscore the social hierarchy based, ultimately, on wealth and access to luxury. Since Dr Primrose's daughters, Olivia and Sophia (their names taken from popular romances), regard the 'accomplishments' of fine ladies with envy, they thoughtlessly imitate their betters, whereas their disgruntled father argues that 'greater refinement would only serve to make their poverty ridiculous, and give them a taste for pleasures they had no right to possess' (54). To claim that politeness and refinement foster equality is disingenuous because it means ignoring the pivotal role of material status in successfully displaying these traits.

Throughout the novel, Goldsmith suggests that by aspiring to achieve the high standards of refinement Dr Primrose's daughters may in fact forsake more vital concerns of morality and good sense. The height of Goldsmith's mockery of the use of art for the sake of an affected display of refinement comes in the chapter that narrates the family's decision (to which Dr Primrose reluctantly submits) to order a family portrait 'to show the superiority of our taste' (86). Unfortunately, after resolving to opt for a 'large historical family piece', the Primroses receive an impressive painting, but one 'much too large to be got through any of the doors'; so, stuck in the house kitchen, the portrait, far from increasing family's reputation, becomes 'the jest of all our neighbours', as the vicar admits (87). Christopher Flint observes that '[the Primrose] family puts art in the service of social competition and a public display of private life'; because their main aim is to compete with the neighbouring Flamborough family and thus gratify the Primroses' vanity, their project fails to provide a thoughtful and accurate depiction of the true value of family: 'Rather than representing structural (or even personal) relations among the sitters, the painting intensifies the discordant and "artificial" roles to which the family aspires, undoing the sentimental oneness the picture was intended to celebrate.'[29] As Flint further notes, because the family portrait is only partly a conversation piece but predominantly employs the methods of 'the life-size allegorical family portrait' (with family members impersonating mythological or allegorical figures), it fails to demonstrate the family's refinement, instead merely flashing the viewer with 'false opulence': 'The Primrose portrait represents an aspiration more than a reality and has little to do directly with the actual economic and political condition of the family.'[30] The flamboyant theatricality of the painted scene contrasts with the modest means of the actual life of the Primroses, with the effect that, by abandoning the pursuit of naturalness typical of the conversation piece, the family fails to present itself as belonging to polite society. The painting in fact testifies to the family's lack of taste, showing no sense of proportion and moderation, such that it serves as a caricature of the family's unrealistic aspirations.

Commenting on Hogarth's satirical depictions of both male and female characters, Linda Walsh speculates that '[the] most important moral value of the eighteenth century was perhaps moderation'.[31] The idea of moderation was typically opposed in the period to diverse manifestations of 'passion' or 'enthusiasm' on the one hand, and 'indulgence' or 'luxury' on the other. In his study of the eighteenth-century concept of beauty, Robert W. Jones sees the 'increased interest in the nature of taste' in the period as an effect of the 'changing patterns of wealth distribution', which made an increasing number of people 'anxious to express their refinement as a means of cultural distinction'.[32] Not so much the pure contemplation of beauty, advocated by Edmund Burke, but rather the desire to earn social distinction through a display of refinement propels an increased interest in the aesthetic notions of beauty and taste. According to Burke, 'contemplation' is necessary to appreciate beauty, which Burke defines as a quality that produces love:

> By beauty I mean, that quality or those qualities in bodies by which they cause love, or some passion similar to it . . . I likewise distinguish love, by which I mean that satisfaction which arises to the mind upon contemplating any thing beautiful, of whatsoever nature it may be, from desire or lust; which is the energy of the mind, that hurries us on to the possession of certain objects, that do not affect us as they are beautiful, but by means altogether different.[33]

Love therefore arises from contemplation. Burke distinguishes it from lust and desire, which strive for possession, and which he qualifies as 'violent and tempestuous passions'.[34] To separate love from desire is perhaps to regulate love, to turn it into a moderate 'passion', in a sense, a passion for 'small objects' that appear beautiful because, as Burke famously stated, 'we submit to what we admire, but we love what submits to us'.[35] As Jones argues, eighteenth-century art theorists were 'highly sensitive to the distinctions of gender', with the female figure frequently representing 'the fear of the effeminacy figured as a loss of restraint and a descent into luxury', although there was also 'a concentration on woman as a sign of true beauty' in the aesthetic theories of the period.[36] Following Burke, it seems that 'true' female beauty would submit to male contemplation and consequently induce love, provided that the male admirer is not thoughtless, or blinded by desire for possession (in which case, he may be content with 'a woman of no remarkable beauty', Burke suggests). The distinction between contemplative love and possessive desire could well serve as a summary for numerous novelistic plots, in which young heroines learn to distinguish passion or mere lust from 'true' love, much as Burke teaches his readers to discern what qualifies as 'beautiful'. Burke attempts to link love with the category of the beautiful in order to associate it with thoughtful moderation, and to dissociate it from both extreme passion and the excesses of luxury, indulgence and effeminacy.[37] The beauty of art, like the beauty of love, should be a matter of inward contemplation, not outward and ostentatious display.

Exposing Hypocrisy: Politeness, Performance, Duplicity

The performative aspect of manners and polite behaviour may suggest a split or discord between outer appearance and hidden motivation or desire. Politeness has also been discussed in certain contrast with sincerity, often in connection with the charge of hypocrisy. As Jenny Davidson writes, 'Manners – the social constraints that check the dictates of individual desire – represent a subtle but pervasive hypocrisy, a form of discipline that exacts certain penalties but also promises social and moral rewards.'[38] Manipulation, coquetry, flattery and hypocrisy may thrive in a social milieu where appearances count and where good manners play a decisive role, which is why novelistic discourse often draws attention to seemingly spontaneous behaviours or bodily reactions as really resulting from studied performance. As Harriet Freke asks provocatively in Maria Edgeworth's *Belinda* (1801): 'I think all our politeness hypocrisy. What d'ye say to that?'[39] Hypocrisy – a more seriously duplicitous form of affectation – may be defined as 'the public falsification of the self', for it concerns the delivery of a convincing and coherent performance that aims at orchestrating a desired public perception.[40] Hypocrites therefore strive to conceal their inadequacies: 'a split in the self', as Jeremy Tambling notes, is 'a split which hypocrisy denies, its characteristic behaviour enacting a desire to present a single identity'.[41] Hypocrisy aims at maintaining a single identity, procuring the appearance of moral coherence and personal integrity, because such an appearance may be requisite for effective deception as well as for political manipulation. In early modern literature, Lucia Nigri points out, 'hypocrisy is associated with wittiness, the adoption of a refined language, and an ability to deceive others through a carefully "targeted" representation of the self'.[42] Machiavelli's advice that a prince may need to employ 'hypocritical manipulation' was partly aimed at reducing 'the need for cruelty', as Demetris Tillyris notes, supporting the argument that hypocrisy may be seen as 'political virtue' (as opposed to 'moral virtue'), which is necessary for 'effecting compromises and building advantageous coalitions', and may 'aid the maintenance of civility amidst conflict'.[43] Hypocrisy might be requisite to avoid direct confrontation: it employs politeness as a policy to maintain social cohesion, albeit at the cost of relinquishing principled morality.

As Davidson argues, for the early novelists such as Henry Fielding and Richardson, who attempted to reinvent the formal character and moral purpose of novelistic discourse, the theme of hypocrisy was 'a central topos for defining and contesting narrative and ethical authority'.[44] In *Tom Jones* (1749), Fielding includes a chapter on the pervasiveness of the metaphor of the world as stage (*theatrum mundi*):

> Some have considered the larger part of mankind in the light of actors, as personating characters no more their own, and to which, in fact, they have no better title than the player hath to be in earnest thought the king or emperor whom he represents. Thus the hypocrite may be said to be player; and indeed the Greeks called them both by one and the same name.[45]

This linguistic slippage is encapsulated, Fielding writes, in the word 'hypocrite' itself – indeed, 'hypocrisy' derives from the Greek term *hypokrisis*, meaning the 'acting of a theatrical part', which suggests putting on a mask or an appearance, as an actor would on stage; this aptly corresponds to the concern with the outward display of inner feelings visible in the literature on politeness, including conduct books, which instruct their readers 'how to act, not how to be'.[46] Hypocrisy disturbs the intimacy between ethics and etiquette, privileging conduct over conscience, appearance over integrity. The vocabulary that Fielding himself employs to highlight the confusion between theatre and reality ('indiscriminately', 'no better title', 'the king or emperor') indicates how a preoccupation with social distinction lies at the heart of his novelistic critique of affectation. Indeed, as Solie Ylivuori explains, 'The problem of hypocrisy, so fundamental to politeness, not only addresses questions of morality and integrity but also closes on philosophical ruminations on identity' – a hypocrite impersonates a coherent character to create a 'false impression', although unlike an actor, the aim is to confound such a performance with the hypocrite's real-life character.[47]

Because politeness serves to avoid conflict and confrontation, a polite society may not prove coterminous with a just or moral one. For more vulnerable social subjects, including women, the culture of politeness promised, as I noted earlier, social exchange freed from brute force, but at the same time polite rituals tended to solidify social hierarchies and discouraged the critique of power relations. When 'politeness became associated with femininity, and women became the paragons of ideal politeness' in the period, the refining role of women was acknowledged; but, somewhat paradoxically, it was appreciated only because women's 'supposedly weaker mental and physical frame became their greatest polite asset, and their civilising function was grounded on their social disadvantages', as Ylivuori puts it.[48] The young, naive and unexperienced heroines in key novels by Charlotte Lennox, Francis Burney, Maria Edgeworth and Jane Austen are often raised in relative isolation, so that, upon entering wider society, they are faced with a formidable task: how to balance their urge to speak their mind and act honestly with the demands of polite or fashionable conduct. Being ignorant

MANNERS, HYPOCRISY AND THE PERFORMANCE OF THE SELF   285

and inexperienced, they become vulnerable to those who know how to exploit societal codes, biases and double standards to their own advantage. There is undoubtedly a price to pay for innocence and idealism, but, these novels tend to argue, there is a still greater price to pay for hypocrisy: the loss of one's integrity and moral standing.

The heroine of Lennox's influential novel *The Female Quixote* (1752), Arabella, may serve as a typical, if slightly exaggerated, example of an innocent young woman whom the novelist perennially confronts with a polite but often morally dubious society. She is raised in 'a Castle' located in 'a very remote Province of the Kingdom', where, living in seclusion with her father, who 'resolved to quit all Society whatever', she acquires idealistic notions about manners and politeness from the 'great Store of Romances' that she peruses in her father's library. Consequently, she becomes 'a strict Observer of romantic Forms' and is gravely disappointed whenever any young gentleman violates 'the Laws of Gallantry and Respect'.[49] Nevertheless, although Arabella seems to be transfixed on forms of address that appear theatrical and outmoded, Lennox introduces an interesting twist to the novelistic treatment of the topic of manners. While a ridiculing parody of the language of French romances – including their somewhat outlandish and heavily codified patterns of courtship – occupies a prominent place in the novel, Arabella's resolute application of the demands of 'romantic Forms' often renders her impervious to the requirements for female submissiveness: 'Although [her] behaviour often appears absurd to her peers, Arabella appropriates for herself the power to stipulate the terms of her relationships with men', as Brean Hammond and Shaun Regan argue.[50] Her expert knowledge of the ways of heroically enamoured gentlemen, although purportedly improbable, allows her to unmask Sir George Bellmour as an impostor – a fortune-hunter who poses as a sentimental lover. After hearing the stories of his former amorous engagements, Arabella accuses him of 'Inconstancy', adding 'the Epithet of Ungrateful and Unjust', and defends her opinion with the following argument:

> For, in fine, Sir, pursued she, you will never persuade any reasonable Person, that your being able to lose the Remembrance of the fair and generous *Sydimiris*, in your new Passion for *Philonice*, was not an Excess of Levity: but your suffering so tamely the Loss of this last Beauty, and allowing her to remain in the Hands of her Ravisher, while you permit another Affection to take Possession of your Soul, is such an Outrage to all Truth and Constancy, that you deserve to be ranked among the falsest of Mankind . . .
>
> Call not, interrupted *Arabella*, that an irresistible Impulse, which was only the Effect of thy own changing Humour. The same Excuse might be pleaded for all the Faults we see committed in the World; and Men would no longer be answerable for their own Crimes.[51]

There is a subtle mitigation of sentimentalism in Arabella's response to Sir George, albeit couched in emotional terms borrowed from the romances she reads. Her severe and unambiguous judgement of his actions surprises Sir George, who attempts to vindicate them by appealing to the passions of the heart. Arabella's argument ultimately points to the ethical responsibility that takes precedence over what Sir George calls 'a powerful impulse': the rules of courtship codified in the idiom of romances empower Lennox's heroine to voice her protest overtly (as Arabella often does) as well as to impose high standards on men, not only in terms of etiquette but, above all, of personal integrity, reliability and sincerity. Although often misguided by the idealised world presented in popular romances, Arabella's quixotic disposition goes beyond a ridiculing parody: as Hammond and Regan assert, 'In her romantic quixotism, what Arabella is able to experience is an alternative world in which women might refuse to comply with their domestication, the rendering of themselves into sweet, submissive, sentimental creatures.'[52]

Catherine Morland, the quixotic reader of Gothic novels in Jane Austen's *Northanger Abbey* (published posthumously in December 1817), to a degree follows the pattern in which the innocent idealism of a young and inexperienced heroine is slightly mocked but also positively contrasted with the opportunism of the wider fashionable society. Like Arabella, many of Austen's youthful heroines are not free from ignorance or prejudice, yet they tend to challenge social hypocrisy by refusing to compromise on what they deem rightful. Intertextually, Catherine Morland is an anti-heroine; in her ordinariness, ignorance and lack of extraordinary beauty or talent she represents the reverse of the heroic names found in earlier literature. Partly like Arabella in *The Female Quixote*, she often appears artless and confused, but, as Margaret Kirkham rightly observes, 'what Austen does is to restrict her heroine's delusions to relatively minor matters, leaving her, with all her youthful thoughts, essentially right in her judgments and feelings on a great many important matters'.[53] The negative parody thus leads to a positive pattern: a non-utopian portrayal of a young girl, clever but lacking in refinement and 'accomplishments'.

To complete the picture one should contrast Catherine Morland with her friend, Isabella Thorpe, whom she first meets at Bath. Importantly, they both read Ann Radcliffe's *The Mysteries of Udolpho* (1794), and they both uncritically admire it, yet their characters are visibly discordant. Isabella may remind readers of Miss Crawford in Austen's *Mansfield Park* (1814); like Mary, she is an urbane, elegant and slightly nonchalant coquette, with a tendency for manipulative behaviour. There is thus plenty of irony when Isabella presents Catherine with her definition of modesty:

> My sweet love, do not be so abominably affected . . . Modesty, and all that, is very well in its way, but really a little common honesty is sometimes quite as becoming. I have no idea of being so overstrained. It is fishing for compliments.[54]

Modesty understood as a mere tactic, as 'fishing for compliments', and Isabella's praise for the effects of 'a little common honesty' wittingly reflect her theatrical pose of unassumed candidness. Importantly, she is also older than Catherine and evidently has much more experience with which to counterbalance the ideas acquired from fiction. The long-running debate on the potentially negative impact of novel reading on a young mind occupied much space in eighteenth-century periodicals. Critics usually quote Samuel Johnson's *Rambler* no. 4 (1750),[55] but the following passage from Eliza Haywood in *The Female Spectator* (1745) focuses on female readers:

> [What] more evidently shows the ill Effects of writing in this manner is, that we often see Girls too young, either to be addressed on the Score of Love, or even to know what is meant by the Passion, affect the languishment they read of, – roll their Eyes, sigh, fold their Arms, neglect every useful Learning, and attend to nothing but acquiring the Reputation of being enough a Woman to know all the Pains and Delicacies of Love.[56]

MANNERS, HYPOCRISY AND THE PERFORMANCE OF THE SELF

Challenging Haywood's assertion, Austen mitigates the ill effects of romantic and passionate writing; there seems to be no correlation between novel reading and personal traits or moral attitudes. Catherine as a younger girl is more prone to misguided reading, but she, and not the hypocritical Isabella, is the main protagonist, who eventually marries happily. Catherine, like Marianne Dashwood, can still learn to be more mature, but Isabella cannot learn to be a little more naive – romantic notions prove less dangerous than the debilitating lack of any idealistic illusions. By having their heroines follow the unrealistic precepts of fictional worlds, Lennox and Austen acknowledge the ignorance of undereducated young women, not their incapacity for judgement or moral impulse. On the contrary, their heroines typically retain enough idealism and honesty to confront openly what they cannot but deem unfair.

In Edgeworth's *Belinda* (a novel praised by Austen in *Northanger Abbey*), the titular young heroine tries to resist the teachings of Mrs Freke, who argues that 'all virtue is hypocrisy', and challenges Mr Percival to prove her wrong. In the chapter entitled 'Rights of Woman' (volume II, chapter VII), she presents an elaborate argument against specifically female hypocrisy, especially as regards 'politeness', 'shame' and 'delicacy':

> 'Your most delicate women are always the greatest hypocrites; and, in my opinion, no hypocrite can or ought to be happy'.
>
> 'But you have not proved the hypocrisy', said Belinda. 'Delicacy is not, I hope, an indisputable proof of it? If you mean *false* delicacy——'
>
> 'To cut the matter short at once', cried Mrs. Freke, 'why, when a woman likes a man, does not she go and tell him so honestly?'
>
> Belinda, surprised by this question from a woman, was too much abashed instantly to answer.
>
> 'Because she's a hypocrite. That is and must be the answer'.
>
> 'No', said Mr. Percival; 'because, if she be a woman of sense, she knows that by such a step she would disgust the object of her affection'.
>
> 'Cunning!—cunning!—cunning!—the arms of the weakest'.
>
> 'Prudence! prudence!—the arms of the strongest. Taking the best means to secure our own happiness without injuring that of others is the best proof of sense and strength of mind . . .'
>
> 'But if you want to know', said Mrs. Freke, 'what I would do to improve the world, I'll tell you: I'd have both sexes call things by their right names'. (209)

For Mrs Freke, any manifestation of shame or delicacy is part of a cunning strategy to conceal one's thoughts and feelings and hence it contradicts the demand for absolute sincerity. She wishes both men and women would 'call things by their right names'. For Mr Percival, in turn, delicacy (arguably one of the code names for politeness) is not a sign of weakness or hypocrisy, but stems from rational prudence designed to 'secure' one's happiness 'without injuring that of others'. The character of Harriet Freke has been discussed as largely transgressive, but also as portrayed somewhat satirically: 'her aberration is especially obvious in her predilection for transdressing, for tall phallic boots in particular. Her vulgar, sadistic behaviour images the experience of living in a "world upside down" where women boldly attempt to usurp male prerogative'.[57] It seems that Mrs Freke's radicalism in detecting cunning and hypocrisy in all forms of politeness cannot be accepted by Belinda, whose characteristic traits include 'persistent adherence to higher moral standards' than in the case of two other major characters in the novel, Lady Delacour and Harriet.[58] At the same time, however, Belinda challenges Mr Vincent, a rich West Indian proprietor, after he voices his indirect criticism of Mrs Freke when praising Creole women, who are 'all softness, grace, delicacy', which he attributes to the indolence and ignorance that attach them 'to domestic life' (209). Although the reader is not invited to treat Harriett's harangue on the ubiquity of hypocrisy seriously, given the generally grotesque presentation of her character, that later conversation, still in the chapter on 'Rights of Woman', challenges the opposite tendency to view both 'delicacy' and 'ignorance' as interrelated, quintessential markers of femininity. If the general trajectory of Edgeworth's novel is to applaud female devotion to family life and domestic bliss, such a devotion needs to follow from a rational and independent choice made by educated women, not imposed by the ideology that commends female ignorance. Likewise, politeness is seen by Mr Percival as a product of rational moral consideration that is requisite not only for sociability but also for fostering ethical conduct and forming valuable personal relations, including in friendship and courtship. Politeness, in his view, is the sign of rationality, not a marker of inferiority or an element of the tactics of an artful, hypocritical performance.

The conversations included in this chapter testify to the fact that gender played an important role in contemporaneous discussions concerning polite behaviour and related topics, such as manners, modesty and delicacy. The chapter's general lesson appears to be that there must be a distinction between men and women, including in terms of their manners and appearance. One may compare Edgeworth's treatment of the topic with the assertion made by Mr Villars in Burney's *Evelina*:

> Though gentleness and modesty are the peculiar attributes of your sex, yet fortitude and firmness, when occasion demands them, are virtues noble and as becoming in women as in men: the right line of conduct is the same for both sexes, though the manner in which it is pursued, may somewhat vary.[59]

The problem in the case of Mrs Freke is that she possesses fortitude and firmness but lacks, according to contemporary standards, gentleness and modesty. With her penchant for cross-dressing and bold opinions, she upsets the demand for that distinction between sexes that Mr Villars ascertains, despite his admission that moral principles for men and women are the same.

Interestingly, in the argumentation both for (Mr Vincent, Mr Percival) and against (Mrs Freke) female delicacy, the concept of happiness plays a crucial role. For Mrs Freke, 'no hypocrite can or ought to be happy' – she sees in absolute sincerity and integrity a *sine qua non* for attaining happiness, simultaneously linking politeness and delicacy with oppression and 'misery': 'This *delicacy* enslaves the pretty delicate dears . . . I hate slavery! Vive la liberté!' (209). To this Mr Percival answers, diplomatically, that he is an advocate not so much for women's rights as for their happiness, as well as 'for their delicacy, as I think it contributes to their happiness'; he later speaks in defence of 'the decent drapery of life', evoking a famous phrase from Edmund Burke's *Reflections on the Revolution in France* (1790), which has painterly connotations, alluding to both dress and the decorative arts. As Claude Rawson explains,

MANNERS, HYPOCRISY AND THE PERFORMANCE OF THE SELF 289

For Swift, as for Burke, the uglier features of the self must indeed be falsified for the sake of decency and public order . . . Reynolds' advocacy of an art in which accidental blemishes and imperfections are removed from the portraiture is the ideal expression of this cast of mind.[60]

The demand for absolute sincerity contrasts with Tambling's argument that a hypocrite is someone who asserts personal integrity, and who claims to be always perfectly honest. Leaving aside more complex political references to the French Revolution made in this chapter, it may be argued that by evoking the question of happiness, including the happiness of women, Edgeworth appears deliberately to shift the focus from the politically charged discussion of rights and from absolutist claims about the moral value of such categories as 'politeness' or 'delicacy' to more pragmatic, even utilitarian, considerations of social relations and personal happiness. The radical critique of hypocrisy is not so much abandoned as mitigated by other factors that a reasonable consideration needs to take into account. If absolute sincerity, practised without any regard for consequences, is neither possible in practical terms nor desirable in moral terms, the charge of hypocrisy should not be indiscriminately applied to all those who act politely or manifest some delicacy.

To conclude, the ambivalence towards politeness in eighteenth-century writing may stem from the contradiction between the need for social integration and cohesion on the one hand, and the reality of social hierarchy and division on the other. Politeness fosters peaceful sociability and promises mutual respect, but it is hardly a tool for challenging inequalities, including in terms of class and gender. Likewise, the period's interest in art and aesthetics testifies to the wish for building the community of taste, though within 'polite society' taste becomes a tool of discrimination rather than inclusion. For some, such contradictions meant that politeness is incurably hypocritical – artificial and illusory rather than artful in any commendable sense. For many authors, including Fielding, Goldsmith, Austen and Edgeworth, politeness is important but remains auxiliary – because it is not a successful self-presentation among polite company that matters most, but a truth-seeking, ethical conduct towards oneself and others.

Notes

1. Sir Walter Scott, 'Emma', *Quarterly Review* (1815): 192–200; reprinted in Harold Bloom, ed., *Jane Austen: Bloom's Classic Critical Views* (New York: Infobase Publishing, 2008), 128–34. This leads Scott into comparing Austen's themes and techniques with the Flemish school of painting: 'The author's knowledge of the world, and the peculiar tact with which she presents characters that the reader cannot fail to recognize, reminds us something of the merits of the Flemish school of painting. The subjects are not often elegant, and certainly never grand; but they are finished up to nature, and with a precision which delights the reader' (133).
2. Ian Watt, *The Rise of the Novel: Studies in Defoe, Richardson and Fielding* (Berkeley and Los Angeles: University of California Press, 1957), 13.
3. John Brewer, *The Pleasures of the Imagination: English Culture in the Eighteenth Century* (Bath: HarperCollins, 1997), 109–11.
4. Solie Ylivuori, *Women and Politeness in Eighteenth-Century England* (London and New York: Routledge, 2019), 21.

5. G. J. Barker-Benfield, *The Culture of Sensibility: Sex and Society in Eighteenth-Century Britain* (Chicago and London: University of Chicago Press, 1996), 59.
6. Barker-Benfield, *The Culture of Sensibility*, 60.
7. Jorge Arditi, *A Genealogy of Manners: Transformations of Social Relations in France and England from the Fourteenth to the Eighteenth Century* (Chicago and London: University of Chicago Press, 1998), 219.
8. Michael McKeon, *The Origins of the English Novel, 1600–1740*, 15th edn (Baltimore and London: Johns Hopkins University Press, 2002), 367.
9. Brewer, *The Pleasures of the Imagination*, 113. Ian Watt discusses how Richardson's *Clarissa* is permeated with 'a deep personal distrust, even fear, of the urban environment', with its heroine being 'a pure country girl', largely ignorant of the ways of the town. Watt, *The Rise of the Novel*, 181.
10. Barker-Benfield, *The Culture of Sensibility*, 248–51.
11. John Mullan, for instance, speaks of 'a gap between ideal and practice' in sentimental fiction, where virtue becomes 'utterly stylized' to comply with 'the habits of sentimental reading'. John Mullan, *Sentiment and Sociability: The Language of Feeling in the Eighteenth Century* (1988; Oxford: Clarendon Press, 2002), 118–20.
12. Dennis M. Welch, 'Blake and the Web of Interest and Sensibility', *South Atlantic Review* 71, no. 3 (2006): 29–33.
13. William Godwin, *An Enquiry Concerning Political Justice*, ed. Mark Philp (1793; Oxford: Oxford University Press, 2013), 133.
14. April London, *The Cambridge Introduction to the Eighteenth-Century Novel* (Cambridge: Cambridge University Press, 2012), 104.
15. Laura Runge, 'Momentary Fame: Female Novelists in Eighteenth-Century Book Reviews', in *A Companion to the Eighteenth-century English Novel and Culture*, ed. Paula R. Backscheider and Catherine Ingrassia (Oxford: Blackwell, 2005), 278.
16. Brewer, *The Pleasures of the Imagination*, 106.
17. Lawrence E. Klein, *Shaftesbury and the Culture of Politeness: Moral Discourse and Cultural Politics in Eighteenth Century England* (Cambridge: Cambridge University Press, 1994), 5.
18. Anthony Ashley Cooper, third Earl of Shaftesbury, *Characteristics of Men, Manners, Opinions, Times*, ed. Lawrence E. Klein (1711; Cambridge: Cambridge University Press, 2000), 398.
19. Brewer, *The Pleasures of the Imagination*, 230. As Linda Walsh documents, debates about the moral value of art significantly contributed to the rise of criticism as an important branch of discursive production; the function of criticism, which both Shaftesbury and Pope recognised and promoted, was that it sought to apply moral concerns to the task of the appropriately guided refinement of taste. Linda Walsh, *A Guide to Eighteenth-Century Art* (Oxford: Wiley Blackwell, 2017), 204–38.
20. Gary Day, *Class* (London and New York: Routledge, 2001), 97.
21. Frances Burney, *Evelina, or the History of a Young Lady's Entrance into the World*, ed. Edward A. Bloom and Lillian D. Bloom (1778; London and New York, 1970), 7–8. The author also underscores that Evelina is 'young, artless, and inexperienced' (8).
22. Burney, *Evelina*, 21.
23. Remy G. Saisselin, *The Enlightenment against the Baroque: Economics and Aesthetics in the Eighteenth Century* (Berkeley, Los Angeles and Oxford: California University Press, 1992), 12–14.
24. David H. Solkin, *Painting for Money: The Visual Arts and the Public Sphere in Eighteenth-Century England* (New Haven and London: Yale University Press, 1992), 86.
25. Solkin, *Painting for Money*, 86.
26. Solkin, *Painting for Money*, 87.

MANNERS, HYPOCRISY AND THE PERFORMANCE OF THE SELF 291

27. Solkin, *Painting for Money*, 87. Solkin interprets the painterly insistence on spontaneity in the Wollaston family painting as suggesting that instinct and inborn qualities rather than forceful or disciplinary measures play a crucial role in shaping polite culture: 'Because [Hogarth] does not arrange his figures as if they were sitting for their portraits, they appear to exist by and for themselves, participating voluntarily in the construction of an all-embracing order that is at the same time beautiful, proper, and enjoyable. Indeed moral and aesthetic propriety would seem to arise spontaneously out of the body's own instinct for delight' (87).
28. Oliver Goldsmith, *The Vicar of Wakefield*, ed. Stephen Coote (1766; Ware: Wordsworth Classics, 1998), 56. Further references parenthetical.
29. Christopher Flint, '"The Family Piece": Oliver Goldsmith and the Politics of the Everyday in Eighteenth-Century Domestic Portraiture', *Eighteenth-Century Studies* 29, no. 2 (1995/96): 129.
30. Flint, '"The Family Piece"', 130.
31. Walsh, *A Guide to Eighteenth-Century Art*, 208.
32. Robert. W. Jones, *Gender and the Formation of Taste in Eighteenth-Century Britain: The Analysis of Beauty* (Cambridge: Cambridge University Press, 1998), vii.
33. Edmund Burke, *A Philosophical Inquiry into the Origin of our Ideas of the Sublime and Beautiful*, ed. Adam Phillips (Oxford and New York: Oxford University Press, 2008), 83.
34. Burke, *A Philosophical Inquiry*, 83
35. Burke, *A Philosophical Inquiry*, 103.
36. Jones, *Gender and the Formation of Taste*, 65.
37. Jones notes that the widespread criticism of luxury articulated by such writers as Thomas Cole (particularly in his *Discourses on Luxury, Infidelity and Enthusiasm* [1761]), John Brown (in *Estimate of the Manners and Opinions of Our Times* [1757]), Samuel Johnson, Edmund Burke and others frequently associated luxury with effeminacy, identifying it with 'an effeminate loss of self-command', 'giddy pleasures of the moment' and 'the twin follies of fashion and commercial affluence'. Jones, *Gender and the Formation of Taste*, 58–61. As Saisselin claims, since the separation of art from mere luxury was a central task of the aesthetic discourses of the time, many aesthetic theories addressed the charge of effeminacy: 'The analysis of the workings of luxury thus merges with a critique of woman: baroque luxury spending had come to be seen as frivolous and feminine. It was also seen as detrimental to the arts.' Saisselin, *The Enlightenment against the Baroque*, 41.
38. Jenny Davidson, *Hypocrisy and the Politics of Politeness: Manners and Morals from Locke to Austen* (Cambridge: Cambridge University Press, 2004), 8.
39. Maria Edgeworth, *Belinda*, ed. Linda Bree (1801; Oxford and New York: Oxford University Press, 2020), 208. Further references parenthetical.
40. Claude Rawson, *Satire and Sentiment, 1660–1830* (New Haven and London: Yale University Press, 2000), 186–7.
41. Jeremy Tambling, *The Histories of the Devil: From Marlow to Mann, and the Manichees* (London: Palgrave Macmillan, 2016), 165. Tambling notes that hypocrisy connects with the comical, both relating to a sense of mismatch, inadequacy or contradiction being exposed: 'Laughter is, and expresses, a double or contradictory feeling' (165).
42. Lucia Nigri, 'Religious Hypocrisy in Performance', in *Forms of Hypocrisy in Early Modern England*, ed. Lucia Nigri and Naya Tsentourou (London and New York: Routledge, 2018), 58.
43. Demetris Tillyris, 'The Virtue of Vice: A Defence of Hypocrisy in Democratic Politics', *Contemporary Politics* 22, no. 1 (2016): 14–16. Still, however, the very distinction between 'moral virtue' and 'political virtue' may suggest a tolerance for double standards.
44. Davidson, *Hypocrisy and the Politics of Politeness*, 112.
45. Henry Fielding, *Tom Jones*, ed. R. P. C. Mutter (1749; London: Penguin, 1985), 299–300. Fielding discusses the topic of hypocrisy in different writings, including the preface to his

earlier novel, *Joseph Andrews* (1742) and in his 'Essay on the Knowledge of the Characters of Men' (1739–40), where he argues that a hypocrite 'is a most detestable character in society', chiefly because the vice of hypocrisy, by posing as virtue, seeks not only to 'derive all honour and reward in this world', but also causes the general inflation in the social respect for virtue, hence it may 'deprive others of the praises due to their virtues'. Henry Fielding, 'Essay on the Knowledge of the Characters of Men', in *The Works of Henry Fielding, Esq.*, ed. Arthur Murphy, 12 vols (London: Millar, 1766), 12:55–6.

46. Davidson, *Hypocrisy and the Politics of Politeness*, 89.
47. Ylivuori, *Women and Politeness*, 22.
48. Ylivuori, *Women and Politeness*, 38–40. As Ylivuori notes, 'attempts to define "the polite" certainly revolve around class, or rather, social hierarchy and power relationships, but not in a straightforward manner. Politeness has often been seen as a culture of common taste and decorum that was used by the middling sort to distinguish themselves, not only from those below them, but especially from those above . . . both positions of superiority and subordination needed to be displayed in the seemingly equal polite interaction' (23). As it typically serves to manifest and sustain social hierarchies, but does so under the guise of equal interaction, politeness at its very core seems to be an embodiment of hypocrisy.
49. Charlotte Lennox, *The Female Quixote, or The Adventures of Arabella*, ed. Margaret Dalziel, intr. Margaret Anne Doody (1752; Oxford and New York: Oxford University Press, 2008), 5–7.
50. Brean Hammond and Shaun Regan, *Making the Novel: Fiction and Society in Britain, 1660–1789* (London and New York: Palgrave Macmillan, 2006), 153.
51. Lennox, *The Female Quixote*, 250–1.
52. Hammond and Regan, *Making the Novel*, 153.
53. Margaret Kirkham, *Jane Austen, Feminism and Fiction* (1983; London: Athlone Press, 1997), 130–1.
54. Jane Austen, *Northanger Abbey* (1817; London: Penguin, 1994), 128.
55. Samuel Johnson, *Selected Writings*, ed. Patrick Cruttwell (London: Penguin, 1986), 150.
56. Eliza Haywood, *Selections from the Female Spectator*, ed. Patricia Meyer Spacks (Oxford and New York: Oxford University Press, 1999), 12.
57. Beth Kowaleski-Wallace, 'Home Economics: Domestic Ideology in Maria Edgworth's *Belinda*', *The Eighteenth Century* 29, no. 3 (1988): 249.
58. Kowaleski-Wallace, 'Home Economics', 242.
59. Burney, *Evelina*, 217.
60. Rawson, *Satire and Sentiment*, 185–7.

17

MUSICAL 'EPIPHANIES' IN THE LATE EIGHTEENTH-CENTURY NOVEL

Pierre Dubois

Introduction

DERIVED FROM THE Greek word *epiphaneia* (ἐπιφάνεια), epiphany means 'appearance', 'manifestation' or 'revelation'. It is originally a religious or mystical term referring to the manifestation of a divinity (such as that of Jesus to the Magi). By extension, in literature, an epiphany consists in a sudden, trivial, evanescent incident, perception or encounter that changes a character's understanding or awareness, to the point that it may affect his or her life and the development of the plot. The paternity of this notion of epiphany in the novel is attributed to James Joyce. In *Stephen Hero* (published posthumously in 1944), the eponymous character experiences a sudden insight one evening as he is passing through Eccles Street in Dublin, 'when a trivial incident set him composing some ardent verses'. Stephen defines what he calls 'an epiphany' as follows:

> By an epiphany he meant a sudden spiritual manifestation, whether in the vulgarity of speech or of gesture or in a memorable phase of the mind itself. He believed that it was for the man of letters to record these epiphanies with extreme care, seeing that they themselves are the most delicate and evanescent of moments.[1]

The suddenness and brevity of the manifestation, which constitutes an illuminating discovery or disclosure of meaning for the subject who experiences it, cancels out and transcends its original triviality. The 'object' or 'fact' that triggers the epiphanic revelation does not matter per se because of its own qualities; instead, it is the very fact that it operates as a catalyst for this revelation that grants it its importance and significance. The object matters less than the perception of it by the subject. As Robert Langbaum remarks, 'epiphany offers an insight into the observer as well as into the object observed'.[2]

Although Joyce was the first to use the term 'epiphany' in this sense, it can be argued that, like other techniques, such as the interior monologue and stream of consciousness, epiphany plays an important role in modern literature generally, and instances of its use can be found in the work of other novelists, such as Henry James, Joseph Conrad, Marcel Proust and Virginia Woolf, among others.[3] Jean-Marc Quaranta argues that the epiphany should be envisaged as a literary practice that is precisely situated in the historical development of literature as it depends on the intellectual context of the late nineteenth century and coincides with the birth of the Proustian novel, influenced as it was by Walter Pater.[4] Conversely, it may be argued that instances of epiphany can be found in earlier literature. At the onset of British Romanticism, Wordsworth tried to capture what he called 'spots of time',[5] that is, moments of spiritual revelation that originated from everyday objects or encounters; this idea was to influence the rise of the notion of epiphany in modern literature.[6] Scenes in which 'epiphanic moments' are staged can also be found in novels of the late eighteenth and early nineteenth centuries. For instance, in Jane Austen's *Emma* (1815), the moment when the heroine visits Donwell Abbey and first grasps the significance of such 'a sweet view – sweet to the eye and the mind. English verdure, English culture, English comfort, seen under a sun bright, without being oppressive', in relation to her emerging feelings for the owner, Mr Knightley, could be described as a full epiphany.[7]

In his introduction to the first edition of *Stephen Hero*, Theodore Spencer remarked that the theory of epiphany 'implies a lyrical rather than a dramatic view of life. It emphasizes the radiance, the effulgence, of the thing itself revealed in a special moment, an unmoving moment of time'.[8] The 'lyrical' quality or dimension of the literary epiphany explains why music can be one of its strongest and most appropriate causes or catalysts. I will argue that this notion had been adumbrated by some English novelists in the late Georgian era and the Regency period, who, each in their own distinctive manner, staged moments of revelation or disclosure, articulated in specific musical scenes, and which may therefore be considered as harbingers of that modernity associated with the Jamesian, Joycean and Proustian epiphany.[9] Focusing on a few examples, I will therefore use the term 'epiphany' in a broad sense and suggest that some late Georgian novelists employed musical epiphanies as a particularly effective device to reveal the importance of the private, inner experience of music, and that this was an integral part of the new role they ascribed to sensibility as an intimate experience.

In *À la recherche du temps perdu*, a 'little phrase' in the fictional Vinteuil sonata triggers strong emotions and reminiscences in Swann through mental associations and he cannot separate the musical phrase from the memory of his love for Odette. Swann's discovery of, and subsequent fixation on, this musical phrase points to the very nature of music as a mysterious, untranslatable medium, the meaning of which can never be precisely explained, making it the ideal vehicle to convey the character's inner feelings and state of mind. Like Walter Pater, who wrote that in music 'the end is not distinct from the means, the form from the matter, the subject from the expression',[10] Proust placed music at the apex of sensorial and emotional experiences and as a model that the other arts ought to emulate.[11]

From an epistemological perspective, such a conception originated from, and depended on, a profound change in the way music tended to be conceived and conceptualised that can be traced back to the second half of the eighteenth century.[12] Philosophers and theoreticians of musical aesthetics, especially in Britain, gradually rejected earlier conceptions of music as one of the sister arts, depending primarily on poetry, and granted it instead its full autonomy as an artistic medium.[13] Music was decidedly not an imitative art, they averred, and its 'meaning' was no longer thought to depend on its subordination to a pre-existing text. This opened the way to a new conception of music considered primarily for its emotional impact and paved the way for the eventual possibility of musical epiphanies to emerge in novels of the second half of the eighteenth century, in which the focus tended to shift from a moral outlook

MUSICAL 'EPIPHANIES' 295

to the expression of the (generally female) character's sensibility through her musical performance or her emotions while listening to music.

One of the conditions required for the musical epiphany to occur is, indeed, that the meaning of music should remain shrouded in mystery. It is music's direct impact on the listener, unmediated by any reference to semantic interpretation, that enables pure emotion to affect the listener irresistibly. The musicalisation of characters' intimate feelings is the necessary condition for the emergence of a musical epiphany. The ability to understand music's ethical intimations is felt spontaneously, intuitively and intimately.

Sterne: Music as a Suppletive to Words

The first 'musical novel' of the period (to use William Freedman's phrase, defining a novel that borrows not only metaphors, but also structural elements, from the art of music[14]) may be considered to be *The Life and Opinions of Tristram Shandy, Gentleman* (1759–67) by Laurence Sterne.[15] The crisis of language is at the core of Sterne's investigation of the power of music as a direct means of communication and of his experimentation in strategies of musicalisation of the literary text.[16] Because language often proves misleading, ambiguous and inadequate, music intervenes to supplement or replace it where a more effective medium is needed to express emotions that words fail to convey satisfactorily. Sterne stages an early example of musical epiphany in the Maria episodes to be found in both *Tristram Shandy* and his later work, *A Sentimental Journey through France and Italy* (1768), in which the respective narrators encounter a forlorn young woman abandoned by her faithless lover, in a picturesque rural setting in harmony with her condition, where she consoles herself with playing mournful tunes on her pipe.[17] In these episodes, the musical metaphor of harmony and vibrations, linked to the moral dimensions of bounty and goodwill, prepares the ground for the epiphany triggered by Maria's pipe. The harmony Tristram feels is not so much the effect of Maria's sad melody per se, as some inner disposition upon which what he hears acts as a catalyst (444–6). Tristram attributes this disposition to some 'secret spring', which implies that it is impossible to explain the real cause of it; this ties in with a definition of the essence of music as a mysterious source of emotion that cannot be rationally accounted for. Tristram's own emotions and moral disposition create the necessary condition for the power of music fully to work on him. What turns the episode into an epiphany is not simply that Tristram should be moved by the music played by Maria, but the fact that her tune enables him to attain a higher degree of response to it and to reach a nobler sphere that is beyond mere 'sentimentality' and partakes of the spiritual. Similarly, in *A Sentimental Journey*, Yorick feels 'undescribable emotions within [him]' when he hears Maria play (94). Again, what Yorick experiences can be said to be an epiphany, as it acts as a catalyst for him to acknowledge the spiritual dimension in human beings. His intentional quest for 'melancholy adventures' makes him 'perfectly conscious of the existence of a soul within [him]'. He declares that he is 'positive he has a soul' (94). Thus, religion is associated with the ability to feel, and music appears as a privileged medium for accessing the nobler spheres of feeling and religious experience.

The moment of epiphany brought about by the musical encounter between Tristram or Yorick and Maria has no lasting effect and may be short-lived, yet it constitutes an important departure from the conventional treatment of musical scenes in earlier

296 PIERRE DUBOIS

English novels. The two parallel episodes foreground music as a crucial accomplice or means to enable an important revelation to be made in trivial circumstances – a revelation that is experienced but not explained, and which remains essentially lyrical, ineffable and evanescent.

Mackenzie and Radcliffe: Music's Forceful but Ambiguous Message

In the wake of Sterne's ground-breaking treatment of music,[18] other British novelists, such as Henry Mackenzie, Ann Radcliffe, Frances Burney and Jane Austen made forays into the use of musical perception and ecstasy as moments of revelation and heightened emotive consciousness. Henry Mackenzie's *Julia de Roubigné* (1777), greatly inspired by Sterne's 'sentimental' mode, is a case in point: music is shown to be a privileged means to express feelings or to access meanings that could not otherwise be formulated verbally.[19] One scene in particular can be read as a kind of epiphany. After having administered the poison with which he succeeds in killing his wife Julia, who he thinks has been unfaithful, Montauban listens to her playing and has belated doubts as to her guilt. Her music seems to be the voice of sincerity and truth, and she looks and sounds so pure and angelic that he begins to think that he may have been mistaken, and that she did not deserve his wrath:

> I went down stairs to let Lonquillez out by a private passage, of which I keep the key. When I was returning to my apartment, I heard the sound of music proceeding from my wife's chamber; there is a double door on it; I opened the outer one without any noise, and the inner has some panes of glass a top, through which I saw part of the room. Segarva! She sat at the organ, her fingers pressing on the keys, and her look up-raised with enthusiastic rapture! – the solemn sounds still ring in my ear! such as angels might play when the fainted soul ascends to Heaven! I am the fool of appearances, when I have such proofs – Lisette is at my door.[20]

His admission that he is 'the fool of appearances' is ambiguous. It may mean that while her playing seems to testify to her innocence, this is misleading since he has proofs of her guilt; conversely, it may mean that the real proof of her innocence is the way she performs such holy, seraphic music, whereas his suspicion was only grounded in false evidence of an inferior cast. As with Maria in Sterne's novels, music thus turns out to be an incontrovertible sign of sensibility and truth. However, while Montauban is on the verge of accessing a revelation thanks to Julia's musical sensitivity, it is too late, and, as the ambiguity of the passage suggests, he is not in a disposition fully to understand or accept music's positive message. The epiphanic impression is thus partly lost on him, but the power of music to reveal truth – for whomsoever is sufficiently attentive – is nonetheless asserted.

It would fall outside the scope of this essay to analyse in detail the numerous scenes in Radcliffe's novels in which her heroines indulge in musical contemplation and are deeply moved by the sounds of music, albeit without any clear understanding on their part of its actual meaning.[21] It is noteworthy that the epiphanic moment of musical ecstasy is often triggered by or associated with a visual perception. Both picturesque scenery and music affect sensitive characters in a similar manner. For instance, in *A Sicilian Romance* (1790), the picture of the still water and the moon that first presents itself to the heroine Julia is soon translated in her mind into a 'pleasing melody', more imagined than real, before she finally hears a song performed by a chorus of boat-men.[22] In such scenes, music is, as it were, the translation into sound of visual percep-tion and it heightens its impact. Music has such a power over the imagination that it imposes itself on the subject and rounds off the moment of epiphany and stasis.[23] The link between visual perception and music is even more evident in *The Castles of Athlin and Dunbayne* (1789), in which Radcliffe associates (in an arguably synaesthetic man-ner) Alleyn's contemplation of the painted portrait of Mary with music, as his 'ear [is] struck with notes of sweet music' while he is in the gallery of pictures.[24] In Radcliffe's intricate literary construct, music is intertwined with visual descriptions and references to nature, and its actual source is not always clear, so that it is permanently shrouded in mystery. It could be argued that Radcliffe adopts an almost 'epiphanic mode', as each of her stories consists in a succession of intense moments of emotion yielding rev-elations that, veiled in obscurity as they are, nevertheless contribute to the characters' progress. These successive musical epiphanies are signs of the characters' exquisite sensibility; they also contribute to the dark Gothic atmosphere of Radcliffe's novels, in which pleasure blends with terror.[25]

Frances Burney: Silence, Femininity and Morality

Although she was less musical than her sisters Esther and Susan, Frances Burney was fond of music and understood its emotional as well as social potential;[26] she made good use of musical scenes in her novels, but followed a different agenda from the authors discussed so far. In her first novel, *Evelina* (1778),[27] references to music remain largely focused on social critique, as found in early Georgian novels by such authors as Henry Fielding and Samuel Richardson. In these, musical scenes generally provided an oppor-tunity to represent the manners of the time, often as the pretext for satirising the behav-iour of the audience. They exacerbated social awareness, made social commentary possible and enabled the author to voice a topical opinion about the very nature of the entertainment depicted. The main target was Italian opera, following the negative out-look expressed by such critics as John Dennis and Joseph Addison.[28] Italian opera was perceived as morally defective and dangerous, a sign of degeneracy and the repository for a harmful foreign influence, and it was therefore dismissed on ideological grounds. The emotional impact of music itself was made subservient to social and moral consid-erations. However, while Richardson, who was Burney's model, mainly insisted on this opera-versus-oratorio dichotomy, denouncing the former and praising the latter – in, for example, *The History of Sir Charles Grandison* (1753), his last novel – the social critique in *Evelina* is targeted at the attitude of the talkative audience, not at the genre of opera itself. The heroine's relatives are the butt of the satire precisely because they still 'appear to echo the opinions of the anti-opera arbiters of public taste from the first quarter of the century', as Leya Landau remarks.[29] Burney suggests that opera may indeed move the listener in a positive way, provided people pay proper attention to the beauty of the music. The moral import of music now depends on the listeners' feelings and their ability to listen, not on a prescriptive discourse.

298 PIERRE DUBOIS

Burney's young heroine loves music, as 'some of the songs [seem] to melt [her] very soul' (37), a clear marker of her 'sensibility'; she is accordingly shocked by the lack of attention and constant talking of the members of the audience around her (38). She is astonished 'to find how little music is attended to in silence; for though every body seems to admire, hardly any body listens' (105). In her diaries, Burney repeatedly denounced noisy audiences.[30] By making precise reference to real works and singers of the time in her novels (such as *Artaxerxes*, or the castrato singer Paccheriotti), she introduced a realism that enabled the contemporary reader to identify with the fictional audience. Readers were thus invited to question their attitudes as potential listeners. It is not so much the characters' ability to express feelings via music as performers that is articulated as their inner emotions and their response to music. The listener's silence, which is the necessary condition for the ability to be moved by music and to experience an epiphany, as we shall see in Burney's *Cecilia*, strangely mirrors music's own non-verbal presence, its power to affect the listener in spite of – or perhaps precisely thanks to – the mysterious, untranslatable character of its very mode of expression. Thus, music pertains intimately to the domain of sensibility and is presented as one of its essential markers.

In *Cecilia* (1782),[31] Burney moves even further away than in *Evelina* from the conventional anti-opera topos, and she associates music with a moment of revelation that amounts to a real epiphany. The heroine, whose name suggests that she is the very embodiment or analogy of music itself, is overwhelmed by strong emotion when she attends an opera rehearsal. As she has never previously been to the opera, she experiences 'a sensation not more new than delightful' and is 'enraptured' by the music (64–5). Thanks to this musical epiphany which creates a receptive context for human compassion, Cecilia 'discovers' the importance of charity during the rehearsal through the attitude of a strange man, Albany, who shares similar emotions. This challenges Megan Grandmont's suggestion that 'the sheer amount of page space devoted to Cecilia's enjoyment of her first opera rehearsal does absolutely nothing to forward the plot of the novel'.[32] The epiphany at the rehearsal affects Cecilia so deeply that it permanently changes her whole attitude, and she consequently applies herself to deeds of charity. The link between music and charity was often asserted in the eighteenth century, not least through great music events such as the Three Choirs Festival. Indeed, Charles Burney, Frances's father, wrote that the 'the true style [of music] for the church' ought to be noble and sober, for then 'it calls to memory nothing vulgar, light or prophane; it disposes the mind to philanthropy, and divests it of its gross and sensual passions'.[33] In a way, Cecilia's sudden realisation, through music, of the importance of devoting herself to acts of charity ties in with Yorick's assertion that he is 'positive he has a soul': music reveals something of a greater import than simply sensorial pleasure or personal gratification. Both true musical appreciation and benevolence towards our fellow human beings are thus bound together and presented as integral constituents of sensibility.

The epiphany is not so much caused by some exterior factor as merely activated by it, for it first requires a predisposition. Cecilia – like Tristram or Yorick in Sterne's novels – has the ideal disposition to be moved by Pacchierotti's singing, whereas the other spectators are there merely for 'a love of company, fashion, and shew' (131) and they do not pay attention to the music itself:

Cecilia was much vexed to find the first act of the Opera almost over; but she was soon still more dissatisfied when she discovered that she had no chance of hearing the little which remained: the place she had happened to find vacant was next to a party of young ladies, who were so earnestly engaged in their own discourse, that they listened not to a note of the Opera, and so infinitely diverted with their own witticisms, that their tittering and loquacity allowed no one in their vicinity to hear better than themselves. Cecilia tried in vain to confine her attention to the singers; she was distant from the stage, and to them she was near, and her fruitless attempts all ended in chagrin and impatience . . . (134)

The ability to experience a musical epiphany is therefore not universal. It is a sign and test of the listener's sensibility and openness to what is on offer, of an individual's inner disposition. Although not very skilled in the art, Cecilia has 'a natural love of music [which] in some measure supplie[s] the place of cultivation', so that what she can 'neither explain nor understand, she [can] feel and enjoy' (65). Quite significantly, it is the music itself, and Pacchierotti's voice and musical expressiveness – the 'refinement of his taste and masterly originality of his genius' (64) – which move Cecilia, not the words (in Italian) of the airs he sings.[34] Let us note, incidentally, that the castrato's high-pitched voice, which would previously have been dismissed as 'effeminate' by the harsh critics of Italian opera, is now perceived by Cecilia as particularly moving and beautiful, which may suggest that it is particularly attuned to feminine sensibility. Although 'the pleasure she received from the music was much augmented by her previous acquaintance with that interesting drama', the real cause of Cecilia's emotion is the singer's 'tone of softness, pathos, and sensibility' (65). The musical message itself, untranslatable as it is, is what matters most, and it enables Cecilia and Albany to meet on the ground of shared sentimental experience.

Cecilia is struck by Albany's 'uncommon sensibility to the power of music' (65), which is similar to hers. This natural disposition of his personality marks him out as someone worth considering and triggers Cecilia's curiosity about him. Burney deftly draws a parallel between the lack of musical sensibility of the other members of the audience and their inability either to perceive Albany's moral virtue, or even to agree on what name to call him by. For some he is the 'man-hater', for others the 'moralist', the 'crazy-man' or the 'bore': 'he is called by any and every name but his own' (66). This suggests that, just as they are deaf to music, these people are blind to Albany's real character. Musical sensibility is thus aligned implicitly with a person's ability to see the world and understand what really matters, which is what defines Cecilia. In the rehearsal scene, musical emotion acts for her as an eye-opener, so to speak: her acute sensibility to the music enables her to see what the others do not. Accordingly, the following day, she decides to perform an act of charity as recommended by Albany after the rehearsal: 'seek the virtuous, relieve the poor, and save yourself from the destruction of unfeeling prosperity' (68). The musical epiphany has had an ethical effect since it motivates a practical decision on Cecilia's part to act generously and relieve misery.

Later in the novel, Albany tells Cecilia his sad story: because he was responsible for the depravation and death of a woman he had loved and then abandoned, he had vowed to lead a life of penance and to devote himself to charity. Significantly, he adds that the only occasional indulgence he allows himself is music, 'which has power to delight me even in rapture! It quiets all anxiety, it carries me out of myself. I forget through it every calamity, even the bitterest anguish' (708–9). In a quasi-circular way, the link between music and charity is thus stated again and reinforced, and this sheds a new retrospective light on the nature of the epiphany experienced by Cecilia during the rehearsal scene at the beginning of the novel. She was not mistaken when she observed Albany's intense emotion as he was listening to Pacchierotti. Without knowing the details of Albany's story at the time, she was sensitive to his response to music, and grasped that there was a close connection between this form of art and morality.

Silent attention to music is presented as a necessary condition for both enjoying it and enabling an epiphany to occur. Cecilia is a silent observer rather than a talkative commentator. This contains an ethical dimension: attention and reserve are presented as necessary to a proper understanding of true moral values as revealed by music. This is why the denunciation of the audience's talkativeness, lack of attention and noise plays an important part in Burney's novels, as *Evelina* suggests. It is interesting to observe that her heroines have both a heightened sensibility and a tendency to remain silent and listen, while so many of the other characters speak profusely and pay little attention to others' feelings or activities. In both Austen and Burney, the most talkative characters are generally the object of ridicule or turn out to be morally defective.[35] In Burney's last novel, *The Wanderer* (1814), published in the same year as Austen's *Mansfield Park*, the musical heroine, Juliet, is defined precisely by her tendency to remain silent, preferring to bear the brunt of some accusation of ill conduct on some crucial occasions rather than to lower herself to justifying her attitude.[36] Silence is a modality of her modesty and good breeding. Following the recommendations addressed to young ladies in the conduct-books of the period,[37] she chooses deliberately to remain silent so as to assert her femininity and to dispute the patriarchal violence of society. Silence, as well as music, acts as a bulwark to protect Juliet against useless talking and noise. In *Cecilia*, the heroine's absorption in the music and Pacchierotti's singing marks her out as different from the rest of the audience, who hardly ever listen to the music, as we have seen. Thus, it might be argued that by endowing the female listener with the ability to remain silent while attending a public musical performance, Burney articulates an implicit gender differentiation as she reappropriates the experience of musical enjoyment within a specifically feminine territory: as the heroine refrains from expressing herself and listens with attention, she shows she is truly at one with the locus of music. Her very silence 'musicalises' her. Juliet's musical performance on the harp, and her retreat into silence when spoken to, are two sides of the same coin, in a sense, or the two complementary forms of the same attitude of restraint and reticence, which were considered to be feminine virtues at the time.[38] Similarly, Cecilia's refusal to indulge in a frivolous conversation and her profound attention during the rehearsal she attends testify to her deeply musical nature.

Jane Austen and the Musical Counter-Epiphany

As in many novels of sensibility of the period – by such writers as Ann Radcliffe, Frances Burney, Jane West, Maria Edgeworth and Elizabeth Inchbald, to name but a few – music plays a prominent role in Jane Austen's novels, but her treatment of the art as a reflection of the protagonists' education and feelings is varied, personal and complex. Several of her female characters play the fortepiano or the harp and sing, some with peculiar talent, but others in a more modest capacity. While Austen's musical scenes contribute to the setting of the social context that her characters inhabit, they are also instrumental in mapping out subtle differences between the young women's personal response to music, either as a means of displaying their accomplishments, or conversely as a more intimate practice through which they express their inner sensibility. Austen consistently expressed reservations towards these female accomplishments and advocated a genuine but moderate involvement of women in music.

It is not really surprising, therefore, that Austen should have approached the idea of musical epiphany from a different angle from that adopted by Sterne and Burney in their novels. While the principle at work – that of a sudden, forceful revelation – is the same, Austen reverses it ironically, or turns it upside down, and creates what could be called 'counter-epiphanies': instead of having a deep, positive and lasting impact on the character concerned, as we have observed with Burney's Cecilia, the moment of revelation through the perception of music proves misleading and illusory – but the psychological mechanism of this misinterpreted and misleading revelation is epiphanic.

One example can be found in *Mansfield Park* (1814), when Mary Crawford seduces Edmund with her harp-playing.[39] The visual impression on him of her beauty when she plays the instrument is almost as important as the music itself. Not unlike Radcliffe, Austen 'paints' the epiphanic moment vividly as if it were a picture or tableau:

> The harp arrived, and rather added to her beauty, wit, and good-humour; for she played with the greatest obligingness, with an expression and taste which were peculiarly becoming, and there was something clever to be said at the close of every air. Edmund was at the Parsonage every day, to be indulged with his favourite instrument: one morning secured an invitation for the next; for the lady could not be unwilling to have a listener, and every thing was soon in a fair train.
>
> A young woman, pretty, lively, with a harp as elegant as herself, and both placed near a window, cut down to the ground, and opening on a little lawn, surrounded by shrubs in the rich foliage of summer, was enough to catch any man's heart. The season, the scene, the air, were all favourable to tenderness and sentiment. (76)

However, it soon appears that this moment of revelation does not yield the whole truth about Mary Crawford but, on the contrary, ensnares Edmund by giving him a misleading impression of her. Her charm, her beauty and her musical abilities do not reveal her true self but conceal her inner moral deficiencies. What is depicted in terms of a musical epiphany is a delusion or a lie. Whereas Juliet's harp in Burney's *The Wanderer* is a sign of her refinement, taste and moral rectitude, Mary Crawford's harp is a lure. Austen uses the conventional musical topos of the harp ironically to denounce and satirise polite forms of superficial, 'sentimental' feeling.[40] In doing so, however, she does concede that music can have an extraordinary power over the imagination and contribute to a person's experience of particularly strong emotions. She does not question the effect of music, but rather the ability of the subject to decipher its meaning accurately. Compelling as it is, the ineffable, non-verbal message music delivers is neither clear, nor easily interpreted. While Burney's Cecilia deduced the importance of good deeds from her musical experience, in *Mansfield Park*, Edmund does not go beyond the surface of the scene that presents itself to him and thus falls victim to mistaken impressions.

Austen had previously presented a similar case of misinterpretation in *Sense and Sensibility* (1811), in which Marianne falls prey to the emotions she feels when she shares moments of musical complicity with Willoughby.[41] This is not an epiphanic 'moment', however, as her feelings develop gradually through repeated exchanges, but

302   PIERRE DUBOIS

here Austen again denounces the dangers of a wrong, emotional or Romantic reading of music. Willoughby uses their shared taste for music as a means to court her. Their romance begins and grows around the fortepiano: 'His society became gradually her most exquisite enjoyment. They read, they talked, they sang together; his musical talents were considerable; and he read with all the sensibility and spirit which Edward had unfortunately wanted' (58).

Marianne's eventual disappointment in love is presented by Austen as a correlative of her blindness to what is actually enacted in their musical exchange. What is at stake is not the love of music itself, but Marianne's excessive and passionate involvement in it. The revelation she believes she has experienced when sharing moments of intense musical emotions with Willoughby turns out to be false and misleading. Like Edmund, Marianne is simply wrong in her interpretation of the moments of musical happiness shared with her first lover. While she does not share similar emotions with Colonel Brandon, who seems cold and detached when listening to her performance, nevertheless he eventually reveals himself to be the more sensitive and benevolent personality. To love music to excess and (mis)interpret its meaning in terms of the promise of a future bond with another person is therefore presented by Austen as dangerous and equivocal.

In *Persuasion* (1817), the ambiguity is of a different kind, but it is nevertheless present. One scene in particular seems to open onto a possible musical epiphany, but it is actually inconclusive, although it paves the way for the happy conclusion of the novel. Near the end, Anne Elliot attends a concert at the Assembly Rooms in Bath. The concert is 'really expected to be a good one' and Anne knows that Captain Wentworth is very fond of music.[42] After a short conversation with him, she is convinced that he 'had a heart returning to her at least; that anger, resentment, avoidance, were no more; and that . . . he must love her' (202). She therefore listens to the first part of the concert with pleasure:

> Anne's mind was in a most favourable state for the entertainment of the evening; it was just occupation enough: she had feelings for the tender, spirits for the gay, attention for the scientific, and patience for the wearisome; and had never liked a concert better, at least during the first act. (203)

Even in a public concert, surrounded as she is by people – including Mr Elliot, who asks her to explain the meaning of the Italian words of a song – Anne concentrates on her sincere love of music and finds happiness in it. As she is now partly reassured as to Captain Wentworth's feelings towards her, and she is determined not to succumb to Mr Elliot's courtship, the scene seems to veer towards a moment of revelation and mutual concord between Anne and the captain, all the more so as we know that, in the past, 'there could have been no two hearts so open, no tastes so similar, no feelings so in unison' as theirs (64). As Miriam F. Hart remarks, Austen's use of the musical term 'unison' is meaningful.[43] It suggests that the relationship between Anne and Wentworth is metaphorically placed under the patronage of musical harmony (implying a thoughtful control of emotions and sensibility) and that the reader can therefore expect the concert to be the occasion of the lovers' reunion. Yet the musical epiphany is partly defeated, since Captain Wentworth, jealous as he is of Mr Elliot's intimacy with Anne, suddenly decides to leave the concert: '"Is not this song worth staying for?" said Anne,

MUSICAL 'EPIPHANIES' 303

suddenly struck by an idea which made her yet more anxious to be encouraging. "No!" he replied impressively, "there is nothing worth my staying for"; and he was gone directly' (190).

So, while on the one hand we may concur with Hart when she writes that 'the musical allusions Wentworth and Anne share culminate in the concert scene, during which the only two educated musicians in the novel meet', on the other, the scene in question ends in discord.[44] Austen plays with the impact of music on the characters and ironically thwarts the reader's expectation by letting Wentworth leave the concert. However, at the end of the novel, when he and Anne are finally reunited, they can retrospectively assess the importance of this concert as a pivotal moment: 'Their first meeting in Milson Street afforded much to be said, but the concert still more. That evening seemed to be made up of exquisite moments' (232). Hart rightly notes that 'music has served as a metaphorical as well as a literal meeting ground for Anne and Wentworth, providing them with language and opportunities to express their passion for one another privately, while in a public setting'.[45] The scene may therefore not be as straightforward and obvious as the rehearsal scene in Burney's *Cecilia*, but it does operate nonetheless in a circuitous, ironical, characteristically Austenian manner.

Conclusion

Although the authors discussed here do not use the term 'epiphany', can these epiphanic musical moments in these novels be considered as real 'epiphanies' in the sense sanctioned by the literary critical tradition inaugurated by Joyce? Admitting that they are, as I have done here, amounts to ascribing to these works a potent role as forerunners of the modernist novel. Music does possess the special power of revealing emotions, feelings and desires more successfully than any other medium. As Labarthe writes about Swann and Vinteuil's musical phrase, music transcends the arbitrariness, transitoriness and fleetingness of the feelings to which it gives substance.[46] Although the effect of such moments of revelation may prompt the character who experiences them to engage subsequently in action, as we saw in the case of Cecilia, the subject is not involved in any activity during the scene. All that he or she does is to keep quiet and listen. While music is being performed, action is partly suspended, which makes it possible for the protagonist to pause, observe and reflect, and to feed on his or her emotions. This is a moment of stasis – an 'unmoving moment of time', to quote Theodore Spencer's phrase once more. Paradoxically, it is in the midst of a social gathering that the heroine attains a state of isolation and estrangement from others within her own thoughts. As she observes silently what is going on, both on stage and around her, she temporarily stops being an agent, turns into a reflective consciousness, and yields to emotional introspection.

What distinguishes what I have called a musical epiphany from musical scenes in which the heroine or some protagonist sings or plays an instrument is precisely the character's active involvement in that performance as opposed to the temporary inactivity belonging to epiphany. This inactivity, however, is far from being passive, since the protagonist experiences a heightened degree of awareness, perception and understanding: they are all attention and yield fully to the regulation of their emotions. The paradox of these musical epiphanic scenes resides in the fact that it is precisely in moments when time is suspended and characters do not perform deliberate actions

304 PIERRE DUBOIS

that they attain the most crucial, and the most enlightening, degree of consciousness (however inconclusive this may prove to be). The musical epiphany, which appears to be as it were a hindrance to the progress of the plot (at least temporarily), reverses priorities and gives precedence to the inner motions of the mind and heart over social gestures and the outward performance of deliberate, practical deeds. Music occupies a place both untranslatable in verbal terms, and independent of the usual logics and workings of plot, but describing a character's response to music contributes more powerfully than any other aspect to the portrait of his or her psychological and emotional nature. Thus, the musical epiphany displaces the centre of gravity of the novel as the characters' actions matter less than their inner feelings. Thanks to the importance given to music in the texts where such epiphanies are staged, sensibility is granted the prime place, and it is little wonder, therefore, that the appearance of epiphanies in the British novel should have corresponded with the rise of the cult of sensibility, while they also foreshadow the workings of the later, modernist literary epiphany.

Notes

1. James Joyce, *Stephen Hero* (c.1904–6; London: Jonathan Cape, 1944, repr. 1969), 216.
2. Robert Langbaum, 'The Epiphanic Mode in Wordsworth and Modern Literature', *New Literary History* 14, no. 2 (1983): 335–58, (338).
3. See, for instance, Morris Beja, *Epiphany in the Modern Novel* (London: Peter Owen, 1971); Jean-Marc Quaranta, 'Impressions obscures et souvenirs involontaire: morphologie de l'épiphanie proustienne', *Bulletin d'informations proustiennes* (1998), 5, https:// hal.science/hal-01773065/document (accessed 20 November 2023).
4. Quaranta, 'Impressions obscures', 5, 7.
5. William Wordsworth, *The Prelude*, ed. Stephen Gill (1805; Oxford: Oxford University Press, 2010), book 11, lines 258, 491.
6. Ashton Nichols, *The Poetics of Epiphany: Nineteenth-Century Origins of the Modern Literary Moment* (Tuscaloosa: University of Alabama Press, 1987).
7. See, for instance, Robert Clark, 'Jane Austen's *Emma*, Adam Smith's "Impartial Spectator", Market Capitalism and Free-Indirect Discourse', *XVII–XVIII. Revue de la société d'études anglo-américaines des XVIIe et XVIIIe siècles* 77 (2020): 39, http://journals. openedition.org/1718/4622 (accessed 20 November 2023).
8. Theodore Spencer, 'Introduction' to the first edition of *Stephen Hero*, 23.
9. Quaranta, 'Impressions obscures', 5, 7.
10. Walter H. Pater, *Studies in the History of the Renaissance* (London: Macmillan, 1873), 135.
11. See, in particular, Marcel Proust, *La prisonnière*, in *À la recherche du temps perdu* (Paris: Gallimard, 1923), II, 70.
12. See, in particular, James Harris, *Three Treatises, Concerning Art; Music, Painting, & Poetry; Happiness* (London: J. Nourse and P. Vaillant, 1744); Charles Avison, *Essay on Musical Expression* (London: C. Davis, 1752–3); James Beattie, *Essays on Poetry and Music as They Affect the Mind* (London: E. and C. Dilly; Edinburgh: W. Creech, 1779); Michel-Paul-Guy de Chabanon, *De la musique considérée en elle-même et dans ses rapports avec la parole, les langues, la poésie et le théâtre* (Paris: Pissot, 1785); Thomas Twining, *Two Dissertations, on Poetical, & Musical, Imitation, in Aristotle's Treatise on Poetry* (London: Payne & Son, et al., 1789).
13. This question is discussed in greater depth in various studies, including Pierre Dubois, *La conquête du mystère musical en Angleterre au siècle des Lumières* (Lyon and Grenoble: Presses Universitaires de Grenoble/Presses Universitaires de Lyon, 2009; Maria Semi,

MUSICAL 'EPIPHANIES'   305

Music as a Science of Mankind in Eighteenth-Century Britain (Farnham: Ashgate, 2012); Marie-Pauline Martin and Chiara Saviettieri, eds, *La musique face au système des arts, ou les vicissitudes de l'imitation au siècle des Lumières* (Paris: Vrin, 2019).

14. William Freedman, *Laurence Sterne and the Origins of the Musical Novel* (Athens: University of Georgia Press, 1978).

15. Laurence Sterne, *The Life and Opinions of Tristram Shandy, Gentleman*, ed. Howard Anderson (1759–67; New York and London: W. W. Norton, 1980). Further references parenthetical.

16. See Pierre Dubois, *Music in the Georgian Novel* (Cambridge: Cambridge University Press, 2015), 87–93.

17. Laurence Sterne, *A Sentimental Journey through France and Italy*, ed. Tim Parnell (1768; Oxford: Oxford University Press, 2003). Further references parenthetical.

18. See, for instance, Freedman, *Laurence Sterne and the Origins of the Musical Novel*; Dubois, *Music in the Georgian Novel*; Werner Wolf, *The Musicalization of Fiction: A Study in the Theory and History of Intermediality* (Amsterdam and Atlanta: Rodopi, 1999).

19. For a detailed analysis, see Dubois, *Music in the Georgian Novel*, 121–31.

20. Henry Mackenzie, *Julia de Roubigné* (London: W. Strahan, and T. Cadell, 1777), 184–5.

21. For a detailed analysis, see Dubois, *Music in the Georgian Novel*, 177–80.

22. Ann Radcliffe, *A Sicilian Romance*, ed. Alison Milbank (1790; Oxford: Oxford University Press, 2008), 58.

23. See Dubois, *Music in the Georgian Novel*, 121–31.

24. Ann Radcliffe, *The Castles of Athlin and Dunbayne. A Highland Story*, ed. Alison Milbank (1789; Oxford: Oxford University Press, 1995), 92. I am grateful to Jakub Lipski for drawing my attention to this passage.

25. See Dubois, *Music in the Georgian Novel*, 194. See also Elizabeth R. Napier, *The Failure of Gothic: Problems of Disjunction in an Eighteenth-century Literary Form* (Oxford: Clarendon Press, 1987), 101, 147.

26. See, for instance, Susan Burney, *The Journals and Letters of Susan Burney*, ed. Philip Olleson (1788; Farnham: Ashgate, 2012).

27. Frances Burney, *Evelina*, ed. Edward A. Bloom and Lillian D. Bloom (1778; Oxford: Oxford University Press, 1982). Further references parenthetical.

28. Joseph Addison and Richard Steele, *The Spectator*: 'No. 5', 6 March 1711; 'No. 18', 21 March 1711; 'No. 13', 15 March 1711; 'No. 29', 3 April 1711. John Dennis, *Essay on the Operas after the Italian Manner* (London: J. Nutt, 1706).

29. Leya Landau, '"The Middle State:" Italian Opera in Frances Burney's *Cecilia*', *Eighteenth-Century Fiction* 17, no. 4 (2005): 670.

30. See, for example, *The Early Journals and Letters of Fanny Burney*, ed. Lars E. Troide, 4 vols (Oxford: Clarendon Press, 1988), 1:367.

31. Frances Burney, *Cecilia*, ed. Peter Sabor and Margaret Anne Doody (1782; Oxford: Oxford University Press, 1999). Further references parenthetical.

32. Megan Grandmont, 'The Power of Her Voice: Music and Patriarchal Politics in Frances Burney's *Cecilia*' (Boston: Archives, vol. 6, no. 22010, 2010), 3/11, https://ejournals.bc.edu/index.php/elements/article/view/9033 (accessed 20 November 2023).

33. Charles Burney, *The Present State of Music in France and Italy; or, the Journal of a Tour through those Countries undertaken to collect Materials for a General History of Music* (1771; London: T. Beckett & Co.; J. Robson and G. Robinson, 1771/73), 152–3.

34. See Landau, 'The Middle State', 673. The opera is *Artaserse* by Ferdinando Gasparo Bertoni, based on a libretto by Metastasio, performed in London, with Gasparo Pacchierotti, in January 1779. Both Susan and Frances Burney greatly admired Pacchierotti. On 13 February 1780, he and Bertoni visited the Burneys and Pacchierotti sang an air from *Artaserse*. Susan wrote: 'I listen'd to him wth a delight wch brought tears to my Eyes – and he was all sweetness

306   PIERRE DUBOIS

and good nature the whole time'; Susan Burney, *The Journals*, 118. These impressions are echoed by Cecilia's own feelings in the novel.

35. See Janis P. Stout, *Strategies of Reticence: Silence and Meaning in the Works of Jane Austen, Willa Cather, Katherine Anne Porter, and Joan Didion* (Charlottesville and London: University Press of Virginia, 1990), 27.

36. See Pierre Dubois, 'Le silence de la musique dans *The Wanderer* de Frances Burney', *XVII–XVIII* 73 (2016): 147–55.

37. See, for instance, Hester Chapone, *Letters on the Improvement of the Mind* (London: J. Walter, 1773); James Fordyce, *Sermons to Young Women* (London: Publisher, 1766); John Gregory, *A Father's Legacy to his Daughters* (London: W. Strahan, T. Cadell, 1774).

38. Dubois, 'Le silence de la musique dans *The Wanderer*', 154.

39. Jane Austen, *Mansfield Park*, ed. John Wilsthire (1814; Cambridge: Cambridge University Press, 2005). Further references parenthetical.

40. See Dubois, *Music in the Georgian Novel*, 288.

41. Jane Austen, *Sense and Sensibility*, ed. Edward Copeland (1811; Cambridge: Cambridge University Press, 2006). Further references parenthetical.

42. Jane Austen, *Persuasion*, ed. Janet Todd and Antje Blank (1817; Cambridge: Cambridge University Press, 2006), 202. Further references parenthetical.

43. Miriam F. Hart, 'Hardly an Innocent Diversion: Music in the Life and Writings of Jane Austen', PhD thesis, Ohio University (1999), 202.

44. Hart, 'Hardly an Innocent Diversion', 205.

45. Hart, 'Hardly an Innocent Diversion', 208.

46. 'La musique révèle: elle révèle la qualité spirituelle d'un art dont la puissance formelle transcende ce que les sentiments auxquels elle donne corps peuvent avoir d'arbitraire, de transitoire, de passager.' Patrick Labarthe, 'Vinteuil ou le paradoxe de l'individuel en art', *Revue d'histoire littéraire de la France* 101 no. 1 (2001): 109.

18

JANE AUSTEN'S ART OF ELOCUTION: DISCERNING FEELING IN *PERSUASION*

Fraser Easton

JANE AUSTEN'S NOVEL *Persuasion* (1817) tells the story of Anne Elliot, a baronet's daughter who, having been convinced some eight years earlier to break her engagement with an impecunious suitor, Fredrick Wentworth, suddenly finds herself thrown his way again. In narrating how the disappointed former lovers are reconciled, Austen makes the ways they test each other's emotional communications, and their own feelings, the central action of the novel.[1] As a part of this dramatisation, I argue that Austen portrays a stark contrast between two eighteenth-century approaches to rhetoric: argumentative and elocutionary. Argumentative rhetoric, like Lady Russell's counsel of prudence to Anne, uses words to communicate information, logic and probabilities to its recipient.[2] It is how Wentworth attempts, unsuccessfully, to dissuade Louisa from her leap on the Cobb. Elocutionary rhetoric, like Mr Elliot's look 'of earnest admiration' at Anne from the top of the beach stairs at Lyme, communicates feelings, especially sexual ones, by way of non-word, bodily elements such as tone and gesture.[3] It is how Anne, after reading Wentworth's letter, reassures him of her reciprocal passion by 'not repulsively' receiving his 'look' (225).[4] While *Persuasion* draws on both kinds of rhetoric during Anne's long journey towards happiness with Wentworth, Austen makes the romantic reconciliation of her two protagonists depend specifically on the art of elocution.[5] Drawing on Laurence Sterne's treatment of the limits of elocutionary reception, Austen casts doubt on notions of sentimental transparency even as she ultimately grants her heroine's wish, for her and Wentworth, that their 'hearts' will 'understand each other' (207).[6]

Critics of *Persuasion* have long called attention to the novel as a sentimental work about bodily feeling (on the one hand) and rhetoric and communication (on the other), but have struggled to explain how these two phenomena are interconnected.[7] In terms of rhetoric and communication, criticism of *Persuasion* approaches the novel almost exclusively in terms of discursive argument, severing rhetoric from the orator's body. For example, Donald Rackin demonstrates the essential role of persuasion and persuadability to the 'moral action' of Austen's novel, but he focuses on how persuasion may draw on 'evidence' and resist 'passion or desire', thereby anchoring Anne's maturation in rational discursive processes.[8] Arthur E. Walzer expands on Rackin's insights by identifying the culturally gendered implications of positive, as well as negative, uses of word-based suasion in *Persuasion*, which he relates to the novel's elevation of Anne's emotional 'persuadability' over Wentworth's rational 'resolve'; however, like Rackin, he too leaves the role of embodied communication unexamined.[9] Similarly, in terms of bodily feeling, critical approaches to the affective dimension of the novel generally proceed without a rhetorical framework, whether argumentative or elocutionary. Adela Pinch brings to view the centrality of the physical body to *Persuasion*, especially Anne's immersive sensitivity (by which others are 'apprehended as insistently sensory phenomena'), but she does not treat these psycho-physical states as themselves rhetorical.[10] Alan Richardson's reading is notable for moving beyond Lockean psychology and the phenomenology of feeling, with which Pinch engages; nevertheless, his concept of 'embodied cognition' remains unrhetorical and does not address the role of feeling in communication in the novel.[11] In elocution, however, feeling and its communication are integrated.

Austen's treatment of argumentative rhetoric in the opening chapters of *Persuasion* paves the way for the novel's turn to elocution. Several critics have noted that the successful arguments for Sir Walter to retrench expenses and for Anne to break her engagement both include emotional appeals (to Sir Walter's self-love and to Lady Russell's affection for Anne). Although such appeals to shared values or admired character, known in rhetoric as appeals to 'ethos', were recognised going back to Aristotle,[12] Walzer and others read them in light of the 'new rhetoric' of George Campbell and Hugh Blair.[13] Campbell, in his *Philosophy of Rhetoric* (1776), sought to revise rhetorical theory in the wake of Locke's view of the relationship between language and knowledge and, in effect, reconcile classical rhetoric with the new learning by subordinating emotional appeals to reason and differentiating rhetoric that convinces the understanding from rhetoric that persuades the will.[14] But in *Persuasion*, Walzer argues, Austen challenges Campbell's preference for rational conviction over emotional persuasion by offering an alternative to a rationalist ethic in rhetorical theory.

In this essay, I situate *Persuasion* in relation to another eighteenth-century line of rhetorical theory, elocution. If Campbell is a central figure to the new rhetoric, Thomas Sheridan is key to the elocutionary movement, both for his insights and his impact. Like Campbell, Sheridan, in *A Course of Lectures on Elocution* (1762), reimagines elements of classical rhetoric (e.g., Quintilian on delivery[15]) in the wake of Locke. Unlike Campbell, however, Sheridan focuses on the non-word elements of delivery, rather than on word-based discourse. Central to Sheridan's understanding of elocution is his argument that while words communicate ideas (as Locke asserted), the effective communication of feeling, emotion and passion requires the use of the non-word elements of delivered speech: tone, gesture, looks and touch.[16] Given the importance of feeling to *Persuasion*, it's significant that, as with Campbell, Austen also reworks Sheridan: specifically, in *Persuasion*, she ascribes an epistemological role to the elocution of feeling. Anne's turn from prudence to romance and the associated limits of rational argument for sexual well-being relies on tone and gesture for the proof of sexual feeling. As I will show, Austen reintroduces a key notion from the new rhetoric – conviction – into her rendering of elocution, thereby endowing the art of bodily rhetoric with an epistemological, as well as affective, significance.

The turn to elocution in *Persuasion* does not arise randomly. With the device of the broken engagement Austen disables word-based language as a means of emotional persuasion, making elocution necessary for Anne and Wentworth: 'How, in all the peculiar disadvantages of their respective situations, would he ever learn her real sentiments?' (180).[17] Even if Anne could surmount the social codes that dissuaded well-born women from articulating their sexual desires, Wentworth no longer trusts her word: looks and tones will have to suffice.[18] And Wentworth's engagement to Louisa limits

JANE AUSTEN'S ART OF ELOCUTION

what he can verbalise. After Louisa and Benwick become engaged, Anne still 'could not understand his present feelings' (168).[19] In this novel, words provide context for the construal of feeling, but they rarely provide its proof. Elocutionary, not argumentative, rhetoric drives the reconciliation plot of *Persuasion*. Wentworth pays as much attention to Anne's 'tones' (226) as to her words at the White Hart Inn, and, after his statement of love in his letter, he waits to receive elocutionary ratification from Anne (225) before daring to converse with her about his feelings for her (226). In this and in so many other scenes in *Persuasion*, it is through elocution that actual felt bodily states (sensibility), including states of sexual desire, are rhetoricised (as tones and gestures) and made available for successful reception as non-word objects of communication.[20]

Although elocution shows how feelings and passions – sensibility – operate through the body as rhetorical events, Austen is deeply aware that elocution's status as an art complicates the notion of a natural language of the body, and the body's infinite configurations complicate its legibility. Austen's awareness reveals the changing ways in which novelists engaged with elocution as an artform. Both Samuel Richardson, in *Pamela* (1740), and Henry Fielding, in *Joseph Andrews* (1742), make relatively uncomplicated use of tone, facial expression and gesture as tools for the representation of character, taking them as largely transparent and legible markers of feeling, as does Frances Burney in *Evelina* (1778). Sterne, in contrast, particularly in *A Sentimental Journey through France and Italy* (1768), explores the limits of elocutionary elements for emotional communication, especially sexual communication, within the emerging novel form.[21] Austen knew Sterne well, as the references to his works in her letters, in *Mansfield Park* (1814) and in *Northanger Abbey* (1817) show,[22] and in *Persuasion* she makes significant intertextual use of her predecessor. Like Sterne's travelling comic parson, Anne must navigate elocutionary expressions of feeling as she travels, not to France and Italy, but to Lyme and Bath. Like Yorick, she translates gestures into extended speeches, attends Italian concerts and has sexually charged encounters in hallways and on stairs. And like *A Sentimental Journey*'s traveller, Anne must govern her sentiments and discern those of others, albeit in a generally serious rather than comic register.

In *Persuasion*, Austen rewrites *A Sentimental Journey*. She simultaneously builds on and departs from Sterne's novel, reworking a humorous enquiry into an explicitly moral drama about how to speak about desire, how to perceive desire (including in oneself), and how to negotiate the lack of a set code for the construal of sexual desire – despite the efforts of elocutionists, life exceeds art. The limits of elocution that Sterne plays for comedy and leaves unresolved, Austen plays for tragedy, before offering her readers a romantic resolution that is achieved by the protagonists testing each other's sexual elocution over time.[23] This emotional trial draws narrator, reader and protagonists into a shared elocutionary reception, not unlike the way in which Sterne concludes *A Sentimental Journey* by breaking the media wall between print and speech, memory and delivery.[24] When Wentworth leaves a letter for Anne to read, it is received by her, the reader and the narrator simultaneously, in the spatio-temporal moment of a single redelivery. The letter is a desperate attempt to clarify Anne's elocutionary actions at the Italian concert in light of her statements (and elocution) when debating Harville at the White Hart Inn. In this moment, Austen repurposes the branching complexities and ambiguities of the Sternean comedy of elocutionary communication and intermediality for pedagogical as well as romantic aims: Anne, Wentworth and even the reader's emotional *Bildung* resides in the elocutionary art of discerning feeling.

Convincing Reasons

The reader first encounters argumentative rhetoric in *Persuasion* with the financial crisis engulfing the Elliot estate. Carefully tailored and timed arguments, based on rational considerations and addressed to the person he really is, move Sir Walter. His persuaders do not deceive him with untrue or unreasonable information or considerations. Lady Russell is the first to attempt to 'persuade' (13) him to a course of action. She uses careful reasoning: 'She drew up plans of economy, she made exact calculations, and . . . she consulted Anne'; together she and Anne place a series of 'regulations' in front of Sir Walter and Elizabeth by which 'in seven years he will be clear' (13). But the reasons they marshal, and the numbers they present, do not 'convince him' (13); indeed, 'he would sooner quit Kellynch-hall at once' (14):

> 'Quit Kellynch-hall.' The hint was immediately taken up by Mr. Shepherd, whose interest was involved in the reality of Sir Walter's retrenching. . . . 'Since the idea had been started in the very quarter which ought to dictate, he had no scruple,' he said, 'in confessing his judgment to be entirely on that side. It did not appear to him that Sir Walter could materially alter his style of living in a house which had such a character of hospitality and ancient dignity to support.—In any other place, Sir Walter might judge for himself; and would be looked up to, as regulating the modes of life, in whatever way he might choose to model his household.' (14)

It is a bravura discursive intervention: Shepherd's speech succeeds where Lady Russell (and Anne) failed: it persuades Sir Walter, moving him to action. But even as the diction of Shepherd's speech is tailored to the snobbery and vanity of his target audience (Sir Walter and Elizabeth), to their 'ethos', a clearly stated and perfectly reasonable rationale grounds it, and the whole speech, made up of appeals to both 'logos' and 'ethos', is carried by words.

The successful persuasion of Sir Walter provides an important counterpoint to Lady Russell's persuasion of Anne. Gillian Beer points out the importance of Lady Russell's 'ethos' on Anne's decision to break off with Wentworth[25] (echoing Shepherd's chameleon-like adoption of Sir Walter's values): 'Lady Russell, whom she had always loved and relied on, could not, with such steadiness of opinion, and such tenderness of manner, be continually advising her in vain' (27). But Lady Russell's argument is also grounded in prudential calculations and reasonable prospects:

> Anne Elliot, with all her claims of birth, beauty, and mind, to throw herself away at nineteen; involve herself at nineteen in an engagement with a young man, who had nothing but himself to recommend him, and no hopes of attaining affluence, but in the chances of a most uncertain profession, and no connexions to secure even his farther rise in that profession; would be, indeed, a throwing away, which she grieved to think of! (26–7)

Anne 'was persuaded to believe the engagement a wrong thing' (27). What is wrong about it is, cleverly, the same thing that is wrong about Sir Walter staying at Kellynch Hall: it is financially imprudent. The compressed indirect account of Lady Russell's argument lists reasons for believing in the improbability of Wentworth's prospects.

Lady Russell may well be motivated by snobbery and rely on discursive emotional appeals in opposing Anne's engagement, but by recounting Sir Walter's financial challenges first, Austen inclines the reader to find Lady Russell's earlier concern (in 1806) for Anne's financial interests seem disinterested and her love of Anne genuine.

By the present day of the novel's action (1814), not only has Anne's relationship to the event of her cancelled engagement changed, so has her relationship to rational argument:

> How eloquent could Anne Elliot have been,—how eloquent, at least, were her wishes on the side of early warm attachment, and a cheerful confidence in futurity, against that over-anxious caution which seems to insult exertion and distrust Providence!— She had been forced into prudence in her youth, she learned romance as she grew older—the natural sequel of an unnatural beginning. (29)

This famous passage speaks to Austen's treatment of argumentative rhetoric in *Persuasion*. Beyond the summary of Anne's situation as a surprising growth into romance from a youth of seeming realism, the narrator invites the reader to consider seriously 'the possible means of persuasion'[26] with a fresh eye, in this case those reasons that Anne can marshal ('over-anxious caution', 'distrust [of] Providence') against her own earlier rejection of an impecunious attachment. Anne's reflection on this topic is partly in the form of an argument from herself to herself – probabilities have been recalculated by the passage of time – but, significantly, the salience of feeling to her situation is weighed differently.

Anne's reasons for trusting early attachment in her rational (imagined) eloquent speech turn the (rational) means of argument against rational discourse per se and in favour of the elocutionary dimension of rhetoric: feelings, not reasons, become their own justification and are added to the means of persuasion; warmth, cheerfulness, confidence and energy ('exertion') all versus anxiety. If arguments of financial prudence (whether borne out or not) are based on the facts of numbers and probabilities, then it makes sense to expect that arguments of romance will be based on the 'wishes' of feelings and passions. The natural realm of this unnaturally recognised rhetoric is elocution. Anne's undelivered, 'could . . . have been' (29) eloquence about prudence and romance marks a crucial pivot in *Persuasion*, one that shifts narrative attention away from a rhetoric focused on reasons communicated via spoken discourse and towards a rhetoric focused on feelings communicated via non-word bodily comportment.

Large Fat Sighings

As an art of the body, elocution proceeds from the lungs, the larynx, the face, the limbs and the hands. Elocution may occur independently of discourse (a shriek, a silent tear), or it may be added to spoken words via pronunciation (variations in tone, volume, speed, pitch, emphasis and rhythm, including pauses) and physical action (variations in facial expression, limbs, hands, posture, as well as tears, blushes, etc.) – in Latin, *pronunciatio et actio*.[27] Austen occasionally underscores the paralinguistic, non-word nature of delivery stylistically. Like Sterne, she uses dashes and aposiopesis to capture such speech effects as velocity and emphasis. *Persuasion* also uses graphically separated, stage-direction-like parentheses to tag key segments of dialogue: thus, in Bath,

312   FRASER EASTON

a speech by Anne to Mr Elliot is delivered '(smiling)' (141); at the concert, a comment
to Wentworth about her time in Lyme is delivered '(with a faint blush at some recollections)' (174); a later speech to Harville is delivered '(with a faltering voice)' (219).[28]
These paralinguistic elements direct the reader's attention two ways: to the drama-like
nature of these dialogues, and to their narrative presentation as delivered speech, like
the speech of an actor. But although the idea of the actor and the acting manual is con-
genial to Austen's understanding of the art of elocution, especially in *Mansfield Park*,
in *Persuasion* she centres elocution within the naturalistic frame of sensibility.

Austen renders the physicality of elocution with care and precision. Pinch astutely
notes how Austen portrays the overstimulation of noise as a physical flow invading
Anne's felt experience.[29] But it is not just noise that flows between people; coherent
elocution does too. As a flow of energy, elocution can be contagious, as when Louisa
speaks 'with enthusiasm' (78) and Anne observes Wentworth 'catching the same tone'
(79). Austen also treats this physicality as a problematic to be explored. Elocution is
both under the orator's control, as when using emphasis in reading aloud effectively,
as Benwick does (94), and outside their control, as when 'Anne's heart beat in spite
of herself, and brought the colour into her cheeks' (158). Elocution is legible (tears of
sadness) and illegible (are the tears of sadness or of happiness?). It is authentic and
it is acted. It is natural and it is cultural. It is well defined (a smile), and it is hard to
define (a smirk). How then can the cause or intent of elocutionary acts be discerned
with confidence?

The challenge of elocutionary reception emerges particularly strongly with Anne's
response to Wentworth's tones and looks in the scene involving the narratorial reaction
to the 'large fat sighings' (63) of Mrs Musgrove. Here Austen inaugurates *Persuasion*'s
exploration of the psychological, social and aesthetic significance of delivery. When
Mrs Musgrove starts lamenting 'poor Richard' (63), Anne notices that

> There was a momentary expression in Captain Wentworth's face at this speech, a
> certain glance of his bright eye, and curl of his handsome mouth, which convinced
> Anne, that instead of sharing in Mrs. Musgrove's kind wishes, as to her son, he
> had probably been at some pains to get rid of him; but it was too transient an
> indulgence of self-amusement to be detected by any who understood him less than
> herself; in another moment he was perfectly collected and serious. (63)

Wentworth's amused and disdainful looks are an instance of his emotions causing the
signalling capacity of his body to escape his control and to reveal impolite feelings,
albeit briefly, before he is again all restrained politeness. Anne's emotional detection
advances Austen's narrative in a variety of ways: first, it reveals Anne's elocutionary
sophistication because she catches the telling, if fleeting, elements in Wentworth's elocutionary performance and has the prior experience to assess them. Second, the reader
sees, through Wentworth's changing demeanour, how elocution is both natural ('curl')
and artificial ('collected').[30] It therefore falls to the recipient of any speech or gesture
to parse out what is spontaneous and what is calculated in its delivery. Third, it is
through an informed elocutionary analysis that Anne hopes to confirm her insights
about Wentworth's facial demeanour. Embodied communication of various kinds, not
discursive reports, are what she uses to determine his 'real sentiments' (180). Fourth,
and finally, Austen describes Anne as 'convinced', going beyond the new rhetoric's

contrast between emotional persuasion and rational conviction to grant epistemological value to the passionate transmissions of elocution.[31]

Whereas Anne's decoding of Wentworth's elocution is presented sympathetically, Mrs Musgrove's unhappiness over the death of her son Richard appears unsympathetically presented, at least at first, filtered through the narrator's ratification of Wentworth's hostile response:

> Mrs. Musgrove was of a comfortable substantial size, infinitely more fitted by nature to express good cheer and good humour, than tenderness and sentiment; and . . . Captain Wentworth should be allowed some credit for the self-command with which he attended to her large fat sighings over the destiny of a son, whom alive nobody had cared for. (63)

In this infamous passage the narrator skewers false sentiment with a fat-shaming animus. The role of cultural aesthetics in perceptions of the body, articulated so comically with the vain Sir Walter's view of physical desire and sexual elocution, reappears here with the negative portrayal of Mrs Musgrove's melodramatic 'body language'.[32] With this conservative formulation, a general point emerges: as embodied rhetoric, cultural assumptions about the body of the orator necessarily contribute to elocutionary reception.

After the parody of Mrs Musgrove's melodramatic feelings, the narrator, uncharacteristically for this novel, breaks into the flow of the narrative with a general pronouncement about bodies and feelings:

> Personal size and mental sorrow have certainly no necessary proportions. A large bulky figure has as good a right to be in deep affliction, as the most graceful set of limbs in the world. But, fair or not fair, there are unbecoming conjunctions, which reason will patronize in vain,—which taste cannot tolerate,—which ridicule will seize. (63–4)

The 'unbecoming conjunctions' arise not from Mrs Musgrove's real or supposed mental grief, her inner life, but from the physical ground available to her for the elocutionary expression of that grief, what Austen metonymically, as well as metaphorically, dubs her 'large fat sighings'. This is not simply a proto-Freudian notion that the body will tell; it reflects seriously on both the physical nature of delivered speech and its cultural framing.

In terms of the reader's reception of the action of the novel, the narrator makes a pedagogical point: individuals elocute with the bodies they have, and, for reasons of cultural context or 'taste', not all elocutionary transmissions will be received with sympathy. The general lesson is that elocutionary reception will be culturally inflected with respect to the body of the sender (among other factors). Elocution goes beyond reason, beyond politeness: to a careful and informed observer like Anne, even Wentworth cannot totally control his own visceral reaction (and thus his own bodily rhetoric) in response to Mrs Musgrove's elocution. Yet Wentworth, who finds the portly Mrs Musgrove falsely emotional, never doubts the emotional authenticity of Benwick, his fellow captain. In a sense, then, even the seemingly spontaneous responsive elocution of bodies like Wentworth's to the elocution of others may have an 'artificial' dimension, one that is conditioned by cultural assumptions and practices, aesthetic or otherwise, about the body of the producer of elocution.

The Misfortune of Poetry

Austen explores another aspect of the artificial/cultural dimension of elocution with her portrait of Captain Benwick. After Anne, Benwick is the figure most engaged with literature, and his calling card is his passionate reading aloud of poetry. Benwick's poetry reading brings another mode of the elocutionary artform into Austen's novel. It also sets up a contrast between Anne, who doubts the value of filtering her own emotions through the stereotyped passions of verse (as seen during her walk to Winthrop [78–9]), and Benwick, whose melancholy appears to be fed from the passages he reads aloud from modern poets such as Walter Scott and Lord Byron. The stylised and melodramatic presentations of feeling in works like *Marmion* (1808) or the *Giaour* (1813) (94) make up for Benwick an anthology with emotional pedagogical force. On the one hand, this evokes a Catherine Morland-like Quixotism, whereby real life is filtered through the emblems of literature, in this case poetry. But on the other hand, it ties back to eighteenth-century elocutionary works, such as John Walker's, that included anthologies of verse, organised according to the specific passions they were felt to carry, for practice in affective reading.[33]

Austen grants Benwick a talent for reading aloud (although perhaps not as talented as Henry Crawford in *Mansfield Park*). Benwick repeats 'with such tremulous feeling, the various lines which imaged a broken heart, or a mind destroyed by wretchedness' (94), that he not only measures up to the standards for effective reading aloud promulgated by elocutionists such as Sheridan and Walker, but he does it too well for Anne's peace of mind.[34] She worries that 'it was the misfortune of poetry, to be seldom safely enjoyed by those who enjoyed it completely; and that the strong feelings which alone could estimate it truly, were the very feelings which ought to taste it but sparingly' (94). Anne famously prescribes Benwick 'a larger allowance of prose' (94) for his everyday consumption, as a kind of desensitising medicine. Desensitising from what? Emotional excess, of course, but also expressive cliché.[35]

Just like Mrs Musgrove, Captain Benwick displays affliction in spades, and Wentworth considers it to be 'impossible for man . . . to be more deeply afflicted' (90) on the death of his fiancée, an opinion Wentworth never abandons, even after Benwick's engagement with Louisa is announced. Benwick is identified with and thrust upon Anne ('he has not, perhaps, a more sorrowing heart than I have' [91]; 'it fell to Anne's lot to be placed rather apart with Captain Benwick' [93]). Among the naval men, Benwick is (with significant dramatic irony) singled out as the stereotypically emasculated man of feeling: he is 'a little man' (91), associates with women, and his name evokes a ribald pun and rhymes with 'Yorick', Sterne's crafty sentimentalist. He lives with and was to be related by marriage to the genuinely feeling Captain Harville, whose name echoes 'Harley', Henry Mackenzie's man of feeling. Rather than dwelling on his small physique, as she does with Mrs Musgrove's large body, Austen uses Captain Benwick's melancholy to emphasise the susceptibility of elocutionary production (as well as reception) to the clichés of taste.

Benwick has learnt to feel by rote. As mentioned above, this replays Austen's critique of quixotism in Catherine's susceptibility to Gothic fiction in *Northanger Abbey*,

JANE AUSTEN'S ART OF ELOCUTION 315

but now the realm of misapprehension is one's inner passions rather than the public actions of others. From another perspective, however, although Benwick's relationship to a collection of feeling passages corrupts his self-delivery through conventionalisation, he happily follows the period's elocutionary pedagogy of placing into memory poetic or other stock literary materials.[36] The implication of Benwick's fate, then, is that conventionalised materials are easily misused and may block rather than enable genuine emotional remembrance (in his case, of his feelings for his deceased fiancée).

Just as Gilbert Austin's illustrations of elocutionary postures (for women, many of them modelled on the actress Sarah Siddons) freeze their performance and put them into memory as conventionalised graphic tableaux, so the poetry collected in works like John Walker's offers a stock anthology of passionate expression for the student of elocution to recite. The anthologising impulse was one facet of the tendency (born of print media) of eighteenth-century elocutionists to develop graphic inscription systems for examples of gestural and acoustic delivery. Joshua Steele's music-like staves for graphing pronunciation, Austin's gestural illustrations and Walker's poetic anthology are all, like Benwick's poetry collection, memory works, which in the context of the novel, via Benwick, and also Mr Elliot's studied 'manner', may be seen as conducive to elocutionary cliché and cant.[37] To properly retransmit the elocution of a remembered feeling, just as to discern it properly, one must break through stock material (a lesson Anne applies to herself on the walk to Winthrop [78–9]), and redeliver a remembered instance of elocution, such as a glance, to yourself. It's Wentworth's fate to experience this dialectic of memory and delivery when he relives the encounter with Mr Elliot on the stairs in Lyme: 'The glances in his heart he bore / Long after they were seen no more'.[38]

Convincing Feelings

The action of *Persuasion* is propelled by the challenge of understanding the 'real sentiments' of others – of translating them, as it were, into consciousness. As we have seen, like word-based communication, elocution is ripe for manipulation and deceit, but also, as a bodily rhetoric, it may reveal the heart despite itself, even to itself. With Anne's encounters with the then-unknown Mr Elliot on the beach steps and in the hotel hallway, immediately preceding Louisa's fall on the Cobb, the bodily communication of desire, its reception and its testing over time come to the fore between Anne, Mr Elliot and Wentworth.

The novel's key moment of sexual elocution occurs when 'a gentleman' (97), Mr Elliot, is 'preparing to come down' just as Anne's party 'came to the steps, leading upwards from the beach' (97). The gentleman

> politely drew back, and stopped to give them way. They ascended and passed him; and as they passed, Anne's face caught his eye, and he looked at her with a degree of earnest admiration, which she could not be insensible of. . . . It was evident that the gentleman, (completely a gentleman in manner) admired her exceedingly. Captain Wentworth looked round at her instantly in a way which shewed his noticing of it. He gave her a momentary glance,—a glance of brightness, which seemed to say, 'That man is struck with you,—and even I, at this moment, see something like Anne Elliot again'. (97)

In this passage, focalised on Anne, Austen orchestrates a complex interaction of glances, recognitions and their narrativisation. The gentleman looks down on the party coming up and sees Anne, appearing healthy from the sea breezes, and casts an eye so glad upon her that even Anne, focused as she has been on a fretful Henrietta and, the night before, the melancholy Benwick, is aware of it and of the feeling of real ('earnest') sexual attraction ('admiration') that it communicates. The narrator is quick to make sure that the reader gets it: 'the gentleman . . . admired her exceedingly'. What does he admire? Her 'animation' of 'eye' as well as 'bloom' of 'complexion' (97): the (unconscious) sexual vitality that Anne's body signals.

Whether Mr Elliot himself is admirable is a matter to be decided: the description of him as 'a gentleman in *manner*' (emphasis added) certainly raises the guard of a re-reader of the novel: just as taste may be put off by an unruly body's elocution, taste may also misjudge the sincerity of a polished orator and his bodily control (in this case, the decorum of his sexual response to Anne). Although he easily dupes Lady Russell, Mr Elliot's gentlemanliness, we learn later, exists only in manner and appearance. Like Anne, the reader will have to learn to distinguish 'real sentiments' from false when elocution is detached from feeling. The other watcher here, Wentworth, observing the interaction between Anne and Mr Elliot, wordlessly communicates his feelings in 'a glance of brightness', one that 'seemed to say, "That man is struck with you,—and even I, at this moment, see something like Anne Elliot again"' (97). The translation from paralinguistic glance to direct discourse is striking. Is Anne reading into Wentworth's look? During the hedgerow conversation, Anne gives more weight to words, to the logic of Wentworth's argument, and to the comparison to the nut, noting only in passing his pregnant 'pause' (82) (an important element of delivery to the elocutionists). But on the beach in Lyme she seems to reverse this emphasis, parsing an entire speech from a single look.[39] As for Wentworth, his recognition in this moment of his own feelings for Anne becomes a kind of 'spot of time' for him, and for the reader, over the course of the second volume of the novel.

Although subsequently overshadowed by Louisa's fall, Austen further underscores the significance of the encounter on the beach steps when, back at the inn, Anne runs into Mr Elliot once again, this time in a hallway:

> Anne in passing afterwards quickly from her own chamber to their dining-room, had nearly run against the very same gentleman, as he came out of an adjoining apartment. . . . It was now proved that he belonged to the same inn as themselves; and this second meeting, short as it was, also proved again by the gentleman's looks, that he thought hers very lovely. (97)

On the stairs, the narrator describes Mr Elliot's non-word look as making it 'evident' to Anne that he fancies her, and Wentworth's own looks are said to confirm this. In the hallway, the diction that Austen uses to describe the effect of Mr Elliot's 'looks' – that they 'proved' his feelings 'again' – clearly separates *Persuasion* from the new rhetoric of Campbell. The hallway episode places passionate communication via non-word elocution firmly ahead of discursive argumentation as a sexual rhetoric – Anne in the hallway is not the same as Anne beside the hedgerow. As seen earlier when Anne is 'convinced' (63) that Wentworth disdained Mrs Musgrove's sentimentality, Austen's diction here ('proved') grants a specifically epistemological value to elocutionary rhetoric, going so far as to equate the proofs of elocution (that he thinks her 'very lovely') with the proofs of direct perception (that he 'belonged to the same inn'). And the epistemological force of elocution is tied back to the recipient's body, too, as something about which one cannot be 'insensible' (97).

Lest readers miss the importance of Anne's encounters with Mr. Elliot, they are referred to again and again in volume two, beginning when Anne and Mr Elliot formally meet in Bath, and Anne, 'smiling and blushing', is amused at 'his little start of surprise' to see who it was whose 'pretty features . . . he had by no means forgotten' (133). The sexual interest between Anne and Mr Elliot is channelled into a semi-courtship: 'They went through the particulars of their first meeting a great many times' (138–9). This sentimental recollection is tied to a memory, at least for Anne, of another participant in the sexual elocution of Lyme: when Mr Elliot confirms to her 'that he had looked at her with some earnestness', readers are informed that 'She knew it well; and she remembered another person's look also' (139). In other words, we see here that Austen tests the power of elocutionary rhetoric partly by mobilising it within an erotic relationship, something that further ties her exploration of elocution back to Sterne's rendering of its limits.

A Sentimental Journey through Lyme and Bath

Anne's translations of elocutionary signals are presented as so sensitive and adept that they evoke those of Sterne's parson, Yorick, particularly on the beach stairs at Lyme. This is an artistically daring gambit, since Yorick's ability as a recipient of elocution is highly ironised by Sterne. Nevertheless, Austen invokes a chapter from *A Sentimental Journey* when Wentworth, a young 'officer' (70), sees Mr Elliot look at Anne in a desirous fashion and Wentworth's 'glance' (97) is translated, seemingly by Anne via the narrator, into direct discourse: '"That man is struck with you,—and even I, at this moment, see something like Anne Elliot again"' (97). In Sterne's important chapter 'The Translation, Paris', Yorick, after observing the gestures of an 'old officer' at the opera, claims that he can 'translate' them into direct discourse, which, exactly like Anne, he proceeds to do.[40] When Yorick takes his seat at the Paris opera, the French officer removes his spectacles and puts them and a small book in his pocket. Sterne continues, in Yorick's voice:

> Translate this into any civilized language in the world—the sense is this:
> 'Here's a poor stranger come in to the box—he seems as if he knew no body; and is never likely, was he to be seven years in Paris, if every man he comes near keeps his spectacles upon his nose—'tis shutting the door of conversation absolutely in his face—and using him worse than a German.' (47)

Both Sterne and Austen mark their protagonists' translation of gesture into words by enclosing the translations in quotation marks, assigning the words for the elocuted gesture to the gesturer as if he were the speaker of them.[41]

As we have seen from her encounters with Wentworth, Anne, too, is confident of her ability to, as Yorick puts it, 'be quick in rendering the several turns of looks and limbs . . . into plain words' (47–8). Much of the *Persuasion* narrator's account of the feelings of others is focalised through Anne via her internally spoken responses

318   FRASER EASTON

('said Anne to herself' [91]) to the elocution of others.[42] In contrast to Anne, Yorick is a very unreliable receiver of elocution – that is part of the comedy of *A Sentimental Journey* – but is Anne's discursive translation not also as freewheeling, if less exaggerated, than Yorick's? The level of detail on the beach steps should give us pause. How confident can we be when we translate elocution into words?[43] When Anne sees Mrs Smith later on in the novel, that lady tells Anne that her 'countenance perfectly informs me' (183) about her feelings of love at the concert the night before – only for Mrs Smith to mistakenly identify Mr Elliot as the object of Anne's elocutionary expression.

Austen's reworking of Sterne in *Persuasion* also evokes, sub rosa, the fortuitous sexual encounter between Yorick and the Marquesina di F*** at 'Martini's concert at Milan' (48). This Italian episode concludes the chapter on 'The Translation, Paris' and waggishly introduces the concept of 'vile' (non-sexual) and 'pleasure' (48) oriented (sexual) translations of the same elocutionary gestures: in other words, Sterne's chapter concludes by highlighting (albeit bawdily) the role of detection in successful elocution. The intertextual relationship is particularly strong here: Anne and Mr Elliot share elocutionary locations (hallways and stairs) with Yorick and the Marquesina di F***; both couples narrowly avoid a collision in a hallway (Anne 'had nearly run against' [97] Mr Elliot; Yorick and the Marquesina di F*** 'flew together to the other side, and then back—and so on—it was ridiculous' [48]); and the sexual communication between each couple is made public when they are on a set of steps or stairs, Anne going up and Yorick going down. Cleverly, it is Wentworth not Mr Elliot who, earlier on, hands Anne into a carriage (84), as Yorick does the Marquesina di F*** (48), although overt recognition of Wentworth and Anne's renewed sexual companionship is deferred to later in the novel.

It is, finally, at a concert of Italian music in Bath that Anne hopes to clear the way between Wentworth and herself now that Louisa (whom Wentworth had been reluctantly courting) and Benwick are engaged. The Italian-ness of the music is mischievously emphasised by Austen in that Mr Elliot, who is there with Anne's party, keeps asking her to translate from the 'concert bill' (176; see also 179). By making this further link to the 'Translation' chapter of *A Sentimental Journey*, Austen does more than emphasise the centrality of elocutionary translation to the romantic plot of her novel. Sterne's ongoing intertextual presence connects the elocutionary love triangle of Anne, Wentworth and Mr Elliot back to the initial encounter in Lyme. It allows us to link Anne with Sterne's Marquesina di F*** as both an object of sexual attention and as a source of her own sexual desire.[44] Like Yorick at his Italian concert, Wentworth makes both a good and a bad translation of Anne's elocution at theirs. The good translation proceeds from Anne's management of her voice and countenance when she and Wentworth first encounter each other 'in the octagon room' (171) just ahead of the concert. While she cannot directly state her own desire for Wentworth, and while she is not certain of his, and despite the 'ceaseless buzz' (173) around them, she does all she can to communicate her feelings in a non-word fashion. The problem for Anne, of course, is that, unlike the Marquesina di F*** (who among other things has her own carriage), she is not able to take control of the scene of her elocutionary communications, as signified earlier on by her passivity in being handed into the Crofts' carriage by Wentworth. The appearance of Mr Elliot at the concert (174) and his elocutionary gestures around Anne – in particular, a proprietary-seeming 'touch

JANE AUSTEN'S ART OF ELOCUTION   319

on her shoulder' (179) – undermine (for the mistranslating Wentworth) Anne's earlier elocution. Her attempts to reassure Wentworth are ignored (180). Wentworth's 'vile' translation at this concert, then, reverses Yorick's 'pleasure' oriented one at his and heightens the tension of Austen's plot by seeming to foreclose Anne's sexual fulfilment because of Mr Elliot's elocutionary interference.

Emotion Recollected

Austen makes time the key dimension through which the significance of elocutionary communication may be stabilised and discerned. Words provide context for, but are not determinative of, elocution. Throughout the second volume, Austen makes Wentworth's education circle around his processing of a moment of delivery – Mr Elliot's look – in memory. For Austen, the elocutionary 'spot of time' takes up the reception, and re-reception in recollection, of human to human, rather than nature to human (as in Wordsworth), emotional encounters: the looks at Lyme, rather than hoots on a lake.[45] But if the scene of and participants in remembered elocution differ between Wordsworth's poetry and Austen's novel, elocution's mode of temporalisation does not. For both authors, the dynamic inward redelivery of a previously received elocutionary element or scene, rather than its static internal inscription, carries passion over time and affirms it.[46] Both authors sediment the time of delivery: what was externally delivered and received becomes an instance of self-delivery when it is internally redelivered at a later time. This temporal layering keeps the other's elocution alive in memory.

If Anne remembers Mr Elliot's look in Lyme, so does Wentworth. After the news of Benwick and Louisa's engagement reaches Anne in Bath, she encounters Wentworth in Molland's shop. When Mr Elliot arrives,

> Captain Wentworth recollected him perfectly. There was no difference between him and the man who had stood on the steps at Lyme, admiring Anne as she passed, except in the air and look and manner of the privileged relation and friend. (167)

In this scene, which takes place before the Italian concert, Wentworth is again attuned to non-word elocutionary signals, in this case of 'air and look and manner' which seem to show that Mr Elliot has supplanted him in Anne's affections. Here too Wentworth makes a 'vile translation' (*A Sentimental Journey*, 48). Unlike Yorick, Wentworth does not pick up on the elocutionary signals of the woman he observes with sexual interest. Of course, readers may recall that Anne prefers 'the frank, the open-hearted, the eager character beyond all others' (151). Mr Elliot is too 'rational': 'There was never any burst of feeling . . . Warmth and enthusiasm did captivate her still' (151). In this comparison of the two men, which divides between them the two aspects of Yorick (his craftiness and his spontaneity), it is the spontaneous elocutionary style (art) of Wentworth that Anne prefers, but also by which she is captivated, that is, sexually persuaded.[47] She feels she can depend upon its 'sincerity' (151). Sincerity, of course, is a slippery concept, perhaps nowhere more so than in *A Sentimental Journey*, which is another reason why Austen's reworking of Sterne in a novel about the elocutionary discernment of true feeling points once more to her questioning of romantic transparency even as she explores Anne's receptive sensibility.

The elocutionary scene at Lyme is recalled with the resolution of the plot of the novel, after a complex scene of indirect, overheard and elocutionary interaction in which Anne speaks with Harville about Benwick and debates the affections of men and women. Wentworth listens in. In his letter to Anne, he asks: 'Can you fail to have understood my wishes?' (222) – the reader knows she is not certain of his wishes at all. As for her wishes, Wentworth writes that 'I had not waited even these ten days, could I have read your feelings' (222). But lest we think that words are the ultimate carriers of feeling, or at least provide its final explication, Wentworth's letter returns the non-word communications on the beach stairs at Lyme to their central role in the novel:

> He persisted in having loved none but her. She had never been supplanted. . . . he had been constant unconsciously, nay unintentionally; . . . he had meant to forget her, and believed it to be done. He had imagined himself indifferent. . . . and only at Lyme had he begun to understand himself.
>   At Lyme, he had received lessons of more than one sort. The passing admiration of Mr. Elliot had at least roused him. (226)

When Wentworth describes what that moment communicated to him, we find that it was 'himself'. Whether we read this as a 'between men' moment, or as a return of Wentworth to himself, we see the effects of internal elocution at work over a period of time. Wentworth's 'glance of brightness' that Anne observed on the beach steps is revealed here to be less a matter of Wentworth suddenly seeing 'something like Anne Elliot again' (97) and more a matter of him understanding 'himself' (226), the external signal of an inner, felt recognition, that of his own authentic desire, much like Emma's arrow of recognition of her own feelings for Mr Knightley. As with Anne's persuasion by external 'warmth and enthusiasm' rather than cold reason, it is an instance of elocution (Mr Elliot's look) that internally rouses Wentworth and leads him to receive his own desire (procedurally the same process as receiving the desire of another) – a necessary precondition for him to be able to signal it to another. And, in the instance on the beach stairs at Lyme, perhaps Anne is right that he also did that with his 'glance'.

First as Comedy, Then as Romance

Persuasion draws energy from *A Sentimental Journey*'s problematisation of elocutionary communication as a transmission between sensible bodies. Bodies, their feelings and their rhetorical expression appear in Austen's novel as subjects of both comedy (Sir Walter, Mrs Musgrove, Benwick and Mr Elliot) and romance (Anne and Wentworth, of course, but also Henrietta and Charles Hayter). In Sterne's innovative fiction, death is played for comic effect and held at bay by someone named, of all things, 'Yorick', but mortality hangs over *Persuasion*, too, and not just at sea, as this is a novel about a sexual death-in-life on land that is happily, if circumstantially, adverted. The challenges of elocutionary reception that Sterne treats comically – the endless infinity of paralinguistic signals and receptions, and their sexual undercurrents (and thus the impossibility, because of nature, of Sheridan's programme of a natural elocutionary legibility),[48] – Austen presents as a problem to be cured by training in the reception of feeling and the passage of time.

Austen's interest in elocutionary rhetoric in terms of a pedagogy of feeling also sets her apart from Sterne. In *A Sentimental Journey*, sentiment, sexual feelings, and the limits of elocution as a means of differentiating between sentimental attachment and sexual desire see little development. 'Real sentiments' remain, in Sterne, mostly hidden. Learning, or not, in contrast, is central to the ways in which Austen's novel mobilises the forms of delivery. The reader, through the narratorial focalisation on Anne, is aware of 'her observations' (76) of those around her. Following the progress of Anne and Wentworth's romance educates the reader, but this romance is in turn a learning experience – a rerun of an earlier failed test – for the lovers for whom direct discursive statements of feeling are impossible because situationally precluded by the broken engagement. So, although elocution may be, for the recipient, a flawed tool (since the elocutionary signal may be insincere, acted, uncertain, stereotyped or accidental and its reception may be prejudiced by inattention, taste or social bias), it is nevertheless a tool – an art – whose reception may be developed and tested, discerned, if you know how. *Persuasion* is, in effect, a guide for the elocutionarily perplexed.[49]

Austen further advances her understanding of the role of elocution in (self-) consciousness by reworking Sterne stylistically. In *A Sentimental Journey*, Sterne has Yorick move from address of others to address of self and back almost seamlessly; Austen picks up on that movement but transfers the address of self to narratorial indirect speech, so that what 'was' delivered by the speaker to themselves becomes delivered 'now' by the narrator to the reader as free indirect discourse.[50] The effect of this narratorial retemporalisation is to draw the reader seamlessly into the internal delivery of the character, creating a mode of cross-temporal focalisation that is not only perspectival (anchored in a point of view) but visceral (a transmission of affective energies).[51] To Austen's debts to Richardson, Fielding and Burney (among others), must be added her engagement with Sterne's innovative treatment of elocution grammatically, as well as thematically, in *A Sentimental Journey*.

Among the critical implications of attending to Austen's art of elocution in *Persuasion* are two that impact an understanding of the novel. First, elocutionary learning is networked throughout, embracing aspects of the narratorial style, the actions of various characters, the consciousness of Wentworth, and the reader's experience of the novel. Sir Walter's fixation with 'natural' beauty, the Crofts' bluntness, Benwick's poetic pastiche, Mr Elliot's mannered politeness, the 'large fat sighings' of Mrs Musgrove – these, as well as Anne's own use of elocution, form her elocutionary *Bildung*, and the reader's. Wentworth's elocutionary education is less closely narrated than Anne's but perhaps is more significant, as he comes to discern his own, as well as Anne's feelings, just as she had learnt to detect ('detected' 63) his. Through the narrator, the reader too is guided to understand the problems of elocution and the receiver's craft – a properly rhetorical one – needed for their resolution.

Second, Austen rewrites the gendered significance of the contingencies of elocutionary events. What in Sterne is a grand tour, a cosmopolitan male-pleasure-centred mobilisation of the art of elocution for sexual opportunity becomes in Austen's hands a domestic excursion, a national female-pleasure-centred experience of the art of elocution for sexual constancy.[52] In effect, Austen uses the pedagogical challenge of the reception of elocution to level the sexes: both are learning, both are testing to find out 'real sentiments' from the signals of others. While some aspects of the final reconciliation are communicated in words, through Anne's debate, Wentworth's letter and their

322   FRASER EASTON

subsequent conversation, the reconciliation follows on from a wrenching moment of elocutionary miscommunication at the Italian concert, and is resolved with a moment of ecstatic elocutionary communication in Charles Musgrove's presence. It is because Wentworth cannot discern Anne's feelings that he writes his letter, and the encounter is predicated on teaching Anne, and us, the emotional equality of men and women via instances of shared delivery. Although, in *Persuasion*, as in *A Sentimental Journey*, elocution cannot, as a tool of passionate communication, be guaranteed by something outside of it (such as the natural body), thanks to time and the accidents of circumstance, it can be tested, and learnt, imparting in Austen's novel the hopeful lesson that men and women may feel together.

Acknowledgement

I would like to thank Camie Kim, Jayne Lewis, Jakub Lipski, Mary Newbould and Terry Robinson for their comments on an earlier version of this essay.

Notes

1. Scholars have long recognised the centrality of communication to *Persuasion* but have often treated it as a thematic, social or physiological matter rather than as a distinct field of contested action. See A. Walton Litz, *Jane Austen: A Study of Her Artistic Development* (New York: Oxford University Press, 1965), 159–60; Alistair M. Duckworth, *The Improvement of the Estate: A Study of Jane Austen's Novels* (Baltimore: Johns Hopkins University Press, 1971), 204–6; Judy Van Sickle Johnson, 'The Bodily Frame: Learning Romance in *Persuasion*', *Nineteenth-Century Fiction* 38, no. 1 (1983): 47–8; John Wiltshire, *Jane Austen and the Body: 'The Picture of Health'* (Cambridge: Cambridge University Press, 1992), 190–3.
2. For some examples of rhetorical readings of *Persuasion* focused on various aspects of argument and discourse (including emotional suasion via words), see Ann Molan, 'Persuasion in *Persuasion*', *Critical Review* 24 (1982): 16–29, and James L. Kastely, '*Persuasion*: Jane Austen's Philosophical Rhetoric', in *Rethinking the Rhetorical Tradition: From Plato to Postmodernism* (New Haven: Yale University Press, 1997), 145–67.
3. Jane Austen, *Persuasion*, ed. Gillian Beer (Harmondsworth: Penguin, 1998, repr. 2015), 97. Further references parenthetical.
4. Non-word looks frame and define Anne and Wentworth's immediate post-letter communications. On joining Anne and Charles Musgrove as they walk back from the White Hart, Wentworth 'said nothing—only looked' (224–5); Anne is just able 'to receive that look, and not repulsively' (225), indicating that she returns his feelings; Wentworth both understands and responds physically: his 'cheeks which had been pale now glowed' (225); in turn, his blush is a physiological signal back to Anne, further confirming to her his desire for her. For an alternative reading of this passage, see Mary Ann O'Farrell, *Telling Complexions: The Nineteenth-Century English Novel and the Blush* (Durham, NC: Duke University Press, 1997), 52.
5. Elocution refers to the rhetorical canon of delivery (the performance of a speech), and includes all the non-word elements of gesture, tone, etc. For an overview of the eighteenth-century elocutionary movement, see Paul Goring, 'The Elocutionary Movement in Britain', in *The Oxford Handbook of Rhetorical Studies*, ed. Michael J. MacDonald (Oxford: Oxford University Press, 2017), 559–68, and Wilbur Samuel Howell, *Eighteenth-Century British Logic and Rhetoric* (Princeton: Princeton University Press, 1971), 143–256. See also Paula McDowell, *The Invention of the Oral: Print Commerce and Fugitive Voices in Eighteenth-Century Britain* (Chicago: University of Chicago Press, 2017).

JANE AUSTEN'S ART OF ELOCUTION 323

6. On elocution and the production of speech in Austen (rather than, as here, its reception), see Patricia Howell Michaelson, *Speaking Volumes: Women, Reading, and Speech in the Age of Austen* (Stanford: Stanford University Press, 2002).

7. Tony Tanner, 'In Between: *Persuasion*', in *Jane Austen* (Houndsmills: Macmillan, 1986), 219, 233, 238.

8. Donald Rackin, 'Jane Austen's Anatomy of Persuasion', in *The English Novel in the Nineteenth Century: Essays on the Literary Mediation of Human Values*, ed. George Goodin (Urbana: University of Illinois Press, 1972), 62, 77, 63.

9. Arthur E. Walzer, 'Rhetoric and Gender in Jane Austen's *Persuasion*', *College English* 57, no. 6 (1995): 689. Cf. Michaelson, who notes the relevance of 'silent gestures' to *Persuasion*, *Speaking Volumes*, 214.

10. Adela Pinch, 'Lost in a Book: Jane Austen's *Persuasion*', in *Strange Fits of Passion: Epistemologies of Emotion, Hume to Austen* (Stanford: Stanford University Press, 1996), 145.

11. Alan Richardson, 'Of Heartache and Head Injury: Reading Minds in *Persuasion*', *Poetics Today* 23, no. 1 (2002): 143.

12. On appeals to 'ethos' and 'pathos' in deliberative persuasion, see Aristotle, *The 'Art' of Rhetoric*, ed. and trans. John Henry Freese (Cambridge, MA: Harvard University Press, 1926), 169–263.

13. Walzer, 'Rhetoric and Gender in Jane Austen's *Persuasion*', 696, 699. See also Elaine Bander, 'Blair's Rhetoric and the Art of *Persuasion*', *Persuasions* 15 (1993): 124–30, and Lynn R. Rigberg, *Jane Austen's Discourse with New Rhetoric* (New York: Peter Lang, 1999), 193–235.

14. Howell, *Eighteenth-Century British Logic and Rhetoric*, 577–90. Howell stresses Bacon's influence on Campbell, but the centrality of the understanding as the 'dominant faculty' (588) in rhetorical address points to Locke's contextual importance.

15. Quintilian, *The Orator's Education*, 5 vols, ed. and trans. Donald A. Russell (Cambridge, MA: Harvard University Press, 2001), 5:85–183.

16. Thomas Sheridan, *A Course of Lectures on Elocution* (London: W. Strahan, 1762), ideas: vii, nonword: x, tone, gesture, etc.: 19.

17. Anne has Wentworth's misunderstanding of her relationship with Mr Elliot in mind, and thus Wentworth's misreading of her feelings.

18. Julia Kavanagh noted early on (*English Women of Letters*, 1862) that 'because she is a woman', Anne 'must not speak' about her feelings. Quoted in Jane Austen, *Persuasion*, 2nd edn, ed. Patricia Meyer Spacks (New York: W. W. Norton, 2013), 221.

19. Earlier in the novel Anne had been surprised at Wentworth's appearance at the Musgroves, thinking that he would avoid her: 'Now, how were his sentiments to be read?' (56).

20. Cf. Paul Goring, *The Rhetoric of Sensibility in Eighteenth-Century Culture* (Cambridge: Cambridge University Press, 2005).

21. See Fraser Easton, 'Yorick's Speech and the Starling's Song: The Limits of Elocution in *A Sentimental Journey*', in *Laurence Sterne's 'A Sentimental Journey': 'A Legacy to the World'*, ed. W. B. Gerard and M-C. Newbould (Lewisburg: Bucknell University Press, 2021), 121–49. The importance of *A Sentimental Journey* to *Persuasion* has not been generally noted by critics. An exception is Christopher C. Nagle who examines the relevance of Sternean sensibility and *A Sentimental Journey* for Austen's last novel in 'The Epistolary Passions of Sympathy: Feeling Letters in *Persuasion* and Burney's *The Wanderer*', *Persuasions* 27 (2005): 88–98 and 'The Social Work of *Persuasion*: Austen and the New Sensorium', in *Sexuality and the Culture of Sensibility in the British Romantic Era* (New York: Palgrave Macmillan, 2007), 97–118.

22. Austen references *Tristram Shandy* in letter 39 to Cassandra, 14 September 1804, in Deirdre Le Faye, ed., *Jane Austen's Letters*, 4th edn (Oxford: Oxford University Press, 2011), 97. Maria cites the starling in Sterne's *A Sentimental Journey* in volume 1, chapter 10 of

Mansfield Park. The narrator refers to 'a chapter from Sterne' (as if in an elocutionary anthology) in volume 1, chapter 5 of *Northanger Abbey*.

23. Van Sickle Johnson notes that 'the lovers . . . seek subtly appealing methods of testing each other's feeling and will', 'Learning Romance in *Persuasion*', 51.

24. Easton, 'Yorick's Speech and the Starling's Song', 141–2.

25. Gillian Beer, 'Introduction' to Austen, *Persuasion*, ed. Beer, xii.

26. Aristotle, *The 'Art' of Rhetoric*, 15.

27. For an inventory of the acoustic elocutionary features of spoken words, see Sheridan, *Lectures on Elocution*, 19. For a systematic documentation of persuasive bodily comportment, see Gilbert Austin, *Chironomia* (London: T. Cadell and W. Davies, 1806).

28. In the context of the theatricals in *Mansfield Park*, Anne Toner relates speech attributions like these to a 'theatrical preoccupation' and calls them 'performative instructions': *Jane Austen's Style: Narrative Economy and the Novel's Growth* (Cambridge: Cambridge University Press, 2020), 144.

29. Pinch, 'Lost in a Book: Jane Austen's *Persuasion*', 155.

30. Austen uses the term 'artificial' in relation to Wentworth's elocution when he offers 'an artificial, assenting smile' (80) in response to one of Mary's outbursts of snobbery; later, Mr Elliot's elocution and conduct are described as 'artificial' (195, 201).

31. Contrast Walzer on a debate between Elizabeth and Darcy from *Pride and Prejudice* in which he finds 'the association of persuasion with emotion and of rationality with conviction' is strongly marked: Walzer, 'Rhetoric and Gender in Jane Austen's *Persuasion*', 695.

32. Terry F. Robinson, 'Deaf Education and the Rise of English Melodrama', *Essays in Romanticism* 29, no. 1 (2022): 2. There is a deep dramatic irony in Wentworth's response to Mrs Musgrove's melodramatic sighs. As Penny Gay observes, at the emotional crux of the novel, Wentworth's letter exhibits 'melodramatic rhetoric', '*Persuasion* and Melodrama', in *Jane Austen and the Theatre* (Cambridge: Cambridge University Press, 2002), 149.

33. Walker offers over 100 pages of poetic passages embodying sixty distinct passions: John Walker, *Elements of Elocution*, 2 vols (London: Printed for the Author, 1781), 2:292–411. Works like Walker's appeared in parallel with the rise of collections of literary beauties, many of which anthologised key scenes from Sterne, including the Starling and Maria episodes from *A Sentimental Journey*. For an alternative reading of feeling and stock literary forms in *Persuasion*, see Deidre Shauna Lynch, 'Jane Austen and the Social Machine', in *The Economy of Character: Novels, Market Culture, and the Business of Inner Meaning* (Chicago: University of Chicago Press, 1998), 207–49.

34. For a valuable account of the elocutionary movement and the cultural salience of reading aloud in this period, see Abigail Williams, *The Social Life of Books: Reading Together in the Eighteenth-Century Home* (New Haven: Yale University Press, 2017), 11–35. Crawford reads Shakespeare to Fanny and Edmund in volume 3, chapter 3 of *Mansfield Park*. On the relationship of elocution to the 'ethos' of women as speakers in *Mansfield Park*, see Michaelson, *Speaking Volumes*, 127–34.

35. Contrast Austen's emphasis on declamatory cliché with Andrew Elfenbein's argument that the elocutionary pedagogy of reading aloud contributed to the Romantic period's notion of the voice as a hermeneutic activity, one that focused on 'textual comprehension' and sought 'a meaningful relation between sound and sense'. See Andrew Elfenbein, *Romanticism and the Rise of English* (Stanford: Stanford University Press, 2009), 112, 113. Again, Austen may have a reworking of melodrama in her sights, where convention determines reading.

36. Memory may be internal, as with Anne's collection of autumnal verses (78), or external, as with Walker's poetic anthology (*Elements of Elocution*, 2:292–411).

37. See the attempts to memorialise the flow of delivery in the musical staves for pronunciation developed by Joshua Steele, *An Essay Towards Establishing the Melody and Measure of Speech to Be Expressed and Perpetuated by Peculiar Symbols* (London: W. Bower and J.

JANE AUSTEN'S ART OF ELOCUTION 325

Nichols, 1775), 40 and *passim*; the plates illustrative of particular gestures and postures, many drawn from theatrical sources, in Austin, *Chironomia*, n.p.; and the anthology of passionate verse in Walker, *Elements of Elocution*, 2:292–411.

38. I adapt the last two lines of Wordsworth's 'The Solitary Reaper' (1807) – 'The music in my heart I bore, / Long after it was heard no more' – to underscore the connection of Wentworth and Wordsworth. For both the speaker of Wordsworth's poem and for Wentworth, despite the differences of theme and circumstance, the redelivery of a previously received moment of emotional elocution feeling is structurally consistent.

39. See also the translation of Harville's 'smile' and nod at the White Hart Inn into direct discourse: '"Come to me, I have something to say"' (217).

40. Laurence Sterne, *A Sentimental Journey and Other Writings*, ed. Ian Jack and Tim Parnell (Oxford: Oxford University Press, 2008), 47. Further references parenthetical.

41. There was a long history in writings about actors of identifying gesture as a universal language; see, for example, Charles Gildon in 1710 (writing as Thomas Betterton, the actor): 'Gesture has therefore this Advantage above mere Speaking, that by this we're only understood by those of our own Language, but by Action and Gesture . . . we make our Thoughts and Passions intelligible to all Nations and Tongues.' Quoted in Robinson, 'Deaf Education and the Rise of English Melodrama', 16. Robinson also suggests, regarding gestural and tonal expression in late eighteenth- and early nineteenth-century melodramas, that 'For contemporaries, melodramatic expression came across as anything but hyperbolic or artificial: it felt strikingly true-to-life' (23).

42. Examples of Anne's internal direct self-address appear throughout the novel; see, for example, her 'We are not boy and girl' speech (207–8).

43. Austen's treatment of the vagaries of elocutionary reception contrasts sharply with the radical Thomas Holcroft's view of theatrical gesture as a means of sincere and transparent emotional communication. Robinson, 'Deaf Education and the Rise of English Melodrama', 31.

44. See Van Sickle Johnson on Anne's sexuality, for example when Wentworth hands her into the Crofts' carriage, 'Learning Romance in *Persuasion*', 54.

45. 'Hoots on a lake' refers to William Wordsworth, 'There was a Boy' (1800), where owls uncannily return a young man's 'mimic hootings' across a lake: William Wordsworth and Samuel Taylor Coleridge, *Lyrical Ballads 1798 and 1800*, ed. Michael Gamer and Dahlia Porter (Peterborough: Broadview Press, 2008), 299. The phrase 'spots of time' comes from book 11 of the 1805 *Prelude*: William Wordsworth, *Wordsworth's Poetry and Prose*, ed. Nicolas Halmi (New York: W. W. Norton, 2014), 353. With her 'retentive feelings' (56), Anne also evokes many spots of time, including Wentworth's 'look' (139) on the beach steps.

46. Wordsworth theorises the redelivery of feeling in the 1800 'Preface' to *Lyrical Ballads*. In developing his formula that good poetry is the 'spontaneous overflow of powerful feelings', Wordsworth adds that 'it takes its origin from emotion recollected in tranquility': Wordsworth and Coleridge, *Lyrical Ballads 1798 and 1800*, 183. The poet re-energises his prior feelings with the act of recollection of a prior experience of elocution (associated with the objects of nature like dancing daffodils), an act which Wordsworth understands in rhetorical terms as the internal redelivery of an earlier instance or scene of received elocution. For Wentworth, Mr Elliot's facial expression at the top of the beach stairs delineates such a scene, marking a spot of time and serving as an occasion for memorial redelivery.

47. Wentworth is not always open and genuine in manner, revealing an element of artfulness in his elocution: with Mrs Musgrove, as we have seen, he adopts a sympathetic manner against his true feelings (63). To Anne's chagrin, this 'open-hearted' man can also, when he wishes, adopt a 'cold politeness' and 'ceremonious grace' (67).

48. Sheridan writes, for example, that tones are 'stamped by God himself upon our natures' (111) and that gesture is 'the hand-writing of nature' (113), while words are a 'work of art, and invention of man' (111).

49. For an alternative view of the moral significance of the novel, grounded in David Hume's views of passion, rhetoric and conversation, see Nancy S. Struever, 'The Conversible World: Eighteenth-Century Transformations of the Relation of Rhetoric and Truth', in *Rhetoric and the Pursuit of Truth: Language Change in the Seventeenth and Eighteenth Centuries* (Los Angeles: The William Andrews Clark Memorial Library, 1985), 98. Struever does not discuss elocution in *Persuasion*, asserting rather that '*pronuntiatio* is not a serious discursive issue for Austen' (97).

50. While there is not space to explore the matter here, the retemporalisation entailed by free indirect discourse is procedurally similar to the dynamics of remembrance we've seen in *Persuasion*'s spots of time.

51. This viscerality is reflected stylistically in moments of rapid syntax; for example, in those moments when Anne is overwhelmed by the sensory phenomena around her, and in Wentworth's letter. On visceral versus theatrical modes of sympathy, see Amit Yahav, 'The Sense of Rhythm: Nationalism, Sympathy, and the English Elocutionists', *The Eighteenth Century*, 52, no. 2 (2011): 181. For a view of Austen's use of free indirect discourse in spatial and perspectival terms, rather than as a cross-temporal transmission, see Cynthia Wall, *Grammars of Approach: Landscapes, Narrative, and the Linguistic Picaresque* (Chicago: University of Chicago Press, 2019), 212–21.

52. The result is an English, if not a British, education, one that domesticates elocutionary forms often viewed as continental; Hugh Blair, for example, notes about gesture that 'The French and the Italians are, in this respect, much more sprightly than we', *Lectures on Rhetoric and Belle Lettres*, 8th edn (New York: Collins & Co., 1819), 335. Cf. Thomas Sheridan, *British Education: Or, the Source of the Disorders of Great Britain* (Dublin: George Faulkner, 1756).

Part IV:

Networks and Interactions

19

Multimedia Coterie Romance

Natasha Simonova

WHILE THE TERMS 'romance' and 'novel' were often used interchangeably in the eighteenth century, by the 1750s there was a general consensus among critics and practitioners of English prose fiction that something had changed. The kinds of romance that had been popular in previous centuries – combining heroic, chivalric and pastoral subgenres and influenced by the rediscovery of ancient Greek fiction – were now held to be decisively out of fashion: in Clara Reeve's term, they were 'exploded', as both overly fanciful and dull in their distance from everyday life.[1] When we think of eighteenth-century fiction, for all of its experimentation and complexity, we do not usually picture heroines named Cleophila or Lindamira being shipwrecked and held prisoner in enchanted towers.

Yet romance in the classic sense did endure in this period, despite – or perhaps even because of – its apparent lack of currency. As Scott Black has argued, the genre can be fundamentally defined by a sense of being out of time, formed through a series of 'temporal knots, loops, or vortices that register and provoke an experience of trans-historical reading'.[2] Where early theorists of the novel insisted on distinctions between 'old' and 'new' species of writing, later reified in accounts of the novel's 'rise', romance serves to break down such models of linear progress altogether. Critics such as Black and Barbara Fuchs have identified its survival as a distinct 'mode' or 'strategy' even within the established canon of novelists such as Henry Fielding and Laurence Sterne.[3] By going beyond that canon to consider a wider range of works and sites of reception, however, I hope to build a more complete picture of romance in the eighteenth century. In this chapter, I argue that it functioned not only as a generic category but also as a 'multimedia' discourse – encompassing texts, visual art, landscape design and forms of what we might now call 'live action role-play'.[4]

The 'imagistic nature' of romance has often been remarked upon, emphasising it as a mode that combined the written and the visual.[5] Several prominent English romances of the early modern period, such as Philip Sidney's *Arcadia* (1593) and Mary Wroth's *Urania* (1621), featured elaborate frontispieces depicting their characters or settings. In France – with which there was a frequent interchange in texts and editions – the link between romance and illustration was even more pronounced. Although Laurence Plazenet cautions that these were far from the *romans illustrés* of the eighteenth century, his study finds that French translations of ancient Greek and English romances, as well as Honoré D'Urfé's influential *L'Astrée*, all appeared in at least one extensively illustrated edition between 1622 and 1637.[6] The vast heroic narratives later in the century, such as *Artamène ou Le Grand Cyrus* and *Clélie*, also included pictorial frontispieces before each of their many volumes.[7]

Carried out by the same elite cadre of artists and engravers, these illustrations helped to establish a consistent visual vocabulary for romance. As Plazenet describes, they combined the suggestion of an ancient setting with anachronisms: the heroines' clothing and hairstyles, for example, evoked both classical statuary and seventeenth-century fashion. The aim was not historical or geographical accuracy but the creation of a coherent fictional universe within which these adventures took place, complete with its own codes and conventions.[8] As we will see, this set of conventions remained distinct and recognisable in the eighteenth century. Despite their differences, for example, both the 1633 and 1733 editions of *L'Astrée* place the characters within similar country-house-style settings, surrounded by billowy-topped trees (Figures 19.1 and 19.2).[9]

The frontispiece to the 1633 edition of *L'Astrée* also resembles that of Wroth's *Urania* in its use of perspective: the apparent directness of the vanishing point contrasts with the details and meanders that fill up the ground before it. In both cases, the foreground elements act as arched gateways that invite the reader into an extensive realm, becoming literal manifestations of what Nandini Das calls the 'fantastic doorways' between real and romance space (Figures 19.3 and 19.4).[10] The romance image thus extends outward into three dimensions: both the stories and the experience of reading them are conceived in spatial terms, as journeys through a fictional 'world'.

Figure 19.1 Honoré D'Urfé, *L'Astrée* (Paris, 1633). Source gallica.bnf.fr / Bibliothèque nationale de France.

Figure 19.2 Honoré D'Urfé, *L'Astrée* (Paris, 1733). Source gallica.bnf.fr / Bibliothèque nationale de France.

Figure 19.3 Honoré D'Urfé, *L'Astrée* (Paris, 1633). Source gallica.bnf.fr / Bibliothèque nationale de France.

Figure 19.4 Mary Wroth, *The Countesse of Montgomeries Urania* (London, 1621). Folger Shakespeare Library, STC 26051 Copy 1.

If romance narrative is imagined as a landscape, it is one that is simultaneously wilderness – extensive, unexpected, rife with possibilities of danger and diversion – and the stylised product of idealising art. In this, I argue, it resembles the eighteenth-century landscape garden with its combination of nature and artificial improvement. Tim Richardson, for example, describes the country-house landscape in the early 1700s as characterised by a kind of 'variety' that is remarkably similar to the structure of romance – it is 'a garden with an episodic nature, surprises, distant prospects suddenly followed by intimate ones . . . different types of terrain and topography' where one might 'wander around as if in a trance'.[11] References to eighteenth-century country houses as 'Arcadia' have become so commonplace as to go largely unexamined.[12]

Of course, actual fashions for landscape design changed considerably over the course of the century, incorporating varying degrees of formal, naturalistic and 'picturesque' scenery. Yet the way that these spaces were conceived and spoken about consistently invoked the timeless (or out-of-time) idea of romance. In 1769, for example, Jemima Grey described Lancelot 'Capability' Brown's planned alterations to her estate at Wrest Park as 'leading me such a Fairy Circle, & his Magic Wand has raised such Landscapes to the Eye . . . with the same Effect as a Painter's Pencil upon Canvass'.[13] In pacing through the grounds with Brown, the still-imaginary landscape is overlaid over the real one in a way that reminds the viewer of her reading and knowledge of visual art, capturing the 'multimedia' experience of romance.

An influential articulation of this affinity between different artforms took place in Joseph Addison's essays on aesthetics in *The Spectator* (1711–12). Here, Addison frequently segues between discussing literature and garden design, with romance serving as the bridge. The 'Pleasures of the Imagination' are portrayed as a series of landscapes in which 'we walk about like the Enchanted Hero of a Romance, who sees beautiful Castles, Woods, and Meadows; and . . . hears the warbling of Birds and the purling of Streams'.[14] Issue 418 depicts a poet as a landscape architect who 'has his choice of the Winds, and can turn the Course of his Rivers in all the variety of *Meanders*, that are most delightful to the Reader's Imagination'.[15] Another essay compares different kinds of garden to different literary genres, aligning 'Bowers and Grotto's, Treillages and Cascades' (the kinds of features that would become ever more popular as the century went on) with the work of 'Romance Writers'.[16]

Perhaps the most direct link between fiction and landscape, however, comes in *The Spectator*'s description of Leonora, a widowed lady whose 'Reading has lain very much among Romances'. The detailed listing of books in her library shapes both her 'particular Turn of Thinking' and her surroundings:

> It . . . discovers it self even in her House, her Gardens and her Furniture . . . [H]er Country-Seat . . . is Situated in a kind of Wilderness . . . and looks like a little Enchanted Palace. The Rocks about her are shaped into Artificial Grottoes covered with Wood-Bines and Jessamines. The Woods are cut into shady Walks, twisted into Bowers . . . The Springs are made to run among Pebbles, and . . . collected into a Beautiful Lake, that is Inhabited by a Couple of Swans, and empties it self by a little Rivulet which runs through a Green Meadow, and is known . . . by the Name of *The Purling Stream*.[17]

Leonora's multisensory created landscape seems to accord perfectly with Addison's articulation of the 'pleasures of the imagination'. Yet because she tries to make the metaphors real, without a suitable degree of detachment from them, *The Spectator* views her activities with a 'Mixture of Admiration and Pity'. In its satire of the female romance reader as overly literal, uncritical and self-indulgent, this portrait therefore falls within the same lineage as the century's most famous such figure: Charlotte Lennox's Arabella in *The Female Quixote* (1752).

Like Leonora, Arabella is defined by her library and her garden. While critical accounts have largely focused on the former, Lennox actually gives the two equal weight in her opening descriptions and the action of the first half of the novel. For the young Arabella, the garden and the library are the intimately connected poles of her life:

> The surprising Adventures with which [her romances] were filled, proved a most pleasing Entertainment to a young Lady, who . . . had no other Diversion, but ranging like a Nymph through Gardens, or, to say better, the Woods and Lawns in which she was inclosed.[18]

As Mary Patricia Martin observes, the Marquis's garden is of the new 'English' style, in which 'the most laborious Endeavours of Art had been used to make it appear like the beautiful Product of wild, uncultivated Nature'.[19] Martin sees

334 NATASHA SIMONOVA

this kind of landscape 'realism' as a symbol for the genre of the novel, contrasted against the 'studied artfulness' of French gardens and French romances.[20] However, it is precisely the stylised wildness of the garden that turns it into a romance space – an 'epitome of *Arcadia*' into which Arabella's father retires like King Basileus, and through which she can range 'like a Nymph'.[21] It is unsurprising that Arabella's first 'love adventure' is with an assistant gardener, whom (still mirroring the plot of Sidney's *Arcadia*) she takes to be a lovelorn nobleman in disguise. Their imaginary amour is inextricable from the landscape, as Arabella sits in arbours and watches him lean against tree trunks: 'She often wondered, indeed, that she did not find her Name carved on the Trees' or 'that he was never discovered lying along the Side of one of the little Rivulets, increasing the Stream with his tears'.[22]

The same vision that turns a country house into an enchanted castle extends to Arabella's perception of herself. As Amelia Dale argues, the description of her father's garden ('Art' made to look like 'Nature') also applies to Arabella's own dress and styling, which painstakingly imitate the flowing, classical *préciosité* of seventeenth-century romance illustrations. According to Dale, it is the pictorial focus of romance that makes Arabella look in the mirror, 'examining and eyeing the desirability of her own body, viewing, reading, and rereading herself'. She then uses her costume as a form of re-enactment, to 'transmute her body into a visual text that reiterates the romance tropes she has consumed and internalized'.[23]

While the other characters react to Arabella's 'singular' dress with bewilderment, however, it would not have been wholly out of place in the real world of the mid-eighteenth century. Between 1730 and 1770, there was a substantial vogue for 'Van Dyke' costume, along with a less specific 'romantic' dress characterised by loose floating draperies.[24] These costumes were used for paintings and masquerades, with the same outfits often serving for both – Horace Walpole described one masquerade as full of 'quantities of pretty Vandykes, and all kinds of old pictures, walked out of their frames'.[25] The combination of seventeenth-century romances' anachronism and the mythologising effects of historical distance resulted in a slippage between the period in which many of the best-known romance texts were written and the (ostensibly ancient/classical) period in which they were set: to dress 'à la Van Dyke' was to evoke both. The fashion for costumed portraits or 'fancy pictures', with their apparent timelessness and idealisation, also accorded exactly with the aesthetics of romance. Heightened by the addition of fanciful names and/or pastoral accessories, the eighteenth-century sitter could imagine herself – and be imagined by viewers – as the embodiment of a fictional heroine, in an artform that fell somewhere between portraiture, illustration and performance.[26]

Several mid-century novelists used scenes of such romance dressing-up in order to set themselves apart from the genre, repudiating it as both absurd and sexually dangerous for women. In Samuel Richardson's *Sir Charles Grandison* (1753), Harriet Byron is persuaded to attend a masquerade in the dress of an 'Arcadian princess', which resembles Arabella's in being close-fitting to the waist and accessorised by a loose floating 'scarf of white Persian silk'. As a bespangled approximation of romance, the costume is simultaneously inaccurate and too accurate: Harriet complains that its exotic glitter 'falls not in with any of my notions of the Pastoral dress of Arcadia', yet she is still punished for assuming the role by being abducted by a would-be ravisher.[27] Oliver Goldsmith's *The Vicar of Wakefield* (1766), meanwhile, mocks the fashion for fancy-dress portraits through a family picture in which the vicar's daughter Olivia appears as an Amazon and her sister Sophia as a shepherdess. The local Squire posing 'in the character of Alexander the great, at Olivia's feet' serves to foreshadow his subsequent seduction of her.[28]

Real female readers, however, were not the 'unthinking receptacles for textual reproduction' that these satirical accounts imply.[29] Their engagement with romance was far more creative and self-aware, and could serve a number of purposes. Julie Eckerle has shown how sixteenth- and seventeenth-century women often drew on romance motifs as 'a useful means of articulating the self' in autobiographical narratives, providing them 'with an imaginative and narrative landscape within which to explore and represent personal experience'.[30] This remained equally true in the eighteenth century, although it might be overlaid with an extra layer of irony. *Don Quixote*, after all, was among these readers' favourite texts – and could be enjoyed by them both as a romance and as a parody.[31] One of them, reading it in 1744, jokes that she is 'almost as much in love with the Don & with Sancho, as they can be with Dulcinea or Dapple': an image that maps her own response onto the comedy of the text without denying the possibility of sincere engagement.[32]

Significantly, this description comes within a series of literary discussions exchanged between like-minded friends. If Arabella's reliving of romance in *The Female Quixote* fails, on the other hand, it may be because (like *The Spectator*'s Leonora) she remains alone in it, despite her attempts to draw other characters into her world. The mother from whom she inherits her romances is dead, while a promising friendship with the Countess – an intelligent, educated woman renowned for her 'Skill in Poetry, Painting, and Music' and able to communicate with Arabella in 'the Language of Romance' – is abruptly curtailed by the narrative.[33] Arabella moves from reading the books to embodying them without ever engaging in other, more conscious forms of creativity. Despite the work and artifice involved, she is always simply dressing rather than dressing up as a heroine. Her vision thus remains self-involved and unproductive – it cannot (unlike Lennox's own parodic rewriting) turn into a form of play.[34]

The missing element, I would suggest, is the idea of the coterie: a collaborative, often playful engagement within a group that had long been central to the romance genre. Romances are filled with scenes of people (especially women) in natural landscapes telling and responding to each other's stories, as well as exchanging literary compositions. The genesis of the texts themselves was imagined in a similar setting – later writers particularly looked back to Sidney composing the *Arcadia* at his sister's country house at Wilton, addressing it to her and a circle of 'fair ladies'.[35] Scholars such as Margaret Ezell, Betty Schellenberg and Michelle Levy have shown that, rather than being eclipsed by the coming of print, this kind of sociable manuscript culture actually extended well into the eighteenth and early nineteenth centuries.[36] The persistence that I argue for romance in this period is inextricable from that context, taking place on the same fringes of the canon and nourished by the same sense of slightly old-fashioned exclusivity.

Christine Gerrard has examined the dynamics of one such eighteenth-century coterie in the 'Hillarian Circle' of writers that included Eliza Haywood, Martha Fowke and Richard Savage, which formed around its founder Aaron Hill in the 1720s. In contrast to contemporary all-male clubs like the Scriblerians, this was a heterosocial gathering that 'operated through a romanticised and often sexually charged mode, in which male and female allure and acts of writing were intimately bound up with each other'.[37]

Although Gerrard examines how sexual tensions eventually led to the splintering of the coterie, I would argue that it was also 'romanticised' in a more generic sense. Its members adopted romance-influenced pseudonyms like Cleanthe, Daphne, Aurelia and Hillarius; Aaron Hill's three daughters (Astrea, Urania and Minerva, all born during this period) ended up actually bearing such names.[38] One member later nostalgically recalled the heyday of the Hillarians through the same fictional lens: 'how like those scenes we read in our youthful days in Sir Philip Sidney's Pastoral Romance!'[39]

The Hillarian circle was further fictionalised in Haywood's *The Tea-Table* (1724–5), although this text was written after her own expulsion from the group. Her fictional community, as Gerrard notes, 'is painted in a romantic, almost chivalric, vein'.[40] The narrative moves from the foibles of contemporary London society to a more idealised world populated by characters named Amiana, Philetus and Dorinthus, whose conversations become a frame for a series of inset amatory fictions and poems submitted to this coterie audience: 'I will read you a Manuscript Novel which I put into my Pocket with a Design to entertain AMIANA with.'[41] The sharing of manuscripts makes the tea table into 'a safe zone for unpolished, emotional, or spontaneous work', which is then discussed collaboratively within the circle.[42]

Ultimately, the Hillarians did not succeed in maintaining the sort of ideal forum that Haywood portrays in *The Tea-Table*. As Gerrard describes, they suffered from 'an oppressive degree of sexual and creative tension', not only in love affairs between the members but also in their competition as professional authors in the marketplace.[43] Even the tea table that Haywood depicts (like the actual meetings of the Hillarians at their London lodgings) constitutes only a small domestic oasis within a cut-throat urban world: Amiana's gathering is constantly interrupted by visitors arriving with mean-spirited gossip. The other-worldly romance atmosphere becomes difficult to sustain in such conditions.

For reasons of both class and geography, the ideal setting for a romance coterie remained the country house. Removed from the city and surrounded by natural scenery, it was an emblem of retreat and classical *otium*, populated by writers who did not need to compete or publish their work for commercial reasons. A depiction of this ideal can be found in Haywood's own *La Belle Assemblée*, translated from *Les Journeés Amusantes* by Marie Angélique de Gomez and published in four volumes between 1725 and 1736. In both the French original and Haywood's translation, the frame narrative features a set of young ladies and gentlemen 'united by their Understandings and Inclinations' who retire from 'the Tumult of a noisy Town' to a country house belonging to one of them, Urania, to find 'additional Inspiration to the Productions of their Wit'. Every evening, they meet in the library furnished by Urania to read, exchange observations on their books, and tell each other romance stories (which, as in *The Tea-Table*, make up the bulk of the narrative).[44]

Despite its obvious idealisation, the gallant mixed-sex circle of *La Belle Assemblée* was in great measure brought to life by a group whose uses of romance will be my focus for the remainder of this chapter. This was the coterie that took shape at Wrest Park in Bedfordshire, owned by the young heiress Jemima, Marchioness Grey and her husband Philip Yorke. Following their marriage in 1740, Wrest brought together Philip, his brother Charles and their Cambridge associates (such as Daniel Wray, John Lawry and Thomas Edwards); Jemima, her aunt Lady Mary Grey (later Gregory) and their childhood friend Catherine Talbot; and eventually the Yorkes' younger sisters, Elizabeth and Margaret. Talbot's journal of a visit to Wrest in 1745 bears a remarkable resemblance

MULTIMEDIA COTERIE ROMANCE 337

to De Gomez and Haywood in its account of days spent in reading, conversation, and exchanges of 'humourous Manuscripts . . . full of Wit & Entertainment'. It was a resemblance of which Talbot herself was very much aware: as well as using coded romance names for her friends and frequently slipping into French, she describes them gathering 'Belle Assemblee-wise in the Library'.[45] Such a textualisation of experience meant that everyday life at Wrest was already part of a conscious literary creation.

The house itself, with its surrounding grounds and gardens, served as both the subject and setting of the coterie's writings. As with many such groups, the same name was used 'for both a set of people and the place in which they met'; their collaborative literary productions were recorded in a volume called *Wrestiana*.[46] Since it was usually visited during the summer parliamentary recess, Wrest represented an escape from the pressures of politics and the frantic activity of London. The coterie gave it the romance name 'Vacuna' after the supposed deity of the place – an obscure Roman goddess whose name was evidently chosen for its resemblance to *Vacation* and therefore *Rest* (as they generally spelled it).[47] Characterised by 'fragrant shade' and 'flowing strain', it was a deliberate ideal separated from other parts of life: as they wrote in *Wrestiana*, 'we flatter our selves that our own way of living here, amidst flowers and fruits, in sober luxury, easy not idle, pleasant not ill-natured, bears some resemblance to the old and true Poetical Description of [the Golden Age]'.[48] Even when these had to be conducted in absence by correspondence, Wrest still served as the imaginative space onto which coterie activity and friendships could be mapped. Writing to Philip Yorke, for example, Edwards describes how 'I make You many mental visits' with 'the plan of Wrest . . . hanging by my bedside', where 'I frequently morning and evening pace over the gardens and cast a look at the Library'.[49]

It was the gardens and the library, once more, that formed the linked focal points of coterie life, combining physical people and places with imaginative expansion. Talbot described Wrest as 'an enchanted Castle . . . The most delightful groves to wander in all day, and a library that will carry one as far as ever one chuses to travel in an evening'.[50] These spaces could easily be moved between depending on the time of day and the weather, with books often taken outside for reading and discussion. The mixing of settings also allowed for a mixing of media in the coterie's pursuits, blending landscape, literature and visual art. In 1748, Jemima proposed a 'Fairy Scheme' to have all her friends gathered 'in *Vacuna's Shades*' in early summer, creating art as they enjoyed each other's company:

> [The gardens] are in some Places really so picturesque, we want some of you Painters to come & draw them . . . Then for your Reward I will assemble all the Beaux-Esprits of my Acquaintance to make Verses upon you in the Employment.[51]

Another letter invites Talbot to view Wrest through a magic telescope, with Grey herself, embedded in the landscape, becoming the object of observation:

> If you follow'd me into the Garden, you would almost take me for a Shepherdess . . . found with my Dog & my Book quite *en Pastorale* among Woods & purling Streams . . . And if you see me now followed in my Walks by a little bounding Fawn (the greatest Beauty you can imagine) you would think me young enough to be even Romantic.[52]

The episode of the fawn illustrates the slippages between reality, composition and the romance personae that the coterie members assumed – just as Wrest became Vacuna, Jemima was 'Graia', Talbot 'Sappho' and Charles Yorke 'Cleander'. In this letter, the fawn's presence allows Jemima to depict herself in the role of a romantic shepherdess; its tragic demise the following year (while an object of real sadness) then continued to serve coterie activity. Talbot was persuaded to write an elegy to it, while a poem in *Wrestiana* addressed 'To Sappho' from a fictional suitor compares Talbot herself to Graia's fawn, 'Whose loss your tunefull Lays deplore'.[53]

The coterie's correspondence and the collection of *Wrestiana* make extensive and varied references to different romance subgenres, ranging from brief flights of fancy to more extended exercises. These often arise in a parodic or mock-heroic mode, highlighting the disjunctures between romance and real life – as when Grey laments that Talbot was able to return home with 'no Recontre! no Enlevement!' despite being 'a fine Lady-Errant travelling the Highways'.[54] Yet, taken together, the attitude is never that of straightforward anti-quixotism. Instead, it operates through layers of irony – acknowledging the attractions of romance adventure as well as its ability to generate the writing through which the coterie constituted itself. As Eckerle has suggested, 'Romancing the self offered a means of problem-solving with the added bonus of wish-fulfillment.'[55] This was true in private journals (where Talbot in particular often used romance discourse as a way of articulating and fictionalising her feelings), but it also applied to the more public and light-hearted ways in which the coterie members romanced each other.[56]

One such narrative from the early 1740s, transcribed by Grey but of uncertain authorship, makes explicit the links between romance and the coterie's interest in early modern history. Written in an imitation of seventeenth-century orthography and claiming to have been found in a dusty drawer at Wrest, this story of 'The beginning & Progresse of the famous amoure between the Lord Viscount F–lkl–nd & the Ladie C–th–r–na T–lb–t' is set in the late 1630s, just before the outbreak of the Civil Wars. While advertised as a *roman-à-clef* or 'Chronique Scandaleuse of the Times', it incorporates Jemima's friends into this setting as 'Catharina Talbot' and 'the Ladie M. Gr-y'.[57] The object of Catharina's 'amoure', however, is not a figure from their real lives but the historical Viscount Falkland, who was the patron of a famous circle of writers at his Great Tew estate. After a daring climb from her bedroom window, Catharina elopes with him to 'Great T-w' in Oxfordshire, where – unconcerned by the resulting scandal – they 'learnte Greeke in a fortnighte', 'read all the beste authores togethere' and turned their house into 'a little College', with Catharina soon taking her degree from Oxford. Her confidante Lady Mary Grey, meanwhile, conceives 'the strongest Platonic Passione imaginable' for Falkland's friend Edward Hyde – later the Earl of Clarendon and the author of the women's favourite account of this period. Refusing proposed marriages with prominent Parliamentarians, both ladies side fervently with the Royalists – a stance that reflected their partisan investment when reading narrative history, which favoured romantic personalities over ideological positions.[58]

This brief text is fascinating for its combination of love affairs with intellectual content – something that romance can evidently capture in a way other genres cannot. What the heroine-readers are truly in love with, it suggests, is the study of a period and the idealised, adventurous version of themselves that they can imagine having been within it. It thus represents a kind of textual equivalent to being painted in 'Van

Dyck' dress (as they also were around this time). Indeed, one of the episodes involves Catharina sitting for her portrait by Anthony Van Dyke, with her lover writing verses upon her picture.

Alongside such *jeux d'esprit*, the Wrest coterie's most extensive textual production – and among the only ones to eventually cross over into the world of print – was the *Athenian Letters*, a collaborative epistolary narrative begun by the Yorke brothers and their friends at Cambridge and first privately printed in four volumes between 1741 and 1743.[59] Set during the Peloponnesian Wars and inspired by *Letters Written by a Turkish Spy* and the *Persian Letters* of Montesquieu and Lyttleton, this work has been read – when it is read at all – as a fairly dry intellectual exercise, which played on the students' knowledge of Greek history and provided a coded vehicle for the Yorkes' political and philosophical views.[60] In fact, however, it is a multivocal text that participates (if not always successfully) in a wide range of mid-eighteenth-century genres, with romance very much a part of the mix. In one of the only sustained discussions of the *Athenian Letters* to date, Jemima Hubberstey describes it as 'an exploratory and sometimes digressive path' through a fictionalised classical world.[61] Reading the text as an Oriental fiction, Hubberstey explores how it breaks down binaries and 'invites an exploration of the strange and the unknown'[62] – a structure that recalls the loops, estrangements and Mediterranean journeys associated with romance.

Elements of romance also emerge within the stories the *Athenian Letters* tell, particularly in the volumes completed after 1741. The same encoding that allowed the contributors to comment on contemporary politics also extended to more personal *roman-à-clef* elements. Daniel Wray, for example, inserts his patrons into the narrative by depicting the union of Orsames with Parmys, the 'most accomplished princess . . . and the greatest succession in the [Persian] empire'.[63] Despite its ultimate success, Philip Yorke and Jemima Grey's marriage at an early age was arranged by their families. Yet Wray romanticises the story, describing how Orsames 'saw and admired her; but . . . formed no other than the distant hope of qualifying himself one day to deserve her'.[64] A subsequent letter from Orsames (also bearing Wray's initial) rhapsodises at length about the beauty, intelligence and character of Parmys, in whom he 'find[s] a perpetual source of delights, a taste for the same amusements, [and] a spirit to invent new scenes of entertainments'.[65] 'Taoces', the couple's villa on the Persian Gulf, becomes an emblem of Wrest itself – although its landscape of 'woodlands, lawns, and water' surrounded by high mountains is intended to provide a variety of exotic scenery rather than an accurate picture of Bedfordshire.[66] Here, Orsames and Parmys are surrounded by 'a select party of friends [who] share with us, and improve the pleasures of the place', including figures clearly representing Mary Grey and Talbot (who contributed to the *Athenian Letters* as 'Sappho'). In contrast to the riot of the court, 'all here is calm and natural; the manners of the last age, set off by the elegance of ours'.[67] However applicable it may be to ancient Persia, this longing for a former golden age combined with modern refinement clearly speaks to the reception of romance in the eighteenth century.

Private jokes and references made their way into the narrative of the *Athenian Letters* and then back again, as coterie members took on elements of their fictional personae. John Lawry wrote to Philip Yorke that the 'relish you shew for your Country residence, and the regret you express at the thought of leaving it are extremely in the manner of Orsames'.[68] A comic dialogue in *Wrestiana* between 'Cleander' (one of

340 NATASHA SIMONOVA

the coterie's names for Charles) and the bookseller Robert Dodsley has him suggesting that 'you may afford us methinks a Frontispiece and a few Vignettes by Gravelot. My Brother will make a tolerable Gobryas, and I think my Air is Grecian enough for Cleander'.[69] Even though they remain imaginary (the real edition was not published by Dodsley and did not include any pictures), such engravings would place the text within the canon of illustrated romances and cement the resemblance between authors and characters. Philip's preface to the 1781 edition speaks of the entire enterprise nostalgically as a kind of enchanted costume party: 'the illusion vanished; it is a masquerade which is closed; the fancy-dresses and the domino's are returned to their respective wardrobes; the company walk about again in their proper habits, and return to their ordinary occupations in life'.[70]

This masquerade would have seemed all the more immersive because of how coterie activity and the narrative of the *Athenian Letters* extended into the Wrest landscape itself. Beginning in the late 1740s, multiple features were added at Philip and Jemima's behest, often accompanied with poems by their friends. These included a Chinese bridge and temple, a cold bath and a hermitage or root house, standing in the 'Mithraic Glade' beside an outsized stone altar. Described as 'Cleander's Altar and Hermitage', these were supposedly built by the protagonist of the *Athenian Letters* and shared in the text's exclusivity.[71] The altar carried inscriptions in ancient Greek and cuneiform ('strange Persick Characters taken out of a Book of Travels'); much to the coterie's amusement, visiting academics and antiquarians took it for genuine but could not interpret its meaning.[72] Hubberstey describes the Mithraic Glade as a practical joke deliberately designed to baffle scholarly authority, but also acknowledges its lingering sense of mystery.[73] It must be experienced, perhaps, in the alternative mode of romance – one that is alive to the real enchantment of the place at the same time as being aware of its playful coterie origins.

Rather than waning through the second half of the century, as one might expect, the interest in romance within the country-house environment continued equally strong in the next generation. The correspondence between Jemima's heiress Amabel Grey and her cousin Jemima Mary Gregory, for example, often adopted a romance diction and persona: 'From the slow-murmuring Streams, & shady Groves of Wrest (or Vacuna if you think that will mend the Stile) the constant-minded Silvia wishes to her friendly Melinda, Health & Happiness.'[74] 'Silvia' and 'Melinda' were not only names they used for themselves, but also the protagonists of the romance texts titled *Arcadia* and *Cythera* that the women worked on together. Their letters include detailed updates on the progress of the 'Knights & Ladies' who were their 'imaginary but intimate Acquaintances', alongside research on the classical Mediterranean setting, exchanges of passages, and debates about how to manage the plot.[75] They also sometimes shared their productions with other members of the family: Amabel records showing sections to her mother and younger sister, who reported that she had 'been employed at Wrest in reading [Sidney's] the Arcadia & am charmed with it, & much wish you to continue yours, as I shall certainly read whatever bears that name'.[76] There was also an occasion when Amabel's husband (usually more interested in hunting) bravely

gallop'd through my Arcadia, being only somewhat disconcerted that I had not compleated the *Reconnoissances*, married my chief Characters & settled them King & Queen in the Course of one Book. – He hung-a-hand on Silvia's long Soliloquy, but spurr'd his Horse & drove through the rest of the Play, but I believe his Speed was quite flagg'd at the end for he never begun the Fairy-Tale.[77]

This passage hints at the generic capaciousness of these romance experiments, involving a mixture of prose, drama, poetry and fairy tales. Indeed, the 'Pastoral Drama' of *Cythera* was eventually performed at a private theatre set up by Amabel's uncle, starring his children and attended by friends and family: 'It seem'd to go off very well', she wrote, '& was very well acted by all. Miss Yorke in Cleone, & Miss Peggy in Melinda, seem'd the most admir'd.'[78]

While these performances turned the text into a spectacle embodied by Amabel's young cousins, the fair-copy manuscripts themselves had already included an element of visualisation. This is evident in Amabel's discussion of the revision of her cousin's *Arcadia*:

> Then you will write it out fair, & afterwards I will execute the Vignette, for which you will leave sufficient Space . . . After this we will do the same with the second Book & I have Figures in my View for the Vignette, which must be Amarilla recovering in the Cave.[79]

More than a decade later in 1786, Amabel would return to the subject of illustrating this particular episode:

> I am going to begin for you a small Drawing of *Amarilla* half dead in the Cave; & I am trying to recollect whether the Cave was at the Back of the Temple, for if it was, the Temple cannot be seen from the mouth of the Cave. I do not know whether the River can be seen, or any other Object but a thick Wood.[80]

Her letters demonstrate a close attention both to the principles of composition (the number and disposition of the 'Figures') and the accuracy of narrative detail. The description recalls the romance illustrations discussed at the beginning of this essay, with their focus on receding prospects: despite being enclosed within the cave, Amarilla would apparently be only a small part of an image filled with architectural and natural objects from the rest of the story.

Amabel Grey's concern with illustration is unsurprising: she was a talented and enthusiastic artist throughout her life, studying drawing with Alexander Cozens and etching with James Bretherton.[81] The previously quoted letter suggests that romance illustrations were a part of the frequent gift-circulation of drawings among her friends and relations. Yet, despite some critical attention to her artistic career, the link between Amabel's art and her romance-writing has not been previously explored. This is partly because the actual illustrations have not survived or been identified – but also because her work, as a lady amateur, has been presumed to be merely 'accurate'. David Adshead writes, for example, that Amabel 'persisted in delineating the specific, producing strictly topographical views rather than idealized or ideal landscapes'.[82] Yet Cozens, her tutor, advocated precisely for originality in composition rather than a strict copying of nature: his method involved starting with rough 'blots' that would then resolve into features combining to form an imaginary landscape.[83] Trained in this style, Amabel records teaching it to a young Scottish lady who 'complain'd of the Masters at Edinburgh for not encouraging Invention'.[84]

Figure 19.5 Amabel Hume-Campbell, Countess de Grey, *View of the Bowling-green Canal, Wrest*. Etching. © The Trustees of the British Museum.

There is also less distance than may appear between Amarilla's cave and the 'beautiful views' of her parents' estates at Wrest and Wimpole that Amabel Grey grew up drawing.[85] As already established, these vistas were themselves an artful, romantic creation designed to create a particular mood and then further 'improved by [Amabel's] ingenuity' in recording them (Figure 19.5).[86] It was these views, with their Gothic ruins and misty treetops, that would be included as part of Josiah Wedgwood's Green Frog Service for Catherine the Great.[87] Their journey to faraway Russia, where Amabel imagined a copy of the folly at Wimpole being 'mounted upon some Hill at *Czarsko Zelo* or any other House with a hard Name that you please', still held a hint of romance wonder in a world of increasingly globalised news and commerce.[88] Like the cross-cultural encounters imagined in the *Athenian Letters*, Wrest would be as exotic to the Empress as the Empress was to it.

Much of our own knowledge of the Wrest coterie comes filtered through a retrospective, elegiac mode, which makes it seem even more like a lost golden age of youth.[89] This associates it further with the nostalgic orientation that was so typical of romance, even at the height of its popularity.[90] As Jemima Grey wrote in 1763 (the beginning of a period when illness and death would decimate the circle): 'I have long thought that the only Rational Amusment in Life was a *Coterie* . . . But Alas! how difficult or rather impossible is it to form or to maintain One' when 'a few Years time will probably . . . leave Voids that never can be replaced'.[91]

Yet there is another kind of time operating here as well – the diffuse, unstructured time of the country house in summer, of the active leisure that defined the restfulness of Wrest. A teenage Amabel, for example, invited Talbot to come and 'take a share in all my Attempts & Designs which are many & various & more than I shall ever accomplish'.[92] There are models of productive work that would regard this admission as a failure – a kind of complacent dilettantism that Talbot herself, drawing on their correspondence, would caution against in her posthumously published 'Dialogues'.[93] Yet Vacuna's way of being 'easy not idle', unlike the enchantment of James Thomson's *Castle of Indolence* (1748), was not opposed to industry as much as to unidirectionality. It was exploratory and frequently diverted from its apparent goals: 'Matters go on in the usual Way', Amabel wrote, 'always busy, & seldom doing what we intend.'[94]

This type of 'unaccommodated' time (undoubtedly privileged as it was) also strongly resembles Black's description of the 'bubbles' and 'relaxed fields' that characterise romance: 'a timescape of holes, loops, and eddies that ripple at the edges of ordinary history'.[95] His image of 'eddies that ripple' recalls the water features that have appeared as a recurrent motif throughout this essay: from the river Lignon winding through the *L'Astrée* frontispiece; to the poet's ability, according to *The Spectator*, to 'turn the Course of his Rivers in all the variety of *Meanders* . . . delightful to the Reader's Imagination'; to the rivulets that Arabella's lover fails to swell with his tears. In his preface to *The Castle of Otranto* (1764), Horace Walpole conceives of the 'fancy' powering romance as a river that is either 'dammed up' (in much 'modern' writing) or set 'at liberty to expatiate through the boundless realms of invention'.[96] Such streams provide not only the visual and auditory effects of sparkling light and water, but also an association with winding motion and wandering – the very opposite of indolence. 'Purling Streams', in particular (as in Leonora's garden, or Jemima's walk with her fawn), are a frequent marker of the 'romancification' of a landscape: a linguistic signal that we have entered a literary, half-metaphorical space, which is the only one in which streams can be said to purl.

It is in this space that the 'adventures' of the coterie occur – a series of imaginative games that are sociable rather than solitary and depend upon the constant interchange of writing. Thus Amabel Grey regales Talbot with a description of a boat being launched on the serpentine canal at Wrest:

> Not sticking in the mud . . . she was brought along shore . . . & had a most prosperous Voyage. The Sun shone . . . the Water & Shores looked more beautiful than ever . . . & being arrived at the open Sea behind the pavilion, we landed under a clump (which I ought to have called a Wood).[97]

This image recalls David Quint's emblem of the romance genre itself as an enchanted boat:

> In its purest form, [it] has no other destination than the adventure at hand. It cannot be said to be off course. New adventures crop up all the time, and the boat's travels describe a romance narrative that is open-ended and potentially endless.[98]

Of course, the potential for endlessness, just like the apparent infinity of a country-house prospect, was an illusion: Amabel's account takes longer than the voyage itself, and its terminus is a clump of trees near her house rather than a wild wood. Yet the interest in romance was not a delusion as Lennox portrays it in *The Female Quixote*,

344   NATASHA SIMONOVA

nor the result (as the Wrest correspondence amply proves) of feminine foolishness or a lack of alternative reading options. It was, rather, a different way of perceiving the world – like a Claude glass for the landscape, which emphasised colours and altered distances into 'a succession of high-coloured pictures . . . like the visions of the imagination, or the brilliant landscapes of a dream'.[99] It is only once we glimpse the multidimensionality of this effect, offering its own unique possibilities and pleasures, that we can begin to understand the significance of romance in eighteenth-century art and fiction.

Notes

1. Clara Reeve, *The Progress of Romance*, 2 vols (Colchester, 1785), 1:79. See also Natasha Simonova, '"A book that all have heard of . . . but that nobody reads": Sidney's *Arcadia* in the Eighteenth Century', *Journal of Medieval and Early Modern Studies* 50, no. 1 (2020): 139–59.
2. Scott Black, *Without the Novel: Romance and the History of Prose Fiction* (Charlottesville: University of Virginia Press, 2019), 1.
3. Barbara Fuchs, *Romance* (London and New York: Routledge, 2004).
4. Although it falls beyond my focus on prose fiction here, eighteenth-century interest in Edmund Spenser's verse romance *The Faerie Queene* also encompassed architecture, sculpture, painting and performance, exerting a strong influence on the design of country-house gardens such as The Leasowes and Stowe. See Hazel Wilkinson, *Edmund Spenser and the Eighteenth-Century Book* (Cambridge: Cambridge University Press, 2017).
5. Corinne Saunders, 'Introduction', in *A Companion to Romance from Classical to Contemporary*, ed. Corinne Saunders (Malden: Blackwell, 2004), 1.
6. Laurence Plazenet, 'Romances sans images? Le roman grec et ses dérivés en France aux seizième et dix-septième siècles', in *Traduire et illustrer le roman au XVIIIe siècle*, ed. Nathalie Ferrand (Liverpool: Liverpool University Press, 2011), 39–52.
7. Plazenet, 'Romances sans images?', 38.
8. Plazenet, 'Romances sans images?', 45–51.
9. Christophe Martin, 'L'illustration de L'Astrée (XVIIe–CVIIIe Siècles)', in *Lire L'Astrée*, ed. Delphine Denis (Paris: Presses de l'Université Paris-Sorbonne, 2008), 201–38.
10. Nandini Das, *Renaissance Romance: The Transformation of English Prose Fiction, 1570–1620* (Farnham: Ashgate, 2011), 17.
11. Tim Richardson, *The Arcadian Friends: Inventing the English Landscape Garden* (London: Bantam, 2007), 7–8, 14.
12. As in the titles of Richardson's *The Arcadian Friends* or Tom Stoppard's play *Arcadia* (London: Faber and Faber, 1993).
13. Jemima Grey to Catherine Talbot, 19 September 1769, Wrest Park [Lucas] Archive, L30/9a/9.125–6, Bedfordshire Archives and Records Service (hereafter cited as Wrest Park MSS).
14. Joseph Addison, 'No. 413', *The Spectator*, 24 June 1712.
15. Joseph Addison, 'No. 418', *The Spectator*, 30 June 1712.
16. Joseph Addison, 'No. 477', *The Spectator*, 6 September 1712.
17. Joseph Addison, 'No. 37', *The Spectator*, 12 April 1711.
18. Charlotte Lennox, *The Female Quixote*, 2 vols (London: A. Millar, 1752), 1:5.
19. Lennox, *Female Quixote*, 1:2.
20. Mary Patricia Martin, '"High and Noble Adventures": Reading the Novel in *The Female Quixote*', *NOVEL: A Forum in Fiction* 31, no.1 (1997): 53.
21. Lennox, *Female Quixote*, 1:2.

22. Lennox, *Female Quixote*, 1:29.
23. Amelia Dale, *The Printed Reader: Gender, Quixotism, and Textual Bodies in Eighteenth-Century Britain* (Lewisburg: Bucknell University Press, 2019), 20, 27.
24. Richard D. Altick, *Paintings from Books: Art and Literature in Britain, 1760–1900* (Columbus: Ohio State University Press, 1985), 26–7; J. L. Nevinson, 'Vogue of the Vandyke Dress', *Country Life* (1959): 25–7; Aileen Ribeiro, 'Some Evidence of the Influence of the Dress of the Seventeenth Century on Costume in Eighteenth-Century Female Portraiture', *Burlington Magazine* 119, no. 897 (1977): 834.
25. Altick, *Paintings from Books*, 27; Ribeiro, 'Some Evidence', 837, 839; Horace Walpole to Sir Horace Mann, 18 February 1742, in *The Yale Edition of Horace Walpole's Correspondence*, ed. W. S. Lewis et al., 48 vols (New Haven: Yale University Press, 1937–83), 17:339.
26. Altick, *Paintings from Books*, 26; Ribeiro, 'Some Evidence', 837, 839.
27. Samuel Richardson, *The History of Sir Charles Grandison*, 7 vols (London: S. Richardson, 1753), 1:115–16.
28. Oliver Goldsmith, *The Vicar of Wakefield*, 2 vols (Salisbury: B. Collins, 1766), 1:161.
29. Dale, *Printed Reader*, 36.
30. Julie Eckerle, *Romancing the Self in Early Modern Englishwomen's Life Writing* (Farnham: Ashgate, 2013), 6, 19–20.
31. Black argues that this kind of self-reflexive double vision, though made explicit in *Don Quixote*, is in fact inherent in romance as a genre; *Without the Novel*, 57–8.
32. Jemima Grey to Catherine Talbot, 1744, Wrest Park MSS, L30/9a/4:7.
33. Lennox, *Female Quixote*, 2:172, 175.
34. Black has recently provided a crucial articulation of romance as play, yet he still ultimately sees it as solitary: adopted from D. W. Winnicott, his model is based on a single child and a mother-observer, rather than a game with multiple participants; *Without the Novel*, 14–19.
35. Will Bowers and Hannah Leah Crummé, 'Introduction', in *Re-Evaluating the Literary Coterie, 1580–1830*, ed. Will Bowers and Hannah Leah Crummé (London: Palgrave Macmillan, 2016), 8.
36. Margaret J. M. Ezell, *Social Authorship and the Advent of Print* (Baltimore and London: Johns Hopkins University Press, 1999); Betty A. Schellenberg, *Literary Coteries and the Making of Modern Print Culture* (Cambridge: Cambridge University Press, 2016); Michelle Levy, *Literary Manuscript Culture in Romantic Britain* (Edinburgh: Edinburgh University Press, 2020).
37. Christine Gerrard, 'The Hillarian Circle: Scorpions, Sexual Politics and Heterosocial Coteries', in *Re-Evaluating the Literary Coterie*, ed. Will Bowers and Hannah Leah Crummé (London: Palgrave Macmillan, 2016), 98.
38. Gerrard, 'Hillarian Circle', 95, 96.
39. Benjamin Victor, *Original Letters, Dramatic Pieces, and Poems*, 3 vols (London: T. Becket, 1776), 1:68.
40. Gerrard, 'Hillarian Circle', 101.
41. Eliza Haywood, *The Tea-Table: Or, A Conversation between Some Polite Persons of both Sexes* (London: J. Roberts, 1725), 19.
42. Catherine Ingrassia, 'Fashioning Female Authorship in Eliza Haywood's *The Tea-Table*', *The Journal of Narrative Technique* 28, no. 3 (1998): 292.
43. Gerrard, 'Hillarian Circle', 102.
44. Eliza Haywood, *La Belle Assemblée: Or, The Adventures of Six Days*, 4 vols (London: D. Browne and J. Brotherton, 1724–36), 1:1–7.
45. Catherine Talbot, 'Journal 28 May–13 June 1745', Wrest Park MSS, L31/106.
46. Bowers and Crummé, 'Introduction', 3. The *Wrestiana* volume is currently in a private collection but will shortly be donated to English Heritage at Wrest Park; there is a microfilm

copy held in the Bedfordshire Archives. I am grateful to Jemima Hubberstey for providing me with images.

47. For a description of the 'Rites of the Goddess' Vacuna as involving 'unbroken Quiet', which first made me understand the pun, see Jemima Grey to Philip Yorke, 13 August [1749], Add. MS 35376, fol.14v, British Library.

48. *Wrestiana*, 55–7, 21.

49. Thomas Edwards to Philip Yorke, 10 August 1745. MS Bodley 1010 fol. 153, Bodleian Library.

50. *A Series of Letters between Mrs. Elizabeth Carter and Miss Catherine Talbot*, 4 vols (London: F. C. and J. Rivington, 1809), 2:57.

51. Jemima Grey to Catherine Talbot, 2 June 1748, Wrest Park MSS, L30/9a/5.69–70.

52. Jemima Grey to Catherine Talbot, 1744, Wrest Park MSS, L30/9a/4.5.

53. *Wrestiana*, 82.

54. Jemima Grey to Catherine Talbot, 27 May 1750, Wrest Park MSS, L30/9a/5.164.

55. Eckerle, *Romancing the Self*, 85.

56. Talbot, 'Journal', Wrest Park MSS, L31/106.

57. Jemima Grey to Catherine Talbot, Wrest Park MSS, L30/21/3:10.

58. See the discussion of Clarendon in Jemima Grey to Catherine Talbot, 14 November 1742, Wrest Park MSS, L30/9a/3:91, and Jemima Grey to Mary Grey, 24 November 1743, Wrest Park MSS, L30/9a/1.18–22.

59. Originally available only to the contributors, they were then reprinted in an edition of 100 copies in 1781 and more widely following Philip Yorke's death in 1792.

60. Schellenberg, *Literary Coteries*, 34–7.

61. Jemima Hubberstey, '"He has so far forgot his native country that even his style is truly attic": Narrative Dis-Orientation in the *Athenian Letters*', *Oxford Research in English* 9 (2019): 73.

62. Hubberstey, 'Narrative Dis-Orientation', 74.

63. Philip Yorke et al., *Athenian Letters: Or, The Epistolary Correspondence of an Agent of the King of Persia*, 4 vols (London: James Bettenham, 1741–3), 3:74.

64. *Athenian Letters*, 3:74–5.

65. *Athenian Letters*, 4:149–50.

66. *Athenian Letters*, 3:223.

67. *Athenian Letters*, 4:150–1. The letter at 3:188–94 relating the failed love of Antiope and Heliodorus also clearly has some *roman-à-clef* meaning, with the description of Heliodorus resembling Wray.

68. John Lawry to Philip York, 6 October 1743, Hardwicke Papers, Add. MS 35605, fol. 163r, British Library.

69. *Wrestiana*, 16.

70. Philip Yorke et al., *Athenian Letters: Or, The Epistolary Correspondence of an Agent of the King of Persia* (London: T. Cadell and W. Davies, 1781), xvi.

71. Thomas Edwards to Daniel Wray, 9 September 1749, MS Bodley 1011, fol. 147, Bodleian Library.

72. Jemima Grey to Catherine Talbot, 14 September 1748, Wrest Park MSS, L30/9a/2.11, and 21 July 1748, Wrest Park MSS, L30/9a/5.87–9.

73. Hubberstey, 'Narrative Dis-Orientation', 72.

74. Amabel Grey to Jemima Mary Gregory, 1772, Wrest Park MSS, L30/23/4.

75. Amabel Grey to Jemima Mary Gregory, 1772–6, Wrest Park MSS, L30/23/1–21.

76. Mary Jemima Grey to Amabel Grey, 5 August 1784, Wrest Park MSS, L30/11/123/16.

77. Amabel Grey to Jemima Mary Gregory, 29 December 1776, Wrest Park MSS, L30/23/20.

78. Diaries of Lady Amabel Yorke [Grey], WYL150/6197/1:34–9, West Yorkshire Archive Service.

MULTIMEDIA COTERIE ROMANCE

79. Amabel Grey to Jemima Mary Gregory, 23 August 1774, Wrest Park MSS, L30/23/13.
80. Amabel Grey to Jemima Mary Gregory, 17 October 1786, Wrest Park MSS, L30/23/67.
81. Kim Sloan, *A Noble Art: Amateur Artists and Drawing Masters c.1600–1880* (London: British Museum, 2000), 149–58; David Adshead, 'Wedgwood, Wimpole and Wrest: The Landscape Drawings of Lady Amabel Polwarth', *Apollo* 143, no. 410 (1996): 31–6.
82. Adshead, 'Wedgwood, Wimpole and Wrest', 33.
83. Sloan, *Noble Art*, 147–9.
84. Amabel Grey to Jemima Mary Gregory, 1772, Wrest Park MSS, L30/23/2.
85. Agneta Yorke to Jemima Grey, 12 July 1768, Wrest Park MSS, L30/9/97/4.
86. Agneta Yorke to Jemima Grey, 10 July 1770, Wrest Park MSS, L30/9/97/8.
87. Amabel's drawings were the source of eleven or thirteen of the final designs (Adshead, 'Wedgwood, Wimpole and Wrest', 31).
88. Amabel Grey to Jemima Grey, 19 June 1774, Wrest Park MSS, L30/9/60/35.
89. Schellenberg, *Literary Coteries*, 37–8.
90. Bowers and Crummé, 'Introduction', 8–9.
91. Jemima Grey to Catherine Talbot, 27 September 1763, Wrest Park MSS, L30/9a/8:135–6.
92. Amabel Grey to Catherine Talbot, 27 August 1767, Wrest Park MSS, L30/21/2/5.
93. Catherine Talbot, *The Works of the Late Mrs. Catharine Talbot* (London: J. F. and C. Rivington, 1780), 212–18.
94. Amabel Grey to Catherine Talbot, 1768, Wrest Park MSS, L30/21/2/10.
95. Black, *Without the Novel*, 3–5, 15.
96. Horace Walpole, *The Castle of Otranto*, 2nd edn (London: Bathoe and Lownds, 1765), vi.
97. Amabel Grey to Catherine Talbot, 29 July 1766, Wrest Park MSS, L30/21/2/3c.
98. David Quint, *Epic and Empire: Politics and Generic Form from Virgil to Milton* (Princeton: Princeton University Press, 1993), 249.
99. Sloan, *Noble Art*, 175; William Gilpin, *Remarks on Forest Scenery*, ed. Thomas Dick Lauder (Edinburgh: Fraser & Co., 1834), 233.

20

THE ART OF READING AND THE EIGHTEENTH-CENTURY NOVEL: THE CASE OF *THE HISTORY OF CHARLOTTE SUMMERS, THE FORTUNATE PARISH GIRL*

Joanna Maciulewicz

VIRGINIA WOOLF, IN the last essay of the second series of *The Common Reader*, entitled 'How to Read a Book', makes an observation that '[t]o read a novel is a difficult and complex art'. The reader, in order to make use of 'all that the novelist – the great artist' offers 'must be capable not only of great fineness of perception, but of great boldness of imagination'.[1] Woolf was not the first writer to recognise the difficulty and complexity of reading novels. In the eighteenth century, the subject of the rules of novel reading was part of the broader debate which began in response to the rapid proliferation of print. As James Raven describes it, if in the last decade of the seventeenth century 'printing was a restricted medium confined to London, Cambridge, Oxford and York', at the end of the next century 'print issued from hundreds of presses operating in London and almost every small town in the country'.[2] The ubiquity of printed texts resulted in a growing number of newly literate readers in need of guidance on how to engage with these publications, and in the growing popularity of a silent, private reading, very distinct from the dominant way of interacting with texts that was still rooted in orality. The novel genre, which was taking shape concomitantly with the growth of literacy and these changes in reading practices, shaped ideas concerning the reader's role in interacting with printed narratives, and the rules of reading and skills needed to perform it well. In this way, it contributed to the development of the art of the novel reading.

The classification of reading as art is evident in many eighteenth-century instructive texts that tried to teach its rules. A good example is Thomas Sheridan's *Lectures on the Art of Reading*, published in 1775, which describes reading as a skill that needs to be mastered and points to the urgency of teaching its rules. Sheridan argues that '[o]f all arts that have been taught mankind, Reading is by much the most general' and that 'it is almost universal [in Britain] since even the children of peasants are introduced in it'. The prevalence of reading, however, did not mean that it was well developed. Sheridan laments that 'there are few that succeed even tolerably in it' and blames 'erroneous and defective' methods of instruction for the poor reading skills of the generally literate British population.[3] This way of writing about reading reflects widespread belief that without proper training it was '"unruly"' as well as 'naïve, non-reflexive, and undisciplined'.[4] Eighteenth-century guides to reading attempted to raise awareness of what

THE ART OF READING 349

the practice of reading actually involves, conceptualising it as 'a skill or craft based on special knowledge'.[5]

Instructions for how to read were included in numerous genres of writing, such as letter-manuals, conduct books, pamphlets, periodicals, plays or fictions,[6] and addressed a wide range of its aspects: grammars, for instance, introduced readers to spelling, etymology, syntax, rhetoric and prosody. Conversation pieces, which Eve Tavor Bannet defines as 'stylized print genres which used the familiar form of conversation to transmit knowledge relevant to the reading and judgment of texts', taught the analysis of characters, genres and styles necessary for interpreting texts.[7] The ubiquity of the theme of reading in eighteenth-century publications provides the firmest evidence for the growing awareness of reading's complex nature, and for the strong conviction of the need to develop a set of skills to perform it correctly.

Instructive works such as these are invaluable sources for studying the eighteenth-century assumptions about reading since they explicitly refer to a practice which, as Roger Chartier put it, is 'always of the order of the ephemeral', 'only rarely leaves traces' and 'is scattered in an infinity of singular acts'.[8] Historians of reading strive to explore those different ways of engaging with texts mainly by drawing on empirical case studies, including trying to retrieve individual stories about reading by analysing marginalia, diaries or commonplace books; however, this evidence gives insight into idiosyncratic reading experiences rather than illuminating the more general nature of how texts were read. Studying the 'prevailing prescriptions of reading' offers a more systematic overview, since they shed light on 'prevailing protocols and practices, and on the social, economic, political and pedagogical functions that contemporaries designed them to serve'.[9] They reflect the variety of reading practices and attempts to regulate the ways readers interacted with written and printed words.

One important theme in the broader debate concerning different ways of reading was that of reading fiction. Instructions for how to do it well were often incorporated into the plots of novels. The most famous examples include Charlotte Lennox's *The Female Quixote* (1752) and Jane Austen's *Northanger Abbey* (written in 1798–9 and published in 1817). Both tell stories of misguided reading to warn readers against the perils of unsupervised and unregulated interactions with fictional narratives, and include dramatised lessons on the rules of interpretation and valorisation of literary genres. The misadventures of Arabella, the protagonist of *The Female Quixote* deluded by heroic romances, and of Catherine, the heroine of *Northanger Abbey*, whose imagination is inflamed by Gothic novels, conclude in lectures about the proper ways of understanding and enjoying fictional narratives. The two naive readers are instructed about the need to confront their descriptions of reality with empirical experience and verifiable factual sources.

Fiction, however, did not only include lessons about interpretation: it also experimented with narrative techniques to explore and expose the role of the reader as it was shaped in complex relationship with a printed narrative. Interest in methods of reading fiction coincided with the growing popularity of silent reading, which brought about radical changes in how readers interacted with texts. Tavor Bannet explains that during the eighteenth century 'perhaps the most obvious meaning of "read"' was '[r]eciting words aloud from a written or printed text'.[10] This was frequently practised in 'a performative church culture' that played a great part in English social life, but, as Abigail Williams demonstrates in *The Social Life of Books*, it was also common in domestic and professional spaces.[11] The prevalence of reading aloud was manifested in the great interest invested in its oral aspects, the 'near obsession with reading aloud' and 'the craze for elocution', to which the print market responded by publishing numerous guides aimed at satisfying the general public's need to hone their skills in delivering oral texts, for instance by adjusting the size and format of printed works to assist 'their suitability for performance'.[12] The turn of the seventeenth and eighteenth century, however, witnessed 'the birth of a generation of silent readers' who were to transform the prevalent model of reading into a mode requiring a different set of skills.[13] Changes in ways of reading, and the advice on how to read fiction designed for silent and solitary reading, were thematised in novels that used self-reflexive techniques to take part in the development of new rules of novel reading.

Novels were particularly well suited to exploring the heterogeneous nature of reading, which could be loud and performative or silent and abstract, because of their affinity with other genres and media. As Marcie Frank observes, 'novels took shape in reference to [theatre]', which 'was the default aesthetic experience of the long eighteenth century'.[14] Fictions and plays functioned in this period as 'contiguous and in many respects symbiotic cultural phenomena'.[15] Print and performance were not seen in terms of 'media opposition', as might be the case now, because for most of the eighteenth century 'reading and seeing plays' were 'mutually enhancing' rather than 'competing activities'.[16] It was as common to read a play as to see it performed, which is evidenced in the catalogues of circulating libraries that listed playbooks next to novels, or in the development of types of drama intended to be read rather performed.[17] The affinity of the two genres led to the conceptualisation of reading as a kind 'mental theatre', and as a convenient form of instruction.[18] The most notable example of the use of the didactic potential of drama in the novel is Samuel Richardson's fiction. The writer was very aware of the powerful influence of drama on its recipients and was wary of its pernicious effects. He believed, however, that 'under proper Regulations, the *Stage* may be made subservient to excellent Purposes, and be an useful Second to the *Pulpit* itself'[19] and borrowed from its aesthetics to teach moral lessons in *Clarissa* (1748), which he described in the postscript as a 'dramatic narrative'.[20] The novel, as a 'cross-generic and intermedial' mode of writing,[21] could freely exploit its own affinity with theatre and drama not only for moral instruction but also to reflect on the ways readers engaged with texts.

The recognition of print's complementarity with other media makes it possible to challenge the frequent claim that print is conducive to absorptive, mindless and passive forms of textual consumption. William Warner argues that the publication formats customarily selected for novels in this period, octavo or duodecimo, encouraged readers to immerse themselves in private, solitary reading, which, in turn, led to their self-obliteration, extinguishing the critical impulse that required detachment and self-awareness.[22] Katherine Mannheimer claims that the typography employed in early novels, most notably in Richardson's fiction, performed the same function. It sustained 'absorptive fantasy' both by employing printing techniques to 'draw the reader deeper into a character's subjectivity' and by drawing attention to the materiality of the book as 'a product of the fictional world' – both were designed to reinforce the 'mimetic illusion', making the reader oblivious of the surrounding reality.[23] It is no accident, then, that absorptive, uncritical reading was associated with realist fiction, which strove to make the reader forget about the constructed nature of the fictional world.

THE ART OF READING   351

The association between absorption, solitariness and realism in the ways in which novels used print was forged in the eighteenth century, which is evident in writings from the period. Vicesimus Knox, for instance, observed in his *Essays Moral and Literary* (1779) that novels, of which he greatly disapproved, 'fix attention too deeply' and incapacitate the mind for 'the painful task of serious study' by 'too lively a plea- sure'.[24] His description of the kind of influence Richardson's fiction exerts upon the reader suggests an emotional engrossment that prevents rational judgement and the dissolution of the boundary between fictional and empirical reality. Readers, 'who naturally pay the greatest attention to the lively description of love, and its effects . . . long to be actors in the scenes they admire'.[25] These novels' modes of publication and the ways they were read made them even more perilous: 'The prudence of their pub- lishers suggests the expediency of making them conveniently portable' so that they can be read in 'the recesses of the closet, [where they] inflame the passions at a distance from temptation, and teach all the malignity of vice in solitude'.[26] The modes of the production and consumption of printed narratives were conducive to uncontrollable immersion in the fictional world, which could potentially corrupt young, impression- able minds.

However, as recent studies repeatedly emphasise, realism was only one among many forms of novelistic writing in the eighteenth century. Patricia Meyer Spacks dem- onstrates in *Novel Beginnings* that the early history of the novel belonged to 'an era of radical literary experiment', characterised by 'an explosion of new energies'.[27] The coincidence of the eclecticism of narrative models in fictional writing with the rapid growth of the number of readers who, as historical studies have shown, developed 'the tremendous diversity of reading practice' and employed 'different reading strate- gies for different texts'[28] was particularly conducive to the development of awareness about the ways novels engaged their readers.

The type of fiction that affords the best insight into understanding the different ways in which readers can engage with the emerging novel genre is one which discourages immersive reading, partly by including self-reflexive comments on the way in which it is written and should be read. Henry Fielding's *The Adventures of Joseph Andrews* (1742) and *The History of Tom Jones, A Foundling* (1749) as well as Laurence Sterne's *The Life and Opinions of Tristram Shandy, Gentleman* (1759–67) are considered clas- sics in the self-conscious tradition of novel writing, but in this mid-century period of the novel's development, characterised by highly experimental and self-aware fiction, numerous other novels also exercised a strong self-reflexive streak. Many were written in imitation of *Tom Jones*, and while some argue that these metanarratives exerted a considerable influence on *Tristram Shandy*,[29] they fell into oblivion due to their self- confessed 'qualitative limitations'.[30] Ian Watt's *The Rise of the Novel*, which promoted realism as the defining characteristic of the novel, influenced a subsequent strand of criticism which held that self-consciousness was a cul-de-sac in the development of the genre. Watt declared it to be an artistic failure since it was designed to 'break the spell of the imaginary world represented in the novel'.[31] Numerous critics have noticed that Fielding shattered the mimetic illusion in his fiction for instructive purposes. John Preston's *The Created Self*, for example, claims that Fielding incorporates readers into his narrative in order to 'school' them,[32] while Henry Power, in his more recent *Epic into Novel*, suggests that Fielding's self-conscious 'commentary is a means by which he can negotiate a relationship with his elusive reader'.[33] The same interest in approaches

352 JOANNA MACIULEWICZ

to novel reading manifested in lesser-known experimental fiction – partly written in imitation of Fielding's narrative models – is often excluded from histories of the novel because of the supposedly derivative nature of this fiction.

Many novels that explored self-conscious narrative techniques were published in the 1750s – long regarded as 'a blank decade in the history of fiction' and 'a low point between the great works of Fielding and Richardson and the *Tristram Shandy* craze'.[34] Until recently they have been viewed as little more than 'literary curiosities' that 'earn rather than invalidate the low repute in which both their first readers and twentieth-century literary critics held them'.[35] However, there is a growing conviction that mid-century fiction deserves serious critical attention so as to improve our understanding of the development of the novel. Thomas Keymer considers the period from 1750 to 1760 to be 'a crucial decade in the history of the novel' because it 'poses an interesting challenge to our assumptions about the genre',[36] Peter Sabor draws attention to the fact that in this period 'a new repertoire of possibilities for the novel was opening up',[37] while Tim Parnell asserts that we should reconsider the relations between Sterne's fictions and the novels of his time to gain a fuller understanding of 'the complex, and still partially mapped, history of the "rise" of the novel'.[38] Narrative experiments were bound to test readerly expectations and customary ways of reading, as well as increasing awareness of the nature of the relationships between the reader, the narrative voice and the characters in the story.

It is noteworthy that mid-century fictions, despite deviating from the realist path, sold remarkably well.[39] One reason for the popularity of this type of novel is precisely the heightened interest it shows in its own audience. Metafictional narratives, Christina Lupton claims, liberate readers from the engrossing 'effects of mimesis', enabling their empowerment: they become 'visible and dialogically active in ways that are normally opposed by the impersonality of print'.[40] Creating a fictional space in which the author, acting in the capacity of the narrator, could negotiate the rules of proper reading seemed to be as appealing as the immersive pleasures of reading realist narratives. The study of self-conscious fiction that has only now been brought to light, such as William Goodall's *The Adventures of Captain Greenland* (1752), Susan Smythies's *The Stage Coach* (1753) and *The Brothers* (1758), and Francis Coventry's *The History of Pompey the Little* (1750), allows us to uncover readers' role in shaping the protocols of novel reading.

The novel that is most frequently mentioned in the context of self-conscious commentary on reading is *The History of Charlotte Summers, The Fortunate Parish Girl*. Its year of composition and publication are uncertain since they are not indicated on the title page. *Charlotte Summers* was most probably published in 1749 or 1750 and it is occasionally credited to Sarah Fielding. It excited little enthusiasm in its own day. Ralph Griffith wrote in *The Monthly Review* that '[A]ll that we can say of this performance, is, that the author has kept his name unknown, which is an instance of his discretion: and that it is sold by Charles Corbet in Fleet-Street.'[41] The indifferent review could not, however, be seen as indicative of the general indifference among its early readers. Lady Mary Wortley Montagu, in a letter to the Countess of Bute dated 16 February 1752, confesses that she 'was not able to quit it until it was read over', although she perceived the deficiencies in character depiction and plot construction. The novel's protagonist displayed the author's lack of skill in drawing a virtuous character, while the story struck Montagu as 'altogether absurd and ridiculous'.[42]

THE ART OF READING 353

Charlotte Summers offers two parallel stories within its framework. One involves the titular protagonist, a poor girl whom Lady Bountiful takes into her family and brings up alongside her own son, Tom. When it turns out that, contrary to her benefactress's designs, Charlotte has engaged Tom's sentiments, she escapes from the house, exposing herself to numerous dangers that threaten her virtue. It was this ill-considered decision to renounce the safety of Lady Bountiful's house that Montagu regarded as absurd. The other, parallel story portrays the narrator's conversations with his readers. This incorporation of discussions about reading within the fictional narrative places the novel firmly in the tradition of printed conversation pieces the popularity of which in the eighteenth century derived from the fact that education was 'heavily dependent on speech and dialogue'.[43] The novel thus operates at the cross-section of genres (since in its use of dialogue it also evokes drama) and media (speech and print), which situates it in a perfect position for commenting upon the variety of reading strategies required by diverse forms of storytelling. It draws attention to the differences between the novel and drama and to the transformations of narration which emerged as a result of the popularisation of silent reading.

Charlotte Summers inherits its interest in reading and readers directly from Fielding's fiction, which it openly imitates. Its author assumes the identity of a son of Fielding's: 'the first Begotten, of the poetical Issue, of the much celebrated Biographer of *Joseph Andrews*, and *Tom Jones*', which explains the likeness of his own work to that of his parent.[44] 'I find so much of his Blood in my Veins, that I have found myself, ever since I was a Boy, under the strongest impulse to mimic every Action of that Gentleman' (1:3–4). In one aspect, however, the imitation of Fielding's fiction surpasses its original. As Wayne Booth noted as early as 1952, *Charlotte Summers* gives much more attention to the subject of reading and the relationship between readers and the narrator. The novel 'go[es] farther than Fielding's [fiction] in the characterisation of the readers', who are 'more various' and 'much more fully endowed with ridiculous characteristics than are Fielding's', and of the narrator, who is described more intimately, and 'in the elaboration of conversations between them'.[45] The extraordinary attention that the novel gives to reading continues to attract critical attention. Keymer states that it 'moves beyond Fielding' by 'intercalating its narrative with imaginary scenes of its own reception',[46] while Sabor notes that *Charlotte Summers*' 'obsession with its own readers goes beyond Henry Fielding to anticipate the self-consciousness of Laurence Sterne in *Tristram Shandy*'.[47] The dramatisation of the interaction between the reader and the narrator in *Charlotte Summers* serves multiple functions. It explores readers' expectations of novels and the misconceptions about what readers seek in such fiction; it displays the diversity of practices of novel reading; it teaches the navigation of a printed narrative; and it instructs readers about how their relation with the narrator has changed in the new kind of fiction that emerged with the rise of silent reading.

Charlotte Summers instructs its readers in these variegated aspects of reading by incorporating or absorbing them into the created world, which at first glance may suggest a metaphorical reference to the immersive effect of reading. The readers of *Charlotte Summers* receive aptronymic names comparable to those given to the characters of the main story. At its opening, they are literally invited into the fictional world. 'You may enter freely', the narrator says, 'I'll conduct you to the Parlour, where you may have the Honour to salute the hospitable Owner of this venerable Mansion' (1:13). As the narrative develops, it turns out that this extension of the fictional world to include its readers is designed not to make them forget about their own world but to make them aware of the transformation of the experience of reading brought about by the growth of literacy and print and the rise of silent reading.

The most significant alteration caused by 'a transition from reading aloud to skilled silent reading' was 'a radical change in the orientation of both writer and reader to the text'.[48] While reading aloud encouraged the reader to assume the role of a mouthpiece, or an impersonator, of the writer, silent reading dissociated the two roles and placed the reader and the narrator in a dialogic relation to one another. The popularisation of silent reading thus led to changes in writing, which in fiction manifested itself in the shift from an intradiegetic to an extradiegetic narrator, and in reading which redefined the relationship of the reader and writer from one of identification to that of 'imaginary conversation'.[49] *Charlotte Summers* illustrates the popularisation of silent reading by dramatising changes in the conceptualisation of the narrator in a mode of fiction which adjusted its model of storytelling to silent reading, and the narrator's relation to the novel's readers and the created world.

The new type of narrator deployed in *Charlotte Summers* is different from the older figure of the storyteller, mainly in that he does not belong in the same world as either the fiction's characters or its readers. This is a convention that a present-day reader takes for granted, but which required a radical adjustment of the conceptualisation of reading from the eighteenth-century audience. The extradiegetic narrator, as Elspeth Jajdelska explains, became 'a new and strange kind of being – not fully embodied, not realised before the reader's eyes as a full participant, yet subject to some limitations in physical time and space and able to address the reader directly, and indeed rather intimately'.[50] *Charlotte Summers* draws attention to the altered nature of the narrator in the new kind of fiction it promoted in a humorous scene in which its narrator put on his 'conjuring invisible Cap, and pop'd in upon the Ladies without their once dreaming that any thing Male was within a hundred Yards of them' (2:155). He plays with this idea of his transformation from the embodied character to the incorporeal voice by reflecting on the privileged position from which he can observe his characters. He looks at Charlotte, who 'had just laced her Stays, her Snowy Bosom all bare, and was preparing the Remainder of her Dress, little suspecting who was near her' (2:156), relishing the proximity that would not be possible for any other character within the narrative. To emphasise the superiority of his vantage point he jokingly alludes to the envy that his position would provoke in Charlotte's suitors, were they to know how close he can approach the girl whom they pursue: 'What would Sir Thomas Bountiful have given to have been in my Place, what would not Mr. Crofts have suffered to have seen her as I did' (2:155). The sexual undertones of the remarks, which the narrator hastens to dismiss by declaring that 'all this Advantage' had 'nothing sensual' in it (2:156), make the entire lesson about the transformation of the narrator in novels intended for silent perusal more entertaining, and in all likelihood more memorable.

Charlotte Summers also illustrates the complications in the narrator's and the readers' spatial positioning inherent in the type of the narrative intended for silent reading. Unlike in the act of oral storytelling, the narrator and the reader of this new kind of fiction do not share the same space. As Jajdelska explains, this creates the need for more explicit indications of location than were necessary in fictions intended for storytelling or reading aloud. *Charlotte Summers* draws attention to the different special positions of the narrator and the reader by the elaborate metaphor of the journey, which is necessary to move the reader to the place of action:

THE ART OF READING 355

> We Are Masters of a Kind of Art Magic, that we have only speak the Word, and,
> *presto*, you are transported, in the very Position you chance to be in at the Time, to
> the Place where we would have you attend us. (1:13)

The explicit references to the place of action and the magical means of the reader's
transportation to it highlight the perspective of the extradiegetic narrator as distinct
from that of traditional storytellers. The narrator first asks for his readers' 'company,
as far as Carmarthenshire, in Wales' (1:13), and then boasts of the power to manipulate time and space: 'Tho the Journey is pretty long, and in the ordinary Way of travelling may take up some Days', it can be shortened to merely 'an Instant' (1:13). When
he becomes impatient with the readers' impolite comments, he points out that they
either have to abide by him, or 'get back to London, on Foot, without seeing the Show'
(1:24–5). The humorous comments on the necessity of transportation points to the
alienation of the narrator and the reader. Writing and print are about distance, which
in print is overcome by a leap of faith and imagination.

This transformation in the role of the narrator in the story designed for silent
reading rather than oral delivery creates a strong antagonism between the storyteller
and the reader. The change in the relationship between them is illustrated in the scene
in which one of the characters tells a story to a live audience. The compliments she
receives leads him to a bitter observation about the different relation between oral
storytellers and their listeners and authors of printed stories and their readers. While
oral stories are usually rewarded with applause for their performance, the authors of
novels cannot count on the same kind reception: 'We Authors are not always treated
with the same Complaisance. Every Reader damns the Blockhead without Ceremony,
and thinks himself obliged to use no Decorum in expressing his dislike' (2:146–7).

The representation of the relationship between the narrator and the reader as that
of opposition rather than identification emphasises the reader's active and critical role
not only in the process of interacting with texts, but also in the process of formulating
the protocol for reading fiction. The novel that, as the author declares, is to serve as
a guide to reading demonstrates that readers are reluctant to accept the rules imposed
on them. This power struggle is evident as early as chapter 1, in a scene in which two
women readers, Beau Thoughtless and 'pretty Miss Pert', fail to thank the narrator for
his 'Pains' (1:24) and complain about his manner of storytelling. They whisper, in a
rather irreverent manner, that, at the opening of the story, rather than reading at length
about 'the old woman' Lady Bountiful, they would like to be introduced immediately
to the heroine of the novel, Charlotte Summers. This unruly behaviour provokes the
narrator to make a declaration about the purpose of his fiction:

> I must inform the pretty Triflers, that I am determined my Readers shall learn
> something in every Chapter, and in this, amongst other Things, they must learn and
> practice Patience, for let them be in never so great a Hurry, to come at the Speech of
> Miss Summers, they cannot come near her, without My Permission, and as I have
> now got them into my Custody, they must travel my Pace . . . (1:24)

The scenes that follow demonstrate that readers are not willing to yield to a new, more
disciplined regime of interacting with fiction and to assume the role of naive, unruly
and docile disciples.

356   JOANNA MACIULEWICZ

They freely express criticisms of plot construction, character drawing and do not allow the narrator to make conventional assumptions about their responses to the text. Mrs Sit-her-time voices, for instance, her dissatisfaction with Charlotte's rejection of Captain Price's suit:

> Oh Pox upon her for a Fool, a Bird in Hand is worth two in the Bush, she should have taken him at any Rate . . . she'll never get such another Match, —but Plague on the Author, what a Pother he has kept about Captain Price, and after all, it has come to nothing, but that the foolish Wench has refus'd him. (2:221)

The author retorts that she might want to have him for herself, 'for I cannot for my Life persuade my Parish Girl to take up with him' (2:221). Widow Lack-it interrupts the concluding chapter, protesting against the narrator's intention to close the story without marrying his heroine off. In an argument that she formulates to encourage the narrator to modify the ending of his narrative, she has a recourse to her own life experience and literary knowledge. She argues that '[i]t is impossible she [Charlotte] can be happy without a Husband' and that 'it's contrary to all Rule to end a History of this kind without marrying the Hero and Heroine' (2:313). The readers of *Charlotte Summers* not only question the narrator's capacity to predict their motivations for reading. When he admonishes Miss Censorious for her taste for scandal, and warns her 'not to run too quick upon a malicious Scent' in making assumptions about Lady Bountiful's unchaste conduct (1:25), the reader takes offence and rebukes him for misjudging her. 'Hang your Impertinence', she says, 'I did not think that she was actually naughty with any of the odious Male Things' (1:25). In this way she asserts her readerly autonomy and questions the narrator's ability to control his readers' responses to the text.

Despite the attempts to educate his readers, the narrator in the end confesses to be a believer in the readerly freedom to pursue one's own feelings as evoked by the encounter with a text. In a chapter ironically entitled 'a Dissertation on the Art of Laughing and Crying', he promises to lay down 'Rules and Precepts, by which the most ignorant may certainly know when they ought to laugh or cry, either at the Incidents in this History, or those of any other Book that is now, or ever shall be written hereafter' (1:215). He recommends it 'to all Gentlemen, Ladies, and others, who want to acquire a thorough Command, either of the merry or melancholy Muscles of their Face' (1:215–16). Yet, the narrator never fulfils the promise. He complains that although, since Solomon, it has been known that there is a time to laugh and there is a time to cry, nobody, not even Aristotle or Horace, bothered to explain 'when a man ought to be merry or sad'. All they did was to formulate the rules for authors instructing them 'when they are to be pleased or displeased with their own Labours', but the audience have never been taught 'when and at what periods they are to exercise their risible and crying Faculties' (1:218). As a result, the same text provokes widely disparate responses, 'to the Scandal of learned Men and the utter Destruction of all Rule and Order' (1:218).

The continuation of the chapter reveals that the lament on the absence of 'the Art of commanding the Muscles of the Face' is nothing but ironic. It is a celebration of the freedom of attachments that readers form with texts and an attack on those who usurp the right to regulate them. The narrator declares that 'every Reader shall only laugh when he is really pleased, and finds the Muscles move that way themselves, and shall cry, sigh or groan just in proportion, as he finds himself sad, moved, or tenderly touched' (1:222). In defence of what he calls 'Muscular Liberty', he attacks critics who stand in the way of the natural response to books. He finds it absurd that a reader 'must wait till the Criticks have examined it [a text] Limb by Limb, before he dare own that he is the least affected with the most tragical Tragedy, that ever was tragedized' (1:224). The reader does not need rules to respond to the text in the manner desired by the author. It is more a question of 'The Laws of Harmony' between the author and the reader, who should be 'tuned to the same Key' (1:226). Reading, then, is described in terms of sympathy and emotional synchronisation rather than as a process regulated by rational rules. Even when emotionally engaging in a text readers seem to preserve their sovereignty. Reading is no longer considered as disciplined or unruly but, rather, as a dialogic relationship between the author and reader that is to unite the two parties in sympathy.

After putting forward this affective theory of reading the narrator assures his readers that, having analysed the two masters of fiction, one the author of *Tom Jones* and the other the author of *Clarissa*, he discovered how they manage to 'usurp such a Dominion over our Hearts and Countenances' (1:220) in such different ways. Their secret, as the narrator describes it, corresponds with Rita Felski's theory of attunement, that is, a kind of attachment which is 'about things resonating, aligning, coming together'.[51] The narrator explains that both Fielding and Richardson,

> while they were writing for the Entertainment of the Public, were pleasing themselves in their different Tastes . . . and as both presented their natural Countenance, we could not help joining in Concert, for Laughing, and Crying, as well as Yawning are both catching, that is, when they are natural and not forced. (1: 221–2)

The best effect reading can have, then, concerns the rapport between the narrator and the reader.

The motivations and expectations which readers should bring to the novelistic text are not the only aspects of reading that *Charlotte Summers* explores. By introducing the character of Arabella Dimple and her maid Polly, who, just like the empirical reader, are in the midst of reading *Charlotte Summers*, the novel draws attention to the different ways novels can be read that require the development of new skills. Arabella reads her novel by herself, but she also has her maid read it for her, which suggests that she is equally experienced in reading both silently and aloud. She had read the first volume in the afternoon, but when she 'is just now stept into Bed' and 'cannot find herself disposed to Rest' (1:67), she asks Polly to read aloud to her. She gives her general instructions about elocution: 'read distinctly, and not as if you were drauling over your Prayers' (1:69) and begins to listen. Polly also demonstrates her understanding about different forms of novel reading. When she discovers that 'her [Mistress is] fast asleep' (1:85), at first she is genuinely surprised: 'Oh la, says she, softly to herself, how can my Mistress fall asleep at hearing this sweet Book read?' (1:85), but soon 'steal[s] away softly' to enjoy reading privately in her bed. The scene of the alternate loud and silent reading highlights the multifaceted and multisensory nature of novel reading, which can be audio-aural or visual, communal and private, and it may require a reader to assume diverse roles involving different sets of capabilities: the more active position of a storyteller and a more passive function of a listener. Polly's deficiencies in elocution and Arabella's falling asleep expose the distinct demands of each kind of reading.

The scene between Arabella and Polly draws attention to yet another aspect of novel reading that poses a challenge: the navigation of the printed text. Reading a printed novel, unlike watching a dramatic performance or listening to a story, makes greater demands on its recipients, who are put in charge of the organisation of the way they follow the story. The sheer length of the novels enforces pauses in their reading and its inevitably punctured nature requires skills in navigating the narrative, the lack of which can result in a disruption of the story's continuity and the reader's disorientation. The narrator frequently alerts readers to the inevitability of interruptions and to disposing of one's powers of concentration wisely, encouraging them to take naps or to otherwise refresh their strength. He also attempts to teach his readers to use the way the novelistic story is organised to find their bearings when they resume reading. At the end of chapter 4, he warns them 'to remember that he left off at the End of the 4th Chapter' (1:67) and illustrates the consequences of failing to take his advice, by dramatising Arabella and Polly's sense of frustration and disorientation, of which the empirical reader, who shares the reading experience with the two women, partakes:

> . . . and, now I think on't, the Author bid me remember, that I left off at the End of — I think it was the 6th Chapter. Turn to the 7th Chapter, and let me hear how it begins—Polly reads, 'Chapter the 7th,–The Death of my Lady Fanciful's Squirrel . . .' —Hold, Wench, you read too fast; and I don't understand one Word of what you are saying . . . I must not have got so far—Look back to the End of that Chapter where the Blookhead of an Author bids us take a Nap, and remember where he left off.—O la, Ma'am, I have found it; here it is. As your Ladyship said, he says . . . (1:68–9)

This passage allows the real or empirical reader to experience the sense of confusion caused by the lack of control of the reading process, and points to the necessity of using the narrator's instructions to develop habits necessary for smoothly reading the novel as a long narrative in print.

The narrator warns the reader against the most instinctive method of availing oneself of the material properties of the novel to mark the point in the story at which that reader arrived. When Polly naively asks whether her 'Ladyship fold[ed] down' where she finished reading, she is scolded and informed that 'the Book is divided into Chapters on Purpose to prevent that ugly Custom of thumbing and spoiling the Leaves' (1:68). The narrator then tries to facilitate the reader's adjustment to the organisation of the narrative in the novel by evoking a familiar experience of the organisation of plays. The 'white Spaces' (1:30) between books and chapters serve the same purposes as the intermissions between acts and scenes, that is, to manage the attention of the audience and to distract them from the necessity of changing the scene or moving the action forward to leave out the 'Ahistorical Years' of the characters' lives (1:31). For audience members it is the time for 'Bows, Smiles, Ogles, Whispers, fluttering of Fans, adjusting of Perukes, Pinches of Snuff and smart Repartee of the Orange Wenches', while readers may use it to take a nap, or 'a Glass of Wine, or [to] eat a Crust of Bread' (1:31). It is essential, however, that readers know how to use these divisions to keep track of the plot. Polly, who has learnt how to navigate the story, is presented to the empirical reader as a model. She reminds herself that she should mind where she interrupts reading: 'I must not lose my Place, nor yet fold down the Leaves; oh, I shall

THE ART OF READING

remember it, for I am just at the End of the Chapter. The sixth Chapter is next . . .' (1:86). To aid her memory in recalling the chapter's number she puts six pins in her sleeve, which the narrator says all readers may imitate. The importance of the right use of chapters to control the process of reading novels is subsequently illustrated with a cautionary tale followed by implicit advice on how to learn the skill of navigating long fictional narratives.

Eighteenth-century writings customarily described novel reading as passive, absorptive and unreflective, but the representation of reading in self-conscious fiction of the period represents it as a practice which requires the development of skills and rules. The study of novels that thematised novel reading gives insight into the formation of the art of reading that was inextricably linked with changes in the modes of interacting with texts accelerated by the explosion of print and literacy, and by the shaping of the generic conventions of the novel, as yet in a highly experimental stage of its development. *Charlotte Summers*, like other metafictional fictions that take interest in methods for reading novels, serves as a guide to novel reading when it shows the ways of orientation within a long, printed narrative, and the significance of imagination in learning the rules of a narrative told by an extradiegetic narrator. It also portrays the art of reading fiction as a complex relationship between the reader and the printed narrative whose rules need to be learnt to experience the pleasures and benefits of imaginative writing.

Acknowledgement

This research was funded by the National Science Centre, Poland, as part of the Opus project number 2020/37/B/HS2/02093.

Notes

1. Virginia Woolf, *The Common Reader. Second Series* (London: Hogarth Press, 1948), 260–1.
2. James Raven, 'The Book Trades', in *Books and Their Readers in Eighteenth-Century England: New Essays*, ed. Isabel Rivers (London and New York: Continuum, 2001), 1–34.
3. Thomas Sheridan, *Lectures on the Art of Reading*, 2 vols (London: J. Dodsley, 1775), 1:1–2.
4. Reinhard Wittmann, 'Was There a Reading Revolution at the End of the Eighteenth Century?', in *A History of Reading in the West*, ed. Guglielmo Cavallo and Roger Chartier, trans. Lydia G. Cochrane (Cambridge: Polity Press, 1999), 290.
5. Eve Tavor Bannet, *Eighteenth-Century Manners of Reading: Print Culture and Popular Instruction in the Anglophone Atlantic World* (Cambridge: Cambridge University Press, 2017), 2.
6. Tavor Bannet, *Eighteenth-Century Manners of Reading*, 1.
7. Tavor Bannet, *Eighteenth-Century Manners of Reading*, 94.
8. Roger Chartier, *The Order of Books: Readers, Authors, and Libraries in Europe between the Fourteenth and Eighteenth Centuries* (Stanford: Stanford University Press, 1994), 1.
9. Tavor Bannet, *Eighteenth-Century Manners of Reading*, 4.
10. Tavor Bannet, *Eighteenth-Century Manners of Reading*, 95.
11. Abigail Williams, *The Social Life of Books: Reading Together in the Eighteenth-Century Home* (New Haven: Yale University Press, 2017), 12.

12. Williams, *The Social Life of Books*, 11, 25, 3.
13. Williams, *The Social Life of Books*, 11.
14. Marcie Frank, *The Novel Stage: Narrative Form from the Restoration to Jane Austen* (Lewisburg: Bucknell University Press, 2020), 2.
15. Gillian Russell, 'The Novel and the Stage', in *The Oxford History of the English Novel*, vol. 2, *English and British Fiction 1750–1820*, ed. Peter Garside and Karen O'Brien (Oxford: Oxford University Press, 2015), 513.
16. Frank, *The Novel Stage*, 6.
17. Russell, 'The Novel and the Stage', 516.
18. Frank, *The Novel Stage*, 3.
19. Samuel Richardson, *The Apprentice's Vade Mecum: or, Young Man's Pocket-Companion* (Dublin: S. Powell, 1734), 17.
20. Samuel Richardson, *Clarissa, or The History of a Young Lady*, ed. Angus Ross (London: Penguin, 1985), 1495.
21. Frank, *The Novel Stage,* 154.
22. William B. Warner, *Licensing Entertainment: The Elevation of Novel Reading in Britain, 1684–1750* (Berkeley, Los Angeles and London: University of California Press, 1998), 132.
23. Katherine Mannheimer, *Print, Visuality and Gender in Eighteenth-Century Satire: "The Scope in Ev'ry Page"* (London: Routledge, 2011), 157.
24. Vicesimus Knox, *Essays Moral and Literary*, 3 vols (London: Charles Dilly, 1779), 2:190.
25. Knox, *Essays Moral and Literary*, 2:187.
26. Knox, *Essays Moral and Literary*, 2:190.
27. Patricia Meyer Spacks, *Novel Beginnings: Experiments in Eighteenth-Century English Fiction* (New Haven and London: Yale University Press, 2006), 4, 2.
28. Ian Jackson, 'Historiographical Review: Approaches to the History of Readers and Reading in Eighteenth-Century Britain', *The Historical Journal* 47, no. 4 (2004): 1050.
29. Thomas Keymer, *Sterne, the Moderns, and the Novel* (Oxford: Oxford University Press, 2002), 58.
30. Christina Lupton, *Knowing Books: The Consciousness of Mediation in Eighteenth-Century Britain* (Philadelphia: University of Pennsylvania Press, 2012), 23.
31. Ian Watt, *The Rise of the Novel: Studies in Defoe, Richardson and Fielding* (Harmondsworth: Penguin, 1957, repr. 1972), 325.
32. John Preston, *The Created Self: The Reader's Role in Eighteenth-Century Fiction* (London: Heinemann, 1970), 116–19.
33. Henry Power, *Epic into Novel: Henry Fielding. Scriblerian Satire, and the Consumption of Classical Literature* (Oxford: Oxford University Press, 2015), 175.
34. Simon Dickie, 'Novels of the 1950s', in *The Oxford Handbook of the Eighteenth-Century Novel*, ed. J. A. Downie (Oxford: Oxford University Press, 2016), 252.
35. Christina Lupton, 'Giving Power to the Medium: Recovering the 1750s', *The Eighteenth Century* 52, nos. 3–4 (2011): 289.
36. Keymer, *Sterne, the Moderns, and the Novel*, 53.
37. Peter Sabor, '"Moral Romance" and the Novel at Mid-Century', in *The Oxford History of the Novel in English*, vol. 1, *Prose Fiction in English from the Origins of Print to 1750*, ed. Thomas Keymer (Oxford: Oxford University Press, 2017), 591.
38. Tim Parnell, 'Sterne's Fiction and the Mid-Century Novel. The "Vast Empire of Biographical Freebooters" and the "Crying Volume"', in *The Oxford Handbook of the Eighteenth-Century Novel*, ed. J. A. Downie (Oxford: Oxford University Press, 2016), 265.
39. Lupton, *Knowing Books*, 25.
40. Lupton, *Knowing Books*, 26.
41. Review of *The History of Charlotte Summers, The Fortunate Parish Girl, Monthly Review*, February 1750.

THE ART OF READING   361

42. Lady Mary Wortley Montagu, *The Letters and Works of Lady Mary Wortley Montagu*, 2 vols, ed. Lord Warncliffe (London: Henry G. Bohn, 1861), 2:218.
43. Tavor Bannet, *Eighteenth-Century Manners of Reading*, 94.
44. *The History of Charlotte Summers, The Fortunate Parish Girl*, 2 vols (London: Printed for the Author, n.d.), 1:3. Further references parenthetical.
45. Wayne C. Booth, 'The Self-Conscious Narrator in Comic Fiction Before *Tristram Shandy*', *PMLA* 67, no. 2 (1952): 181.
46. Keymer, *Sterne, the Moderns, and the Novel*, 58.
47. Sabor, '"Moral Romance" and the Novel at Mid-Century', 591.
48. Elspeth Jajdelska, *Silent Reading and the Birth of the Narrator* (Toronto: University of Toronto Press, 2007), 6.
49. Jajdelska, *Silent Reading and the Birth of the Narrator*, 6.
50. Jajdelska, *Silent Reading and the Birth of the Narrator*, 182.
51. Rita Felski, *Hooked: Art and Attachment* (Chicago and London: University of Chicago Press, 2020), 42.

21

THE EIGHTEENTH-CENTURY NOVEL AND THE SOCIABLE ARTS

Emrys D. Jones

Introduction: Defining the Sociable Arts

WHEN READING KATE RETFORD's landmark study of the eighteenth-century conversation piece, it is striking how closely the critical discourse on this distinctively sociable genre of visual art parallels scholarly debate about the 'rise' of the novel. In both cases, historians must reckon with the modernity and novelty of the cultural products under consideration. Like the novel, conversation pieces have often been explained as representing the new-found influence and affluence of a burgeoning middle class, who wished to celebrate their communal identities and to extol more general 'values of taste, hospitality and sociability' through group portraiture.[1] But also like the novel, the scope of the conversation piece's social gaze and ideological force far exceeds the bounds of a single class interest. The success of both forms resulted from their 'ability to serve a wide variety of groups and concerns'.[2] Their respective formulations of sociability were concomitantly multifaceted, at once promoting certain ideals of social conduct and allowing these ideals to be scrutinised, their artifice and their performativity exposed through each form's flexible relationship to verisimilitude.

The paintings considered in Retford's book do not behave exactly like novels, nor should we expect them to do so. As Jakub Lipski has recently outlined in his work on pictorial discourse and the eighteenth-century novel, the era itself was replete with arguments for the fundamental difference between visual and textual forms, even as many contemplated and capitalised upon the 'sister arts' theory of intermedial affinities.[3] Lipski quotes Sir Joshua Reynolds's most strident refutation of the idea that one art's particular mode of imitating or deviating from nature might 'bear transplantation to another soil'.[4] And indeed, the kinds of distance and 'stiffness' that Retford identifies as characteristic of the conversation piece's sociable scenes appear to prove this point.[5] The social lessons imparted when artists such as Arthur Devis or Charles Philips painted a gathering of family or friends must necessarily differ from those available in a written narrative, if only because the viewer has no way to access the substance of the conversation being depicted. Thus, Retford regards the paradoxical uneasiness of the conversation piece's sitters less as a by-product of widespread class anxiety than as an indication of the form's underlying method and signifying strategies:

> Conversation pieces such as the portrait of the Cromwell and Thornhill families are dumb shows, wordless scenes in which 'expressive' 'gestures' and 'actions' denote

THE SOCIABLE ARTS   363

communication and narrative. . . . They display, above all, the forms of conversation, abstracted from its words and subject matter, and with little, if any, attempt
to suggest actual exchange of spoken sentences. These portraits present schematic
displays of sociability, which separate out the poses and gestures intended to convey generic sentiments from the specifics of conversational exchange which those
poses and gestures were intended to frame.[6]

We are far removed here, it would seem, from the essential characteristics of the novel
form as Jane Austen would famously celebrate them in the fifth chapter of *Northanger
Abbey* (pub. 1817): the 'most thorough knowledge of human nature, the happiest
delineation of its varieties, the liveliest effusions of wit and humour' cannot be comfortably accommodated in a visual form so devoted to external gesture and social
formula.[7]

Nonetheless, it is worthwhile considering the eighteenth-century novel's conception
of the sociable arts alongside the formal workings of the conversation piece because the
two media share a fascination with how sociability informs art, and vice versa. In even
defining what the sociable arts encompass for the purposes of this essay, we should be
open to the term's productive ambivalence, as it can denote both the art of navigating
the social world and the cultural vessels – the paintings and texts themselves – which
foregrounded that art and were to a great extent propelled by it. The novel and the conversation piece were sociable artforms in the sense that they took sociable relations as
their chief subject matter, but also because they were designed to stimulate conversation,
to serve as tokens of sociable exchange. As Abigail Williams has written of specifically
domestic sociable contexts, '[t]he spectacle of the reading woman and the conversation
that her book furnished her with were typically ways in which visitors were to evaluate
a person and a home'.[8] The idea of reading as a spectacle and of the book as a social
tool brings the novel closer to Retford's view of the conversation piece than we might
first have anticipated. It also parallels work by Peter de Bolla and others that considers
portraits as 'prompts for conversation, and the process of their making . . . a textual
one'.[9] The novel's displays of sociability might not generally be as 'abstracted' as those
Retford finds in the conversation piece, but awareness of the form's own potential for
social credit, its fluctuating meaning and value within social settings, adds to the impression that it does more than simply document sociable custom. Its accounts of eighteenth-
century sociable life are necessarily self-reflexive in a similar sense to that adopted by
Lipski in his work: rather than settling on a particular version of sociability and advocating for it from an authoritative, neutral position, novels frequently interrogate their
own relationship to sociability, inviting comparison with other artforms, such as the
conversation piece, in the process.[10]

This chapter will proceed to examine the work of three eighteenth-century novelists with the intention not of pinpointing a consistent attitude to sociability within
the form, but of revealing the kinds of interrogatory, often ironic energy with which
authors engaged with sociable possibilities. Daniel Defoe, Charlotte Lennox and Frances Burney wrote at profoundly different moments, with different understandings of
the form they were in the process of constructing. But for each, notwithstanding prose
fiction's apparent promises of intimacy and of individualism, the novel emerges first
and foremost as a means to probe sociability's value, to anatomise the sociable arts
and expose literature's own complicated relationship to them.

Crusoe and the Sociable Arts

It is unfortunate, but perversely amusing, that the prototypical hero of the eighteenth-century novel, as he has been enshrined in critical and pedagogical tradition and admired by generations of readers, should be a man alone on a desert island. Robinson Crusoe was the perfect figurehead for Ian Watt's appraisal of the novel form as 'individualist and innovating', but he does not superficially convey, any more than the novel which introduces him does, the form's investment and interest in sociability.[11] Of the many problems and oversights that have been identified in Watt's arguments since his work's publication more than sixty years ago, his relative neglect of the novel form's sociable dimensions is hardly the most egregious.[12] In a charitable reading, his understanding of individualism must itself encompass a sociable spirit, in that the characters created by Defoe and by Watt's other chosen few were 'to be regarded as particular individuals in the contemporary social environment'.[13] However, it is still necessary to push back against the implication that isolation and solitary reflection were somehow inherent in the earliest examples of the form, or that an interest in these topics was incompatible with a wider attention to the sociable arts. Even as he describes himself as being *'divided from Mankind, a Solitaire, one banish'd from humane Society'*, Crusoe thinks about his predicament in relation to what he has lost.[14] His banishment only makes sense in the context of his earlier commercial ambitions, as a yearning for company.[15] Though at other parts of the novel and its two sequels he revises his attitude towards solitude, alternating between utopian views of its benefits and a deep aversion to its constraints, he is at all times shaped as a sociable being.[16]

I have written elsewhere about the loneliness of Defoe's *Journal of the Plague Year* (1722) and the deep ambivalence with which that book's hero, H. F., confronts the risks and potential blessings of sociable life.[17] We might think about Crusoe in similar terms, adopting Jason Pearl's view that he is punished for the sin of 'unguarded sociability, an incautious openness to the potentially corrupting influence of others'.[18] If this is indeed the case, then it makes not for an antisocial novel per se, but one which attempts to scrutinise the sociable arts from a distance, to judge appropriate degrees of guardedness and formality, letting society reclaim Crusoe and his island only gradually, in safe measures. And seen in such a light, the novel can be read much as Retford reads the conversation piece, with an awareness of how frequently it defers the actual act of conversation, its privileging of forms, poses and actions over and above the ostensible substance of sociable relationships.

When Crusoe first uses the word 'sociable' during the account of his island years, it is in order to insist that he requires no sociability at all. Resignation to God's will made his life 'better than sociable', he assures us, and

> when I began to regret the want of Conversation, I would ask my self whether thus conversing mutually with my own Thoughts, and, as I hope I may say, with even God himself by Ejaculations, was not better than the utmost Enjoyment of humane Society in the World. (160)

For all the apparent submissiveness of this passage, it is perhaps significant that it is phrased as a question, one posed by Crusoe to himself in the moment of his deepest isolation, and not directly answered by the text or by the unfolding of his fortunes.

THE SOCIABLE ARTS 365

After all, he can only 'hope' that his cries to God constituted a conversation of sorts. If we as readers sense that the issue of his sociable needs has not been fully addressed or resolved by the end of the sentence, then that feeling will likely be exacerbated by his next invocation of sociability a few pages later, upon the return of the parrot he had taught to speak at an earlier stage in the text. Thanks to Crusoe's efforts, Poll has become 'a sociable Creature', waking up his erstwhile tutor with cries of '*Robin, Robin, Robin Crusoe*' (168–9). Eric Jager has written of this episode that Crusoe's initial alarm at hearing his name spoken results from an othering of the character's voice, a threat to the selfhood that he is so painstakingly constructing in the text and on the island.[19] But the description of the parrot as sociable, particularly so soon after Crusoe's attempted repudiation of 'humane Society' and its enjoyments, also serves to ironise the notion of sociability itself. On the one hand, Poll fulfils the need that Crusoe tried to insist he did not have – a need for companionship and conversation, albeit stilted. On the other hand, like the participants in a conversation piece, the parrot offers the pure forms and gestures of sociability abstracted from the reality of social interaction or the possibility of ulterior motives. Thus, when Crusoe describes him as 'honest Poll' the phrase is effectively meaningless, removed as it is from the anxieties attendant on human sociability.

Crusoe has taught his parrot at least some of the sociable arts, and in doing so has exposed the limitations of those arts as they can be represented or relayed through language. When, shortly after Poll's reintroduction, Crusoe portrays the usual scene at his island dinner table, we again find sociable rules and gestures oddly aestheticised, drained of emotional or moral value even as they assume supposed political value. Again, the parrot plays a crucial role in the process:

> It would have made a Stoick smile to have seen, me and my little Family sit down to Dinner; there was my Majesty the Prince and Lord of the whole Island; I had the Lives of all my Subjects at my absolute Command. I could hang, draw, give Liberty, and take it away, and no Rebels among all my Subjects.
>
> Then to see how like a King I din'd too all alone, attended by my Servants, *Poll*, as if he had been my Favourite, was the only Person permitted to talk to me. (175)

Crusoe's metaphors of kingship, command and rebellion are so eye-catching that it is easy to miss the more commonplace, pseudo-sociable aspects of this tableau. Lipski has rightly noted how the passage anticipates the heyday of the conversation piece, and he views it as 'a climactic point in Robinson's compensatory practices'.[20] It is worth examining in more depth exactly how such a pictorial connection is established. Before Crusoe launches into his ever more boastful claims to absolute power, he begins with himself and his 'little Family', a claim which, while already metaphorical, seems positively modest beside the monarchical aspirations that rise in its wake. Moreover, though Crusoe does not explicitly construct the scene as a painting, one wonders if some of his violent and dictatorial language might yield other meanings, subtly summoning thoughts of an artistic work's production and consumption. His entourage might be 'Subjects' posing for a painter. His own power to 'hang' and to 'draw' the members of his court might put him in the shoes not just of a bloodthirsty tyrant but also of an artist, or the commissioner of an artist, who captures a group likeness for hanging on his wall. The parrot's privilege in this scene is to carry out the act of

366 EMRYS D. JONES

conversation single-handedly, but if his status as 'Favourite' did not already signal the likely hollowness of his contributions, our previous familiarity with the limitations of Poll's repartee must surely do so.[21] We are shown a conversation piece in which no conversation is really taking place, where the central figure is in fact 'all alone' despite being surrounded by his household. It testifies to a fascination with sociable form, its performativity and fragility. It takes Crusoe's very particular experience of aloneness, and through it confronts the distance and discomfort that were integral even to far more conventional depictions of sociability.

The novel is sociable precisely because it recognises what is formulaic and wilfully inauthentic in the sociable arts. Nowhere is this more apparent than in Crusoe's eventual interactions with other humans on the island. When he rescues his soon-to-be servant Friday, the earliest part of their relationship is of course dominated by the making and reading of physical gestures, substitutes for spoken conversation which threaten to make spoken conversation redundant. We are given little detailed explanation of what these gestures involve. Crusoe makes 'Signs' for Friday to step forward, 'which he easily understood', and he in turn seems to understand – or at least assumes he understands – Friday's ensuing genuflections as a 'token of acknowledgment for . . . saving his Life' (241).[22] Signs proliferate over the following few pages. Friday laughs as a 'Sign of Triumph', but accompanies this laughter 'with abundance of Gestures which I did not understand' (242). Indeed, there is much arbitrariness concerning which signs can be deciphered and which defy interpretation, Crusoe's ability to fathom Friday's meaning being partly dependent on his existing frame of reference, but also prone to convenient lapses. Their near confrontation over Friday's persistent cannibal appetites epitomises the improvisational, scarcely dependable nature of their communications:

> I found *Friday* had still a hankering Stomach after some of the Flesh, and was still a Cannibal in his Nature; but I discover'd so much Abhorrence at the very Thoughts of it, and at the least Appearance of it, that he durst not discover it; for I had by some Means let him know, that I would kill him if he offer'd it. (246)

This passage is overflowing with different, though practically indistinguishable, forms of 'discovery'.[23] The process by which Friday has made his 'hankering Stomach' known to Crusoe is presumably different from that 'least Appearance of it' which would be summarily and lethally punished. In Crusoe's vague, almost nonchalant reference to his 'Means' of instruction, we likewise see just how haphazard his signage really is.

Observing similar kinds of awkwardness in such descriptions, Jason Farr has commented that the use of gesture 'undermines the assumed sovereignty of the would-be ruler, Crusoe, even as it helps him to consolidate authority'.[24] One might reach similar conclusions about its relationship to the sociable arts, in the sense that the exchange of signs both is and is not sociable, muddling Crusoe's own sociable credentials at the very moment he tries to assert them. He often seems more comfortable with his oddly indeterminate signs than with speech itself. His default conversational mode is one of fact-finding and attending to practicalities, followed by indefinite delay – a trajectory neatly encapsulated in his later rescue of a Spaniard on the beach:

> I lifted him up, and ask'd him in the *Portuguese* Tongue, What he was? He answer'd in Latin, *Christianus*; but was so weak, and faint, that he could scarce stand, or

THE SOCIABLE ARTS 367

speak; I took my Bottle out of my Pocket, and gave it him, making Signs that he should drink, which he did; and I gave him a Piece of Bread, which he eat; then I ask'd him, What Countryman he was? And he said, *Espagniole*; and being a little recover'd, let me know by all the Signs he could possibly make, how much he was in my Debt for his Deliverance; *Seignior*, said I, with as much *Spanish* as I could make up, we will talk afterwards; but we must fight now[.] (278–9)

Admittedly, there are pressing practical and narrative reasons for the curtailment of this rather faltering, multilingual conversation, but one cannot escape the sense that, after gleaning the required information and acquiring a new ally, Crusoe is glad of the opportunity to postpone further dialogue. He may pride himself on his dominion over the island and its inhabitants, but his use of signs rarely brings him closer to them either emotionally or morally. When he reflects during his early observations of Friday that non-Europeans may in fact be 'more ready to apply' God's social gifts – 'the same Affections, the same Sentiments of Kindness and Obligation' that have been bestowed on his countrymen (248) – it only heightens the impression that he is distanced from the actual practice of sociability, that he may seek to identify or instil the sociable arts in others, but cannot fully embody them himself. In all of this, even though we return to the figure of the isolated and lonely Crusoe, we see his loneliness as in some sense a corollary of the early novel's sociable interests. Conversation is deferred and gestures dominate, as in painted conversation pieces, precisely because the application of the sociable arts is a separate matter from the personal experience of sociability itself.

Quixotism and Sociability

What we are dealing with in Crusoe's social awkwardness may be a variation of what Immanuel Kant would eventually describe as 'unsociable sociability', an attempt to navigate the intrinsic resistance and competition that he understands as informing human social behaviour.[25] As J. B. Schneewind puts it, unsociable sociability's main function for Kant was 'as a permanent spur to personal and social improvement', but this optimistic perspective is not borne out straightforwardly in Defoe's novel, nor perhaps in most British novels of the eighteenth century.[26] Crusoe does not teach or advocate for the sociable arts in a way that clearly demonstrates their value, nor is either he or the reader necessarily improved by observing their artifice. In fact, enjoyment of the novel might stem from the spectacle of the sociable arts being mishandled, of unsociable sociability that does not inherently tend towards a refinement of morality but instead emphasises the novel form's affinity with social disjuncture and miscommunication. In Charlotte Lennox's *The Female Quixote* (1752), that affinity becomes the basis not only for the reader's amusement and the heroine's resistance to personal improvement, but for sustained consideration of how the sociably situated novel must differ from earlier types of prose fiction.

Lennox's heroine, Arabella, has a strong command of certain sociable arts and is entirely oblivious to others. With a social understanding that has been overwhelmingly moulded by the conventions of seventeenth-century French romance, she cannot fully master the sociable modes of the more realist novel she unwittingly inhabits. However, she is surprisingly well equipped, in her naivety, to expose the falseness of sociability as it is practised by those around her, and to model, at least until her eventual re-education, a more ingenuous and morally consistent kind of sociable art. David Marshall has argued that Arabella's misreading of the world arises from her existence within 'a realm of likenesses, copies, patterns, simulacra, playacting, and representations', and that she thus demonstrates 'the dangers of viewing the world as if it were art'.[27] But Arabella is, at the same time, much less artful in her sociable interactions than most of the characters who surround her. Possibly because she does not recognise the distinction between reality and art that others would insist upon, she often approaches sociability as if it were a natural, instinctive occupation. She has Crusoe's sense of isolation but little of his wariness. If, as her cousin and future husband believes, her 'absurd and ridiculous Notions' are owing to 'the Solitude' of her upbringing, then that solitude is also a platform from which the novel can interrogate the sociable world's own absurdities.[28]

Arabella's detachment from the more contrived and calculated sociable arts is on full display during an early excursion to the races. Accompanied by her aforementioned cousin, Charles Glanville, and his sister Charlotte, Arabella panics the former and riles the latter by speculating about the concealed identities of the jockeys, whom she imagines must be 'Persons of great Distinction' (1:125). As so often in the novel, the envious Charlotte responds with insult and sarcasm, but these forms of sociable manoeuvre are completely lost on Arabella, who is 'so wholly taken up with the Event of the Races' that she gives 'but very little Heed' to her cousin's remarks (1:126). It instead falls upon Charles to condemn Charlotte for 'the Liberty she took' (1:127). The individual who is theoretically more socially aware, with a far greater command of diverse sociable arts, is hereby set at a social disadvantage, though this scarcely seems to discourage Charlotte in her ensuing interactions, for she again reaches for a strategy of facetious rudeness when an old friend of her brother's, Sir George, then arrives on the scene:

> ... Miss *Glanville* was quite overjoyed, hoping she would now have her Turn of Gallantry and Compliment: Therefore, accosting him in her free Manner, Dear Sir *George*, said she, you come in a lucky Time to brighten up the Conversation: Relations are such dull Company for one another, 'tis half a Minute since we have exchanged a Word. (1:127)

It is Charlotte's own sense of proper sociable conduct, and her frustration that Arabella should receive praise while flouting convention, that paradoxically leads her to abuse the sociable arts far more gravely than Arabella ever would. Charlotte is like a sitter for a family portrait who breaks the unspoken rules of the conversation piece by drawing attention to the dullness of the company she keeps. In adopting a 'free Manner', albeit one leavened with wit and bathos, she risks undermining the very basis of sociable exchange. This allows Arabella to become an unexpected spokeswoman for sociable propriety and the value of patience in social settings, as she remarks that Charlotte has 'so strange a Disposition for Mirth, that she thinks all her Moments are lost, in which she finds nothing to laugh at' (1:127). Such a judgement speaks to Arabella's faulty education, of course, in that her ideals of female propriety are dictated by the lofty demeanour of fictional princesses, but she is also, ironically, closer to a successful navigation of the sociable world in this moment thanks to her ignorance of the artistry it too often demands. That it should be Charlotte's disposition rather

THE SOCIABLE ARTS

than Arabella's that is singled out for its strangeness only highlights what is volatile and potentially alienating in sociability.

If it were not already clear from this episode, the point is made explicitly later in the novel that Arabella is opposed to conversation built on raillery:

I am of Opinion, Sir, said *Arabella*, that there are very few proper Objects for Raillery; and still fewer, who can railly well: The talent of Raillery ought to be born with a Person; no Art can infuse it; and those who endeavour to railly in spite of Nature, will be so far from diverting others, that they will become the Objects of Ridicule themselves.

Many other pleasing Qualities of Wit may be acquired by Pains and Study, but Raillery must be the Gift of Nature[.] (2:144)

It is understandable that Arabella should object to this sociable mode in which Charlotte excels, since its insincerity is at odds with everything she prizes most in her fictional exempla. Her hostility towards it is also rooted in her more general suspicion of artfulness, the sense that, notwithstanding her inability to discern truth from artistic likeness, she nonetheless puts the utmost premium on what is natural and effortless in human behaviour. In this, she contradicts the arguments of the third Earl of Shaftesbury, who had advocated for 'ridicule itself' as a means by which to arrive at truth.[29] She also overlooks what is unnatural and arguably ridiculous in her own approach to sociability. Indeed, it is highly ironic that, at the very moment she decries the role of art in sociable exchange, she is in fact closely paraphrasing a conversation from one of her beloved prose romances, a discourse on raillery from the ninth volume of Madeleine de Scudéry's *Artamène* (1649–53). One section of that dialogue that she tellingly does not quote contrasts the imperfectly imitative qualities of conversation with the proliferation of interchangeable copies that is supposedly possible in visual art:

It is not with Rallarie as with pictures, which sometimes are copied so like the original, that one cannot know the copie from its original; but in matter of Rallarie, there is no imitating another, and therefore let him never attempt it.[30]

Had Arabella recalled and dwelt a little longer on this contrast, she might have considered the ways that her own conversation is artful despite itself: even as she imitates Scudéry's Euridamia, she inevitably shows some degree of sociable independence and particularity, whether through her omissions or through the absurdity of her imitations themselves. She will eventually be cured in the novel's penultimate chapter through the intervention of a learned 'Divine' who asserts that 'the Likeness of a Picture can only be determined by a Knowledge of the Original' (2:318). This statement itself seems to adapt and qualify the line from de Scudéry that Arabella had neglected in her earlier discourse. Marshall sees it as emphasising the allure of 'empty fiction' and the danger that Arabella becomes an 'empty fiction' herself,[31] but it also, from the perspective of sociability, highlights the futility of searching for originals at all. Imitation offers no secure foundation for sociable interaction because it always entails eccentricity and clumsy reproduction. On one hand, quixotism liberates Arabella from sociable artifice. At the same time, it accentuates her literary and social difference.

370 EMRYS D. JONES

Arabella sees the danger of making oneself ridiculous through misjudged raillery, but she does not and cannot account for the other forms of ridicule to which she is vulnerable simply by virtue of her entry into the sociable world. At various points in the novel, she is reliant on the patience and generosity of others in forgiving her faults. Especially noteworthy insofar as it reflects on this character's ambivalent relationship to the sociable arts is the intercession on Arabella's behalf of an unnamed Countess during her stay at Bath in the later stages of the novel. Encouraged both by Charlotte's malicious gossip-mongering and by widespread jealousy of Arabella's 'uncommon Beauty', the 'fair Defamers' of the town vie with each other in their 'contemptuous Jests' (2:229). Arabella's embarrassment has become social capital for others to trade upon, until, that is, the Countess declares herself 'in her Favour':

> A Person of the Countess's nice Discernment could not fail of observing the Wit and Spirit, which tho' obscur'd, was not absolutely hid under the Absurdity of her Notions. And this Discovery adding Esteem to the Compassion she felt for the fair Visionary, she resolv'd to rescue her from the ill-natur'd Raillery of her Sex; praising therefore her Understanding, and the Beauty of her Person with a Sweetness and Generosity peculiar to herself, she accounted in the most delicate Manner imaginable for the Singularity of her Notions, from her Studies, her Retirment [sic], her Ignorance of the World, and her lively Imagination. (2:230)

Just as methods of sociable discovery had been crucial, albeit vaguely delineated, in Crusoe and Friday's early relationship, here Arabella has the Countess's 'Discovery', and her 'nice Discernment', to thank for her reputational rescue. What exactly is being discovered, and how? It is, after all, Arabella's underlying sociable virtues that win the Countess to her cause, the 'Wit and Spirit' that emerge despite her absurdity, and that are in some sense mirrored by the 'Sweetness and Generosity' of the Countess herself. The 'Singularity' of Arabella's notions can likewise be balanced out only by the avowed peculiarity of the Countess's kindness. She has the sociable authority and consistent command of the sociable arts that Arabella lacks; she uses her 'most delicate Manner' to salvage the quixote's dignity. The Countess thus serves as a reminder not only that Arabella possesses sociable talents which may not be obvious to the untrained eye, but also that the application of art is essential in combating social prejudice and cruelty, that natural, ingenuous behaviour is rarely protection enough. As the novel oscillates between condemnation of overly cynical sociability and its own mockery of Arabella's innocence, it is through figures like the Countess that it offers hope for a more stable and fruitful configuration of sociable artistry.

Agreeable Sociability in *Evelina*

The title character of Frances Burney's *Evelina* (1778) may not cultivate her understanding of the sociable arts from quite the distance that Crusoe experiences by way of shipwreck or that Arabella does through her chronic misreading. This work, described by Jon Mee as offering 'something of a conspectus of the conversable worlds of the early 1770s', is ostensibly more grounded, less outlandish in its portrayal of sociability than some earlier iterations of the realist novel.[32] However, the sociable arts as they are conceived and represented in *Evelina* retain a sense of contradiction, a resistance

THE SOCIABLE ARTS   371

to full understanding or ownership, that ensures it has more in common with Defoe's
and Lennox's works than may first be obvious. This arises in part from Evelina's own
awkward situation. In the uncertain legitimacy of her parents' marriage and the insecurity of her claims to aristocratic heritage, she endures what Betty Rizzo regards as a
kind of 'social suspension': she is, 'like Burney, uncomfortably poised in a world that
can sense [her] fineness but cannot identify [her] entitlement to it'.[33] Beyond Evelina's
personal circumstances, though, the novel frequently implies that certain types of discomfort and abstraction are intrinsic to the sociable arts, that they will always demand
a separation of performance from intent, regardless of who is enacting or observing
them. As Mee has observed, Burney paves the way for Jane Austen in at once valoris-
ing and critiquing the 'flow of talk' that upholds polite society.[34] We can understand
conversation in this context as something of a test, what Katie Halsey and Jane Slinn
describe as 'a struggle with oneself and one's conversational partner to discover truths
about both self and other'.[35] But Burney also capitalises on the novel form's particular
and long-standing capacity to see sociability from inside and outside simultaneously,
to view the conversation piece while also commenting on its contrivances.

When she first meets her future husband, Lord Orville, and is asked to dance by
him, Evelina is incapable of 'entering into conversation', 'seized with such a panic,
that I could hardly speak a word'.[36] This moment, reminiscent in its way of Crusoe's
struggles to converse, sets the tone for many of the novel's subsequent evocations of
sociability, descriptions in which Evelina may tell us about the practice of the sociable
arts but rarely seems to recreate or fully inhabit any given sociable encounter. Shortly
after her initial panic attack, Lord Orville manages to calm her nerves and to impress
her with his sociable virtues, but as in a conversation piece, these are rendered through
and as external gesture, with very little sense of what is actually being spoken: 'His
conversation was sensible and spirited; his air and address were open and noble; his
manners gentle, attentive, and infinitely engaging; his person is all elegance, and his
countenance, the most animated and expressive I have ever seen' (1:36–7).

It is tempting to say that Evelina is distracted by exteriors, that she is so engaged
by Orville's conversation and by his powers of attentiveness that she does not herself attend to the substance of what he says, at least not sufficiently to relay it to the
novel's readers or the recipient of her letter, the Reverend Villars. But a reading that
dismisses her praise for Orville as merely superficial, the product of awestruck excitement, overlooks the considerable challenge of doing justice to sociable arts which
must by necessity combine performance with an appearance of effortlessness. Mee has
written of the above passage that Burney 'struggled to convey [the] idea of easiness in
Orville's dialogue', and this is certainly true, but we should not on that basis disregard
the conversation as seen at one remove.[37] Gesture, manner and countenance cannot
be subordinated to speech. Exteriors, if they are exteriors, cannot be neglected, but
must be read and might be misread, such are the demands of the sociable world. When
Orville's conversation is again singled out for commendation later in the novel's first
volume, it is again from a distance, with an emphasis on instinctual courtesy that at
once underscores and effaces the sociable artist's actual labour:

> The conversation of Lord Orville is really delightful. His manners are so elegant,
> so gentle, so unassuming, that they at once engage esteem, and diffuse compla-
> cence. Far from being indolently satisfied with his own accomplishments, as I have

372 EMRYS D. JONES

already observed many men here are, though without any pretensions to his merit, he is most assiduously attentive to please and to serve all who are in his company; and, though his success is invariable, he never manifests the smallest degree of consciousness. (1:119)

The entire passage is a rather precarious balancing act, no less for the ever-observant Evelina than for Orville himself. Her disclaimers – about his lack of pretension and 'consciousness'; about the possibility of serving one's company without demeaning or too obviously exerting oneself in the process – suggest the oxymoronic qualities of the sociable arts, which may indeed prove nigh impossible to convey in recorded conversation.

Orville's name, as well as playing on ideas of urbanity ('ville') that run throughout Burney's novel,[38] might also carry a slight mythological echo. It links him to Orpheus, the ancient Greek bard who, by virtue of his exceptional musical skill, is able to charm his way into the underworld in hopes of rescuing his bride, Eurydice, from death. It seems no coincidence that precisely this story should be the subject of a firework display which Evelina watches at Marybone (i.e., Marylebone) pleasure gardens in the novel's second volume, shortly before she herself is plunged briefly into London's underworld and accidentally fraternises with a pair of likely prostitutes. Evelina's story will end more happily than Eurydice's, in part because Lord Orville – much unlike Orpheus – fails in 'distinguishing' her while he walks past (2:197). But the alignment of his character with the most celebrated poet of Greek myth, however ironic its implications, can add to our understanding of Orville as artist. Orpheus is the classical epitome of song's persuasive and almost sociable powers: not only does he win over the rulers of the underworld thanks to his art, but after losing Eurydice for a second time, he uses his song to gather a circle of trees, animals and birds around him as an audience.[39] Orpheus's chief failing is his inability to restrain curiosity and emotion, to hide what motivates his art in the first place. He cannot help but look back at his love Eurydice as they ascend to the living world, and being seen condemns her to a second death. Orville, as a consummate performer of the sociable arts, will not fall into the same trap thanks to exactly that lack of consciousness which Evelina values in him. He practises his art without seeming to commit himself to it. When, on a rare occasion, he too clumsily distinguishes himself from those around him, he chastises himself for it. In the third volume, having shamed Mr Coverley and Lord Merton for their trifling activities, he asks Evelina who most deserves rebuke, 'those who adapt the conversation to the company, or, those who affect to be superior to it' (3:42). It is pretty clear that he regards the latter as the more serious social transgression, even when conversational intervention is morally justified. '[S]o unseasonable a gravity' has no place in Orville's usual sociable repertoire, and he holds himself to blame for allowing it to surface (3:43).

Burney's novel cannot behave with any consistency as Orville aspires to behave. Though certain passages abstract the sociable arts in the manner of a conversation piece, Evelina is also drawn to reflect on her own exclusion and on the manifold ways that her friends and acquaintances fail to respect the signs and gestures that ought to underpin their sociable interactions. The xenophobic Captain Mirvan violates sociable decency repeatedly, but in recounting his transgressions, inviting judgement and covertly encouraging amusement from her readers, Evelina perhaps conducts herself in an even more suspect fashion. She is unable to emulate Lord Orville's detachment

THE SOCIABLE ARTS

373

when brushing past conversational awkwardness and instead fixates on all that she should be saying, the apologies that have no place in these tableaux:

> As the husband of Mrs Mirvan had borne so large a share in this disagreeable altercation, Lord Orville forbore to make any comments upon it; so that the subject was immediately dropt, and the conversation became calmly sociable, and politely chearful, and, to every body but me, must have been highly agreeable:—but, as to myself, I was so eagerly desirous of making some apology to Lord Orville . . . that I hardly ventured to say a word all the time we were walking. (1:97–8)

Much as in *The Female Quixote*, what is agreeable for the reader of the novel is for the most part very different from what is held agreeable in the sociable scene itself. It is in the nature of novelistic narrative and characterisation that we remain aware, along with our guide Evelina, of what the sociable arts cannot easily acknowledge: absurdity, insecurity, the impossibility of true speech. This awareness may itself provide the basis for sociable solidarity and communal identities, a phenomenon that Alexis Tadié has identified as an intrinsic element in the disrupted and eccentric conversations of Laurence Sterne's fiction.[40] It may also be possible even within the tradition of the painted conversation piece. Retford recognises in William Hogarth's *The Hervey Conversation Piece* (1738–40) a strain of 'aristocratic waggishness' that makes the viewer complicit in its practical jokes and operates in a similar satirical vein to moments in Henry Fielding's fiction.[41] However, in going beyond the anticipation of sociable malfunction to consider the anxiety and embarrassment of its aftermath, the novel's dual investment in the appeal and inadequacy of the sociable arts is more pronounced.

Conclusions

While it is dangerous to extrapolate general truths about the novel form from three such different texts, this chapter has aimed to convey at least some of the ironic and self-reflexive power integral to the relationship between eighteenth-century fiction and the era's sociable custom. I have shown the kinds of distancing prompted by fiction's consideration of the sociable arts, and the way that this distancing parallels that found in painted conversation pieces. But I have also demonstrated how the novel allowed for more extensive and subversive interrogations: interrogations of what really constituted sociable virtue, of how it could fluctuate between the artificial and ingenuous, and of how it so often came into focus, paradoxically, through evocations of solitude or alienation. Crusoe, Arabella and Evelina may inhabit thoroughly different sociable worlds and fare quite differently in their navigation of them. Yet in their struggle to read and make the appropriate signs, to fill the right silences and leave others unremarked, they each embody both a debt to sociable art and a disquiet at its influence.

Notes

1. Kate Retford, *The Conversation Piece: Making Modern Art in Eighteenth-Century Britain* (New Haven: Yale University Press, 2017), 9; Retford summarises here arguments from David Solkin, *Painting for Money: The Visual Arts and the Public Sphere in Eighteenth-Century England* (New Haven: Yale University Press, 1993).

2. Retford, *The Conversation Piece*, 11.
3. Jakub Lipski, *Painting the Novel: Pictorial Discourse in Eighteenth-Century English Fiction* (New York and London: Routledge, 2018), 3–9.
4. [Sir Joshua Reynolds], *A Discourse, Delivered to the Students of the Royal Academy . . .*, *December 11, 1786* (London: Thomas Cadell, 1786, repr. 1787), 22; later edition quoted in Lipski, *Painting the Novel*, 8.
5. Retford, *The Conversation Piece*, 9; Retford builds here on observations made by earlier theorists of the genre, including Mario Praz, *Conversation Pieces: A Survey of the Informal Group Portrait in Europe and America* (London: Methuen, 1971), 128.
6. Retford, *The Conversation Piece*, 67.
7. Jane Austen, *Northanger Abbey*, ed. James Kinsley and John Davie (1817; Oxford: Oxford University Press, 2003), 24.
8. Abigail Williams, *The Social Life of Books: Reading Together in the Eighteenth-Century Home* (New Haven and London: Yale University Press, 2017), 49.
9. Peter de Bolla, 'Portraiture as Conversation', in *The Concept and Practice of Conversation in the Long Eighteenth Century, 1688–1848*, ed. Katie Halsey and Jane Slinn (Newcastle upon Tyne: Cambridge Scholars Publishing, 2008), 175; see also, in the same volume, Ludmilla Jordanova, 'Picture-Talking: Portraiture and Conversation in Britain, 1800–1830', 151–69.
10. On the self-reflexivity of the eighteenth-century novel, itself conducive to 'the inter-artistic analogy', see Lipski, *Painting the Novel*, 13.
11. Ian Watt, *The Rise of the Novel: Studies in Defoe, Richardson and Fielding* (London: Chatto & Windus, 1957), 13.
12. For a snapshot of the various critiques that Watt's work has received over the decades, see Lennard J. Davis, 'Who Put the *The* in *the Novel*? Identity Politics and Disability in Novel Studies', *NOVEL: A Forum on Fiction* 3, no. 3 (1998): 317–18; this article also provides the starting point for Nicholas Seager, *The Rise of the Novel: A Reader's Guide to Essential Criticism* (Basingstoke: Palgrave Macmillan, 2012), 1.
13. Watt, *The Rise of the Novel*, 19.
14. [Daniel Defoe], *The Life and Strange Surprizing Adventures of Robinson Crusoe* (London: Printed for W. Taylor, 1719), 76. Further references parenthetical. Lipski has observed in his own recent work on Crusoe's sociability that the banishment described in this quotation is the only disadvantage of shipwreck not effectively counterbalanced by 'a corresponding advantage' when the hero takes stock of his situation. See Jakub Lipski, '*Robinson Crusoe*: Speech, Conversation, Sociability', in *British Sociability in the European Enlightenment: Cultural Practices and Personal Encounters*, ed. Sebastian Domsch and Mascha Hansen (Cham: Palgrave Macmillan, 2021), 189–90.
15. On Crusoe's longing 'for someone to relieve his solitude', see Maximillian Novak, '"The Sum of Humane Misery"?: Defoe's Ambiguity toward Exile', *Studies in English Literature, 1500–1900* 50, no. 3 (2010): 610.
16. On Crusoe's capacity to view the island, in hindsight, as 'both a prison and a sanctuary', see Jason H. Pearl, 'Desert Islands and Urban Solitudes in the "Crusoe" Trilogy', *Studies in the Novel* 44, no. 2 (2012): 137.
17. Emrys D. Jones, *Friendship and Allegiance in Eighteenth-Century Literature: The Politics of Private Virtue in the Age of Walpole* (Basingstoke: Palgrave Macmillan, 2013), 50.
18. Pearl, 'Desert Islands and Urban Solitudes', 128.
19. Eric Jager, 'The Parrot's Voice: Language and the Self in Robinson Crusoe', *Eighteenth-Century Studies* 21, no. 2 (1988): 326–7.
20. Lipski, '*Robinson Crusoe*: Speech, Conversation, Sociability', 192.
21. On the long-standing association of court favourites with political corruption, see J. H. Elliott and L. W. B. Brockliss, eds, *The World of the Favourite* (New Haven: Yale University Press, 1999).

THE SOCIABLE ARTS 375

22. On ambiguity and potential misunderstanding in Crusoe's exchanging of signs with Friday, see Jason S. Farr, 'Colonizing Gestures: Crusoe, the Signing Sovereign', *Eighteenth-Century Fiction* 29, no. 4 (2017): 556.

23. The *OED*'s definition 5.b. for 'discover' seems most relevant here: 'To reveal or manifest (an attribute, quality, circumstance, etc.), unconsciously or unintentionally, esp. by one's actions or behaviour; to allow to be seen or observed; to evince.'

24. Farr, 'Colonizing Gestures', 541.

25. Immanuel Kant, 'Idea for a Universal History with a Metropolitan Aim' (first published in *Berlinische Monatsschrift* iv, 11 November 1784), as translated in Kant, *Anthropology, History, and Education*, ed. Günter Zöller and Robert B. Louden (Cambridge: Cambridge University Press, 2007), 107–20; I have discussed the concept further in Emrys D. Jones, 'Friendship and Unsociable Sociability in Eighteenth-Century Literature', in *British Sociability in the Long Eighteenth Century: Challenging the Anglo-French Connection*, ed. Alain Kerhervé and Valérie Capdeville (Woodbridge: Boydell Press, 2019), 199–218.

26. J. B. Schneewind, *Essays on the History of Moral Philosophy* (Oxford: Oxford University Press, 2009), 331.

27. David Marshall, *The Frame of Art: Fictions of Aesthetic Experience, 1750–1815* (Baltimore: Johns Hopkins University Press, 2005), 148.

28. [Charlotte Lennox], *The Female Quixote; or, the Adventures of Arabella*, 2 vols (London: A. Millar, 1752), 2:122. Further references parenthetical.

29. Anthony Ashley Cooper, third Earl of Shaftesbury, 'Sensus Communis, An Essay on the Freedom of Wit and Humour', in *Characteristics of Men, Manners, Opinions, Times*, ed. Lawrence E. Klein (1711; Cambridge: Cambridge University Press, 1999), 30.

30. As translated in F. G. Gent., *Artamenes, or The Grand Cyrus*, 10 vols (London: Humphrey Moseley, 1653), 9:142 [misnumbered as 152].

31. Marshall, *The Frame of Art*, 166.

32. Jon Mee, *Conversable Worlds: Literature, Contention, and Community, 1762 to 1830* (Oxford: Oxford University Press, 2011), 102.

33. Betty Rizzo, 'Burney and Society', in *The Cambridge Companion to Frances Burney*, ed. Peter Sabor (Cambridge: Cambridge University Press, 2007), 146.

34. Mee, *Conversable Worlds*, 211.

35. Katie Halsey and Jane Slinn, 'Introduction', *Concept and Practice of Conversation*, ed. Halsey and Slinn, xvii.

36. [Frances Burney], *Evelina, or, A Young Lady's Entrance into the World*, 2nd edn, 3 vols (1778; London: T. Lowndes, 1779), 1:36. Further references parenthetical.

37. Mee, *Conversable Worlds*, 120.

38. See Samuel Choi, 'Signing Evelina: Female Self-Inscription in the Discourse of Letters', *Studies in the Novel* 31, no. 3 (1999): 266.

39. As recounted in Book X of Ovid's *Metamorphoses*; see Rolfe Humphries, trans., *Ovid: Metamorphoses* (1955; Bloomington: Indiana University Press, 2018), 234–8.

40. Alexis Tadié, *Sterne's Whimsical Theatres of Language: Orality, Gesture, Literacy* (Aldershot: Ashgate, 2003), 46.

41. Retford, *The Conversation Piece*, 304.

22

NOVELS, PAINTINGS AND THE HALF-TRAINED EYE IN MID-EIGHTEENTH-CENTURY READING CULTURE

Paul Goring

IN 1722 THE painter and art theorist Jonathan Richardson published his *An Account of Some of the Statues, Bas-reliefs, Drawings and Pictures in Italy &c. with Remarks*. Richardson was, by that time, a highly respected portraitist and, with his earlier *Essay on the Theory of Painting* (1715) and other published discourses, he was on his way to becoming the leading British writer on the visual arts of the early eighteenth century.[1] His new work on the art of Europe came charged with the clout that he had already established for himself, but there was an aspect of its composition that put pressure on his authority: Richardson had never travelled to see the works he was writing about. He did recognise that this could be regarded as problematic. 'That I should write upon what I never Saw, may appear strange to some', he observed in the preface.[2] But he insisted that his project was validated by his excellent sources: his son, another Jonathan, had been on an extensive Grand Tour to Italy and had provided copious written observations, and these were supplemented by Richardson's wide reading in existing publications and through his study of prints and drawings, a large collection of which he had amassed himself. Fuelled by the vicarious experience that these materials gave him, he confidently offered his tour of Europe's artistic treasures to the British public, feeling qualified to describe and pass judgement with an extraordinary attention to detail. He finds Raphael's frescoes in the Vatican, for example, inferior to the cartoons by the artist at Hampton Court, for they 'are not so Gay, and Pleasing; which is Partly Owing to the Colouring' – colouring which he had never seen himself.[3]

This chapter addresses this issue of not having seen paintings in relation to literary pictorialism and the writing and reading of prose fiction in Britain during the middle decades of the eighteenth century, from around the time Jonathan Richardson was writing to around 1770. From the standpoint of the modern accessibility of art, including our easy saturation in colour photographic reproductions of paintings from around the world, it considers connections between fiction and painting in relation to the idea that access to painting, although it was becoming more widespread, remained relatively limited and exclusive during much of the early phase of the novel's fabled 'rise'. Could a novelist in the 1720s allude or refer to, say, Raphael or his frescoes and expect the reference to be meaningful for most readers? What sort of opportunities for making such references arose in the subsequent decades? How dependent was the appreciation of literary pictorialism upon experience and knowledge of the visual arts? The period under scrutiny here is that which, concerning painting, largely preceded the broad 'education of the eye', as Peter de Bolla has termed the growth and social spread of visual aesthetic awareness and associated debates about what constituted the ability to see – or rather to see with propriety. Did appreciation of the visual depend upon learning and wide ocular experience – including exposure to a canon of original paintings – or rather upon an innate, untutored sensitivity to what lay before the eye? These were the 'two poles', de Bolla argues, 'in the debate over visual culture' – one which embraced not only painting but also landscape, architecture and other visual cultural forms, and which intensified in the latter half of the eighteenth century in part because of the growing public accessibility of painting.[4] Those questions were voiced in the earlier period, but the context for the debate was different, particularly before 1760, because most Britons enjoyed little exposure to paintings, not only to those works lodged in Europe, but also to those imported into Britain or produced there, and this, it will be suggested here, had consequences for the ways in which painting could be deployed as a point of reference in fiction. Such a view of the level of public awareness of painting is contestable: some historians and critics, as will be seen, prefer to see a more rapid democratisation of visual culture from early in the century – due, in part, to the circulation of engravings – which enabled knowledge and experience of painting to spread and become a type of public currency or field of reference. Here it will be suggested that a shared awareness of painting typically constituted only an experimental, cautiously deployed currency in the communication between early novelists with 'sister arts' interests and their manifold readers. The works of such novelists disclose a sense of a growing but yet-to-be embedded public awareness of painting and of the evolving canon of 'great' painters and paintings. At the same time, they often display an investment in sharing the pleasure of looking at paintings, and as such may be seen as participants in the spread of visual culture and of discussions concerning how it can be appreciated.

Jonathan Richardson is not a figure directly involved in this story of the early intermingling of the novel and painting, but his discourse on Italian art (including the manner of its writing and the fact of it being a written text) is nonetheless enmeshed in correlative intermedial issues, and it is notable that it appeared at a time when prose fiction was becoming increasingly popular within the literary marketplace and was beginning to develop its rapport with the visual arts. As well as Richardon's *Account*, 1722 saw the publication of Daniel Defoe's *Moll Flanders* and *Colonel Jack*, Eliza Haywood's *The British Recluse*, Penelope Aubin's *The Noble Slaves* and other works that were contributing to the establishment of 'the novel' as an acknowledged literary form. From early on, as many critics have shown, this genre attached itself to the visual arts and demonstrated keen pictorial aspirations: it was a form of entertainment which, by means of different literary techniques, would regularly aim to prompt the visual imaginations of its readers, encouraging them to think in terms of pictures while following the strings of printed words beneath their eyes. The novel genre, critics have argued, developed in a self-nourishing relationship to the work of visual artists, with some of its central characteristics emerging as counterparts to tendencies within earlier and contemporary work in paint. Maximillian E. Novak, for example, points out in an essay on Defoe's relationship to the visual arts that 'realistic prose fiction . . . developed almost simultaneously with the new realism in painting', particularly that of Dutch artists.[5] Defoe, Novak argues, forged a realist mode of writing that was not just like a verbal form of Dutch painting, in terms of what is represented and the amount of detail provided, as has long been observed, but that was also indebted to the work of Dutch artists in terms of both its properties and purpose. In the most significant recent intervention in the field – Jakub Lipski's *Painting the Novel: Pictorial Discourse in Eighteenth-Century English Fiction* (2018) – it is further argued that 'pictorial and meta-pictorial content' contributed to the process of generic definition taking place within early novelistic performances. The many references and connections to painting that appear in fictions which may be seen partly as literary experiments, Lipski argues, contributed to 'a generic agenda': painting, in addition to invigorating literary pictorialism, helped eighteenth-century authors of prose fiction determine what it was they were doing.[6] Richardson, then, was writing at a key moment in the history of the novel's evolution, but the suggestiveness of his work extends beyond temporal coincidence.

The novel's pictorialism rests on a firm faith in ekphrasis – that is, the power of verbal language to convey or suggest the visual, whether it be a scene or a work of art – and here Richardson's armchair or virtual tourism provides a striking demonstration of that faith in action.[7] In his earlier *Essay on the Theory of Painting*, Richardson had, in fact, deemed verbal language to be ambiguous and 'very imperfect' when compared with the language of the painter: 'Words paint to the Imagination', he observed, 'but every Man forms the thing to himself in his own way.'[8] In the later *Account*, though, we find him promoting the ekphrastic writing of his son as an adequate surrogate (when augmented with prints) for his own experience of seeing, and if Richardson Jr could be seen to 'write visually' with such clarity and vividness, so too could the imaginative authors of early novels. The *Account* itself was also an expression of confidence in ekphrasis. It did not include illustrative plates and so Richardson's powers of description were vital. Illustrations would soon become more common in publications about the visual arts. Ingrid R. Vermeulen has shown that '[i]n the course of the eighteenth century, more and more art reproductions were gradually integrated in the text in practically all the genres of the art literature, comprising biographies, collection catalogues and monographs on schools'.[9] For Richardson, though, the burden of representation rested upon the word.

Most importantly here, though, Richardson's dependence upon his son's accounts points to the issue already noted: that extensive exposure to paintings (of any kind, but particularly European Old Master works) was a privilege of the few at this time; knowledge of the visual arts based on first-hand encounters with a wide body of paintings was rare. If Britain's leading art theorist had not seen the artworks that were coming to be regarded as the main achievements in an emerging history of European art to which he himself was a contributor, what type of access to and knowledge of the visual arts might have been possessed by the broader population, including those people who read novels? An equally important question is how, in subsequent years, did such access change and develop and thus alter the conditions in which the writing and reading of prose fiction was conducted? Opportunities to experience the visual arts undoubtedly increased in the decades after Richardson was writing, and there was consequently a significant 'rise of art-historical consciousness', as Chia-Chuan Hsieh has termed it in an important essay that addresses levels of awareness of the visual arts and the social reach of such awareness in Britain from 1707 to 1764.[10] It is well recognised that there was a general expansion of the arts, with access to painting increasing and reaching further down the social hierarchy. Almost certainly the most important innovation here was the introduction in 1760 of annual public exhibitions arranged by the Society for the Encouragement of Arts, Manufactures and Commerce and the Society of Artists of Great Britain. The significance of these exhibitions both for the viewing public and British painters has led David Solkin boldly to declare that '[t]here is no more important date [than 1760] in the entire history of British Art'.[11] But prior to 1760, art-historical consciousness was already growing in part due to the increasing availability of engravings of paintings, not only copies of older works but also those printed in tandem with the making of modern paintings (the mode of production pursued, most notably, by Hogarth), which, if not fostering historical consciousness, still cultivated interest in visual aesthetics. Hsieh dates the beginning of the proliferation of printed versions of paintings to the 1720s when 'Old Master paintings in private collections were increasingly . . . engraved and published'.[12] Amid these developments in the consumption of the visual arts, what type of 'language of painting' could be incorporated into novels? In the communication taking place between authors of fiction and the multiple unknown readers who might pick up their works, what foundation of knowledge or experience of the visual arts could be assumed to be in place? These are questions which have received little attention in critical accounts of the early novel's pictorialism, but it is worth enquiring into the level of experience or knowledge of painting that was enjoyed by readers of novels – or by the imagined readers that novelists considered as their public – for it can help to illuminate the way in which the discourse of painting became incorporated as a part of the language of fiction.

What follows here takes the form of two broad overviews: first, an examination of the challenges involved in seeing an extensive body of paintings, including printed copies, and of the exclusivity of exposure to the medium of paint in Britain before the introduction of public exhibitions; second, a whistle-stop tour through a selection of novels from the 1720s to the 1770s, in which sister arts connections – that is, possible influences from the world of painting as well as explicit references to painters and painting – are read as possible gauges of public art-historical consciousness. Novelists considered here include Daniel Defoe, Jonathan Swift, Eliza Haywood, Richard Graves, Henry Mackenzie, Frances Sheridan, Charles Johnstone, Laurence Sterne and – an outlier in terms of the overall argument here – Henry Fielding. This flitting approach to the period's fiction precludes a deep examination of any one novel, but it allows for the identification of a recurrent literary trait which is dubbed here the 'supplemented reference' – a reference which is not left to stand alone demanding readerly knowledge but rather comes packaged with self-explanation – and this repeated feature of mid-eighteenth-century novels is read as a sign of a culture with a burgeoning but far from established broad public knowledge of painting.

The Limits and Growth of Art-Historical Consciousness

The experience that Richardson's son was able to enjoy certainly placed him firmly within a small elite: among those Britons who had the wealth needed to experience the works that were considered the highest achievements within the visual arts, almost all of which were found abroad. In the early eighteenth century, Britain had no widely respected native school of painting and while some of the movable works of European art had been brought over the Channel – principally by aristocratic buyers for private display – there were few opportunities to see major works in Britain. Continental

380   PAUL GORING

travel – the Grand Tour – remained the primary means of access to eminent painting, and it demanded not only huge resources in terms of time and money but also powerful social connections. The 'principal way to familiarize oneself with works of art', Vermeulen writes,

> was by traveling to European countries, and in particular Italy, to visit the churches, libraries, studios, auction houses, galleries and palaces in which they were stored. Scholars such as De Piles, d'Argenville, Bottari and Luigi Lanzi (1732–1810) often acknowledged travel as a precondition for trustworthy observations on art. Yet, the access to the treasure houses was not always a matter of course, and often had to be organized via influential acquaintances on the basis of recommendation letters or under the guidance of local connoisseurs.[13]

Privilege, then, did not expunge difficulty, but the keenest tourists did manage to experience many of the artistic treasures of the Continent, and one consequence of their efforts was that an increasing number of paintings – both originals and copies – were bought or commissioned and sent to Britain by travellers interested in adorning their homes on their return. There were also dedicated art dealers who pushed the international trade in paintings and other artworks, and they found a profitable market in Britain, particularly for Italian works. There are surviving records of the importation of paintings from the Continent, on the basis of which Ian Pears has charted a gradual if uneven increase between 1722 and 1774, with around a thousand paintings, about half from Italy, entering the country per year at the end of that period.[14]

Britain was accumulating a scattered stock of paintings in private hands, then, but it is unlikely that many of those works would have been widely seen. If sold at auction – as many of the imports were – then the paintings would have had a type of public viewability.[15] Auctions have consequently been regarded by some critics as significant precursors to the later exhibitions, as events through which painting became a public matter with significant social reach. At a general level, auctions did raise the profile of painting, but given the fleetingness of such sales, individual paintings sold in this way were not in the public eye for long, and those attending auctions were for the most part from the upper social stratum. William Hogarth's depiction of an 'Auction of Pictures', from around 1730, showing a gathering of well-dressed potential bidders, certainly suggests that, in his time, auctions were hardly for the *poloi*.[16]

In fact, with regard to the experience of the visual arts available to less advantaged Britons, while it is agreed that there was a significant growth of the arts, the extent of that growth and how far it reached in terms of social class remains a matter of debate. On the one hand, there is the view put forward by John Brewer and others that growing prosperity produced a population that hungrily consumed cultural products of all kinds and that, while the lowest orders could not afford to be regular cultural consumers, spending on culture spread significantly through the ranks, particularly in urban communities. Brewer is keen to emphasise that enjoying the arts 'was emphatically not confined to the aristocracy', and nor was it purely a development in Britain: 'all over Europe artisans and merchants, shopkeepers and farmers, lawyers, doctors and minor clergy bought books, collected prints to display in their parlours and dining rooms and, when they could, attended dances, plays and concerts'.[17] Brewer identifies in Britain a 'pent-up demand for European painting' which produced a buoyant market satisfying an 'enthusiasm for art [that] extended down the social scale'. Acknowledging that 'rich aristocrats made the most spectacular purchases', he notes that 'many clients were of much humbler origin' and sees the 'depth of the market' as explicable partly 'by the low prices of most pictures'.[18]

A more cautious view is put forward by Robert Hume who, on the basis of close examination of eighteenth-century incomes and prices, claims that 'pretty consistently between 1688 and 1801, no more than about 3 percent of the families in England and Wales had sufficient income to purchase more than a bare minimum of "cultural" products'.[19] With regard to paintings, Hume suggests that it was rare for most people to encounter originals prior to the public exhibitions that began to be arranged in London from 1760. 'Until relatively late in the century', he writes, 'most Londoners would have had little or no opportunity to see paintings.'[20] Actually owning paintings was the preserve of the very few, with prices that 'can be shocking' early in the period and which 'boggle the mind' later in the century.[21] Puncturing Brewer's idea of what constitutes a 'low price', Hume's calculations show that 'buying or commissioning paintings is definitely the territory of elite culture: only the decidedly rich could have afforded to do so'; painting was 'basically unavailable to almost everyone'.[22] More people saw paintings than owned them, of course, and works displayed in private homes could be viewed by visitors and also by those members of the lower classes who served the wealthy and cleaned up after them. In fact, the culturally educated servant became a minor 'type' in the period. James Townley's farce *High Life Below Stairs* (1759), for example, features a servant of a duke who, with connoisseurial arrogance, complains to a servant in another household, 'You have a damn'd vile Collection of Pictures I observe, above Stairs, . . . Your 'Squire has no Taste. . . . There is not an original Picture in the whole Collection.'[23] The comic quality of this character type, though, rests on the idea that a servant with deep experience and knowledge of the arts is an aberration.

Like Hume, Ronald Paulson has argued for the exclusivity of the medium of paint, particularly before the mid-century, suggesting that it was basically not a part of 'popular culture'. Reflecting on the type of visual cultural experience that would have been available to most Londoners in, roughly, the second quarter of the century, Paulson suggests that '[t]hey probably never saw a painting'. He points to 'a few places, such as St. Paul's, Greenwich Hospital, St. Bartholomew's Hospital and the Foundling [Hospital]', where paintings could be seen (with a visit requiring 'an act of will'), but otherwise most Londoners' exposure to images created in paint would have been largely restricted to 'the signboards and shop signs that cluttered the streets of London . . . painted arms on coach doors, decks of cards, and other common images'. They would sometimes see 'engravings (including engraved copies of paintings)',[24] and there were other visual cultural forms that were more widely accessible, such as illustrated broadsides, woodcuts, stained-glass windows in churches, and other images in public meeting places that could be seen freely or cheaply. But paintings were simply not a part of common experience, and there were few opportunities, therefore, to hone the more advanced kind of visual literacy that some paintings – when compared with, say, a shop sign – demand of their viewers.

The prints that Paulson refers to were, indeed, the prime medium for the dissemination of the visual arts in the period, and as the example of Richardson's writing on

European art suggests, they were highly respected as a vehicle for the remediation of painting. A chapter dedicated to 'the Usefulness and Use of Prints' appeared in *The Art of Painting*, a treatise of 1706, originally published in French, by the painter and critic Roger de Piles. He, like Richardson, regarded prints as essential tools for the accumulation of knowledge and expertise, both for practitioners in the art of painting and those seeking to appreciate visual art in an informed way. Acknowledging the expense of collecting paintings and the difficulty of seeing several in one place, de Piles commends the opportunities offered by print collecting:

> one may easily see the Works of several Masters on a Table, one may form an Idea of them, judge by comparing them one with another, know which to chuse, and by practising it often, contract a Habit of a good Taste.[25]

With such faith in engravings, writers like Richardson and de Piles were celebrating the way in which print technology had, to use Walter Benjamin's famous phrase, placed works of art firmly in an 'Age of Mechanical Reproduction' – an age in which artworks could proliferate, be dispersed internationally and gain a broader public, due to the busy turning of the presses.[26] The reproduction of paintings was, of course, 'semi-mechanical' rather than mechanical: it demanded the work of a draughtsman and engraver prior to the printing process, and there are consequently sometimes striking differences between engravings and original paintings, as well as between different engravings of the same painting (an obvious demonstration of which is found in those engravings offering a mirror-image version of a painting).[27] It is appropriate, in fact, to see many engravings more as interpretations than copies of the paintings from which they spring. But art enthusiasts like Richardson and de Piles who made use of prints, either for pleasure or study, seem to have been content to overlook the distortions involved in remediation, as well as the absence of colour, as the usefulness of prints outweighed the limits of their fidelity to the original works to which they gave a form of vicarious access. Indeed, absorbing images through engravings was not necessarily seen as inferior to the experience of seeing an original painting. When Richard Steele claimed in a 1711 *Spectator* essay that an 'Engraver is to the Painter, what a Printer is to an Author' he was expressing the view that the essence of a painting is eminently reproducible – not lodged inexorably within the paint of a unique original but, rather, ripe for the work of the good copyist and the printer.[28]

This was a position that would sometimes be challenged. For example, the French aesthetician Charles Batteux, whose work was translated into English, pointed to the inherent limitations of 'a mere print' which lacked the 'perfect coloring which belongs to art alone'.[29] Furthermore, as access to original works of art increased, the idea that paintings could truly be appreciated through prints lost some of its credibility, particularly in elite circles, and seeing original works became de rigueur in the business of art appreciation and connoisseurship. A particularly telling example of this is found in the fact that anyone wishing to be nominated for membership of the Society of Dilettanti – Britain's foremost elite club for (male) art lovers, founded in the 1730s – had to have travelled to Italy and met an existing member there in order to be considered.[30] This was a club rule that basically restricted membership to those who had been on a Grand Tour, and it underlined the idea of first-hand viewing of the Italian Old Masters as a necessary basis for true connoisseurship. It was an expression of what Harry Mount

NOVELS, PAINTINGS AND THE HALF-TRAINED EYE 383

describes as the 'determination on the part of the social elite to preserve their own private enclave' within the business of cultural consumption and appreciation.[31] Still, in humbler circles print versions of Old Master works continued to be highly valued. As a mid-century proponent of the art of engraving wrote, 'all the celebrated Performances and Inventions of the most eminent Masters, are exceedingly well imitated, and reduced to so small a Size, as to be communicable to the whole World'.[32]

Because of their greater accessibility, prints have been seen to have had a key role in creating a foundation for the novel's embrace of the sister art of painting, with prints and novels being regarded as twin, mutually developing products of the printing press, with an intimate form of that twinning found in novels illustrated with plates based on paintings; some editions of Samuel Richardson's *Pamela* (1740), for example, included engravings based on paintings by Francis Hayman. Lipski recognises the importance of prints in his study of the early novel's pictorial discourse. He leans towards Brewer's view of the growing reach of the arts as he depicts a culture of art-aware authors and readers; he points to 'the gradual democratization of connoisseurship and visual experience' and to how works of art 'were made universally available' and 'were no longer targeted at the upper class exclusively'. Painting was 'largely commoditised', firstly through auctions but also by becoming 'part of the rapidly developing print culture'. '[T]he public experience of a piece of painting', he writes, 'was very often mediated by widely circulated engravings'.[33] Lipski presents an account of the novel's early development taking place in a culture in which writers and readers acquired a high level of art literacy – and the print is key to the creation of that culture. But his point that this was a 'gradual' process is important to emphasise, and some caution regarding the reach of prints may also be useful to apply, including that suggested by Robert Hume's attention to the high price of culture. Hsieh's study of art-historical consciousness suggests that, in the early years of the century, there were relatively few works that circulated widely in engraved form. Her focus is on the publication of prints of the Raphael cartoons at Hampton Court, which did indeed become available 'in various formats and at a wide range of prices', but these reproductions constituted an exception rather than a norm: the cartoons stood out as by far 'the most widely "visible" works of an Old Master in early eighteenth-century England'.[34] From the 1720s, Hsieh's discussion shows, copies of an increasing number of paintings began to circulate, but this marks the early stages of the growth of a popular art-historical consciousness which could not be said to be widely established until later. Hsieh is not concerned with the novel, but an important implication of her chronology of the rise of visual arts literacy is that authors of fiction in the 1720s – even if they had themselves enjoyed direct access to the paintings, which was the case for Defoe and Swift – could not assume a broad base of visual arts knowledge in their imagined readers. In subsequent years the proliferation of prints facilitated the spread of such knowledge, but still the actual collecting of prints in the manner of Jonathan Richardson or de Piles remained predominantly a gentlemanly and aristocratic pursuit.[35] Prices were not so very low. When, in the mid-century, William Gilpin wrote one of the first guides to print collecting, *An Essay on Prints . . . to which are Added, Some Cautions that May be Useful in Collecting Prints* (1768), he described the practice as an 'elegant amusement', and his advice on buying prints was pointedly pitched to a readership with considerable disposable income.[36] The illustrated works of art criticism and history that, as Vermeulen has shown, began to be produced in the years after Jonathan Richardson was writing also tended to be

384   PAUL GORING

high-priced, luxury publications. The commoditisation of culture through print was
not for all.

It is, of course, impossible accurately to map the reach of art-historical consciousness and its status within the evolving communities of eighteenth-century
novel readers. The main point here is that that consciousness was something that
was 'rising', to use Hsieh's term, together with the popularisation of the novel
genre. There was a movement towards the visual arts becoming 'universally available', as Lipski puts it, but that took time, and, for much of the eighteenth century,
novelists – whatever their own exposure to the arts – could not have written with an
idea of their readership as being comprehensively steeped in visual culture. And that
sense of a readership with a developing consciousness of the visual arts is indeed
suggested when we begin to consider the particularities of novelists' use of painting
within their fictions, including inconspicuous absorption of aspects of this sister art
as well as overt references to painting and to specific painters.

Quiet Sister Art Relations in Two Early Fictions

In his preface to *The Fortunate Mistress* (1724), the novel popularly known as
Roxana, Defoe declared that, for his work to be improving for his readers, vice had
to be *'painted in its Low-priz'd Colours'*.[37] This direct, if unspecific, allusion to the art
of painting is unusual in the work. It is a fiction that makes only slight explicit reference to painting: it contains a handful of mentions of 'pictures' – as furnishings and
portraits of characters – but Defoe shows little interest in name-checking recognised
artists, as some later novelists would, while on those occasions when the word 'paint'
occurs it most often means make-up (which is unsurprising in a novel concerned with
the value and sexual power of appearances). At the textual surface level of *Roxana*, in
other words, there is quietness or near silence regarding the art of painting. More an
absence than a presence, such quietness might not seem to call out for examination,
but it becomes significant – and arguably eloquent regarding Defoe's sense of his readership – when it is considered alongside the fact that aspects of *Roxana* may actually
have been shaped by a profound and intimate relationship to contemporary trends in
the medium of paint.

This claim regarding *Roxana* is a result of historically contextualised interpretation, and the main critical intervention here is made by Lipski who, in *Painting the
Novel*, offers a very extensive, chapter-length study of *Roxana*, arguing that 'for Defoe,
the fine arts, and especially seventeenth- and eighteenth-century realist and allegorical
painting were a significant point of reference in his attempt to conceptualise the novel
form'.[38] Making the case, Lipski gives particular attention to two passages in *Roxana*,
describing them as 'word-paintings' which are 'inscribed in the text itself'. He argues
that one of them, a long description of Roxana in a state of misery, is analogous to
Dutch depictions in paint of the trials of the biblical Job, while the other, an account
of Roxana finely dressed in a more fortunate state, is comparable with the genre of
'the *turquerie* portrait'.[39] Regarding the latter, he points to the 'exotic fascinations'
of, notably, George I and Lady Mary Wortley Montagu, which triggered an Orientalist fashion for lavish Turkish dress and for portraits in which sitters would pose in
such dress. Roxana's description of herself, including a detailed account of her being
'dress'd in the Habit of *a Turkish Princess*',[40] may be read as a verbal counterpart to

such portraits, Lipski argues, and it contains a range of highly pictorial techniques and characteristics.[41] For example, how Roxana draws attention to her own posture, as well as framing devices, such as her being seen in her finery through a doorway, lend a tableau quality to the depiction. Of central importance is the amount of material detail that Defoe has Roxana convey in her account of her garb. 'The Dress was extraordinary fine indeed', she recalls,

> the Robe was a fine *Persian*, or *India* Damask; the Ground white, and the Flowers blue and gold, and the Train held five Yards; the Dress under it, was a Vest of the same, embroider'd with Gold, and set with some Pearl in the Work, and some *Turquois* Stones; to the Vest, was a Girdle five or six Inches wide, after the *Turkish* Mode; and on both Ends where it join'd, or hook'd, was set with Diamonds for eight Inches either way, only they were not true Diamonds . . .
>
> The Turban, or Head-Dress, had a Pinacle on the top, but not above five Inches, with a Piece of loose Sarcenet hanging from it; and on the Front, just over the Forehead, was a good Jewel, which I had added to it.[42]

Such detail may certainly be said to lend vividness and visual suggestiveness to the work, and in his consideration of both this and the Dutch-style 'word-painting' Lipski is persuasive in his identification of likenesses between Defoe's verbal descriptions and the respective genres of painting. He additionally points to the fact that the first edition of the work (and many subsequent editions) included an engraved frontispiece depicting Roxana in her Turkish dress, which, while probably not arranged by Defoe, is nonetheless a striking part of the book, and one with the potential to imprint 'itself on the reader's perception of the ensuing narrative'.[43] What is most important for the present discussion, though, is the fact that in the descriptive passages Defoe does not underscore or make explicit connections to these genres of painting; his 'word-paintings' are devoid of direct invocations of the art of painting. If painting was indeed 'a point of reference' for Defoe and contributed to his authorial process, its manifestation in the pictorial depictions of Roxana is implicit – lodged quietly in the extensive description, possibly as a type of deep allusion, noticeable by some but not all readers, with a connection perhaps triggered by seeing the engraved frontispiece. There is no overt invitation to readers to connect the artforms, or, it can be said, no indication of an expectation that readers are familiar with *turquerie* portraiture or Dutch genre painting that may be underpinning these passages.

Studies of further works of fiction from the 1720s have pointed to other connections (or possible connections) to the visual arts which, on the surface level of the fiction, are manifested with a comparable type of discretion. It has been argued, for example, by Murray Roston – a doyen of verbal-visual studies – that Jonathan Swift's adoption of particular narrative perspectives in *Gulliver's Travels* (1726) points to his 'belong[ing] very centrally to immediately contemporary trends in landscape painting'.[44] In terms of viewpoint, Roston argues, Swift's creation of Gulliver as an elevated observer of the diminutive Lilliputians is a literary counterpart to Canaletto's 'veduta' paintings which depict, from a particular distance, urban scenes crowded with human figures. Swift and Canaletto were at work at more or less the same time, and Swift, Roston implies, could well have been aware of Canaletto, whose works were reaching Britain since they were popular purchases for Grand Tourists when in Italy.[45] (Canaletto later

386 PAUL GORING

moved to and worked in England, but this was after *Gulliver's Travels*.) Positing an influence of painter upon author as a possibility rather than a certainty, Roston's main point is that Swift and Canaletto were, in their different media, basically in tune with a type of perspectival zeitgeist, and he does not suggest that knowledge of Canaletto had a significant role in the early reading of *Gulliver's Travels*. Swift's work makes no reference to Canaletto; it requires no familiarity with the painter in order to be understood or appreciated. Perhaps readers with an awareness of Canaletto might sense a transmedia echo – and thereby enjoy a different, possibly enriched reading experience – but, like the 'word-painting' passages in *Roxana*, *Gulliver's Travels* does not, by means of the perspective in the Lilliput sections, necessarily invite reflection upon the visual arts as a part of the reading process.

What is significant, then, about these examples of textual reticence regarding painting – in fictions that are arguably deeply influenced by painting – is that neither Defoe nor Swift actually requires of readers even a basic art-historical consciousness. If there is a sister arts relationship at work in these cases from the 1720s, it resides primarily in the processes of composition. Regarding consumption, readers are invited to activate their visual imaginations in the encounter with verbal pictorialism, but they are not pointedly alerted to any authorial influence from the world of painting. The works offer ocular pleasure but do not require that a reader is, in de Bolla's terms, a 'knowing viewer' – one 'trained in the correct ways of looking and legitimated by the institutions of cultural evaluation'.[46] Indeed, the pictorialism of the works is open to readers (or listeners, if the fiction was read aloud) from among those less privileged Britons who, as Paulson suggests, may never have seen a painting.[47]

'Supplemented References' to Painters and Paintings in Mid-Century Fiction

The affinities that Lipski and Roston identify are very different in terms of palpability in the fictional text from, say, the intermedial reflections in the introductory dedication to *Ferdinand Count Fathom* (1753), in which Tobias Smollett declares that 'A Novel is a large diffused picture, comprehending the characters of life, disposed in different groupes, and exhibited in various attitudes',[48] or the moment in Haywood's *The History of Jemmy and Jenny Jessamy* (1753) when a character writes 'This puts me in mind of a very just as well as beautiful Hieroglyphic, which I once saw among the paintings of Titian.'[49] These passages explicitly direct readers towards the visual arts, with Smollett gesturing to no specific artist but to a very particular type of character-filled painting, while Haywood's character refers directly to a particularly celebrated painter. Writing around three decades after Defoe and Swift, here Smollett and Haywood appeal directly to readerly awareness of the arts. Indeed, the passages may be said to hail or interpellate readers, embracing them as fellows in a community of cultural consumers. Such references may be read as signs of a widening social spread of interest in the visual arts, but still, it is noticeable that neither passage actually demands that readers bring a store of knowledge to the text in order to comprehend it. Smollett, described by Novak as 'the first important novelist to link' painting and prose fiction, presents a comparison which is unspecific and self-explanatory.[50] The passage probably brought the popular works of Hogarth to the minds of many early

NOVELS, PAINTINGS AND THE HALF-TRAINED EYE

readers; when Smollett was writing in the early 1750s, no living artist was better known in Britain than Hogarth, in large part because of the wide circulation of prints of his works, and indeed many of his narrative pieces have the sort of composition – with groups of characters 'exhibited in various attitudes' – that Smollett invokes. But the passage does not demand being read in such a specifically associative way; indeed, it would make sense to a reader who has never heard of Hogarth.

In a different way, Haywood's reference to Titian is accommodated to a wide range of readerly knowledge. After mentioning Titian, the character offers a long ekphrastic account of the 'beautiful Hieroglyphic' she recalls seeing in his painting:

> the capital figures in the piece were two Cupids, the one coming down from Jupiter in a milk-white robe, his sparkling eyes wide open, and garlands in his hands of fresh and unmix'd sweets, ready to crown the brows of every faithful votary:—the other in a garment of a dusky yellow, spatter'd all over with black, seem'd ascending from the earth, — condens'd vapours encircled his head,—a bandage cover'd his eyes, and in his impure hands were wreaths of half-shed faded roses, thinly blended with thorns and prickly briars.[51]

Haywood, in other words, does not let the name of Titian stand in isolation but rather supplements the reference, bridging the gap between her character, who has had the privilege of seeing original Titians, and readers with differing levels of access to the arts. Those who have seen the works of Titian are offered a type of double pictorialism – reference plus description – while those who have not are spared the potential alienation of a reference with no resonance by means of ekphrasis. Indeed, those readers are invited to feel enfranchised within the exclusive world of paint and canvas by means of a reference to an Old Master whose name is probably recognised but whose works they may never have seen.

Surveying actual mentions of painters in novels from the mid-eighteenth century reveals that this type of 'supplemented reference' is common, with the elaboration of what is implied by means of a reference to a specific painter emerging almost as a new novelistic convention or trope. Smollett, like Haywood, refers to Titian, grouping him together with Raphael and Guido Reni in a passage in *The Adventures of Roderick Random* (1748). He does not expand upon a particular image as Haywood does, but there still is a form of readerly guidance in the manner in which the artists are brought into the novel. The reference appears late in the narrative in a passage which develops the traditional idea of the expressive superiority of the image over the word when Roderick, the protagonist-narrator, is trying to convey the sight of his future wife, the beautiful Narcissa, recovering from a faint:

> O! that I were endowed with the expression of a Raphael, the graces of a Guido, the magick touches of a Titian, that I might represent the fond concern, the chastened rapture, and ingenuous blush that mingled on her beauteous face, when she opened her eyes upon me, and pronounced, 'O heavens! is it you!'[52]

There may be some wryness at work here – a knowing sense of the fine line between a sincere attempt to appreciate different painters and pompous prattle. But the passage is not so clearly satirical as to shut down the possibility of a more serious function: a

388 PAUL GORING

presentation to readers of a pictorial account of the facially expressed emotions that Roderick feels unable to describe, together with suggestions of what the trio of Old Masters could have brought to the representation, albeit that the painters' powers are conveyed in terms that are more suggestive than explanatory in a specific way. Smollett, it may be said, leaves no ekphrastic 'work' to be performed by extratextual knowledge of any of the painters, and indeed the passage offers a shorthand guide to qualities associated with those painters. Returning to Hsieh's phrase, it builds art-historical consciousness more than it demands it.

In the same novel, Smollett also refers to Hogarth (as he also would in *Peregrine Pickle* [1751] and *Humphry Clinker* [1771]).[53] The naming of his contemporary appears within another deployment of the 'words cannot convey . . .' trope, and here the narrator offers a more elaborate description of what he supposedly struggles to describe. Roderick is about to be shaved by the barber's apprentice Hugh Strap when he tells him something shocking:

> It would require the pencil of Hogarth to express the astonishment and concern of Strap, on hearing this piece of news; the basin in which he was preparing the lather for my chin, dropped out of his hands, and he remained some time immoveable in that ludicrous attitude, with his mouth open, and his eyes thrust forward consider-ably beyond their station; but remembering my disposition, which was touchy and impatient of controul, he smothered his chagrin, and attempted to recollect himself.[54]

Here again there is an expansion on a reference with description: the invocation of Hogarth prepares the ground for Roderick's attempt to convey an image of Strap, but it does not take the place of ekphrasis. For the informed reader, the artist's name pro-vides a signal of a visual genre – comic caricature – that Smollett is about to attempt in words with his description of droll action (the dropping of something), the stretching of reality which caricature requires (with the eyes 'beyond their station'), together with an explicit call to see the figure as 'ludicrous'. It is another passage, though, that does not actually require an informed reader – and indeed if there were readers in 1753 who were unfamiliar with Hogarth, Smollett's description could have functioned as a type of gloss on the name.

Further examples of the 'supplemented reference' trope are found in novelists' embrace of the seventeenth-century continental landscape painters – notably Claude Lorrain, Nicolas Poussin and Salvator Rosa – who, from the mid-century, were becom-ing increasingly popular in Britain.[55] Claude Lorrain, for example, makes a sudden appearance in *The Spiritual Quixote* (1773), a satire of Methodism by the clergyman and author Richard Graves. The painter is called upon by Graves not in the description of a landscape but as the basis for a simile deployed to convey the power of a smile:

> Mrs. Rivers received Wildgoose, as her husband's friend, with a sweet smile; which, like the sun-shine so much admired in the landscapes of Claude Lorraine, diffused an additional chearfulness over every other object.[56]

Again there is a type of interpellation at work with a construction that suggests a shared familiarity with the artist and with a 'much admired' characteristic of his work, but for any uninitiated reader the passage clearly explains the force of what has been

NOVELS, PAINTINGS AND THE HALF-TRAINED EYE

introduced for the purposes of comparison. The passage is gently educational – not openly didactic, but indirectly explanatory in a way which is informative while fostering a sense of community built around the enjoyment of art. While such references helped to establish the name of Claude Lorrain as a touchstone for ideas of 'the beautiful' in landscape, mentions of Salvator Rosa were tied to a wilder, more threatening conception of landscape. Henry Mackenzie, a contemporary of Graves, referred to Rosa in *The Man of Feeling* (1771) – a work often regarded as the apogee of mawkish sentimentalism – when the protagonist Harley, walking in a remote rural setting, encounters a prostrate figure:

> An old man, who from his dress seemed to have been a soldier, lay fast asleep on the ground; a knapsack rested on a stone at his right hand, while his staff and brass-hilted sword were crossed at his left.
> Harley looked on him with the most earnest attention. He was one of those figures which Salvator would have drawn; nor was the surrounding scenery unlike the wildness of that painter's backgrounds. The banks on each side were covered with fantastic shrub-wood [. . .] A rock, with some dangling wild flowers, jutted out above where the soldier lay; on which grew the stump of a large tree, white with age, and a single twisted branch shaded his face as he slept.[57]

The mention of the painter points both back and forwards here, rounding off Mackenzie's description of the figure and providing a frame of reference for the elaborate landscape description that follows. It is another reference to a painter which forges a knowing relationship between narrative and reader – suggesting their sense of community as members of an art-aware public, all on first-name terms with 'Salvator' – without actually requiring a knowing reader since knowledge is offered in the passage itself. Describing a scene declared to be like the work of Rosa, Mackenzie is indirectly providing an ekphrastic description of the work of Rosa.

It should be acknowledged that not all novelists followed this tendency to provide explicatory supplementation of their references to painters. Henry Fielding seems to have expected more knowledge of the arts in the readers of *Tom Jones* (1749) when he has his narrator observe:

> Vanbrugh and Congreve copied Nature; but they who copy them draw as unlike the present age, as Hogarth would do if he was to paint a rout or a drum in the dresses of Titian and of Vandyke. In short, imitation here will not do the business. The picture must be after Nature herself.[58]

Familiarity with Hogarth is assumed in *Tom Jones*, both here and elsewhere. For Fielding's narrator, in fact, the artist is 'my friend Hogarth' (echoing Fielding's well-documented friendship with the artist in life) and readers of the work are expected to be able to visualise a character when told that 'she exactly resembled the young woman who is pouring out her mistress's tea in the third picture of the Harlot's Progress'.[59] And that expectation of learning also extends further to a basic sense of art-historical chronology and to the visual gap between the contemporary world and the paintings of Van Dyke and Titian. Fielding's assumption or construction of an idea of a learned reader here provides a useful reminder of the dangers of generalising

390 PAUL GORING

about 'the novel' during specific phases of the history of the genre: authors imagined or constructed their readers in different ways and there was more than one way in the mid-eighteenth century to refer to painting and painters. Still, while not universally adopted, the supplemented reference, which Fielding does not provide here, may still be identified as a recurrent trope forming part of a common register which hails readers of many kinds with varying levels of familiarity with the arts.

Conclusion

The narrative register of which the supplemented reference is a part can be described in terms of what it is: accommodating, accessible, explanatory. But it may also be seen in terms of what it is pointedly not – alienatingly connoisseurial – and, by way of conclusion, it is worth pointing briefly to fiction's active resistance to the more abstruse forms of art appreciation, for this was another way in which the novel, as it developed its intimate relationship with painting and participated in the growth of art-historical consciousness, situated itself within a popular rather than elitist cultural stratum and made room for readers who had limited access to the arts. Satire was crucial here, with many novels staging opposition to the exclusivity, characteristics and tone of elitist art appreciation by holding connoisseur or pseudo-connoisseur characters up to ruthless ridicule. Smollett, for example, offered a vivid portrait of connoisseurial absurdity in *Peregrine Pickle* in the character of Pallet, a painter as well as a false critic 'with an eternal rotation of tongue, floundering from one mistake to another'. In the depiction of this character, Smollett pushes the listing of artists and their qualities seen in *Roderick Random* to a point where mockery is clear, with Pallet cataloguing the virtues of 'the divine Raphael, the most excellent Michael Angelo, Bona Roti, the graceful Guido, the bewitching Titian, and above all others, the sublime Rubens'. To avoid any doubt of the work's distancing of itself from such discourse, Smollett has his narrator add that Pallet 'would have proceeded with a long catalogue of names which he had got by heart for the purpose, without retaining the least idea of their several qualifications'.[60]

There were many further representations of the type. For example, in *Memoirs of Miss Sidney Biddulph* (1761), Frances Sheridan depicts a 'stiff, conceited, overbearing, talkative, impertinent coxcomb', and shows the character haughtily misjudging 'a fine landscape of Claude Lorrain': 'looking through his fingers, as if to throw the picture into perspective, that is a pretty good piece, said he, for a copy'.[61] Ever pompous and typically wrong, connoisseurs were given a rough ride by eighteenth-century novelists. Charles Johnstone, like Sheridan, presents a scornful attitude to such types in *Chrysal; Or, The Adventures of a Guinea* (1760–5), in a depiction of a high-ranking military man whose art obsession leads him to neglect his duties: 'Pictures! painting is the sole object of his admiration, the only knowledge he values himself upon . . . name *Rembrandt* or *Titian*, and he immediately gives you a dissertation on their excellencies, and the difference of their schools!' Johnstone's narrative offers clear-cut judgement of the man: 'Such absurd passions are always the objects of artifice and imposition.'[62]

Critical probing of connoisseurship also formed a strand in the authorship of Laurence Sterne, in both *The Life and Opinions of Tristram Shandy, Gentleman* (1759–67) and his later *A Sentimental Journey through France and Italy* (1768), and it included sceptical examination of some of the printed tracts and treatises associated with 'high' art appreciation. A well-known passage in the first volume of *Tristram Shandy*, for example, mocks a systematic manner of judging the quality of a painting – 'the painter's scale, divided into 20' – which had been developed by Roger de Piles and subsequently commended by Jonathan Richardson in his *Argument on behalf of the Science of a Connoisseur* (1719). Offering wry mockery of art criticism, Sterne has his narrator measure his own writing against the scale, finding that 'the out-lines will turn out as 12,—the composition as 9,—the colouring as 6,—the expression 13 and a half,—and the design . . . I think it cannot well fall short of 19'.[63] Sterne also evolved different and subtler ways of expressing suspicion of exclusive aesthetic discourse. *A Sentimental Journey* is a type of Grand Tour tale which seems to teeter on the brink of the connoisseurs' world, only to pull itself back and onto more common ground. Sterne's narrator, Yorick, has been described by one critic, Brian Michael Norton, as 'a connoisseur of painting, casually referencing the work of Raphael and Guido',[64] but importantly Yorick's references are not rarefied or abstruse; they do not require a connoisseurial reader. When Yorick invokes Guido Reni in a description of the head of a monk, he shows the same tendency to refer to and then elaborate as has been seen in other authors of fiction:

> It was one of those heads, which Guido has often painted—mild, pale—penetrating, free from all common-place ideas of fat contented ignorance looking downwards upon the earth—it look'd forwards; but look'd, as if it look'd at something beyond this world.[65]

But Sterne's work goes further than offering this conventional form of access and, as Norton argues very persuasively, it situates itself to one side of connoisseurship as it pursues an alternative interest in 'the aesthetics of everyday life', with a narrator who 'endeavors to expand the realm of the aesthetic, to find value in humble things'.[66] Indeed when the name of Raphael enters the narration, it actually appears as part of an argument made by Yorick against looking at works of visual art when there is as much to be gained by looking instead at our immediate circumstances and the people who might be encountered therein. Yorick is in Paris when he mentions Raphael as he is explaining his manner of gaining pleasure to a Count:

> I have not seen the Palais royal,—nor the Luxembourg—nor the Façade of the Louvre—nor have attempted to swell the catalogues we have of pictures, statues, and churches—I conceive every fair being as a temple, and would rather enter in, and see the original drawings and loose sketches hung up in it, than the transfiguration of Raphael itself.[67]

When Sterne wrote this passage he had, in fact, become something of an art connoisseur himself. After a long career as a rural clergyman with an amateur interest in painting, his success in middle age as an author of fiction brought new opportunities and social elevation; he was able to indulge in a type of belated Grand Tour through France and Italy and to fraternise with the upper classes, including many of the art enthusiasts who filled the ranks of the Society of Dilettanti.[68] In life he had become a mingler within London's cultural elite, conversing knowledgeably on paintings and prints, but in *A Sentimental Journey* – a fictionalised rendering of his own travels – he avoids a connoisseurial tone in the chosen narrative register and indeed offers a type of manifesto which promotes the idea that rich aesthetic experience may be gained without coming into contact with great art. The passage also contains a degree of wit and sexual innuendo – in Yorick's declaration of a desire to 'enter in' to 'every fair being' – but such energies do not necessarily undermine the argument in which they are threaded. Sterne described his work in a letter to his publisher as 'likely to take in all Kinds of readers', and its undemanding approach to the arts may be deemed a part of the democratic openness which he points towards here.[69] It provides a reminder that there is much that can be enjoyed without seeing great art – and also that among the 'all Kinds of readers' who picked up novels in a period when accessing art was far from straightforward there were many who had not had that privilege.

Notes

1. David Solkin deems Richardson's writing on art to be his 'most important legacy'. David H. Solkin, *Art in Britain, 1660–1815* (New Haven: Yale University Press, 2015), 71.
2. Jonathan Richardson, *An Account of Some of the Statues, Bas-reliefs, Drawings and Pictures in Italy &c. with Remarks* (London: J. Knapton, 1722).
3. Richardson, *An Account of Some of the Statues*, 198. It should be noted that Richardson's son is also credited as an author – the title-page presents the work as by Jonathan Richardson 'Sen and Jun' – but it is the senior Richardson who commands the narrative (as suggested by the first-person singular in the earlier quoted passage) and he who, rhetorically at least, takes on the role of 'seer'.
4. Peter de Bolla, *The Education of the Eye: Painting, Landscape, and Architecture in Eighteenth-Century Britain* (Stanford: Stanford University Press, 2003), 16.
5. Maximillian E. Novak, 'Picturing the Thing Itself, or Not: Defoe, Painting, Prose Fiction, and the Arts of Describing', *Eighteenth-Century Fiction* 9, no. 1 (1996): 3.
6. Jakub Lipski, *Painting the Novel: Pictorial Discourse in Eighteenth-Century English Fiction* (New York and London: Routledge, 2018), 1.
7. In strict uses 'ekphrasis' refers to the transformation of visual works of art into creative verbal forms, or as James Heffernan puts it, in a neat distillation of the term's nuances, 'ekphrasis is a kind of writing that turns pictures into storytelling words'. James A. W. Heffernan, 'Ekphrasis: Theory', in Gabriele Rippl, *Handbook of Intermediality: Literature – Image – Sound – Music* (Berlin: De Gruyter, 2015), 48. As Heffernan notes, though, there is little consensus in applications of the term and it is sometimes used to refer to verbal description of the visual more generally.
8. Jonathan Richardson, *An Essay on the Theory of Painting* (London: John Churchill, 1715), 5.
9. Ingrid R. Vermeulen, *Picturing Art History: The Rise of the Illustrated History of Art in the Eighteenth Century* (Amsterdam: Amsterdam University Press, 2010), 10.
10. Chia-Chuan Hsieh, 'Publishing the Raphael Cartoons and the Rise of Art-Historical Consciousness in England, 1707–1764', *The Historical Journal* 52, no. 4 (2009): 900. The phrase 'art-historical consciousness' is used subsequently without quotation marks, but it should be acknowledged that it is borrowed from Hsieh throughout.
11. Solkin, *Art in Britain*, 151.
12. Hsieh, 'Publishing the Raphael Cartoons', 920.
13. Vermeulen, *Picturing Art History*, 8.
14. Ian Pears, *The Discovery of Painting: The Growth of Interest in the Arts in England, 1680–1768* (New Haven and London: Yale University Press, 1988), 207–10.
15. Pears gives an account of art auctions, a marked increase in which occurred from the 1680s. Pears, *Discovery of Painting*, 57–67.
16. Ronald Paulson, *Hogarth: His Life, Art, and Times*, 2 vols (New Haven and London: Yale University Press, 1971), 212–13.

NOVELS, PAINTINGS AND THE HALF-TRAINED EYE 393

17. John Brewer, *The Pleasures of the Imagination: English Culture in the Eighteenth Century* (New York: Farrar, Straus and Giroux, 1997), xviii–ix.
18. Brewer, *The Pleasures of the Imagination*, 204–5.
19. Robert D. Hume, 'The Value of Money in Eighteenth-Century England: Incomes, Prices, Buying Power – and Some Problems in Cultural Economics', *Huntington Library Quarterly* 77, no. 4 (2014): 377.
20. Hume, 'Value of Money', 392.
21. Hume, 'Value of Money', 390.
22. Hume, 'Value of Money', 407, 413.
23. James Townley, *High Life Below Stairs* (London: printed for J. Newbery, 1759), 35.
24. Ronald Paulson, *Popular and Polite Art in the Age of Hogarth and Fielding* (Notre Dame and London: University of Notre Dame Press, 1979), 31.
25. Roger de Piles, *The Art of Painting* (London: J. Nutt, 1706), 60.
26. Benjamin's 'The Work of Art in the Age of Mechanical Reproduction' (1939) is included in Walter Benjamin, *Illuminations*, ed. Hannah Arendt, trans. Harry Zohn (London: Fontana, 1992). Benjamin is primarily interested in photography, but noting that '[i]n principle a work of art has always been reproducible' (212), he gives some attention to earlier techniques of reproduction, including stamping and printing.
27. Such differences are well illustrated by examples reproduced in Vermeulen, *Picturing Art History*.
28. Richard Steele, 'No. 226', *The Spectator*, 19 November 1711.
29. Charles Batteux, *A Course of the Belles Lettres: Or the Principles of Literature. Translated from the French of the Abbot Batteux*, 4 vols (London: B. Law and Co., 1761), 1:92.
30. Bruce Redford, *Dilettanti: The Antic and the Antique in Eighteenth-Century England* (Los Angeles: The J. Paul Getty Museum and the Getty Research Institute, 2008), 2.
31. Harry Mount, 'The Monkey with the Magnifying Glass: Constructions of the Connoisseur in Eighteenth-Century Britain', *Oxford Art Journal* 29, no. 2 (2006): 182.
32. Anon., *Sculptura-Historico-Technica: Or, the History and Art of Ingraving* (London: S. Harding, 1747), 1.
33. Lipski, *Painting the Novel*, 4.
34. Hsieh, 'Publishing the Raphael Cartoons', 911.
35. See Antony Griffiths, 'Print Collecting in Rome, Paris, and London in the Early Eighteenth Century', *Harvard University Art Museums Bulletin* 2, no. 3 (1994): 37–58. Griffiths does not address the social rank of collectors head on, but his discussion points clearly to the well-heeled status of collectors in the period.
36. William Gilpin, *An Essay upon Prints*, 2nd edn (London: J. Robson, 1768), iii. Gilpin's preface indicates that the work was mostly written at least fifteen years before the 1768 publication.
37. Daniel Defoe, *Roxana*, ed. David Blewett (Harmondsworth: Penguin, 1982), 36 (italics original).
38. Lipski, *Painting the Novel*, 25.
39. Lipski, *Painting the Novel*, 33–4.
40. Defoe, *Roxana*, 214.
41. Lipski, *Painting the Novel*, 35.
42. Defoe, *Roxana*, 215.
43. Lipski, *Painting the Novel*, 28.
44. Murray Roston, *Changing Perspectives in Literature and the Visual Arts, 1650–1820* (Princeton: Princeton University Press, 1990), 155.
45. In a chapter on Swift and painting, Joseph McMinn makes no mention of Canaletto, but he does show that Swift took an interest in the visual arts and attended a number of notable auctions. Swift's chief interest, McMinn suggests, lay in portraits, mostly of people he knew. Joseph McMinn, *Jonathan Swift and the Arts* (Newark: University of Delaware Press, 2010), 127–47.
46. De Bolla, *The Education of the Eye*, 16.

47. On the social consumption of books in the period, including the enfranchisement within literary culture of the illiterate by means of reading aloud, see Abigail Williams, *The Social Life of Books: Reading Together in the Eighteenth-Century Home* (New Haven: Yale University Press, 2017).
48. Tobias Smollett, *The Adventures of Ferdinand Count Fathom*, ed. Damian Grant (Oxford: Oxford University Press, 1978), 2.
49. Eliza Haywood, *The History of Jemmy and Jenny Jessamy*, 3 vols (London: T. Gardner, 1753), 2:257.
50. Novak, 'Picturing the Thing Itself, or Not', 3.
51. Haywood, *Jemmy and Jenny Jessamy*, 2:257–8.
52. Tobias Smollett, *The Adventures of Roderick Random*, ed. Paul-Gabriel Boucé (Oxford: Oxford University Press, 1999), 406.
53. Smollett's references to and representations of Hogarth are discussed in Ronald Paulson, 'Smollett and Hogarth: The Identity of Pallet', *Studies in English Literature, 1500–1900* 4, no. 3 (1964): 351–9.
54. Smollett, *Roderick Random*, 283.
55. On the growing popularity of these painters, see the tables in Pears, *The Discovery of Painting*, 220–1, and James Stourton and Charles Sebag-Montefiore, *The British as Art Collectors: From the Tudors to the Present* (London: Scala, 2012), 116.
56. Richard Graves, *The Spiritual Quixote; Or, The Summer's Ramble of Mr. Geoffry Wildgoose*, 3 vols (London: J. Dodsley, 1773), 2:7.
57. Henry Mackenzie, *The Man of Feeling*, ed. Brian Vickers, intr. and notes Stephen Bending and Stephen Bygrave (Oxford: Oxford University Press, 2001), 63–4.
58. Henry Fielding, *The History of Tom Jones*, ed. R. P. C. Mutter (Harmondsworth: Penguin, 1985), 610.
59. Fielding, *Tom Jones*, 63.
60. Tobias Smollett, *The Adventures of Peregrine Pickle*, 4 vols (London: Printed for the Author, 1751), 2:64–5.
61. Frances Sheridan, *Memoirs of Miss Sidney Bidulph*, ed. Patricia Köster and Jean Coates Cleary (Oxford and New York: Oxford University Press, 1995), 24.
62. Charles Johnstone, *Chrysal; Or, The Adventures of a Guinea*, 2nd edn, 2 vols (London: T. Becket, 1761), 1:85–6.
63. Laurence Sterne, *The Life and Opinions of Tristram Shandy, Gentleman: The Text*, ed. Melvyn New and Joan New, 2 vols, The Florida Edition of the Works of Laurence Sterne (Gainesville: University Press of Florida, 1978), 1:16. Sterne's sources and the manner of his satire here are discussed in R. F. Brissenden, 'Sterne and Painting', in *Of Books and Humankind: Essays and Poems Presented to Bonamy Dobrée*, ed. John Butt (London: Routledge & Kegan Paul, 1964), 97–8.
64. Brian Michael Norton, 'Laurence Sterne and the Aesthetics of Everyday Life', in *Sterne, Tristram, Yorick: Tercentenary Essays on Laurence Sterne*, ed. Melvyn New, Peter de Voogd and Judith Hawley (Newark: University of Delaware Press, 2016), 220–1.
65. Laurence Sterne, *A Sentimental Journey through France and Italy and Continuation of the Bramine's Journal*, ed. Melvyn New and W. G. Day, The Florida Edition of the Works of Laurence Sterne (Gainesville: University Press of Florida, 2002), 8.
66. Norton, 'Sterne and the Aesthetics of Everyday Life', 223.
67. Sterne, *A Sentimental Journey*, 111.
68. Paul Goring, 'Sterne's Subscribers and the Society of Dilettanti', *The Shandean* 27 (2016): 57–81.
69. Laurence Sterne to Thomas Becket, 3 September 1767, in *The Letters. Part 2: 1765–1768*, ed. Melvyn New and Peter de Voogd, The Florida Edition of the Works of Laurence Sterne (Gainesville: University Press of Florida, 2009), 616.

Part V:
Adaptations and Afterlives

23

FROM VISUAL TO MATERIAL CULTURE: THE AFTERLIVES OF FRONTISPIECES TO *ROBINSON CRUSOE*

Nathalie Collé

Introduction

IN 1933, WHEN presenting the task of the bibliographer with regard to works of imagination containing illustrations, Edgar Breitenbach insisted that '[w]orks only once or rarely illustrated should only be dealt with at length if the quality of the illustrations justifies this', and that '[s]uch editions as are not illustrated by sequences of pictures but only by a frontispiece, vignettes and so forth should be mentioned briefly'.[1] In Breitenbach's view, then, the frontispiece image, like 'vignettes and so forth', has no intrinsic interest in the illustrated fictional work. It may matter when associated with a sequence of pictures, but it does not hold great significance as an individual image. It is, at best, a pendant to a series of book illustrations. In contrast to Breitenbach's view, other scholars, such as Gérard Genette,[2] have foregrounded the value of para-textual components in general, while others still have emphasised the value of visual components, and especially of frontispieces. Janine Barchas, for instance, devotes a full chapter of *Graphic Design, Print Culture, and the Eighteenth-Century Novel* to 'the genre of the frontispiece' and 'its rhetorical status' in the print culture of the eighteenth century.[3] She notes that editorial practice concerning modern editions and reprints of eighteenth-century novels has not paid enough attention to 'the genre's original appearance as a printed book, ignoring its layout, prefatory puffs, end matter, and graphic design and dismissing its punctuation and ornamentations as "accidentals"'. To her, 'the insipid uniformity of modern paperback editions of eighteenth-century fiction' is both a distortion and a diminishment of 'the early novel's graphic diversity', and a testimony to the difficulty of 'resurrect[ing] the genre's lost visual dynamism'.[4]

Barchas's work in *Graphic Design* focuses mostly on the frontispiece portrait of the author, which emerged in England as a prominent feature of book production during the seventeenth century.[5] Her analysis of this phenomenon highlights parallels between eighteenth-century portraiture and literary innovation within the compass of the printed book.[6] In her study of the 'graphic anatomy' and 'graphic genomics' of the novel, the frontispiece figures among what she identifies as the six significant visual features that attended the reading of early novels, along with title pages, non-pictorial illustrations, ornamentation, punctuation and catalogues.[7] Although these elements have mostly disappeared from modern editions, resulting in our unfamiliarity with them, they originally played a key role, not only in 'the novel's printed look' but also in 'the novel's textual body', and the book's formation as an aesthetic whole. Moreover, Barchas claims, frontispieces 'demand a special visual-verbal consideration' vital to informing our understanding of how far the early British novel 'depends for its literary effects upon its graphic appearance as a printed book'.[8] Gladly, the interaction between text, book production and reception has become a cornerstone of eighteenth-century studies.

While Barchas rightfully acknowledges that the frontispieces found in eighteenth-century novels 'disappear and re-appear, along with other under-studied paratexts and original print features',[9] they also reappear in numerous other forms and contexts besides. She also leaves aside the crucial question of the relationship between a frontispiece – and the complex interpretations it invites – and any other illustrations in the volume in which it appears, besides observing that there was a significant expansion of book illustration mid-century, meaning that booksellers were not reluctant to invest in such visual material per se even if the authorial frontispiece itself witnessed a decline in popularity.[10] The book industry certainly invested heavily in series of illustrations meant to feature in the body of the text rather than at its outskirts, moving away from presenting the frontispiece as the main (if not the only) iconographic and visual component of the novel, a shift in the production of English novels highly visible from the mid-eighteenth century to the mid-nineteenth century, and even towards its latter decades.

This chapter is directly concerned with the visual and material reappearance of eighteenth-century frontispieces in interartistic and intermedial creations that testify to the eighteenth-century novel's circulation in varied and multiple forms. It shifts attention from what Barchas considers to be 'print culture's appetite for graphic design and visual novelty' towards the appetite of both polite and popular cultures for the refashioning of iconic book images inspired by frontispieces into a wide variety of visual and material artefacts.[11] The essay is interested not so much in how the arts operate within the space of the novelistic text and genre, but rather in how they function beyond that space, in both visual culture and material culture, to reconsider interartistic connections between the novel and its iconographic, visual and material expressions. The aim is to assess the lasting influence of the novel in forms other than the text and the book, and in places beyond its original contexts of production and reception.

Iconic Frontispieces: From One Prototype to the Next

One of the most famous frontispieces, if not the most famous ever attached to an eighteenth-century novel, is undoubtedly John Clark and John Pine's 1719 engraved interpretation of Robinson Crusoe after an unknown artist for the first edition of Defoe's novel, which was published in London in April 1719 by William Taylor (Figure 23.1). David Blewett calls it the 'haunting portrait of Crusoe' and sees in it 'a powerful influence on Crusoe portraiture ever since'.[12] According to Robert Folkenflik, too, it is 'arguably the most iconic book illustration of an eighteenth-century novel', which, as well as being frequently reprinted as the sole image accompanying the first edition, became 'the model' for the visualisation of Crusoe.[13] Folkenflik highlights the long-lasting visual power of Clark and Pine's original, as well as its effective intervisual legacy in later reconfigurations. A frontispiece may indeed become a visual icon and remain a constant source of inspiration for iconographic and, more largely, visual retellers in a wide variety of contexts, including stage play directors, film producers

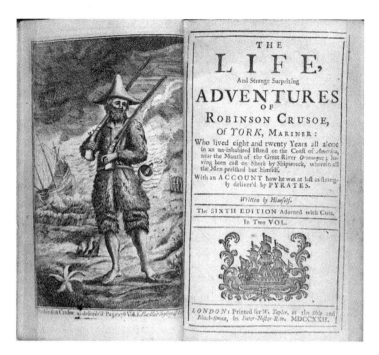

Figure 23.1 Unknown artist, frontispiece to *The Life and Strange Surprizing Adventures of Robinson Crusoe of York, Mariner* (London: W. Taylor, 1719). Etching by John Clark and John Pine. Courtesy of Beinecke Rare Book and Manuscript Library, Yale University.

and game designers.[14] It may also become the basis for an array of material refashionings, which are indebted not so much to the source text they incarnate but rather to its original iconographic interpretation(s).

Clark and Pine's frontispiece image has been widely examined and discussed in the scholarship devoted to Defoe, *Robinson Crusoe* and eighteenth-century book illustration more widely. Blewett's pioneering analyses have been taken up and debated by numerous critics, including Barchas, Helen Cole and Folkenflik.[15] For Blewett (quoted by Barchas), this frontispiece 'offers us a compression of various events in a single picture', according to an eighteenth-century illustrative style which Barchas calls 'allegorical summary'.[16] She considers Clark and Pine's image to be an 'old-fashioned frontispiece' that encapsulates the entire story, and which 'looks backwards to the text's literary heritage rather than forwards to a new print culture paradigm'.[17] It therefore seems to be at odds with Defoe's 'modernist realism and novelistic ambitions'; and yet it is almost alone among eighteenth-century novelistic frontispieces in having attained a canonical status of its own.[18]

In her analysis of frontispieces to English fiction from 1690 to 1740, Cole uses Defoe's *The Life and Strange Surprising Adventures of Robinson Crusoe* and Giovanni Paolo Marana's *Letters Writ by a Turkish Spy* as examples of where 'a novel's frontispiece engraving has been repeated across eighteenth-century editions', creating an enduring afterlife for an illustration originally allied to a specific novel. By mid-eighteenth century, she explains, new editions of the *Letters* and *Robinson Crusoe* 'came with frontispiece

400 NATHALIE COLLÉ

designs that had little changed in decades'.[19] Although indebted to the practice of recycling images used by earlier printers – as evidenced by the tenacity of the frontispiece design to many editions of John Bunyan's *The Pilgrim's Progress* from the seventeenth century onwards – such 'repeated images' appear 'at their boldest and most anomalous' in the eighteenth century, as 'their repetition seems to contradict the period's perception of itself as restlessly inventive'.[20]

Blewett explains that Clark and Pine's frontispiece was continually reprinted in all authorised editions of the text over the next sixty years and had 'a lasting influence on Crusoe portraiture' – despite the fact that it 'poses several problems of interpretation'.[21] Pat Rogers notes that most abridgements of *Robinson Crusoe* 'have one initial cut [which] corresponds to the illustration in the first edition (1719)', and which repeat 'crucial factors in the design'.[22] Cole adds that 'approximations' of this image were published in both authorised and unauthorised editions over subsequent decades, giving the portrait universal recognisability, even beyond its source text.[23] Both Blewett and Cole refer, like others before and after, to A. Edward Newton's 1925 famous and enduring statement on Clark and Pine's design:

> This illustration has outlasted several centuries of criticism. We always look for it and are disappointed when we do not find it. . . . It has come to be the accepted portrait; no legend is required: one knows that he is looking at Robinson Crusoe.[24]

As Cole remarks, it was not rare to see a graphic image reappear in several editions of a literary work, yet 'the scale of the repetition' is outstanding in the case of *Robinson Crusoe*. Even though certain narrative moments repeatedly attract the attention of illustrators – as the numerous iconographic interpretations of Crusoe's discovery of the footprint or of Friday's willing submission to his saviour later testify – it is more unusual to see frontispiece illustrations that depict a narrative moment or a scene 'take hold lastingly'. When they do, they typically 'inspire varied, distinctive interpretations' rather than demonstrate 'the steady adherence to a visual paradigm'.[25]

In trying to understand the uncommon lifespan of the Crusoe frontispiece in a context that indicates 'the fleeting nature of much literary illustration', as well as '[a] fascination with novelty' in 'most aspects of eighteenth-century cultural life', Cole turns to material culture specialists.[26] Relying on Maxine Berg's analysis of luxury and pleasure in the period, she equates readers with other types of consumer, books with goods and fiction with a product, and concludes that readers, like other consumers, desired novelty and aspired to variety.[27] Cole opposes the reality of publishers' and booksellers' practices, and the evidence of bibliography, to the uncertainty of authorial involvement in and readerly response to the image of what Blewett terms 'the timeless figure of the castaway'.[28] The commercial context, on the one hand, 'provides the best evidence of a positive reception for frontispiece designs', as such extensive repetition of the same image indicates that it was unlikely to have met with an unfavourable response. On the other hand, whether or not a reader liked or even became attached to a particular image was effectively down to 'booksellers' commercial thought processes' about what might sell.[29]

In Cole's conception, 'Crusoe's mournful figure in his signature goatskin clothing identified a brand that could be *Robinson Crusoe* the novel, the writing of Daniel Defoe or even fiction itself' – including unauthorised versions of the work: the famous woodcut

portrait of Crusoe as the frontispiece to such a volume unjustifiably yet assuredly introduced it as Defoe's original text.[30] The frontispiece's association with misleading selling
tactics, however, pertains to Defoe's authentic work for some critics. In Folkenflik's view,
the inclusion of a frontispiece illustration of the eponymous character in the first edition
of *Robinson Crusoe* supports the notion that this is 'a counterfeit autobiography rather
than as a novel', just as 'the first-edition illustrations of *Gulliver's Travels* (1726) accompany its parody of *Crusoe* to suggest a travel book or autobiography'. Folkenflik argues
that, typically, frontispiece portraits of the author predominantly fronted posthumous
collected works, whereas few novels represented their fictional first-person narrators at
the outset, as this would break the illusion of reality. Their booksellers opted instead
for illustrations that drew from the fictional narrative itself. Clark and Pine's image of
Crusoe, therefore, is 'a clever case of the frontispiece portrait as part of the illusion'.[31] As
Blewett and others have noted, a slightly revised and anonymous version of the image
appeared in the sixth edition of the novel, published in 1722, with an altered background
(a rougher sea, darker and stormier sky and battered ship) which, leaving Crusoe 'looking
curiously unperturbed',[32] creates further interpretative problems in suggesting his 'psychological detachment from his own story'.[33] This version also figured in the chapbooks
and penny novels of the nineteenth century, in which it announced the seafaring component of the story.[34]

The first French translation of *Robinson Crusoe*, which appeared in 1720, included
another frontispiece portrait of Crusoe by the distinguished French engraver Bernard
Picart (Figure 23.2), along with a series of six unsigned and inferior engravings, probably not by Picart himself. According to Blewett, Picart 'was clearly familiar with Clark
and Pine's engraving', as the choice of subject and several details indicate; furthermore,
Pine 'was almost certainly a former pupil of his'. Blewett finds Picart's engraving '[t]
echnically superior' and more accurate in detail, having 'the benefit of familiarity with
the text', which it follows more closely 'in the details of Crusoe's appearance'. But for
all their differences, Blewett suggests that the two frontispieces 'are alike in creating
an enduring visual image of the extraordinary figure who so impressed himself upon
the European imagination'.[35] Folkenflik also comments on Picart's use of Clark and
Pine's image as a model, such as in its rendering of Crusoe's 'elegantly placed feet and
a few other details in the portrait largely drawn from the novel's earliest description of
Crusoe on his island'.[36] According to Folkenflik, however, Picart 'is not more accurate'
than Clark and Pine in his depiction; rather, he simply 'engraves the better-known
description of Crusoe with his "*Mahomatan* Whiskers" and "Muschatoes", saw
rather than sword, and umbrella'.[37] Picart also introduced the parasol, another iconic
element in future representations of Crusoe on the island, both visual and material.

Picart's visual image of Crusoe endured throughout the eighteenth century in regular editions, as well as in pirate versions and chapbooks. It was later remodelled by
Thomas Stothard, who first produced seven drawings for Defoe's novel in two volumes,
in James Harrison's reprint series *The Novelist's Magazine* in 1781, and then contributed a new set of drawings engraved by Thomas Medland for a 1790 edition published by John Stockdale. In the 1790 Stockdale edition – which, according to Blewett,
offers 'the first English pictorial treatment of *Robinson Crusoe* as a progress', one that
'de-emphasi[ses] the solitary aspect' and illustrates 'more social scenes'[38] – the frontispiece to volume 1 no longer pictures the stranded and island-established Crusoe, but the
young and insecure man taking leave of his distressed parents. The iconic figure appears,

Figure 23.2 Bernard Picart, frontispiece to *La Vie et les avantures surprenantes de Robinson Crusoe* (Amsterdam: L'Honoré & Chatelain, 1720). Engraving. Courtesy of Beinecke Rare Book and Manuscript Library, Yale University.

however, towards the end of the island section of the novel, featuring as an attendant illustration now integrated into a pictorial narrative. It was restored to frontispiece status in the 1804 Stockdale edition, and reproduced in later editions, with other illustrations, engraved by Charles Heath the elder and published by Cadell and Davies (Figure 23.3). For Folkenflik, this new portrait is an imitation of Clark and Pine's frontispiece, while for Jakub Lipski it represents 'another memorable pictorial moment' from the novel itself (like the discovery of the footprint, the meeting with Friday or the building of the ship), one which reverses the perspective of Crusoe as the focaliser.[39] In addition, the background 'against which Crusoe poses' omits the sea, sky and ship and 'shows no human interference whatsoever'; his figure therefore 'merges with the background – an effect achieved by the engraver's use of the same technique for the castaway's outfit and the leaves of the trees behind him', according to Lipski.[40] The result is that, '[r]ather than showing how Robinson transformed the space' (notably through the palisade, which represents Crusoe's colonialising and territorial impulses), apparently 'the space transformed the man and gave birth to a new "natural" Crusoe'.[41] Since the island no longer shares the background with the sea, sky and ship – as in the earlier two illustrations – the seafaring elements have vanished; the island itself has become the subject of the composition, and the figure of Crusoe himself, combining elements drawn from both the Clark and Pine and the Picart images, is now fused with rather than set against his environment. Thus, the originally 'foregrounded Crusoe', with the sinking ship on one side and his cave set into the hillside on the other, 'emphasizing their centrality to his survival', is

Figure 23.3 Thomas Stothard, *Robinson Crusoe in his island dress* (1782), engraved by C. Heath, in *Robinson Crusoe* (London: T. Cadell & W. Davis, 1820), facing p. 92. Engraving. Private collection.

now represented as having adapted to his new milieu.[42] Moreover, in the Stockdale edition, the original 'author' portrait has given way to a conversation piece, the frontispiece to volume 1 picturing young Crusoe facing his distressed parents, while the frontispiece to volume 2 represents Crusoe's return to the island and encounter with the Spaniards. Together, Blewett notes, the two frontispieces depict 'tender moments' and 'enlarg[e] the degree of intimacy and affection in the story'.[43]

'Probably *because* they idealized Crusoe's life on the island', in Blewett's words, Stothard's designs, re-engraved by Remi-Henri-Joseph Delvaux, were chosen by the French publisher Charles Panckoucke for a 1799–1800 edition of *Robinson Crusoe* produced in Paris and prefaced by the approbative 'Jugement de Jean-Jacques Rousseau sur Robinson'. They were complemented by additional scenes, including an image that features 'the more-or-less obligatory portrait of Crusoe in his goatskins'.[44] This former frontispiece portrait now turned 'plot-inspired illustration', to use Teri Doerksen's phrase, reappeared in various subsequent editions with yet further new illustrations.[45] Two editions published by Stockdale in 1804 give the image pride of place; the more expensive volume inserts it in the body of the text, although it does not appear in the opening list of plates, whereas the smaller and cheaper volume elevates it to the status of a frontispiece. Although '[a]n unexciting design, even by Stothard's standards', according to Blewett, it is 'remarkable' in showing 'the extraordinary hold of the original frontispiece upon the expectation of readers'.[46] Sometimes entitled or captioned 'Robinson Crusoe in his island dress', Stothard's drawing was not only reinstalled as a frontispiece in various nineteenth- and early twentieth-century editions; it also appeared as a loose print in portfolios of assorted images. For instance, a copy of Stothard's portrait engraved by Charles Heath was published by Cadell and Davies in their 1820 edition of *Robinson Crusoe*, but also as a stand-alone image that now forms part of a set of thirty-five prints and photographs of various subjects held in the Upcher Collection at Sheringham Hall, Norfolk. The portrait has therefore lived a life of its own independent from Defoe's text and from his published editions of it, testifying to the power of the iconic Crusoe beyond its original contexts of circulation and reception.

From Print Culture to Material Culture, or from Visual to Material Icons

The ongoing pictorialisation of Crusoe through frontispieces and attendant illustrations has thus relied on three major eighteenth-century sources and models: Clark and Pine's 1719 original interpretation, Picart's 1720 version and Stothard's 1790 reinterpretation. There is indeed not one 'model for the visualization of Crusoe';[47] there are in fact three, and those three have had long-lasting visual power and provided an effective intervisual legacy for publishers and readers alike. All three book illustrations have become visual icons and constant sources of inspiration for iconographic, visual and material refashioners of *Crusoe*. Anyone seeing an image of Crusoe modelled on one or the other of these three prototypes will immediately recognise the face and figure of the adventurer, whether the viewer knows *Robinson Crusoe* or not. 'No legend is required', to repeat Newton's words, and that statement holds true whether the face and figure appear in books or elsewhere, that is, in literary culture, in visual culture or in popular culture. Like the authentic author portraits that fronted texts from the early days of printing, and which were sometimes cut out from books and 'sent along with letters, pasted to walls, [or] individually sold', the fictional author portraits that accompanied early novels have also had 'a life apart from book[s]', in various forms and media.[48] They have also no doubt been used as extra-illustrations in extra-illustrated or grangerised books.[49]

The most famous materialisation of Robinson Crusoe in non-book form is, perhaps ironically, the bronze statue erected to Alexander Selkirk, or Selcraig (1676–1721), the Scottish sailor who was allegedly Crusoe's prototype (Figure 23.4). Situated at the site of Selkirk's original house on Main Street in Lower Largo, a coastal village in Fife, Scotland, 'this real-life Robinson Crusoe, looking out to sea', is evidently modelled on the iconic frontispieces discussed here, in particular Stothard's.[50] It shows Selkirk clad in goatskins, wearing a rounded hat, beard and whiskers, holding a musket, and with axe, pistol and sword attached to his belt, awaiting rescue from the Juan Fernandez Islands off the coast of Chile. The half-tone statue was created by Thomas Stuart Burnett, donated by David Gillies of Cardy House – a manufacturer of nets and a descendant of the Selkirks – and unveiled by Lady Aberdeen in December 1885. The unveiling was accompanied by a procession and speeches that took place in front of a large crowd, and occasioned street decorations and celebrations.[51] Signposts in the village present the piece as 'the Robinson Crusoe statue', and Lower Largo as the 'Birth Place of "Robinson Crusoe"', thus conflating eighteenth-century history and fiction in the eyes and minds of both locals and visitors.

In October 1987, this iconic statue was removed from its niche in the Crusoe Buildings on Main Street and taken to Perthshire for restoration by Bill Hepworth of the Alyth Art Foundry. Before returning home, the Selkirk/Crusoe statue 'went on an adventure' to the Glasgow Garden Festival, which ran from 26 April to 26 September 1988. It was placed at ground level in the 'Water and Maritime' themed section of the festival, alongside tall ships, navy ships and water sports, an area designed to display Scotland's rich history of maritime trade and exploration. Deprived of its intended elevated position, it was set against a new background and painted green.[52]

Like all the other statues in the exhibition, Selkirk/Crusoe did not make the same impression on the Glasgow Garden Festival visitors as it had done and has continued to do on Largo visitors and locals. According to local bloggers, 'Largo folks were relieved

Figure 23.4 Statue of Alexander Selkirk at the site of his original house on Main Street, Lower Largo, Fife, Scotland (1885). Photograph by Sylvia Stanley (23 September 2009). Sylvia Stanley, CC BY-SA 3.0, https://creativecommons.org/licenses/by-sa/3.0, via Wikimedia Commons.

to see him return home, restored to his normal colour!'[53] Thus, the book-frontispiece-turned-statue has itself become iconic, but it is also site-dependent in order to make the strongest impression: if its iconographic predecessor was meant for the specific niche of a book intended for a frontispiece or other illustration, then the statue is meant for the niche of a building and is strongly associated with a specific place. The statue, it seems, and the man/character it represents, belongs to Largo rather than to literary history and culture.

The Selkirk/Crusoe statue has enjoyed its own afterlives in visual and material cultures, beyond its existence in the two locations discussed so far. For example, a picture of its unveiling adorns the Crusoe Hotel in Largo. In addition, black and white, as well as colour postcards of the statue have been manufactured and sent around the world; they are now collectible items that are occasionally available on e-commerce websites such as eBay. In 1963, West Yorkshire graphic artist Paul Sharp produced a small pen and ink drawing representing the statue on site, seen from the street and from behind a group of three consisting of a man, two children and two cats. In 1886, an engraving of the statue by William Ballingall, a local of Largo, had served as an illustration to an issue of *Home Words*, a monthly religious Victorian penny magazine. It presents the statue on a pedestal, not at its actual location but set against a mountainous background that slightly recalls Clark and Pine's original scene, rather than Stothard's. The magazine illustration reintroduces the island location component of both the story and the original book frontispieces, and it presents the Stothard-inspired figure of Selkirk/Crusoe inland, looking out to the horizon.

A Stothard-and-Picart-inspired Crusoe also occupies the foreground of the relief plaque that enhances the wall of a small cafe in Queen's Gardens in Kingston upon Hull (usually abbreviated to Hull), an English port city in East Yorkshire (Figure 23.5). The 'run down, somewhat seedy establishment . . . with a tacky sign' is associated with pop music via Mick Ronson, a local musician who played with David Bowie, while the five-foot-high plaque is a celebration of Robinson Crusoe's departure from Hull on 1 September 1651, according to Defoe's account. The plaque is accompanied by the following inscription:

> Robinson Crusoe, most famous character in fiction, sailed from here September 1st, 1651. Sole survivor from a shipwreck, he was cast up on a desert island where he spent 28 years, 2 months and 19 days. An example of resolution, fortitude, and self-reliance. 'Had I the sense to return to Hull, I had been happy'.[54]

It was designed by local artist Harry Ibbetson, paid for by public subscription and unveiled by the Lord Mayor, Alderman Lionel Rosen, on 21 May 1973. It has also found an afterlife in a limited edition, amber earthenware replica made by Eastgate Pottery, Withernsea, East Yorkshire and sold by former Hull department store Hammonds, with

Figure 23.5 Robinson Crusoe monument, in what is now Queen's Gardens, Hull but what would then have been Queens Dock (1973). Photograph by Steve F-E-Cameron (2007). Steve F-E-Cameron (Merlin-UK), CC BY-SA 3.0, http://creativecommons.org/licenses/by-sa/3.0/, via Wikimedia Commons.

a card giving details about it.[55] In both items, Crusoe is pictured in the foreground with his iconic attributes, including his dog, while the background emphasises the seafaring element (the sea and the ship) as well as the island location (the mountains) with birds linking the two.

Some reinterpreters of the iconic frontispiece(s) have dispensed with the background altogether, focusing on the character only. The creator of the Café Martin Robinson Crusoe, number 22 of a series of 24 gilded plastic 'Sports' figurines dating back to 1958, chose to give shape to Stothard's Crusoe, with rags, musket, gourd, back basket and parrot. A late eighteenth-century French creation now sold as an antique proposed an unusual combination of Picart's parasol with the later iconographic motif of the parrot, along with musket, belt knife and gourd – all iconic elements of Crusoe portraiture now assembled in a gilded bronze and mother-of-pearl decorative figurine.[56] With this figurine, the 'background' is now provided by the place or environment where the object is displayed rather than by the artist, consisting of open space rather than the engraved lines that compose a fixed backdrop for the figure of the castaway in a book illustration. The context of display and of perception is therefore changeable, insofar as the figurine is likely to be placed (and therefore seen and interpreted) in different places and environments. Altogether, these multiple figurines testify to Crusoe's image's adaptability to interpretative mediums and changing contexts of reception.

The material embodiments of Crusoe, then, often rely on its original representations in graphic and visual culture, which they sometimes combine. But in examples such as the bronze figurine, these former frontispiece(s)-turned-objects become homely goods intended for decoration and display. Other bronze or lead figurines of Crusoe, as well as home-made dolls, have indeed been produced and sold worldwide as collectible pieces, testifying to the lasting popularity of the story and of its archetypal character with consumers, if not always readers of Defoe. The one-dimensional images previously inscribed on paper become three-dimensional visual artefacts that occupy private spaces, serving decorative and affective functions rather than purely literary and editorial ones.

The early frontispieces to *Robinson Crusoe* also inspired nineteenth- and early twentieth-century French artists working to attract Parisians and tourists to the *guinguettes*, those popular destinations for day trippers looking for an exotic place for 'ample drinking, simple eating and lively dancing'.[57] Traditionally, *guinguettes* were located next to a river or a lake in the Parisian suburbs. In 1848, Joseph Gueusquin, an experienced cabaret manager, changed the concept and built 'a suite of interconnected tree houses in a majestic chestnut tree' situated in a forest southwest of Paris, which he named 'Au Grand Robinson'. According to a blog post on the website *Images Musicales*, Gueusquin 'had confused Daniel Defoe's *Robinson Crusoe* who lived in a cave and "The Swiss Family Robinson" who lived in a tree house as described by Johann Wyss in his book from 1813'.[58] He and his successors capitalised on the popularity of the story and myth of Robinson Crusoe. It is said that, alonsgide the Parisian elite, a Spanish king and a Russian tsar visited the place. 'Au Grand Robinson' was renamed 'Le Vrai Arbre Robinson' in 1888, and eventually transformed into a ranch baptised 'Robinson Village' in the 1960s, swapping 'the spirit of Robinson Crusoe' for 'that of the American Wild West', before eventually closing down in 1976.

Three statues were created in the 1930s to serve as signs on the facades of the huts of the *guinguette* and to attract clients, thus evoking the original association between frontispieces and architecture. The first statue was the work of Henri Le Pecq. It was made around 1930 to serve as a sign for Le Vrai Arbre de Robinson, which was then run by Noël Ratti, and installed after the Liberation of France from German occupation during the Second World War. It was later bought by the Robinson *guinguette*'s direct competitor and finally donated to the city of Le Plessis-Robinson (originally Plessis-Piquet but officially renamed after Le Grand Robinson in 1909 – just as Juan Fernandes was renamed 'Robinson Crusoe Island' in the 1960s). When Le Vrai Arbre closed in 1966, its historic competitor, Le Grand Arbre, bought the statue. Its last owners, Monsieur and Madame Fayoux, donated it to the town of Plessis-Robinson. It has adorned Robinson's garden since its opening in 1999.[59]

Ever since the establishment opened in 1848, the exotic figure of Robinson Crusoe was used to attract customers. Over the years, three statues were added to the *guinguette*'s entrance. Noticeably, the three Robinson Crusoe statues that were made to front the various buildings of the Robinson *guinguette* are all direct descendants of the early frontispieces to the novel, and they all display the iconic attributes of Crusoe: the goatskins and boots, the hat, the parrot and the parasol or musket. One of them introduces the character of Friday to the scene, walking behind Crusoe and dressed in leopard skin. Another offers a variation on Crusoe's traditional front-facing pose, presenting instead a semi-profile, emphasising the parrot in a theatrical gesture.

The statues were photographed and turned into postcards for tourists to buy – postcards being another form of iconographic afterlife of the original frontispieces. The caption of a postcard representing the statue of Crusoe and Friday reads: 'Venez, Joyeux Amants, Robinson vous invite sous ses Ombrages frais à lui rendre Visite' (Come, Happy Lovers, Robinson invites you under his cool Shades to visit him).

For visitors, the statues therefore served as an invitation to enter the buildings, as much as (or perhaps even more so than) the original fictional universe they stood for – just as the original book frontispieces had done. The statues fronting the *guinguette* indeed find a fascinating echo in original, architectural frontispieces, those elements that framed and decorated the main or front door to a building. As French philosopher, historian, semiologist and art critic Louis Marin reminds us, the term 'frontispiece' was 'imported into the book, or at its frontier, from the field of architecture'. It was subsequently used to refer to 'a kind of pictorial preface, a picture at the threshold of the book and at the threshold of the reading of the book'.[60] It stands as the 'main and frontal face of a volume, which it illustrates', in all the meanings of the term, including by granting it 'lustre, price and value'.[61] The frontispiece highlights both the title and the work, having an economic and an aesthetic impact, as well as an interpretative one.[62] Being possibly the first image in a series, which it opens and prefaces or prefigures, the frontispiece literally puts to the fore certain aspects of the work, which it thus illustrates as well.[63] Graphic frontispieces are therefore keys to the books and texts they accompany, and, in the case of the novel, entrance doors to the fictional universes they precede and announce. In Genette's terms, they are 'thresholds of interpretation'.[64]

Conclusion

The history of the Robinson *guinguette* and of the Parisian city that welcomed its huts and statues, as well as the history of the numerous artefacts that have been created and sold worldwide based on images of Crusoe, testify to the long-lasting popularity and far-reaching effects of eighteenth-century novelistic frontispieces. These frontispieces' first move away from print culture into visual and material cultures was through separately printed or cut out pictures being framed and used as posters. Their refashioning into images of all sorts has helped to perpetuate literary characters and scenes through time, beyond the book market and literary sphere, and into both polite and popular cultures. Originally elements of 'the graphic packaging and repackaging' of books, frontispieces testify as much to 'the troublesome mutability of the printed book' as to that of the novel's 'graphic genetics'.[65] In addition to their mutation in iconographic contents, they have produced a wide variety of visual and material afterlives for favourite novels, modifying their own genetics in the process, as well as that of novelistic characters and scenes. They have also mutated from pictorial book illustrations to material three-dimensional objects. They are therefore what I call 'extended illustrations' in the sense that they materialise beyond the book and the page, and 'expanded illustrations' in the sense that they materialise in forms other than the iconographic.

Frontispieces not only formed part of the emerging, developing and maturing novel's material embodiment as a printed book and of its presentation as an illustrated text; they also contributed to the shaping of the material, visual and textual identity of the novel genre, and to the lasting popularity of its favourite texts. In whatever form they took and style they displayed, frontispieces participated in the emergence of the novel as both genre and artefact. They provided a visual co-text for its developing narrative and evolving contents, in all imaginable forms, including very material ones. To be sure, the textual ingenuity and experimentation typical of the eighteenth-century novel found an echo in the visual ingenuity and experimentation of its accompanying frontispieces, as well as in the material ingenuity of their numerous afterlives. Originally 'pictorial preface[s]' or 'picture[s] at the threshold' of books and texts, frontispieces to eighteenth-century fiction mutated into a variety of material postfaces, or 'afterfacts – artefacts of the afterlife' (in Tom Blackburn's words) of literary texts.[66] They have perpetuated these texts far beyond their original contexts of production and reception, and they have brought them to recirculate in sometimes strange and surprising forms. The study of frontispieces and of their place and role in the history of the novel is therefore an interdisciplinary endeavour that involves bibliography, book history and print culture, as well as visual and material cultures.

Finally, the publication and post-publication histories of *Robinson Crusoe* illustrate the fact that favourite frontispiece images came to be reissued, copied, imitated, transformed and then recast in forms and contexts other than, and with effects different from, those originally intended. The question we may ask, in the end, is whether the history of the numerous artefacts based on book images of Crusoe testifies to the popularity and persistence of eighteenth-century novel frontispieces in general, or of *Robinson Crusoe*'s in particular. To my knowledge, the only equivalent in terms of lasting popularity and appeal was the original frontispiece to the seventeenth-century predecessor to the English novel, that is, Robert White's sleeping portrait of John Bunyan's *Pilgrim's Progress* (1678), which was also reissued, copied, imitated, transformed and recast in other contexts, forms and media – though in a more limited range than Crusoe's frontispiece images. Bunyan's *Progress* being a precursor of the novel rather than a novel per se, the comparison does not allow us to draw conclusions that are specific to the eighteenth-century novel. Yet it attests to the visual power of some frontispieces in relation to certain fictional works, and to their malleability and adaptability when subject to various intentions and recipients, in various media.

Undoubtedly, the mythical status of grand narratives such as *Robinson Crusoe* and, previously, *The Pilgrim's Progress*, together with the iconic dimension of their central characters, have inspired and guaranteed their ongoing visual and material refashioning and adaptations. In other words, it is the (literary history and canon-induced) mythical status of these narratives, combined with the (book illustration-induced) iconic status of their protagonists, that has ensured their long-lasting and widespread existence and popularity in multiple forms and media. In the case of *Robinson Crusoe*, one example lies in the picturesque Robinson huts that appeared in late eighteenth-century gardens,[67] or, more recently, the Robinson bungalows and restaurants that have opened throughout the world and which a visitor can rent or book in a couple of clicks on the Internet. One, relatively recent, example is the Crusoe Cabana Deluxe restaurant and lounge that opened in Wynwood, Miami, in Florida, on 25 May 2022. The food is meant to 'provoke[e] reaction, and mak[e] every guest feel like a mariner', while the decor is 'designed to transport [you] into the 1700s landing on a remote tropical desert island along with Crusoe himself'. Guests are 'lured to embark on . . . a culinary and sensory voyage, drawing inspiration from the famed novel', in 'an ambience straight out of Crusoe's odyssey'.[68] The aim is to transport the visitor into Crusoe's world and time in order for him or her to live the ultimate Crusoe experience in a visual, tactile, gustative, olfactory and auditory way – yet another, multiple form of literary afterlife.

To be sure, not many eighteenth-century novels and their illustrations ever exerted such universal appeal as *Robinson Crusoe* and its illustrations, and not all eighteenth-century frontispieces were matter for visual appropriation and material adaptation. Adaptation certainly allows, and perhaps also encourages, mobility between texts and images of all types, but recognisability cum iconicity is undeniably one of the key factors of the post-book afterlife and popularity of novels and of their characters: it seems, indeed, that not all texts and images are equal in this respect. Recognisability and iconicity are undoubtedly the assets of such worldly stories and figures as Bunyan's Christian and Defoe's Crusoe (and Selkirk, for that matter), guaranteeing commercial success to the visual appropriators and material refashioners who have continually capitalised on them – even at times when and in spheres where the original texts no longer seem to be read or have been subsumed by their adaptations. At a present-day point when *Robinson Crusoe* is consumed and experienced as much as it is read, if not more, it seems fair to assert that recognisability and iconicity, and the type of identification that both allow, are the bedrocks on which the ongoing commercialisation of Crusoe images and artefacts has relied, and the foundations on which the enduring postmodern reappropriation of the early book images has rested. In other words, the early frontispieces to *Robinson Crusoe* are the bases on which Crusoe's multiple afterlives have thrived and Crusoe's brand name has rested.[69] They are also perhaps, in some cases, people's first and only entries into the original 1719 text.

Notes

1. Edgar Breitenbach, 'The Bibliography of Illustrated Books: Notes with Two Examples from English Book Illustration of the 18th Century', in *A History of Book Illustration: 29 Points of View*, ed. Bill Katz (Metuchen and London: Scarecrow Press, 1994), 299.

This chapter was originally published in *The Library Association Record* II (1935): 176–85.

2. Gérard Genette, *Paratexts: Thresholds of Interpretation*, trans. Jane E. Lewin (Cambridge: Cambridge University Press, 1997).

3. Janine Barchas, *Graphic Design, Print Culture, and the Eighteenth-Century Novel* (Cambridge: Cambridge University Press, 2003), 21. Most of the arguments developed in this chapter previously featured in Barchas's 'Prefiguring Genre: Frontispiece Portraits from *Gulliver's Travels* to *Millenium Hall*', *Studies in the Novel* 30, no. 2 (1998): 260–86.

4. Barchas, *Graphic Design*, 6.

5. Barchas, *Graphic Design*, 21. According to A. Hyatt Mayor, the genre emerged much earlier than that as '[m]any grand manuscripts in antiquity and the Middle Ages began with a full-page frontispiece showing the author at his desk. The first elaborate printed frontispiece alluding to the author was designed by the Dutch artist Erhard Reuwich for Breydenbach's *Pilgrimage to the Holy Land* (Mainz, 1486)'. *Prints & People: A Social History of Printed Pictures* (Princeton: Princeton University Press, 1971), 'Title page and frontispiece', n.p. (ills. on pages 211–14).

6. Barchas, *Graphic Design*, 20, 22.

7. Barchas, *Graphic Design*, 7.

8. Barchas, *Graphic Design*, 7–8.

9. Barchas, 'Prefiguring Genre', 264.

10. Barchas, *Graphic Design*, 59.

11. Barchas, *Graphic Design*, 41.

12. David Blewett, 'The Iconic Crusoe: Illustrations and Images of *Robinson Crusoe*', in *The Cambridge Companion to 'Robinson Crusoe'*, ed. John Richetti (Cambridge: Cambridge University Press, 2018), 159, 160.

13. Robert Folkenflik, 'The Rise of the Illustrated English Novel to 1832', in *The Oxford Handbook of the Eighteenth-Century Novel*, ed. J. A. Downie (Oxford: Oxford University Press, 2016), 313.

14. The British Library website presents it as the 'iconic frontispiece' that 'shows Crusoe in his goatskin jacket and cap, with guns slung over his shoulders'. 'First edition of Daniel Defoe's *Robinson Crusoe*, 1719', https://www.bl.uk/collection-items/first-edition-of-daniel-defoes-robinson-crusoe-1719 (accessed 22 November 2023).

15. See, by David Blewett, *The Illustration of* Robinson Crusoe, *1719–1920* (Gerrards Cross: Smythe, 1995); 'Robinson Crusoe, Friday, and the Noble Savage: The Illustration of the Rescue of Friday Scene in the Eighteenth Century', *Man and Nature / L'homme et la nature* 5 (1986): 29–49; 'The Illustration of *Robinson Crusoe*: 1719–1840', in *Imagination on a Long Rein: English Literature Illustrated*, ed. Joachim Möller (Marburg: Jonas Verlag, 1988), 66–81; and, more recently, 'The Iconic Crusoe: Illustrations and Images of *Robinson Crusoe*'. See also Helen Cole, 'From the Familiar to the New: Frontispiece Engravings to Fiction in England from 1690 to 1740', *Journal for Eighteenth-Century Studies* 39, no. 4 (2016): 489–511.

16. Barchas, *Graphic Design*, 29.

17. Barchas, *Graphic Design*, 46, 47.

18. Barchas, *Graphic Design*, 47, 48.

19. Cole, 'From the Familiar to the New', 489.

20. Cole, 'From the Familiar to the New', 489–90.

21. Blewett, *The Illustration of* Robinson Crusoe, 27. These problems are discussed by Cole and Folkenflik.

22. Pat Rogers, 'Classics and Chapbooks', in *Books and Their Readers in Eighteenth-Century England*, ed. Isabel Rivers (Leicester: Leicester University Press and St Martin's Press, 1982), 30.

23. Cole, 'From the Familiar to the New', 492.
24. A. Edward Newton, 'Introduction' to Henry Clinton Hutchins, Robinson Crusoe *and Its Printing, 1719–1731: A Bibliographical Study* (New York: Columbia University Press, 1925), xvii. According to Cole, '[t]he frontispiece representations of Mahmut and Crusoe circulated widely enough to have been recognisable almost as celebrity portraits'. See 'From the Familiar to the New', 499.
25. Cole, 'From the Familiar to the New', 494.
26. Cole, 'From the Familiar to the New', 494, 496.
27. Maxine Berg, *Luxury and Pleasure in Eighteenth-Century Britain* (Oxford: Oxford University Press, 2005), 86. Cole, 'From the Familiar to the New', 496–7.
28. According to Cole, '[i]t is not certain that Defoe played any direct part in choosing whether or not his work should be illustrated and, if he did, in what manner. His consent could be inferred from the unusual degree of "visual novelty" in evidence throughout his published oeuvre, and this is in fact Barchas's argument (*Graphic Design, Print Culture, and the Eighteenth- Century Novel*, p. 41)'. 'From the Familiar to the New', 499n58. Blewett, *The Illustration of* Robinson Crusoe, 30.
29. Cole, 'From the Familiar to the New', 498–9.
30. Cole, 'From the Familiar to the New', 500–1.
31. Folkenflik, 'The Rise of the Illustrated English Novel', 308–9.
32. Blewett, *The Illustration of* Robinson Crusoe, 29.
33. Barchas, *Graphic Design*, 47.
34. On this subject, see Andrew O'Malley, 'Poaching on Crusoe's Island: Popular Reading and Chapbook Editions of *Robinson Crusoe*', *Eighteenth-Century Life* 35, no. 2 (2011): 23–4, and Michael J. Preston, 'Rethinking Folklore, Rethinking Literature: Looking at *Robinson Crusoe* and *Gulliver's Travels* as Folktales: A Chapbook-Inspired Inquiry', in *The Other Print Tradition: Essays on Chapbook, Broadsides, and Related Ephemera*, ed. Cathy Lynn Preston and Michael J. Preston (New York: Garland, 1995), 19–73.
35. Blewett, *The Illustration of* Robinson Crusoe, 31–2.
36. Folkenflik, 'The Rise of the Illustrated English Novel', 313.
37. Folkenflik, 'The Rise of the Illustrated English Novel', 313.
38. Blewett, *The Illustration of* Robinson Crusoe, 49–50.
39. Folkenflik, 'The Rise of the Illustrated English Novel', 313; Jakub Lipski, 'Picturing Crusoe's Island: Defoe, Rousseau, Stothard', *Porównania* 25, no. 2 (2019): 87.
40. Lipski, 'Picturing Crusoe's Island', 87.
41. Lipski, 'Picturing Crusoe's Island', 87–8, 96.
42. Kevin MacDonnell, 'Beneath Defoe's Island: Imperial Geopolitics and the Inorganic Economy in *Robinson Crusoe*', *Philological Quarterly* 99, no. 1 (2020): 7.
43. Blewett, *The Illustration of* Robinson Crusoe, 52.
44. Blewett, *The Illustration of* Robinson Crusoe, 58.
45. Teri Doerksen, 'Framing the Narrative: Illustration and Pictorial Prose in Burney and Radcliffe', in *Book Illustration in the Long Eighteenth Century: Reconfiguring the Visual Periphery of the Text*, ed. Christina Ionescu (Newcastle upon Tyne: Cambridge Scholars Publishing, 2011), 463–500.
46. Blewett, *The Illustration of* Robinson Crusoe, 60.
47. Folkenflik, 'The Rise of the Illustrated English Novel', 313.
48. Sarah Howe, 'The Authority of Presence: The Development of the English Author Portrait, 1500–1640', *The Papers of the Bibliographical Society of America* 102, no. 4 (2008): 467.
49. On the phenomenon of extra-illustration, see, for instance, Lucy Peltz, *Facing the Text: Extra-Illustration, Print Culture, and Society in Britain, 1769–1840* (San Marino: Huntington Library Press, 2017); Luisa Calè, 'Extra-Illustration and Ephemera: Altered Books

and the Alternative Forms of the Fugitive Page', *Eighteenth-Century Life* 44, no. 2 (2020): 111–35; and 'Extra-Illustration in Non-Traditional Contexts: Charting New Avenues for Research in Illustration Studies', ed. Christina Ionescu, special issue of *Journal of Illustration* 8.2 (2022).

50. David Ross, 'Lower Largo, Fife', *Britain Express*, https://www.britainexpress.com/attractions. htm?attraction=5017 (accessed 22 November 2023).

51. 'Alexander Selkirk Statue Unveiling', *Vintage Lundin Links and Largo*, 11 December 2013, https://lundinlinks.weebly.com/blog/alexander-selkirk-statue-unveiling (accessed 22 November 2023). The plaque beneath the statue reads, 'In memory of Alexander Selkirk, mariner, the original of Robinson Crusoe who lived on the island of Juan Fernández in complete solitude for four years and four months. He died 1723 of HMS *Weymouth*, aged 47 years. This statue is erected by David Gillies, net manufacturer, on the site of the cottage in which Selkirk was born'.

52. For a photograph of the statue, see http://www.drookitagain.co.uk/coppermine/display-image-59-6938.html (accessed 22 November 2023).

53. 'Crusoe Statue at Glasgow Garden Festival', *Vintage Lundin Links and Largo*, 11 May 2017, https://lundinlinks.weebly.com/blog/crusoe-statue-at-glasgow-garden-festival (accessed 22 November 2023).

54. 'Glamrock Meets Robinson Crusoe: No Contest', *Hull and Hereabouts*, https://hulland-hereabouts.wordpress.com/tag/mick-ronson/ (accessed 22 November 2023).

55. 'Robinson Crusoe Limited Edition Plaque Eastgate Pottery Withernsea Hull Defoe', *Worth-Point*, https://www.worthpoint.com/worthopedia/robinson-crusoe-limited-edition-470894373 (accessed 22 November 2023).

56. 'Figure in Gilded Bronze and Mother of Pearl of Robinson Crusoe', *Proantic*, https://www. proantic.com/en/display.php?id=516912 (accessed 22 November 2023).

57. 'Le Voyage à Robinson', *Images Musicales*, 7 May 2017, https://blog.imagesmusicales.be/ le-voyage-a-robinson/ (accessed 22 November 2023).

58. 'Le Voyage à Robinson'.

59. 'La statue de Robinson', https://www.plessis-robinson.com/decouvrir-la-ville/visitez-le-plessis-robinson/parcours-du-patrimoine/des-guinguettes-aux-cites-jardins/la-statue-de-robinson.html (accessed 22 November 2023).

60. Louis Marin, 'Préface-image: le frontispice des *Contes* de Perrault', *Europe* 739–40 (1990): 114. See also 'Les enjeux d'un frontispice', *L'Esprit créateur* 27, no. 3 (1987): 49–57.

61. Marin, 'Préface-image', 114 and 'Les enjeux', 49–50.

62. Marin, 'Les enjeux', 50.

63. Marin, 'Les enjeux', 50.

64. Genette, *Paratexts: Thresholds of Interpretation*.

65. Barchas, *Graphic Design*, 13, 12 (referring to Adrian Johns, *The Nature of the Book: Print and Knowledge in the Making* [Chicago: University of Chicago Press, 1998]), and 14.

66. Tom Blackburn, '*Macbird!* and *Macbeth*: Topicality and Imitation in Barbara Garson's Satirical Pastiche', *Shakespeare Survey* 57 (2004): 137.

67. On this subject, see Jakub Lipski, *Re-Reading the Eighteenth-Century Novel: Studies in Reception* (London and New York: Routledge, 2021), 16–18.

68. Tripadvisor, 'La Cabaña de Cruoses', Malaga, Andalucia, https://www.tripadvisor.fr/ Restaurant_Review-g187437-d12220653-Reviews-La_Cabana_de_Crusoes-Estepona_ Costa_del_Sol_Province_of_Malaga_Andalucia.html (accessed 22 November 2023).

69. On this question, see, in particular, Andreas K. E. Mueller and Glynis Ridley, eds, *Robinson Crusoe After 300 Years* (Lewisburg: Bucknell University Press, 2021), and Jakub Lipski, ed., *Rewriting Crusoe: The Robinsonade across Languages, Cultures, and Media* (Lewisburg: Bucknell University Press, 2020).

24

TEXT TRANSFORMED INTO SILKWORK: BRITISH NEEDLEWORK PICTURES AND THE ADAPTATION OF *CHARLOTTE AT THE TOMB OF WERTER*

Sandro Jung

WITHIN A SHORT time of its publication, Johann Wolfgang von Goethe's 1774 novel, *Die Leiden des jungen Werther*, triggered an extensive creative engagement in terms of literary imitations in Britain: in addition to an extensive body of Werter poetry, between 1785 and 1800 six novels in imitation of the German work were issued.[1] One of the most popular, *Letters of Charlotte during Her Connexion with Werter* (1786), was also translated into French and German, while *The Female Werter. A Novel* had been translated from French.[2] Goethe's work was revisited and recreated as part of a larger cultural process that involved the polygeneric and multimedial reworking and transformation of eighteenth-century fiction in Britain: novels 'were adapted, appropriated, and otherwise re-presented'.[3] In the process, novelistic characters appeared in different media and through varying interpretive lenses that conditioned multifarious understandings of them and the works that first introduced them to readers. These characters, as David Brewer shows, represented 'a starting point – a common reference, but one perpetually inviting supplementation through the invention of additional details and often entirely new adventures'.[4] British audiences became widely familiar with Goethe's Werter through translation, the first rendering into English of *Die Leiden des jungen Werther* by Daniel Malthus, *The Sorrows of Werter: A German Story*, appearing in 1779. Apart from inspiring a range of imitations, it also generated numerous objects of Wertheriana, media that fed, amplified and directed the ways in which readers made sense of *Werter* as a sentimental work.[5] Objects featuring scenes from the novel – and especially Charlotte at Werter's tomb – were produced not only in the eighteenth-century German-speaking world but also as far from Germany as China, where, within a decade of the publication of the work, a porcelain dish and a bowl featuring a vignette depicting Charlotte at the tomb were manufactured and exported to Europe.[6] The illustrations adorning these objects held stories that the beholders needed to contemplate and unravel, establishing in the process their relevance for an understanding of *Werter*.

Goethe's transmedial afterlife was not a unique phenomenon but coincided with the manufacture of objects that were inspired by English literary works: Laurence Sterne's *A Sentimental Journey through France and Italy* (1768), for instance, triggered the production of as diverse a literary material culture as that of *Werter*. Literature was experienced intermedially, and iterations of popular works occurred in a range of different forms – from monumental artworks to small-scale personal objects. In fact, the sentimental and mourning-related vignettes by which Sterne's novel was widely recognised functioned as metonymic devices that frequently conveyed textual knowledge through visual media. The story of Maria of Moulines, which had first been introduced in *Tristram Shandy* but was revisited and invested with greater affective-sentimental power in *A Sentimental Journey*, gave rise to visualisations that were adapted by makers of literary material culture in ways that are closely connected with those utilised for the visual remediation of scenes from *Werter*. According to Peter de Voogd, Maria was the 'most popular subject' among the scenes from *A Sentimental Journey* selected by artists, and her character, usually accompanied by her pet dog, 'sat for almost one third of all illustrations'.[7] It became a favourite subject among collectors of prints as well; one of these prints, published by William Wynne Ryland in April 1779 and based on a design by Angelica Kauffman, served numerous women as a design which they transmediated in hand-crafted silkworks.

Recognising the multimedial nature of objects through which literary works could be experienced, this chapter will examine the remediation, as well as adaptation, of the scene in which Charlotte mourns Werter. A micro-sequel to Goethe's work, Charlotte's attendance at the tomb follows the deceased's suicide, which, in turn, was the result of Charlotte's non-reciprocation of his passion. The discussion will contextualise the sentimental vignette in light of the memorialising literary culture of late eighteenth-century Britain, as part of which two vignettes from Sterne in particular – the gift exchange between Yorick and Father Lorenzo, including the former's commemoration of the latter, as well as Yorick's encounter with Maria – were repeatedly adapted medially.[8] It will also focus on two engraved designs by John Raphael Smith and by Robert Smirke and the ways in which they render Werter's tomb scene. Beyond the medium of the print on paper, both Smirke's and Smith's designs were appropriated by women who created silkworks based on these literary illustrations that reflected 'the [material] entanglements of texts and textiles'.[9]

While existing scholarship has recognised that literary subjects 'are to be found in needlework',[10] there has not been any previous study of how the silkworker's mediation of the visualised literary work affects textual meaning-making. And yet, these silkwork pictures individuated and personalised the previously mechanically reproduced images, offering contextual interpretations of Charlotte and her relationship with Werter through specific colour schemes. According to Crystal Lake, the 'material literacy embodied in the embroidered works ... foregrounds a material poetics where it was possible to prioritize the associative relationships between objects, images and ideas'.[11] Occasionally, too, the makers of silkworks reinscribed the referentiality of memorial design by introducing the names of deceased real-life individuals into spaces (such as funereal tablets and plaques) that previously featured a literary figure's name.[12] The transmediation of designs as silkworks adjusted and altered the meaning of illustrations,[13] since the cultural practices involved in the individualised production of these objects of literary material culture differed from those of printing exact copies. Silk embroidery was a frequently used text-technology which allowed women to create furnishings for the home that carried relationally constructed meanings. These were shaped by the embroiderer's dialogue not only with the iconic work copied and the text invoked by this illustration, but also by the manner in which illustrations were realised, for these embroidered pictures reflected the material literacy of their makers, 'who mobilized their knowledge of making to comment upon, judge and inform their own activities as consumers', and especially as makers and readers of literary material culture.[14] At the same time, the silkworkers' strategies involved in translating the monochrome print design into a polychrome speaking picture entailed their use of 'the needle *as* the pen', needlework pictures representing the product of 'a coded practice' as part of which women makers shape meaning through how they embroider the silk substrate.[15]

The transmediation of prints depicting mourning scenes involving Werter and Charlotte needs to be understood in the context of the production of literary visual culture at the end of the eighteenth century. That visual culture centrally engaged with literature: at the high end of academy painting in the form of historical-narrative works exhibited at the annual exhibitions of the Royal Academy, and at the more affordable end through reproductions of paintings in the form of furniture prints intended for collectors' portfolios or for framing in domestic spaces.[16] Visual culture remediated literary works, in the process, through the selection of scenes and the characterisation of individual figures, promoting interpretations that circulated in the cultural domain of those viewing these artworks. For literature was not only read typographically: it could also be experienced at exhibitions, in print shops and, in large groupings and series, in the literary galleries of the 1790s devoted to works such as William Shakespeare's, John Milton's *Paradise Lost* and James Thomson's *The Seasons*.[17] These different spaces and modes of display facilitated an experience of literary works that was frequently intermedial, catalogues featuring excerpts of the literary work visualised and pictures being glossed through labels on the frames, for instance.

The largest number of iconic engagements, however, occurred within the pages of the codex of literary editions and miscellanies through the medium of book illustration.[18] Both the designs for book illustrations and for prints had a far greater pervasiveness than unique artworks, not only because they could be mechanically reproduced in large numbers but also because they frequently enjoyed a life beyond the medium of paper – on objects for which they were not originally produced. Illustrations of literature (and especially of well-known novels such as *Robinson Crusoe*, *A Sentimental Journey* and *The Vicar of Wakefield*) found application on objects ranging from ceramics to furniture, where various transfer processes were used to copy the existing image onto a new substrate.[19]

The 1780s and 1790s marked a period following the inception of the Royal Academy in which so-called 'cabinet pictures' were produced: because of their significantly smaller size, compared with large historical canvases, these pictures recommended themselves for display in smaller rooms or in groups. In their needlework pictures of literary works women often copied popular prints based on the formal styles of Kauffman and Charles Reuben Ryley. Among other novelistic works, the former produced designs of two Sternean scenes, whereas the latter illustrated two scenes from *Werter* and various moments from *Joseph Andrews*.[20] In silkwork versions of such prints, makers displayed their skill in embroidery and water-colour painting, the latter used especially for fine details such as facial expressions and hands. But they also personalised design through their own discriminating choice of colours, polychromatic nuance and additional shading. Silkwork pictures, in this respect, represented personal accomplishment indicative of the level of material literacy and proficiency a maker had achieved. They were decorative objects that had been produced at leisure, in the process highlighting the maker's social status and skill in producing an *objet d'art* for domestic ornamentation. But silkworks – through the selection of the visual subject – also constituted objects of discernment. The literary text visualised through embroidery displayed in the home served as an expression of literary taste. How pervasive the presence of embroidered pictures was in the homes of the middling sort is evidenced by their being rooted in a skill identified with female formal accomplishment.

The production of embroidered pictures was taught in schools for girls, as is demonstrated by a poem of 1769 entitled 'On Seeing a Picture wrought in Silk by Miss Ann Walford, at Mrs. Aylmer's Boarding-School, at Withim in Essex'.[21] In 1790, Mrs Tanner's 'School for Young Ladies' advertised its teaching of 'all Sorts of Needle-Work, Painting upon Silk and Gauze',[22] enabling its pupils to paint on silk in watercolour those parts of the image (such as faces and hands) that were not commonly embroidered. An alternative existed for those who did not want to undertake the application of watercolours, or who chose not to trace painstakingly the lines of the printed design. Aimed at those who could afford to purchase prepared substrates for their leisure activities, silk for embroidery, with the pattern already applied, was readily available from numerous artisans, including the London 'Embroiderer, Fancy Worker, and Pattern Drawer', H. Sass. He retailed 'the greatest assortment of beautiful Subjects and Designs, drawn by the best masters of figures, with Face and Hands painted on Silk or Satin, ready drawn for embroidery and Prints or Paintings to work from'.[23] Likewise, among his assortment, the London 'carver and gilder, looking-glass manufacturer, printseller and Picture Frame Maker' J. Freeman had 'Drawings on Silk, for embroidery or print work' for sale.[24] In Birmingham, Allen Everitt, 'Painter and Drawing Master', 'neatly executed' 'all Kinds of Drawing for Needle-work',[25] giving his customers the option to propose a particular subject. Sass, Freeman and Everitt were advertising in the 1790s, the decade in which an unprecedented number of literary prints that could then be transferred as patterns onto silk was published. Their advertisements indicate that embroidered pictures derived from printed designs were enjoying popularity on a scale that warranted the ready production of silk featuring patterns for embroidery as well as painted details. The manufacture and sale of such silk substrates testifies to the transmedial uses of print designs, and their transfer onto a material that could then be transformed medially and expressively by embroidery. The commercial preparation of silkgrounds featuring literary subjects indicates that works such as *Werter* and *A Sentimental Journey* were recognised as particularly apt for domestic use. They were celebrated instances of sensibility and, as such, expected to be suitable for the female silkworkers' contemplation, at the same time that they were brought to life through colour schemes to be selected by each silkworker.

The production of silkworks ranged from those small-format designs based on cabinet pictures to larger and more ambitious compositions, the latter category frequently being showcased as artworks on their own terms rather than as derivative. In fact, dedicated exhibitions of sophisticatedly executed embroidered pictures took place, as is evidenced by a description in 1809 of an exhibition displaying the work of Mary Linwood (1755–1845). Linwood had organised exhibitions of her work since 1798, and she would continue to do so until at least 1812.[26] The reviewer of the 1809 exhibition noted that the pictures displayed were 'executed with the nicest judgment', resulting

418   SANDRO JUNG

in artefacts of an astonishingly 'highly-finished state'.[27] They represented curiosities, resembling 'the richest painting', yet differed from them through their technique and medium, which were both associated with feminine application.[28] In fact, Linwood's embroidered pictures represented 'a performance of femininity',[29] the expert female embroiderer, whose name was commonly publicised, elevating needlework to the status of art. The fineness of the silk thread replaced the brushstrokes of the painting. Where colours would have been mixed, the female silkwork maker created intricate multi-colour patterns, at times overlaid with watercolour, which sought to evoke the brilliance of the painting. Silkwork embroidery thus entailed an appropriation of the effect of the painted medium.

The production of embroidered literary pictures was widespread. In fact, in addition to those in public collections, more than forty versions of Kauffman's *Shakespeare's Tomb* print, which was first published in August 1782, have been traced at auction sales in the past five years.[30] It should be borne in mind that they were produced by different women, mostly in Britain but, at times, also in America. These surviving silkworks share one feature: they are framed, protecting the delicate silk ground from handling, soiling and destruction. Silkworks based on prints of literary works – besides *A Sentimental Journey* and *Werter* – include Jean-François Marmontel's 'Adelaide, or the Shepherdess of the Alps',[31] scenes from Geoffrey Chaucer's *Canterbury Tales*,[32] Torquato Tasso's *Gerusalemme Liberata*,[33] Edmund Spenser's *The Faerie Queene*,[34] Shakespeare's plays,[35] Thomson's *The Seasons*[36] and Sir Walter Scott's *Lady of the Lake*.[37] Literally hundreds of examples have survived, if no doubt a fraction of those produced at the end of the eighteenth and the start of the nineteenth centuries. What is striking and apparent from this short list of works is the transnational subject coverage, ranging from British and French to Italian and German texts. As such, silkwork pictures of scenes from these texts are an index to their cultural currency at the time. Their framing, frequently in ornate *verre églomisé* frames, testified not only to their decorative-ornamental function within the domestic space where they were displayed; it also monumentalised them as part of cultural narratives of female accomplishment and alternative modes of reading – the viewer not only recognises the subject depicted but also embeds it within a recalled story. It was, after all, the identification of the subject (and, implicitly, the print) which tied these silkworks to a literary culture as part of which they functioned as extensions of literary meaning.

Goethe's *Werter* was one of the most frequently selected works for British silkwork pictures. Those examined here were based on separately issued furniture prints. At the same time, one book illustration – the frontispiece to the 1797 edition of William James's *The Letters of Charlotte, during her Connexion with Werter* (originally published in 1786) – also, albeit less extensively, served needleworkers as a model for their silkwork productions.[38] Goethe's work focused on the frustrated passion of the eponymous hero, in love with Charlotte. She, however, prefers Albert, whom she has consented to marry. Despairing, Werter commits suicide, his death and burial concluding the novel:

> At twelve Werter breathed his last. . . . and in the night the body of Werter was buried in the place he had himself chosen. The Steward and his sons followed him to the grave. Albert was not able to do it. Charlotte's life was despaired of. The body was carried by labourers, and no priest attended.[39]

Werter's suicide triggered an extensive discussion of the protagonist's morality. As an 'antidote' to Goethe's novel, which he denominates 'an apology for the horrible crime of Suicide', James's *Letters of Charlotte* set out to counteract the perceived irreligious tendency of the German work.[40] In his preface, he promises the reader that, unlike *Werter*, *Letters of Charlotte* will not 'wound delicacy, or pervert sentiment', nor will it 'militate against the precepts of religion'.[41] According to Orie William Long, James 'considered Goethe's novel altogether from the ethical standpoint', his principal aim being to caution overzealous readers against following Werter's pernicious example by indulging their sensibility unrestrainedly.[42]

In contrast to James's novel, *The Confidential Letters of Albert* (1790) offered an account of Werter's fate from the perspective of Charlotte's husband, who argues against 'that high degree of sensibility' that results in the derangement of Henry, a local youth in love with Charlotte and subsequently 'confirmed in insanity'.[43] In contrast to Henry, Werter is beloved by Charlotte, who, however, honours Albert's prior claim on her, and marries him. While Albert's letters extol the 'unimpassioned temperament' that regulates his early love for Charlotte, they also later reveal his jealousy, especially once he learns after Werter's suicide that his wife loved him.[44] *The Confidential Letters of Albert* introduces a vignette of Charlotte at the tomb, the young woman in decline and destined for an early grave: Albert relates to his correspondent that 'her sad soul hovers perpetually over the tragic fate of Werter, and her steps involuntarily haunt the mournful spot that holds his mangled form'.[45]

The figure of Charlotte at the tomb was also central to the numerous elegies on Werter that were published in Britain in the 1780s. In the 1785 poem 'The Sorrows of Charlotte at the Tomb of Werter', the speaker finds herself at his resting place, 'His loss . . . ever [to] deplore', for her 'heart is o'erburthen'd with woe'; but she is also certain that they will meet again after death, 'never to part'.[46] 'An Elegy upon Charlotte and Werter', published in the *Hibernian Magazine* in 1787, focused on Charlotte's lament and her self-reproaches:

> For oh! My Werter's number'd with the dead,
> And leaves me here his hapless fate to mourn.
> Wretch that I am! the sole and very cause,
> That life and Werter should be now no more.[47]

The poet imagines the scene of Werter's burial, a description of which Goethe did not provide in his work, in the process impressing on the reader the power of friendship that induced Albert to introduce an ekphrastic device narrating Werter's 'fate':

> Beneath two limes, expanding far around,
> Poor, hapless Werter, and his relics lay,
> And o'er him Albert rais'd a sacred mound,
> Whose sculptur'd marble does his fate display.[48]

Werter-mania went beyond poems commemorating the love of Werter and Charlotte, as well as the latter's mourning. Manufacturers of literary material culture produced objects that not only visualised scenes occurring in the work but also produced imaginative expansions of the narrative that centralised Charlotte after Werter's death.

These objects included the Derby Porcelain Manufactory's statuette entitled 'Charlotte weeping for Werter' dating from the mid-1780s. Numerous pieces of mourning jewellery, including rings and medallions – such as Turner & Co.'s pottery, and Josiah Wedgwood's stoneware and jasperware plaques and cameos, the latter based on 'a design by [Elizabeth Upton,] Lady Templeto[w]n',[49] who also created designs based on *A Sentimental Journey* – were manufactured in the 1790s. A 'Miniature' by W. V. Bouquet entitled *Charlotte decorating the tomb of Werter* was displayed at the Royal Academy's 1786 exhibition.[50] The producers of these examples of literary material culture drew on earlier practices involving the making of textual tie-ins, for instance, the ways in which Samuel Richardson's *Pamela* (1740) had been visualised and adapted for the embellishment of snuffboxes and fans.[51] But unlike illustrations of *Pamela*, those visualisations that remediated *Werter* and Sterne's Maria focused on scenes of sensibility, commemoration and mourning.

As with *A Sentimental Journey*, print sellers issued numerous engravings depicting scenes from *Werter*, the most frequently illustrated being that of Charlotte mourning.[52] John Raphael Smith produced a design (measuring 402 × 355 mm) entitled *Charlotte at the Tomb of Werter* (Figure 24.1) that he engraved and published in London on 17 October 1783.[53] The design sold at 7s 6d for the monochrome version and at 15s for a printed version in colour.[54] It was re-engraved in Augsburg in 1790 and reissued in London, with the vegetation realised distinctly differently, by F. R. Cooke in 1792.[55] In the same year, it was republished once more in Germany by Martin Engelbrecht, albeit much reduced in size (190 × 143 mm), the design attributed to Thomas Stothard.[56]

Figure 24.1 Stipple print of *Charlotte at the Tomb of Werter*, engraved by J. R. Smith (1783). Reproduced from a copy in the author's collection.

The artist's scene introduced a bonneted Charlotte looking sadly upon a large urn placed on a pedestal, which is inscribed with Werter's name, a weeping willow in the background underscoring the melancholy atmosphere. Charlotte is holding a book, which is still half open, her reading having been interrupted by contemplating the memorial symbol in front of her. In the print, the book's spine features '[Friedrich Gottlieb] Klopstock',[57] the German poet of the epic, *The Messiah* (1748–73), and of sacred odes Goethe greatly admired, and who is also referenced in *Werter*: after a thunderstorm, Werter and Charlotte view the refreshed natural environment and are moved by its splendour and sublimity, which reminds them both of Klopstock, and culminates in the young man rapturously imprinting a kiss on Charlotte's hand. Whereas their reference to Klopstock results in a moment of intimacy and closeness, the visually represented scene involves a different, non-reciprocating nearness, signalling a moment of stasis, even of paralysis: Charlotte appears to be incapable of advancing in order to seek the proximity to Werter that is now forever lost to her. Such was the demand for Smith's design that it was widely adapted: beyond its use by silkworkers, it also featured on an item of jewellery, a late eighteenth-century mourning brooch.[58]

Robert Smirke's design based on the same subject (measuring 268 x 193 mm) was engraved by Robert Samuel Marcuard and published in 1785 by James Walker, as well as re-engraved in France as *Charlotte au tombeau de Werther* (Figure 24.2).[59] Smirke's *Charlotte at the Tomb of Werter* does not depict a large and centralised urn but a tomb proper, upon which Charlotte is scattering flowers. The small urn placed on the tomb does not identify Werter by name. Unlike the female figure in Smith's illustration, that

Figure 24.2 Intaglio print of *Charlotte at the Tomb of Werter*, engraved by R. S. Marcuard (1785). Reproduced from a copy in the author's collection.

in Smirke's print is looking down towards the tomb in which the deceased's body has been placed. Her raised right foot indicates her motion towards his final resting place. Whereas Smith had offered an infantilised version of Charlotte, who is dressed as a mourner, Smirke's Charlotte exudes sadness, engaged as she is in a final mourning tribute. But her figure also conveys eroticism. The painter closely reworked Kauffman's print of Shakespeare's tomb in which she had rendered a classically dressed woman with wings on her head, whom the lines of verse beneath the image identify as Fancy. Strewing flowers on the tomb, Fancy is not a mourner but a devotee of Shakespeare, an idealised, allegorical female. The tomb bears a plaque featuring Shakespeare's name.

The influence of Kauffman's design cannot only be seen in Smirke's tomb scene commemorating Werter: her illustration was also transmedially used on a fan leaf of 1790, although the manufacturer had the engraved image adapted, removing the wings from Fancy's head and replacing Shakespeare's name on the tomb with two crossed trumpets. The appropriation of the design continued, as makers of silkwork pictures adopted it to commemorate Werter's death, replacing Shakespeare's name with that of Goethe's character. Subsequently, another silkwork maker substituted Shakespeare and Werter with (William) 'Cowper', the poet, who had died in April 1800.[60]

Both Smith's and Smirke's designs drew on the memorial iconography of earlier prints and designs for memorial jewellery, including Kauffman's *Shakespeare's Tomb*, and both served needleworkers as models for their silkwork pictures. One of the designs probably provided the basis of a silkwork that a mother encountered on accompanying her daughter to boarding school:

> after the first salutations were over, the matron fixed her eyes upon some work'd picture subjects in the parlour; and pointing to one more attractive than the rest, ask'd 'what is that?' 'That,' replied the tutoress, 'is Charlotte at the tomb of Werter.'[61]

The school's parlour serves as an exhibition space in which the students' embroidered pictures are displayed: the silkworks are not only the product of the young women's application but also the result of the school's teaching. They thus represent achievement in two respects. The use of Charlotte at the tomb as a subject testifies to the scene's sentimental and fashionable currency. The picture appeals to the mother visiting the school for aesthetic reasons, the realisation of the design in coloured silk thread introducing a uniqueness (distinct from the monochrome print) that brings the mourning scene to life. That the tutees in schools for young women undertook a range of designs in silkwork is evidenced by a young Dublin woman, Eliza Farran. While a pupil at a girl's boarding school, she executed a silkwork of *Charlotte at the Tomb of Werter*, a task that took her from May to July 1790. She embroidered other designs, too, including Griselda returning to her father, Ferdinand and Miranda, and Lord Thomas and Fair Ellinor.[62] These designs were largely of a literary nature and most likely were inspired by communal readings of these works in the boarding schools where the silk pictures were undertaken.

That Smith's design was of a mourning scene proper is reinforced through the strategies that the makers of silkwork versions of it adopted; the majority bestowed a mourning habit on Charlotte by realising her cape in black.[63] One example (Plate 14) also adds a black hat, as well as cuffs rendered in the same colour. To a viewer, these black elements would unmistakably identify the female figure as a mourner, especially since the use of black in such concentration is unusual in a silkwork; the maker of this embroidered picture used felt in addition to silk thread to produce the comparatively large area of the cape. By contrast, Plate 15 shows a silkwork that offers a more sophisticated strategy, in that the hem of the cape is framed with a lighter colour, which also makes the hood visible: in the previous needlework picture (Plate 14), the hood had been obscured by the block of black used for the cape. In Plate 15, the hat is only fringed with black, a device constituting another common feature of mourning apparel. Using black so centrally in these two pictures emphasises its symbolic significance, which makes unmistakable the meaning of the scene.

Like Plate 14, Plate 15 also offers foliage identifiable as willow to convey the predominant modes of sadness and lament. All the silkworks discussed here are close copies of Smith's design, featuring the urn bearing Werter's name. Only Plate 15 replaces the hat Charlotte had worn in the printed design. Each version reproduces the name of the deceased, but in Plate 15 the silkworker increases its size. In doing so, the urn becomes a focal point. This is amplified by the inclusion of text on the pedestal, which was not part of Smith's illustration, and which has been added by the maker of the silkwork: 'Oh! May the interventions of Charlotte / plead for the decay of Reason in Werter'. The lines enrich Charlotte's characterisation, as in her visit to the tomb she possibly intends to pray for the deceased. She is rendered holding a book, but it is no longer recognisable as a work by Klopstock and could instead be interpreted as representing a prayer book, underscoring Charlotte's petition to her maker. The producer of the silkwork has thus appropriated the space of the pedestal not to commemorate Werter, but to appeal to the reader-viewer attentively examining the embroidered picture. It is a message meant to elicit sympathy for Charlotte's 'interventions', her prayers, as Werter's suicide was perceived to be a mortal sin and unforgivable. While not defending the deceased's action that led to his demise, the maker of the silkwork holds out hope that Werter's 'decay of Reason' represented a corrosive illness born from his unregulated passion for Charlotte. In other words, his death was not the result of a wilful, deliberate and premeditated ending of his life, even though he was fully conscious of his actions and their ramifications for his soul. The addition of the lines complicates the scene, transforming it from a contemplative mourning tableau into one where Charlotte's mourning and the inscription on the pedestal are intended to affect readers by inducing them to sympathise with the once-ill Werter. The silkwork, while anchoring the scene in Goethe's novel, expands the story, assigning to Charlotte a pivotal role in Werter's rehabilitation.

In contrast to the silkworks depicting the scene already discussed, Plate 16 does not strikingly differentiate Charlotte from the funereal monument. Quite the opposite. It aligns the stone structure and the young woman through the earthen-grey colour used for both. The stasis of the scene is reinforced through a sense of petrifaction, Charlotte literally appearing to have turned to stone, only her face differentiated from the remainder of her person through the fleshy tints added in watercolour. It is her facial expression that particularly draws the reader-viewer's attention. The aureate colouring of the background (and especially the golden fringing of the foliage) that had already characterised Plate 15, as well as the more centralised focus on Charlotte and the tomb, frame the scene in a way that celebrates the deceased; at the same time, the naturalistic manner of the colouring of Plate 14 being replaced by earthen and golden tones in Plate 16 also underscores the nobility of sentiments conveyed by Charlotte's mourning.

424   SANDRO JUNG

In contrast to these silkworks depicting Charlotte at the tomb, an American maker of a less elaborate and sophisticated silkwork based on the same design, albeit reversed in the embroidered picture, offers a fundamentally different colour scheme that is not in tune with the chromatic characterisation of the mourning apparel provided by other embroidered versions of the design (Plate 17).[64] Unlike the other examples discussed, the use of watercolour on Charlotte's face is not of the standard that induced Emily Leigh Lowes to class literary silkworks as part of the 'painted faces' period of embroidery.[65] In fact, this absence of painting as an expressive medium assigns more significance to the colouring adopted. The most striking colours to be used in the figure are red and pink, life-affirming colours that echo a description in *Werter* of Charlotte wearing pink ribbons. In fact, these ribbons possess particular significance, since following Werter's first encounter with the young woman he describes her to his correspondent as 'dressed in a plain white gown with pink ribbands'.[66] Pink and red possessed symbolic associations with the sacred, red-coloured silk thread frequently being used in religious and pastoral embroidery.[67] Red – achieved either through madder or cochineal – was 'the most difficult, and thus, most costly color to reproduce', its use in embroidery thus being especially, symbolically meaningful.[68] The combination of the light beige and red/pink used for Charlotte approximates her appearance to that of a bride. The scene, in this respect, potentially presents a reimagining of her encounter with Werter, who is represented by an oversized version of the urn and rendered in the same colour as Charlotte's dress. The use of dark green for the foliage of the willow and the outlines of the urn, as well as Werter's name, connect the two modally. But the colour also introduces an organicity that bestows a contemplative agency onto the monument when viewed by Charlotte, who now pledges herself to his memory.

By introducing Charlotte in the manner by which she was characterised before Werter's suicide, the maker of the silkwork may have sought to present her as virginal and devoted to the deceased, an alteration of the narrative by which the associative presence of Albert as Charlotte's husband – Charlotte being depicted here as virginal – no longer affects the viewer's understanding of the relationship between Charlotte and Werter. At the same time, the cause of the latter's death being rooted in Charlotte's marriage to another is negated by the manner in which the young woman is introduced through the colour scheme of her garments. The choice of colour and the evocation of a pre-marital Charlotte allow the reader to sustain the illusion that Werter's death was not a suicide motivated by disappointment in love, but by an unlucky event preventing his marriage to Charlotte. This illusion did, in fact, circulate in adaptations of Goethe's work, including an epitome published by T. Sabine. Sabine's twenty-seven-page *Werter and Charlotte* concluded by allowing a final union of Charlotte, who 'every morning visited it [the tomb], and gathered the choicest flowers to strew upon it':

> Thus she continued mourning, and her frame consuming, till at last she sunk into the arms of death, and to the last she called on Werter, by whose side she was laid, at the request of his friend, who had gained the secret of their loves by some papers he had left behind.[69]

Her frequent visits to the tomb may thus be understood as a form of pledge through which Charlotte binds herself to Werter.

BRITISH NEEDLEWORK PICTURES

425

Another silkwork based on the same design also prominently deploys the colour red, a shade of maroon or blood red, as part of the dress Charlotte is wearing, although the life-affirming connotation of the colour is offset by the beige-grey tones that predominate in the young mourner's apparel (Plate 18). Whereas in the American silkwork the realisation of the face was schematic, little effort having been made to produce the effect of nuanced tonality seen in other versions, in this production the finely rendered face is expressive of sadness and sorrow. The alignment of Charlotte's eyeline with the inscription of the name 'Werter' on the urn, much more so than in the rendering of the scene previously discussed, creates a connection through which the mourner's facial expression should be understood. The name on the urn serves as a prosthetic placeholder both for the bodily existence of the deceased young Werter and for Charlotte's emotional investment. The careful execution of details allows the reader to trace Charlotte's expression, but also to identify the foliage of the weeping willow as seemingly moving, nature paying a silent tribute to Werter's memory, as well as to Charlotte's connection with him. In a more pronounced manner than in the previous example, this silkwork is a sophisticated painterly rendering where the watercolour painting used for the face and the detailed realisation of the foliage are deliberately deployed to create inter-iconic symbolic rapport.

Even though Smirke bestowed the same title as Smith on his design, the manner in which Charlotte was rendered by makers of silkwork pictures based on Smirke's print differs strikingly from the strategies adopted by those remediating the earlier artist's design. Despite the presence of the tomb that is inscribed with Werter's name, the female figure who strews flowers on it is not clearly defined as a mourner. Rather than aligning himself with the funereal symbolism of Smith's work, Smirke followed the example of Kauffman's print. Silkworks based on Smirke's design were routinely characterised by ornate colour schemes, avoiding a sombreness that might contribute towards turning Fancy into a sepulchral figure. While some makers realise the composition in earthen tones of browns, yellows or gold,[70] as with designs based on Smith's image, others use striking colours such as red for Fancy's dress,[71] a colour that also usually reappears in the flowers she strews onto the tomb and that, as 'a sacred colour',[72] lends the figure an elevated status. Reds and golds predominate for Fancy, while on occasion light blues (at times, in combination with gold) are also used for her garments.[73]

Based on my findings, Smirke's design appears to have been less commonly adopted by makers of needlework pictures than Smith's. While the design served at least one maker of a silk and hair picture – combining black and white silk, as well as dark hair – as a model for her production,[74] most silkworks based on it are strikingly polychromatic, thereby contrasting with the subdued colour schemes of silkworks of Smith's design: the young woman is dressed in blue in both silkworks introduced here, a colour denoting high rank and nobility. She is potentially a version of Kauffman's Fancy. The tomb, which occupied a prominent position in the engraved print of Smirke's design, has receded to the background, owing to the colour of silk thread used to realise it, in addition to its reduction in size. In the process, the figure dressed entirely in blue gains a significance of her own. Read through the lens of Kauffman's Fancy, she is a muse-like figure paying homage to the deceased Werter, without having enjoyed the personal connection with him that Charlotte had entertained. Removed from the paratextual framework of Smirke's print, the identity of Charlotte needs to be inferred, but the cues provided by the makers of silkworks align with the colourful depictions of the allegorical Fancy of embroidered pictures of Kauffman's design. They transform the scene into a pseudo-classical visitation, rather than an intimate scene of personal recollection. The silkwork in Plate 19 demonstrates the same strategy as that used in transmedial renderings of Smith's work, to transform the vegetation background of Smirke's print by featuring an aureate colour scheme that removes the scene from the storyworld of Goethe to that of a mythical realm in which Werter is commemorated by the goddess of the imagination. The real acts of sad and painful commemoration and mourning central to Smith's illustration are thus no longer foregrounded. By not introducing any religious intertext, as represented by the book that Smith's Charlotte was holding, the subject of the deceased's suicide is not implicitly introduced here either.

The second silkwork based on Smirke's design (Plate 20) bestows on Charlotte a much fuller head of hair. No longer clad in blue only, but in a dress that combines cream colour with light blue, including blue shading on the sleeves and a blue ornamental accessory on the young woman's torso, Charlotte is embedded in a landscape that differs strikingly from that depicted in Plate 21. The foliage is lusciously executed, and in great detail, in shades of green and gold. The picture's profusely depicted vegetation, as well as the absence of a clearly demarcated foreground and background, highlights the seclusion of this setting, but also Charlotte's immersion within it. Beyond this absorptive quality, however, Smirke's design does not offer a meaningful expansion of the work, such as suggesting why Charlotte attends the tomb, as Smith had done in his amplification of the Charlotte–Werter story.

In contrast to the silkworks depicting Charlotte at the tomb, those based on *A Sentimental Journey* and inspired by Kauffman's design of Maria show a greater range of colour schemes – despite the fact that Sterne had offered a clear visual representation of Maria's apparel, including the colour of her dress (white) and the ribbon 'which fell across her shoulder to the waist'.[75] The ribbon in Sterne's description is 'pale green', a colour Kauffman also retained in her original polychrome painting of the design on copper, which was subsequently engraved as a copperplate print. Silkworkers often chose green for the ribbon, too, suggesting an effort on the part of those with detailed textual knowledge to synchronise their work with Sterne's description (Plate 21).[76] Less commonly, pink or red were selected instead of green, thus differing from Sterne's characterisation, but conveying similar associations of purity and sacredness as communicated by the colour schemes of silkworks depicting Charlotte. Silkwork renderings of the design strive for accuracy in copying Kauffman's realisation of Sylvio, Maria's pet dog, but they vary in the colour patterns their makers adopt for the pastoral background. Settings of earthen and aureate tones predominate, in which the greens of the vegetation are unobtrusively added. At times, the scene is entitled 'Contemplation', without indicating that it is rooted in Yorick's account of Maria.[77] The young woman's posture, her head resting on her left hand, is not unmistakably expressive of the sadness Sterne's vignette conveys. Rather, as realised in silkworks, Maria frequently appears to be asleep rather than melancholy, the addition of Sylvio and her flute being such characteristic attributes to allow the scene's identification as belonging to *A Sentimental Journey*. In the process, this representational ambiguity, like that of Smirke's design via the medium of silkwork, allows different readings which are usually directed through colour symbolism.

To a greater extent than silkworks of Kauffman's Maria, the transmedial use of the *Werter* designs by Smith and Smirke enabled the women responsible for these embroidered pictures to devise strategies that clarified and, moreover, directed meaning. These makers understood needlework 'as a *form of* discourse' with which they could amplify the meaning of the designs they transferred onto silk ground.[78] Since the prints on which these silkworks were based visualised a moment not in fact mentioned in the novel, the scene of Charlotte at the tomb represented an expansion of Werter's story that was imagined differently by the two visual artists. They created two incarnations of Charlotte that have little in common, a difference highlighted by the strategies the silkworkers adopted to render Smith's figure as a mourner and Smirke's as a pseudo-allegorical figure. It has been noted that the 'textile arts can be rhetorically meaningful both through their products and their practice', including the ways in which beholders engaged with the narratives embroidered.[79] Like the mother encountering a silkwork rendering of Charlotte at the tomb in the parlour of her daughter's boarding school, others, such as the protagonist of Caroline Matilda Warren's *The Gamesters; or Ruins of Innocence* (1805), attributed meaningfulness to the visualisation in relation to their own lives and romantic connections. For Warren's protagonist had produced 'an unfinished drawing' of the same subject, understanding the scene depicted not only in relation to Goethe's story but also in relation to her own longing. Rather, the character had undertaken the drawing while trying 'to amuse herself on the day preceding the one fixed for her marriage with Evander' whom she loved.[80] In this respect, the indissoluble romantic connection Charlotte retains with Werter in Smith's image likely served as a lens through which to view her own love for Evander, underpinning the design. Unlike the drawing and the monochrome prints of Smith's and Smirke's illustrations, however, the silkworks were characterised by polychrome execution, the differently coloured silk threads creating maps of meaning that would be exhibited in the domestic realm, where these embroidered pictures intersected with other symbolically inscribed material culture.

The use of colour symbolism in silkworks testified to their makers' recognition of visual conventions as well as to how they could be reinforced. While the majority of silkworks of Smith's work I have encountered represent the elegiac mode of the scene through the addition of sadness-evoking willows, others significantly adapted the original design: as we saw, one maker added text on the pedestal of the urn whereby she explained Charlotte's role as intercessor. The inscription complicates the straightforward scene of mourning by resisting framing Werter's suicide as a moral question. Smith's rendering had successfully muted Charlotte's beauty, and casting her in black or other subdued colours aligned her with the colour of the tomb, recontextualising her meaning. She is an erotic object no longer. By contrast, Smirke's muse-like figure, even though modelled on Kauffman's Fancy, is more erotically introduced. She is a dynamic individual, full of life, and not paralysed by grief, as Smith's contemplative Charlotte is. None of the silkworks are exact copies of one another: they are individual realisations of a scene that is extratextual, following on from the end of Goethe's narrative. Reinforcing the moral casting of Charlotte, on the one hand, as well as the devotional-erotic characterisation of her allegorical persona on the other, silkworkers adapted the visual artists' designs to interpret a figure whose characterisation in *Werter* was ambivalent.

Silkworks represented individualised mediating platforms for the promotion of textual knowledge within the domestic space where these embroidered pictures were both made and displayed. Scenes from *Werter* and *A Sentimental Journey* were particular favourites in Britain: they were brought to life by the silkworker's engagement with the embroidered design, but also through a mental dialogue with the source text and its images. As such, literary silkworks functioned as personalised versions of iconic interpretations of literature that were more widely disseminated through the printed visual culture on which these handcrafted needlework productions were based. At the end of a century when literary material culture was increasingly manufactured through mechanical processes involving transfer-printing, silkwork pictures of character vignettes constituted an important mode of literary reception: they relied on individuals to make decisions as part of the faction, which affected how their productions could be understood as literary epitexts, but also as equally capable of highlighting or critiquing aspects of the works illustrated.

Notes

1. I adopt the historical English spelling of 'Werter', rather than the German 'Werther'.
2. The remaining novels imitating *Werter* were: *Eleanora, from the Sorrows of Werter* (1785), *The Confidential Letters of Albert. From his First Attachment to Charlotte to Her Death* (1790), *The Slave of Passion; or, the Fruits of Werter* (1790) and *Werter and Charlotte. A German Story, Containing Many Wonderful and Pathetic Incidents* (c.1800).
3. Daniel Cook and Nicholas Seager, 'Introduction', in *The Afterlives of Eighteenth-Century Fiction*, ed. Daniel Cook and Nicholas Seager (Cambridge: Cambridge University Press, 2015), 2.
4. David A. Brewer, *The Afterlife of Character, 1726–1825* (Philadelphia: University of Pennsylvania Press, 2005), 2.
5. To date, the critical-creative afterlife of *Werter* has predominantly been studied in terms of literary works imitating the novel, although the way in which Goethe's work affected literary-textual practice, rather than inspired imitations only, has recently begun to be examined. For a survey, which also includes some information on the visual fortunes of *Werter*, see Georg Jaeger, *Die Leiden des alten und neuen Werther: Kommentare, Abbildungen, Materialien zu Goethes Die Leiden des jungen Werthers* (Munich: Hanser, 1984). See also Andrew Piper and Mark Algee-Hewitt, 'The Werther Effect 1: Goethe, Objecthood, and the Handling of Knowledge', in *Distant Readings: Topologies of German Culture in the Long Nineteenth Century*, ed. Matt Erlin and Lynn Tatlock (Rochester: Camden House, 2014), 155–84.
6. A late eighteenth-century cup and saucer produced in Jingdezhen (Jiangxi province) depicts an image, realised *en grisaille*, of Charlotte leaning on a pedestal with an urn, the pedestal featuring an oval plaque with 'Werter' inscribed on it (see the British Museum's collections, museum number Franks.880.+).
7. Peter de Voogd, 'Sterne and Visual Culture', in *The Cambridge Companion to Laurence Sterne*, ed. Thomas Keymer (Cambridge: Cambridge University Press, 2009), 150.
8. See W. G. Day, 'Sternean Material Culture: Lorenzo's Snuff-box and His Grave', in *The Reception of Laurence Sterne in Europe*, ed. Peter de Voogd and John Neubauer (London and New York: Continuum, 2004), 248, 252–4.
9. Crystal B. Lake, 'Needlework Verse', in *Material Literacy in the Eighteenth Century: A Nation of Makers*, ed. Serena Dyer and Chloe Wigston Smith (London and New York: Bloomsbury, 2020), 36.
10. Margaret Jourdain, *The History of English Secular Embroidery* (London: Paul Kegan, Trench, Trubner and Co., 1910), 117.

11. Lake, 'Needlework Verse', 36.
12. A silkwork in my collection introduces a tombstone behind a female figure weeping, the tombstone being inscribed with 'In Memory of Anna Rowley'.
13. See Sandro Jung, *Eighteenth-Century Illustration and Literary Material Culture: Richardson, Thomson, Defoe* (Cambridge: Cambridge University Press, 2023).
14. Serena Dyer and Chloe Wigston Smith, 'Introduction', in *Material Literacy in the Eighteenth Century: A Nation of Makers*, ed. Serena Dyer and Chloe Wigston Smith (London and New York: Bloomsbury, 2020), 1.
15. Heather Pristash, Inez Schaechterle and Sue Carter Wood, 'The Needle as Pen: Intentionality, Needlework, and the Production of Alternate Discourses of Power', in *Women and the Material Culture of Needlework and Textiles, 1750–1950*, ed. Maureen Daly Goggin and Beth Fowkes Tobin (Aldershot: Ashgate, 2009), 14, 15.
16. Richard D. Altick, *Paintings from Books: Art and Literature in Britain, 1760–1900* (Columbus: Ohio State University Press, 1985).
17. Walter Pape and Frederick Burwick, eds, *The Boydell Shakespeare Gallery* (Bottrop: Peter Pomp, 1996); Luisa Calè, *Fuseli's Milton Gallery: Turning Readers into Spectators* (Oxford: Oxford University Press, 2006).
18. See Ian Haywood, Susan Matthews and Mary L. Shannon, eds, *Romanticism and Illustration* (Cambridge: Cambridge University Press, 2019); Sandro Jung, *James Thomson's* The Seasons, *Print Culture, and Visual Interpretation, 1730–1842* (Bethlehem: Lehigh University Press, 2015).
19. Scenes from *Robinson Crusoe* featured extensively on early nineteenth-century ceramics, including, at the high end, French porcelain vases and, at the lower end, children's crockery and alphabet plates. Numerous silkworks of Maria of Moulines survive, as do jasperware objects (such as medallions) of the character. Differently coloured engraved fan leaves, dating to 1796 and depicting three scenes from *A Sentimental Journey*, are held by the Victoria and Albert Museum (accession number: E.2245–1920; accession number: E.3185–1938 [two copies]) and the British Museum (registration number: 1891,0713.419). Illustrations of moments from Goldsmith's novel were transfer-printed onto creamware jugs. On *Robinson Crusoe* and illustrated material culture, see Jung, *Eighteenth-Century Illustration and Literary Material Culture*, 60–9.
20. Ryley's paintings were displayed at the Royal Academy exhibition of 1785 and published, on 1 December 1785, as companion cabinet prints by S. Watts, 'A Visit to the Woman of the Lime Tree' and 'The Last Interview between Charlotte and Werter'.
21. *The Town and Country Magazine* 1 (1769): 712.
22. *Sheffield Register*, 27 August 1790.
23. *Caledonian Mercury*, 16 April 1792.
24. *Norfolk Chronicle*, 10 January 1795.
25. *Aris's Birmingham Gazette*, 12 March 1798.
26. See *Exhibition of Miss Linwood's Pictures in Needle Work* (at the Hanover-Square Concert Rooms, 1798); *Miss Linwood's Gallery of Pictures in Worsted: Leicester Square* (London: Rider and Weed, 1812).
27. *The Lady's Monthly Museum, or Polite Repository of Amusement and Instruction* 6 (1809): 315.
28. The reviewer of the 1811 edition noted in relation to the usefulness of embroidery work: Linwood's 'works exhibit . . ., in a moral point of view, how much may be accomplished by unremitting industry, and how satisfactory and laudable it is always to be usefully employed'. *The Linwood Gallery of Pictures in Needlework* (London: J. Harris, 1811), 8.
29. Pristash, Schaechterle and Wood, 'The Needle as Pen', 17.
30. Victoria and Albert Museum (accession number: 39–1874; accession number: 1743–1869); Cooper Hewitt Smithsonian Design Museum (object ID: 18482601; accession

number: 1974–100–12); Lady Lever Art Gallery (see Margaret Swain, *Embroidered Georgian Pictures* [Oxford: Shire Publications, 1994], 14).

31. One of these silkworks (based on a Kauffman print of 1794, published by William Dickinson) is reproduced on the title page of Swain's *Embroidered Georgian Pictures*; another is held by the Lady Lever Art Gallery. Another engraving of 'Adelaide' produced in 1784 by Francesco Bartolozzi was also copied for silkworks.

32. Francesco Bartolozzi's 1784 engraving of 'Griselda returning to her Father' served as the basis for subsequent silkworks. See Swain, *Embroidered Georgian Pictures*, 11.

33. Silkworks were produced of Kauffman's Erminia print, but a more complex composition utilising Kauffman's design, integrating it in a larger scene, was also undertaken.

34. James Birchall's 1783 print of Kauffman's *Una and the Lion* design was used for silkworks.

35. 'Lear and Cordelia in Chains', based on a design by Thomas Stothard (Victoria and Albert Museum, accession number: T.449–1977). Two examples of Ferdinand and Miranda are reproduced in Swain, *Embroidered Georgian Pictures*, 10–11.

36. A silkwork in my collection (based on John Raphael Smith's 1780 print) visualises Thomson's tale of Palemon and Lavinia. Two other embroidered pictures (based on illustrations – one also rendering the Palemon and Lavinia story – in the 1792 edition of *The Seasons*, co-published by Peter Hill and J. Strachan & W. Stewart) sold at Sotheby's on 25 June 2001.

37. A silkwork featuring Scott's subject is held by the Royal Museum of Scotland.

38. The two silkworks I have traced of this design (one sold at Sotheby's in 2015) both change significant details of the frontispiece illustration, including the shape of the urn, as well as removing the fencing surrounding Werter's tomb. The silkwork makers thus eliminate the physical barrier between Charlotte and Werter. A version of the design, credited to Burnet Reading as both designer and engraver, was also issued as a small print by R. Wilkinson on 1 September 1785. The oval depicting the scene of the kneeling Charlotte in front of the tomb features, next to the title ('Charlotte at the Tomb of Werter'), four lines of text: 'At Werter's Tomb beneath a Willow plac'd. / Fair Charlotte sits in Contemplation chaste. / What to defend thy Life, O Youth She lent. / Thy misplac'd Passion shows by dire Event'. A copy of the print is held by Freies Deutsches Hochstift / Frankfurter Goethe-Museum (Kunstsammlung: III–03222).

39. Johann Wolfgang von Goethe, *The Sorrows of Werter: A German Story*, 2 vols (London: J. Dodsley, 1780), 2:172.

40. William James, *Letters of Charlotte, During Her Connexion with Werter*, 2 vols (London: T. Cadell, 1786), 1:vii, ii–iii.

41. James, *Letters of Charlotte*, 1:i, ii.

42. Orie William Long, 'English and American Imitations of *Werter*', *Modern Philology* 14, no. 4 (1916): 13.

43. *The Confidential Letters of Albert; from His First Attachment to Charlotte to Her Death* (London: G. G. J. and J. Robinson, 1790), 13, 23.

44. *The Confidential Letters of Albert*, 17.

45. *The Confidential Letters of Albert*, 179.

46. 'The Sorrows of Charlotte at the Tomb of Werter', *The European Magazine* 7 (1785): 261–2, lines 4, 20, 24.

47. 'An Elegy upon Charlotte and Werter', *The Hibernian Magazine* 17 (1787): 157, lines 23–6.

48. 'An Elegy upon Charlotte and Werter', lines 41–4.

49. *The Wedgwood Handbook: A Manual for Collectors* (London: George Bell and Son, 1875), ix.

50. *The Exhibition of the Royal Academy. The Eighteenth* (London: T. Cadell, 1786), 10.

51. See Thomas Keymer and Peter Sabor, *'Pamela' in the Marketplace: Literary Controversy and Print Culture in Eighteenth-Century Britain and Ireland* (Cambridge: Cambridge

BRITISH NEEDLEWORK PICTURES 431

University Press, 2005), especially 143–6. Also, Jung, *Eighteenth-Century Illustration and Literary Material Culture*, 11–24.

52. A list of the subjects of prints produced in late eighteenth-century London is given in Johann Wilhelm Appell, *Werther und seine Zeit: Zur Goethe-Litteratur* (Oldenburg: Schulzesche Hofbuchhandlung und Hof-Buchdruckerei, 1896), 16–17.

53. Smith was known to have devised the design for the print. See *Manuel des Curieux et des Amateurs de l'Art* 9 (1808): 282.

54. *Caledonian Mercury*, 24 April 1784.

55. An undated version was also engraved in London by Francesco Bartolozzi (see the copy held by the Freies Deutsches Hochstift / Frankfurter Goethe-Museum (Kunstsammlung: 14518).

56. This version of the design is held by the Freies Deutsches Hochstift / Frankfurter Goethe-Museum (Kunstsammlung: III–14848). The urn does not feature Werter's name.

57. Julia Frankau, *An Eighteenth-Century Artist & Engraver: John Raphael Smith. His Life and Works* (London: Macmillan & Co., 1902), 90.

58. Victoria and Albert Museum accession number: 942–1888.

59. A copy of this version is held by the Freies Deutsches Hochstift / Frankfurter Goethe-Museum (Kunstsammlung: III–00099).

60. I have a silkwork adapting Kauffman's design and featuring Cowper's name in my collection.

61. *Derby Mercury*, 25 August 1791.

62. Swain, *Embroidered Georgian Pictures*, 11–12. These pictures illustrated scenes from Boccaccio's *Decameron*, Shakespeare's *The Tempest* and the tragic ballad of 'Lord Thomas and Fair Ellinor'.

63. My examination is based on eight copies held by Leicester Museum (reproduced in Swain, *Embroidered Georgian Pictures*, 15), the Museum of Early Southern Decorative Arts (accession number: 4251, Plate 17), the copies in my collection (Plates 14, 16 and 17), two sold at auction (on bidsquare.com; at Tovey's Needlework, Textiles and Clothing auction, 6 December 2019, lot 2803) and one for sale (Plate 15) from a specialist seller (Needlework Antiques). The silkwork sold by Tovey's featured Charlotte wearing a black hat and black shoes. The silkwork picture sold on bidsquare.com rendered Charlotte's cape in the same manner as that of Plate 15, but added a black hat, with white fringe, a black book and red shoes.

64. The silkwork is held by the Museum of Early Southern Decorative Arts (accession number: 4251).

65. Emily Leigh Lowes, *Chats on Old Lace and Needlework* (London: T. F. Unwin, 1908), 335.

66. Goethe, *The Sorrows of Werter*, 1:43.

67. See Maureen Daly Goggin, 'The Extra-Ordinary Power of Red and Eighteenth- and Nineteenth-Century Needlework', in *The Materiality of Color: The Production, Circulation, and Application of Dyes and Pigments, 1400–1800*, ed. Andrea Feeser, Maureen Goggin and Beth Fowkes Tobin (Aldershot: Ashgate, 2012), 30, 36, 40.

68. Goggin, 'The Extra-Ordinary Power of Red and Eighteenth- and Nineteenth-Century Needlework', 31.

69. *Werter and Charlotte: A German Story, Containing Many Wonderful and Pathetic Incidents* (London: T. Sabine, undated), 27.

70. One of the silkworks in the Victoria and Albert Museum has this colour scheme (accession number: 39–1874).

71. I have two versions in my collection, in which red is centrally used for elements of Fancy's dress. There is a similar silkwork in the Victoria and Albert Museum (accession number: 1743–1869).

72. Goggin, 'The Extra-Ordinary Power of Red and Eighteenth- and Nineteenth-Century Needlework', 40.

73. I have such a version in my collection.
74. Lowes, *Chats on Old Lace and Needlework*, 344. The hair picture is reproduced on page 345.
75. Laurence Sterne, *A Sentimental Journey through France and Italy and Continuation of the Bramine's Journal*, ed. Melvyn New and W. G. Day, The Florida Edition of the Works of Laurence Sterne (Gainesville: University Press of Florida, 2002), 150. On the visualisation of the scene, see W. B. Gerard, *Laurence Sterne and the Visual Imagination* (Aldershot: Ashgate, 2006), 125–73.
76. I have two such examples in my collection.
77. I have one such silkwork in my collection.
78. Pristash, Schaechterle and Wood, 'The Needle as Pen', 14.
79. Pristash, Schaechterle and Wood, 'The Needle as Pen', 16.
80. Caroline Matilda Warren, *The Gamesters; or Ruins of Innocence* (Boston: J. Shaw, 1828). 252.

25

EXTRA-ILLUSTRATION AND THE SEDUCTION OF A 'STANDARD' TEXT: JAMES COMERFORD'S EROTIC BOOKS

Helen Williams

Introduction

THE HISTORY OF erotic reading has long been one of supposition and theorisation. As Karen Harvey has argued, few owners of erotic texts identify themselves.[1] Victorian book collector James Comerford was an exception, inscribing his name on his copy of *A Voyage to Lethe* (1741). The book claims to be authored by the pseudonymous Captain Samuel Cock and, with a mock imprint common of the genre, pretends to be published by '*J. Coneybeare* in *Smock-Alley* near *Petticoat-Lane* in *Spittlefields*', though it was probably printed by John Hughs of Holborn.[2] Like the imprint, which amuses through its punning on what lies beneath smocks and petticoats, this is a work which perceives readerly pleasure as emerging from the imagination's response to words, principally those which metaphorically invoke the sexualised female body through topography. Comerford's copy is of interest as a unique material artefact of the history of sexuality, for Comerford was a prolific extra-illustrator, adding printed engravings to many of his books.

What we now call 'extra-illustration' is a process of appending new media – predominantly visual matter such as engraved images and printed ephemera – to a printed book, in a process that makes original connections between related topics.[3] Extra-illustration emerged from the eighteenth-century hobby of print collecting and allowed prolific collectors to showcase their prints in volumes in a manner which, for a while, enhanced their monetary value.[4] It was popular from the 1770s to the 1850s, and eighteenth- and nineteenth-century extra-illustrated volumes survive in their thousands.[5] But it was also, and continues to be, derided, and the value of such books plummeted from the mid-nineteenth century onwards.[6] This essay joins a growing body of research in the field of extra-illustration. Recent studies have likened the process to hypertext, drawing interesting links between well- (and less well-) chosen images and their new contexts.[7] They have so far tended to focus on the classic examples of extra-illustration – multi-volume Bibles, Shakespeare collections and folio works of biography or topography – providing a solid foundation for the field, and they have analysed the volumes' manifestation of literary engagement and connoisseurship, intentions often attributed by scholars to extra-illustrators.[8]

For the first time, this essay considers extra-illustration by James Comerford. Comerford was born in Holborn. By profession he was a notary, and in December 1840 he was elected a Fellow of the Society of Antiquaries.[9] He was, like his father, a book collector. At the end of the nineteenth century, William Roberts reported that Comerford 'had an exceedingly fine library, which consisted for the most part of topographical works, many of them on large paper with proof-plates'.[10] Following his death at the age of seventy-six in 1881, his books were sold in 1882 at Sotheby's across thirteen days, realising over £8,000.[11] Books holding his heraldic bookplates (with the notoriously untranslatable motto 'So Ho Ho Dea Ne', which is possibly an old war cry) are now sought-after collectors' items.[12] Comerford's extra-illustration practice encompasses a range of books, many of topographical interest, and is probably best represented by his copy of Henry Campkin's *Grub Street (Now Milton Street) London* (1868), which was gifted to him by the author on 14 September of that year, subsequently disbound and then collaged with letters, prints, drawings and relevant articles from newspapers.[13]

Many of Comerford's extra-illustrated volumes are held by the British Library and have thereby made their way onto digital platforms such as Google Books and Eighteenth-Century Collections Online (ECCO), as well as the British Library's own webpages. Some of the titles Comerford owned and extra-illustrated have subsequently become rare and significant sources for literary scholarship on romance, sexuality, erotica and popular culture, but his role in their creation as extra-illustrated works has so far gone unnoticed. Comerford's production of his own unique, highly stylised volumes through the process of extra-illustration evidences his own reading and reception of his book collection, his diverse extra-illustrative practice, and has also in some sense shaped the discipline of eighteenth-century studies, mediating our access to an eighteenth-century past. In the case of Comerford's books, at least two have become the most commonly used editions of eighteenth-century literary works which are otherwise out of print, functioning as digital surrogates which do not make clear their hybrid status as nineteenth-century extra-illustrated works.

This essay asks, what happens when the extra-illustrated text becomes the standard text? It considers two of Comerford's extra-illustrated books held by the British Library. They are single volumes which he disbound and individually rebound to accommodate loose or repurposed prints. The first book is *Voyage to Lethe* (1741), a rare anonymous erotic work in the 'Merry Land' tradition of metaphorical topographies of female bodies. The second is a copy of John Cleland's *The Romance of a Day; or an Adventure in Greenwich-Park, Last Easter* (1760), the first of four novellas that appeared in the 1760s and were subsequently reprinted together as the *Surprises of Love* in 1764. It offers a titillating story of class transgression and an insight into a now-canonical author's wider body of work. These eighteenth-century books feature Comerford's distinctive bookplate and have had plates added to them, bound within the work, sometime in the nineteenth century. They have both, in some sense, also become representative texts. Comerford's extra-illustrated copies of *Voyage to Lethe* and *Romance of a Day* are the texts available via a subscription to ECCO, and the latter is also freely available on Google Books.

A Voyage to Lethe

A Voyage to Lethe has attained a sort of mythic status in the history of erotic books. First published in 1741, it reappeared with a Glasgow imprint in 1756, allegedly 'Printed for Mrs. Laycock, at Mr. Clevercock's, in Smock-Alley'. Comerford was not its

EXTRA-ILLUSTRATION AND THE SEDUCTION OF A 'STANDARD' TEXT 435

only nineteenth-century fan, as the text was reissued for Victorian collectors in a limited edition run of 200 by the popular publisher of pornography Edward Avery.[14] The text's narrative describes sex and sexualised bodies in ways that encourage an imaginative visualisation. For instance, the protagonist explores a Palace, 'the Seat of Pleasure, inhabited by a kind of Deity, call'd *Voluptuaria*',[15] who shows him around 'a noble spacious Gallery of Capital Pictures', hung with portraits and tapestries of amorous individuals and couples:

> I am sorry it is not in my power to describe all the various whimsical Attitudes they were in; at the same time, I lamented very much my Inability to take a Draught of them; but I have since been informed, that one Sig^r. *Aretino*, an *Italian* Virtuoso, has amply supply'd that Deficiency, and that there are few of the politer Cabinets of *Europe*, but what are stock'd with Copies of them in *Mezzotinto*. (34)

In 1524 the satirist Pietro Aretino had composed verses to accompany a series of prints of sixteen sexual positions by Marcantonio Raimondi after Giulio Romano: *I Modi* (*The Ways*), also known as *The Sixteen Pleasures*. The result was a second edition, but this time the volume combined text with printed images, which became known as *Aretino's Postures* (1527). The zeal with which the authorities attempted to suppress these works, and the counter-zeal with which printers strove nevertheless to circulate this material – which went through approximately twelve different generations of replication[16] – meant that 'Aretino's *Postures*' became a byword for print pornography and was widely recognised as a project 'perhaps unprecedented in Italian engraving of secular subjects'.[17] Although *Lethe*'s traveller is unable to provide us with visuals, he relies upon our knowledge of and perhaps even access to a private practice of erotic connoisseurship in a satirical jibe at the European aristocracy and their appetite for such materials. The text's simultaneous reliance on and exploitation of common eighteenth-century pictorial tropes provided a strong rationale for Comerford's showcasing of his own print collection through extra-illustration. Reversing the process by which Aretino supplied text for images, Comerford supplied images for texts.

In his discussion of the erotic text of the Romantic period, Bradford Mudge borrows Roland Barthes's *Pleasure of the Text* and his theorisation of the erotic as to be glimpsed in the interstices:

> Not to be confused with the schoolboy's desire to have the body fully exposed eroticism is thus transformed from a problem of knowledge and possession – of knowing/seeing/having the body of the beloved – into a problem of imagination and relinquishment – of seeing what is to be seen and imagining what is not and letting go of the illusion of mastery.[18]

This applies not only to Romantic-era erotic writing, but also to the medium of the eighteenth-century book (and especially that which holds the erotic or romantic tale), where it is not the text itself that is the ultimate referent, but what its materiality leaves concealed. Desire emerges in the gaps between the pages. Nowhere is this more apparent than in the extra-illustrated text. No matter how fulsomely the narratives are illustrated, there remain incongruities between plate and text, and plate and subsequent plate, which only further displaces the reader, and perhaps the creator, from the illusion of mastery or possession. As Kathleen Lubey suggests, 'Sexual encounters

436   HELEN WILLIAMS

push intimate fictions toward their most literary; for they call on readers to imaginatively supplement the partial and highly stylized narratives of eroticism on their own.'[19] But both Mudge and Lubey are concerned with the reading of text rather than the reading of both text and image, and neither considers readers responding to text by producing their own new combinations of text and image. Comerford's extra-illustrated books reveal a reader enthusiastically accepting that invitation to 'imaginatively supplement . . . narratives of eroticism' though dismantling and then reassembling works of fiction.

Comerford's copy of *Voyage to Lethe* is a first edition from 1741 in a fine green leather three-quarter binding with marbled paper sides and matching endpapers. 'Voyage to Lethe – 1741' is stamped in gold on the spine, sandwiched between two fleurons and gold tooling. The binding itself evidences Comerford's investment in what had originally been a fairly inexpensive publication, taking ownership of the book in a manner which enhances its fetishistic status as extra-illustrated work. It is the most extra-illustrated of the texts discussed here, featuring eighteen images appended to a work of only 84 pages. By comparison, *The Romance of a Day* includes nine images in a work of 81 pages (see Appendix A and Appendix B). The volume opens with a fold-out map of love, *A Map or Chart of the Road of Love, and Harbour of Marriage* (1748), by 'T. P. Hydrographer' (Plate 22; Appendix A.1[20]). The map serves as a sort of key to the text, mirroring the narrator's voyage 'down the *Midway*', 'entring the Bay' (14), being entertained by '*Voluptuaria*' (67), then visiting '*Buttock-land*' and 'the Streights of *Hymen*' before making 'Cape *Virginia*', then finding himself at 'Despair Island' and 'Agonia' where the company quits the ship for '*Lethe*' (68). After visiting Lethe (a satirical space of forgetfulness where visitors come to abandon thoughts of their spouses and their morals), and a counterpoint well of remembering (under the protection of the goddess Nervami, where the King himself comes to remember his people), Cock returns home, marries a wealthy widow and, being 'very happy' (84), has no further need to visit Lethe. Cock's voyage shares similarities with the map's depiction of the 'Road of Love', which recommends passage via 'Cuckoldom Bay', through the 'Harbour of Marriage' to, ultimately, hopefully, 'Felicity Harbour', though there are also dangers to be aware of, as the verse suggests:

A Thousand Dangers here they run
What Points, What Rocks, what Sands to shun!
Lock'd in the winding Coast, how vain!
Are wishes to return again! (n.p.)

The proximity between the text and the image is striking, and although the image is not an exact depiction of the text it may have been inspired by it, given its focus and the date of its publication, seven years after the *Voyage*.

We then encounter as a mock frontispiece an engraving of 'Captain Jam[s] Cook, F.R.S.' (Figure 25.1; A.2). This print surprisingly suits its new location, due to the similarity of 'Cook' to 'Cock', the explorer's staff, which takes on new significance in this copy, and the contemporary association between travelling to exotic locations and sexual freedom. The printed caption to the image has been amended by hand to 'Captain Sam[l]. Cock, F.R.S.', to associate the image more closely with the protagonist

Figure 25.1 A print serving as a 'frontispiece' to Comerford's *Voyage to Lethe* (1741): H. Dodd, engraved by Andrew Birrell, *Captain James Cook, F.R.S.* (amended by hand to 'Saml. Cock') (1785). British Library General Reference Collection Cup.1001.c.4. By permission of the British Library.

of the *Voyage*. When Cock's ship lands among a 'Parcel of Lovers' (23–4), Comerford inserts the *Inhabitants and Monuments of Easter Island* (1798) (A.8), after Gaspard Duché de Vancy. This stereotypical representation of semi-naked indigenous people among fully clothed colonisers was originally designed for Jean-François de Galaup de La Pérouse's *A Voyage Round the World, in the Years 1785, 1786, 1787, and 1788* (1798), and in its idealism it portrays what Comerford longs for Cock to find rather than what the text describes, that is, the realities of matrimonial bickering and the long voyage to find an eroticised safe 'harbour'. Comerford's juxtaposition of Cook with La Pérouse betrays a Victorian sensibility, revealing the extra-illustrator recontextualising historical narratives with the so-called benefit of hindsight – particularly through the consolidated appreciation and national memory of Cook's voyages – and in an entirely different market for books and prints from that which might be presumed from the date on the title page of the volume.

Many of Comerford's prints were taken from magazines and volumes of fiction. This was the case for an illustration originally intended for Voltaire's short story, *Jenni, ou Le sage et l'athée*, in an edition of *Romans et contes* (1778) (A.4).[21] Voltaire's *Jenni* is a short story about an Englishman embroiled in the Spanish Inquisition. The episode depicted in Comerford's illustration is related by a woman, Dona Las Nalgas, who describes her desire to see the naked body of an imprisoned English heretic, since English heretics had been described by their Inquisitors as monstrous, having 'the tails

438 HELEN WILLIAMS

of monkeys, the paws of bears, and the heads of parrots'. Las Nalgas and Dona Boca Vermeja plant themselves in a closet adjoining Jenni's bathroom and, as he emerges from the water, they are pleasantly surprised at his physique. The image, designed by Jeanne Deny after Charles Monnet, shows Jenni's head turned towards the women, whom he discovers watching him bathe, and in the process showcases to the reader the body that the women have been admiring. In Comerford's volume, the image faces the textual description of Samuel Cock, 'the youngest of twelve Sons and ten Daughters (all born and christen'd) of *Sampson Cock* of *Coney-Hatch*, Esq; by my Mother, his first Cousin, a celebrated Toast in her Time; of the *Laycock* Family, settled at *Cunning-ton* in *Huntingdonshire*' (4). It serves to idealise the physique of the male character who is about to engage in a series of erotic encounters. Some of Comerford's prints were stand-alone collectors' items, like the folded colour print of Thomas Rowland-son's *Love in a Tub or a Cure for a Cold* (1802) (A.3), featuring a couple with bare legs bathing their feet together by the bed while a woman brings them a warming pan and a posset. Julie Peakman has described this image as a depiction of 'plebeian sex', showing ordinary people rather than typical depictions of sex, involving the nobil-ity at play.[22] It is also an image that privileges a female perspective, with the women seemingly catching each other's eyes, suggesting an added element of voyeurism and a female gaze, which is echoed in the illustration from *Jenni*.

Love in a Tub appears after the mock subscribers' list, which names 'The Rev. Mr. *Slowcock*' as by far the most generous subscriber, who 'for himself and Parish-ioners' pledges 3,000 copies of the *Voyage*, 'to bind up with the Octavo Edition of *Pamela*'. This comic paratext is another important moment where the text hints self-consciously at its own materiality and its propensity to be bound at the will of the purchaser, being sold sewn or in sheets, as was the custom in the eighteenth cen-tury. Indeed, extra-illustration becomes an extra stage beyond bookbinding, which Julia Miller has called the last vestige of 'un-mass-production for the many'.[23] Com-erford responds to the paratextual '*Slowcock*' with the bold insertion of *Love in a Tub*, which suggests how far the extra-illustrated work acts as a historical palimp-sest, and creates new intertexts for the *Voyage* long after Richardson's 1740 novel through the practice of binding the text with prints of the eighteenth and early nineteenth centuries.

Perhaps the most significant prints in the volume are those that currently remain unidentified, including what could be a rare Thomas Rowlandson print, of Venus embracing Cupid on a Velázquez-like bed with a cherub voyeur (Figure 25.2; A.9). It may have had a caption at some stage, and perhaps identified its makers, but the manner of its binding makes it almost impossible to know. The 'Rowlandson' Venus faces the *Voyage*'s description of 'the Entrance into the Gulf of *Venus*, . . . built on the *Terra firma* of *Buttock-Land*, by some Geographers call'd *B-llock-Land*' (27–8). The cherub's view of Venus's buttocks, while we see Venus from the front, perhaps suggested the juxtapo-sition with the text describing the foundations of the 'Gulf of *Venus*', rather than the image's disturbing eroticised depiction of children. In what is perhaps a neater connec-tion with the text, at a mention of the goddess 'Dildona', Comerford includes a small, almost square, print of a woman sitting by a kitchen table while dinner steams beside her (Figure 25.3; A.12). She has raised her skirt and is masturbating with the carrots. Com-erford's extra-illustration makes the works of well-known artists just as important to the text as those of their lesser known or in this case unidentified contemporaries, with each insertion offering a valid and different way of reading the text in hand.[24]

EXTRA-ILLUSTRATION AND THE SEDUCTION OF A 'STANDARD' TEXT 439

Figure 25.2 Thomas Rowlandson? after Velázquez, a Venus embracing Cupid (n.d.), facing p. 29 of Comerford's *Voyage to Lethe* (1741). British Library General Reference Collection Cup.1001.c.4. By permission of the British Library.

Figure 25.3 Unidentified erotic print of a woman masturbating with carrots, extra-illustrating Comerford's *Voyage to Lethe* (1741), facing p. 35. British Library General Reference Collection Cup.1001.c.4. By permission of the British Library.

440 HELEN WILLIAMS

Comerford's extra-illustration, in his specific selection and insertion of pertinent prints, was not only a process that determined new codex-homes for loose prints but also one which rehomed prints originally included in other volumes, as was the case for the *Jenni* image and that of the Rapa Nui scene. Two prints in Comerford's *Voyage to Lethe* were originally produced for the *Rambler's Magazine; or, the Annals of Gallantry, Glee, Pleasure, and the Bon Ton, etc.* (1783–90): *A Jew Turning to a Christian* (October 1784) (A.14), depicting a couple on a sofa, and the *Three Gracelesses* (April 1784) (A.18), showing a trio of dancing naked women with a male fiddler and voyeur. An erotic periodical aimed at a nominally male readership, the *Rambler's Magazine* aimed to 'undraw the Hymenieal curtain, to unravel the amours of the imprudent and voluptuous; or the neglected wife, and the too-importunate suitor'.[25] One of the ways in which it did so, designed to be most aesthetically appealing to readers, was to print one of the above or similar images as a frontispiece to an issue, with the accompanying piece of text printed deep within the issue. The texts tended to be dialogues which gave life to the image. The price of the Jewish man's liaison with the Christian woman is his conversion, which he undertakes enthusiastically, with the tale's antisemitism rendered transparent. For the three 'Gracelesses', an orgy is described at C—n [Carlton] House, involving a thinly veiled Lord Bute, Charles James Fox, and three women, 'Perdita' (Mary Robinson), 'The White Crow' (Maria Corbyn) and 'The Green Linnet' (probably Gertude Mahon, or the 'Bird of Paradise'):

> *Perdita.* How does your lords-p approve my *movements*? I think I *keep time* tolerably well.
>   *Lord B.* A perfect *time-piece!* A man that cannot find out the longitude with such an assistant, must keep a devilish bad reckoning.
>   *The white Crow.* I think our dancing is infinitely superior to your music.— What a large aukward instrument you have got!—'Tis enough to terrify a moderate woman to look at it!—I wish you would take the filthy thing out of my sight— . . .
>   *Carlo Khan.* Ladies, you are certainly mistaken—I think it is a *noble instrument*— but if you rather choose to be amused by something in the diminutive way, I have got a cremona in miniature *(pulling out a wretched meagre instrument).* How do ye approve of its dimensions, ladies?—It is extremely brisk and entertaining, and will make up, by its activity, for every deficiency of length or bulkiness.[26]

Alongside its text, the image in its original context satirised Fox's collaboration with female canvassers during the 1784 election. But because of the generic faces of the women it is likely that the names were applied to the risqué image after production, to add extra contemporary appeal as the magazine was finalised for the press. In its new context in Comerford's *Voyage*, the illustration aligns with the text's description of 'a promiscuous Circle of beautiful young Damsels, Wives, Widows, Prudes, Coquets, and others, committing all the Extravagancies as at the *Floral* Games of old; running naked around the Idol, kissing and sucking the decorating Shrub with all the Marks of a furious Adoration' (65–6), a party which Captain Cock enthusiastically joins.

The *Rambler's Magazine* combined erotic fiction with the scandal of the day. According to one newspaper, it had 'a wonderful circulation among 'prentice boys, indecent rakes, and profligates'.[27] The plates were later acquired by publisher William Benbow, who reprinted them with some fresh text in a revamped *Rambler's Magazine; or Fashionable Emporium of Polite Literature* (1822–3). Benbow had opened a shop on the back of the periodical's success, but was taken to court in May 1822 by the Society for the Suppression of Vice, where the prosecution argued that the work 'was calculated to inflame passion and to throw chastity into disgrace'. The court heard examples of the obscene libels in question, including a song from the *Magazine* and an extract of a French novel Benbow was about to publish. They also looked at the *Magazine*'s prints. The inspection and reading of these sources were reported to have 'occupied an hour'. Benbow's lawyer, Charles Phillips, offered an eloquent defence, arguing that not once had the Society prosecuted a man of their own social standing, aiming always at working men such as Benbow, 'a humble, unprotected man', apparently for fear of their own hypocrisy coming to light. He suggested that they 'overlooked the titled and the opulent':

> They would not aim at high game, lest some hoary hypocrite amongst themselves should meet the punishment he deserved. . . . His candidate had been obliged to leave his house in the Strand because he had been persecuted by another gang, who procured him to be imprisoned for ten months, and then turned him out of his dungeon, his last shilling gone, and family brought to ruin. These were the modern champions of Christianity.

Benbow was found not guilty.[28] Though he was saved by the eloquence of his defence, and the hypocrisy of his prosecution, that his images were considered as examples of obscene libel suggests the subversiveness of Comerford's collection.

We cannot know whether Comerford bought discrete copies of books and periodicals and then reassembled them in ways which extra-illustrated some texts while depriving others of their original image. What is more likely is that he purchased prints, separately or in bulk, from a seller or multiple sellers who profited from an eighteenth-century marketplace in which prints were often detached from and circulated separately from their original works. In the case of the illustrations from the *Rambler's Magazine*, as well as from its rival the *Wit's Magazine* (1784–5), Comerford's extra-illustration participated in an untold hierarchy of printed texts, taking apart some works in order to enhance others, in a culture in which periodicals were considered disposable and ephemeral, while their images could, detached, continue to circulate.

The Romance of a Day

In Comerford's *Voyage to Lethe*, we can discern certain propensities in his choice of prints: a tendency to privilege voyeurism, and to combine exploration with erotica; but Comerford's illustrative focus as an interactive reader is quite different in his copy of John Cleland's *Romance of a Day*.[29] What Comerford seemed to find interesting about the *Romance of a Day* was the situation of its romantic comedy within a recognisable urban milieu. Indeed, while Cleland's romantic short stories are rarely considered in scholarship, as Hal Gladfelder points out, they were his most commercially and critically successful works.[30] Comerford added several plates to Cleland's story. The first illustration takes its position as a frontispiece. It is currently unidentified, but it does accurately portray the fact that the text features four main characters, two of each sex (Figure 25.4; B.1): in this case the characters are Letitia and Frederic of the nobility, and

Figure 25.4 Unidentified print of a group of people by a riverside facing the first page of Comerford's *Romance of a Day* (1760). British Library General Reference Collection 1459.a.60. By permission of the British Library.

their servants Tom and Deborah. However, the picture inaccurately suggests that the heroine of the tale will be approached by admirers of both sexes, given the image's portrayal of her outstretched arms while her hands are kissed by a man and a woman. The three most prominent figures are dressed in the highest fashion, whereas Cleland's four protagonists appear in servant dress. The image was likely chosen because of its depiction of a woman being seduced in an urban riverside location. The woman's status and confused air is appropriate enough for this tale of a Greenwich adventure, in which the noble hero and heroine pretend to be of the working classes in order to enjoy a day out.

Many of the prints Comerford binds to this erotically charged novella are topographic, setting the scene of the action. The first of this kind is *A View of Greenwich Park on Whitsun-Monday* (1802) (B.2), taken from the *European Magazine*, and folded between the pages dealing with Frederic's appearance at the holiday festivities. Of all the images appended to the text this is the most relevant to its content and setting. The Greenwich Observatory in the far-right corner ties the engraving to the immediate context of Cleland's story, in which Frederic passes around half an hour 'on the lawn at the bottom of the hill in the park, just under the observatory in a circle formed by a number of young persons of both sexes' (7). The expanse of lawn in the image provides space for freedom of expression while the shaded areas by the trees conceal romance, sex and crime.

The text describes Frederic's subaltern disguise, which shows off his 'eyes of the first lustre, a head of fine black hair negligently tied behind . . ., a free easy shape, perfectly well-fashioned legs, . . . [and] a manly air diffused over all' (7). In short, 'The

EXTRA-ILLUSTRATION AND THE SEDUCTION OF A 'STANDARD' TEXT   443

young man of distinction still peeped through this occasional under-dress' (6). The central focus of the magazine image is a musician with a music box, who gazes out at the viewer while being surrounded with diverse entertainment. There are boxers surrounded by a crowd of armed men, women and couples dancing, with one woman experiencing a wardrobe malfunction, and what seems to be a heterosexual dalliance against a tree, all of which establish Greenwich as a place of frolic and sexual freedom for the lower classes. The image itself follows a tradition of visual representations of festive abandon, like Rowlandson's *Vauxhall Gardens* (1785) and William Hogarth's *Southwark Fair* (1734), engravings which exploit the fact that locations such as the pleasure gardens, and temporary holidays including fairs, proffered opportunities for transgression of all kinds. The engraving depicts Greenwich Park as a place where the 'subaltern class' can let their hair down on holidays away from the policing eyes of the nobility. Its insertion within Cleland's text portrays the place as if perceived through the eyes of Frederic, the noble interloper, who sees it as a hunting ground:

> Already then he was looking round, like an eastern monarch in the midst of his seraglio, for his favorite sultana of the moment, to whom he should graciously throw the handkerchief, and consecrate the rest of the evening to less innocent diversion. (9)

Frederic sees Greenwich Park as an Orientalised, eroticised landscape of possibility, just as it is framed within the print. Comerford's extra-illustration therefore positions the reader as that 'eastern monarch', looking around at the activities depicted in the print in order to identify the activities described in the text.

The image helps to set the scene for what is arguably this short story's most erotic moment:

> he had amused himself with the various shapes into which the native coquettry of the female sex broke forth on this occasion in this subaltern class. The half-advances and half-repulses of some, the skittish wildness or the tractable tameness of others, the gentle glow in all of working nature, yet exalted by the conspiring heat of the weather and exercise, opportune trips and provoking falls on the green on purpose to be taken up again by so pretty a fellow as Frederic; all this scene, in short, of low, if what is natural can be called low, merriment had not even unsensually affected him. At his age, it was scarce possible, without being moved, to take and give so many kisses, and toy with so many girls, whose pure beauties of flesh and blood, were such, as that he must have been more or less than man to have withstood their impressions. (8–9)

Cleland builds the erotic tension as Frederic finds himself ready to leave the park with any willing companion. But this is a moment interrupted by Comerford's insertion (at the word 'conspiring', which breaks over pages 8–9) of another topographical print, *A View of London from One-Tree-Hill in Greenwich-Park* (B.3), probably from *The Gentleman's Magazine* of January 1754. It was derived from another engraving originally published in 1744 after a painting by Peter Tillemans of around 1730, and later widely adapted and populated with different characters. It depicts the hill upon which we have learnt that Frederic played 'hunt the handkerchief' with the young women, and 'occasionally made excursions up the hill, and run or rolled down the slope of it with more than one giggling hoyden' (8). But the scene in the image is altogether more respectable. It is not the occasion of a holiday, but of a regular day, with respectable families and couples walking across a considerably less busy landscape, which is orderly and spacious, and notably quieter. It is a reminder, perhaps, of Frederic's out-of-placeness at the Easter holiday given his social class which is both inherited and embodied, what Cleland calls the 'fortune and figure of Frederic' (78). Taken together, the two images of Greenwich Park show the world in which Frederic finds himself, and that to which he belongs. In one sense, the Tillemans image functions as a sort of blank canvas for the erotic tension of the scene, and in another replicates the suspense wrought by Cleland on a textual level, when he delays Frederic's intended departure – and the implied consummation of his desire – by the arrival of Letitia:

> Nothing kept him in suspence but the variety of such as without too much vanity, he had reason from broad hints, to imagine, would not tear his eyes out, if he should offer his service to them. He was in this quandary, when a sudden buz interrupted it; a buz such as runs through any assembly of people at the first appearance of an interesting figure. (9–10)

The narrator proceeds to explain the presence of Letitia, a disguised wealthy heiress lured into a frolic at the park by her servant, Deborah – a forty-year-old, charmless, gullible woman who believes a suitor will propose to her there. Here, Comerford inserts an image of a ship with Greenwich Hospital in the background (B.4). This illustration was taken from *London and its Environs Described* (1761). The image is in one sense bathetic, mirroring Cleland's own deferral of his intricately wrought sexual tension to flash back to the reasons for Letitia being in the park. To a reader like Comerford the print perhaps contributed to the ability of the text to prompt the imagination to set the scene, evidencing his range of interests as collector and as reader. At this point in the text we learn that, before leaving, Deb (much like Comerford's image) had 'extolled so much the pleasure of the walk, of the sight, and of the evening' (22) that Letitia agrees to accompany her in a serving girl's disguise, provided her father does not find out. The women embark upon their scheme, prompting the reader to anticipate sexual danger in the locale Comerford illustrates.

Back in the present, Frederic asks Letitia to dance, prompting a friendship between the two, while his servant Tom is tasked with taking care of Deborah. Comerford tips in another image of Greenwich just at the moment that the four potential lovers approach 'the park-door which opens into the avenue leading to the town' (42). Comerford's insertion of *The Ancient Palace at Greenwich, called Placentia, the Birth-Place of Queen Elizabeth*, after James Basire the Elder, probably from *Vestuta Monumenta* (1767) (B.5), takes us through that portal. The text interrupted by the image describes the crossing of the threshold, and the moment when they leave the park for the town: 'Tom had officiously stepped before, and held it open for them to pass' (42–3), at which point Letitia asks Deborah where they are going: 'Only, said she, just to take a walk down the town, give a look at the Thames, and then return home' (43). Cleland's forty-year-old virgin is now at the bidding of Tom, an accomplished player and prankster, who has exploited her willingness to be wooed in order to construct an elaborate ruse to enable Frederic to have time alone with Letitia.

The figures of Tom and Deborah bring such light relief to the tale that they are in danger of becoming its true heroes. When the characters take their walk by the river,

EXTRA-ILLUSTRATION AND THE SEDUCTION OF A 'STANDARD' TEXT   445

following a secluded route perhaps not unlike Comerford's image of *Placentia*, the group are seemingly forced to take refuge at a tavern because Tom has suddenly put his comedic skills to use and pretended to faint in the street (43–4):

> Tom as they were passing before the door of a tavern there, plaid off such a stage-trick, which he had been meditating for the service of his master, and for which he had somewhat prepared Deborah by telling her he found himself taken of a sudden, in a manner quite unusual to him, and that he was afraid he had walked too much in the sun that day. The twice too tender Deborah was greatly alarmed at this, but much more so, when just before the door, he fainted away. He was too good a comedian not to act this to the life. Deborah screamed out for help, and presently two or three waiters came out, and desired the company to walk in. (43–4)

Frederic is made aware of the ruse by a wink, while Letitia does not suspect the trick. Deborah, however, is full of 'exclamations and tears, though they formed rather a kind of comic distress, the expression of which did not add much to her beauty' (44). Deborah's despair at the scene prompts Comerford to insert an unidentified illustration resembling those found in some eighteenth-century editions of comic drama. The plate features two women looking down from a balcony at three men gesticulating in the street (Figure 25.5; B.6), similar in style to that which serves as Comerford's frontispiece. The image somewhat imperfectly reflects Cleland's narrative. The obviously rich clothing of the characters in the image contrasts with the subaltern disguises of Cleland's protagonists. One of the men could potentially be interpreted as being on the verge of fainting, but he is quite upright, and not at all like Tom, 'who lay on the ground unrecovered from his swoon' (44). Nevertheless, the fairly standard architecture of the backdrop and the figures' animated expressions may have appealed to Comerford as an appropriate means of illustrating this important moment.

More significantly, the image marks a generic pivot in the story. Cleland's hitherto erotic adventure moves to the realm of comedy, which Comerford recognises with a transition from topographical to comedic prints. Deborah's tears, it seems, stem less from the fact that she might lose Tom as a prospective husband than that she might never get married at all, 'and for a husband she was now so thoroughly a-gog, that rather than not make sure of one, it is not at all clear that she would not have taken up with the antientest private pensioner in Greenwich Hospital' (45). The comedic circumstances continue when Letitia's father interrupts Frederic's attempted conquest at the inn, a moment marked by Comerford with a print entitled *The Unexpected Meeting* (B.7): Jean Michel Moreau le Jeune's frontispiece to *L'École des femmes* (1662) from the *Œuvres de Molière* (1773). In the context of Cleland's story, the image aligns Letitia's father with Molière's Arnolphe, the scheming guardian in a tricorn, who (at least initially, for Cleland) threatens to come between the lovers. The resolution of Cleland's tale, with Letitia and Frederic discovering each other's noble birth, and therefore their ability to continue their courtship, is recognised by Comerford through his insertion of another print, *La confiance des belles âmes* (B.8) from Jean-Jacques Rousseau's *Julie: or la Nouvelle Héloïse* (1761), in which Julie introduces her former tutor and lover, Saint-Preux, to her husband, the noble Monsieur de Wolmar, at the entrance to their estate. As both the tone and the title of the image suggest, the picture is one of trust and confidence, of two men becoming acquainted through a virtuous woman. The Rousseauvian intertext

Figure 25.5 Unidentified print of two women looking from a balcony onto three men in a city street, extra-illustrating Comerford's *Romance of a Day* (1760), facing p. 45. British Library General Reference Collection 1459.a.60. By permission of the British Library.

implies an insurmountable class barrier between the lovers that is ultimately resolved by Cleland. Comerford's Cleland, then, is a hybrid of mid-eighteenth-century sentiment undercut by late seventeenth-century comedy.

The idealised match between the main (upper class) protagonists in Cleland's narrative is not only socially conservative but also potentially generative of income through the consolidation of two neighbouring estates, a fact which Comerford's topographical insertions serve to enhance. Frederic's initial reprimand by Letitita's father for his indiscretion with his daughter (whose upper-class identity he soon recognises) is 'closed with a kind of desire of better acquaintance, not without a broad hint of the convenience of a match between their children, on condition of the parties liking one another' (76). While these estates are not described in the text, the romance fetishises the underclasses as all the while it consolidates the power of the landowners, a fact that Comerford underlines through the extra-illustrative parallels he makes between *Julie* and Cleland's neat conclusion to the *Romance of a Day*.

Cleland's *Romance of a Day* is a topography of romance and a romance of topography, and ultimately manifests an erotics of landowning which contributes to the pleasure of the ending, consistently promoted by Comerford as extra-illustrator in his additions of landscape scenes. There is a self-consciousness in both Cleland's short stories and Comerford's extra-illustration. The narrator of Cleland's *Romance of a Day* reflects upon the predictable nature of his story's conclusion:[31]

EXTRA-ILLUSTRATION AND THE SEDUCTION OF A 'STANDARD' TEXT 447

But, alas! nothing sublunary is susceptible of perfection, or I should not have on this occasion to deplore the unutterable woe of the unfortunate Mrs. Deborah. For, would you believe it, notwithstanding the known infallibility of dreams; notwithstanding the laudable industry with which she had labored for the verifying her's, insomuch that malice itself cannot say it was her fault that it was not verified; notwithstanding the likelihood of her turning out a most loving wife to whoever should make the experiment, and that Tom, the dear object of her wishes, could not be suspected of such nicety as to reject a virgin whom Letitia's good-nature was ready to make a sort of fortune to him; the match between this illustrious pair did not take place, and in not taking place, besides the feelings it must give for the disappointed fair one, violates all the rules of romance: but how can I help it? Truth is above every thing; that rogue Tom had a wife and two children. (79–80)

Cleland's witty insertion of himself as author into the text, playing upon the pretence that his characters are beyond his power, transforms what had so far been circumstance-based humour into a more literary pleasure, one to which Comerford enthusiastically responded and through which he – like Cleland – reminds us of his authority over this volume.

Comerford's prints as appended to both *Voyage to Lethe* and the *Romance of a Day* range from topographic to erotic, novelistic to comedic, and demonstrate the breadth of his collection, revealing Comerford's wide-ranging interests, some clearly salacious but others more anodyne. Comerford's extra-illustrated volumes function in one sense as repositories serving to represent and contain that range, to some degree irrespective of the book's content, or at least, in the case of the *Voyage to Lethe* and the *Romance of a Day*, of their more erotic content. This leads us to consider the conversation between word and image that an extra-illustrated work seems to invite. In each of Comerford's books, the text itself seems to be enhanced by the images interspersed within it, which superimpose a specific interpretation or which exaggerate author-initiated tension. Comerford's extra-illustration reveals the ways in which bibliographical history recreates the seeming power balance in word–image relations, challenging logocentrism, and in fact serves to create a new version of 'the book' itself.

'Standard Copies' and Eighteenth-Century Works Online

Comerford, as a prominent Victorian collector of eighteenth-century literature, has exerted an unexpected impact upon the discipline of eighteenth-century studies today, since his volumes have become part of a national collection. Because these titles are rare, with few alternative copies available to consult, it has been difficult for readers to identify them as extra-illustrated. Provenance, and the quirks of a specific reader-owner, are not always visible in library catalogues, and are almost always absent in their digital surrogates. Comerford's extra-illustrated texts evidence a kind of editorial process through which he creates his own version of these works: not only do these books elucidate his activities and interests as a collector – what he read, what he kept – but they also capture the processes of selection and organisation of which image to use and where, such that he becomes both editor and creator. His copies have become the unique vehicles by which certain texts have been made available to a wider public, which in turn can invoke the dangers of careless assumptions about 'the' text and its history, when in the case of Comerford's extra-illustration the issue of provenance should always be paramount.

448 HELEN WILLIAMS

One of the seductions of the digital archive is that it tempts us to view its surrogates as standard copies. But it is as important to remember the production histories of databases as it is those of the physical book. As Lucy Peltz has pointed out, many collections holding extra-illustrated books

> lack the protocols for noting the distinctive characteristics of particular volumes. Part of the problem is that the materials do not fit established categories: they are neither book nor album nor print collection, and yet they are simultaneously all three. The consequence is that extra-illustrated books are often overlooked, misunderstood or, in many cases, broken up for the prints and drawings they contain.[32]

Extra-illustrated volumes face further challenges in digital corpora of major library collections. The main dataset for our field, Eighteenth-Century Collections Online, is composed of digital facsimiles of 'The Eighteenth Century' microfilm collection originally published by Research Publications (now PSM, part of Gale publishing company). The microfilms were predominantly produced from the holdings of the British Library. Copies of rare books in that repository, therefore, have been microfilmed and then digitised. While they have individual Gale Document Numbers, and the full citation option allows us to identify the Source Library as the British Library, the identifying information of the specific copy – including the British Library catalogue number of that item, as well as other copy-specific information such as provenance – is not available as part of the ECCO metadata. The result is that the images are divorced from any sense of a book as a unique physical artefact, and subsequently they become presented as standard editions: a subversion of an existing collection by a new one that ignores provenance. Comerford's copies of Cleland's *Romance of a Day* and of the anonymous *Voyage to Lethe* are presented on ECCO complete with Comerford's appended engravings, which appear without commentary. The overexposed quality of microfilm images means that, for instance, the ECCO edition of Comerford's *Voyage to Lethe* disguises the fact that some of the engravings have been folded in the middle and tipped in, some are hand-coloured, and some displayed in window mounts. Their nineteenth-century material qualities – and Comerford's interventions into each codex – are rendered invisible by the poor contrast.

The seduction of reading these texts as standard – whether in the flesh, as material books, or in digital form – is richly demonstrated by the reception of *Voyage to Lethe*, which, as a rare book, survives in its first edition in only three UK collections, and nine in North America. It has featured in histories of sexuality by Karen Harvey and Julie Peakman as an important, because rare, example of erotica from the first half of the eighteenth century. Perhaps it is doubly appealing in Comerford's version, with its rare erotic images. As evidence of erotic reading, Comerford's *Voyage* has carried more weight for eighteenth-century erotica than for its nineteenth-century moment of extra-illustration. It is a text in disguise, not unlike Cleland's protagonists. Harvey analyses Comerford's *Voyage to Lethe* in her study of women's spaces as repositories of pleasure in the eighteenth century.[33] Writing that the images 'were inserted by a later bookseller or reader late in the century', Harvey does not identify the illustrations as Comerford's interventions, nor as extra-illustration as such, and reads the text as a product of the eighteenth century.[34] Peakman has imagined that there were multiple copies of Comerford's *Voyage to Lethe*, writing that

EXTRA-ILLUSTRATION AND THE SEDUCTION OF A 'STANDARD' TEXT   449

The bound versions of *Voyage to Lethe* carried similar drawings undertaken on voyages round the Pacific, such as 'Monuments on Easter Island' (1744–97) made by William Hodges, draughtsman for James Cook on the Endeavour, although these were later additions to the text. These covert messages contained in *Voyage to Lethe* would have been obvious to eighteenth-century readers. Indeed, the picture of Captain Sam Cock is none other than Cook himself.[35]

Comerford's piecing together of erotic text with erotic image may have been inspired by a lust for the eighteenth century, but, in fact, there were no eighteenth-century readers of Comerford's *Voyage to Lethe*. Comerford was born in the nineteenth century, and his *Voyage to Lethe* was not produced until at least after 1822, the date of its earliest illustration, when Comerford himself was aged around fifteen. While conceding that the images were later additions to the bound volume, Peakman nevertheless reads the map and the Cook/Cock 'frontispiece' as integral to the eighteenth-century experience of that text.[36] But Comerford's *Voyage to Lethe* represents an enhanced gathering of obscene printed materials, which is far from representative of the standard copy of this erotic book, and evidences a nineteenth-century reading of eighteenth-century erotica.

Comerford's copies present us with an engaging research and teaching opportunity. His pasted-in prints create intertextual connections in the interstices of the text. These are volumes which become out of time, via a nineteenth-century reading moment, and finally transposed into a digital present. They tell multimodal histories of literature and sexuality, of print production, collecting and ephemera, and present to us unexpected narratives of comparative literature and reading history spanning centuries. The illustrations defer gratification, extend the text, explore its complexities and ambiguities, and at times either heighten or dampen the narrative's sexual potential. They demonstrate Comerford's identification of the interstices of the erotic text as opportunities for extra-illustration, and they see him participating in the pleasure of the text by adding to it sedimentary layers of print matter which help shape their original narratives for future readers.

Appendices: James Comerford's Extra-Illustrated Books

These Appendices list the prints appended to the two books once owned by James Comerford discussed in this essay and identify the locations of the prints within the texts. Where possible, they identify the designer, the engraver and the publisher of an image, as well as its original publication context. They provide references to the digital surrogates of Comerford's books as well as to each of the identified images in either their original contexts or in museum/printshop holdings. Some remain a mystery to be solved by future readers.

Appendix A

Prints in Comerford's *Voyage to Lethe* (1741), British Library General Reference Collection Cup.1001.c.4.
Comerford's copy is available via Eighteenth-Century Collections Online, Gale Document number GALE|CW0115703237.

Table 25.1 Prints in Comerford's *Voyage to Lethe* (1741)

Item	Artist	Title	Publication details	Type	Links to colour images of alternative copies
1. Folded within front endpapers	T. P. Hydrographer [Pseud.]	*A Map or Chart of the Road of Love, and Harbour of Marriage*	London: Laurie and Whittle, 1748 [amended by hand to '1741']. See Plate 22.	Hand-coloured engraving	British Library, https://www.bl.uk/collection-items/map-of-the-road-of-love
2. Facing title-page	Designed by H. Dodd, engraved by Andrew Birrell	*Captain James Cook, F.R.S.* [amended by hand to 'Saml. Cock']	London: Fielding, 1785. See Figure 25.1.	Engraving	Royal Museums Greenwich, item 2 at https://www.rmg.co.uk/collections/objects/rmgc-object-107043
3. Folded between the subscribers' list and the Introduction	Thomas Rowlandson	*Love in a Tub or a Cure for a Cold*	London, 1802.	Aquatint	Meisterdrucke Kunstreproduktionen, https://www.meisterdrucke.uk/fine-art-prints/Thomas-Rowlandson/1116754/Love-in-a-Tub-or-a-Cure-for-a-Cold%27.html
4. Facing p. 5	Jeanne Deny after Charles Monnet	*Jeune homme à sa toilette*	Bouillon: Société typographique, 1778. Originally included in François-Marie Arouet dit Voltaire, *Romans et contes*, vol. III, *Jenni ou Le sage et l'athée*, facing p. 6 [annotated on reverse in pencil 'Voyage, P. 4']	Engraving	See Florence Fesneau, 'Les secrets plaisirs de la voyeuse au temps des Lumières', *Lumen*, 37 (2018), 182
5. Facing p. 7		*The Unwelcome Visitor*	*The Rambler's Magazine* (November 1784). Accompanies a narrative entitled 'Further Adventures of Kitty Pry', pp. 452–5		

6. Facing p. 13		[A woman sitting on a man's knee, his hand up a her skirt, kissing in a chair by the fire]	Unidentified		
7. Facing p. 23	Published by William Benbow	*A Jew Turning to a Christian*	*The Rambler's Magazine* (October 1784). Accompanies a dialogue entitled 'A Jew Turning to a Christian', pp. 404–5	Engraving	A variant is available at HathiTrust, https://catalog.hathitrust.org/Record/002560130
8. Folded between pp. 24 and 25	After Gaspard Duché de Vancy	*Inhabitants and Monuments of Easter Island*	London: G & J Robinson, 1798. Produced for Jean-Francois de Galaup de La Pérouse, *A Voyage Round the World' in the Years 1785, 1786, 1787, and 1788* (London: Stockdale, 1798) [annotated in pencil on reverse, 'Capt. Cock']	Engraving	British Museum, https://www.britishmuseum.org/collection/object/P_1948-0120-24
9. Landscape format, facing p. 29	[Thomas Rowlandson? after Velázquez]	*Bonansoni?* [illegible] [Venus embracing Cupid on a bed, while a cherub looks on beneath a drape]	Unidentified. See Figure 25.2	Engraving	
10. Facing p. 31		[Bare-chested woman interrupted in breastfeeding by a gesticulating man – baby looks up at him]	Unidentified	Engraving	

(*Continued*)

11. Facing p. 33		*A Fine Subject on the Carpet*	Frontispiece to *The Rambler's Magazine: Or, the Annals of Gallantry, Glee, Pleasure and the Bon Ton* (May 1783). Accompanies an account of a divorce case entitled 'Further Evidence upon Mrs. Williams's Trial', p. 164–7.	Copperplate engraving	
12. Facing p. 35		[Woman masturbating with carrots]	Unidentified. See Figure 25.3		
13. Facing p. 36		*The Peeper, or a Stolen View of Lady C-'s Premisses*	*The Rambler's Magazine: Or, the Annals of Gallantry, Glee, Pleasure and the Bon Ton* (June 1783). Accompanies a story entitled 'The Peeper; or, a Stolen View of Lady C-'s Premisses', pp. 224–5	Copperplate engraving	
14. Folded between pp. 33 and 37	Published for Harrison, 1784	*The Dog*	*The Wit's Magazine; or, Library of Momus*, vol. 2.5 (November 1784), facing p. 430. Accompanied by a long poem entitled 'The Dog, A Tale. By W. Whitehead, Esq. Poet-Laureat', pp. 431–3	Copperplate engraving	HathiTrust, https://catalog.hathitrust.org/Record/012406810
15. Facing p. 39, the title-page to Hudibrasso		*The Banquet of Love*	*The Town and Country Magazine, or, Universal Repository of Knowledge, Instruction, and Entertainment*, vol. 11 (September 1779), facing p. 481. Accompanies 'The Banquet of Love. A Short History, Founded in Truth', pp. 481–2	Copperplate engraving	HathiTrust, https://catalog.hathitrust.org/Record/000493943

16. Facing p. 41	Charles Spooner	*Love and Wine*	London: Robert Sayer, 1787 (print number 112). The original includes the following verse: Heighten'd by Bacchus see the Amorous Pair, How soft her Looks – how negligent his Air. Pleasure at present thrills thro' every Vein, But ah! such Transports often end in Pain.	Mezzotint	Yale University Library, https://findit-uat.library.yale.edu/catalog/digcoll:550955
17. Folded between pp. 62 and 63	Thomas Rowlandson after Giovanni Battista Cipriani	*Two Nymphs Bathing, One Washing the Other's Foot*	[London,] 1799 [annotated on reverse in pencil 63, i.e. the page number]		The Metropolitan Museum of Art, https://www.metmuseum.org/art/collection/search/788126
18. Facing p. 67	Published by Bird	*The Three Gracelesses*	Frontispiece to *The Rambler's Magazine: Or, the Annals of Gallantry, Glee, Pleasure and the Bon Ton* (April 1784). Accompanies a dialogue entitled 'The Three Gracelesses; or, The Naked Jig, a Frolic, as it was Performed at C—n House', p. 145		Google Books, https://books.google.co.uk/books?id=8xlOAAAAcAAJ&source=gbs_navlinks_s

HELEN WILLIAMS

Appendix B

Prints in Comerford's *Romance of a Day* (1760), British Library General Reference Collection 1459.a.60.

Comerford's copy is available via *ECCO*, Gale Document Number GALE|CW0116857452, and via Google Books, https://www.google.co.uk/books/edition/The_Romance_of_a_Day/Wg9mAAAAcAAJ?hl=en&gbpv=1

Table 25.2 Prints in Comerford's *Romance of a Day* (1760)

Item	Artist	Title	Publication details	Type	Links to colour images of alternative copies
1. Facing p. 1		[A group of four people, finely dressed, on a street by a river. One woman is kissed on each hand by a man and a woman, while a second man looks on, surprised.]	Unidentified. See Figure 25.4	Engraving	
2. Facing p. 7	Engraved by S. Rawle from an Original drawing by J. N. Esq. R.A.	*A View of Greenwich Park on Whitsun-Monday*	London: Sewell, 1802. Originally printed for the *European Magazine* (May 1802), facing p. 385. Accompanies the poem, 'Greenwich Park: or, Whitsun Monday. [With a View taken on the Spot by J.N. Esq. R.A.]', by 'SENNED' [pseud.], pp. 385–7, of which the following is an extract: In spacious circle near yon tree The merry lads and lasses see. One smart damsel, passing round, Just without its ample bound, Drops the handkerchief—and mark! 'Tis nearest to that jemmy spark. Bounding like the nimble fawn, See the nymph spring o'er the lawn, While the swain pursuing hard, Anxious for the sweet reward, The panting fugitive does bring, Blushing, to the joyous ring, 'Midst laughing lads and titt'ring misses Takes his well-earn'd prize of kisses.	Engraving	HathiTrust, https://babel. hathitrust.org/cgi/pt?id=nj p.32101065086405&view =1up&seq=9.

(Continued)

3. Folded. Between pp. 8–9.		*A View of London from One-Tree-Hill in Greenwich Park*	London, 1754. A later version of a plate originally printed for *The Gentleman's Magazine* (January 1754), facing p. 37	Engraving	HathiTrust, https://babel.hathitrust.org/cgi/pt?id=mdp.39015013472850&view=1up&seq=9
4. Landscape. Facing p. 23		*Greenwich Hospital*	*London and its Environs Described* (London: Dodsley, 1761), vol. 3, facing p. 69	Copperplate engraving	Google Books, https://books.google.co.uk/books?id=WnhbAAAAQAAJ&source=gbs_navlinks_s
5. Landscape. Facing p. 43	After James Basire the Elder	*The Ancient Palace at Greenwich, called Placentia, the Birth-Place of Queen Elizabeth*	A few versions of this print exist. One was produced for *Vestuta Monumenta* (7 vols, 1747–1904) published by the Society of Antiquaries: Vol. 2 (1767), plate 25	Engraving	See, for example, Royal Museums Greenwich, https://www.rmg.co.uk/collections/objects/rmgc-object-155595
6. Facing p. 45		[Two young men gesticulate with a third man who leans on a stick, in a city street, while two women look on from a balcony.]	Unidentified. See Figure 25.5	Engraving	
7. Facing p. 68	After Jean Michel Moreau le Jeune	*The Unexpected Meeting*	Actual source unidentified. The reverse of this image, and perhaps its source, can be found in Bret, ed., *Œuvres de Molière*, 6 vols (Paris: Compagnie des Libraires Associés, 1773), entitled 'L'École des femmes', and engraved by Denis Née	Engraving	One version is available at Utpictura18, https://utpictura18.univ-amu.fr/notice/9559-lecole-femmes-moliere-ii-1773-moreau-jeune. Another title-less version is visible at the British Museum, https://www.britishmuseum.org/collection/object/P_1914-0228-2861

8. Facing p. 73	Hubert François Bourguignon d'Anville, dit Gravelot	*La confiance des belles âmes*	Jean-Jacques Rousseau, *Julie ou la Nouvelle Héloïse* (1761), vol. 4, p. 69. Neither the versions engraved by Chaffard nor Jacob Folkema look quite the same as Comerford's copy, which must be by another engraver	Engraving	A similar but not exact image is available at Musée d'art et d'histoire, Ville de Genève, https://www.mahmah.ch/collection/oeuvres/illustration-pour-jean-jacques-rousseau-julie-ou-la-nouvelle-heloise-planche-7
9. Facing p. 74	After Jean Michel Moreau le Jeune	*The Parting Lovers (Le Dépit Amoureux)*	The version used by Comerford appeared in the *Universal Magazine* (August 1776), facing p. 76. It accompanies 'The Parting Lovers: A Dramatic Tale'. The original includes the following verse: When Manly saw the Maid prepare to part A deadly cold ran shiv'ring to his heart: She thrice essay'd to speak: but thrice in vain: For sobs and sighs her fault'ring voice restrain. The image was taken from Moreau's illustration to the *Œuvres de Molière*, 6 vols (Paris: Compagnie des Libraires Associés, 1773), vol. 1, facing p. 247, which was engraved by A. J. Duclos	Copperplate engraving	Google Books, https://books.google.co.uk/books?id=Iy82AAAAMAAJ&source=gbs_navlinks_s

Notes

1. Karen Harvey, *Reading Sex in the Eighteenth Century: Bodies and Gender in English Erotic Culture* (Cambridge: Cambridge University Press, 2004), 61.
2. According to annotations on the British Library copy of *Voyage to Lethe* ([London?]: 1900?), British Library General Reference Collection Cup.1000.aa.10.
3. Lucy Peltz, *Facing the Text: Extra-Illustration, Print Culture, and Society in Britain 1769–1840* (San Marino: Huntington Library, 2017), 1.
4. Peltz, *Facing the Text*, 4.
5. Peltz, *Facing the Text*, 5, 4.
6. Peltz, *Facing the Text*, 4.
7. Gabrielle Dean, '"Every Man His Own Publisher": Extra-Illustration and the Dream of the Universal Library', *Textual Cultures* 8, no. 1 (2013): 57–71.
8. See, for example, Ann Lewis, 'Extra-Illustrating Rousseau's *Julie, ou La Nouvelle Héloïse*: The Case of the Defer de Maisonneuve Edition (1793–1800)', in *Extra-Illustration in Non-Traditional Contexts: Charting New Avenues for Research in Illustration Studies*, ed. Christina Ionescu, Special Issue of *Journal of Illustration* 8, no. 2 (2021): 251–80; Naomi Billingsley, '"The Great Bowyer Bible": Robert Bowyer and the Macklin Bible', in *The Unique Copy: (Extra-)Illustration, Word and Image, Book History, and Print Culture*, ed. Christina Ionescu, Special Issue of *Journal of Illustration* 8, no. 1 (2021): 51–80; Erin C. Blake and Stuart Sillars, eds, *Extending the Book: The Art of Extra-Illustration* (Washington, DC: Folger Shakespeare Library, 2010); Peltz, *Facing the Text*.
9. *Proceedings of the Society of Antiquaries of London* 8 (1881): 522. *Society of Antiquaries, Minute Book* 38 (date): 83, 102. *London Directory* (1851): 1511, 1841 and 1851 censuses, National Archives, HO 107/684/17, f.17; HO 107/1493, f. 377. See also John Ashdown-Hill, 'The Bosworth Crucifix', *Leicestershire Archaeological & Historical Society Transactions* 78 (2004): 83–96.
10. William Roberts, *The Book-Hunter in London: Historical and Other Studies of Collectors and Collecting* (Chicago: McClurg, 1895), 86.
11. Roberts, *The Book-Hunter in London*, 86.
12. Catalogue B172, *Blackwells Rare Books: Antiquarian and Modern*, 57, https://ilab.org/assets/catalogues/catalogs_files_1111_catalogue_b172.pdf (accessed 23 November 2023).
13. As Karen Harvey has demonstrated, the map and the travel book became 'suitable models for erotic depictions of sex' in the eighteenth century: 'In erotica, narrative leads to mapping with hardly a shift in register.' Karen Harvey, 'Spaces of Erotic Delight', in *Georgian Geographies: Essays on Space, Place and Landscape in the Eighteenth Century*, ed. Miles Ogborn and Charles W. J. Withers (Manchester: Manchester University Press, 2004), 131, 132.
14. According to annotations on the version of the floral endpaper in the British Library copy. *Voyage to Lethe* ([London?]: 1900?), British Library General Reference Collection Cup.1000.aa.10.
15. James Comerford's illustrated copy of *A Voyage to Lethe* (London: Coneybeare [Hughs], 1741), British Library General Reference Collection Cup.1001.c.4., p. 28. Further references parenthetical.
16. James Grantham Turner, 'Marcantonio's Lost Modi and their Copies', *Print Quarterly* 21, no. 4 (2004): 384.
17. Turner, 'Marcantonio's Lost Modi and their Copies', 363.
18. Bradford K. Mudge, 'How to Do the History of Pornography: Romantic Sexuality and its Field of Vision', in *Historicising Sexuality*, ed. Richard C. Sha, *Romantic Circles Praxis* (2006), https://romantic-circles.org/praxis/sexuality/index.html (accessed 28 November 2023).
19. Kathleen Lubey, *Excitable Imaginations: Eroticism and Reading in Britain, 1660–1760* (Lewisburg: Bucknell University Press, 2012), 5.

20. This – and subsequent references – refer to the numbered items within the table in each appendix.
21. For reasons of economy, I only include here images which are either adapted or unique. Please see the appendices for a list of links to versions of the images discussed here.
22. Julie Peakman, *The Pleasure's All Mine: A History of Perverse Sex* (London: Reaktion, 2013), 31.
23. Julia Miller, *Books Will Speak Plain: A Handbook for Identifying and Describing Historical Bindings* (Ann Arbor: Legacy Press, 2018), 164n255.
24. Stuart Sillars, 'Extra-Illustrated Shakespeares', in *Extending the Book: The Art of Extra-Illustration*, ed. Erin C. Blake and Stuart Sillars (Washington, DC: Folger Shakespeare Library, 2010), 14–18, 16.
25. Advertisement, 1783. British Library General Reference Collection Cup.820.a.12.
26. 'The Three Gracelesses; or, The Naked Jig, a Frolic', *Rambler's Magazine* (April 1784), 145.
27. *Chester Courant*, 31 July 1804, n.p.
28. *London Moderator and National Adviser*, 17 July 1822, n.p.
29. James Comerford's extra-illustrated copy of John Cleland, *The Romance of a Day; or an Adventure in Greenwich-Park, Last Easter* (London: Pottinger, 1760). Further references parenthetical.
30. Hal Gladfelder, *Fanny Hill in Bombay* (Baltimore: Johns Hopkins University Press, 2012), 195.
31. See also Gladfelder, *Fanny Hill in Bombay*, 198.
32. Peltz, *Facing the Text*, 4.
33. Harvey, *Reading Sex in the Eighteenth Century*, 170.
34. Harvey, *Reading Sex in the Eighteenth Century*, 13.
35. Julie Peakman, *Mighty Lewd Books: The Development of Pornography in Eighteenth-Century England* (Basingstoke: Palgrave Macmilla, 2003), 105.
36. Peakman, *Mighty Lewd Books*, 106, 103.

26

EIGHTEENTH-CENTURY FICTION AND THE ART OF GRAPHIC SATIRE, FROM CHARACTER TO CONSTELLATION

Brigitte Friant-Kessler

THE CONNECTION BETWEEN eighteenth-century fiction, political caricature and graphic satire covering more than three centuries contributes to the reception of eighteenth-century writers. Probing literature through the prism of graphic satire, I suggest, correlates with a constellation of connections which need to be brought to prominence, and for which cultural, sociological, political, aesthetic and material aspects need to be taken into consideration. The following investigation into eighteenth-century novels and their links with graphic satire supplements existing critical work, but situates itself more specifically in the wake of David Francis Taylor's inquiry into a literary history of caricature and its paradigm. Studies of eighteenth-century adaptation – such as Daniel Cook and Nicholas Seager's edited collection *The Afterlives of Eighteenth-Century Fiction*, or Jakub Lipski's *Painting the Novel* – all highlight the legacy and enduring popularity of Georgian fiction across media, and pinpoint links with politics, across time and space.[1] They allow us to chart the itineraries of particular titles, as well as the artistic modes in which literary works, whether canonical or not, are presented to a readership or to an audience.

Caricature is an art in its own right.[2] As noted by Vic Gatrell concerning its practice in England in the eighteenth century, 'At first the art was received as nothing more noxious than the establishing of a witty equivalence between reality and its grotesque exaggeration . . . thereafter it fused with more elaborate parodic, witty or ironically punning forms of representation.'[3] It has ramifications with high art and classical portraiture, which it generally subverts, and resonates with symbolic, philosophical and religious beliefs, alongside theories relating to the body, such as physiognomy or phrenology, which are rooted in the history of science. Individual styles, fluctuating aesthetic tenets and important social changes are reflected in political graphic satire. Satirical imagery may find sources of inspiration in book illustration, which it can revisit and adapt to comment on specific policies and political decisions. While most examples of the genre resort to the grotesque, the scatological and scurrilous visual idiom found in the prints of late Georgian England, which the Victorians judged coarse and abusive, remains a cultural and aesthetic landmark. Printshops gained in popularity in the latter part of the century and contributed to the dissemination of satirical iconography. Furthermore, satirical prints by artists such as James Gillray and the Cruikshanks remained a high-end market commodity. As collectibles, from the early eighteenth century to the present day original satires and political cartoons have been auctioned, exhibited and purchased by private collectors, as well as museums or galleries.[4] From Georgian satirists who engaged in offending personalities, including the royal family and its entourage, to the apparently politer Victorians, and then back to the more violent modes of attacking politicians that took hold from the 1970s onwards, British graphic satire and political caricature has undergone significant changes over the course of more than three centuries,[5] mostly due to shifts in circulation, format, print technology and historical events. Globalised print markets, changes in graphic styles and technology, editorial policies and the space allotted to cartoons in the press have further shaped a multifaceted graphic and textual ecosystem, which influences correlations between eighteenth-century fiction and political caricature.

While some fictional works have always been discarded by satirists and deemed unfit for caricature, other titles have, on the contrary, established an enduring presence as literary parodies. Satirical prints and political cartoons based on or inspired by fictional characters and scenes function as a kind of visual shorthand for the fictional source, but they are also autonomous artworks. Taylor's research has shown to what extent Shakespeare, Milton and Swift were brought to participate in what he describes as 'literary politics'. In fact, Shakespeare's plays and Jonathan Swift's *Gulliver's Travels* (1726) are still frequently used by political cartoonists. They have, in addition, been given a transnational and global treatment across the Anglophone world, a process which is now fully incorporated in the reception studies of authors and artists alike.

In *The Afterlife of Character*, David Brewer posits degrees of detachability in relation to fictional characters.[6] Brewer's investigation into the phenomenon of literary characters who transcend the works in which they originate and go on to lead separate lives in sequels, spin-offs and (sometimes) radically new cultural contexts also applies to graphic satire. A political caricature may be seen as a literary adaptation, or at least as a spin-off derived from or loosely inspired by literature, which is refracted in the visual satire, often in a fragmented manner (by citation, passing textual reference in the caption, parodied character or scene).[7] For fictional characters to migrate from literature into political satire, they need to be detached from the strands and strings of the narratives in which they originally act as puppets to approximate universal types, while also retaining certain traits and specificities belonging to the fictional representation of those characters. Simultaneously, the satirical discourse in prints or cartoons is strengthened by the opportunity given to the reader/viewer to re-experience something of the pleasures of the fictional world. Once it is recognised, parody buttresses the satirical attack and reinforces its efficacy by playing on the common ground shared between satirists and their audience. This might explain why only a limited number of fictional characters and scenes match caricaturists' expectations, but also why the same protagonists – Robinson Crusoe, Lemuel Gulliver – are repeatedly reprised and passed on from one generation of cartoonists to the next as part of a graphic and cultural heritage. Conversely, characters or works by eighteenth-century authors such as Henry Fielding, Samuel Richardson, Tobias Smollett or Jane Austen have never been used in political parodies, as they do not appear to fulfil the necessary prerequisites to occupy a space in graphic satire. It would seem that adventure stories, romance and sentimental fiction are ill suited to the genre.

The crux for fictional characters to migrate into graphic satire is to be both typical and topical, that is to say to represent a type, which is akin to an allegorical mode, and yet simultaneously to be adaptable so they can be reconfigured in a specific context. Nathalie Zimpfer argues that Swift's satire, in particular *Gulliver's Travels*, is ambivalent and that a 'juxtaposed vision, although more disturbing, yields more faithful results than relentlessly single vision'.[8] This may also account for its malleability, which allows it to oscillate between acerbic political satire and children's literature, a view supported by Jonathan Coe, for instance.[9] Gulliverised figures in graphic satires usually tap into the first voyage to Lilliput and are shown as imprisoned or constrained individuals. They may also metaphorise states and signify the fight of the powerless, whoever they may be, against the powerful. In a different vein, Daniel Defoe's *Robinson Crusoe* (1719) blends several genres: its island setting and the hero's relationship with Friday, or even the footprint in the sand, are both polysemous and symbolic. Zimpfer further suggests that Defoe's and Swift's texts are 'antagonistic parables of British Empire',[10] but when we look at satires in which colonialism is attacked, be it by referencing Gulliver or Crusoe, this opposition seems to dissolve.

Crusoefied political figures generally indicate isolation, and when depicted with Friday there tends to be a colonialised subtext. However, Gulliver-themed graphic satires also allegorise de-colonialisation. For this essay, I adopt a critically dialectic approach, from fiction to graphic satire and back again, in order to address a twofold question: what does eighteenth-century fiction do to/with caricature and political satire, and what does graphic satire do to/with eighteenth-century fiction? I first discuss *Robinson Crusoe* and *Gulliver's Travels*. The corpora of graphic satire derived from those two narratives seem to be boundless and they epitomise longevity in terms of literary dissemination in political satire. *Robinson Crusoe*, a non-satirical piece of fiction in the first place, has been adapted in a wide range of media and formats, and it has come to be the source of at least three constantly revisited motifs in political caricature corresponding to emblematic scenes: isolation (a single character, usually sitting on a small rock island), the Crusoe–Friday duo, which mostly signifies inequality in political or diplomatic relationships, and, thirdly, the 'footprint scene' which, as I shall explain, tends to convey an acute sense of territorial property. *Gulliver's Travels*, on the other hand, was designed for satirical purposes from the outset. The efflorescence of Gulliver-based satire in Britain really began with Gillray's anti-Napoleonic prints. The motif has been recurrently revisited by cartoonists to this day, as shown by, for instance, Dave Brown's 2023 *Rishi Gulliver and the King of Bullyingnag* cartoon, which parodies Gillray's 1803 *Gulliver and the King of Brobdingnag*, itself a parodic image.[11] *Gulliver's Travels* has been adapted in print, on stage, on screen and in comic book format, and heavily sanitised as children's literature in abridgements that excise the third and fourth voyages, along with removing rude or scatological passages. Political caricature is but one of the multiple transmedial, transgeneric and transnational trajectories of that work and Defoe's *Robinson Crusoe*.

To enlarge the spectrum of ways in which fiction and the art of caricature intersect, I scrutinise writers' portraits in the second section of this discussion because they reflect celebrity culture and show a different facet of eighteenth-century public figures. Sometimes an author's celebrity was directly linked to their engagement in politics, which is the case of Henry Fielding and Tobias Smollett, and the reason behind their depiction in satirical prints, or what M-C. Newbould names 'a disembodied presence'. While Austen as a writer was not involved in politics or public affairs, two fairly recent political cartoons of 2013 and 2017 revisit her likeness reproduced on a banknote.

THE ART OF GRAPHIC SATIRE

This depiction opens avenues for yet another connection between fiction and satire, through paper money iconography. At the periphery of the constellation that couples fiction and graphic satire are artistic modes that exist neither as stand-alone satirical prints nor as political cartoons, and which are explored in the third section of this chapter. They may, nonetheless, convey a satirical discourse that is concealed beneath the surface of seemingly non-political narratives. To shed light on more rhizomatic connections, I examine how cartoonist, illustrator and writer Martin Rowson straddles graphic creation as a homage to Gillray in a film adaptation of the Austenian spin-off *Pride and Prejudice and Zombies*, and how he adapts and updates *Gulliver's Travels* as a graphic novel, which doubles as a caustic anti-Blair recrimination.

Character Migration and Emblematic Scenes: Crusoefied Leaders and Gulliverised Politics

Both Defoe's *Robinson Crusoe* and Swift's *Gulliver's Travels* 'have long been universally recognised as adaptable works, and have thus provided material that is endlessly subject to appropriation even when it is not read or presented in its original fictional shape', notes Lipski.[12] During the latter part of the nineteenth century and up to the present day, most British press organs (*The Daily Mirror*, *The Evening Standard*, *The Evening Magazine*, *Punch*, *Private Eye*) have used iterations of scenes based on Crusoe as a castaway or involving Gulliver, mostly in Lilliput and more rarely in Brobdingnag. Across the Atlantic, we find a similar pattern as shown, for instance, by a certain Trump-Gulliver figure.[13] Emblematic scenes such as Crusoe in the company of Friday, the footprint in the sand or, for Swift's tale, Gulliver tied to the ground and assaulted by Lilliputians have since their inception functioned like pegs onto which a large array of satirical discourses can be hung and reinterpreted according to a particular context or event. Those scenes are underpinned by a visual and verbal rhetoric, which takes the original prose fiction from which they derive in a variety of directions. Literary parodies used for political satire in the English-speaking world have shaped a parallel graphic canon in which *Robinson Crusoe* and *Gulliver's Travels* have had a significantly enduring presence.[14] Famous cartoonists and artists such as E. H. Shepard, Bernard Partridge, Leslie Illingworth in the 1930s and 1940s or Nicholas Garland in the 1970s, up to more contemporary graphic satirists like Steve Bell, Martin Rowson, Dave Brown or Peter Brookes, to name but a few, have all at some point produced political cartoons that parody classics, including *Robinson Crusoe* and *Gulliver's Travels*.

Crusoe and Gulliver are endowed with such a degree of plasticity, and at the same time reducibility, that they can be easily remodelled and adapted. They incarnate values and symbols, but can also still be identified with the literary work in which they originate, which is an essential aspect for satire that comments on policies and politics with the assistance of literary parody. Cartoons and caricature may be seen as having a similar dynamic to that of emblematic coding,[15] as well as being artforms which rely on corporeal, linguistic and metaphorical distortions. The conjoined use of hyperbolic rhetoric, hybridity and enunciative disjunction, alongside the play on scale, proportion and size are part and parcel of caricature.[16] The specific moments in these two narratives that inspire political caricaturists have gained the status of iconic

464 BRIGITTE FRIANT-KESSLER

scenes. They are formulaic and can be used as a globalised visual shorthand. There is no need to represent a human figure to evoke Crusoe, as exemplified by the frontispiece to the series of nine illustrations after Thomas Stothard for the Cadell and Davies edition of *Robinson Crusoe* published in 1820. The title page of that edition is adorned with a single vignette described by the curators of the British Museum as follows: 'a wooden scarecrow dressed in a tunic and hat of fur and animal skins, with sword, palm umbrella, net, gun, spade and axe'.[17] The absence of an actual portrait or human figure registers the possibility of imagining Crusoe in almost any garb within these parameters, originally derived not only from Defoe's text, but from its most famous and most enduring illustration, which first appeared in 1719. Given such a flexibility, caricature stands as the visual gap-filler of a space left open to a multiplicity of interpretative discourses.

Furthermore, 'islandness', which is paradigmatic in both Crusoe's and Gulliver's narratives, is malleable and, according to Emmanuelle Peraldo, the 'malleability of insular space makes all displacements possible', and thus such fictional worlds lend themselves to being transferred in politics.[18] Political figures represented as Crusoe after the shipwreck are often dressed in the same attire as the fictional character as depicted in perhaps the most iconic illustration of the work, the frontispiece to the 1719 edition by John Clark and John Pine, featuring Robinson with his standard accoutrements – goatskin clothes, umbrella, parrot, saw and two guns – which conjures what David Blewett calls a 'haunting portrait'.[19] This type of portrait-making bears signs of emblem book semiotics and, as such, has frequently migrated into graphic satire. Political isolation, forced exile or banishment are encompassed in the process of Crusoefication in topical satires. While Taylor notes there is no satire derived from Defoe in Britain from 1760 to 1830, there are, however, examples of Crusoe-inspired satires which appeared in continental Europe.[20] The case of Napoleon, first on Elba (1814), then on the island of St Helena (1815–21), is particularly compelling in this context. British satirists used *Gulliver's Travels* for their anti-Napoleonic prints, but those working in France and Germany turned to Crusoe to ridicule Little Boney's exiles.

Both imperial exiles triggered a spate of satirical prints based on the analogy between Defoe's character and the former emperor's situation as an isolated ruler fallen from grace. Prints depicting a Crusoefied Napoleon were popular in France and Germany. A satire by the French printmaker and engraver Jacques Louis Constant Le Cerf, inspired by a theatrical Robinsonade staged in Paris in 1805, depicts Napoleon as *Le Robinson de l'Ile d'Elbe*.[21] This satirical representation operates as a stark counterpoint to the aesthetics of the classic painterly portraiture associated with the former emperor and mocks any sense of grandeur. An anonymous print, dated 1815, *Le Nouveau Robinson de l'Isle Ste Helene*, features a dejected Napoleon, in tattered attire, who stares at a rather aggressive-looking bird of prey.[22]

Along a similar parodic pattern, the German caricaturist Johann Michael Voltz also represents a tattered and Crusoefied Napoleon on St Helena (Plate 23). Entitled 'Der neue Robinson auf der einsamen Ratten Insel im Süd-Meere, St Helena genannt' (The new Robinson on the lonely rat island in the south seas named St Helena), the satire depicts a sad-looking Napoleon, sitting on a drum, and surrounded by rats, some of which are shown nibbling away at his fur and what is left of his regalia (sceptre, orb). The former emperor, now devoid of any authority, laments the loss of his distinctive bicorn hat at la Belle Alliance, his headquarters before the battle at Waterloo

THE ART OF GRAPHIC SATIRE   465

in 1815. The Jacobin hat is compared to a night cap by a speaking parrot, which overtly mocks the exiled ruler and reduces his name to the moniker 'Nap'. This form of metaphorical and verbal belittlement echoes Gillray's visual 'Little Boney' in the palm of the Brobdingnagian King George III, which Voltz adapted in another of his anti-Napoleonic satires. The analogy with Crusoe is conveyed by Defovian props: a gun, tools and an umbrella. Voltz topped it with an eagle figure, a symbol of imperial power since ancient Rome. The Latin phrase 'Sub umbra alarum tuarum' (under the shadow of Thy wings) inscribed on the rim of the umbrella is originally from Psalm 17:8 but it is equally used as a heraldic motto on royal coats of arms (Queen Isabella of Spain) and city armouries (Nuremberg). The German anti-Napoleonic miniature Robinsonade subverts these symbolic codes of power and conjures a series of parallel cultural references that resonate with one another, among which are Napoleon at Elba satires, illustrations of *Robinson Crusoe* and his bestiary, as well as several other St Helena satires depicting Napoleon (1815–16) before an army of more or less anthropomorphic rodents. Rats, interestingly, reconnect these political satires to the Defovian narrative, but also to Selkirk and Dampier, as these animals ran rampant on ships and were metaphysically perceived as a divine plague.[23] Conversely, Voltz's Crusoefied Napoleon isolated on a rat-infested island, the comical parrot-castaway dialogue and the ironically used biblical fragment are part of an agenda in support of the European allies (Britain, Germany, Austria) who brought down the 'Corsican Tiger'[24] and can ultimately underscore his defeat by circulating satirical images thanks to a transnational network in the print market.

American and Canadian cartoonists have revisited Crusoe in subsequent periods, thereby adding one more stone to the edifice of this book's global reception and its worldwide popularity. Magazines like *Harper's Weekly* or *Puck* have on several occasions presented cover illustrations or centrefolds with satirical cartoons based on Defoe's eponymous character. A case in point is Charles W. Fairbanks, Vice-President of the United States of America (1905–9) under Theodore Roosevelt, who stood as a standard punchbag of the satirical magazine *Puck* for being taciturn. He is represented as a castaway on the cover of the issue published on 3 January 1906 in an image by Joseph Keppler Jr captioned 'Robinson Crusoe Fairbanks' (Plate 24).[25] The Crusoefication of the American politician by the artist is made clear through the combination of an island setting and a verse. The quatrain printed at the bottom of the page is taken from the first stanza of William Cowper's 1782 poem *The Solitude of Alexander Selkirk*, in which the poet imagines a monologue by Selkirk, the real-life castaway on whom Defoe's fictional Crusoe was modelled.[26] The poem begins with 'I am monarch of all I survey' and celebrates in high spirits territorial conquest, but since Fairbanks worked against Roosevelt's policies the chosen lines mirror how he suffers the pangs of loneliness due to his political failure:

O Solitude! where are the charms
That sages have seen in thy face?
Better dwell in the midst of alarms,
Than reign in this horrible place.

Keppler drew his Crusoefied Fairbanks with a fur hat, a beard and a somewhat oversized moustache, which match that of Crusoe in the illustrations by George Housman

Thomas for the 1863 Cassel edition, but also Fairbanks's photographic portraits.[27] Book illustration for the novel once again migrates into caricature as a mirror image, even if the original novelistic context, or its subsequent aesthetic repackaging in new editions, is not necessarily part of the viewer/readership's interpretative toolkit. For those who are equipped with knowledge of this frame of reference, however, the politician's posture and his surroundings in the new visual adaptation of Defoe's fiction, and of its later adaptations in the form of book illustrations, prompt a connection that remains intelligible, and which adds a further level of satirical humour.

The relationship between Robinson and Friday is another popular motif in political cartoons as it offers the opportunity to comment on personalities as well as nations.[28] The Crusoe island motif remained a thread running from the colonial expansion belonging to Wilhelm II's imperial ambitions, which led to his alienation from Germany's European counterparts, to a parallel isolationism occasioned, again, by Germany's aggressive colonisation of global territories in the context of the Second World War and Adolph Hitler's ideological despotism, in company with fascist allies. In Britain, Bernard Partridge appropriates the character in a satirical cartoon published in *Punch* on 16 December 1942, in which Hitler as Crusoe sits under a palm tree next to Mussolini as Man Friday. Partridge drew John Bull and Stalin as Christmas baubles dangling from the leaves, embodying the Anglo-Russian alliance. This scene of political isolation is ironically captioned 'The Festive Season'. The Crusoe–Friday companionship has continued to run as a thread in graphic satire, responding to new political contexts and the close (but inherently imbalanced) power dynamics of the alliances that belong to them, while also being adapted from a different angle and given a further ironic twist. When transposed into political arenas, though, depending on which side of the political divide one stands, Crusoe may be perceived either as a hero or an anti-hero.

Crusoe's discovery of the footprint on the beach is the third most significant episode in the narrative repeatedly used in the satirical press.[29] The case of two *Punch* cartoons from the 1940s shows that artists rely on the iconic templates of book illustration and refashion them to fit their own topical contexts, which makes those cartoons comprehensible in a broad sense while their topicality is nowadays only remotely graspable. In other words, the literary reference prevails upon the event, and fictional elements become interchangeable props. E. H. Shepard, whose name is generally associated with the children's literature success *Winnie-the-Pooh*, also worked for *Punch* and published two Crusoe-based cartoons in the 1940s. As is often the case, cartoonists reuse similar tropes time and again. Shepard published his first Crusoe-inspired satire in *Punch*, dated 10 December 1941, shortly after the Pearl Harbor attack.[30] Titled 'Robinson Kurusu', the cartoon combines literary parody of Defoe's emblematic scene with comment on the complex diplomatic situation between Japan and the United States. A stereotypically Asian-looking Crusoe is depicted with a parrot bearing a Nazi swastika. Saburō Kurusu is recorded in history as Japan's ambassador to Nazi Germany and was the Japanese envoy who tried to negotiate peace with the Americans. Crusoe/Kurusu, reinforced by a pun on the pronunciation of the Japanese name, is shown in the context of the Japanese-Thai conflict; this is the reason why, while dazed by a giant American leg, he ironically exclaims, 'And I thought it was only a footprint', which echoes the bewilderment of Defoe's character who describes the footprint as 'an apparition' or some 'dangerous creature'. Interestingly, in this cartoon, Defoe and Swift are conjured as a pair, rather like a miniature graphic 'Gulliverian Robinsonade':

THE ART OF GRAPHIC SATIRE   467

the hyperbolically large leg of Uncle Sam stepping on Thailand may well be a visual hint at *Gulliver's Travels*, which underscores the anti-Axis satire as the Japanese forces invaded (small) Thailand a few hours after Pearl Harbor. It references Defovian and Swiftian topoi in one single image.

Gulliver's Travels is, indeed, prominent among eighteenth-century novels that have inspired political satire well beyond their first moment of appearance and into subsequent centuries. The first and second voyages are the main sources for adaptation. Critical literature on Gulliver in political satire abounds, and the character has never ceased to inspire visual satirists, from Hogarth's famous mock illustration *Lemuel Gulliver's Punishment*, published in December 1726, to twenty-first-century adaptations, even expanding into complete graphic narratives, such as Martin Rowson's 2012 *Gulliver's Travels, Adapted and Updated*, to which I shall turn later. Even the Victorian era, the leading cartoonists of which (John Leech, George du Maurier, John Doyle who signed himself H.B., John Tenniel) turned away from eighteenth-century satirical styles to make caricature a respectable form of art, found Gulliver palatable enough.[31] Beyond their immediate function in the narrative, Crusoe and Gulliver are frequently used as metaphorical substitutes for nations or specific communities. A distinctive interplay between miniature worlds and a giant character, an oversized political figure or entity captured and subjected to the assault of powerless little people, a giant figure straddling continents like a colossus or hauling ships, or on the contrary, a diminutive figure facing giant-looking observers:[32] all these are cues that signal a Gulliver-themed visual rhetoric intertwined with the topicality of a political event that form visual contexts in which Gulliver is either called upon, cited or referenced in absentia.

A brief survey of Gulliver-themed popular cartoons is proof of the wide transnational dissemination of this visual rhetoric. While most images are based on scenes from the first voyage to Lilliput – mainly Gulliver tied to the ground and assaulted by the Lilliputians – a few also exploit the moment with the fleet of Blefuscu. Some explore the notion of awakening and breaking free from bondage in different political contexts. Honoré Daumier, for instance, published two satirical lithographs for the French periodical *Le Charivari*, one depicting a large Gulliverian figure tied to the ground ('Lilliputiens essayant de profiter du sommeil d'un nouveau Gulliver', 20–21 May 1850), then, a year after, a second cartoon showing the awakening ('Une panique des Lilliputiens qui ont essayé de garrotter le Suffrage universel pendant son sommeil', 28 June 1851), which causes his Lilliputian enemies, in this case President Thiers[33] and his acolytes, to flee in panic (Figure 26.1). Gulliver's body is inscribed with the word 'suffrage', indicating that it is an allegorical representation of the people's power to vote, which was seriously jeopardised at that point.[34] The upheavals of the 1950s and 1960s, during which African nations under French rule strove to become independent, led Leslie Illingworth to create, in 1953, 'Gulliver Africanus', which represents the whole continent awakening. Reminiscent of caricatures that anthropomorphise geographic maps, Gulliver's body is shown contorted so as to fit the shape of Africa.[35] These few examples are indicative of the plasticity of Gulliver in political cartoons, which transcend Swift's fictional world yet keep echoing its universality. They also show the longevity of Gulliverised politicians and politics, across different countries – and show, above all, that the motif is far from extinct in political caricature.

Figure 26.1 Honoré Daumier, *Une panique de Lilliputiens qui ont essayé de garotter le Suffrage universel*, *Actualités* no. 158. G 2857. Published in *Le Charivari* no. 179, 28 June 1851. © Paris Musées. Musée Carnavalet – Histoire de Paris.

Fiction, Fame and Satire: Politicised Writers' Portraits

Visual representations of authors rather than works can also intersect with graphic political satire. Literary figures such as Henry Fielding and Tobias Smollett, whose works and characters are not given prominence in graphic satire, themselves appear or are alluded to in satirical prints because they engaged in the political debates and feuds of their times. Beyond his career as a novelist, Fielding published pamphlets, edited newspapers, and wrote essays, as well as satirical plays. Smollett was the editor of the *Briton*, a pro-Bute satirical newspaper towards the end of the Seven Years' War (1756–63). Whenever these two authors are represented, or mentioned in satirical prints, they are depicted amongst groups of politicians and participants in political controversies and not necessarily directly in relation to their literary works; they are nevertheless inherently bound up with their novels as the sometimes quixotic embodiments of their authors' fame. Fielding's and Smollett's public figures in satires are the cogs and wheels of a huge eighteenth-century fame machine, which heralds the beginning of celebrity culture.[36]

Now mainly remembered for his literary output, Fielding enjoyed a multifaceted career and was a high-profile figure in London political and journalistic circles. Strictly speaking, there are no political satires related to any one of his novels comparable to those inspired by *Gulliver* or *Crusoe*. His name, however, or rather his journalistic persona, can be associated with at least one satirical print. *The Jacobite's Journal* first

THE ART OF GRAPHIC SATIRE 469

appeared on 5 December 1747 and ran until 5 November 1748, under the title-page legend *By John Trott-Plaid Esq* who ironically occupies the position of (mock-)editor.[37] Published with the mock-signature 'I. Trott-Plaid invt.' on 13 February 1747, which is a falsified date designed to give the impression the print is a first state variant of '*The Humours of the Westminster Election or the scald-miserable Independant Electors in the Suds*', the satire entitled *Jaco-Independo-Rebello-Plaido* ridicules a group of politicians involved in the Westminster election that year and adds several characters dressed in tartan-patterned clothes. It parodies the print dated July 1747. Since Trott-Plaid appears as the designer of the plate, it may have been published around the same date as the first issue of the *Jacobite's Journal*, in any case between July and December 1747, or possibly even in 1748 but not in February. The comparison between the two prints further highlights an anti-Scottish and anti-Catholic agenda. As several critics have demonstrated, Fielding's political anti-Jacobite stance percolated into the fictional world of *Tom Jones* (1749), the plot of which features several hints at the '45 Jacobite Rebellion, though not without a degree of ambivalence.[38] The satirical print and the *Jacobite's Journal* form part of that literary and political constellation.

After Fielding's newspaper was discontinued, a poem dated 1748 and published in the *London Evening Post* critically assesses Fielding's persona by merging the author of the novels and the journalist in the pseudonym. While the trio footman-wench-priest refers to *Joseph Andrews* (1742), Trott-Plaid clearly alludes to the editor of the *Jacobite's Journal*:

> *Low Humour*, like *his own*, he once express,
> In *Footman, Country Wench*, and *Country Priest*:
> But all who read, must pity, or must snore,
> When TROTT-PLAID's *humble Genius* aims at *more*.[39]

The *London Evening Post* had been lambasted in the *Jacobite's Journal* in the form of a headpiece designed by Hogarth, which depicts an ass chewing the paper and led by a rope over which the *London Evening Post* is draped.[40] Anti-Catholic clues pervade the scene: the friar, the woman in tartan dress wearing a crucifix. In November 1748, *The Gentleman's Magazine* reprinted an epitaph, with a similar set of verses alluding to Fielding's plays, but also thieves and rogues in his prose:

Epitaph *from* Old England, Nov. 20

> Beneath this stone
> Lies *Trotplaid John*
> His length of chin and nose;
> His crazy brain,
> *Unhum'rous* vein
> In verse and eke in prose.
> Some plays he wrote,
> Sans wit or plot,
> Adventures of inferiors!
> Which, with his lives
> Of *rogues* and *thieves*,

Supply the town's posteriors.
But ah, alack! He broke his back,
When politics he tried:
For like a —— He play'd his part,
Crack'd loudly, stunk, and died.[41]

This satirical and evidently scatological poem connects Trott-Plaid from the *Jacobite's Journal* with *Tom Jones* and *Joseph Andrews*, and thus, like the verse printed in the *London Evening Post*, unites at once the novelist, the journalist and political graphic satire, albeit by following a long, winding path.

Like Fielding's, Tobias Smollett's fiction, whether in the picaresque vein or that of the adventure narrative, did not generate responses from graphic satirists, despite the biting wit found in works such as *Roderick Random* (1748), *Peregrine Pickle* (1751), *Ferdinand Count Fathom* (1753) or *Humphry Clinker* (1771). While his fiction did not resurface in graphic satire, the author himself featured in many prints, probably owing to the prominence he gained from his political journalism. Satirical prints associated with the Scottish politician John Stuart, third Earl of Bute and his ministry were issued towards the end of the Seven Years' War, several of which depict Smollett, sometimes simply identified by the initial 'S'.[42] As a Scotsman, Bute had gained the support of Smollett, as editor of the *Briton*, but also other personalities such as the actor, playwright and editor of the *Auditor*, Arthur Murphy. Anti-Bute prints were often tainted with Scotophobia. In this context, a generic tartan patterned outfit was used to target Smollett too, as is the case in the Shakespeare-inspired print, published in 1762, entitled *The Tempest or Enchanted Island*.[43] Smollett, in tartan dress in the foreground, lies on the floor, beside Murphy, and they are mauled by a lion in what is evidently a setting of a disenchanted and perturbing island, which satirises Bute's politics. Elsewhere Smollett is dressed in fine clothes, and, if anything at all, only a tartan waistcoat adds the Scottish touch. In the engraved headpiece of 'The Evacuations, or An Emetic for Old England Glorys', dated December 1762 – another anti-Bute attack, following the Peace of Paris negotiations, which led Britain to lose several important territories[44] – Smollett stands next to Bute and Henry Fox, 1st Baron Holland, on a mountebank stage.[45] A reverse copy of that print has been renamed 'The Evacuation, or An Emetic for Old England, by a Scot' (Figure 26.2). Smollett's graphic persona holds a doctor's cane to his nose and is surrounded by figures incarnating Fox with a clyster-pipe in hand, who holds a bag with Smollett's prescription, and Bute depicted with zoomorphic heads, as masks.[46] This print's scatological overtones perhaps unintentionally resonate with Smollett's fictional works, which often exploited the comical effects derived from enema, emetics or bodily purges and 'soupe maigre', for instance in *Roderick Random* or *Humphry Clinker*: although these works do not provide the source of inspiration for such graphic satires, their preoccupations are inherently bound up with the figure of Smollett the journalist, and the doctor-turned-novelist.

Beside citation, a character or a scene elicited in the viewer's mind and the recognisable features of a celebrity writer of the day, the connection between literary politics and parody can be modelled on a previously existing work of art, too, which itself may or may not be intended as parodic. In contemporary political caricature Dave Brown, famous for his Rogues' Gallery cartoons, draws on well-known artworks, which he reframes, both in a literal and a figurative sense. Banknote iconography is an

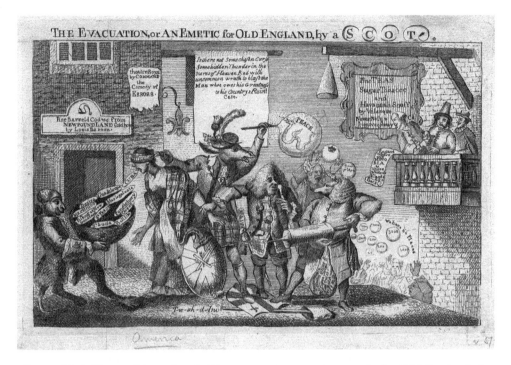

Figure 26.2 George Townshend, *The evacuation, or, An emetic for Old England, by a Scot* (1762). Courtesy of the Lewis Walpole Library, Yale University.

artistic subgenre in its own right. The example in Plate 25, a cartoon by Peter Brookes which parodies banknote portraiture, shows how Regency literature through a writer's portrait can provide the foundation for biting political satire. The kind of portraiture executed for a banknote is at the other end of the spectrum of writers' visual representations in the satires targeting Fielding or Smollett previously discussed. The rendering is usually realistic and devoid of facial distortions or the grotesque elements found in caricature. From a technical viewpoint, designing paper money calls for a crossover competence of graphic design, usually an engraver's skills, a training in applied arts and a sense of composition put in the service of highly symbolic and widely circulated imagery which cannot be detached from an array of social, political and economic issues. Studies in banknote iconography or stamp iconography show that this is an arena where portraiture and politics are often intertwined, with literary or artistic portraits statistically popular choices.[47]

Authors such as Smollett, whose notoriety was gained in part through his public prominence in the context of what was still, after all, a fairly small world of political journalism in the eighteenth century, as well as his undoubted celebrity as a novelist, have slipped from the currency of popularism compared with other novelistic contemporaries. By contrast, Jane Austen enjoys a present-day popularity far exceeding that of almost any writer of her period, and her portrait has become an iconographic reference point of that popular currency. According to Marin Marian-Bălaşa, there is a 'political narrative' in banknotes, and she uses the expression 'talkative money'.[48] Both concepts fit the characteristic effect achieved by Jane Austen's portrait as it appeared on the first polymer British £10 note, designed in 2013 but issued on 14 September 2017. This portrait of Austen is known to have been based on a sketch by her sister Cassandra, which was later reworked for the 1870 edition of *A Memoir of Jane Austen*.[49] On the final version of the note, the portrait is rearranged in a complex graphic environment in which every detail by and large resonates with Austen's writing activity: quills from Chawton House in Hampshire; her brother's home, Godmersham Park, which she visited often, and which is thought to have inspired some of her novels; and a quotation from *Pride and Prejudice*: 'I declare after all there is no enjoyment like reading!' However, that particular sentence, which accompanies the portrait, must not be taken at face value. It is ascribed to Miss Bingley in chapter 11, when she is trying to get Darcy's attention and only pretends to be interested in books.

As a banknote design, the bill and its aesthetics articulate the convergence of the writer's face, and the materiality related to writing (desk, quill). All these details put together help to construct the feel of an imaginary writer's house on/in paper. In view of its mode of circulation and the elements of its design, the banknote virtually becomes a portable miniature museum. Erudite Austen readers and scholars may at this point recall Austen's own words from a letter to her nephew: 'What should I do with your strong, manly, spirited Sketches, full of variety and Glow? – How could I possibly join them on to the little bit (two inches wide) of Ivory on which I work with so fine a Brush, as produces little effect after much Labour?'[50] In comparing writing fiction with miniature painting on ivory, Austen invokes a specific technique often favoured by banknote designers too.[51] The Austen banknote also symbolically stands as a chosen piece of national heritage. The currency of her work and iconic portrait disseminated, ironically enough, in the form of currency also perhaps unwittingly underscores the financial and economic discourses threaded throughout her novels. Finally, the denomination may also be a hint at the £10 the booksellers Crosby and Co. offered for *Susan*, the first version of *Northanger Abbey* in 1803.[52] The overall design strengthens a sense of the writer's profession and the idea that she has in the course of centuries become the incarnation of a nation's beloved author while 'the portrait on a banknote identifies not only the banknote itself but also attempts to represent the very (idea of a) strong and stable state'.[53]

It is precisely this sense of stability that is questioned, indeed profoundly shaken and tangentially jeopardised, in Peter Brookes's caricatures of the Austen £10 note. Two parodies by Brookes (2013, 2017) take the banknote portrait and the surrounding emblems as springboards for political satire. Austen's private family portrait is extracted from the literary historical arena and is treated like a public blank space, which can be filled in accordance with the cartoonist's agenda. Brookes's 2017 cartoon was published in *The Times* and came out shortly after the note entered official circulation. The satire attacks Theresa May. In a carnivalesque twist, the parodied opening line of *Pride and Prejudice* deftly mimics eighteenth-century typographical games with asterisks, sometimes used to avoid accusations of libel by partially eliding a person's name while also leaving it easily decipherable: 'It is a truth universally acknowledged that I am well and truly f***ed'. The writer's portrait is still recognisable, but it has been grotesquely hybridised with that of Conservative prime minister Theresa May, whose long eagle-beak Pinocchio nose and rapacious squint are reminiscent of Gerald Scarfe's caricatures of Margaret Thatcher. In the centre of the note, a miniaturised

THE ART OF GRAPHIC SATIRE 473

May figure wearing her distinctive leopard-skin pumps lies on the ground in tears. The quill as a symbolic emblem of handwritten fiction has been turned into a weapon: five magnified quills protrude from May's back, like the arrows of a Saint Sebastian martyrological effigy. In the background, a House of Parliament in ruin has replaced the stately home.

Not only does the caricaturist parodically transmogrify paper money iconography, but by doing so he also latches on to the art of literary politics through a dual process of featuring a well-known remediated portrait and repurposing the iconic Regency writer in the context of political caricature twice in the same decade. It is not a universally acknowledged portrait, but it has far wider popular currency than, say, Smollett's or Fielding's. By replacing the cultural and literary filigree of the banknote, the caricaturist is effectively making Austen's portrait literally talk back to us, while also echoing her novels. In a self-reflexive fashion, the satire channels an indictment of May's responsibility for poor governmental stewardship of the nation, something that is metonymically encapsulated in the very heritage incarnated by the first Austen-based note, which is itself parodied. The original sketch had been tampered with in the first place. Its afterlife via the note has been tailored to suit an editorial and political comment, which brings the banknote to represent 'talkative money' with several narrative strands.[54]

A cartoon's hybridity and its multilayered subtexts form in their own way part of a literary and visual constellation. The enduring artistic heritage splices the visual representation of literary figures and a long tradition of literary politics, particularly in British caricature. Austen, otherwise absent from political parody, has been widely mythologised, and the cultural weight of her fiction is made palpable on the materiality of the banknote through her portrait and all the elements surrounding her portrait.[55] By fusing visual satire and writerly portraiture mediated in the form of banknote iconography, Brookes's twenty-first-century cartoons contribute to the myth-making surrounding this particular author and her posthumous celebrity. A parody of Austen's portrait as found on the banknote is tied to caricature as an art that, in Gatrell's words, is 'a modernized form of an ancient effigy magic delivered against otherwise unassailable enemies . . . [a] symbolic defilement anciently embedded in ritual destructions of the defamatory image'.[56] In this instance, former British prime minister Theresa May is symbolically defiled for her inability to redress economic failure, something which is made even more spectacular through the ripple effect of Austen's iconic likeness on a banknote, then repurposed in the realm of literary politics. Alongside quotations, fragments and emblematic phrases lifted from literary works, portraits are stepping stones towards paths that indirectly lead fiction to political caricature. The question, however, is always one of more or less hidden clues.

Cameo Caricature, Easter Eggs and Motley Mediascapes

Pride and Prejudice and Zombies (2009) is a mashup of Austen's Regency novel, advertised on the front cover as co-authored by Jane Austen and Seth Grahame-Smith.[57] The transmedial repackaging of the mashup is an aftering of an afterlife of Austen's text. If we consider neo-Regency novels as part of a larger phenomenon, this book-to-film adaptation falls into the category of neo-Regency narratives, in word and/or image.[58] The movie blends semi-comical horror fiction with a heritage film setting. The parody is set against the backdrop of a pseudo-Regency environment threatened by a deadly plague, which turns invaders into zombies. Critics such as Francesca Guidotti argue that Austen's novel easily accommodates elements of monstrosity,[59] which the mashup consciously brings to the fore.[60] Guidotti further claims that the inclusion of the zombies came as a natural ingredient, as they were already there in the subconscious of Austen's original.[61]

The title sequence of the 2016 film *Pride and Prejudice and Zombies* calls for attention in the context of this essay as it is underpinned by a multifaceted perspective on fiction and graphic satire, in which Gillray's political caricature is pastiched by Martin Rowson, whose skills as political cartoonist and Gillray expert were sought after by the art director.[62] The final animated format relies on the artistic interplay between novels, print culture and Regency satire as it comprises allusions to that historical context. Different media interact with Rowson's Gillrayesque illustrations to create the illusion of theatrical depth, and add a tri-dimensional perspective to the satirical elements. The graphic CGI (computer-generated imagery) montage borrows from the aesthetics of puppet theatre and is a *trompe l'oeil* tunnel book.[63] Austen's narrative reimagined by Grahame-Smith as a spin-off, subsequently repackaged in a film, is peopled with zombies and pseudo-Austenian characters prone to cannibalistic feastings. In the title sequence, an audience attuned to Gillray's satirical prints will identify scenes reminiscent of *Temperance enjoying a Frugal Meal*, *A Family of Sans Culottes* (full title '*Un petit souper, a la Parisienne; - or - a family of sans-culottes refreshing, after the fatigues of the day*') alongside a pastiche of *The Plum-Pudding in Danger*, all of which are selected for their brutal Gallophobic stance and which are in keeping with the theme of predacious man-eating.[64]

Regarding the multimedia design for the title sequence, Gillray's graphic virtuosity and visual rhetoric, even if pastiched, coalesces with the *mise en abyme* of three adaptations in one: tunnel book layout on screen, an aftering of Austen's fiction, and pastiched illustrations of Gillray's prints. Anti-Revolutionary representations in Gillray's period were a visual response to the fear-ridden atmosphere generated by the aftermath of the execution of the French king Louis XVI in 1792, and the Terror that reigned during that decade. In *Pride and Prejudice and Zombies* on screen, horror film cannibalism and the pastiche of eighteenth-century graphic satire intermingle, and zombie film aesthetics vies with neo-Georgian caricatural grotesque in the title sequence, which blurs high–low boundaries, as does the textual mashup. Rowson, however, renders the mashing-up more complex in that he places George Osborne (former Chancellor of the Exchequer) as a cameo appearance among the dead zombies.[65] Rowson's additional nod to an artist whom he frequently names 'the father of British caricature', together with a form of Easter egg game,[66] extends the satirical network surrounding Austen's narrative from the late Georgian period to that of David Cameron's Coalition government (2010–15).

Revisiting Gillray in this manner puts Austen's fiction at the centre of a constellation of different media and discourses, which connect her novel to the history of print culture, politics and caricature. For all the delights they afford, however, watching the film's opening few minutes, designed to get the viewer into the mood of the film, does not accommodate establishing Gillray as a graphic source for the audience. In fact, viewers will probably feel alien to most such imagery since spotting these art references requires previous knowledge of Georgian visual culture. Pastiched Gillray iconography, repurposed in the context of a mass culture product like *Pride and Prejudice and Zombies* on film nonetheless reveals the long-lasting popularity of Austen's fiction, alongside Austen-based spin-offs. Like neo-Georgian fiction, which is characterised by 'a dual approach which combines a concern with the past and with the present,'[67] *Pride and Prejudice and Zombies* adapted for the screen, and then graphically illustrated by an artist like Martin Rowson, showcases embedded levels of pastiche and parody the ramifications of which are connected to a larger network of adaptations to which it implicitly belongs. Such a view supports the claim for an enduring presence of the (long) eighteenth century in our contemporary graphic and literary cultures, insofar as it allows for the widening of the scope for potential intersections, for instance, between Austen, satire and the art of caricature.[68] Literary spin-offs and parodied caricature are also part of the constellation in which Austen's comedy of manners as found in *Pride and Prejudice*, and Gillray's prints, which are themselves so frequently enmeshed in a complex web of literary and artistic allusions, can echo one another.

If a graphic animated sequence suggests one way of expanding adaptation networks,[69] graphic narratives, which incorporate editorial cartooning in cameo appearances, are yet another area where prose fiction and the art of caricature can converge. To go back to Swift's Gulliver, explored at the beginning of this chapter, Rowson's *Gulliver's Travels, Adapted and Updated* is not only an artistic and visual afterlife of Swift's text, it is also explicitly rooted in Rowson's political stance of anti-Blair satire.[70] His updated adaptation capitalises on the political satire of *Gulliver*, which is brought to the fore in a twofold manner: it takes an eighteenth-century fiction with lasting popularity as a springboard for revitalising Swift's text, and it simultaneously attacks British politics and the policies of former prime minister Tony Blair, particularly vilified for having betrayed his own Labour voters and for having lied about the Iraq War. In other words, Rowson's updating of Swift's prose features a modern 'splendide mendax'.[71] In the graphic narrative, one Dr Lionel Gulliver accidentally lands in Lilliput in 1997, where he comes across a Tony Blair-esque character (Figure 26.3).[72] Drawn with big ears sticking out, Blair's body and his often exuberant podium gestures are grafted onto the fictionalised prime minister in the graphic novel, all of which apes very closely attitudes and speech manners of the actual prime minister in office from 1997 onwards, mostly as observed during annual Labour Party Conferences.[73] In the first voyage to Lilliput, the cartoonist uses stylistic details from his own political cartoons and introduces topical 'visual journalism' in his fictional reimagining.[74] The emphasis is laid on the art of persuasion, the ambivalence of discourse in Lilliput, alongside mendacious eloquence and theatrical emotions during speech delivery, a topos that is not too commonly present in Gulliver-themed graphic satire. Lilliput in Rowson's updated adaptation is in the hands of a Rupert Murdoch-looking oligarch, which is another cameo caricature. Gulliver observes the disastrous effects of a stifling state propaganda supported by the media, and based on gullibility, in keeping with Swift's satire. The graphic novel comes across as a visual tribute to Swift interspersed with self-reflexive lifts from Rowson's graphic archive.[75]

Martin Rowson has illustrated and transposed all four voyages, each in a distinctive graphic style, adapting them so that Swift's potent satire is not only perceptible, but literally magnified tenfold. To follow Philippe Kaenel's view on the French illustrator and caricaturist Jean Ignace Isidore Gérard, better known as Jean Jacques Grandville, we can say of Rowson's adaptation of Swift that, 'to understand the illustrator's work, we must first turn to the political cartoonist'.[76] Rowson appropriates *Gulliver's Travels* and distils his own ethical discourse, situating the narrative in a

Figure 26.3 Martin Rowson, *Gulliver's Travels Adapted and Updated* (2012), page 18. Courtesy of Martin Rowson.

modern world where technology is the mother of all vices (social networks, tabloids, human trafficking). In that respect, the comic book format of Rowson's twenty-first-century *Gulliver's Travels* constitutes a graphic polyphony and a dialogical space, in Bakhtin's sense, where the productive hybridity of graphic satire and comics shapes a new mediascape. This graphic heterogeneity proves doubly fertile by reviving press cartoons and Augustan fiction. At the crossroads of an enduring piece of classic literature, a long tradition of political satire inspired by literary works and comics as a medium, a circulatory constellation emerges, which takes into account a modernised Gulliver, where the representation of politics and media allows the original Swiftian rhetoric to be redeployed. Like the Swiftian model, Rowson's narrator decides to make his story memorable, but in 'the defining media of the age'.[77] The 2012 adaptation is therefore not only about Swift's content but also about using it to articulate reflexivity regarding the medium itself, something which eighteenth-century novelists strived to do and frequently experimented with.

Conclusion: Graphic Constellation and Eighteenth-Century Novels Redux

This survey of eighteenth-century novels and graphic satire over an extended period yields only a handful of emblematic scenes, characters and a limited number of authors culled from a body of works spanning from 1719 to 1819. We may thus have the impression that eighteenth-century fiction as seen through the lens of caricature and graphic satire resembles the circulation of a redux version of a large and cumbersome canon, with some works over-represented, but with several major texts and writers from that period never having featured in political satire. Such an overall vision of paucity, though, begs for nuance. The notion of redux may indeed apply to brief formats like single-sheet satires and editorial cartoons as opposed to extended multi-page formats, but its etymology equally implies returning from and to the past. Rather, the art of graphic satire, like other forms of adaptation, 'plays a harlequin role'[78] in that it distils and refracts, in a rhizomatic fashion, memorable fictional fragments, references authors, sometimes indirectly, and simultaneously accrues a vast parallel graphic canon. Paradoxically, as it were, this contributes to bringing those works and authors back, and makes them more monumental, and thus, more perennial as cultural objects, at least in the English-speaking world. The constellation I have tried to chart is one of interconnected, yet not identical areas where the role of artists, authors, their fiction and its connections with politics are constantly redefined and/or revived. From embedded and encrypted political caricature to revisited and repackaged eighteenth-century satire, the part played by expanded networks (afterlives, literary spin-offs, cameo appearances and mashup poetics) begs for attention by adopting inter-transmedial angles to explore graphic artforms as echo chambers of literary pieces, with which we converse via the images. Graphic satire related to novels and novelists is like a vehicle that can take us back and forth between the past and several temporal frames, including the present day, while fictional worlds from the eighteenth century talk back to us when they are reconfigured as graphic novels, banknotes, or indeed political cartoons.

Notes

1. David Francis Taylor, *The Politics of Parody: A Literary History of Caricature, 1760–1830* (New Haven and London: Yale University Press, 2018); Daniel Cook and Nicholas, eds, *The Afterlives of Eighteenth-Century Fiction* (Oxford: Oxford University Press, 2015); Jakub Lipski, *Painting the Novel: Pictorial Discourse in Eighteenth-Century English Fiction* (New York and London: Routledge, 2018). M-C. Newbould explores adaptations of Laurence Sterne's fiction in a variety of media, which range from theatrical plays to visual reworkings, such as illustration and graphic satire. See M-C. Newbould, *Adaptations of Laurence Sterne's Fiction: Sterneana, 1760–1840* (Farnham: Ashgate, 2013).
2. On Caricature as an art, see, for instance, Laurent Baridon and Martial Guédron, *L'art et l'histoire de la caricature* (Paris: Citadelles et Mazenod, 2021).
3. Vic Gatrell, *City of Laughter: Sex and Satire in Eighteenth-Century London* (London: Atlantic Books, 2006).
4. The difference I make between stand-alone satirical prints and cartoons in the press stems from the history of the word 'cartoon', which only came into usage after the mid-nineteenth century. In 1843, John Leech published 'Substance and Shadow' as Cartoon no.1 in *Punch*. This representation of social satire triggered the change in the meaning of the word 'cartoon'.
5. For a detailed survey of changes in Victorian satire, see Henry J. Miller, 'John Leech and the Shaping of the Victorian Cartoon: The Context of Respectability', *Victorian Periodicals Review* 42, no. 3 (2009): 267–91.
6. David A. Brewer, *The Afterlife of Character, 1726–1825* (Philadelphia: University of Pennsylvania Press, 2005).

7. For a discussion of the dissemination of literary works through fragments and citations, see the notion of 'disembodied presence' in Newbould, *Adaptations of Laurence Sterne's Fiction*, 208–12. See also Brigitte Friant-Kessler, 'The Art of Cursing: The Circulation of Shandean Fragments in Pamphlets and Prints (1815–1821)', *XVII–XVIII. Revue de la société d'études anglo-américaines des XVIIe et XVIIIe siècles* (2010): 257–77, https://doi.org/10.3406/xvii.2010.2492 (accessed 23 November 2023).

8. See Nathalie Zimpfer, 'The World, Gulliver, and the Critic', *XVII–XVIII. Revue de la société d'études anglo-américaines des XVIIe et XVIIIe siècles*, 77 (2020), http://journals.openedition.org/1718/5982 (accessed 23 November 2023).

9. See for instance, Vanessa Guignery, 'An Interview with Jonathan Coe – Looking Backwards and Forwards', *Études britanniques contemporaines* [online], 54 l(2018), http://journals.openedition.org/ebc/4396 (accessed 12 December 2023); Jonathan Coe, 'Writing a Children's Book for Our Turbulent Times', *The Guardian*, 18 November 2017, https://www.theguardian.com/books/2017/nov/18/jonathan-coe-gullivers-travels-broken-mirror?utm_source=esp&utm_medium=Email&utm_campaign=Bookmarks+-+Collections+2017&utm_term=253002&subid=19126853&CMP=bookmarks_collection (accessed 12 December 2023). Both articles refer to Coe's 2013 *Marginal Notes* in Jonathan Coe, 'Jonathan Swift: *Gulliver's Travels*'. Written for the Guidizio Universale, 2007, *Marginal Notes, Doubtful Statements* (London: Penguin ebooks, 2013). On Gulliver's adaptability and its ambivalence, see, for instance, David Bywaters, '*Gulliver's Travels* and the Mode of Political Parallel during Walpole's Administration', *ELH* 54, no. 3 (1987): 717–40.

10. Nathalie Zimpfer, 'The World, Gulliver, and the Critic', *XVII–XVIII* [online] 77 (2020), http://journals.openedition.org/1718/5982 (accessed 9 December 2023).

11. The cartoon was published as part of the Rogue's Gallery series, 4 February 2023. See, for instance, Brown's parody of Gericault's painting *The Raft of the Medusa*, https://www.lambiek.net/artists/b/brown_dave.htm (accessed 10 December 2023).

12. On the topic of appropriation, see Jakub Lipski, *Re-Reading the Eighteenth-Century Novel: Studies in Reception* (London and New York: Routledge, 2021), 89–104, 90.

13. Lipski's essay on the Age of Trump offers an illuminating view on Gulliver-based cartoons and visual satire on Donald Trump, in particular images with a Trump agenda, which revisit Swift. See Lipski, *Re-Reading the Eighteenth-Century Novel*, 89–104, 93.

14. Alongside Crusoe and Gulliver, we note other literary sources from the Anglophone world that are frequently referenced in caricature: Shakespeare's plays, King Arthur's legend, *Frankenstein*, Dickens, *Oliver Twist*'s emblematic 'Oliver asks for more' scene, as well as Lewis Carroll's *Alice* books. Captions may sometimes allude to famous poems or parody famous quotes, which include passages from the Bible or classics, like Milton.

15. Early modern emblem books may be seen as predecessors of political cartoons in which text, image and meaning are interdependent and comprehension is conditioned by the context.

16. On Swift's satire and the notion of 'enunciative disjunction', see Nathalie Zimpfer, 'Orgueil et démesure, ou la satire swiftienne', *XVII–XVIII. Revue de la société d'études anglo-américaines des XVIIe et XVIIIe siècles* 71 (2014): 209–30.

17. A copy of that print is held at the British Museum. See Museum Number Qq,14.219.1-9, https://www.britishmuseum.org/collection/object/P_Qq-14-219-1-9 (accessed 24 November 2023).

18. 'Islandness' and/in Robinsonades is discussed by Emmanuelle Peraldo, 'Introduction: 300 Years of Robinsonades', in *300 Years of Robinsonades*, ed. Emmanuelle Peraldo (Newcastle upon Tyne: Cambridge Scholars Publishing, 2020), 1–13. See also, David Taylor's chapter '*The Tempest*; or The Disenchanted Island', devoted to satirical prints based on Shakespeare's play, in David Francis Taylor, *The Politics of Parody: A Literary History of Caricature, 1760–1830* (New Haven and London: Yale University Press, 2018), 71–100.

THE ART OF GRAPHIC SATIRE 479

19. David Blewett, 'The Iconic Crusoe: Illustrations and Images of Robinson Crusoe', in *The Cambridge Companion to 'Robinson Crusoe'*, ed. John Richetti (Cambridge: Cambridge University Press, 2018), 159.

20. Taylor, *The Politics of Parody*, 19.

21. See British Museum (Number 2002,0224.8), https://www.britishmuseum.org/collection/object/P_2002-0224-8 (accessed 24 November 2023).

22. See British Museum (Number 1868,0808.8280), https://www.britishmuseum.org/collection/object/P_1868-0808-8280 (accessed 24 November 2023).

23. On rats and Crusoe, see Lucinda Cole, 'Crusoe's Animals, Annotated: Cats, Dogs, and Disease in the *Naval Chronicle* Edition of *Robinson Crusoe*, 1815', *Eighteenth-Century Fiction* 32, no. 1 (2019), 55–78. In Defoe's original novel, Crusoe attributes his victory over rats to Providence when he salvages a bag of grain. As a counterpoint to this, in Michel Tournier's *Robinson ou la vie sauvage*, Friday takes rats as pets.

24. See, for instance, the print *The Corsican Tiger at Bay*, by Thomas Rowlandson (1808), accession number 59.533.2069, https://www.metmuseum.org/art/collection/search/812092 (accessed 24 November 2023).

25. *Puck* 58, no. 1505, 3 January 1906. The artist, Udo Keppler Jr, who went by the name of Joseph Keppler after 1894, was the son of the Austrian-born cartoonist Joseph Keppler, who was also the founder of *Puck Magazine* (1871–1918). The magazine's editorial line was generally known to be in favour of Teddy Roosevelt in the run-up to the 1908 election.

26. The full original title of Cowper's 1782 poem is 'Verses supposed to be written by Alexander Selkirk, during his solitary Abode in the Island of Juan Fernandez', in *The Complete Poetical Works of William Cowper*, ed. H. S. Milford (London: Henry Frowde, 1905), 311–12.

27. One such illustration by George Housman Thomas, engraved by Butterworth and Heath, is 'Crusoe and Friday', in *The Life and Strange Surprising Adventures of Robinson Crusoe of York, Mariner. Related by himself*. With upwards of One Hundred Illustrations (London: Cassell, Petter and Galpin, 1863–4) 133, https://victorianweb.org/art/illustration/cassell/36.html (accessed 24 November 2023). The introduction to that edition presents William Cowper's poem by insisting on 'the touching lines in which Cowper supposes Alexander Selkirk records his feelings', xiii.

28. A good example of how the history of nations or communities can be connected with Defoe's characters is Thomas Nast's full-page cartoon for *Harper's Weekly* 14, no. 685, 12 February 1870, p. 112, captioned 'Robinson Crusoe Making a Man of his Friday', published in the context of the assimilation policy of the government of the United States. Nast depicts the American president, Ulysses Grant, as Crusoe, dressing almost forcibly an Indian Chief (Friday) in European American-styled clothes, which reflects the attempt of the federal government to assimilate Native Americans and impose Christian norms and ethics on them, in the same way Robinson Crusoe intends to educate Friday. See Library of Congress, Thomas Nast, *Robinson Crusoe making a man of his Friday* / Th. Nast, 1870, https://www.loc.gov/item/2003653580/ (accessed 24 November 2023).

29. The surprising effect of the footprint in the sand often articulates anxieties related to the infrigement of diplomatic dispositions, the trespassing of a given territory, and precariousness, which is a threat. In the database of the University of Kent cartoon archive, one notices that between 1972 and 1997, several cartoons by Nicholas Garland, for instance, take their cue from that scene, to comment on domestic and international periods of crisis. He draws Ian Smith during the Rhodesia crisis in 1972, then uses the trope again in 1973 and 1987. In 1997, he published a cartoon in which the word 'resign' inscribed in the footprint looks menacing as it points to a trial of strength over offshore funds allegedly held by Geoffrey Robinson, Tony Blair's Treasury Minister.

30. The second was published in *Punch* in 1948 and features a Crusoe-type figure in the Arctic zone on the Falkland Islands, a disputed territory in the aftermath of the war.

31. See, for instance, the lithograph by the Irish artist H.B. (John Doyle), 'Gulliver Capturing the Enemies Fleet', dated 29 May 1846, from the series entitled *Political Sketches by H.B.* (no. 865). Prime Minister Robert Peel (Gulliver) is shown hauling ships named after politicians who opposed his policy in favour of free trade, in the context of the repeal of the Corn Laws. A copy is held at the National Gallery of Victoria, Melbourne and can be viewed here: https://www.ngv.vic.gov.au/explore/collection/work/28211/ (accessed 24 November 2023). For a more detailed study on Victorian caricature, see Henry J. Miller's arguments about shifts in satire, 'John Leech and the Shaping of the Victorian Cartoon: The Context of Respectability', *Victorian Periodicals Review* 42, no. 3 (2009): 267–91.

32. One of the few Brobdingnag-themed satires after Gillray's period is a 1906 scene by Keppler Jr, 'Gulliver Cleveland and the Wall Street Brobdingnagians' (*Puck* 58, no. 1508, 24 January 1906), which depicts a diminutive American President Grover Cleveland being scrutinised by four giant Wall Street finance tycoons among which are John Rockefeller or Pierpont Morgan: https://www.loc.gov/resource/ppmsca.26028/ (accessed 24 November 2023). Keppler was probably aware of an earlier Gulliverised Cleveland, drawn by Bernhard Gillam: 'Gulliver-Cleveland takes possession of the enemy's fleet and deprives them of their strength' (*Puck* 17, no. 432, 17 June 1885) iterates Gulliver towing the Blefuscuan fleet for Lilliput, https://www.loc.gov/item/2011661756/ (accessed 24 November 2023).

33. The same French President Thiers, interestingly, is depicted as a constrained Gulliver in a cartoon by John Tenniel for *Punch* entitled 'Little Gulliver' (*Punch*, 1 February 1873). As a president, Thiers was continuously under attack from activists and factions in the opposition.

34. On 27 September 1866, Daumier published a lithograph in *Le Charivari*, titled 'Renouvelé de Gulliver'. That new giant Gulliverian figure was the Prussian emperor Wilhelm II, violently taking hold of diminutive people and bruising them deliberately. Between 1850 and 1868, the Gulliver motif was recurrently used by Daumier. He further published cartoons in *Le Charivari* related to the unification of Italy by Garibaldi (*Italy awakening*, 1859) and the revolution in Spain (*In Spain. The Giant and Pygmies*, 1868), featuring giant figures in postures that closely resemble his Gulliverian prints.

35. For such caricatures, see, for instance, the series by Robert Dighton, *Geography Bewitched! or, a Droll Caricature Map of England and Wales*, c.1793.

36. On the notion of fame and celebrity culture with reference to Laurence Sterne, see Thomas Keymer, *Sterne, the Moderns and the Novel* (Oxford: Oxford University Press, 2002), and Frank Donohue, *The Fame Machine: Book Reviewing and Eighteenth-Century Literary Careers* (Stanford: Stanford University Press, 1996). See also Julia H. Fawcett, 'Creating Character in "Chiaro Oscuro": Sterne's Celebrity, Cibber's *Apology*, and the Life of *Tristram Shandy*', *The Eighteenth Century* 53, no. 2 (2012): 141–61.

37. See Bertrand Goldgar, 'Fielding's Periodical Journalism', in *The Cambridge Companion to Henry Fielding*, ed. Claude Rawson (Cambridge: Cambridge University Press, 2007), 109–21, 116.

38. For detailed studies of Fielding's anti-Jacobite stance and its connections to the novel *Tom Jones*, see, for instance, Anaclara Castro-Santana, 'Henry Fielding's Theatrical Reminiscences: Another Look at Sophia Western as Jenny Cameron', *Studies in Eighteenth-Century Culture* 50 (2021): 187–212; Jill Campbell, *Natural Masques: Gender and Identity in Fielding's Plays and Novels* (Stanford: Stanford University Press, 1995); Peter Carlton, '*Tom Jones* and the '45 Once Again', *Studies in the Novel* 20, no. 4 (1988): 361–73.

39. *London Evening Post*, 28–30 July 1748.

40. The following explanation is given for the design: 'The woodcut headpiece, designed by Hogarth, relates to an episode during the Jacobite Rising of 1745 when the Scottish sergeant, Dickson, and a female drummer rode ahead of the main Jacobite army into Manchester, boasting that the locals had not put up any resistance, only for the Jacobites to be driven north a few days later.' Details are provided by a note on the headpiece, https://

THE ART OF GRAPHIC SATIRE 481

www.rct.uk/collection/913457/a-design-for-the-headpiece-to-the-jacobites-journal (accessed 24 November 2023).

41. *The Gentleman's Magazine* 18 November 1748, XXIII: 'Exit of the Jacobite Journal, with the author's epitaph', 515.

42. The search yields around thirty hits alone in the British Museum database and the Lewis Walpole Library. On the series of anti-Bute prints by Paul Sandby, with reference to Scottishness and Smollett, see also Ann V. Gunn, 'The Fire of Faction: Sources for Paul Sandby's Satires of 1762–63', *Print Quarterly* 34, no. 4 (2017): 400–18. Gunn notes that 'Smollett is identified by name or by publication' (414).

43. *The Tempest or Enchanted Island* (1762), https://www.britishmuseum.org/collection/object/P_1868-0808-4223 (accessed 24 November 2023).

44. The Peace of Paris or Treaty of Paris, which officially ended the Seven Years' War, was signed on 10 February 1763 but negotiations were well under way by the end of 1762. The terms of the Treaty were especially harsh on British dominions, literally expelled by Britannia in the print. Bute's government was held responsible for the loss.

45. Another anti-Bute print entitled '*The Mountebank*' (1762), which depicts Smollett on stage as a zany quack with a fool's cap, and a copy of the *Briton* in his pocket. The Lewis Walpole Library, call no. 762.05.00.20, https://collections.library.yale.edu/catalog/10713058 (accessed 24 November 2023).

46. Paul Sandby (?), *The Evacuations or An Emetic for Old England Glorys* (1762), https://www.britishmuseum.org/collection/object/P_1904-0819-712 (accessed 24 November 2023). The British Museum catalogue note specifies: 'To the left are Tobias Smollett wearing a tartan waistcoat, sniffing a doctor's cane and taking Britannia's pulse (in the second state, a copy of the Briton protrudes from his pocket), and Henry Fox preparing to administer a large clyster; he holds a heavy bag with a prescription from Smollett reading, "Soupe Maigre / Ry Caledon: cacoeines aa / Ligna Calcea: Q: S:/ fiat onixt / Pro Brit Anus / T[obias]. S[mollett]. M. D".'

47. For a detailed study on that topic, see Virginia Hewitt, *The Banker's Art: Studies in Paper Money* (London: British Museum Press, 1995).

48. Marin Marian-Bălaşa, 'Music on Money: State Legitimation and Cultural Representation', *Music in Art* 28, no. 1/2 (2003): 173–89.

49. 'Austen-Leigh commissioned a professional artist, James Andrews of Maidenhead, to execute a portrait from the sketch, and this then provided the model for a steel engraving . . . ; in its Victorian refashioning, the face is softer, its expression more pliant, and the eyes only pensively averted . . . As visual biographies the two tell quite different stories, whatever claim either might make to be representing a human original.' James Edward Austen-Leigh, *A Memoir of Jane Austen and Other Family Recollections*, ed. Kathryn Sutherland (Oxford: Oxford University Press, 2002), xlv.

50. Jane Austen to James Edward Austen-Leigh, 16 December 1816, Add MS 89437, British Library.

51. The French banknote designer Pierrette Lambert, born in 1928, is also a miniature artist. See 'Pierrette Lambert', *Les Billets de France*, https://billetsdefrance.com/artists.php?name=Lambert%2C+P (accessed 24 November 2023). For a study on a large corpus of eighteenth-century novels in relation to miniature painting, see, for instance, Anne Bandry-Scubbi and Brigitte Friant-Kessler, 'Peindre en corpus: Miniatures et roman anglais féminin (1751–1834)', in *Palette pour Marie-Madeleine Martinet*, ed. Françoise Deconinck-Brossard and Liliane Gallet Blanchard (2016), http://www.csti.paris-sorbonne.fr/centre/palette/index.html (accessed 24 November 2023).

52. See Jane Austen, *Selected Letters*, ed. Vivian Jones, letter no. 46 (Oxford: Oxford World's Classics, 1998), 117–18: 'Wednesday 5 April 1809, In the Spring of the year 1803 a MS. Novel in 2 vol. entitled Susan was sold to you by a Gentleman of the name of Seymour, &

the purchase money £10. recd at the same time.' In the rest of the letter, however, Austen complains about her book not having been published.

53. Marian-Bălaşa, 'Music on Money', 174.

54. *Debased Currency* is part of a series of several cartoons by Brookes that parody banknotes or coins.

55. A French 50 franc note with Antoine de Saint-Exupéry featured the writer, the most famous illustration from *The Little Prince*, and a drawing from the narrative with the elephant swallowed by the boa.

56. Gatrell, *City of Laughter*, 227. Gattrell aligns with Ernst Gombrich who theorised image-magic in a seminal essay. E. H. Gombrich, 'The Cartoonist's Armory', *South Atlantic Quarterly* 62, no. 2 (1963): 189–228.

57. Jane Austen and Seth Grahame-Smith, *Pride and Prejudice and Zombies* (Philadelphia: Quirk Books, 2009). The novel was adapted for the screen in 2016.

58. On the concepts of neo-Regency and neo-Georgian, see Jakub Lipski and Joanna Maciule-wicz, 'Introduction: Delineating the Neo-Georgian', in *Neo-Georgian Fiction: Reimagining the Eighteenth Century in the Contemporary Historical Novel*, ed. Jakub Lipski and Joanna Maciulewicz (London and New York: Routledge, 2021).

59. Francesca Guidotti, 'Mashing Up Jane Austen's Classics: *Pride and Prejudice and Zombies & Mansfield Park and Mummies*', in *Thinking Out of the Box in Literary and Cultural Studies*, ed. Rocco Coronato, Marilena Parlati and Alessandra Petrina (Padua: Padova University Press, 2021), 125–47.

60. For another mashup in the same vein, and by the same American publisher as *Pride and Prejudice and Zombies*, see Ben H. Winters, *Sense and Sensibility and Sea Monsters* (Philadelphia: Quirk Books, 2009). Austen's Dashwood sisters are sent away from their home to live on a dangerous island infested with hammer-head sharks and monstrous creatures.

61. Guidotti, along with Seth Grahame-Smith, argues that the regiment of soldiers in Austen's novel is a group of predators who are subconsciously hungry for souls and bodies. The overall argument relies on the gaps Austen left in her fiction about historical events. Simi-larly, Guidotti supports her view by saying that 'If *Pride and Prejudice* can be read as a "conservative" and "anti-Jacobin novel", the mashup is even more so: greedy zombies are a degraded version of the Third Estate, symbolic villains with no property of their own, con-stantly and insatiably hungry. These zombies are presented as a mass underclass.' Guidotti, 'Mashing Up Jane Austen's Classics', 133. The claim of zombification, however, first and foremost originates in Grahame-Smith's desire to produce a counter-narrative to Austen, and an American one at that.

62. For more details on the technical aspects of the title sequence, as well as hidden visual jokes, there is an interesting interview with Ben Smith, the director, and Martin Rowson as illustrator: Will Perkins, 'Pride and Prejudice and Zombies', *Art of the Title*, 5 April 2016, https://www.artofthetitle.com/title/pride-and-prejudice-and-zombies/ (accessed 24 November 2023).

63. Tunnel books, also known as peep shows, are made of cut-paper panels, stuck together so as to create the illusion of depth and perspective. Sometimes called stage books, they are often described as a format which predates virtual reality. Tunnel books have been a popular form of entertainment based on optical illusion since the mid-eighteenth century. In the history of tunnel books, Martin Engelbrecht, an engraver and print-seller born in Augsburg, is a name to remember. In the bookbinding and bookmaking tradition, tun-nel books remain spectacular works of art, by virtue of combining storytelling and the physicality of a three-dimensional stage set or diorama. See, for instance, 'The Dance of the Tunnel Book', https://library.si.edu/digital-library/exhibition/paper-engineering/dance-tunnel-book (accessed 24 November 2023).

THE ART OF GRAPHIC SATIRE

64. James Gillray, *A Voluptuary under the Horrors of Digestion* (1792), https://www.british-museum.org/collection/object/P_1868-0808-6219 (accessed 24 November 2023).

65. Beside Osborne, Rowson also hid the filmmaker among the zombies he drew. On Rowson and drawing George Osborne, see Mark Reynolds, 'Martin Rowson Draws Up a Storm', *Bookanista*, bookanista.com/martin-rowson (accessed 24 November 2023). This interview with the cartoonist took place in the context of *The Coalition Book*, published by SelfMadeHero in 2014: 'As I mention in the book, cartoonists do get involved in this weird kind of Stockholm syndrome where we fall in love with our victims. In 2004 every single fibre of my being wanted Bush to lose, except my over-active satire gland which just loved drawing his eyebrows like mad chinchillas on his forehead. I love drawing George Osborne – and I despise him more than anybody in politics in the last thirty years.'

66. In computer software and media, an Easter egg is usually a hidden surprise, joke, image or secret feature.

67. See Lipski and Maciulewicz, 'Introduction', 2.

68. A similar rationale underpins the two volumes on Hogarth's 'enduring presence'. See Caroline Patey, Cynthia E. Roman and Georges Letissier, eds, *Enduring Presence: William Hogarth's British and European Afterlives* (Frankfurt am Main: Peter Lang, 2021).

69. On the notion of expanding adaptation networks, see, for instance, Kate Newell, *Expanding Adaptation Networks: From Illustration to Novelization* (London: Palgrave Macmillan, 2017).

70. After *The Life and Opinions of Tristram Shandy* (first edition 1996), *Gulliver's Travels Adapted and Updated* (2012) is the second venture by Martin Rowson into novel-to-comic book adaption of an eighteenth-century work. Both projects display an idiosyncratic inclination for a particular author. On Rowson's graphic style in the use of blackness in his *Gulliver's Travels*, see, for instance, Brigitte Friant-Kessler, 'L'encre et la bile: Caricature politique et roman graphique satirique au prisme de *Gulliver's Travels Adapted and Updated* de Martin Rowson', in *L'Image railleuse: La satire visuelle du XVIIIe siècle à nos jours*, ed. Laurent Baridon, Frédérique Desbuissons and Dominic Hardy (Paris: Publications de l'Institut national d'histoire de l'art, 2019), https://books.openedition.org/inha/9465 6219 (accessed 24 November 2023).

71. Blair as B-LIAR seemed aptly associated with Gulliver depicted as *splendide mendax*.

72. Often set in dystopian environments, Rowson's editorial cartoons, mostly published in *The Guardian*, *The Scotsman*, the *Tribune* and *The Mirror*, followed Blair's political trajectory.

73. Photographs of the 2005 Annual Labour Conference in Brighton, 28 September 2005, like, for instance, those taken by Rupert Rivett, and the subsequent editorial cartoon by Rowson in *The Guardian* (28 September 2005) show striking similarities with Blair's body language and attitudes when he delivers a speech and those found in the Blair-esque character of the 2012 graphic novel. The clone-looking audience, wearing identical smiley masks in the cartoon, is also present in the comic book adaptation.

74. On Rowson's own definition of an editorial cartoonist as a 'visual journalist', see, for instance, Martin Rowson, 'We, the Cartoonists, are the True Outsiders of Journalism', *The Political Cartoon Society*, https://www.original-political-cartoon.com/cartoon-history/we-cartoonists-are-true-outsiders-journalism/ (accessed 24 November 2023).

75. Rowson is, however, not the first cartoonist and illustrator to smuggle political caricature into an adaptation of *Gulliver's Travels*. Chris Riddell's 2004 illustrations to *Gulliver's Travels* (retold by Martin Jenkins) stages a cameo caricature of Blair in Balnibarbi. In the foreword to the edition published by Candlewick Press in 2004, Riddell explains how he combined political cartooning and children's book illustration: 'My favourite picture is the portrait of the politician being subjected to rough treatment to keep him honest. I drew a caricature of Tony Blair, the politician I have drawn the most often in my career,

who would have benefited from Swiftian treatment.' Chris Riddell, 'Foreword', in Martin Jenkins, *Jonathan Swift's Gulliver* (Somerville: Candlewick Press, 2004).

76. Philippe Kaenel, *Le Métier d'illustrateur, 1830–1880, Rodolphe Töpffer, J. J. Grandville, Gustave Doré* (Geneva: Droz, 2004), 300.

77. The final pages of the graphic novel are devoted to an auctorial persona (Martin Rowson) presented as a mediator between the reader and Gulliver who insisted his adventures be told in comic book format.

78. On adaptations and the notion of the 'harlequin role' played by adaptations, see Newbould, *Adaptations of Laurence Sterne's Fiction*, 10.

27

CONTEMPORARY ART AND THE EIGHTEENTH-CENTURY NOVEL

Amelia Dale

CONCEPTUALLY ORIENTED ART has a history of adapting eighteenth-century fiction. Contemporary gallery art has regularly repurposed and translated eighteenth-century writing across media; and, by moving from one medium to another, it illuminates, under strange light, certain elements and structures of the eighteenth-century novel. I will not provide an exhaustive catalogue of appearances of eighteenth-century novels within contemporary visual art; instead, I will closely examine how three prominent contemporary visual artists rework eighteenth-century fiction, namely John Baldessari, Meg Cranston and Paul Chan. All three artists are concerned with translating aspects of the reading experience across media.

John Baldessari's lithograph series and artist book *The Life and Opinions of Tristram Shandy, Gentleman* (1988) places Laurence Sterne's text alongside found film stills and photographs, suggesting proximities between eighteenth-century fiction and conceptual art practice. Meg Cranston's *The Complete Works of Jane Austen* (1991), a large inflatable sculpture filled with the precise amount of air the artist imagines she would need to inhale in order to read Austen's oeuvre, evokes the imagined space novel reading creates. Paul Chan's e-rewritings of the Marquis de Sade's works – particularly *Les 120 Journées de Sodome ou l'école du libertinage* (written 1785) – in his installation 'Sade for Sade's Sake' (2009), simultaneously write and sculpt literary character. Codex book morphs into film, sculpture, 'fontwork' and back to book again.[1] For Garrett Stewart, ideas transgressing across different media is key to 'Conceptualism 2.0' – the art that follows the 'first wave' of conceptualism.[2] Taking these works into account, this essay analyses how the citational and self-reflexive practices of eighteenth-century writers, which frequently foreground the novel as a material and visual object, have been refracted through the transmediality of contemporary conceptual art. The eighteenth-century novel's materiality, mediation and formal organisation is written anew through the medial disruption of recent art history. By reworking the eighteenth-century novel within other mediums, contemporary art presents us with a unique picture of the specificity of the experience of reading a prose narrative within a codex book.

While the terms 'contemporary art', 'postmodern art' and 'conceptual art' are sometimes used loosely and interchangeably, each is simultaneously yoked to a specific historical period and particular artistic practices. So, even though 'conceptual art' can be closely associated with artistic movements in the 1960s and 1970s, such as the Art & Language group, it also denotes a specific practice, one which emphasises ideas over

AMELIA DALE

material, meaning over 'content' or craft.[3] To quote Sol LeWitt's 1967 'Paragraphs on Conceptual Art':

> In conceptual art the idea of concept is the most important aspect of the work. When an artist uses a conceptual form of art, it means that all of the planning and decisions are made beforehand and the execution is a perfunctory affair. The idea becomes a machine that makes the art.[4]

Conceptual art subordinates the content or matter of the work to its overarching idea, to the point where the content itself might be emptied out, sometimes to the point of vanishing. 'Contemporary' might seem to merely refer to art made recently and can indeed refer to art from the late 1980s onwards, when the category of the 'contemporary' begins to supplant the increasingly obsolescent idea of the 'postmodern'.[5] Yet contemporary art is not only a period designation but also a kind of art. Not all art made now is contemporary art. The art that dominates contemporary gallery spaces and the art market is 'an art premissed on the complex historical experience and critical legacy of conceptual art', particularly conceptual art's treatment of media.[6] The crossing or transference between different media – what Stewart calls 'transmedia', and what fluxus artist Dick Higgins described as 'intermedia' – is a staple of contemporary art.[7]

The eighteenth-century novel is multiplied across media in contemporary visual art. The artworks I discuss take up the experience of reading and move it beyond the paper book-object. They relocate eighteenth-century print to the rooms of the art gallery, hanging on the gallery wall as diagrammatic mappings or sections of extracted text to be read and viewed. They construct sculptures and name the sculptures after books and characters. Or, outside the gallery space, they write programs and make files that intervene in our contemporary, screen-oriented consumption of text, and contrast the eighteenth-century book object with the PDF or the Microsoft Word document. Stewart notes that as a result of their intermedial situation, contemporary gallery objects tend to become 'fine-grained reports on their own medial constitution'.[8] They can reveal something tangible about the materiality of the medium, or something else entirely through the way they navigate these medial crossings.

Stewart's comment on contemporary art also holds true of much eighteenth-century fiction. It often involves self-reflexive experimentation in print, through typographic innovation, and in anticipating its own reception, marketing, reading, circulation and disposal. Thomas Keymer, among others, notes the prevalence of mid-eighteenth-century texts that reflect on their material situation as printed objects. Read along these lines, Laurence Sterne's intermedial, novel-like book *The Life and Opinions of Tristram Shandy, Gentleman* (1759–67) is simply the most famous example of a self-reflexive mid-eighteenth-century text.[9] The extent to which eighteenth-century fiction's medial self-reflexivity is analogous to that of more recent experiments in art is a fraught question. There are key differences in context, in reception, in motivation between medial self-reflexivity in eighteenth-century print and the intermedial crossings of contemporary conceptualism. Still, it remains the case that contemporary art perceives a sufficient relation between itself and eighteenth-century fiction to reference and appropriate it.

Illustrating *Tristram Shandy*: Book as Citational Collage

Tristram Shandy is widely referenced and appropriated in works of contemporary art, reflecting its popular reputation as an anachronistic early work of intermedial experiment.[10] Take, for instance, the Lisbon exhibition 'PICTURES and CREAM, The confidential report of the life and opinions of Tristram Shandy & friends, Volume 1', curated by Paulo Mendes (9 July–26 September 2015), which in the exhibition's press release asks questions about the relationship between reading a book and viewing an artwork in a gallery space:

> How to transform a book into an exhibit? ——————— And a gallery into a book? How might a book shed its primary vocation of being read to be transformed into a complex spatial object? ——————— Would it be possible to three-dimensionalize a book into an exhibition-installation? ———————
>
> ———————————————————————
> ———————————————————— [11]

The promotional material frames these questions with dashes and ends with a series of lines, resembling the punctuational and typographic peculiarities that animate *Tristram Shandy*. We could dwell here on the implicit position – particularly startling given the references to *Tristram Shandy* – that a codex book has neither three dimensions nor a complex spatiality. Another approach, however, is to note how this exhibition, and the examples I will discuss below, demonstrate, in their movement between prose fiction and visual art, how reading is a complexly spatialised, embodied process. At the same time, like any adaptation across media these artworks interpret and selectively occlude elements of the works they adapt. They are concerned with identifying within the eighteenth-century novel the aesthetics of the contemporary.

John Baldessari (1931–2020) was among the artists in Mendes's exhibition. Baldessari had a long-standing interest in *Tristram Shandy* and was involved in several Shandy-related art projects for the Laurence Sterne Trust.[12] Baldessari's oeuvre straddles both 1960s and 1970s conceptual art and the 'conceptualism 2.0', or postconceptualism, of contemporary art.[13] Baldessari's work is persistently interested in the nature of the book object. Among his most famous works is the 'Cremation Project', where he cremated all the artworks in his possession that he had made between May 1953 and March 1966. He kept the ashes in 'a bronze urn in the shape of a book suitable for your library shelf'.[14] Baldessari's 'Cremation Project' tips the question about how to turn a book into an exhibit on its head, reducing a collection of possible exhibits into ashes, themselves enclosed within a book-like object.

In 1988 Baldessari created a series of thirty-nine photo-collage 'illustrations' of Sterne's work, commissioned by Andrew Hoyem of Arion Press. Five of the collages became large-scale lithographic prints, while the collection of thirty-nine photographs and text was published as part of a limited 400-copy, three-volume edition.[15] The three volumes, enclosed in a slipcase, consisted of a volume of Baldessari's 'illustrations', with concertina-like folds; a one-volume edition of *Tristram Shandy*; and a volume with a biographical essay on Sterne by Melvyn New, a Sterne scholar, previously printed in the *Dictionary of Literary Biography*.[16] New, despite collaborating on the project, later authored a journal article attacking Baldessari's 'illustrations' of

Tristram Shandy and comparing them unfavourably with William Hogarth's.[17] He has since repeated his critique in multiple forums.[18] Most of New's objections come from considering Baldessari's work as illustrations and viewing them as failing to subordinate themselves adequately to Sterne's text. New's privileging of word over image, writer over artist, needs to be reconsidered if we are to discover what contemporary art does with eighteenth-century fiction. Within Sterne studies, scholars such as Brigitte Friant-Kessler and W. B. Gerard have situated Baldessari's collages within a rich visual history of illustrations and artworks inspired by Sterne, most of which do not have a Hogarthian, or even a hobby-horsical fidelity to Sterne's letter.[19] Yet New's opposition to Baldessari's practice also points to larger issues at stake in these artworks: like any adaption of a text into a different medium, they take a position on the texts that they appropriate and offer a reading of them.[20] Between book art and wall art, Baldessari's collages take *Tristram Shandy*'s intermediality and citationality as a starting point from which they broach their own preoccupations from within the aesthetic of the contemporary.[21]

Baldessari's artworks quote and reframe text from *Tristram Shandy*, placing selected passages alongside repurposed images. Baldessari's use of found image and text echoes how Sterne reuses other writers' words in *Tristram Shandy*. Sterne acknowledges some sources, such as Miguel de Cervantes, and silently incorporates passages from others, such as Robert Burton's *Anatomy of Melancholy*.[22] Textual recycling is hardly unusual in eighteenth-century fiction, with Shandyesque antecedents such as Thomas Amory's *The Life of John Buncle, Esq.* (1756) similar in how they recycle long passages from other writers.[23] Denis Diderot's *Jacques le Fataliste* (published 1796) ostentatiously incorporates and rewrites sections from *Tristram Shandy* itself. More generally, eighteenth-century texts are rife with hidden quotations and phrases borrowed from other sources.[24] However, when reading eighteenth-century fiction as it is refracted through the lens of conceptualism, as Baldessari's treatment of *Tristram Shandy* encourages us to do, some forms of textual recycling appear more relevant than others: namely, those passages which overtly reflect upon the act of textual repurposing, where plagiarism becomes part of the narrative. This kind of citational writing is conceptual writing.

Contemporary conceptual writing occasionally brushes shoulders in the same reified gallery spaces as conceptual art, which it takes as a model. Paul Chan, as we will see, is both a conceptual artist and a conceptual writer, as, arguably, are Baldessari and Cranston. Like conceptual art, conceptual writing can be aligned with both a specific group and period, and with a certain practice. It is associated with a circle of North American poets including Kenneth Goldsmith, Vanessa Place and Christian Bök, who were particularly prominent in the first decade and a half of the twenty-first century. The conceit of conceptual writing is that it takes the practices of conceptual art and applies them to writing: the content of the writing is subordinated to an overarching idea. It usually involves repurposing text sourced from elsewhere or generating writing via mechanical processes.

As a practice, conceptual writing necessarily exists before and beyond Goldsmith's circle. In the influential anthology *Against Expression* (2011), which Goldsmith edited with Craig Dworkin, they bolster their argument for 'uncreative writing' with examples from art and literary history. Dworkin identifies Baldessari's word paintings as an important precedent for conceptual writing.[25] The anthology

CONTEMPORARY ART AND THE EIGHTEENTH-CENTURY NOVEL   489

also includes a passage of Diderot's *Jacques le Fataliste*'s repurposing of text from *Tristram Shandy*. For Goldsmith and Dworkin, 'Diderot's plagiarism ... brings together both the narrative structure and uncreating aspects of *Jacques*, collapsing form and content'.[26] Sterne's use of Burton works similarly, particularly the passage where Tristram declaims against plagiarism with text borrowed from *The Anatomy of Melancholy*, using recycling to make a point about recycling.[27] Vanessa Place and Robert Fitterman identify this passage as conceptual writing in their manifesto *Notes on Conceptualisms* (2009).[28] Like Baldessari's collages, and other conceptually minded acts of plagiarism, what matters is not so much what the recycled text is, but how it is reframed.

Other examples that support Baldessari's (as well as Place's and Fitterman's) suggestion of a conceptual Sterne include *Tristram Shandy*'s missing chapter 24 of volume 4 which Nicholas Nace, himself a conceptual poet, notes is the only portion of the text that Tristram labels an 'experiment'. For Nace, 'What we see in the chapter's absence are the results of absence itself when carried by the printed artefact.'[29] The absence of a chunk of pages, which Tristram tells the reader he has 'torn out' (1:372), forces into the foreground the printed book's materiality and its production. Different from yet related to the marbled page, which is unique across each copy of each early edition, the absent pages for chapter 24 – marked by a jump in page numbers between the close of chapter 23 and the first page of chapter 25 – press against the distinctions between manuscript and print, text and copy; they first appear to be a binder's error, not uncommon in copies of eighteenth-century books, yet are revealed by Tristram to be an 'experiment', involving a negation of content, with meaning orbiting around the missing chapter's 'chasm' (1:372). The chasm continues to mark the rest of the volume, triggering a subsequent reversal of the standard recto/verso page numbering. *Tristram Shandy* here, as throughout, experiments with the conventions of the printed book, refusing to let the reader ignore its constitution as an embodied, material object.[30]

Baldessari's artwork reworks *Tristram Shandy*'s missing chapter and typographical elisions. Sterne's work has two blank pages, experiments with blank space and the placement of text on the page, and frequently refrains from spelling out words or phrases, offering instead dashes and asterisks. Baldessari arranges absences: blanks over faces, bodies without heads, space beneath text, clothes without bodies, text decontextualised from its source. This is perhaps most overt in the collage that incorporates the text describing Tristram's anticipation of writing about Toby's amours with Widow Wadman (Plate 26). As with the other prints, Baldessari places text from *Tristram Shandy* (with an accompanying citation, providing a page reference) alongside black and white photographs:

–and the thing I *hope* is, that your worships and reverences are not offended—if you are, depend upon't I'll give you something, my good gentry, next year, to be offended at—that's my dear *Jenny's* way—but who my *Jenny* is—and which is the right and which is the wrong end of a woman, is the thing to be *concealed*–it shall be told you the next chapter but one, to my chapter of button-holes,–and not one chapter before.

These references in the text to 'the thing to be *concealed*' are accompanied by what appears to have been a photograph of a couple embracing in a bed. The viewer's eye

490 AMELIA DALE

can detect traces of bodies, shadowy shapes remaining amongst the rubbings, but ultimately their faces and torsos are only visible as something that has been erased. In both Sterne's text and Baldessari's collage there is the shape, or the shadow of an image; but in *Tristram Shandy* the description of the amours is not destroyed, it is withheld, in a novelistic narrative strategy (or an ironic gesture towards one) that impels the reader to continue reading, to continue turning pages. When this print is excerpted and viewed in isolation from the sequence, on a gallery wall, or indeed, in the image reproduced for this essay, Baldessari's erasure of the people in the image – like Tristram's removal of chapter 24 – is a permanent withholding of material. Yet when it is viewed in the concertina-folded volume of illustrations, or in a gallery as the eighteenth entry in a series, it foreshadows images of a couple embracing and kissing in a later illustration (the twenty-eighth, accompanying a passage beginning with 'Now I see no sin in saying'). Baldessari's illustrations, like the voluminous, serially published work they excerpt, derive meaning from seriality and sequence.[31] Red lines mark out a space of erasure within an irregular pentagon, within which the only thing not rubbed out is an arm of one of the lovers. The arm could be read as a visual phallic pun, crossing genders as well as media in its provision of a visual equivalent to the suggestive association Sterne's passage makes between button-holes and female body parts. Yet the arm also extends itself into a hand in the image directly below, where a hand holds a pen, a hand that could be that of a writer or an artist. Both writer and artist make marks on paper with ink, something *Tristram Shandy* repeatedly reminds the reader, perhaps most overtly with the blank page, where, exclaiming 'here's paper ready to your hand', Tristram tells the reader to 'paint' Widow Wadman 'to your own mind'. The reader is given space to create either a visual or verbal substitute to the description Tristram withholds (2:566–8). This is an instruction Baldessari would follow in his contribution to the Laurence Sterne Trust project 'Paint Her to Your Own Mind'.[32]

The analogy between a printed codex book and an artist's canvas or sketchpad is continued, in a larger sense, by Baldessari's collages, which move between the body of a book and the gallery space, taking paragraphs from *Tristram Shandy* and pressing them against the gallery wall. Many of the passages that Baldessari selects stress the way Sterne looks beyond print to other forms: music, theatre, oratory and painting, while Baldessari's collages themselves are constructed across multiple media, with his use of found images pointing to post-eighteenth-century media: photography and film. In Plate 26, Tristram's (eventually temporary) withholding of narrative matter finds its visual analogue in the artist's erasure of part of an image, in this case, two faces. The omission of a face in a photograph is something of a Baldessarian signature, though here, unlike many of Baldessari's works, and indeed images from this series, the faces are not blanked out with a coloured dot.

Baldessari's collages, with their selection of Shandean extracts, participate in the history of compiling extracts from *Tristram Shandy* and the author's other works in anthologies, such as the popular *Beauties of Sterne* series published by George Kearsley in numerous editions from the 1780s onwards.[33] The collages are also part of a rich history of using Sterne's work as the basis for visual elaborations, taking their cue from *Tristram Shandy*'s narration: its self-consciousness, its citationality and its ostentatious fragmentation. Throughout *Tristram Shandy*, Tristram breaks off in his narration and directs the reader to the gaps in the text, to the things 'to be *concealed*' (1:401). W. B. Gerard and Elizabeth Harries both connect *Tristram Shandy*'s fragmented description with theories of visual perception.[34] The rich visual history of Shandean afterlives suggests how *Tristram Shandy*'s fragmentation impels visual elaborations and readers to fill in Sterne's foregrounded gaps. Baldessari's collages, as we have seen, are self-conscious about how they visually elaborate upon narratorial fragmentation. Baldessari's collaged transmedial illustrations with their repurposed text and images is just one instalment in a catalogue of works which extend Sternean text via visual art.

The Works of Jane Austen's Readers

Jane Austen is not routinely connected to conceptual experimentation in the same way as Sterne. Her works' association with contemporary visual arts appears, at first glance, to be of a different kind. There is no shortage of Austen-related art, but it often appears outside galleries: in public sculptures, such as the painted bench 'Sitting with Jane' series (2017); through the rich history of illustrating her work; and most overwhelmingly, at the present time, through fan communities in digital spaces.[35] The popularity of film and television adaptations of Austen means that they are often the starting point from which her characters are drawn, painted and otherwise reimagined by fans. Typical Austen art online is fan-generated, conspicuously intimate and mediated by Austen's adaptation in other media, particularly films and television series. While Sterne and, for that matter, Sade – the subject of our third case study – enjoy a degree of notoriety in the contemporary moment, their names are not synonymous with massive and commercially significant popular interest like 'Austen' is. Yet, just as Sterne and Sade complement their influence on vanguardist art with a pop culture presence, so Austen is far from absent from conceptually oriented art or writing.

The work of Meg Cranston (born 1960), a frequent Badessari collaborator, features within the gallery system.[36] Her egg-like sculpture *The Complete Works of Jane Austen* (1991, Plate 27), is a 457 cm diameter balloon filled with the 100,000 litres of air she estimates it would take for her to read Austen's complete works. In an interview conducted while Cranston was making the artwork, she explains, 'It's based on my body. I read, depending on the book, a page every two minutes. Every minute I'm exchanging sixteen breaths of air, 8 L.'[37] Cranston's work is both an arithmetic monument to and a spatialisation of the experience of reading, of the time it takes, its embodied nature and its capacity to create worlds. Consider the topology of the balloon, its flatness when it is deflated, but how, when invested with the air of a person's body – in this case, specifically Cranston's reading body – it grows until it fills the room. The balloon becomes a potential analogy for the way the flat surface of the page of a novel conjures up, via the reader's temporal and embodied investment, something that has the quality of space.

While Cranston's method can ostensibly be applied to any author – one can imagine 'The Complete Works of Charles Dickens', for instance – Austen is the single author Cranston chooses to sculpt via balloon. There are complex resonances in the choice. Its shape as a confined, portable space, large but limited, perhaps suggests the way Austen's novels can appear – sometimes deceptively – as enclosed, self-contained worlds. Austen's facetious comment in a letter to her nephew, James Edward Austen, dated 16 December 1816: 'the little bit (two Inches wide) of Ivory on which I work with so fine a Brush, as produces little effect after much labour', has 'been intoned and recycled with the utmost seriousness, inviting readers to envision her as a miniature, modest, familial author'.[38] For instance, Charlotte Brontë famously wrote to George Henry Lewes on 12 January 1848 that Austen presents 'a carefully-fenced, highly cultivated garden with neat borders and delicate flowers – but no glance of a bright vivid physiognomy – no open country – no fresh air – no blue hill – no bonny beck'.[39] The idea of Austen as a self-contained domestic writer working on a limited canvas continues to be queried by Austen scholars, who argue her work intervenes in debates surrounding empire, war, abolition and revolution. However, Brontë's comments are also part of a long-standing tradition of understanding Austen's work as characterised by constraint and circumscribed spaces. *Mansfield Park* (1814), for example, is a novel of enclosures and borders, while the eponymous heroine of *Emma* (1815) never leaves the small town of Highbury. Generally speaking, the heroines of Austen's novels are confined by their class and gender to the domestic sphere. Cranston's spherical balloon evokes these associations between femininity and enclosed spaces. When placed indoors, it potentially becomes a literalised domestic sphere. When approached as a sculpture of the imagined spaces that a novel opens up, secreted between the page and a reader's mind, it could be said to be a room of one's – the reader's – own.

In her history of Austen's reception, Devoney Looser notes how, across her reading history, '[o]ne near constant is that her imagined intimacy with audiences has been described as of the coziest, quotidian, familial kind'.[40] It is hard to imagine a space cosier or more feminised than an interior of an egg. The colour of Cranston's egg means it resembles a chicken rather than a human egg. Eggs are contained within the space of a hen's body and then beneath a brooding hen. Within the confines of a fertilised egg a chick gestates and grows. Eggs are familiar and quotidian as household pantry staples; they are also familiar in the sense that they are to do with the family, with matters of birth and reproduction. In *Tristram Shandy*, for instance, Tristram begins his fictionalised autobiography '*ab Ovo*' – from the egg – commencing at the moment of his conception (1:5). Both Cranston and Sterne draw on long histories of using biological birth as an allegory for artistic production. A related trope metaphorically describes an image or idea birthed from the brain. For example, also in *Tristram Shandy*, Tristram narrates his father Walter's metaphorical 'begetting' of a 'hypothesis', and describes Walter as being 'gone with this [hypothesis] about a month' (1:177). Walter's intellectual pregnancy is juxtaposed with the events surrounding Tristram's birth. With complex gendered resonances, Cranston's art suggests how novels, and Austen's work in particular, might give life to something beyond themselves.

The idiosyncratic arithmetic involved in determining the volume of Cranston's balloon echoes Austen's complex novelisation of scale. Yoon Sun Lee describes Austen's novels as 'scale-making projects', noting how carefully they map and measure subjectively experienced units of space and time.[41] Cranston, basing the mathematics of the sculpture on her own body, echoes how Austen merges time and space with characters' consciousness. In Austen's novels, the experience of time and space is subjective, embodied and inflected by gender and class. This is seen, for instance, in the conversation between Darcy and Elizabeth in *Pride and Prejudice* (1813) about whether 'fifty miles' is a '*very* easy distance' or not: Darcy, more mobile through his gender and wealth, believes it to be so, to the surprise of Elizabeth. Elizabeth comments that the 'far and the near must be relative, and depend on many varying circumstances'.[42]

Austen's careful treatment of space is also inflected by the wider contemporary contexts of the British empire. This was perhaps most influentially articulated by Edward

Said, in his reading of how *Mansfield Park* tracks 'very precisely' a series 'of both small and large dislocations and relocations in space'.[43] Through her narrativisation of space, Austen connects 'the actualities of British power overseas to the domestic imbroglio within the Bertram estate'.[44] Said's reading, and those in its wake, stress how Austen's circumscribed domestic spaces only initially appear to be self-contained, isolated and insulated. Mansfield Park, like England, enriches itself through 'overseas sustenance'.[45] When considering how imperialism marks Austenian space it becomes significant that Cranston's sculpture seems to mirror the colour of her white skin. On the one hand, this could further associate the artwork with Cranston's reading body. Yet it also reminds us of how Austen's interiors are the interiors of empire, and more broadly, of the gendered and racialised geography of European empire, which places the white woman in a domestic interior at its centre, while men project outwards, expanding the empire's project into dark exteriors all the while 'yearning for home and whiteness'.[46] Cranston gives us both a cosy and a hollow shell of female whiteness sitting in the locus of empire.

Such a reading is only possible because the title of this sculpture, *The Complete Works of Jane Austen*, comically posits a commutability between moderately large balloon and Austen's corpus. The titular juxtaposition of balloon and oeuvre, via a title that suggests the work is textual, presents the artwork as an emptying out of content. Unlike Baldessari – and, as we will see, Chan – who evoke eighteenth-century print's self-reflexivity in their own transmedial incorporation of print, in Cranston's sculpture print is not present. Instead, the work deals in air, space and shape. It is a sculpture, after all. The title *The Complete Works of Jane Austen* prompts the viewer to reflect simultaneously upon the nature of sculpture and of the novel. Similar to Baldessari's book-shaped urn, containing the ashes of his renounced works, or the various 'bookworks' which Stewart tracks in contemporary art – works which use book forms 'either imitated or mutilated, replicas of reading matter or its vestiges' – Cranston's work concerns itself with translating aspects of the experience of reading across media, and she makes this act of translation more apparent through resolutely refusing text, emptying out character, narrative and prose.[47] Cranston's sculpture evokes the experience of reading books but cannot be read like one. The title, suggesting a collection of books, denotes instead a balloon. A body of writing becomes air. Book becomes equivalent to balloon.

Sade and Post-Digital Character

Bodies, textual surfaces and the space of the gallery also come into play in 'Sade for Sade's Sake', a monumental project Paul Chan (born 1973) premiered in the 2009 Venice Biennale. The centrepiece of the installation was a five-hour and forty-five-minute video projection, involving silhouettes of near life-size figures, convulsing and interconnecting via a vast number of sexual acts. Donatien Alphonse François, Marquis de Sade has an afterlife intimately connected to avant-garde art – even more so, perhaps, than Sterne – recently traced in Alyce Mahon's book, *The Marquis de Sade and the Avant-Garde*. Sade features heavily in twentieth-century art as an embodiment of artistic, sexual, intellectual and political licence.[48] Chan's work, however, is more interested in Sade as a writer and in translating formal aspects of Sade's writing across media. As with Cranston's sculpture, Chan's video reflects on the durational nature of reading. The length of the video

494 AMELIA DALE

projection echoes the time it takes to read Sade's *Les 120 Journées de Sodome, ou l'École du libertinage* [120 Days of Sodom or the School of Libertinage] (1785). Chan says:

> if one approaches Sodom less as a story than as a poem, the work changes. Reading it with an ear for rhythm rather than narrative coherence transforms Sodom into something strangely, and compulsively, readable. It is as if what is most provocative about Sodom isn't the story at all but how it is written in the cadence of a relentless sexual compulsion. The rhythm is what animates the work.[49]

Across Chan's corpus of work, from his early animation and film works to the more recent gyrating 'breathers' or inflatable moving sculptures, he is interested in marking movement, rhythm and time, as this film does with differently animated bodies and more placidly floating squares. Towards the end of the video cycle the silhouetted bodies begin to fragment. They are still shuddering and thrusting, but they begin breaking down, disintegrating into arms, legs, torsos, penises in what, in a write-up of the exhibition, Chris Reitz calls 'sexual graphemes'.[50]

In the same installation, human-high ink drawings also present themselves as sexual graphemes, offering an obscene phrase or a word for each letter of the alphabet (Plate 28). Each of these drawings stands for a different Sadean 'font', downloadable from Chan's 'National Philistine' website at the time of the exhibition and sold as a separate CD-ROM entitled *Sade for Fonts Sake* (2009; later reissued 2011).[51] Chan had been experimenting with 'Alternumerics' or using font programs as the basis for art from the early 2000s. A PDF with the filename 'FAQ on Alternumerics' announces: 'By replacing individual letters and numbers (known as alphanumerics) with textual and graphic fragments that signify what is typed in radically different ways, Alternumerics transforms any computer connected to a standard printer into an interactive artmaking installation.'[52] While Chan's earlier fonts experiment with different forms of writing and the space of a page, producing a scribble or a diagram for a particular letter, and have different themes, the fonts associated with the Sade project – each of their titles prefaced with 'oh' – relentlessly operate around sexual exclamations.

These fonts, when downloaded, are variations of the Century Schoolbook typeface, but modified so that a letter or number corresponds to a sexually suggestive phrase. Character, Deidre Lynch argues, is bound to the technologies of writing and print; she draws together the associations of the word 'character' with the way 'character' can also describe a letter or a written sign.[53] Chan's fontworks play on the conceptual overlaps between character and person: the way character involves both writing and a figure with human-like qualities.[54] Chan's font drawings are called 'bodies' in their title, which is emphasised by the shoes at their base and their human height (Plate 28).[55] Through collapsing body into page, Chan's work draws on the long-standing metaphorical link between the paper page, impressed by print, and sexually penetrated flesh, an association which colours eighteenth-century ideas of the reading body.[56] Black and white, and with flat, one-dimensional torsos, Chan's font bodies seem to negotiate a space between 'character' as text on paper, 'character' as sign, 'character' as function, and yet also 'character' as human-like figure through their embodied presence within the gallery space. Like Baldessari's collages they move between the paper surfaces interior to the physical book and paper mounted to a gallery wall, yet here, though they are framed, they are not quite pictures on a wall; instead, they are angled against it, sculptural beings with shoes.

CONTEMPORARY ART AND THE EIGHTEENTH-CENTURY NOVEL 495

As software programs or 'Alternumerics' they directly reflect upon the digital mechanisms of print, yet the 'bodies' of the fonts in the installation bear the marks of the hand of the artist. As with Baldessari's collages – themselves echoing Sterne's intermedial play between manuscript and print – Chan's font bodies situate writing and drawing alongside print. Their use of handwritten script potentially evokes the surface of the scroll of *Les 120 Journées*. Sade wrote in secrecy during his imprisonment in the Bastille on a roll of paper made up of individual pieces of paper smuggled into the prison and glued together. The complex history of the work's belated publication and censorship plays out across the multiple surfaces of Chan's installation.

The Alternumerics each represent a particular character or personality: several are characters from Sade's works (Justine, Juliette), but the series also contains fonts that describe other personalities – such as 'young Augustine' and 'Monica' – and writers, such as 'Gertrude' [Stein]. The reference to Monica Lewinsky, with a font where multiple letters correspond to tentative questions (b='like this?', k='like that?'), might appear at first glance to be a dated joke. Yet it cogently draws a parallel between the totalising power enjoyed by the Sadean libertine and the United States president, and, in reframing Lewinsky as a Sadean female victim, it registers her treatment in late twentieth-century culture as a young woman who became an object of widespread sexual derision and attack.

At the same time that Chan's fontworks arguably serve as a literalisation of the notion of 'character writing', they also adapt an aspect of Sade's writing, perhaps most prominent in his *Les 120 Journées*, where characters are rendered as entities with genitals and orifices operating within a set, performing specific sexual functions, arranged in various configurations and relations with each other. *Les 120 Journées* involves four libertines who select from their subjugated group of four daughters, eight young girls, eight young boys, eight men, four older women and four female storytellers, with the libertines organising smaller subsets for specific acts. A drafted section of *Les 120 Journées* is overt about the way characters become mathematical entities subject to sexual combinatorics: '46. He has girls A and B shit. Then he forces B to eat A's turd, and A to eat B's. Then both A and B shit a second time; he eats both their turds.'[57] This might be why Chan describes *Les 120 Journées* as having 'the narrative quality of a user's manual for some accounting software'.[58] In Chan's work, character becomes font, or more precisely a procedure or a function where one input (letter typed into the keyboard) produces a specific output (a sexual word or phrase). For example, if we take the beginning of the sentence 'In Chan's work, character becomes font', and render it using the font 'Oh Blangis', titled after the primary libertine in *Les 120 Journées*, it becomes something else (Figure 27.1).

Frig that crack and lips and hit your mouth, balls and laugh, cock and hit that, rub your mouth, rub your cock and hole and fuck your mouth, mound, fuck your cock and hit your nose and fuck your ass and slit and hit your crack and hole and laugh,

Slut, hit that, rub your crack and ass and

Figure 27.1 The phrase 'In Chan's work, character becomes font' rendered according to the Alternumeric 'Oh Blangis'. Courtesy of the artist and Greene Naftali, New York.

These fontworks express a kind of Sadean haunting of private digital spaces and screens, appearing in a word processor and turning nondescript text into barely readable repetitive smut. Chan used the fonts as the basis for further written work, a pornographic version of Plato's dialogue, *Phaedrus*, as *Phaedrus Pron* (2010), which moves between eighteen different Oh-fonts. Gertrude Stein's 'Composition as Explanation' and John Maynard Keynes's 'How to Organize a Wave of Prosperity' in 2008 both received similar treatments, in PDFs uploaded to Chan's website.[59] The book associated with the Sade exhibition, *The Essential and Incomplete Sade for Sade's Sake* (2010), includes twenty-one 'poems' written using different Oh-fonts, each titled with both the name of the font and the text they transform.[60] These poems and PDFs are examples of conceptual writing; they use pre-existing text and digital processes to generate writing.[61] While Baldessari's artistic repurposing of text was an influential precursor to the conceptual writing movement, Chan's Sadean 'Alternumerics' were produced at its high point.

On one level, Chan's fonts offer a procedure for or method of writing, of the generation of text, with poetic line breaks produced via digital means. Since any slab of text can be transformed into a set of textual ejaculations using one of these fonts, this method provides an implicit prompt for further writing. But there are other ways that these fonts' functions can be read. Their conversion of print into a string of ejaculations or expletives offers a form of post-digital analogy for Sade's own practice of avidly absorbing and studying the Richardsonian sentimental novel only to produce *Justine*. On another level, we could think about how these fontworks reflect the narrative movements of *Les 120 Journées*, the libertines' selection of one or various subjugated subjects, their obsession with degrading their victims, and their final murderous mauling of the subjugated bodies.

Chan's Sadean fonts position Sade's late eighteenth-century productions alongside the digital processes of contemporary print. More broadly, much of Chan's work uses contemporary digital challenges to the codex book to reflect upon the history of print technology.[62] This is seen, for example, in Chan's e-library, titled *My Own Private Alexandria*, an idiosyncratic selection of audiobooks that he read himself and which he made available from his website. Relatedly, Chan founded and worked as editor of the experimental publishing company Badlands Unlimited, its motto to 'make books in an expanded field', which published, alongside more conventional books, a stone slab with an ISBN.[63] Chan's interest in the book object is emphatic in book-oriented works, such as *New New Testament* (2014) and the book *Wht is a Book* (2011), which involves an abundance of quotations from Andrew Pettegree's monograph on early European print.[64] Chan uses illustrations from the 1797 edition of *Juliette* in the e-books *How to Organize a Wave of Prosperity Pron* (2008), *Composition as Explanation Pron* (2008) and *The Essential and Incomplete Sade for Sade's Sake* (2010), sampling material from the eighteenth-century printed novel object and repurposing it for an e-reading screen.

Whereas Baldessari's collages elaborate on and eroticise Sterne's bawdy treatment of gaps on the page, Chan's works take the more overtly sexual work of Sade to probe his formal qualities: medium, narrative structure and characterisation. In both artists' work, sex intersects with medium. Yet the crucial differences between the two echo those between Sterne and Sade. While Sterne sometimes teasingly suggests to his reader that potentially any object (whiskers, noses, buttonholes) or ellipsis can signify something sexual, Sade's *Les 120 Journées* is far more explicit and relentless in its treatment of sex

CONTEMPORARY ART AND THE EIGHTEENTH-CENTURY NOVEL 497

acts. Chan's work views Sadean sex as a set of grammatical functions that can potentially be deployed in a commentary on politics, empire and war. His interest in form and rhythm creates a distance and a formality in his engagement with Sade. The video projection of the convulsing silhouettes is carefully poised so that the viewer cannot tell if what they are witnessing is an atrocity or an ecstatic scene of sexual liberation. Yet Chan, by juxtaposing a 1797 illustration to *Juliette* with a photograph taken of the abuse of prisoners in Abu Ghraib, stakes out a clear position, associating Sadean libertinism with war crimes. Chan reads Sade as a writer who 'consistently used war and other forms of social conflict as the setting for his stories of debaucheries, as if to suggest that one always begets the other', and asserts that *Les 120 Journées* is a story about 'war profiteers'.[65] The inclusion of images of abuse at Abu Ghraib is more than a glancing reference point, and should be read in terms of Chan's long-standing anti-war work and active resistance to the atrocities of the United States' 'War on Terror'. He worked in Iraq as part of an anti-war group in December 2002, which, after Chan's departure from Iraq in January 2003, 'helped expose what would eventually be called, simply, Abu Ghraib. War is abominable enough. But this photo and others like it embody what is arguably most unbearable about the violence in war: it harbors a sexual dimension'.[66]

Chan's politicised updating of the Sadean libertine parallels Pier Paolo Pasolini's repositioning of *Les 120 Journées* in his film *Salò, or the 120 Days of Sodom* (*Salò o le 120 giornate di Sodoma*, 1975) in 1944, in a country estate in Salò, Benito Mussolini's last stronghold. Chan comments, '[i]f Sade illuminated Abu Ghraib for me, it was Pier Paolo Pasolini who helped me do the same for Sade'.[67] Pasolini's 'update' on *Les 120 Journées*, as well as transposing the time, place and political context, involved updating the methods of killing and torture to more modern judicial forms of execution, such as the electric chair.[68] Analogous to the newer technologies of killing and torture documented in *Salò* and in images from Abu Ghraib are the newer technologies Chan and Pasolini use in their Sadean adaptations: film, photography and, for Chan, digital animation and computer programming. Technological developments proffer new ways in which bodies, text and narrative can be processed and painfully dismantled.

Conclusion

The installation 'Sade for Sade's Sake', like much contemporary gallery art, attempts to project a reading experience into a gallery space. It also became a reading experience itself: repackaged as a book, published by Chan's then-new press, Badlands Unlimited, the gallery experience was remediated in print and e-book form, allowing the reader to read a viewing of Chan's representation of his reading. Like Cranston's sculpture, Chan's work involves a depiction of the artist's reading experience. For Chan, these movements across multiple media are not just meditations on mediation but carry the weight of works about sexual torture. Chan's encounters with Sade culminated in a retirement from art. In 2012, he talked about being 'fucking ruined' by the Sade project:

> I did a project on the Marquis de Sade and he just fucking ruined me. I couldn't look at porn, I didn't want to think about sex, I didn't want to look at lights, or video. I didn't want to look at anything. I was done. And so at the end of 2008 I thought well fuck it I'm just not going to do anything.[69]

In various comments about his retirement from art, Chan attributes it to a range of factors – exhaustion, weariness with the gallery system – but here the weariness is tied directly to two things: Sade and Chan's media (lights and video). Moving eighteenth-century fiction across media can produce fascinating art that lays bare structures of character and narrative rhythm. It can also force you into early retirement.

For the reader of eighteenth-century fiction, contemporary art's transmedial adaptations, like those into film or theatre, offer interpretations of their source text. The present remakes the past, seeking continuities, whether between Sade's fiction and US imperial atrocities, or Sterne's medial self-reflexivity and conceptualist self-consciousness. When tracking these transpositions of eighteenth-century fiction across media and history, it is striking what is omitted as much as what is brought forward. Yet if any works are self-conscious about their selection and omission of content it is these. Perhaps this is most overt in Cranston's work, a sculpture of space and air, which sets out how these medial shifts involve a necessary emptying out of content, of text. Chan's fonts strip back the narrative and descriptive trappings of character to present it as both a function and a prompt for writing, while Baldessari's illustrations parallel their games of erasures and omissions with Sterne's own chasms. Reading's embodied and spatialised nature comes to the fore in all three artworks, with Baldessari's parallels between reading and viewing, Cranston's sculpting of the reading body's breath and Chan's movements between gallery installation and an e-reading screen. From book to gallery, from paper to e-reader, these works are works about media. They sculpt, print and program the reading body's encounter with print, and by so doing, present before our eyes the eighteenth-century novel within a new scene of reading.

Notes

1. The back of Paul Chan's CD-ROM, *Sade for Fonts Sake* (National Philistine, 2009), containing Chan's font-based conceptual art, describes the different fonts as 'fontwork'.
2. Garrett Stewart, *Transmedium: Conceptualism 2.0 and the New Object Art* (Chicago: University of Chicago Press, 2017).
3. For a discussion of the complications and potential anachronisms inherent in the term 'conceptualism', see Terry Smith, 'One and Three Ideas: Conceptualism Before, During, and After Conceptual Art', *e-flux Journal* 29 (2011), https://www.e-flux.com/journal/29/68078/one-and-three-ideas-conceptualism-before-during-and-after-conceptual-art/ (accessed 24 November 2023).
4. Sol LeWitt, 'Paragraphs on Conceptual Art', in *Conceptual Art: A Critical Anthology*, ed. Alexander Alberro and Blake Stimson (Cambridge, MA: MIT Press, 1999), 12. First published in *Artforum* 5, no. 10 (1967).
5. Pamela M. Lee, *New Games: Postmodernism after Contemporary Art* (New York and London: Routledge, 2013).
6. Peter Osborne, 'The Postconceptual Condition: Or, the Cultural Logic of High Capitalism Today', *Radical Philosophy* 184 (2014), https://www.radicalphilosophy.com/article/the-postconceptual-condition (accessed 24 November 2023).
7. Stewart, *Transmedium*, 5; Dick Higgins, *Horizons, the Poetics and Theory of the Intermedia* (Carbondale: Southern Illinois University Press, 1984).
8. Stewart, *Transmedium*, 2.
9. Thomas Keymer, *Sterne, the Moderns, and the Novel* (Oxford: Oxford University Press, 2002). See also Janine Barchas, *Graphic Design, Print Culture, and the Eighteenth-Century*

Novel (Cambridge: Cambridge University Press, 2003); Christina Lupton, 'Giving Power to the Medium: Recovering the 1750s', *The Eighteenth Century* 52, nos. 3–4 (2011): 289–302. Examples include the frontispiece to John Kidgell's *The Card* (1755) and Henry Fielding's errata list to *Joseph Andrews* (1742).

10. Some of numerous examples include Scott Myles, 'Full Stop (The Life and Opinions of Tristram Shandy, Gentleman)', 2006, chromogenic print, National Galleries Scotland; Mai-Thu Perret, 'A tolerable straight line (Shandy II)', 2014, neon, Simon Lee Gallery.

11. 'PICTURES and CREAM, The confidential report of the life and opinions of Tristram Shandy & friends, Volume 1: A project curated by Paulo Mendes for Cristina Guerra Contemporary Art', Christina Guerra Contemporary Art, 2015, https://www.cristinaguerra.com/en/exhibition/pictures-and-cream-the-confidential-report-of-the-life-and-opinions-of-tristram-shandy-amp-friends-volume-1/ (accessed 24 November 2023).

12. 'Paint Her to Your Own Mind', The Laurence Sterne Trust, Shandy Hall, 2016, https://blankpage147.wordpress.com/participating-artists/; 'Emblem of My Work', The Laurence Sterne Trust, Shandy Hall, 2011, http://emblemofmywork169.blogspot.com/ and 'The Black Page', The Laurence Sterne Trust, Shandy Hall, 2009, http://blackpage73.blogspot.com/ (all accessed 24 November 2023).

13. At the same time, Baldessari cannot be grouped without qualification with the 'official' incarnation of 1960s–1970s conceptual art. He was dismissed, for instance, by Joseph Kosuth as not making 'actual conceptual art': 'the amusing pop paintings of John Baldessari allude to this sort of work by being "conceptual" cartoons of actual conceptual art'. Joseph Kosuth, 'Art after Philosophy', in *Art After Philosophy and After: Collected Writings, 1966–1990*, ed. Gabriele Guercio (Cambridge, MA and London: MIT Press, 1991), 29.

14. *A Brief History of John Baldessari*, directed by Henry Joost and Ariel Schulman (Supermarché, 2011), 2:36.

15. Andrew Hoyem, 'Working Together: Collaboration in the Book Arts', *Visible Language* 25, no. 2–3 (1991): 209–10.

16. Melvyn New, 'Laurence Sterne', in *Dictionary of Literary Biography 39: British Novelists 1600–1800*, ed. Martin C. Battestin, 2 vols (Detroit: Gale, 1985), 2:471–99.

17. Melvyn New, 'William Hogarth and John Baldessari: Ornamenting Sterne's *Tristram Shandy*', *Word & Image* 11, no. 2 (1995): 182–95. His distaste for Baldessari's 'illustrations' was shared by Sean Shesgreen in a review of New's article. Sean Shesgreen, 'William Hogarth and John Baldessari: Ornamenting Sterne's *Tristram Shandy*', *The Scriblerian and the Kit-Cats* 31, no. 1 (1998): 23.

18. Melvyn New, 'Taking Care: A Slightly Levinasian Reading of *Dombey and Son*', *Philological Quarterly* 84, no.1 (2005): 77–9; Melvyn New, 'John Baldessari and Laurence Sterne', *The Shandean* 31 (2020): 29–42.

19. Brigitte Friant-Kessler, 'Synaesthetics and Laurence Sterne's Fiction', *Interfaces* 36 (2015): 150–1; W. B. Gerard, *Laurence Sterne and the Visual Imagination* (Aldershot: Ashgate, 2006), 83–8. For eighteenth-century and early nineteenth-century visual adaptations of Sterne, see M-C. Newbould, *Adaptations of Laurence Sterne's Fiction: Sterneana, 1760–1840* (Farnham: Ashgate, 2013), 153–214. See also W. B. Gerard and Brigitte Friant-Kessler, 'Towards a Catalogue of Illustrated Laurence Sterne', *The Shandean* 16 (2005): 18–69; *The Shandean* 17 (2006): 35–72; *The Shandean* 18 (2007): 56–87; *The Shandean* 19 (2008): 90–110.

20. Tellingly, contemporary illustrations of Sterne which New does approve of are Tom Phillips's frontispieces for the Folio Society edition of *Tristram Shandy*, which, for New, convey the 'Scriblerian nature' of the work, agreeing with his general position that *Tristram Shandy* engages predominantly with earlier traditions and texts. New, 'John Baldessari and Laurence Sterne', 40–2.

21. Andrew Ellam makes a similar point. See Andrew Ellam, 'From Sterne to Baldessari: The Illustration of *Tristram Shandy*, 1760–1996', 1999, https://web.archive.org/web/20070308063238/http://www.aellam.net/ts/index.html (accessed 24 November 2023).

22. Pointed out by John Ferriar, *Illustrations of Sterne: With Other Essays and Verses*, 2nd edn, 2 vols (London: T. Cadell and W. Davies, 1812), 1:94–5; see Melvyn New, 'Introduction' to *Tristram Shandy, Notes to Tristram Shandy* by Melvyn New with Richard A. Davies and W. G. Day, The Florida Edition of the Works of Laurence Sterne (Gainesville: University Press of Florida, 1984), 12–24.

23. Moyra Haslett, 'Introduction' to *The Life of John Buncle, Esq*, by Thomas Amory (Dublin: Four Courts Press, 2011), 18, 23; Helen Williams, *Laurence Sterne and the Eighteenth-Century Book* (Cambridge: Cambridge University Press, 2021), 155–6.

24. See for example, Amelia Dale and Nicola Parsons, 'Pornographic Celebrity and the Characters of *Harris's List*', *The Eighteenth Century* 63, no. 1–2 (2022): 51, 54–5.

25. Craig Dworkin, 'The Fate of Echo', in *Against Expression: An Anthology of Conceptual Writing*, ed. Craig Dworkin and Kenneth Goldsmith (Evanston: Northwestern University Press, 2011), xxii–iii.

26. Craig Dworkin and Kenneth Goldsmith, eds, *Against Expression: An Anthology of Conceptual Writing* (Evanston: Northwestern University Press, 2011), 186.

27. Laurence Sterne, *Tristram Shandy: The Text*, ed. Melvyn New and Joan New, 2 vols, The Florida Edition of the Works of Laurence Sterne (Gainesville: University Press of Florida, 1978), 1:408. Further references parenthetical.

28. Vanessa Place and Robert Fitterman, *Notes on Conceptualisms* (New York: Ugly Duckling Presse, 2009), 46.

29. Nicholas D. Nace, 'Unprinted Matter: Conceptual Writing and *Tristram Shandy*'s "Chasm of Ten Pages"', *The Shandean* 24 (2013): 31.

30. For discussion of the missing chapter beyond Nace, see Peter de Voogd, '*Tristram Shandy* as Aesthetic Object', *Word & Image* 4, no. 1 (1988): 385; Amelia Dale, *The Printed Reader: Gender, Quixotism, and Textual Bodies in Eighteenth-Century Britain* (Lewisburg: Bucknell University Press, 2019), 86–7. Helen Williams studies Sterne's engagement with eighteenth-century print technology and print conventions in *Laurence Sterne and the Eighteenth-Century Book*.

31. For Sterne's use of seriality and time, see Thomas Keymer, 'Dying by Numbers: *Tristram Shandy* and Serial Fiction (1)', *The Shandean* 8 (1996): 41–67; 'Dying by Numbers: *Tristram Shandy* and Serial Fiction (2)', *The Shandean* 9 (1997): 34–69.

32. Artists and their 'pages' are not matched up on the website; however, 'Page 60' contains Baldessari signature elements, using a found, black and white photograph, with coloured dots covering faces. 'Page 60', in 'Paint Her to Your Own Mind', 10 July 2016. https://blankpage147.wordpress.com/2016/07/10/94/ (accessed 24 November 2023).

33. See, for example, *The Beauties of Sterne: Including all his Pathetic Tales, and Most Distinguished Observations on Life. Selected for the Heart of Sensibility* (London: T. Davies, J. Ridley, W. Flexney, J. Sewel and G. Kearsley, 1782).

34. Gerard, *Laurence Sterne and the Visual Imagination*, 19–20; Elizabeth W. Harries, *The Unfinished Manner: Essays on the Fragment in the Later Eighteenth Century* (Charlottesville: University Press of Virginia, 1994), 45–7.

35. For example, the search term 'Jane Austen' results in 5,200 'Deviations' in the online art community DeviantArt, https://www.deviantart.com/search?q=%22Jane%20Austen%22 (accessed 24 November 2023).

36. Meg Cranston, 'A Remembrance of John Baldessari by Otis Fine Arts Chair Meg Cranston', *Otis News* (14 January 2020), https://www.otis.edu/news/john-baldessari-otis-college-fine-arts-meg-cranston (accessed 24 November 2023). Cranston, with Hans Ulrich Obrist, edited Baldessari's complete writings. Hans Ulrich Obrist and Meg Cranston, eds, *More*

CONTEMPORARY ART AND THE EIGHTEENTH-CENTURY NOVEL 501

Than You Ever Wanted to Know About John Baldessari, 2 vols (Zurich: JRP|Ringier, 2013).

37. Saul Ostrow, 'Assemblage, Bricollage, and the I: Meg Cranston, Melissa Kretschmer and Maya Lin', *BOMB* 35 (1991): 22.

38. Jane Austen, *Jane Austen's Letters*, ed. Deirdre Le Faye, 4th edn (Oxford: Oxford University Press, 2011), 337; Devoney Looser, *The Making of Jane Austen*, 2nd edn (Baltimore: Johns Hopkins University Press, 2019), 5.

39. Charlotte Brontë, *Selected Letters of Charlotte Brontë*, ed. Margaret Smith (Oxford: Oxford University Press, 2007), 99.

40. Looser, *The Making of Jane Austen*, 4.

41. Yoon Sun Lee, 'Austen's Scale-Making', *Studies in Romanticism* 52, no. 2 (2013): 171–95.

42. Jane Austen, *Pride and Prejudice*, ed. Pat Rogers (Cambridge: Cambridge University Press, 2006), 201.

43. Edward W. Said, *Culture and Imperialism* (New York: Vintage, 1993), 84.

44. Said, *Culture and Imperialism*, 95.

45. Said, *Culture and Imperialism*, 89.

46. Richard Dyer, *White* (London and New York: Routledge, 1997), 36.

47. Garrett Stewart, *Bookwork: Medium to Object to Concept to Art* (Chicago and London: University of Chicago Press, 2011), xiii.

48. Alyce Mahon, *The Marquis de Sade and the Avant-Garde* (Princeton and Oxford: Princeton University Press, 2020), 1.

49. Paul Chan, 'A Harlot's Progress: On Pier Paolo Pasolini' (2013), in *Paul Chan: Selected Writings 2000–2014*, ed. George Baker, Eric Banks, with Isabel Friedli and Martina Venanzoni (Münchenstein and New York: Laurenz Foundation, Schaulager, and Badlands Unlimited, 2014).

50. Chris Reitz, 'Paul Chan's Sade for Sade's Sake', *Idiom*, 30 November 2009, https://www.idiommag.com/index.html%3Fp=827.html (accessed 24 November 2023).

51. 'Sade for Fonts Sake (free)', accessed through the Wayback Machine, https://web.archive.org/web/20130615051639/http://www.nationalphilistine.com/oh/ (accessed 24 November 2023). Chan took his website offline in 2014. See 'National Philistine, 1999–2014', https://web.archive.org/web/20140414223711/http://www.nationalphilistine.com/ (accessed 24 November 2023).

52. Paul Chan, 'FONTS AS THE PENULTIMATE INTERACTIVE ART FORM, SECOND ONLY TO SEX', 'National Philistine', accessed via the Wayback Machine, https://web.archive.org/web/20070804063533/http://www.nationalphilistine.com/alternumerics/FAQ_alternumerics.pdf (accessed 24 November 2023).

53. Deidre Lynch, *The Economy of Character: Novels, Market Culture, and the Business of Inner Meaning* (Chicago and London: Chicago University Press, 1998), 34–5.

54. See John Frow, *Character and Person* (Oxford: Oxford University Press, 2014).

55. In multiple interviews, Chan mentions that he has a shoe fetish and so incorporates them whenever he can into his artwork. See, for example, 'Conversation: Paul Chan', Guggenheim Museum, at 10:28, https://www.youtube.com/watch?v=Wdmh1ODVUmc (accessed 24 November 2023).

56. Dale, *The Printed Reader*, 9–11.

57. Marquis de Sade, *The 120 Days of Sodom or the School of Libertinage*, trans. Will McMorran and Thomas Wynn (London: Penguin, 2016), e-book. 'Il fait chier une fille A et une autre B; puis il force B à manger l'étron de A, et A de manger l'étron de B; ensuite elles chient toutes deux, et il mange leurs deux étrons.' Marquis de Sade, *Les Cent Vingt Journées de Sodome ou l'école du libertinage* in *Œuvres*, vol. 1, ed. Michel Delon (Paris: Gallimard, 1990), 315.

58. Chan, 'A Harlot's Progress'.

59. Paul Chan, *Phaedrus Pron* (New York: Badlands Unlimited, 2010), Paul Chan, *Composition as Explanation Pron* ([New York]: National Phillistine, 2008); Paul Chan, *How to Organize a Wave of Prosperity Pron* ([New York]: National Phillistine, 2008).

60. Paul Chan, *The Essential and Incomplete Sade for Sade's Sake* (New York: Badlands Unlimited, 2010).

61. Brian Stefans describes Chan as a 'conceptual writer of sorts'. Brian Stefans, 'Third Hand Plays: The Comedy of Exhaustion', *Open Space*, San Francisco Museum of Modern Art, 2 August, 2011, https://openspace.sfmoma.org/2011/08/third-hand-plays-the-comedy-of-excess/ (accessed 24 November 2023).

62. For a discussion of Chan's work with books, see Sven Lütticken, 'Paul Chan's Book Club', in *New New Testament*, ed. Paul Chan (Münchenstein and New York: Laurenz Foundation, Schaulager, and Badlands Unlimited, 2014), 1017–32.

63. 'About', 'Badlands Unlimited' November 2018, accessed via the Wayback Machine, https://web.archive.org/web/20190601112920/https://badlandsunlimited.com/about (accessed 24 November 2023).

64. Pul Chn [Paul Chan], *Wht Is a Book?* (New York: Badlands Unlimited, 2011); Andrew Pettegree, *The Book in the Renaissance* (New Haven: Yale University Press, 2011).

65. Chan, 'A Harlot's Progress'.

66. Chan, 'A Harlot's Progress'. For Chan's anti-war work, see Paul Chan, 'Portrait of a Day in Baghdad' (2004), in *Paul Chan: Selected Writings 2000–2014*, ed. George Baker, Eric Banks, and with Isabel Friedli and Martina Venanzoni (Münchenstein and New York: Laurenz Foundation, Schaulager, and Badlands Unlimited, 2014); the film *Baghdad in No Particular Order* (January 2003) and *RE:THE_OPERATION* (2002), both a single channel video and a set of desktop replacement icons for MAC and PC; and Chan's untitled video of Lynne F. Stewart, the New York lawyer convicted of aiding Islamic terrorism (2006).

67. Chan, 'A Harlot's Progress'.

68. Pasolini mentions this in an interview with Gideon Bachmann, 'Pasolini on de Sade: An Interview During the Filming of *The 120 Days of Sodom*', *Film Quarterly* 29, no. 2 (1975–6): 41–2. Surviving production photos show an electric chair, but it was deleted or is otherwise missing from the final film.

69. This was at the Contemporary Artists' Book Conference, part of Printed Matter's NY Art Book Fair, 28 September, 2012. 'Paul Chan at the NY Art Book Fair, 2012', A YouTube videoposted by James Mitchell, at 4:11, https://www.youtube.com/watch?v=LmHXSqvy9q8 (accessed 24 November 2023).

28

INVOKING THE IMPLIED VIEWER IN THE EIGHTEENTH-CENTURY NOVEL ON FILM

Jennifer Preston Wilson

ANY ACCOUNT OF the early novel and its afterlives faces a problem of terminology, since the era of the novel's popular emergence featured multiple ideas and names for its proliferating fictional kinds. Alternately called (to paraphrase Henry Fielding) histories, adventures, romances, tales and epic poems in prose – among other variations – the fictional accounts we now group under the term 'novels' had not yet coalesced as a form in the eighteenth century. By 1760, the year that George Colman the Elder published his 'Preface' to the dramatic afterpiece *Polly Honeycombe*, he portrays the novel as just stepping out as the new kid in town:

> But now, the dear delight of later years,
> The younger Sister of ROMANCE appears:
> Less solemn is her air, her drift the same,
> And NOVEL her enchanting, charming, Name.[1]

Even though 'NOVEL' is introduced into society in these lines, at the same time a familial 'drift' erases some of her individuality. The speaker's willingness to be charmed by either sister perhaps conveys the most important point of the passage, as the eighteenth century marks a media moment when audiences relished intertextual appropriation and adaptation of characters, stories and images, unconstrained by our current conceptions of copyright law.[2]

Recent work in adaptation studies explores the eighteenth century as a teeming site of creative revisioning along much the same lines. David Brewer's concept of 'imaginative expansion' examines the cultural phenomenon of wanting 'more' from characters. He argues that this era's 'persistent fantasy that literary characters were both fundamentally inexhaustible and available to all' encouraged the invention of further performances for these fictional figures roaming the textual commons.[3] Anticipating fan fiction of today, Brewer offers a sociable model that places emphasis on the 'social canon' above authorial control.[4] Meanwhile, in the essay collection *The Afterlives of Eighteenth-Century Fiction*, Daniel Cook and Nicholas Seager connect contemporary methods of multi-platform adaptation with flourishing eighteenth-century practices of remediation, with wide-ranging chapters considering how fictions reappear in later texts as well as recycle earlier forms.[5] Their collection identifies 'adaptation as an ongoing process within a larger matrix of allusion and invocation rather than a product'.[6] More specifically examining film adaptation, Robert Mayer's *Eighteenth-Century Fiction on Screen* adopts a

504   JENNIFER PRESTON WILSON

reading theory approach to circumvent the 'fidelity' trap that so frequently privileges novels as 'original' 'source' material to their film adaptations. Mayer interweaves the theories of Hans-Robert Jauss, Stanley Fish and Harold Bloom to argue that every adaptation is a reading, or a 'creative act that in "concretizing" a work remakes it and indeed remakes the artistic field in which it appears'.[7] In this essay, I will build on this idea of remaking, attending to design features that shape how a new audience will experience the adaptation. Audience awareness, always of course a factor in the creative process, dominated eighteenth-century critical concerns about fiction's moral influence over readers and also loomed large in twentieth-century film's dependence on box office numbers. In both contexts, we find auteurs responding to these pressurised conditions by creating distinctive artistic works dependent upon numerous gaps and ironies that their audiences must work through and learn from.[8] To illustrate this parallelism that spans 200 years, I will focus upon Henry Fielding's and Tony Richardson's versions of *Tom Jones*, both of which self-consciously build towards metafictional themes, making the very conditions of their audience reception into creative means.

While remediated narratives proliferated in the eighteenth century, readers' intense enjoyment of texts generated much critical concern. How would that deep immersion in popular stories affect their understanding of the world? With even more specific alarm, male critics figured 'the reader' as female, naive and likely to imitate what she reads. In his sermon 'On Female Virtue' of 1766, James Fordyce channels these stereotypes as he decries books

> which contain such rank treason against the royalty of Virtue, such horrible violation of all decorum, that she who can bear to peruse them must in her soul be a prostitute, let her reputation in life be what it will.[9]

To ward off the attractive power that bad examples might hold over impressionable minds, Samuel Johnson urges in *Rambler* No. 4 (1750) that

> authors are at liberty, though not to invent, yet to select objects, and to cull from the mass of mankind those individuals upon which the attention ought most be employed; as a diamond, though it cannot be made, may be polished by art.[10]

Johnson here figures authorship as curating the best examples from life in order to provide spiritual guidance. Although every era features some degree of didacticism in its art, at a time when the most popular published material was still the sermon,[11] attentiveness to the formative influences of fiction on readers was a common rallying cry. Self-reflective awareness of these critical constraints became a standard feature in the mid-century novel as new publications were careful to position themselves as offering an innovative solution to the problem of seductive forms; these interventions embedded the debate about media consumption within structures such as direct address to the reader, self-conscious theorising, and paratextual signalling, among other means.

Twentieth-century critics returned to this question of the nature of the reader's role in fiction, as interest in theorising the novel gained ground against the New Critical preferencing of poetry. Wolfgang Iser's landmark book *The Implied Reader* (1974) looks at how the reader is invited into playing a more active, conscious role within the story formation of early English fiction. He presents the emergent novel as a co-creative process: the reader actively participates in the production of the text by filling in its areas of indeterminacy, thus 'realizing' the meaning of the work.[12] As Robert Folkenflik puts it, 'For Iser a novel is a lit kit, complete with instructions that the reader constructs.'[13] Iser contends that this interactivity emerged from readers' search for reassurance against the distress of predestination;[14] he builds support for this claim with analysis of John Bunyan's *Pilgrim's Progress* (1678) where engagement with exemplarity occurs alongside study of human anguish and the search for signs.[15] The implied reader, Iser argues, occupies a place of potentiality amid these forces, just as 'theological withholding of certitude stimulates human self-assertion'.[16] In Fielding's *Tom Jones* (1749), this potentiality lies between the author–reader dialogue, which continually offers interpretive guidelines, and the 'whole repertoire of norms' depicted in the book, none of which encompasses the conduct of the hero;[17] this gap necessitates constant adjustment by the reader as new information comes forward. Iser depicts the reading experience as active and adaptive: 'We look forward, we look back, we decide, we change our decisions, we form expectations, we are shocked by their nonfulfillment, we question, we muse, we accept, we reject; this is the dynamic process of recreation.'[18] Throughout the long eighteenth century, the novel foregrounds this dynamic process of learning that occurs through the act of reading.

Iser's interest in the reader as an active participant in making the meaning of a novel swept through literary studies in the 1970s and continues to inform ethical, cognitive and affect theories today. Iser's method can also be found in the rhetorical approaches to cinema narration developed by critics such as Seymour Chatman and David Bordwell. Bordwell follows Iser in arguing that 'filmic narration is best considered as a process' wherein 'A film cues the spectator to execute a definable variety of *operations*.'[19] As he further discusses the 'operations' of hypothesis making and testing that the viewer carries out, Bordwell utilises the terminology of Reid Hastie who identifies discrete cognitive processes that engage the viewer. Bordwell puts it all together to stress the perceptual-cognitive activity of the audience:

> The viewer builds the fabula on the basis of prototype schemata (identifiable types of persons, actions, locales, etc.), template schemata (principally the 'canonic' story), and procedural schemata (a search for appropriate motivations and relations of causality, time, and space).[20]

His practice as outlined here resembles Iser's description of the reader's restless search to reconcile individual and type, behaviour and norm, exception and probability. Seymour Chatman augments Bordwell's model, calling attention to the fact that readers do not create meaning by themselves. Chatman thus adds the functions of the 'Presenter' (the filmic narrator – 'a composite of a large and complex variety of communicating devices') and the 'Inventor' (the implied author) as forces that shape interpretation.[21] Using these models of rhetorical narration, I will argue that Tony Richardson's *Tom Jones* (1963) effectively involves its viewers in navigating three central questions that Fielding presents to his readers: problems of authority, experience and closure.

Problems of Authority

The opening sequence of Richardson's adaptation mimics the undercranked camerawork and melodramatic acting of silent era films in order to literalise the same faults in Tom's adoptive father, Squire Allworthy of Paradise Hall, that also destabilise his portrayal in Fielding's novel. The movie thus instantly establishes a visual gap between Allworthy's charity and his powers of observance. As the film begins, Allworthy has just arrived home, where the animated greetings of the whole household serve to establish his virtues and most of all his 'good Heart', as elaborated by Fielding's narrator.[22] Yet the film also shows the problems inherent in goodness as Allworthy stands stock still, frozen by 'surprize' when he gets ready to sleep and finds an abandoned infant in his bed (29). In acting out the keyword that the book's narrator repeatedly associates with Allworthy's detachment and obtuse understanding of the people he should deal with fairly as magistrate,[23] the movie quickly consolidates a concern about his competence. Allworthy merely stares at the baby, wondering, as the intertitle proclaims, 'How did it get here?' Meanwhile, Mrs Wilkins acts with great dispatch during his frozen puzzlement, proposing and fetching culprits. Although we share Squire Allworthy's gaze and humane fascination with the infant Tom as a long close-up allows the credits to roll, we also reel from the breakneck speed with which supposed 'justice' has been served. Allworthy's divergent presentation as both caring and careless thwarts his immediate identification by the audience through what Reid Hastie calls 'prototype schemata', wherein 'individual members of a class [are sorted] according to some posited norm'.[24] Moreover, an underlying irony develops between silent film conventions, with their clearly drawn heroes, villains and rubes, and the complex mixture of satire and romance in the Presenter's exposition. Allworthy's household seems infused with a stilted lack of subtlety as we become aware that we need to consider the moral implications of character, and the vestiges of this 'primacy effect' linger over the rest of the performance.[25]

Fielding's text foregrounds the gap between Allworthy's much touted goodness and his faulty judgements through his long exhortations on the serious consequences of sin as juxtaposed with his repeated inability to forecast human behaviour. Allworthy's earnestness and generosity emerge when he takes the time to try to reason with wayward individuals. The reader registers these qualities in Allworthy's lecture to Jenny Jones, but must also grapple with the narrator's indication that the good man's moralising is a matter of taste and should only be read by 'those who relish that Kind of instructive Writing' (36). He continues his dismissiveness when he later refuses to include Allworthy's admonition to Tom since 'it is unnecessary to insert it here, as we have faithfully transcribed what he said to *Jenny Jones* in the first Book' (126). By undermining his own example of goodness, the narrator portrays Allworthy as ineffectual and passive; as Eric Rothstein has argued, the narrator 'distinguishes himself as one who can grasp and adapt the law, the laws of human nature and of "history" writing, in contradistinction to Allworthy's damaging naiveté'.[26] Allworthy is isolated (and thus is repeatedly 'surprized' at others' behaviour [36, 65]), lets others set the terms of discussion (such as Blifil's insistence on secrecy [97]) and does not engage in second rounds of questioning when he needs more information (as when Square recasts Tom's behaviour as appetitive rather than charitable [128]). In this latter instance, Square's rhetoric 'stamped in the Mind of *Allworthy* the first bad Impression concerning *Jones*' (128). Allworthy's impressionable qualities have been interpreted by critics as both terrible weaknesses and as evidence of his Christian innocence, showing the space for interpretation built into his portrayal; Rothstein claims the narrator creates an 'ethical refuge' for Allworthy in order to enhance his own authority, while J. Paul Hunter asserts that Allworthy reprises Parson Adams's childlike goodness in *Joseph Andrews* (1742), a figure intended for comic effect and designed to prevail over time.[27] Regardless of which view we follow, the narrator's repeated undercutting of his own example of virtue creates an odd ethos that makes us read more warily. His short-changing of Allworthy makes it seem as if he had no choice of character selection and must merely make do with the materials he has been allotted, ultimately calling his own authority into question.

If Allworthy's portrayal presents a chasm between his professions and actions, the much-analysed narrator of the novel diverges and contradicts at every turn. Henry Knight Miller calls the narrator 'a rhetorician'; Jill Campbell analyses his speech as the chief example of Bakhtin's heteroglossia in a text that abounds with an 'almost riotous profusion of forms of speech'; and many have identified him as the principal character of the whole book.[28] Despite the narrator's volubility and distinctive stamp upon the relation of Tom's story, though, the reader repeatedly comes up short against the narrator's pointed vagueness, periphrasis and flat-out refusals to comment on 'Matter[s] which we cannot indulge our Reader's Curiosity by resolving' (129). Experiencing such junctures of non-narrative narration is felt by readers as both a flaunting of authority and an insight into its inner workings.

In Richardson's film, a non-diegetic 'Commentator' voice intervenes with similarly shifting and ambiguous observations that function as a gap between politeness and truth. The technique of over-narration typically goes against the principles of cinematic depiction, as found in George Bluestone's distinction that 'between the percept of the visual image and the concept of the mental image lies the root difference between [film and novel]', and the associated argument that films should and cannot try to mimic their written pre-texts.[29] The booming presence of the Commentator's voice therefore disrupts film art purity and perhaps engages with some of its primal fears; Sarah Kozloff contends that film theory's insistence on the image above all else derives from 'the need to divorce film from the theater, its parent and competitor'.[30] The transgressive quality of the Commentator consequently helps to establish the inherent contradictions about its authority and motivations. Because it would be unfeasible in cinema to have a voiceover intervene as often as Fielding's narrator does, the Commentator instead specialises in equivocation, a technique that stresses a disjunction between order and cover-up. After the opening sequence with Allworthy, for instance, the Commentator indicates that 'Our hero grew apace',[31] and a double wipe replaces the highlighted face of the hungry baby with a close-up of Tom, aged eighteen, as he strides through the darkened woods. Though the newly introduced voiceover speaks in a resonant baritone with the full assurance of authority, he does not advance our sorting of Tom's character via Bordwell's prototype schemata. Even in his first four words we hear an ironic inversion of the concept of 'growth', and some equivocation in the term 'apace', which might mean 'speedily' but could also mean simply 'of the pace of men'.[32] Which interpretive path should we take? Is Tom an extreme example or merely an ordinary man? These complications proceed further as Tom is called a 'bad' hero before that blame is pushed far off onto the biblical Adam's initial poor decision-making.[33] Through double entendre, proverbial expressions and shifts of register, the Commentator problematises a clear and immediate understanding of character, making the viewer learn by experience, much as the hero must.[34] When we hear the familiar phrase that 'The weeks passed and Molly grew apace too . . .',[35] we move to condemn Tom as morally responsible, but when we at last discover that Mr Square is the father, we must modulate our response once more.

Special narrative effects further condition us to accommodate the authoritative view in both versions of *Tom Jones*. Where Fielding's novel uses burlesque diction to frame a close-up depiction of the ridiculous, Richardson's film enlists still frames to render an analogous effect in the visual realm. In both, slowing down forward movement of the action provokes the audience to microscopic and macroscopic analysis and disrupts a plot-centric mindset. Fielding's exaggerated, animalistic imagery, for instance, makes us reconsider what we may call 'love' when it is defamiliarised as 'the Desire of satisfying a voracious Appetite with a certain Quantity of delicate white human flesh' (176). The imagery of destruction to the point of satiety that comes across in this burlesque effect makes us pause and reconsider characters' motivations; the image is slightly nauseating, but also slightly amusing because it seems to anticipate the cliché of 'wolfing down' one's food. Fielding justifies burlesque in the realm of diction alone in the famous 'Preface' to *Joseph Andrews*, contending that in small doses it provides 'wholesome physic for the mind'.[36] He is careful, though, to distinguish his use of it from the entire 'species of writing' called the burlesque, which he equates with the art of caricature aimed to 'exhibit monsters, not men'.[37] In this instance, the burlesque causes us to zoom in on everyday behaviours, such as talk about 'love', and consider them more closely. Fielding's narrator also exploits the passage for rhetorical purpose, conceding the appetitive aspects of some human behaviour in order to argue that benevolent love exists as well. The distinction is an important touchstone for Fielding, one that he developed earlier in his *An Essay on the Knowledge of the Characters of Men* (1742), which distinguishes good humour, or the 'Triumph of the Mind, when reflecting on its own Happiness', from the truly amiable and selfless traits of good nature.[38] The burlesque thus serves as a 'tell' to help us recognise the selfishness behind what is good feeling, not good nature.

Tony Richardson also deploys strategic exaggeration to emphasise the overlapping qualities of man and beast, stopping diegetic progress with a framed portrait to let us consider human nature. When the camera pauses upon the sleeping figures of Squire Western and his bulldog and holds them statically framed, we experience satire by analogy – Western lives his life in a directly appetitive and experiential way without higher judgemental functions, much like his dogs do – but the filmmakers go one step further and simultaneously suggest William Hogarth's well-known self-portrait with his pug, Trump. In this painting, Hogarth self-consciously draws the viewer's attention to the similar countenances of man and pet to create a sense of emotional connection between the two figures;[39] the film instead emphasises naturalism, framing Western as 'caught napping' and inadvertently revealing his real nature. This still moment moves outward from instantaneous individual satire to critique of wider roles, including country squires, John Bull Englishmen and eventually human nature itself. In so doing, the film practises the 'vital plasticity of relationship between moral urgency and urbane detachment' that Claude Rawson identifies as central to the authorial command displayed in Fielding's work.[40] As the camera asks us to contemplate Squire Western, it at once reveals a societal problem and allows us to stand apart from it in laughter.

If insertions of burlesque and still frame present a loaded narrative moment when the narrator/Commentator insists that the audience 'look at this', even more disconcerting are his constant and sometimes unwonted fourth wall breakages and assertions of confidence and complicity. The audience scarcely knows what to do with these nar-ratorial claims of relationship. As Hunter elaborates, these familiar addresses make 'so many categories for the Reader—the "judicious Reader", the "curious Reader", the "expectant Reader", the "candid Reader", and many, many more—Fielding both comprehends and excludes every real reader'.[41] All these glances out at the audience make us self-conscious about our role and just what is expected of us. While the novel's narrator tends to call out our cognitive capacities, both complimenting and laughing at us by calling us 'sagacious',[42] Richardson's camerawork likewise puts us on the spot. At different times, its multiple eyeline shots bring us to look directly at a frightened thrush, a winking owl and a 'hungry' Tom Jones, munching a handful of birdseed while talking about the appetites of the Seagrim girls. All of these gazes seem to equate us with alternately fearful, over-knowing and carnal creatures. As our eyes lock with theirs, we are shaken out of immersion in the story and feel called out for being what we are.

Problems of Experience

Fielding locates contemporary concerns about the vulnerability of the reader at the very core of his novel. As he presents the problems of the self and its search for guid-ance, however, he offers no easy answers, placing an ironic emphasis on extremes. His narrator maps out the perils of both adhering too strictly to models and also of overweighing the particulars of one's own experience. By delineating these contradic-tory routes to despair, he mocks the didactic formulae of the eighteenth century and opens an uncharted *via media* that requires regular readjustment. Such questions pre-dominate in the middle section of the novel, finding allegorical reinforcement in the wandering journey of Tom, cast out from his 'father' Allworthy's house and separated from his beloved Sophia. As we are aware of our hero's alienation alongside our own search for meaning, Fielding's narrator argues that models of perfect human behaviour actually undermine our motivation towards self-improvement; he contends that when presented with an exemplar, a reader will most likely 'be concerned and ashamed to see a Pattern of Excellence, in his Nature, which he may reasonably despair of ever arriving at' (338). This explanation of motivational psychology, taken all by itself, does seem reasonable; common sense coincides with cognitive science to show that incremental improvements underwrite long-term change. However, readers also weigh the timing of this insight, coming as it does right after Tom's betrayal of Sophia at Upton. The 'rule' that we respond more favourably to natural, mixed characters rather than paragons seems offered as cover for Tom's indiscretion, rather than judiciously asserted as a foundational principle. Moreover, the narrator has recently told us of Tom's encounter with just such a mixed character, the Man of the Hill, whose history has proven unhelpful in providing a model. Even though steeped in empirical detail, the Man's life story is merely used by him as confirmation bias for his misanthropy, showing us that experience also has shortcomings as guidance.

Richardson's film aligns with the novel in spoofing the ineffectuality of extreme precepts and models, as both works encourage the audience to think outwards to their own previous experience and encounters with overbearing didacticism. While simplistic models of virtue perhaps even make us worse, negative examples do affect us strongly for the very reason of our spectatorial self-involvement. Our fear of the pain we might suffer through similar error effectively encourages avoidance behaviours that will not soon be forgotten. Where we all are most blind, though, is in the interpretation of our own experience. This problem underlies the Man of the Hill's misanthropy, portrayed in the novel as a lengthy interpolated tale. The Man universalises his lived reality to assume that his view must prevail everywhere, and no external input can penetrate his set ideas. Since the Man of the Hill episode is regularly cut in abridged versions of the novel, it must come as no surprise that Richardson's film does not include it, but instead finds an effective way to perform his cynicism within the dramatic irony of the churchyard battle. The misanthropic Man, whose life story parallels that of Tom, has renounced the world because of the question of design: 'how a benevolent Being should form so foolish, and so vile an Animal' as humankind (312). A version of his complaint creeps into the Commentator's rhyme before the epic contest is about to begin:

> Let dogs delightful bark and bite, for God has made them so,
> Let bears and lions growl and fight for 'tis their nature to,
> But ladies you should never let such angry passions rise,
> Your little hands were never made to tear each others' eyes[43]

No sooner is this conduct rule articulated, though, than it is broken. The film's instant contradiction leaves the viewer to grapple with the dramatic irony that so dismays the novel's Man. How are we to reconcile the discrepancy between human potential and actuality? By dramatising such high–low contrasts, the film delays our identification of what Bordwell calls 'template' schemata where the audience tries 'to presuppose a particular master schema, an abstraction of narrative structure which embodies typical expectations about how to classify events and relate parts to the whole'.[44] Much like Fielding's narrator, the film resists easy answers about its rules and structure.

In the novel, Tom attempts to undercut the Man's logic, but gets trapped in dramatic irony himself. Tom reasons that the Man's life circumstances, while unfortunate, stem from bad luck and a corrupt environment, thus invalidating his experience as a foundation for general pronouncements about humanity. Instead, Tom urges that 'nothing should be esteemed as characteristical of a Species, but what is to be found among the best and most perfect Individuals of that Species' (313). While Tom calls the man 'unfortunate' and 'incautious' – and therefore non-'characteristical' – he fails to see that these descriptors fit his own life story. We realise this irony all the more powerfully when, immediately after talking with the Man, Tom acts incautiously for good (saving Mrs Waters from Northerton) and for ill (forsaking Sophia for the pleasures of the moment). He, too, might be deemed 'unfortunate' for being led by the turn of events into error.[45] Fielding's narrative leaves this dramatic irony for the reader's judgement to sort out, but we too are caught in the trap of reasoning by experience. How can we subtract chance and environment from what is characteristic of human life when we are caught within the play of these factors ourselves?

Richardson's film manifests the problem of judging by experience by establishing multiple lines of sight for the viewer. He builds a visual rhetoric that draws us close to Tom's experience in London at the same time that we are aware of spectatorial erotics at work. Repurposing Fielding's allusions to the artworks of his friend and colleague Hogarth, Richardson draws *mise en scène* elements directly from the artist's *Progress*

INVOKING THE IMPLIED VIEWER 511

narratives to narrate with a Hogarthian 'slant' and make us aware of our participatory role in the hero's downfall.[46] This movement from general satire on humanity in the countryside to the particular degradation of the individual in the city supports the Man's view that London is the site of higher-order vices 'of a relative kind; such as Envy, Malice, Treachery, Cruelty, with every other Species of Malevolence' (290). We are plunged not only into the wickedness of the big city, but into a complicated awareness of its both moralised and eroticised imagery, a pattern elaborated in Mark Hallett's model of the 'doubled reading' provoked by Hogarth's works. Hallett's method acknowledges the complex 'pictorial borrowing' practised by graphic satirists of Hogarth's time, especially 'discourses in contemporary culture that dealt with the sexually commodified body of the prostitute, and that oscillated between demonizing that body as an emblem of metropolitan corruption and dramatizing its concurrent status as a fetishized site of urban erotics'.[47] As if to amplify the problem of our visual engagement, our auditory companion, the Commentator, grows cold and circumspect in the new setting. After skewering the 'notorious Lady Bellaston',[48] he steps back to a more infrequent factual function, merely reading out the contents of letters and identifying new characters.

Indeed, with the Commentator's withdrawal, Lady Bellaston steps forward as surrogate author, scripting the lives of Tom and Sophia as sexual commodities. Our spectatorial circuit coincides with hers in a troubling way as her focalisation takes over the slant of the film. Lady Bellaston, who excels in the cruelties 'of a relative kind' that so disturb the Man of the Hill, is quite at home in London. Her cool self-assurance puts the implied viewer on alert when, the morning after the masquerade, we find her ordering new clothes for Tom. As he is measured, our hero stands in the same slump-shouldered posture as Tom Rakewell in the first plate of his story, hand extended in useless expostulation.[49] Lady Bellaston, by orchestrating this makeover, sets her lover on what we can clearly identify as the path to his dissolution. As we are drawn into Tom's polished and eroticised new look, we are made uncomfortable with awareness that our gaze coincides with Lady Bellaston's, even though we also know that her voyeurism is being satirised. In tracing Hogarth's appropriations from high art as well as pornographic prints, Hallett links the power of Hogarth's plates to their disturbing investigation of 'the relationships between pleasure and warning' (100).

Lady Bellaston likewise serves as instigator of Sophia's ruin, as her false concern for her house guest's welfare makes her reach out and caress Sophia's cheek with her feather pen, a compromised display of interest parallel to Mother Needham's appraisal of the London newcomer, Moll Hackabout.[50] The quick turnaround that occurs in Plate II of *A Harlot's Progress*, where Moll is an already established mistress, is mirrored in Bellaston's immediate enlistment of Lord Fellamar to rape Sophia. The very pen that strokes the girl's cheek also writes an invitation for her assailant to wait upon Lady Bellaston's orders. As our eyes also appraise Sophia, we enter the sexually commodified economy that is being perpetrated and critiqued here. Christine Riding suggests that 'While Moll [Hackabout] and Tom [Rakewell] are flawed in themselves, Hogarth makes it clear that they are by no means alone as transgressors within a world that is, by turns, self-serving, indifferent, and unforgiving.'[51] We are made to feel very much a part of that world in Richardson's film, and our entanglement makes corruption seem inevitable.

Richardson's film thus visualises and makes us even more uncomfortable with an ethical dilemma also figured in the novel. Fielding's narrator, through an early form of free indirect discourse, brings us close to the logic of sin practised by the worldly players of London, and most of all by the demirep, Lady Bellaston. In this way of thinking, Harriet Fitzpatrick's acquisition of a 'Vice-Husband' as lover and protector is legitimised by the term (399). The same is also true for Mr Fitzpatrick who, unable to locate his partner in holy matrimony, takes Mrs Waters to fill that 'vacant . . . Office' (593). This language of 'acting' wife or husband, while a satire on the human tendency to legitimise one's selfish desires, also becomes problematic because readers begin to naturalise characters' identities in these terms. In addition to showing how easily language can obscure vice, the novel documents how quickly mere circumstance can lead to compromising appearances. We are repeatedly shown, for example, how accidents place Sophia in jeopardy of being seen as a fallen woman: first on a literal level when she falls from her horse and her naked lower half is exposed to bystanders (371), then in a comparative fashion when a landlord identifies her as Jenny Cameron (372), and ultimately in an (almost) irrevocable manner when Lady Bellaston encourages Lord Fellamar to be 'a Man of Spirit' and rape her (514). The narrator in this last instance trains us to expect the spectacle of Sophia's ruin, promising that this will be 'the most tragical Matter in our whole History' (515). This troubling cue to read forward to the destruction of Sophia forms a pact of mutual interest that informs other permutations of Fielding's business ventures. Lance Bertelsen has shown how Fielding's Universal Register Office functioned as a 'quasi-brothel', commenting that 'Perhaps Fielding was simply wise enough to know that all worldly relations involve usage, and canny enough to rationalize that the potential sexual usage of domestic service was generally better than the assured sexual usage of prostitution.'[52] In marrying his own housekeeper after the death of his wife, Charlotte, Fielding seems to have followed this train of thought. Bertelsen also documents Fielding's double language in the court reportage of *The Covent Garden Journal* where 'Fielding's descriptions of young prostitutes suggest that the intersecting languages of law and sympathy may act textually to provoke the same subversive erotic charge they seek legally to muffle.'[53] The equally compromised presentation of Sophia's body as the site of lewd jokes, misrecognitions and 'Design' engages the audience within a dialectic between righteousness and titillation that brings us into an ethical quandary (513).

The evils done by Lady Bellaston, and supported by the social system in which she (and we) circulate, are wrapped up in the polite behaviours of shopping, letter writing, social calling and taking tea in both book and film. In *Knowledge of the Characters of Men*, Fielding calls this false front 'the Art of Thriving' and contrasts its drive for 'private distinction' from the Stoic concept of living 'as fellow-citizens of the world'.[54] His cultural analysis reveals the hypocrisy behind seemingly communal and civil activities. Richardson's work also excels at confronting us with the ethics of private distinction. When Lady Bellaston's spending spree is over and a transformed Tom raps on her door with his new cane, we come face to face with the human costs of her establishment. Along with Tom, we watch the door open and gaze into the surprised face of a black servant who registers the same astonished look as a similar character in Plate II of *A Harlot's Progress*. Not only does the presence of this enslaved boy signal Lady Bellaston's involvement in colonial exploitation, his resemblance to Hogarth's figure critiques her cultural capital as well. The similar luxurious fabrics on the footboy and on Tom suggest that both wear livery for their Lady and are, in fact, owned by her. As David Dabydeen observes, Hogarth depicts 'a society scarred by commercialism, the cash nexus replacing human relationships . . . In other words, people are always seen in relation to *things*, a relation that is indicative of the depersonalization of human life.'[55] Bellaston's whole household reflects this inhumane way of being, its entrance hall filled with nude statuary and mirrors, objectifying items that emphasise image, not life.

Problems of Closure

Problems of authority and experience – of who and what models we can trust and of how to account for our participation in the very economy we are attempting to judge – are the crux of both novel and film. Rather than resolve this puzzle, the endings to both works perpetuate it, which seems fitting given Tom's reprieve and the perpetuation of his life. Fielding's *Tom Jones* may feature a display of order and completion in the final pages, described by Dorothy Van Ghent as a 'Palladian mansion',[56] but the reader's experience does not collate so symmetrically into a grand facade. We have repeatedly been brought up short and stopped by ironies, ambiguities, blind spots, compromised perspectives and further entanglements, often abetted by our 'friend' the narrator (10). The appearance of harmonious arrangement at the end of the novel therefore might be effectively juxtaposed with its theme of incompleteness. K. G. Simpson finds that 'The "plot" of narrator–reader relations leads to the conclusion that any fixed and single view-point is necessarily inadequate to cope with judgement of the complexity and flux of experience.'[57] In other words, readers are encouraged by their progress through the text to develop some knowledge of their human capacities and their limits. In the end, they know that the narrator's great revelation of Tom's birth history could hardly have been foretold based on the information given, and, despite the pleasing architecture of his plot, the narrator has his vagaries and limits as well.

If Fielding's narrator creates a balanced and probable ending that turns upon our spectatorship and some good acting by the narrator, Bridget Allworthy, Jenny Jones and the like, Richardson's film flips that paradigm. He uses a single actor's capacity to play multiple roles to break rules about the conservation of character and the boundaries of an independent work of art.[58] Careful viewers of Richardson's adaptation may already have noticed its allusion to the 1953 film of John Gay's *The Beggar's Opera* (1728) in the double-casting of the actor who plays the Beggar, Hugh Griffith, as Squire Western.[59] Although Griffith's Beggar is soft-spoken and his performance of Western is raucous, both characters are enthusiasts, merging life with their art or sport. Both, too, disrupt the operations of the corrupt capital punishment system: the Beggar by scripting a reprieve for Macheath and Western by riding up and rescuing Tom himself. When the drunken squire intervenes at the very moment when Tom is dangling in the noose, the film flaunts Aristotelian rules of unity, paralleling the meta moment in *The Beggar's Opera* film where Macheath, played by Laurence Olivier, convinces the author of his story to change the ending. In each case, the hanging is underway when suddenly Griffith's intense face intervenes as death and fate are denied. The film's self-consciousness at this moment 'rests on the fact that the medium permits a given signifier – an actor – to signify more than one character'.[60] In this way, Richardson's work creates an expansive effect at the end, much like the unfolding facade of Fielding's Palladian manor. In both instances, we are aware of the art involved in bringing us to this vista as we move towards resolution.

514 JENNIFER PRESTON WILSON

The film then likewise reprieves our guide, the Commentator, who signals that we are nearing the close. His expostulation that 'To die for a cause is a common evil, to die for nonsense is the devil' shucks off Lady Bellaston's interpellated plotting of Tom and Sophia's 'Progress' towards dissolution.[61] With this rejection of tragedy, the film effectively sides with its protagonist and yet comes to rest upon a final double irony. As J. Douglas Canfield has argued, the wish-fulfilment quality of the conclusion to *The Beggar's Opera* undercuts the rest of its plot by forging a pact of 'mutual interest' between the taste of the town and the author.[62] Richardson's final note is also double-voiced, aware of the marketplace and yet artistically suitable. Breaching what James Phelan calls the 'probability code' through its codeswitching with another work, the film models openness and then leaves the final thinking about it, appropriately, to the viewer.[63]

Maintaining a metafictional self-consciousness, Henry Fielding's *Tom Jones* and its film adaptation by Tony Richardson fashion appealing works that promote awareness of the cognitive effects of narrative transactions. The book and film teach us to question authority, putting us on guard against expecting too much of goodness or underestimating language's capacities for deception. In a more positive light, they also train us to stay alert for breakthrough moments of insight into other people's characters or the roles we play ourselves. They encourage scepticism about our self-involvement, especially when we think we have a moralising or experiential edge over others. Finally, and fittingly, these two works provoke our awareness of the multiplicity of views required in good judgement. Much as narrative forms adapt and remediate other works, accurate thinking requires the processing of multiple perspectives.

Tony Richardson's *Tom Jones* does not stand alone as a film adaptation that turns the eighteenth century's concern for the reader to artistic use. Over just the last few decades, similar awareness of the intertwined powers of irony, didacticism and the implied viewer manifests in movies such as Ang Lee's *Sense and Sensibility* (1995), Patricia Rozema's *Mansfield Park* (1999), Robert Zemeckis's *Cast Away* (2000), Michael Winterbottom's *Tristram Shandy: A Cock and Bull Story* (2005) and Joe Wright's *Pride and Prejudice* (2005). All of these adaptations come from auteurs who are willing to take conceptual risks that activate the viewers' involvement in the narrative. Richardson's Academy Award winning *Tom Jones* can now be seen as a forerunner of these millennium-era films in its vision of how eighteenth-century fictions can make us think critically about our own media moment.

Notes

1. George Colman (the Elder), 'Prologue to *Polly Honeycombe*, A Dramatic Novel of One Act (1760)', in *Novel Definitions: An Anthology of Commentary on the Novel 1688–1815*, ed. Cheryl L. Nixon (Peterborough: Broadview Press, 2009), 218. A portrayal of 'Mrs Novel' also appeared earlier in Henry Fielding's *The Author's Farce* (1730) as an allegorised depiction of Eliza Haywood. Through the rest of this essay I will use the word 'novel' to designate early prototypes of what has now become a familiar form, although acknowledging the complex language of literary modes in the eighteenth century.
2. For a discussion of the ripple effects of the Queen Anne Law of 1710, see William B. Warner, *Licensing Entertainment: The Elevation of Novel Reading in Britain, 1684–1750* (Berkeley: University of California Press, 1998), 134–5.

INVOKING THE IMPLIED VIEWER 515

3. David Brewer, *The Afterlife of Character, 1726–1825* (Philadelphia: University of Pennsylvania Press, 2005), 10.

4. Brewer, *The Afterlife of Character*, 16–19.

5. Daniel Cook and Nicholas Seager, 'Introduction', in *The Afterlives of Eighteenth-Century Fiction*, ed. Daniel Cook and Nicholas Seager (Cambridge: Cambridge University Press, 2015), 1–3.

6. Cook and Seager, 'Introduction', 1–2.

7. Robert Mayer, 'Introduction: Is There a Text in the Screening Room?', in *Eighteenth-Century Fiction on Screen*, ed. Robert Mayer (Cambridge: Cambridge University Press, 2002), 7.

8. For a full account of Henry Fielding as auteur, see Ian A. Bell, *Henry Fielding: Authorship and Authority* (New York: Longman, 1994).

9. James Fordyce, '"On Female Virtue", Vol. 1 of *Sermons to Young Women* (1766)', in *Novel Definitions*, ed. Nixon, 265.

10. Samuel Johnson, '*The Rambler*, No. 4 (March 31, 1750)', in *Novel Definitions*, ed. Nixon, 150.

11. John Brewer, *The Pleasures of the Imagination: English Culture in the Eighteenth Century* (New York: Farrar, Straus and Giroux, 1997), 172.

12. Wolfgang Iser, *The Implied Reader: Patterns of Communication in Prose Fiction from Bunyan to Beckett* (Baltimore: Johns Hopkins University Press, 1974), 37.

13. Robert Folkenflik, 'Wolfgang Iser's Eighteenth Century', *Poetics Today* 27, no. 4 (2006): 679.

14. Iser, *The Implied Reader*, xiii.

15. Iser, *The Implied Reader*, 2–5.

16. Iser, *The Implied Reader*, 24.

17. Iser, *The Implied Reader*, 52.

18. Iser, *The Implied Reader*, 288.

19. David Bordwell, *Narration in the Fiction Film* (Madison: University of Wisconsin Press, 1985), xi, 29.

20. Bordwell, *Narration in the Fiction Film*, 49.

21. Seymour Chatman, *Coming to Terms: The Rhetoric of Narrative in Fiction and Film* (Ithaca: Cornell University Press, 1990), 133–4. Chatman launches his discussion of adaptation with a quotation from Iser that privileges the imaginative experience of fiction over film. Chatman retorts, 'Are narrative gaps solely ones of picturing – in other words, are films "gapless" because visually explicit?' He goes on to use Iser's model to show how filmic gaps stimulate 'the conceptual imagination', 162.

22. Henry Fielding, *Tom Jones*, ed. Sheridan Baker, 2nd edn (1749; New York: W. W. Norton, 1995), 28. Further references parenthetical.

23. Freezing characters in this emotion is a favourite Fielding device, most notably employed when Joseph Andrews repulses Lady Booby's advances by referencing his virtue. We might see this technique as one of many ways that Fielding's theatre experience leads him to think about how emotions are registered on the body for comedic effect, an intermedial quality that already hints at the possibilities of still frames in cinema. Henry Fielding, *Joseph Andrews*, ed. Homer Goldberg (1742; New York: W. W. Norton, 1987), 32–3.

24. Bordwell, *Narration in the Fiction Film*, 34.

25. Meir Sternberg defines primacy effect as 'a frame of reference to which subsequent information [is] subordinated as far as possible'. Meir Sternberg, *Expositional Modes and Temporal Ordering in Fiction* (Baltimore: Johns Hopkins University Press, 1978), 94.

26. Eric Rothstein, 'Virtues of Authority in *Tom Jones*', *The Eighteenth Century* 28, no. 2 (1987): 107.

27. Rothstein, 'Virtues of Authority in *Tom Jones*', 106; J. Paul Hunter, *Occasional Form: Henry Fielding and the Chains of Circumstance* (Baltimore: Johns Hopkins University Press, 1975), 121.

28. Henry Knight Miller, 'The Voices of Henry Fielding: Style in *Tom Jones*', in *The Augustan Milieu: Essays Presented to Louis A. Landa*, ed. Henry Knight Miller, Eric Rothstein and G. S. Rousseau (Oxford: Clarendon Press, 1970), 267. Jill Campbell, 'Fielding's Style', in *Approaches to Teaching the Novels of Henry Fielding*, ed. Jennifer Preston Wilson and Elizabeth Kraft (New York: MLA, 2015), 124–5.

29. George Bluestone, *Novels into Film* (Baltimore: Johns Hopkins University Press, 1957), 1.

30. Sarah Kozloff, *Invisible Storytellers: Voice-Over Narration in American Fiction Film* (Berkeley: University of California Press, 1989), 9.

31. John Osborne, *Tom Jones: A Film Script* (New York: Grove, 1965), 13. Much of the success of Richardson's project stems from Osborne's skill in finding rich and concise analogues for Fielding's epic techniques.

32. *OED*, s.v. 'apace', https://www-oed-com.proxy006.nclive.org/view/Entry/9010?redirected From=apace#eid (accessed 28 October 2021).

33. Osborne, *Tom Jones: A Film Script*, 13.

34. I here diverge from Martin Battestin's assertion that the Commentator unambiguously expresses 'wry amusement and affection for the character [of Tom], controlling our attitude toward him'. I do, however, find Battestin's larger thesis that the film's camerawork is 'technically analogous to Fielding's stylistic mannerisms and his own distinctive narrational devices' quite compelling. Martin C. Battestin, 'Adapting Fielding for Film and Television', in *Eighteenth-Century Fiction on Screen*, ed. Mayer, 91–2.

35. Osborne, *Tom Jones: A Film Script*, 31.

36. Fielding, *Joseph Andrews*, 5.

37. Fielding, *Joseph Andrews*, 5.

38. Henry Fielding, *An Essay on Knowledge of Characters of Men*, in *Miscellanies by Henry Fielding, Esq.*, ed. Henry Knight Miller, 3 vols (Middletown: Wesleyan University Press, 1972), 1:158.

39. William Hogarth, *The Painter and his Pug*, Tate Gallery, https://www.tate.org.uk/art/artworks/hogarth-the-painter-and-his-pug-n00112/ (accessed 26 November 2023).

40. C. J. Rawson, *Henry Fielding and the Augustan Ideal Under Stress* (Boston: Routledge & Kegan Paul, 1972), 245.

41. Hunter, *Occasional Form*, 164.

42. This is the first of over twenty references to the reader's sagacity. For analysis of this motif and its satire on Richard Bentley, see Henry Power, 'Henry Fielding, Richard Bentley, and the "Sagacious Reader" of *Tom Jones*', *The Review of English Studies* 61, no. 252 (2010): 749–72.

43. Osborne, *Tom Jones: A Film Script*, 33.

44. Bordwell, *Narration in the Fiction Film*, 34.

45. Sheldon Sacks argues that Tom and the Man of the Hill are 'disparate' because Tom would never steal from his roommate as the Man does. I agree that there are important differences between their characters, but that their significant shared traits (including self-blindness) obstruct their own thriving. Sheldon Sacks, *Fiction and the Shape of Belief* (Berkeley: University of California Press, 1964), 202.

46. 'Slant' is Seymour Chatman's term for 'the narrator's attitudes and other mental nuances appropriate to the report function of discourse', as opposed to the Hollywood 'seamless style'. Chatman, *Coming to Terms*, 143.

47. Mark Hallett, *The Spectacle of Difference: Graphic Satire in the Age of Hogarth* (New Haven: Yale University Press, 1999), 98, 100.

48. Osborne, *Tom Jones: A Film Script*, 132.

INVOKING THE IMPLIED VIEWER

49. William Hogarth, *A Rake's Progress*, Plate I, in *Engravings by Hogarth*, ed. Sean Shesgreen (New York: Dover, 1973), 28.
50. William Hogarth, *A Harlot's Progress*, Plate I, in *Engravings by Hogarth*, ed. Shesgreen, 18.
51. Mark Hallett and Christine Riding, *Hogarth* (London: Tate Publishing, 2006), 73.
52. Lance Bertelsen, *Henry Fielding at Work: Magistrate, Businessman, Writer* (New York: Palgrave Macmillan, 2000), 53–6.
53. Bertelsen, *Henry Fielding at Work*, 24.
54. Fielding, *Characters of Men*, 154.
55. David Dabydeen, *Hogarth's Blacks: Images of Blacks in Eighteenth-Century English Art* (Athens: University of Georgia Press, 1987), 11.
56. Dorothy Van Ghent, *The English Novel: Form and Function* (New York: Harper & Row, 1953), 80.
57. K. G. Simpson, 'Technique as Judgement in *Tom Jones*', in *Henry Fielding: Justice Observed*, ed. K. G. Simpson (Totowa: Barnes & Noble, 1985), 169.
58. Judith Bailey Slagle and Robert Holtzclaw offer an analysis of how Richardson 'made a movie about making movies' in 'Narrative Voice and "Chorus on the Stage" in *Tom Jones* (1963)', in *The Cinema of Tony Richardson: Essays and Interviews*, ed. James M Welsh and John C. Tibbetts (Albany: State University of New York Press, 1999), 194.
59. *The Beggar's Opera*, directed by Peter Brook (Warner Bros., 1953), 1:33.
60. This quotation from Chatman is made in reference to *The French Lieutenant's Woman* (1981). Chatman, *Coming to Terms*, 165.
61. Osborne, *Tom Jones: A Film Script*, 180.
62. J. Douglas Canfield, 'The Critique of Capitalism and the Retreat into Art in Gay's *Beggar's Opera* and Fielding's *Author's Farce*', in *Cutting Edges: Postmodern Critical Essays on Eighteenth-Century Satire*, ed. James E. Gill (Knoxville: University of Tennessee Press, 1995), 323–4.
63. James Phelan, *Somebody Telling Somebody Else: A Rhetorical Poetics of Narrative* (Columbus: Ohio State University Press, 2017), 49.

Notes on Contributors

Katherine Aske is Lecturer of English at Edinburgh Napier University. Her research examines understandings of female beauty within eighteenth-century literature and cultural history. She has published on the subject of beauty, including an article in the *Journal for Eighteenth-Century Studies* examining cosmetics in Jonathan Swift's poetry. Her forthcoming monograph, *Being Pretty in the Eighteenth Century: A Cultural History of Female Beauty*, is under contract. With the support of a British Academy Small Research Grant, Aske is currently working in the medical humanities, exploring beauty and the origins of dermatology in the long eighteenth century.

Georgina Bartlett is a music historian researching the intersections between stage music and street song in London around the turn of the nineteenth century. She received her Bachelor's and Master's degrees from the University of Miami, studying under Professor Karen Henson, and she wrote her doctoral dissertation at the University of Oxford under the supervision of Professor Suzanne Aspden. She has lectured at Oxford's Faculty of Music and has held a Junior Teaching Fellowship at the Ashmolean Museum and a lectureship at St Peter's College, Oxford. She is currently a lecturer at University College, Oxford, running the Academic Transition Support Programme.

Ashleigh Blackwood is Lecturer in Professional Practice at the University of Sunderland. She specialises in cultural co-creation, health and medical cultures of the long eighteenth century. Ashleigh was Co-Investigator of the Wellcome Trust project 'Thinking Through Things: Object Encounters in the Medical Humanities', a project which explores the visual and material aspects of studying health, and she has published on a variety of themes including anatomy, obstetrics, mental health, sleep, and women's roles within medicine. Her monograph *Reproductive Health, Literature, and Print Culture, 1650–1800: Everybody's Business* is forthcoming.

Katharina Boehm is Professor of English Literature at the University of Passau. She is the author of *Charles Dickens and the Sciences of Childhood: Popular Medicine, Child Health and Victorian Culture* (2013). She has edited a number of essay collections and co-edited, with Victoria Mills, a special issue of *Word & Image*, 'Mediating the Materiality of the Past, 1700–1930' (2017). Her articles on antiquarianism, material culture

NOTES ON CONTRIBUTORS

and the novel have appeared in *SEL, Studies in the Novel, Victorian Review, Textual Practice* and *Modern Philology*. She is completing a book on the novel and antiquarian practices in the long eighteenth century.

Nathalie Collé is Professor of English Literature at the Université de Lorraine (IDEA), France, specialising in the illustration of classics. The fields covered by her research include book history, print culture, visual culture and material culture. She has published 'Wayfaring Images: The Pilgrim's Pictorial Progress' in *The Oxford Handbook of John Bunyan* (2018), the 'Introduction' to *The Pilgrim's Progress. By John Bunyan. With the Watercolour Illustrations by William Blake* by The Folio Society Ltd (2020), and 'Author-Portraits of Milton, Authorship, and Canonization' in *Global Milton and Visual Art* (2021). She is the co-founder and co-director of BPTI (Book Page Text Image, formerly Book Practices & Textual Itineraries), a collection devoted to book history, textual scholarship and illustration studies (EDUL).

Daniel Cook is Associate Dean of Education and Reader in English Literature in the School of Humanities, Social Sciences and Law at the University of Dundee. He is the author of *Walter Scott and Short Fiction* (2021), *Reading Swift's Poetry* (2020) and *Thomas Chatterton and Neglected Genius, 1760–1830* (2013). His most recent books include *Scottish Poetry, 1730–1830* (2023), *Gulliver's Travels: The Norton Library* (2023), *The Cambridge Companion to Gulliver's Travels* (with Nick Seager, 2023) and *Austen After 200: New Reading Spaces* (with Annika Bautz and Kerry Sinanan, 2022).

Amelia Dale is Lecturer in Eighteenth-Century Literature at the Australian National University's School of Literature, Languages and Linguistics and co-editor of *The Shandean*. She is the author of *The Printed Reader: Gender, Quixotism, and Textual Bodies in Eighteenth-Century Britain* (2019) which was shortlisted for the BARS first book prize. She is currently working on a large collaborative project on *Harris's List of Covent-Garden Ladies* (1760–94) with Nicola Parsons. Recent work appears in *Eighteenth-Century Fiction, The Eighteenth Century: Theory and Interpretation, The Shandean, Romanticism, The Library* and the *Australian Humanities Review*.

Joseph Drury is Associate Professor of English at Villanova University. He received his BA from the University of Oxford, his MA from Queen Mary, University of London, and his PhD from the University of Pennsylvania. He is the author of *Novel Machines: Technology and Narrative Form in Enlightenment Britain* (2017), as well as several articles and book chapters exploring eighteenth-century literature's engagement with the history of aesthetics, science, technology, gender and sexuality, and material culture. He is currently at work on a monograph about the emergence of 'the whimsical' as an aesthetic category in the long eighteenth century.

Pierre Dubois is a retired professor of eighteenth-century English studies. He has written numerous papers and several books in both French and English on eighteenth-century English music and literature. These include a study on aesthetic theories of music in eighteenth-century Britain, *La conquête du mystère musical en Angleterre au siècle des*

Lumières (2009, Research Prize of the French Societé des Anglicistes de l'Enseignement Supérieur in 2010), *Music in the Georgian Novel* (2015), *Dr Charles Burney and the Organ* (2021) and *Claude Balbastre – un virtuose au siècle des Lumière* (2021).

Fraser Easton is Associate Professor of English at the University of Waterloo. His literary and historical work has appeared in *Past and Present, Studies in Romanticism, Textual Practice, Genre, Eighteenth-Century Fiction* and *Studies in Eighteenth-Century Culture*. His essays on the literary reception of elocution have appeared in *Reading Christopher Smart in the Twenty-First Century, Mocking Bird Technologies,* and *Laurence Sterne's 'A Sentimental Journey'*. With Ian Balfour, he is editor of and contributor to a collection of essays on Christopher Smart (including a new, posthumous article by Geoffrey Hartman) forthcoming in *Eighteenth-Century Studies*.

Chris Ewers is Senior Lecturer in Eighteenth-Century Literature at the University of Exeter. His monograph *Mobility in the English Novel from Defoe to Austen* was published in 2018. He has also written articles on Henry Fielding, Thomas Love Peacock, Sir Walter Scott, Robert Bage, Sir John Hill, Laurence Sterne and Agatha Christie. He has published work on the representation of sport in films such as *Rocky, The Wrestler* and *This Sporting Life*. He is currently writing a book about temporality in the long eighteenth century, which looks at conceptions of the 'moment' and its relation to libertinism, street poetry, the novel, slavery and architecture.

Marcie Frank is Professor in the English Department of Concordia University in Montreal where she teaches mainly eighteenth-century British literature. *The Novel Stage: Narrative Form from the Restoration to Jane Austen* was published in 2020. She is currently working on two projects: one that considers contemporary autofiction in the long history of the novel, and the other, funded by the Social Sciences and Humanities Research Council of Canada, that develops situation as a cross-media narrative concept. 'Situation: A Narrative Concept', co-authored with Kevin Pask and Ned Schantz, is forthcoming in *Critical Inquiry* in summer 2024.

Brigitte Friant-Kessler is Emerita Researcher at the Université Polytechnique Hauts-de-France, Valenciennes, where she currently coordinates a transdisciplinary project about the visual and cultural heritage of the French spa town Saint-Amand-les Eaux. She is a Sterne scholar who specialises in inter-transmedial studies. Her academic interest lies in graphic arts (book illustration, satirical prints, graphic novels, web comics). In 2019 she launched, with Anne Chassagnol (Paris 8), an international research project (conferences, publications) on literature and tattoos. With Emanuele Arioli, she co-edited *Arthur Transmedial* (2023) on adaptations of King Arthur's legend in a variety of media (music, games, comics and caricature). Recent book chapters and essays discuss Sternean tattoos, *Gulliver's Travels* as graphic novel, theatre and caricature, political cartoons and comics. She often contributes to exhibition catalogues and works with museum curators as an academic consultant.

Paul Goring is Professor of Literature and Culture at the Norwegian University of Science and Technology in Trondheim. He has long-standing interests in relations between literature and the visual arts and performance which he has earlier explored in essays

NOTES ON CONTRIBUTORS

521

on Virginia Woolf and Laurence Sterne as well as in *The Rhetoric of Sensibility in Eighteenth-Century Culture* (2005). He has ongoing projects on eighteenth-century theatre, particularly the work of the actor and playwright Charles Macklin, and is also a researcher on a collaborative project exploring European lotteries. In this capacity he is researching the representation of lotteries on stage as well as the selling of paintings and entire art collections by means of lottery in the eighteenth and nineteenth centuries.

Mascha Hansen is Lecturer in British Literature at the University of Greifswald, Germany. She is a member of the GIS Sociabilités/Sociabilities and its flagship project, the DIGITENS (*The Digital Encyclopedia of British Sociability in the Long Eighteenth Century*), and has recently edited a collection of essays, *British Sociability and the European Enlightenment: Cultural Practices and Personal Encounters* (with Sebastian Domsch, 2020). Her research interests range from eighteenth-century women's novels, autobiographies and letters – particularly those of the bluestockings – to women's involvement in science and education, their medical history and their visions of the future. Her current project is a digital edition of the German correspondence of Queen Charlotte.

Emrys D. Jones is Senior Lecturer in Eighteenth-Century Literature and Culture at King's College London. He has published widely on representations of sociability in eighteenth-century poetry and prose, and he also specialises in the development of celebrity culture throughout the period. He is the author of *Friendship and Allegiance in Eighteenth-Century Literature* (2013), and the co-editor of several essay collections on related topics. He co-edits the journal *Literature and History* and serves as reviews editor for the *Journal for Eighteenth-Century Studies*. Alongside these roles, he maintains an interest in the representation of eighteenth-century culture in contemporary film and television.

Sandro Jung is Distinguished Professor of English and Comparative Literature at Fudan University. He is also Past President of the East-Central American Society for Eighteenth Century Studies. He is the author of, among others, *David Mallet, Anglo-Scot: Poetry, Politics, and Patronage in the Age of Union* (2008), *The Fragmentary Poetic: Eighteenth-Century Uses of an Experimental Mode* (2009), *The Publishing and Marketing of Illustrated Literature in Scotland, 1760–1825* (2017), *Kleine artige Kupfer: Buchillustration im 18. Jahrhundert* (2018) and *Eighteenth-Century Illustration and Literary Material Culture* (2023).

Elizabeth Kraft is Professor Emerita of the University of Georgia. She is the co-editor (with E. Derek Taylor and Melvyn New) of Samuel Richardson's *Sir Charles Grandison* (2022) and the editor of *The Cultural History of Comedy in the Age of Enlightenment* (2020). She has published widely in the field of eighteenth-century British literature and is the author of several monographs, including *Women Novelists and the Ethics of Desire* (2008) and *Restoration Stage Comedies and Hollywood Remarriage Films* (2016). She has essays forthcoming on Robert Burns, Samuel Richardson, Daniel Defoe and Christian Isobel Johnstone, and is currently completing her edition of Anna Letitia Barbauld's literary criticism.

Jakub Lipski is University Professor in the Department of Anglophone Literatures, Kazimierz Wielki University in Bydgoszcz, Poland. Before obtaining his PhD in English

522   NOTES ON CONTRIBUTORS

Literature, he studied English, Cultural Studies and Art History. He is the author of *Castaway Bodies in the Eighteenth-Century English Robinsonade* (2024), *Re-Reading the Eighteenth-Century Novel: Studies in Reception* (2021), *Painting the Novel: Pictorial Discourse in Eighteenth-Century English Fiction* (2018) and *In Quest of the Self: Masquerade and Travel in the Eighteenth-Century Novel* (2014). His research interests include eighteenth-century English fiction and culture, word and image crossovers, as well as reception and adaptation studies.

Joanna Maciulewicz is University Professor and Head of the English Literature of the Eighteenth and Nineteenth Centuries and Print Culture Research Unit at the Faculty of English at Adam Mickiewicz University in Poznań, Poland. She is the author of *Representations of Book Culture in Eighteenth-Century English Imaginative Writing* (2018) and co-editor (with Jakub Lipski) of *Neo-Georgian Fiction: Reimagining the Eighteenth-Century in the Contemporary Historical Novel* (2021). She is associate editor of *Studia Anglica Posnaniensia*. Her research interests focus on the development of the early novel in the context of print culture in eighteenth-century England, the transnational history of early modern fiction and Anglo-Spanish literary relations.

Hannah Moss works in the heritage industry, having completed her PhD studies at the University of Sheffield in 2020. Her thesis, titled 'Sister Artists: The Artist Heroine in British Women's Writing, 1760–1830', interrogates the ways in which women writers of the long eighteenth century respond to one another in the characterisation of artists in their works. Hannah's interdisciplinary approach saw her organise the Women and the Arts conference held at the University of Sheffield in 2019 in order to bring art historians and literary critics together. Alongside Joe Bray she is co-editor of *The Edinburgh Companion to Jane Austen and the Arts* (2024).

Mary Newbould is currently Assistant Professor at Kazimierz Wielki University in Bydgoszcz, Poland, having taught and researched at the University of Cambridge for many years. She specialises in eighteenth-century literature and visual culture, with a particular interest in Laurence Sterne, and in literary afterlives. Her monograph on Sternean adaptations appeared in 2013; she co-edited (with W. B. Gerard) an essay collection on Sterne's *A Sentimental Journey* in 2021, and (with Helen Williams) *Laurence Sterne and Sterneana*, an Open Access dataset hosted by Cambridge Digital Library. She is an editor of the international Sterne journal *The Shandean*.

Frédéric Ogée is Professor of British Literature and Art History at Université Paris Cité. His main publications include two collections of essays on William Hogarth, as well as *'Better in France'? The Circulation of Ideas across the Channel in the 18th Century* (2005), *Diderot and European Culture* (2006; repr. 2009) and *Thomas Lawrence, le genie du portrait anglaise* (2022). His next book, *J. M. W. Turner, les paysages absolus*, will come out in October 2024. In 2006–7 he curated the first-ever exhibition on Hogarth for the Louvre museum. From 2014 to 2017 he was a member of Tate Britain's Advisory Council.

Natasha Simonova has worked as a lecturer and researcher at the Universities of Edinburgh, Cambridge and Oxford. Her publications include studies of the early novel, the reception of Philip Sidney's *Arcadia* and the works of Samuel Richardson, including a monograph on prose fiction sequels in the seventeenth and eighteenth centuries (*Early Modern Authorship and Prose Continuations: Adaptation and Ownership from Sidney to Richardson*, 2015). She is a section co-editor for the *Palgrave Encyclopedia of Early Modern Women's Writing* and is currently working on a trade biography of female letter-writers among the Grey family of Wrest Park.

Przemysław Uściński is Assistant Professor at the Institute of English Studies, University of Warsaw, and the editor of *Anglica. An International Journal of English Studies*. He has published a number of articles on British literature and culture in the long eighteenth century, including studies of the English novel, parody, satire and Romantic poetry. His book *Parody, Scriblerian Wit and the Rise of the Novel* was published in 2017. His current research focuses on colonial history, nature and travel in eighteenth-century discourses, Romantic peripatetic poetry and travel writing. In 2022 he co-edited the volume *Travel and Otherness in Nineteenth-Century British Writing*. He also co-organises the *Warsaw Literary Meetings* seminar cycle and the conference series *From Queen Anne to Queen Victoria*.

James Watt is a professor in the Department of English and Related Literature and Director of the Centre for Eighteenth Century Studies at the University of York. His most recent book is *British Orientalisms, 1759–1835* (2019), and he has edited *The Citizen of the World* as part of the *Collected Works of Oliver Goldsmith*, ed. Michael J. Griffin and David O'Shaughnessy (2024). With Alison O'Byrne he is the co-editor of the essay collection *Discovering Britain and Ireland in the Romantic Period: Grand Tours* (2025).

Helen Williams is Associate Professor of English Literature at Northumbria University and a British Academy Innovation Fellow working in collaboration with the Worshipful Company of Stationers. Helen specialises in eighteenth-century book history and the novel. She is the author of *Laurence Sterne and the Eighteenth-Century Book* (2021) and co-director with Mary Newbould of the *Laurence Sterne and Sterneana* dataset hosted by Cambridge Digital Library. She is a co-editor of *Memoirs of a Woman of Pleasure* (2018) and of the forthcoming *Cambridge Edition of the Correspondence of John Cleland*. Helen's current work explores eighteenth-century women in the book trades.

Jennifer Preston Wilson is Professor of English at Appalachian State University and co-editor, with Elizabeth Kraft, of *Approaches to Teaching the Novels of Henry Fielding* (2015). She has written on film adaptations of *Robinson Crusoe* (in *Rewriting Crusoe: The Robinsonade Across Languages, Cultures, and Media*, 2020) and *The Madness of King George* (in *The Cinematic Eighteenth Century: History, Culture, and Adaptation*, 2018), as well as on Thing Theory (in *Laurence Sterne's A Sentimental Journey: A Legacy to the World*, 2021) and cognitive approaches to literature (*Journal of the Short Story in English*, A. S. Byatt Special Issue, 2021). Her current project, 'Teaching Anne Finch in "Partisanship in Restoration and Eighteenth-Century Britain"', has recently been published on *ABO: Interactive Journal for Women in the Arts, 1640–1830*.

INDEX

References to figures are in *italics*. References to plates are in ***bold italics***.

Abington, Frances, 44
Adam, James, 10, 110, 119
Adam, Robert, 10, 110, 111, 119
adaptation
  in the eighteenth century, 460, 503
  practice of, 15, 262, 410, 461, 474
  and print culture, 485, 487–8
  theories of, 410, 460
  in the twentieth century, 15–16, 467,
    474–5
  see also contemporary visual art; film; Goethe,
    Johann Wolfgang von; graphic satire;
    Shakespeare, William; Sterne, Laurence
Addison, Joseph
  critique of opera in the works of, 237, 297
  on physiognomic theory, 142, 143
  'The Pleasures of the Imagination', 5, 89–90,
    105, 333
  on puppetry, 233
  on the spectator figure, 26
  see also Spectator, The; Steele, Richard
Adeline de Courcy (anon.), 131
Adventurer, The, 146, 152
Adventures of Dick Hazard, The (anon.), 132
Adventures of Mr. Loveill, The (anon.), 134
Adventures of Peregrine Pickle, The (Smollett)
  gendered statuary tropes in, 135–7
  medical debates in, 69, 77–8, 82
  satire of connoisseurship in, 390
Adventures of Roderick Random, The (Smollett)
  anatomical debates in, 69, 72–3, 75
  artists referenced in, 387–8, 390
  maternal imagination in, 77
  referenced in broadside ballads, 254
aesthetics
  debates surrounding, 5–8
  in fiction, 184–9
  and pleasure, 90
  and race, 12–13
  theories of, 5, 6–8, 166, 180–1

treatises on, 5, 89–90, 105, 333
and visuality, 377, 378–9
see also beauty; Burke, Edmund; taste;
  ut pictura poesis; whimsy
affect
  and elocution, 308, 321
  and gender, 62
  and music, 216–18, 220
  and the novel, 307–8
  and reading experience, 28, 218, 219, 314
  and sensibility, 262
  theories of, 279–80, 282, 283, 284, 321,
    357
  and the visual arts, 403, 407
  and whimsy, 207–8
afterlives, literary
  in anthologies, 177
  digital, 15
  of frontispieces, 399–400, 404–10
  in graphic satire, 460–2
Aikin, John, 211
Albinus, Bernhard Siegfried, *Tabulae Sceleti
  Musculorum Corporis Humani*, 68, 70, 71
Ames, Joseph, 160
Amory, Thomas, *The Life of John Buncle,
  Esq.*, 488
anatomical art, 69–70, 74, 80, *80*, 82
anatomical debates, 178, 186, 315, 490
antiquarianism
  and collections, 55
  and domestic tourism, 55–6
  female antiquaries, 54–5, 56, 60
  and gender politics, 62–3
  and the Gothic, 53, 56, 117
  and handicrafts, 14, 54
  and household objects, 60
  in the mid-eighteenth century, 54–7
  and the novel's emergence, 53
  see also *Millenium Hall* (Sarah Scott); Society of
    Antiquaries of London, the; Stonehenge

INDEX

Apuleius, *Metamorphoses*, 239
Arabian Nights' Entertainments, The, 40, 47–8
Aravamudan, Srinivas, 38, 40, 47
Arcadia, 105, 176–7, 332, 334–5, 340–1
architecture
  aesthetics of, 110
  and architects, 111–12
  Classical, 110, 111–16, 117
  concept of, 108–9, 117
  country houses in literature, 112, 113–16, 120, 336–7, 340, 342–3
  and the early novel, 108, 112, 113, 114–16
  and Enlightenment education, 185
  gendered perceptions of, 116
  Gothic, 110–11, 116–19
  and great houses, 108–9
  as high art, 109–10, 116
  links with literary movements, 110–12
  in the novel, 14, 119–21
  Palladianism, 111, 113–14, 120, 513
  Rococo-Gothic, 200–1, 207
  see also Austen, Jane; *Tom Jones* (novel, Henry Fielding)
Aretino, Pietro, 435
arts, the
  and class, 12
  collection and display of, 2, 152, 156, 157–8, 159, 160–1, 162–5, 168–9, 170, 180, 183
  and collective labour, 10
  and correspondence, 8–9, 204, 237
  definitions of, 11, 110
  feminisation of, 11, 54
  the fine arts *see* fine arts, the
  and gender, 11–12
  hierarchisation of, 5
  and interartistic discourse, 1–3, 4, 5–6, 7–8, 9
  and intermediality, 9, 24–5, 362–3, 377, 386–7, 398, 415, 416, 486, 487, 488, 495
  popular forms of, 2
  professional vs amateur, 58
  and race, 12
Ashmolean Museum, Oxford, 2, 55
Athenian Letters, 339–40, 342; *see also* Yorke, Charles; Yorke, Philip
Aubin, Penelope, *The Noble Slaves*, 377
Aubrey, John, 159
audiences
  for antiquarianism, 54, 55
  in the eighteenth century, 5, 10
  for fiction, 30, 178, 262, 503–5, 509
  for film, 504–10
  of Gothic fiction, 118
  for music, 225, 297–8, 299, 300

for Shakespeare, 264–9
for theatre, 229, 231–4, 237, 240
  see also readers; *Tom Jones* (film, Tony Richardson)
Austen, Jane
  architecture in the works of, 113, 115–16, 120
  art inspired by, 15, 463, 473–5, 485, 491–2
  and domesticity, 491–2
  Emma, 294
  empire in the works of, 492–3
  in graphic satire, 15, 462, 471–3
  influence of Sterne on, 309, 311–12, 317–19, 320–1
  music in the works of, 296, 301–3
  Northanger Abbey, 2, 286, 349, 363
  and the novel's emergence, 10
  Pride and Prejudice, 115–16, 120, 472, 492
  reviews of, 16, 277
  Sense and Sensibility, 93, 301–2
  see also Mansfield Park (Austen); *Persuasion* (Austen)
authorship
  and anonymity, 10, 24, 26, 131, 132, 245
  and classical authors, 3
  and gender, 24, 25, 33
  and moral purpose, 40, 348, 349
  and pseudonymity, 57, 240, 336, 433, 469
  see also frontispieces
Avery, Edward, 435

Bage, Robert, *The Fair Syrian*, 14, 39, 41, 44–6
Bakhtin, Mikhail, 117–18
Baldessari, John, 15
  'Cremation Project', 487
  The Life and Opinions of Tristram Shandy, Gentleman, 485, 487–8, 489–91, 495, 496, **Plate 26**
  see also Sterne, Laurence
Ballaster, Ros, 26, 29, 40, 46
Bannet, Eve Tavor, 23, 26, 27, 349
Barbauld, Anna Letitia
  'The Origin of Song-Writing', 211, 218
  on poetry, 178
  theory of the novel of, 3, 211, 217
  see also Clarissa (Samuel Richardson)
Barchas, Janine, 220, 397–8, 399
Barker, Jane, *A Patch-Work Screen for the Ladies*, 14, 70–1, 72, 79, 82
Basire the Elder, James
  The Ancient Palace at Greenwich,, 444
  Vestuta Monumenta, 444
Batteux, Charles, 382

INDEX

Beattie, James, *The Minstrel*, 186–7
beautiful, the
  as aesthetic category, 12, 57–8, 90–1, 140–1,
    142, 146, 241, 282–3
  and architecture, 109–10
  and landscape, 183–4, 198–9, 206, 333–4,
    342–3, 388–9
  and race, 12, 47
  see also Burke, Edmund; Hogarth, William;
    Radcliffe, Ann
beauty
  and appearance-character relationships, 142–3,
    145–6, 150, 151–2
  in book illustrations, 141, 143, 149
  and contemplative love, 282–3
  and cosmetics, 150–1
  in the early novel, 140, 141
  and facial expression, 142–3, 146, 149–50, 152
  in fiction, 140, 141, 143–6, 147–9, 150–2, 151
  and gender, 14, 57, 104, 128, 140, 141, 205,
    387–8
  and hair, 148, 150, 197, 205, 330
  notion of 'complete' beauty, 14, 140–1, 147–9,
    150–1, 152, 200, 334
  and physiognomy, 142, 143
  in relation to virtue, 140–1, 143–5, 146, 147,
    148, 151
  and social identities, 141–2, 150
  and taste, 282–3, 291n27
  theories of, 140, 141, 282–3
Beckford, William, 46–7, 48, 111
  and Fonthill Abbey, 39, 46–8, 115, *115*, 119
  and sexuality, 39, 46–7
  see also architecture; Gothic fiction;
    Orientalism; *Vathek* (Beckford)
Behn, Aphra, 108
  and drama, 27–9, 91
  embodiment in the works of, 27–9, 30
  The Emperor of the Moon, 27–8
  The History of the Nun, 28, 29
  and interartistic discourse, 3, 12
  invisibility and gender in the works of, 27–9,
    32, 34
  literary allusions in, 14, 27
  The Luckey Chance, 27, 28
  and the novel's emergence, 2, 4
  Oroonoko, 3, 12, 28–9, 34
  racial discourses in the works of, 12–13, 34
  The Rover, 27, 91
  see also Fielding, Henry; Haywood, Eliza;
    Invisible Spy, The (Haywood)
Bell, Steve, 463
Benbow, William, 440–1
Bentley, Richard, 201, 516n42
Bentley, Thomas, 179
Berkeley, George, 198–9, 205

Bickerstaff, Isaac, *The Sultan*, 41, 44–6
Birch, Thomas, 160
Blair, Hugh, 251, 308
Blake, William, 8–9
Blenheim Palace, 55, 90, 111, 120, 180
Blondel, James Augustus, 75–6
body, the
  anatomical studies of, 68
  in anatomical prints, 69–70, 74, 80, *80*, 82
  anatomy of, 70–1, 72, 74, 79, 82
  and appearance-character relationships, 142–3,
    145–6, 150, 151–2
  and body snatching, 73–4
  and dissection, 70, 71, 73–4
  and empirical enquiry, 89, 93
  and gendered statuary metaphors, 123, 124,
    125, 126–7
  and interiority, 70–1, 72, 74, 79, 82
  metaphorical topographies of, 434
  and physiognomic theory, 142, 143
  and self-awareness, 100–1
  and sensibility, 100, 101, 102–4, 317, 320, 392
  as site of commercial exchange, 93–4, 95–9,
    104, 105, 511–13
  topographical descriptions of, 13
  see also embodiment; medicine; statuary
Bordwell, David, 505, 507, 510
Boswell, James, 178
Brady, Patrick, 195–6
Bramble, Matthew, 44
Brewer, David, 67, 414, 461, 503
Brewer, John, 10, 277, 278, 279, 380–1, 383
Bridgeman, Charles, 90
British Critic, The, 177
British Museum, the, 2, 55
British Novelists, The, 17n12, 190n15, 226n1
broadside ballads
  'Answer to the Cabin Boy', 246
  audiences of, 244–5, 249–50, 255–6
  and ballad singers, 256–7
  collections of, 244–5, 246, 257n8
  cultural complexity of, 245–50
  figure of 'Jack Tar' in, 253, 255
  format of, 244, 245, 247, 250
  'The Heart That Can Feel for Another', 255
  hybrid forms of, 244, 246–9
  illustrations to, 247–9, 248, 254–5, 256
  'Lovely Nan', 247, 249, 253
  moral function of, 250, 251, 252, 253, 255
  in oral culture, 245–6
  and popular theatrical songs, 250–1, 253
  and print culture, 244, 245, 246
  sentimentalism in, 15, 253–7
  stories in, 245, 249, 250
  'Tom Bowling', 253–5
  'True Courage', 255–6

INDEX

Brontë, Charlotte, 492
Jane Eyre, 41
Brookes, Peter
Debased Currency, 471, 472–3, **Plate 25**
graphic satire of, 463
Brown, Dave
and banknote iconography, 470–3
political caricatures of, 462, 463, 470
Brown, Lancelot 'Capability', 10, 90, 201, 332
Bunyan, John, *The Pilgrim's Progress*, 400,
409–10, 505
Burke, Edmund
aesthetics in the works of, 89
on beauty, 140, 141, 148, 282–3
*A Philosophical Enquiry into the Origin of our
Ideas of the Sublime and Beautiful*, 7, 140
Burke, William, 73–4
Burney, Frances
and father-daughter plots, 267, 268
masquerades in the works of, 94
and musical appreciation, 298, 300
musical epiphanies in the works of, 296,
297–300, 301
and the novel's emergence, 10
sensibility in the works of, 262, 263, 271–2
sentimental novels of, 262, 268, 271
Shakespeare's influence on, 262, 264, 265–6
and statuary metaphors, 123
theatricality in the works of, 263
The Wanderer, 268, 300, 301
see also *Camilla* (Frances Burney); *Evelina*
(Frances Burney)
Burney, Sarah Harriet
Clarentine, 262, 269
Country Neighbours, 262, 263, 271, 272
and father-daughter plots, 267, 269–70
Geraldine Fauconberg, 269
and reading Shakespeare, 270, 271
sensibility in the works of, 262, 263, 271–2
sentimental novels of, 262, 269, 271
Shakespeare's influence on, 262, 264, 265, 269,
270–1
The Shipwreck, 270–1
Traits of Nature, 269–70
writing career of, 269
Burton, John, 82
Burton, Robert, *The Anatomy of Melancholy*,
488, 489
Byron, George Gordon, Lord, 48, 314

cabinet pictures, 416
Camilla (Frances Burney)
father-daughter plots in, 267
as novel of manners, 263
ridicule of sensibility in, 263, 268
Shakespearean references in, 267–8

Campbell, Colen, *Vitruvius Brittanicus*, 110
Campbell, George, 308
Campbell, Robert, 205
Campkin, Henry
Grub Street (Now Milton Street) London, 434
see also Comerford, James
capitalism
and commercialised pleasure, 92, 103, 208
and the family unit, 92–3
and gender, 92–3, 99, 111
see also body, the; consumerism; luxury;
pleasure
Carter, Elizabeth, 218
friendship with Catherine Talbot of, 56, 59
'Ode to Wisdom', 216, 218–9
see also Richardson, Samuel
Castle of Otranto, The (Horace Walpole)
animated artworks in, 127–8, 156, 166, 171
and antiquarianism, 53
architecture in, 116–17, 119
narrative function of images in, 155–6
patriarchal inheritance in, 116–17, 156
portraiture in, 127–8
preface to, 343
and the uncanny, 127, 166
Cecilia (Frances Burney)
father-daughter plots in, 268
musical epiphanies in, 298–300, 301
see also Shakespeare, William
Chan, Paul
anti-war work of, 497
artistic career of, 15, 493–4, 497–8
as conceptual writer, 488
and film, 493–4, 497
Les 120 Journées de Sodome, 485, 494, 495–7
My Own Private Alexandria, 496
reading experience of, 493–4, 497
Sade for Fonts Sake, 494–5, **Plate 28**
'Sade for Sade's Sake', 485, 493–7
Charles II, King of England, 91–2, 105
'Charms of Silvia, The', 215, *215*; see also *Pamela*
(Samuel Richardson)
chinoiserie, 197, 207
Cibber, Colley
The Provok'd Husband, 268–9
and Shakespeare adaptations, 266
Civil War, the (English), 168, 221, 338
Clarissa (Samuel Richardson)
architecture in, 108, 113, 120, 216
and drama, 350
epistolary form of, 91
and gender politics, 127, 129–30, 131, 132,
136, 211, 220
and the lifelike corpse motif, 127, 128, 129, 131
music in, 14, 211, 216–20
'Ode to Wisdom' in, 216–17, 218–20, *220*

528 INDEX

Clarissa (Samuel Richardson) (*cont.*)
  revised edition of, 136
  sentimental affect in, 211, 216–20, 357
  sexual violence in, 99, 127, 129
  statuary metaphors in, 14, 126–7, 128, 129,
    130, 132
  see also Barbauld, Anna Letitia
Clark, John, 398–401, 399, 404, 464; *see also*
  Pine, John; *Robinson Crusoe* (Defoe)
classical antiquity
  and architecture, 110, 111–16, 117
  and the novel, 111–16
  and Dialogues of the Dead, 239
  in the eighteenth century, 1–2, 3
  in fiction, 239
  and gender, 59
  and interartistic discourse, 1
  and rhetoric, 308
  and romance, 336, 339
  and statuary, 58, 123, 330
  and the visual arts, 334, 442
  see also neoclassicism
Claude glass, the, 183, 344; *see also* Lorrain,
  Claude
Cleland, John
  The Memoirs of a Woman of Pleasure, 23,
    31, 95
  see also *Romance of a Day, The* (Cleland)
Cole, William, 156, 172
Coleridge, Samuel Taylor, 113, 176, 177–8
Collier, Jane
  The Cry, 131
  *An Essay on the Art of Ingeniously
    Tormenting*, 11
  see also Fielding, Sarah
Colman the Elder, George, *Polly Honeycombe*,
  503
Comerford, James
  book collection of, 433–4, 447
  extra-illustration practices of, 15, 433–4,
    435–6, 437–40, 441–7
  illustrated prints belonging to, 449–53,
    454–7
  see also Campkin, Henry; *Romance of a Day,
    The* (Cleland); *Voyage to Lethe, A* (anon.)
conceptual art, 485–6, 488
conceptual writing, 488–9, 496
Confidential Letters of Albert, The, 419; see also
  Die Leiden des jungen Werther (Goethe)
Congreve, William, 389
  'Of Pleasing, An Epistle to Sir Richard Temple',
    160–2
  The Way of the World, 91
connoisseurship, 2–3, 12, 123–5, 137, 155, 159,
  166, 168, 171, 180, 198, 205, 228–9, 239,
  380–3, 390–2, 433–5

Constant Le Cerf, Jacques Louis, 464
consumerism
  and anatomical knowledge, 68, 95
  and cultural consumers, 2, 5, 10, 386, 400
  and gender, 198, 202
  and hedonism, 199, 204–5, 208
  and luxury, 197, 198, 206–7, 400
  and the print trade, 383–4
  and the sex trade, 97–9, 103, 104
  see also capitalism; Haywood, Eliza; whimsy
contemporary visual art
  and adaptations of eighteenth-century novels,
    15, 485–6, 498
  definitions of, 485–6
  movements of, 486
  see also Baldessari, John; Chan, Paul;
    conceptual art; conceptual writing; Cranston,
    Meg; Sterne, Laurence
conversation
  the art of, 110, 198, 280–1, 368–9, 371–3
  and communication, 101–2, 103, 234, 236,
    317, 321–2, 363, 364–7
  and gender, 278–9, 284, 286, 287–9
  and isolation, 364–5
  literary, 60–1, 336–7, 349
  and politeness, 60–1, 110, 132, 144–5, 197–8,
    279, 280–1, 288, 371–2
  and sexuality, 95, 101–2, 133, 288
  and sociability, 103, 279, 280–1, 300, 371
  see also elocution; *Evelina* (Frances Burney);
    Robinson Crusoe (Defoe); sociability;
    spontaneity
conversation pieces
  as artistic genre, 282
  parallels with the novel, 362–3
  performance of sociability in, 15, 362, 363,
    365–6
  and portraiture, 280–1, 362, 363, 373,
    Plate 13
  and reading practices, 349, 353
  social commentary in, 362–3
Covent Garden Theatre, 241
Coventry, Francis
  The History of Pompey the Little, 352
  on realism in the novel, 40
  and satire of rococo, 200–2, 204, 207
Cowper, William, 422, 465
Cozens, Alexander, 341
Cranston, Meg, 15, 485, 488
  The Complete Works of Jane Austen, 485,
    491–2, *Plate 27*
Crébillon *fils*, Claude-Prosper Jolyot de
  Les Egarements du cœur et de l'esprit, 101
  The Sopha, 24
Critical Review, The, 48, 177
Cumberland, Richard, *The West Indian*, 252

INDEX
529

Daniell, Thomas and William, *Views of Calcutta*, **Plate 2**

Daumier, Honoré, 467, 480n34
Une panique de Lilliputiens, 467, 468

Davidson, Jenny, 265, 283, 284

De Arte Graphica (Fresnoy), 5; *see also* Dryden, John; sister arts, the

de Bolla, Peter, 9–10, 11, 114, 120, 363, 377, 386

Defoe, Daniel
the body in the works of, 93–4
Colonel Jack, 109, 377
and the history of the novel, 4, 100–1, 112–13
A Journal of the Plague Year, 364
literary pictorialism in the works of, 13
masquerades in the works of, 94–5
pleasure in the works of, 91–5
prefaces to the works of, 250
and realist prose fiction, 377–8
sexual politics in the works of, 92
and spirituality, 24
A Tour Thro' the Whole Island of Great Britain, 112
and the visual arts, 15, 39, 377–8
see also *Fortunate Mistress, The (Roxana)* (Defoe); *Moll Flanders* (Defoe); Orientalism; *Robinson Crusoe* (Defoe)

Devis, Arthur, 362

Dibdin Sr, Charles, 247, 249, 253–6

Dickens, Charles, 491

Diderot, Denis
admiration for Greuze of, 97
Jacques le Fataliste, 488, 489
Le Rêve de d'Alembert, 100
Les Bijoux indiscrets, 24
and self-awareness, 100–1

Die Leiden des jungen Werther (Goethe)
adaptations of, 414–15, 418–20
character of Charlotte in, 415, 418–21
and mourning jewellery, 420, 421, 422
phenomenal success of, 15, 414, 419–20
prints illustrating scenes from, 415, 416, 418, 420–1, 420, 422, 426–7, **Plates 14–16**
remediations of, 414, 415, 418–20
silkworks based on, 415–16, 417, 418, 422–6, 427–8, **Plates 14–20**
translations of, 414

digital resources (scholarly research), 15, 434, 447–9

Dodd, H., 437

Dodd, William, 264

Doody, Margaret Anne, 4, 220, 224, 267

Doort, Abraham van der, *A Catalogue and Description of King Charles the First's Capital Collection*, 162; *see also* Walpole, Horace

drama
as artform, 1
didactic potential of, 350
and embodiment, 27, 29
print-performance relationship, 350
and the visual arts, 1, 27
see also Behn, Aphra; Burney, Frances; Burney, Sarah Harriet; Haywood, Eliza; Shakespeare, William; theatre

Drury Lane (Theatre Royal), 44, 105, 241, 275n53

Dryden, John, 5, 180, 221, 225
and statuary metaphors, 126
translation of Ovid by, 125
see also Fresnoy, Charles Alphonse du

D'Urfé, Honoré, *L'Astreé*, 329, 330, *330*, 331, 343

Edgeworth, Maria, 284, 300
Belinda, 283, 287–9

ekphrasis
in broadside ballads, 249
as literary technique, 184, 378
theories of, 378, 392n7
see also Haywood, Eliza; sister arts; *ut pictura poesis*

Ellison, Ralph, *The Invisible Man*, 33

elocution
and anthologisation, 315
the art of, 11, 15, 307, 309
and body language, 313, 315, 317–19
and communication, 313–14
the elocutionary movement, 308
and feelings, 307, 308–9
paralinguistic aspects of, 311–12, 316, 320
and reading aloud, 246, 349–50
and rhetoric, 307, 308, 309, 311, 321
and sentimentalism, 307, 314, 316–19, 321
and sexuality, 307, 308–9, 315–17, 318, 319
and taste, 314–15
temporal aspects of, 319–20

Elstob, Elizabeth, 56

embodiment
and disembodiment, 33–4
in drama, 27, 29
and gendered authorship, 33
and invisibility, 24, 25–7, 29
representations of women's bodies, 67–8
see also Behn, Aphra; *Invisible Spy, The* (Haywood); *Persuasion* (Austen)

emotion
in artworks, 130–1, 425
and body language, 28, 101–2
and elocution, 307, 308
excesses of, 130–1, 314
and the limitations of language, 6, 308–9

530 INDEX

emotion (*cont.*)
  and music, 183, 211, 221–2, 294–5, 297,
    301–3
  philosophical treatments of, 117
  in relation to sensibility, 278, 285
  and statuary metaphors, 130–1, 132
  and the visual arts, 7
  see also affect; elocution; musical epiphanies;
    sensibility
empiricism
  and anatomical study, 74, 80
  empirical inquiry, 10, 75, 89, 93, 95, 105, 185
  in philosophy, 4, 99
  and readers, 349, 351, 357, 358–9
Enlightenment, the
  and aesthetics, 89–90
  and the body, 100
  and cultural experiences, 11
  and education, 185
  and Orientalism, 40, 48
  and sentimentalism, 251
ephemera
  and broadside ballads, 245, 257n8
  and classical antiquity, 123
  and extra-illustration, 433, 441, 449
  and fashion, 198, 200
  and reading, 349
epiphany, definition of, 293
  see also musical epiphanies
epistolary fiction
  formal constraints of, 145
  forms of, 30–1
  narrative techniques of, 140, 143, 145, 148,
    251–2, 254–5
  and the novel's emergence, 91
  and sentimental novels, 251, 252
  see also Clarissa (Samuel Richardson); Evelina
    (Frances Burney)
erotica
  collections of, 433–4, 447
  history of, 433
  and illustrative prints, 438, *439*
  in magazines, 440–1
  and obscenity trials, 441
  and print culture, 441
  readers of, 433
  in *The Wit's Magazine*, 441
  see also Comerford, James; extra-illustration
Etherege, George, *The Man of Mode*, 91
Evelina (Frances Burney)
  appearance-character relationships in, 146
  body language in, 309
  classical references in, 372
  concept of beauty in, 14, 140, 141, 147–8
  conversation in, 371, 372–3
  epistolary form of, 143, 145

  and father-daughter plots, 267, 268
  music in, 297–8
  politeness in, 280, 288
  sociability in, 15, 370–3
  statuary metaphors in, 125, 126
  and theatre, 267
  see also masquerades; pleasure gardens; theatre
exhibitions
  of artworks, 165, 380, 381, 416
  of contemporary art, 487, 494, 496
  and museum culture, 2, 55
  of silkworks, 417–18, 420, 422
  and the viewing public, 71, 279, 378–9
  see also Royal Academy, the
extra-illustration
  collections of, 433, 434
  history of, 433–4
  practice of, 160, *161*, 433–4
  in relation to digital resources, 15, 434, 447–9
  and standard copy texts, 434, 447–9
  see also Comerford, James; erotica; Walpole,
    Horace

Favart, Charles-Simon, 41
Female American, The (anon.), 125
Female Quixote, The (Lennox)
  appearance-character relationships in, 151–2
  and female novel readers, 286, 349
  the figure of 'complete' beauty in, 14, 140, 141,
    150–1, 152
  and intermediality, 15
  landscape gardens in, 333–4
  quixotism in, 285–6, 314, 334, 335, 367–9
  and romance fiction, 202, 204, 333–5
  sociability in, 15, 367–70
  and whimsy, 202, 333
Female Werter. A Novel, The, 414; see also
    Die Leiden des jungen Werther (Goethe)
Fielding, Henry
  adaptive practices of, 30–1, 228, 240
  Amelia, 134
  approach towards hypocrisy of, 284
  business ventures of, 512
  *An Essay on the Knowledge of the Characters
    of Men*, 508, 512
  and fictional representations of ghosts, 29, 30
  in graphic satire, 462, 468–70
  invisibility in the works of, 27, 29–31
  masquerades in the works of, 94, 240, 511
  metafictional commentaries of, 2–3, 27
  political journalism of, 468
  and realist prose fiction, 30, 40, 201
  Shamela, 30–1, 145
  and statuary's comic effects, 123–4
  theatrical experiments of, 29–30
  Tom Thumb, 29, 30

and the visual arts, 2–3, 14, 389–90
and William Hogarth, 3, 510–11
see also *Gulliver's Travels* (Swift); *History of the Adventures of Joseph Andrews, The* (Henry Fielding); *Invisible Spy, The* (Haywood); *Tom Jones* (novel, Henry Fielding)
Fielding, Sarah, 352
  The Cry, 131
  see also Collier, Jane; *History of Charlotte Summers, The* (Fielding, Sarah ?)
film
  adaptations of eighteenth-century novels, 16, 474, 491, 503–4, 514
  and audience reception, 504
  and conceptual art, 485, 490
  Gothic frameworks of, 172
  and graphic satire, 475
  the implied viewer in, 16, 504–5, 511, 514
  narration in, 505–9, 510–12, 513–14
  and transmedial adaptation, 473–5, 498
  see also *Tom Jones* (film, Tony Richardson)
fine arts, the, 8, 11, 176, 197, 279, 384; see also painting; sculpture
Flint, Christopher, 282
Folkenflik, Robert, 398, 399, 401, 402, 505
Fonthill Abbey see Beckford, William
Fordyce, James, 'On Female Virtue', 349
Fortunate Mistress, The (*Roxana*) (Defoe)
  alternative endings to, 38, 40–1
  costume in, 38, 44, 46, 94–5, 384–5, **Plate 1**
  frontispiece to, 385, **Plate 1**
  and libertine culture, 91, 92
  and literary pictorialism, 384
  and the novel's emergence, 40–1, 91, 94–5, 384
  references to painting in, 39, 384–5, 386
  Roxana's character in, 92
  sexuality in, 14, 31, 38–9, 44, 92
French Revolution, the, 117, 185, 253, 289, 474
Fresnoy, Charles Alphonse du, *De Arte Graphica*, 5
frontispieces
  afterlives of, 15, 399–400, 404–10
  and authorial portraits, 397, 401, 404
  as branding tools, 385, 400–1
  design of, 403
  and the eighteenth-century novel, 409–10
  and interartistic discourses, 397–8
  and intermediality, 398, 404–10
  material afterlives of, 399–400, 404–10
  and the novel's materiality, 397–8
  in romances, 329–30
  scholarship on, 397
  see also *Fortunate Mistress, The* (*Roxana*) (Defoe); *Robinson Crusoe* (Defoe); *Romance of a Day*

Gainsborough, Thomas
  aesthetics of, 104

Elizabeth and Mary Linley, 104–5, **Plate 7**
The Mall in St. James's Park, 104, **Plate 6**
Mr and Mrs Andrews, 104
Mrs. Mary Robinson (Perdita), 105, **Plate 9**
Mrs. Richard Brinsley Sheridan, 105, **Plate 8**
  and portraiture, 104–5
  style of, 104
  training of, 104
Gallagher, Catherine, 24, 25, 34
galleries
  expansion of, 2
  in Gothic fiction, 170, 172
  and the Grand Tour, 380
  literary, 416
  and private art collections, 110
  see also Royal Academy, the
Garrick, David
  acting style of, 264
  Florizel and Perdita, 264–5
  Shakespearean adaptations by, 264, 265, 266–7
  as theatre manager, 44, 105
Gay, John
  ballad operas of, 252
  The Beggar's Opera, 93, 250, 513–14
  poetry of, 11
gender
  and artistic practice, 11–12
  and authorship, 24, 25, 33
  and consumerism, 198, 202
  and conversation, 278–9, 284, 286, 287–9
  feminisation of the arts, 11, 54
  politics, 127, 129–30, 131, 132, 136, 211, 220
  and handicrafts, 59–60
  and musical appreciation, 300
  and politeness, 278–9
  and reading practices, 286, 349, 504
  and statuary tropes, 123–4, 129, 131, 132, 134–6
  see also beauty; embodiment; gender (female)
gender (female)
  and advice manuals on the arts, 57–8
  and anatomical studies, 68
  coquetry, 198, 202, 286
  and dangers of novel reading, 286, 349, 504
  and domesticity, 58–60, 61
  and economic autonomy, 92–3
  and father-daughter plots, 265, 267, 269–70
  female antiquaries, 54–5, 56, 60
  invisibility of women, 11–12, 24
  and the male gaze, 11–12, 123, 124, 125–6
  and medical practice, 67, 68, 69, 75–7, 82
  and motherhood, 92
  self-creation and physical appearance, 150
  and statuary metaphors, 123, 124, 125, 126–7, 132
  women as artistic creators, 12
  see also beauty; body, the; marriage

532 INDEX

genius, 58, 187
Gentleman's Magazine, The, 469–70
George IV, King of England, 46, 104, 105
Gibbes, Phebe, *Hartly House, Calcutta*, 14, 39,
  48–51
Gillray, James
  adaptations of the works of, 463, 474–5
  allusions in the works of, 474
  anti-Napoleonic satire of, 462, 465
  collectability of, 460–1
  The Contrast, or Things as they Are, 117, **Plate 10**
  political satire of, 460–1, 462, 465, 474
  see also Rowson, Martin
Gilpin, William, 56
  An Essay on Prints, 383
Glorious Revolution, the, 89, 91
Godwin, William, 278
Goethe, Johann Wolfgang von, 421; *see also*
  Die Leiden des jungen Werther (Goethe)
Goldsmith, Kenneth, 488–9
Goldsmith, Oliver
  'Chinese Letters', 41
  The Citizen of the World, 48
  An Essay on the Theatre, 252
  sentimental novels of, 251
  The Vicar of Wakefield, 15, 278, 281–2, 334–5,
    416
Goodall, William, *The Adventures of Captain
  Greenland*, 352
Gothic, the
  and antiquarianism, 53, 56, 117
  in architecture, 14, 56, 110–11, 116–19
  and body snatching, 73
  and the novel's emergence, 10
  Rococo-Gothic architecture, 200–1, 207
  theories of, 56, 59, 110–11, 117, 166–7
  see also Strawberry Hill
Gothic fiction
  animated artworks in, 127–30, 156, 166, 170–1
  castles in, 117–19
  chronotopes of, 117–18
  dangers of for female readers, 349
  and female interiority, 116
  lifelike corpse motifs in, 127, 128–9
  queerness in, 47
  relationship with the plastic arts of, 127
  statuary metaphors in, 123, 127–30
  and the uncanny, 127, 166
  see also *Castle of Otranto, The* (Horace
    Walpole); Lewis, Matthew Gregory;
    Radcliffe, Ann; *Vathek* (Beckford)
Gothic Revival, the, 201
Grahame-Smith, Seth, *Pride and Prejudice
  and Zombies*, 473, 474, 482n61; *see also*
  Austen, Jane
Grand Tour, the, 1–2, 112, 123, 380, 382, 391
graphic satire

  as an artform, 460
  and banknote iconography, 462–3, 470–1,
    Plate 25
  broadsides as, 246
  collectability of, 460–1
  fictional characters in, 461–2
  inspired by eighteenth-century fiction, 15,
    460–3, 476–7
  and Napoleon Bonaparte, 464–5, **Plate 23**
  novelists depicted in, 462, 468–71
  and political caricatures, 460, 461
  see also Brookes, Peter; Gillray, James;
    Gulliver's Travels (Swift); Hogarth, William;
    Robinson Crusoe (Defoe); Rowson, Martin
Gravelot, Hubert-François, 103–4, *144*
Graves, Richard, *The Spiritual Quixote*, 388
Gray, Thomas, 166, 168, 169
Gregory, Jemima Mary, 340
Greuze, Jean-Baptiste, 97
Grey, Amabel Hume-Campbell, Countess de,
  340–2, *342*, 343
Grey, Jemima, Marchioness, 336, 337, 339, 342–3
Grose, Francis, 'Antiquarians Peeping into
  Boadicia's Night Urn', 60
Gulliver's Travels (Swift)
  abolition of excessive language in, 238–9
  afterlives of, 228–9, 240–1, 461, 462, 463–4,
    466–7
  architecture in, 228, 233, 234, 235–6
  the arts in, 228, 239–40, 385–6
  and Dialogues of the Dead, 239
  first illustrations to, 401
  in graphic satire, 15, 461, 462, 463–4,
    466–7
  Gulliver as character in, 228, 229, 232–5,
    241
  musical performance in, 235–6, 238
  and the novel's emergence, 3, 229
  performative arts in, 228, 229, 230, 236–9
  poetry in, 236, 240
  politics in, 230–3, 239–40
  popular entertainments in, 14, 228, 229
  puppetry in, 233, 234, 237–8
  rope-dancing in, 230, 231, 240–1
Gwyn, Nell, 92, 105, **Plate 4**

Hagstrum, Jean, 10
Handel, George Frederick
  Alexander's Feast, 220–1, 222–4, *223*, 225
  see also *History of Sir Charles Grandison, The*
    (Samuel Richardson)
handicrafts
  and antiquarianism, 54
  domestic, 58– 60, 61
  and economic exchange, 62–3
  feminisation of, 54
  and gender, 59–60

INDEX

in relation to literary practices, 60–1
in traditional historiographies, 54, 58, 61
see also antiquarianism; *Millenium Hall* (Sarah Scott); silkworks
Hare, William, 73–4
Harvey, William, 68, 79
Hatchett, William, 24, 30
Hawkesworth, John, 146, 152
Hayman, Francis, 383
Hays, Mary, 251
The Memoirs of Emma Courtney, 131
Haywood, Eliza
Anti-Pamela, 30, 31, 145
The British Recluse, 377
decorative arts in the works of, 205–6
dramatic career of, 23–4
The Dramatick Historiographer, 23
and erotica, 24
Fantomina, 109, 197, 203–5
The Female Spectator, 23, 26, 197–8, 199, 202–3, 286
and the Hillarian circle, 335–6
The History of Jemmy and Jenny Jessamy, 386, 387
The History of Miss Betsy Thoughtless, 134, 197, 198, 205–6
invisibility in the works of, 24, 25–7, 29, 34
La Belle Assemblée, 336
Love in Excess, 91
masquerades in the works of, 94
Memoirs of the Court of Lilliput, 240–1
and the novel's emergence, 4, 377
The Parrot, 23
and readerly awareness of the arts, 15, 386, 387
and statuary's comic effects, 123–4
The Tea-Table, 336
use of ekphrasis by, 387
and whimsy, 197–8, 199, 202–3, 206, 207, 208
A Wife to be Lett, 27
see also Fielding, Henry; *Invisible Spy, The* (Haywood)
Hazlitt, William, 262
Henley, Samuel, 48
Higgins, Dick, 9
Highmore, Joseph, 99, 143
history
and antiquarianism, 53
and historical fiction, 53
marginalisation of women in, 54, 58, 59
political and military histories, 59, 60
theories of, 61
and women's material practices, 59–60
see also antiquarianism
History of Charlotte Summers The (Fielding, Sarah ?)
and conversation pieces, 353
critical reception of, 352
generic hybridity of, 353

as imitation of Henry Fielding's fiction, 353
narrative structure of, 353, 354–7
and the printed text, 358–9
the reader in, 15, 353–7
and reading practices, 355–9
History of Sir Charles Grandison, The (Samuel Richardson)
Alexander's Feast in, 220–1, 222–4, 223, 225
gender in, 221–2, 224–5
masquerades in, 334
opera vs oratorio in, 297
and the restorative powers of art, 224–5
song in, 211, 221–2
History of the Adventures of Joseph Andrews, The (Henry Fielding)
expression of feelings in, 309
the figure of 'complete' beauty in, 140
format of, 31, 91
in graphic satire, 469, 470
illustrations of, 416
and interartistic discourse, 2–3
and the novel's emergence, 40, 91, 351
as parody of *Pamela*, 30
preface to, 2–3, 508
and realist prose fiction, 40
sexuality in, 99
and statuary's comic effects, 132–3
Hobbes, Thomas, *Leviathan*, 91
Hodges, William, 49
Hogarth, William
Before & After, 95–7, 96
aesthetic theories of, 157
The Analysis of Beauty, 90, 157, 205
anti-connoisseurship of, 205, 279
'Auction of Pictures', 380
'Credulity, Superstition and Fanaticism', 41, 42
engagement with anatomy of, 69
as an engraver, 379
The Four Stages of Cruelty, 68, 73, 74
graphic narratives of, 8, 95–9, 157
graphic satire of, 469, 511
A Harlot's Progress, 92, 95, 97, 98, 511, 512
The Hervey Conversation Piece, 373
High Life Below Stairs, 381
Lemuel Gulliver's Punishment, 467
Marriage A-la-Mode, 97, 111, 112
Mary Toft (Tofts) appearing to give birth to rabbits, 75, 76
public awareness of, 386–7, 388, 389
references to in Fielding's works, 3, 510–11
self-portrait by, 508
Southwark Fair, 443
William Wollaston and his Family in a Grand Interior, 281, **Plate 13**
Hsieh, Chia-Chuan, 378, 379, 383, 384, 388

534   INDEX

Hume, David, 62, 89, 99, 251, 279
  An Enquiry Concerning Human Understanding, 7
Hutcheson, Francis, 99, 251

iconotexts, 8, 9
illustrations
  of beauty, 141, 143, 149
  for broadsides, 247, *248*
  and engraving, 420
  to medical texts, 68, 70, 80
  in the romance genre, 329–30, *330*, *331–2*,
    340, 341–2, *342*
  and silkworks, 415–16
  and visual culture, 416
  see also extra-illustration; frontispieces; print
    culture; *Robinson Crusoe* (Defoe); Wroth,
    Mary
image
  and narrative, 155–8
  and the visual imagination, 69–70, 74, 160
  word-image debates, 5, 6–7, 8–9, 10, 49
  see also extra-illustration; illustration
imagetext, 8, 9
imagination, the
  and empirical enquiry, 89
  and erotica, 435–6
  freedom of, 185
  and hedonism, 199, 204–5, 208
  maternal, 69, 75–7, 82
  theories of, 5, 89–90, 105, 333
  visual, 377–8
imperialism
  British, 39
  in contemporary art, 497
  eighteenth-century, 14, 462, 492–3
  and India, 39, 48–51
  see also Austen, Jane; Gibbes, Phebe;
    Orientalism
implied readers, 16, 504–5
implied viewers, 16, 504–5, 511, 514
intermediality
  and the arts, 9, 24–5, 362–3, 377, 386–7, 398,
    415, 416
  in contemporary art, 486
  and frontispieces, 398, 404–10
  and the novel, 309, 350, 377, 386, 486, 487,
    488, 495
  theories of, 9, 15, 362
invisibility
  in drama, 27, 29
  literary allusions to, 27–9
  as narrative strategy, 25–6, 29, 34
  in relation to visibility, 24, 32–3
  see also *Invisible Spy, The* (Haywood)
Invisible Spy, The (Haywood)
  and drama, 23, 24

  and gender, 25–6, 31
  generic range of, 23, 24, 34
  as libertine erotica, 23–4, 31–2
  literary allusions in, 27, 29
  narrative structure of, 14, 24, 25–7, 29, 34
  as secret history, 23
  see also Fielding, Henry
Iser, Wolfgang, 504–5

Jacob, Hildebrand, *Of the Sister Arts*, 6, 7
Jacobite Rebellion, the (the Jacobite Rising),
    206–7, 469
Jacobite's Journal, The, 468–9
James, William
  *The Letters of Charlotte, during her Connexion
    with Werter*, 418, 419
  see also Die Leiden des jungen Werther
    (Goethe)
Johnson, John, 245
Johnson, Samuel
  definition of art of, 11
  Dictionary, 11, 109, 110
  The History of Rasselas, Prince of Abissinia, 40
  novel criticism of, 279
  The Rambler, 40, 286, 349
  and reading practices, 178
  on Shakespeare, 262
Jones, Inigo, 110
Joyce, James, 293

Kames, Henry Home, Lord, 89
  Elements of Criticism, 6, 99
Kauffman, Angelica, 180
  adaptations of the works of, 415, 416, 426
  Shakespeare's Tomb, 418, 422, 425
Kent, William, 90, 110
Keppler Jr, Joseph, 'Robinson Crusoe Fairbanks',
    465–6, *Plate 24*
King, Kathryn R., 23, 24, 26, 29
Knox, Vicesimus, 351

landscape
  artistic depictions of, 183, 344, 442–4
  in the early novel, 108
  literary depictions of, 176, 181–3, 333
  naturalness of, 333–4
  and romance fiction, 329, 330, 332–4,
    341–2, *342*
  and sociability, 337
  and topography, 442–4
  see also beautiful, the; Claude glass, the;
    erotica; picturesque, the; Radcliffe, Ann
landscape gardening
  aesthetic debates surrounding, 110, 155, 200–2,
    203, 204, 207, 280
  Arcadian, 105, 176–7, 332, 334–5, 340–1

INDEX

and pleasure, 90, 280, 337, *Plate 3*
practice of, 90, 280, 332, 410
and relation to nature, 90, *Plate 3*
as sister arts, 9, 10, 196
see also Bridgeman, Charles; Brown, Lancelot
  'Capability'; Kent, William; Repton,
  Humphry
language
  figurative, 238–9
  the inexpressibility topos, 5–6
  limitations of, 6, 7, 100, 102, 295, 296
  non-verbal communication, 6–7, 100, 102–3,
    309, 321
  non-verbal expression of erotic feelings, 102–3,
    309, 321
  and verbal-visual debates, 5–8
  see also body, the; *ut pictura poesis*
Lawrence, Thomas, 105
Lely, Sir Peter, 91–2, *Plate 4*
Lennox, Charlotte, 284, 287, 363, 370–1; see also
  Female Quixote, The (Lennox)
Lessing, Gotthold Ephraim, *Laocoon*, 7, 8, 157
Lewis, Matthew Gregory
  The Monk, 128–30, 132, 168
  and statuary metaphors, 123, 128–9
LeWitt, Sol, 486
Life and Opinions of Tristram Shandy,
  Gentleman, The (Baldessari) *see* Baldessari,
  John
Life and Opinions of Tristram Shandy,
  Gentleman, The (Sterne)
  adaptations of, 488, 489
  the body in, 68
  childbirth in, 79, 81–2, 492
  and limitations of language, 5, 6, 102
  missing chapter of, 489, 490
  musical epiphanies in, 295–6, 298
  and the novel's emergence, 351, 353, 486
  reproduction in, 68, 69, 81–2
  satire in, 81–2, 390–2
  and textual recycling, 488–9
  visual and typographic experimentation in, 6,
    67–8, 486, 487, 489, 490, 495
  see also Baldessari, John; Smellie, William
Linley, Elizabeth, 104–5, *Plate 7, Plate 8*
Linwood, Mary, 417–18
Lipski, Jakub, 127–8, 147, 176, 184, 362, 378,
  383, 384–5, 402
literary criticism
  and comparative studies, 8, 195–6
  of the eighteenth-century novel, 3
literary pictorialism, 6, 10, 12–13, 377, 378–9,
  386, 387
Locke, John, 89, 99, 308
  An Essay concerning Human Understanding,
    4–5, 77

Lorrain, Claude, 176–7, 180, 181, 182–4, 388–9;
  see also Claude glass, the
Loutherbourg, Philippe-Jacques de (Philip James),
  39, 46; *see also* Beckford, William
luxury, 93, 197–8, 206–7, 278, 280–1, 282–3,
  291n37, 400; *see also* pleasure; whimsy

Machiavelli, Niccolò, 283–4
Mackenzie, Henry, 15, 379
  Julia de Roubigné, 296
  The Man of Feeling, 251–2, 314, 389
  and the sentimental novel, 251–2, 296
  and the visual arts, 379, 389
  see also Rosa, Salvator
McKeon, Michael, 17n14, 35n5, 290n8
Macklin, Charles, 264
Malthus, Daniel, *The Sorrows of Werter: A*
  German Story (translation), 414; see also *Die*
  Lieden des jungen Werther (Goethe); Goethe,
  Johann Wolfgang von
Manley, Delarivier, 4
Mann, Horace, 167, 168; *see also* Walpole,
  Horace
manners
  and artificiality, 277, 278, 283
  definition of, 262
  in the eighteenth century, 277–8
  and performativity, 263, 277, 283
  and politeness, 278–9
  and sentimental novels, 262, 263, 268,
    271, 278
  see also politeness
Mansfield Park (Austen), 14, 514
  architecture in, 14, 109, 113, 116, 120
  elocution in, 312, 314
  gender in, 286
  music in, 301
  references to Sterne in, 309
  spatiality in, 492, 493
Marana, Giovanni Paolo, *Letters Writ by a*
  Turkish Spy, 399–400
Marmontel, Jean-François, 41, 44
marriage
  and domesticity, 93
  economics of, 92, 93, 97, 111, *112*
  eighteenth-century social conventions of, 126,
    160
  and gender politics, 92, 93, 99, 111, 135–7
  as market, 97–9, 111–12, 116
  and social stability, 120
  and statuary metaphors, 126
masquerades
  and balls, 94, 166
  dangers of, 32, 38, 44, 203, 222
  in literature, 91, 94–5, 240, 334, 511
  as social practice, 197, 198, 278, 334, 340

INDEX

medicine
  and anatomical studies, 68, 71–2, 73–4, 80, *80*
  in the British military, 72, 73
  and dissection, 70, 71, 73–4
  and midwifery, 68, 75, 78, 79–82
  and the nervous system, 100
  and reproduction, 67–9, 75–8, 79, 82
  the visual imagination and anatomical art, 14,
    68–70, 74, 80, *80*, 82
  see also *Adventures of Roderick Random,
    The* (Smollett)
Meissonnier, Juste-Aurele, 197
Mendes, Paulo, 487
meta-pictorialism, 378
Millenium Hall (Sarah Scott)
  and antiquarianism, 14, 54, 62–3
  gender in, 54, 57, 62–3
  and handicrafts, 14, 53–4, 57–9, 60–1
  narrative structure of, 56–7
  socio-economic structure of, 62–3
Mills, Charles W., 24
Moll Flanders (Defoe)
  architecture in, 109, 113
  and commerce, 92–3, 94, 511
  cross-dressing in, 94–5
  and gender, 93, 94, 511
  and the novel's emergence, 91, 377
Montagu, Edward Wortley, 46
Montagu, Elizabeth, 56, 58, 59–60, 179
Montagu, George, 169
Montagu, Mary Wortley, Lady, 46, 50, 352
Montagu House, 2, 55; *see also* British Museum,
    the
morality
  and broadsides, 250
  dangers of novel reading, 286, 349, 504
  and gender, 140–1, 143–5, 146, 147, 148,
    151
  and motherhood, 92
  in popular culture, 250
  and religion, 212–13
  Restoration, 91–2
  and sentimental literature, 99, 251
  and sociability, 277
  and taste, 150, 198
  in the visual arts, 95–7, *96*
Moreau le Jeune, Jean Michel, *L'École des
    femmes*, 445
Morrissey, Lee, 110
museum culture, 2, 55; *see also* galleries
music
  and charity, 298–9
  eighteenth-century conceptions of, 294–5
  and emotion, 183, 294–5, 297, 301–3
  in fiction, 235–6, 238, 300–1
  organ, 221
  and sensibility, 295, 298, 299

and silent listening, 298, 300
  as social critique, 297
  and verbal insufficiency, 295, 296
  see also affect; Austen, Jane; emotion; *Gulliver's
    Travels* (Swift); opera; Radcliffe, Ann; song
musical epiphanies
  definitions of, 294–5, 303–4
  in fiction, 15, 296, 297–300, 301–4
  and sensibility, 295, 298, 299
  and the visual arts, 297
  see also affect; Burney, Frances; music;
    Radcliffe, Ann; Sterne, Laurence
Mysteries of Udolpho, The (Radcliffe)
  aesthetic development in, 185–9
  architecture in, 119, 171, 185
  Coleridge's review of, 177–8
  composition of, 182
  enlightened reason in, 128, 171, 185–6
  and Gothic fiction, 14
  and imaginative freedom, 185
  landscape in, 187–8
  poetic excerpts in, 177–8, 184, 185,
    186–7
  statuary in, 128, 171
  the visual arts in, 180

neoclassicism
  in architecture, 49, 105, 110, 111, 112
  in the eighteenth century, 1–2
  in philosophy, 89–90
  and reason, 235
New, Melvyn, 487–8
Newton, Isaac, 89
  Opticks, 5
Noggle, James, 11
novel, the
  definitions of, 2, 3–4, 16, 23 16
  and formal realism, 3, 40, 201, 250, 351,
    377–8
  historical emergence of, 3–4, 40, 90–1, 94, 377,
    503
  and improbability, 201–2
  individualised experience in, 4, 10, 40, 91,
    108
  interartistic discourse in, 2–3, 7, 10–11
  links to the theatre of, 263
  material packaging of, 9
  multimedial reworkings of, 414–15
  non-verbal communication in, 6, 7
  pictorial metaphors in, 3, 377–8
  in relation to romance, 3, 4
  self-conscious narrative techniques in, 351–2,
    486
  sister arts discourse in, 5, 6–7, 8–9, 10–11, 123,
    157, 362, 383

O'Keeffe, John, *Poor Soldier*, 252

INDEX

opera
comic, 252
criticisms of, 237, 279, 297
critiques of Italian, 237, 279, 297
English, 252–3
in fiction, 214–16, 298–9
and literary adaptations, 252
and opera glasses, 237
and oratorio, 217, 221, 297
as a 'total work of art', 184
see also Gay, John; Handel, George Frederick
oral culture
and broadside ballads, 245–6
and reading aloud, 246, 349–50
Orientalism
and domestic realism, 40, 48
and exotic dress, 38, 46, 384–5, *Plate 1*
in fiction, 38–41, 46, 47–8
and graphic satire, 41, 43–4, *43*, 46
narrative traditions of, 41–3
and seraglio figures, 39, 46–7
and sexuality, 14, 39, 45, 46–8
and slaves, 41, 44–6
Turkey and the Near East, 39
see also *Arabian Nights' Entertainments, The*;
    Fortunate Mistress, The (Roxana) (Defoe);
    Gibbes, Phebe
Ovid, 125

painting
annual exhibitions of, 165, 376, 378–9
and art-historical consciousness, 378–9, 383–4
and canon formation, 377
and connoisseurship, 390–1
engravings of, 379, 381
exclusivity of access to, 376–7, 378, 379–81,
    382–3
and importation of European art, 123, 380
and print collections, 381–2, 383–4
references to in novels, 156, 376–7
and sister arts discourse, 5, 6–7, 8–9, 10, 123,
    157, 362, 383
see also conversation pieces; portraiture
Palladianism, 111, 113–14, 120, 513
Palladio, Andrea, 111
Pamela (Samuel Richardson)
adaptations of, 30–1, 145, 252, 420
architecture in, 113
epistolary form of, 91, 143, 145
and erotica, 438
gender in, 125, 143–5, 146
illustrations to, *144*, 383
marriage in, 211–12
opera in, 214–16
paintings of, 99, 143
physical beauty in, 14, 140, 141, 143–5, 146,
    147, 152

as sentimental novel, 251
sexual violence in, 99, 126, 144
and social manners, 278, 309
statuary metaphors in, 126, 133
see also Highmore, Joseph; psalmody
Partridge, Bernard, 466
Pasolini, Pier Paolo, *Salò*, 497
Peacock, Thomas Love, 119
Perrault, Charles, 'The Sleeping Beauty in the
    Wood', 129–30
Persuasion (Austen)
argument in, 307, 308, 310–11
body language in, 307, 317–19
elocution in, 307, 308–9, 311–12, 313–14, 320–2
embodied communication in, 307–8, 311–14
influence of Sterne on, 309, 317–19, 320–1
musical epiphanies in, 302–3
publication of, 2
and sexuality, 307, 308–9, 315–17, 318, 319
Philips, Charles, 362
philosophy
in the eighteenth century, 4–5, 69–70, 75
empirical, 99
moral, 99, 141, 145, 251
of race, 24, 40
in relation to literature, 5, 89, 152, 251
in relation to visual culture, 5, 7, 61, 140
sentimental, 251, 253–4, 255
Picart, Bernard, 401, *402*
pictorialism *see* literary pictorialism
picturesque, the
in landscape gardening, 332, 410
and musical affect, 295–7
and print culture, 54
and tourism, 56
in visual culture, 110, 337
see also Gilpin, William
Piles, Roger de, 382, 383, 391
Pilkington, Laetitia, 240
Pine, John, 398–401, *399*, 404, 464; *see also*
    Clark, John; *Robinson Crusoe* (Defoe)
Piozzi, Hester Lynch Thrale, 179
pleasure
and aesthetic theories, 5, 14, 89–90, 105,
    333
and commerce, 92
and entertainments, 94
and fantasy, 198–9, 203–4
and hedonism, 199
and libertinism, 91
during the Restoration, 91, 277–8
and sensibility, 99, 100, 101, 105
see also erotica; luxury
pleasure gardens (London)
Ranelagh, 41, 94, 104
Vauxhall, 41, 94, 104, 443
in the visual arts, 94, 443

INDEX

poetry
  estate poems, 112
  and imagination, 183
  in novels, 177–8, 184, 185, 186–7, 236, 240
  relationship to painting of, 5, 6–8, 53, 157
  and sister arts discourse, 5, 6–7, 8–9, 10, 123,
      157, 362, 383
politeness
  eighteenth-century, 277–8, 280
  and elocution, 312
  and enlightenment, 278–9
  in fiction, 278, 280, 281–2, 283, 287–9
  and gender, 285–7, 288–9, 367–9
  and hypocrisy, 283–5, 287–8
  ideals of, 279–80
  and performativity, 283, 284
  role of the arts in, 15, 279
  and sensibility, 278
  and sociability, 277, 278, 279, 280–1
  and social hierarchies, 281–2, 284, 289
  and taste, 279, 280, 282–3
  and theatricality, 277, 278, 279–80
  see also conversation; manners; Shaftesbury,
      Anthony Ashley Cooper, Third Earl of;
      sociability
Pope, Alexander
  adaptations by, 228, 240
  and antiquarianism, 58
  The Dunciad, 26, 58
  An Epistle to Burlington, 49, 112
  interest in architecture of, 111, 112
  and Italian opera, 279
  and taste, 290n19
pornography, 435; *see also* erotica
Portland, Margaret Bentinck, Duchess of, 56,
      59–60
portraiture
  in aesthetic theory, 166, 180–1
  and animation, 127–8, 156, 166, 171
  and authorial frontispieces, 397, 401, 404
  and conversation pieces, 280–1, 362, 363,
      373
  in fiction, 127–8
  during the Restoration, 91–2, *Plate 4*
  and romance, 334
  see also *Castle of Otranto, The* (Horace
      Walpole); Gainsborough, Thomas; painting;
      Reynolds, Sir Joshua; Walpole, Horace
print culture
  and access to paintings, 381–2, 383–4
  and adaptation, 485, 487–8
  and collective labour, 10
  and freedom of the press, 89
  growth of, 2, 348
  and the novel, 397–8
  in popular culture, 244

  and print collections, 381–2, 383–4, 433
  see also extra-illustration; graphic satire;
      Hogarth, William
Proust, Marcel, 293, 294
provincialism, 54, 278
psalmody, 14, 212–13, 217; see also *Clarissa*
      (Samuel Richardson); *Pamela* (Samuel
      Richardson)
Punch, 466

race
  aestheticisation of otherness, 12–13
  in the arts, 12
  depictions of blackness, 13
  in fiction, 12
  and invisibility, 24, 33
  see also Behn, Aphra; Gibbes, Phebe;
      imperialism; Orientalism
Radcliffe, Ann
  admiration for Claude Lorrain of, 176–7, 180,
      181, 182–4
  anthologisation practices of, 178, 186
  appreciation of landscape of, 176, 181–2
  biography of, 178–80, 181
  The Castles of Athlin and Dunbayne, 184–5,
      297
  commercial awareness of, 177, 179
  Gaston De Blondeville, 179, 183
  and heroines' aesthetic development, 184–9
  and imaginative freedom, 185
  The Italian, 179, 182
  A Journey Made in the Summer of 1794,
      176–7, 179, 182, 183
  knowledge of the arts of, 179–81
  musical epiphanies in the works of, 296–7
  pictorialism in the works of, 176, 181–2
  The Poems of Mrs. Ann Radcliffe, 189
  poetic practices of, 177–8, 184, 185, 186–7
  professional standing of, 176, 179
  and romance, 176–7
  A Sicilian Romance, 181–2, 297
  three-part sister arts model of, 176–7, 182,
      183–4, 189
  the 'total work of art' notion of, 14, 176
  and tourism, 176–7, 179, 180, 182
  see also *Mysteries of Udolpho, The* (Radcliffe)
Rambler's Magazine, The, 440–1
readers
  fictional role of, 252, 504–5
  and growth in literacy, 2
  implied, 16, 504–5
  knowledge of the arts of, 379, 386–8
  relationship with the narrator of, 354–7
reading
  aloud, 246, 349–50
  as an art, 15, 348–9

challenges of, 348
dangers of, 286, 349, 504
durational nature of, 485, 491, 493–4
and extradiegetic narrators, 354–6
fictional representations of, 353
and growth in literacy, 278, 348, 354
instructions for in fiction, 349, 355–9, 504–5
and performance, 350
practice of, 2, 351–2
private, 348, 349, 350–1, 354
and self-conscious novels, 351–2, 353, 357, 359
uncritical, 350–1
and viewing artworks, 349, 487, 497
realism
formal, 4, 30
limitations of, 3
in the novel, 3, 40, 201, 250, 351, 377–8
and the novel's emergence, 350–1, 359
and Orientalism, 40, 48
in painting, 377–8
and verisimilitude, 53
Reeve, Clara
The Old English Baron, 168
and pictorialism, 3
The Progress of Romance, 3, 23
religion, in the eighteenth century, 212–13
Rembrandt, Harmenszoon van Rijn, 4
Repton, Humphry, 10
Restoration, the, 91–2, 277–8
Reynolds, Sir Joshua
Discourses on Art, 7–8
and the Royal Academy, 7, 27, 49, 104, 199
theory of painting of, 199–200, 205, 279, 362
rhetoric
and appeals to ethos, 308
and argument, 307, 308, 310–11
and elocution, 307, 308, 309, 311, 321
embodied, 313–15, 320
literary applications of, 23, 41, 45, 308–9, 321
and narration in film, 505, 506–7, 508, 510–11
theories of, 308, 316–17
in the visual arts, 110, 349, 397, 427, 467,
474, 476
see also elocution
Richardson, Jonathan (Senior)
An Account of Some of the Statues, 376, 378
*Argument on behalf of the Science of a
Connoisseur*, 391
art criticism of, 376, 377
and ekphrasis, 378
Essay on the Theory of Painting, 5, 376
print collections of, 376, 381–2, 383
Richardson, Samuel
and didacticism, 30–1, 130, 140, 146, 350–1
domestic realism in the works of, 40
ekphrasis in the works of, 126, 378

literary criticism of, 211
moral purpose in the works of, 113, 130, 136,
141, 143–5, 146, 212, 217
and the novel's emergence, 10
prefaces to the works of, 250
and sentimental fiction, 251
statuary metaphors in the works of, 123, 126–7,
130, 136–7
theme of hypocrisy in the works of, 284
see also Barbauld, Anna Letitia; *Clarissa*
(Samuel Richardson); *History of Sir Charles
Grandison, The* (Samuel Richardson);
Pamela (Samuel Richardson)
Richardson, Tony see *Tom Jones* (film, Tony
Richardson)
Robertson, David, 62
Robinson, Mary (Perdita), 93, 105, *Plate 9*
Robinson Crusoe (Defoe)
afterlives of, 15, 399–400, 404–10, *405, 406*
architecture in, 109, 113
branding of, 400–1
character of Friday in, 12–13
and conversation pieces, 403
editions of, 401–3
French editions of, 401, *402,* 403
frontispiece to, 398–9, *399, 400, 402*
in graphic satire, 15, 461, 462, 463–6, *Plate 23*
illustrations to, 398–401, *399, 403,* 404, 407,
416, 463–4
and the novel's emergence, 3, 91
sociability and isolation in, 15, 364–7
see also Picart, Bernard; Pine, John
rococo
and the decorative arts, 199–200, 205
definition of, 196
in the eighteenth century, 195, 196–7
in fiction, 197
in garden design, 104, 200, 201, 204, 207
literary scholarship on, 195–6, 197
in the visual arts, 104, 105, 195
and whimsy, 14, 196–7
see also Haywood, Eliza
Rococo-Gothic architecture, 200–1, 207
romance
and chivalry, 130, 134–5, 177, 329, 336
classical, 329, 330
and costume, 334–5, 337, 339
and coteries, 334–40
and country house settings, 336–7, 340, 342–3
in the eighteenth century, 329, 343–4
and fantasy, 338–9
and frontispieces, 329–30
and gender, 124, 126, 129–31, 132, 134–6
and Gothic fiction, 56
illustrations to, *330, 331–2,* 340, *341–2, 342*
in landscape, 329, 330, 332–4, *341–2, 342*

540 INDEX

romance (*cont.*)
multimediality of, 329, 332–3
and the novel, 3, 4
in portraiture, 334
in relation to statuary metaphors, 130–1, 134
temporality of, 342–3
see also *Athenian Letters*; Radcliffe, Ann; Wrest
Park (coterie of)
Romance of a Day, The (Cleland)
extra-illustrations to, 15, 434, 436, 442, *442*,
443–4, 445–6, *446*, 448, 454–7
frontispiece to, 441–2, *442*, 445
see also Comerford, James
Romanticism, 278
Rosa, Salvator, 388, 389
Rouquet, Jean-André, 196–7
Rousseau, Jean-Jacques, 90
Julie, 445–6
Rowlandson, Thomas
and anatomy, 69
depictions of Venus by, 438, *439*
graphic satire of, 41, 43–4, *43*
Love in a Tub, 438
'Turkish Ambassador introduced to the Duke of
N—', 41, 43–4, *43*
Vauxhall Gardens, 443
Rowson, Martin
adaptive practices of, 463, 474
Gulliver's Travels, Adapted and Updated, 467,
474–6, *476*
political satire of, 463, 467, 474
Roxana (Defoe) see *Fortunate Mistress,
The (Roxana)* (Defoe)
Royal Academy, the
annual exhibitions of, 378–9, 416
foundation of, 7, 104, 199, 279
and moral instruction, 279
Royal Society, the, 90
Ryland, William Wynne, 415
Ryley, Charles Reuben, 416

Sabine, T. see *Werter and Charlotte*
Sade, Donatien Alphonse François, Marquis de
afterlives of, 15, 491, 493
*Les 120 Journées de Sodome ou l'école du
libertinage*, 485, 494, 495
see also Chan, Paul; Pasolini, Pier Paolo
Savage, Richard
The Authors of the Town, 26
and the Hillarian circle, 335
Scott, Sarah
and antiquarianism, 56, 58, 60
and domestic handicrafts, 54, 58–9
A Journey through Every Stage of Life, 62
see also handicrafts; *Millenium Hall
(Sarah Scott)*

Scott, Walter
literary criticism of, 16, 176, 182, 277
Waverley novels of, 53, 110
sculpture
and animacy, 123, 127, 135, 171
art of, 123, 124
classical, 123
collections of, 2, 58, 155, 165, 171
in contemporary art, 485, 486, 491–3, 494,
497, 498
definitions of, 124
in fiction, 123, 125, 126–9
in Gothic fiction, 123, 127, 135, 171
market for, 2
and the visual arts, 69, 123, 196, 197
see also statuary
Selkirk, Alexander, 404, *405*, 465; see also
Robinson Crusoe (Defoe)
sensibility
and the body, 100, 101, 102–4, 317, 320, 392
and civility, 278, 281
dangers of, 185–6
definitions of, 263
in the eighteenth century, 89, 99–100, 262–3,
294
in fiction, 15, 151–2, 262–3, 264, 268, 271–2,
294, 300
language of, 262, 263, 271–2
moral value of, 150
and musical appreciation, 295, 298, 299
and the nervous system, 100
and pleasure, 99, 100, 101, 105
and queerness, 207
in relation to reason, 89, 99–100
in the visual arts, 132, 149
sentimental fiction
and epistolarity, 251, 252
and father-daughter plots, 265, 267, 269–70
formal features of, 251
and gender, 263–4, 265, 266–8, 269–72, 278
as genre, 251–2, 263–4
and manners, 262, 263, 268, 271, 277, 278
narrative methods in, 252
Sentimental Journey through France and Italy, A
(Sterne)
access to the arts in, 391–2
afterlives of, 414–15, 417, 418, 426, 427–8,
Plate 21
body language in, 100, 101, 102–4, 317–19,
320, 392
eroticism in, 102–3, 309, 321
illustrations to, 416
as literary influence, 309, 317–19, 320–1
musical epiphanies in, 295–6, 298
publication of, 99
satire in, 390

INDEX

541

sentimentalism
  in broadside ballads, 253–7
  definitions of, 263
  development of, 99–100
  in fiction, 251, 253, 278
  and moral formation, 99, 251
  and the 'noble savage', 251
  in philosophy, 100, 251
  in theatre, 251, 252, 264, 265, 266
sexuality
  and cross-dressing, 94–5
  and elocution, 307, 308–9, 315–17, 318, 319
  homoeroticism, 47, 198
  homophobia, 39, 43–4
  and libertine culture, 91–2, 277–8, *Plate 4*
  and Orientalism, 14, 38–9, 44, 45, 46–8, 49–50
  in sentimental fiction, 102–4, 309, 321, 392
  and whimsy, 200
  women's sexual freedom, 92
  see also erotica; gender; Sade, Donatien
    Alphonse François, Marquis de
Shaftesbury, Anthony Ashley Cooper, Third
  Earl of, 99, 142–3, 152, 251, 279; *see also*
  politeness; sociability
Shakespeare, William
  eighteenth-century adaptations of, 262, 264–5
  eighteenth-century reading of, 270, 271
  ghosts in the works of, 27
  influence of, 262, 264, 265
  King Lear, 266–7
  Othello, 50, 267–8
  performances of the works of, 264, 265, 266–7
  in political cartoons, 461
  Romeo and Juliet, 268
  sentimentalism in productions of, 264, 265, 266
  The Tempest, 270–1
  Twelfth Night, 270–1
  visual afterlives of, 418, 422, 425
  The Winter's Tale, 124–5
  see also Burney, Frances; Burney, Sarah Harriet;
    Garrick, David; Kauffman, Angelica; theatre
Shelley, Mary, *Frankenstein*, 73, 172
Shepard, E. H., 466
Sheridan, Frances, 15, 379, 390
  Memoirs of Miss Sidney Biddulph, 390
Sheridan, Richard Brinsley, 105
Sheridan, Thomas, 308, 348–9
Siddons, Sarah, 270, 273n15, 273n19, 315
Sidney, Philip
  Arcadia, 329, 334, 335, 336, 340
  on interartistic discourse, 1, 5
silkworks
  based on illustrations, 415–16, 425–7,
    Plates 19–20
  and chromatic characterisation, 422–4, 427,
    Plates 14–16

exhibitions of, 417–18
as female accomplishment, 417, 418, 422
as an individualised medium, 415–17, 427–8
and literary adaptations, 415–18, 422–6,
  427–8, *Plates 14–20, Plate 21*
mourning-related vignettes in, 415, 416, 422–5,
  426–7
and schooling, 417, 422
and textual meaning, 415–16, 417, 418, 427
use of colour in, 422–3, 424–5, 427, *Plates
  17–18*
see also Goethe, Johann Wolfgang von;
  Kauffman, Angelica; Smirke, Robert; Smith,
  John Raphael; Sterne, Laurence
sister arts, the
  criticisms of, 7–9
  and interartistic discourse, 1, 7–9, 362
  landscape gardening, 9, 10, 196
  and the novel, 5, 6–7, 8–9, 10–11, 12, 123,
    157, 362, 383
  painting, 5, 6–7, 8–9, 10, 123, 157, 362, 383
  poetry, 5, 6–7, 8–9, 10, 123, 157, 362, 383
  statuary, 123
  theories of, 5–7, 9–10, 158
  and *ut pictura poesis*, 1, 5, 7, 10, 157, 158
  and verbal-visual debates, 5–7, 8, 9–10
  see also *De Arte Graphica* (Fresnoy);
    Hildebrand, Jacob; Kames, Henry Home,
    Lord
Sixteen Pleasures/Aretino's Postures, The, 435;
  see also Comerford, James; erotica
Smellie, William, 68, 79–80, *80*, 81, 82
Smirke, Robert, *Charlotte at the Tomb of Werter*,
  415, 421–2, *421*, 425–7, *Plates 19–20*
Smith, Adam, 99, 251
Smith, John Raphael, *Charlotte at the Tomb of
  Werter*, 415, 420–1, *420*, 422, 426–7,
  Plates 14–16
Smollett, Tobias
  The Adventures of an Atom, 43
  The Expedition of Humphry Clinker, 39, 41–3, *43*
  Ferdinand Count Fathom, 3, 386
  in graphic satire, 462, 468, 470, 471, *471*
  masquerades in the works of, 94
  and medical knowledge, 69, 72, 75–6, 81, 82–3
  and the novel's emergence, 10
  pictorial metaphors in the works of, 3
  political journalism of, 470
  and readerly awareness of the arts, 15, 386–8
  and statuary's comic effects, 14, 123–4
  see also *Adventures of Peregrine Pickle, The*
    (Smollett); *Adventures of Roderick Random,
    The* (Smollett)
Smythies, Susan
  The Brothers, 352
  The Stage Coach, 352

542 INDEX

sociability
  as an art, 11
  moral value of, 277
  in the novel, 278–9, 362–3, 364–73
  and politeness, 278–9
  practice of, 94, 104, 109, 142
  and unsociability, 367
  in the visual arts, 362–3
  see also conversation; conversation pieces;
    Evelina (Frances Burney); *Female Quixote,*
    The (Lennox); *Robinson Crusoe* (Defoe)
Society of Antiquaries of London, the, 54
Society of Dilettanti, the, 382, 391
song
  emotion expressed in, 211, 221–2
  moral purpose of, 212, 217
  in the novel, 211, 216–20
  and representations of gender, 211
  restorative powers of, 224–5
  as sociable practice, 211–16, 217
  see also broadside ballads; Handel, George
    Frederick; opera; psalmody; Richardson,
    Samuel
Sorrows of Werter: A German Story, The
  (translation), 414; see also *Die Leiden des*
  jungen Werther (Goethe)
Southey, Robert, 48
spatiality
  narrativisation of, 492, 493
  in relation to temporality, 7, 157
  and *ut pictura poesis*, 157
Spectator, The, 89, 142, 146, 333, 382
Spence, John, 158
Spence, Joseph, 149–50
spontaneity, 101, 196, 278–81, 283, 291n27, 295,
  312, 313–14, 319, 325n45, 336; *see also*
  conversation; elocution; musical epiphanies;
  sensibility
Stationers' Company, The, 244, 249
statuary
  and animacy, 127–8, 129–30, 171
  art of, 124
  classical, 123
  and collecting, 2, 58, 155, 165, 171
  in comic fiction, 14, 123–4, 131–4
  and the female body, 123, 124, 125,
    126–7, 132
  and gendered agency, 14, 123, 124–5, 126,
    129, 131, 132, 134–6
  in Gothic fiction, 128–30, 132, 171
  and lifelike corpse motifs, 127, 128, 129, 131
  and literary afterlives, 404–5, *405*, 407–8, 420
  and the male gaze, 123, 124, 125–32
  as metaphor for emotional overload, 130–1, 132
  in the novel, 123, 133–4, 232
  and pseudo-chivalric romance, 134

  in public spaces, 123
  and sexual violence, 123, 124, 126, 127,
    128–9, 130, 135–6
  and supplication, 126–7
  see also Clarissa (Samuel Richardson); Goethe,
    Johann Wolfgang von; Lewis, Matthew
    Gregory; Ovid; sculpture; *Tom Jones* (novel,
    Henry Fielding)
Steele, Richard, 89, 146, 152, 382; *see also*
  Addison, Joseph; *Spectator, The*
Sterne, Laurence
  adaptations of, 15–16, 485, 487–8, 489–91,
    495, 496, *Plate 26*
  anthologisation of the works of, 490
  the body in the works of, 68
  body language in the works of, 100, 101, 102–4,
    317–19, 320, 392
  and body snatching, 73
  influence on Jane Austen of, 309, 311–12,
    317–19, 320–1
  and the limitations of language, 295
  and medical knowledge, 14, 69, 78–80, 82–3
  music in the works of, 15, 295–6, 298
  and the novel's emergence, 10, 351, 353, 486
  and sensibility, 99, 100, 101, 105
  and suspended narrative endings, 103–4
  see also Life and Opinions of Tristram Shandy,
    Gentleman, The (Sterne); *Sentimental*
    Journey through France and Italy, A (Sterne)
Stevenson, Robert Louis, 'The Body Snatcher', 73
Stewart, Garrett, 485, 486
  Stonehenge, 55–6
Stothard, Thomas, 401, 420, 464
Stowe (landscape garden), 55
Strawberry Hill, 117, *118*, 201, 207; *see also*
  Gothic, the; Walpole, Horace
Stuart, James, 179
Stubbs, George, 82
Stukeley, William, 55, 56
sublime, the
  as aesthetic category, 110, 115, 181–2, 207,
    218
  in architecture, 111, 114, 115
  in landscape, 181–3
  in song, 218
  theories of, 7, 110, 207
  in the visual arts, 390
  see also beautiful, the; Burke, Edmund
Swift, Jonathan
  adaptations of, 30
  afterlives of, 33
  the body in the works of, 93
  knowledge of the arts of, 228, 385–6
  on music, 235
  and the novel's emergence, 3, 229
  'Ode to Sir William Temple', 232

and politics, 229, 230–3, 239–40, 461
portrait of, 180
and public knowledge of the arts, 379, 383
A Tale of a Tub, 3
see also *Gulliver's Travels* (Swift)

Talbot, Catherine, 56, 59, 336, 337, 339, 343
Talfourd, Thomas Noon, 'A Memoir of the Author, with Extracts from her Journals', 179–80, 181, 182; *see also* Radcliffe, Ann
taste
  and architecture, 110, 118, 207
  and the arts, 279
  and the body, 100
  and civic humanist discourses, 198–9, 201, 203–4, 205
  concept of, 155, 195–6, 201–2, 205, 280–1
  development of, 186, 188
  in the eighteenth century, 2
  elitism of, 207, 213, 280–2, 289
  and elocution, 313, 314–15, 316
  emancipatory potential of, 200
  in fiction, 197–8, 199
  and gender, 11–12, 58, 141, 143, 151
  moral value of, 151, 201, 219, 279
  and musical appreciation, 301–2
  and painting, 199–200, 205
  and politeness, 279
  and reading, 178
  and sentimentality, 100
  and whimsy, 197–202, 205–6
  see also aesthetics; genius
Tatler, The, 146, 152; *see also* Steele, Richard
temporality
  and elocution, 319–20
  in narrative structure, 342–3
  in relation to architecture, 116–17, 119–21, 155
  in relation to spatiality, 7, 157
  and *ut pictura poesis*, 157
  in the visual arts, 157, 168–70, 172
theatre
  audiences for, 229, 231–4, 237, 240
  and the novel, 23, 24, 263
  Restoration, 91, 278–9
  and sentimentalism, 251, 252
  and stagecraft, 27
  see also drama; Garrick, David; *Invisible Spy, The* (Haywood)
Thomson, James
  Britannia, A Poem, 185
  The Castle of Indolence, 343
  The Seasons, 186, 416, 418
Tillemans, Peter, 444
Tom Jones (film, Tony Richardson)

audience awareness in, 504, 505, 506, 508–10, 513, 514
  and closure, 513–14
  implied viewer in, 16, 504–5, 511, 514
  and problems of authority, 505–9, 514
  and problems of experience, 509–13, 514
Tom Jones (novel, Henry Fielding)
  anti-Jacobite message in, 469
  appearance-character relationship in, 145
  architecture in, 14, 113–14, 120, 513
  beauty in, 14, 140, 141, 148–9, *149*
  the body in, 511–13
  format of, 91
  ghosts in, 24
  hypocrisy in, 284
  and narrative authority, 507
  readerly awareness of the arts in, 389–90
  and the reading experience, 114, 505, 509
  references to Hogarth in, 510–11
  and self-conscious narrative, 2, 351, 357
  sexuality in, 99
  statuary metaphors in, 133–4
tourism
  continental, 1–2, 112, 123, 380, 382, 391
  domestic, 55, 124
  in the novel, 2, 177
  picturesque, 56
  in romance, 177
  virtual, 378
  see also Claude glass, the; Grand Tour, the; Radcliffe, Ann; Sterne, Laurence
Townshend, George, *The evacuation*, 470, *471*
Trahndorff, K. F. E., 176
Trapp, Joseph, *Praelectiones poeticae*, 6–7
travel writing
  forms of, 100–1, 102, 176–8
  as genre, 100, 176
  and the novel, 40, 56–7, 99
  in relation to the arts, 1–2, 11, 181–4
  in relation to travel, 56
  see also Radcliffe, Ann; *Sentimental Journey through France and Italy, A* (Sterne)
Turner, Daniel, 75, 76
Turner, J. M. W., 10, 105

urbanism
  and architecture, 109, 230, 236, 239
  and the broadside ballad, 245, 246
  and commerce, 91, 92–3
  and sentimentalism, 278
ut pictura poesis, 1, 5, 7, 10, 157, 158

Van Aken, Joseph, *An English Family at Tea*, 280–1
Van Dyck, Sir Anthony, 180, 334, 338–9
Vanbrugh, Sir John, 111, 112

INDEX

Vathek (Beckford)
architecture in, 48, 109, 119
literary influences on, 47–8
Orientalist tropes in, 39, 47–8
see also *Arabian Nights' Entertainments, The*;
Orientalism
Vertue, George
and antiquarianism, 56
*Original Drawings of Heads, Antiquities,
Monuments, Views, &c.*, 162, 163–4
see also Walpole, Horace
Vesalius, Andreas, 70, 71
visual culture
as academic discipline, 13–14, 398
access to in the eighteenth century, 376–7,
378–9, 379–81
eighteenth-century, 9–10, 14, 68–9, 73, 114,
121n14, 376–7, 416, 474–5
the eye as the primary sense organ, 4–5
and literary engagement, 416
and readerly awareness of the arts, 386–8
see also painting; portraiture; print culture
visual imagination, the, 68–70, 74, 80, 82, 160, *161*
visuality
and aesthetic awareness, 377, 378–9
and art-historical consciousness, 378–9, 383–4
and the novel, 14
and ocularity, 9–10
in relation to perception, 4–5
and verbal-visual debates, 5–8
Vitruvius, *De architectura*, 111, 119
Voltaire
Jenni, 437–8, 440
Nanine, 252
Voltz, Johann Michael, *Der neue Robinson*,
464–5, *Plate 23*; see also *Robinson Crusoe*
(Defoe)
Voyage to Lethe, A (anon.), 15, 433, 434–5,
436–41, 437, 447, 448–53, *Plates 22–3*;
see also Comerford, James

Wall, Cynthia, 108, 109, 114–15
Walpole, Horace, 14
Aedes Walpolianae, 156, 157–9
Anecdotes of Painting, 156, 159–60, 166
and animate artworks, 127–8, 156, 166, 170–1
'Book of Materials', 156, 158, 160, 165, *170*, 171
collections of, 155, 156–8, 159, 162, *163–4*
A Description of Strawberry Hill, 155, 156,
158, *161*
ekphrasis in the writings of, 155, 156–7, 159
exhibition catalogues of, 159–60
extra-illustration practices of, 14, 155, 160, *161*
handwritten annotations by, 160–4, *163, 164*
and Houghton Hall, 169
interest in architecture of, 111

and King Charles I's art collection, 168–9, 170
knowledge of the arts of, 155
and narrative appeal of the visual arts, 155–6,
157, 159, 162–5, 167, 172
portrait of Lord Falkland, 156, 157, 166,
Plate 11
portraits of Bianca Cappello, 166–8, *Plate 12*
sketches by, 170–1, *170*
and Strawberry Hill, 117, *118*, 201, 207
and temporality in the visual arts, 155,
168–70, 172
and the uncanny in the visual arts, 166, 170–1
use of anecdotes of, 159, 165
word-image practices of, 14, 158, 160, *161*
see also *Castle of Otranto, The* (Horace
Walpole); Doort, Abraham van der; Gothic,
the; Gothic fiction; Vertue, George
Walpole, Sir Robert, 117, 157, 232
Warren, Austin, 8, 9
Warren, Caroline Matilda, *The Gamesters*, 427
Watt, Ian, 4, 30, 113, 250, 277, 351, 364
Watteau, Jean-Antoine
The Embarkation for Cythera, 94, *Plate 5*
influence on Gainsborough of, 104
Webster, John, *The Duchess of Malfi*, 77
Wedgwood, Josiah, 179, 420
the Green Frog Service, 112, 342
see also Gothic, the
Wellek, René, 8, 9, 195
Wendorf, Richard, 10
West, Benjamin, *The Raising of Lazarus*, 180–1
whimsy
and aesthetic judgement, 197–8, 199, 200–2,
333
and aesthetics, 197–8, 199, 200–2, 207–8, 333
and consumerist hedonism, 199, 204–5, 208
definitions of, 195, 196
in the discourses of taste, 197–202
in the eighteenth century, 196–7
and female sexuality, 202–3, 206, 207, 208
and the figure of the coquette, 198, 202
and luxury, 197, 206–7
and the rococo, 14, 196–7
and sexual desire, 200
see also luxury; architecture; spontaneity
Williams, Abigail, 246, 349–50, 363
Willoughby, Cassandra, 60
Wit's Magazine, The, 441
Wollstonecraft, Mary
Mary: A Fiction, 131
A Vindication of the Rights of Woman, 46
Woman of Colour, The (anon.), 13
Woolf, Virginia
and epiphanies, 293
and novel-reading, 348
Orlando, 33, 34

Wordsworth, William, 10, 294
World, The, 200–2, 204, 207
Wotton, Sir Henry, 111, 112
Wrest Park (coterie of), 15, 336–44
Wrestiana, 337, 338, 339–40
Wroth, Mary, *Urania*, 329, 330, 332
Wycherley, William, *The Country Wife*, 91

Yorke, Charles, 336, 337, 338, 339–40; see also *Athenian Letters*; Wrest Park (coterie of)
Yorke, Elizabeth, 336; *see also* Wrest Park (coterie of)
Yorke, Margaret, 336; *see also* Wrest Park (coterie of)
Yorke, Philip, 336, 339–40; see also *Athenian Letters*; Wrest Park (coterie of)